Readings in
Introductory Sociology

Dennis H. Wrong

Harry L. Gracey

Readings in **Introductory Sociology**

MACMILLAN PUBLISHING CO., INC.

NEW YORK

THIRD EDITION

Copyright © 1977, Macmillan Publishing Co., Inc.

Printed in the United States of America

Earlier editions copyright © 1967 and 1972 by Macmillan Publishing Co., Inc.

Macmillan Publishing Co., Inc.
866 Third Avenue, New York, New York 10022

Collier Macmillan Canada, Ltd.

Library of Congress Cataloging in Publication Data

Wrong, Dennis Hume, (date)   comp.
  Readings in introductory sociology.

  Includes bibliographical references.
  1. Sociology—Addresses, essays, lectures.
I. Gracey, Harry L., joint comp. II. Title.
HM66.W73 1976   301'.08   76-959
ISBN 0-02-430700-9

Printing: 1 2 3 4 5 6 7 8   Year: 7 8 9 0 1 2 3

Preface

Most introductory sociology courses today include consideration of the nature of man as now conceived by sociologists; the basic concepts and perspectives of sociology as the scientific study of man's social life; some reference to the most enduring ideas of the founders of the field and their successors, the "second generation" sociologists; and, usually central to the course, analyses of the important institutions, organizations, and processes of modern Western society. This book covers all of these topics, with a large number of substantial readings on each. The teacher can, therefore, either use it to supplement his textbook, selecting from among the readings we offer in each of these areas, or adopt it as his text, using the introductions to help present a systematic overview of the field and the selections to provide basic facts, concepts, and theories that he will develop in his lectures.

Nearly a third of the readings in this edition of the reader are new, some of them dealing with topics not covered in previous editions and some of them replacing earlier selections. We have included, for the first time, readings on crime and deviance by adding an entire new section with a short introduction and contributions by Daniel Bell, Gresham Sykes, and Erving Goffman. Other subjects neglected in previous editions but covered in this edition are sex roles (Suzanne Keller), contemporary American religious consciousness (Robert Bellah), and the professions (Eliot Freidson).

Parts One and Two have been changed only slightly for this edition. We have added a theoretical analysis of institutionalization from Peter Berger and Thomas Luckmann's influential book *The Social Construction of Reality* in Part One and eliminated the separate section on social change, as Parts Two and Three deal heavily with social change in accounts of the creation of industrial society and the evolution of "postindustrial" society. Kingsley Davis's review of the world population explosion now appears in Part Three. In Part Two we have substituted a selection by Marx himself on alienation in industrial society for the old secondary summary of his views.

In addition to the new readings already mentioned, we have added a number of selections in Part Three. We have included a recent discussion of life in suburbia by Herbert Gans and an analysis of planned new communities by Lawrence

Susskind in the section on the community and have added a selection by Reinhard Bendix on the bureaucratization of industry in the bureaucracy section. We have substituted a survey of contemporary ethnicity world-wide by Nathan Glazer and Daniel Moynihan for their previous survey of race and religion in New York City. This new article now matches in scope Everett Hughes's treatment of race relations. We have added Michael Harrington's discussion of the American working class to the section on stratification and inequality and, also, substituted a recent treatment of stratification by Dennis Wrong for an earlier one by him. The section on the political economy has been strengthened by the addition of articles by Robert Boguslaw on the impact of computer technology on work relations, Dennis Wrong on democratic politics, and Christopher Lasch on the causes of modern revolutions and the obstacles to revolution in our advanced industrial societies.

In the introductory part "What Is Sociology?" we present two readings that discuss the subject matter of sociology, the methods of study, and the status of sociology as a humanistic discipline—part of our age-old search for knowledge of ourselves. These readings are preceded by an introduction that brings in some aspects of the historical development of the field and changing concepts of its nature and purpose.

Part One, "Basic Concepts and Perspectives of Sociology," contains explanatory and analytic articles on the concepts—including human evolution, social action, symbolic communication, the self, norms, roles, values, groups, institutions and institution building—that have become the common tools of sociological analysis. In addition to introducing the particular readings in the section, the introduction to Part One discusses the uniqueness of human nature and conduct within the perspective of biological evolution and summarizes the interrelations among the basic concepts of sociology. The concepts covered can be seen to range from the microsociological to the macrosociological, from those used to describe and analyze face-to-face interaction to those applied to organized social groups and the structure of whole societies. These readings will be especially valuable to teachers using this book as a basic text, for here the student is given the distinctively sociological perspective on the life of the "human animal." We want to point out, however, that the selections in Part One do not simply give textbook expositions of the basic concepts: they also provide critical examinations of these concepts and examples of their use in sociological analysis. This part, therefore, should be a valuable addition to the standard textbook expositions of the basic concepts. As a whole, it will give the student an appreciation of the wide range of sociological interest and the broad scope of sociological inquiry.

Part Two, "Industrial Society and the Origins of Sociology," provides substantial selections from the works of the classical sociologists, a feature not found in other anthologies. These readings depict the historical origins of scientific sociology in the "age of revolution" when Western society was in the process of transformation from a rural-agrarian life to today's urban-industrial world. The selections include discussions of the concepts and theories that the classical sociologists developed to comprehend this transformation. Many of these are still very much at the heart of sociology, including alienation, anomie, social class, conflict, the Protestant ethic, industrialization under capitalism in the West, and the meaning of science for modern life. These readings can be used as a unit to provide a historical introduction to sociological analysis or individually and in conjunction with those sections of Part Three that give contemporary applications of these and related concepts and theories. The introduction to Part Two provides a brief summary of the central ideas of each selection, places the whole unit in historical perspective, and points out the contemporary relevance of the ideas discussed. This discussion—plus the fact that many of the concepts and ideas included are not only part of sociology today but have found their way into popular discourse (witness the revival of interest in the concepts of alienation and anomie)—puts an understanding and appreciation of classical sociology well within the capacities of today's students.

Part Three, "Sociology of Contemporary Society," constitutes two thirds of the book, reflecting the emphasis of most introductory courses. Here is the important "payoff" of the sociological enterprise: making sense out of life in today's society. Each section of this part is an interrelated group of essays analyzing a particular aspect of contemporary social life. Each section has a basic theme, or set of interrelated themes, that the selections develop with regard to that area of social life. These themes include the urbanization and metropolitanization of community life; the bureaucratization of organizational life in advanced societies; the developing patterns of ethnic and race relations in modern societies; the characteristics of social class in American society and the changing nature of its stratification system; the interrelations of government, business, and the military establishment in the political economy of modern Western societies; and the consequences for the individual of living in modern society. The introduction to Part Three reviews the topics covered while the separate introductions for each of the sections forecast for the student some of the themes and ideas that will be met there. The student thus enters each section prepared for its basic ideas. The sections themselves have been arranged in a logical sequence, from the simpler to the more complex topics, and the readings in each section have been ordered from the general to the specific.

Several sociological topics often given separate treatment in anthologies and textbooks are included in this reader, although grouped differently. Population, for example, will be found discussed in Kingsley Davis's article in Part Three. Social-psychological topics are considered throughout the book. These include the treatment of the relationship between personality and role performance in Part Two, Weber's famous discussion of the relationship between the values of the Protestant and his behavior as a capitalist, and, in the entire second section of Part Two, discussions by the classical sociologists of the influence of society and culture on personality. Socialization is discussed in the first section of Part Three, notably in Harry Gracey's article on the kindergarten and Ulf Hannerz's article on growing up in the Washington D.C. black ghetto. Considerations of the consequences of social arrangements for the lives of individuals are scattered throughout the readings in Part Three, and the final section on "The Effects of Social Change" specifically concentrates on how trends in American society and culture affect the behavior and personality of contemporary Americans. Social psychology, as the study of the interrelation of personality and social structure, is thus one of the themes pervading the entire book.

Sociologists traditionally have been concerned with the emerging trends of change in society, as well as with its origins and contemporary structures and operation. A preoccupation with the shape of things to come is one of the defining characteristics of the works by the classical sociologists that we have excerpted for this book. We have included readings that, in addition to analyzing present-day social realities, attempt to project the direction of change in contemporary society. Such attempts to anticipate the future draw on verified sociological knowledge of both the past and the present in order to establish the limits within which future changes are likely to take place. Sociology, as the study of social life, cannot ignore the shape of the future at a time when all people are conscious of unceasing social change as the central, disturbing fact of contemporary life.

Sociology is a subject vital to the intelligent understanding of life in society today. We have been guided in our selection of material by a desire to show the student the crucial relevance of sociology to his understanding of the world we live in. A special effort has been made to find intelligent and intelligible analyses of the central areas of social experience for people living in today's advanced societies. We hope in this way to make sociology worthy of the respect of our students.

We want to thank the authors and publishers of our selections for permission to reprint their material, thus making them more readily available to the beginning student. We also want to thank our editor at Macmillan, Mr. Kenneth Scott, for his labors on behalf of this third edition.

D. H. W.

H. L. G.

Contents

Part Two
Industrial Society and the Origins of Sociology

Introduction

Part Three
Sociology of Contemporary Society

Introduction

What Is Sociology?

INTRODUCTION

Sociology is very much a product of modern history, seeking to provide new answers to old questions as well as answers to the new questions posed by the social changes and contacts between previously isolated peoples that have become the background of daily life in the twentieth century. Of course, long before 1837, when Auguste Comte coined the term *sociology*, the Greek philosophers, the Church Fathers, and the thinkers of the Enlightenment—to mention only the most outstanding figures of Western intellectual history—reflected on the origins and foundations of human society. Indeed the first amateur sociologist was the tribesman who first perceived in the social relations of his fellows an enduring pattern or structure that outlasted the particular individuals composing it at a given time.

In spite of their many penetrating insights into human customs and institutions, the early philosophers and theologians generally regarded human social relations as part of a divinely ordained cosmic order or as the expression of a fixed and timeless human nature. The political philosophers and classical economists, who were the immediate precursors of the founding fathers of sociology, had a narrow view of the social bonds uniting men, seeing them almost exclusively as political and economic relations. Thus Hobbes, Locke, Rousseau, and the other great seventeenth- and eighteenth-century political theorists thought of the relation between man and society largely in terms of the relation of the state to its subjects. Adam Smith and the classical economists, on the other hand, saw the contractual relations between traders in an exchange economy as the prototype of all social relations. Only after the social consequences of the great political and economic revolutions of the late eighteenth and early nineteenth centuries became fully evident was it possible for the structure of social relations to be perceived as an *autonomous* realm, a "variable" partially independent of political regimes and market relations. The disintegration of traditional European institutions as a result of the French Revolution and the industrial revolution made visible the existence of an order in men's social behavior that was independent of the statecraft of rulers and that could not be seen as the manifestation of an unchanging human nature.

The thinkers who were the first to conceive of the social order as a larger whole encompassing the state, the economy, and all the other institutions of society are the men we honor today as the founding fathers of sociology: Henri Saint-Simon and Auguste Comte in France, Herbert Spencer in England, and Karl Marx in Germany. Comte and Spencer in particular saw the necessity for developing a new intellectual discipline—sociology—which would study the social order and seek to discover general principles and laws underlying it.

The historical changes which gave birth to sociology as a new perspective—and, eventually, a new discipline—have continued at an accelerating rate to transform Western industrial societies. Indeed, machine technology, the concentration of more and more people in large cities, representative government, the nation-state as the dominant form of political organization, and the substitution of secular values for religiously inspired ones are now spreading around the world. The conception of sociology as a continuing effort to understand these societal changes, from the time of the founding fathers to the present, has served as the main organizing principle of this book.

If sociology originated as a response to the birth pangs of the modern world in Western Europe, it is also true that the discovery of the "social" as an independent force shaping human experience had implications transcending the specific historical conditions under which it occurred. The sociological perspective has cast light on traditional as well as on modern societies, and it has also illuminated age-old questions about the nature of human nature and the origins of man and society. The sociological perspective has influenced the work of other social scientists and that of philosophers and historians as well. Indeed practitioners of these disciplines have made many important contributions to sociology itself.

C. Wright Mills points out in our first reading that the enormous variety of social worlds that men have created has been the major stimulus to the social sciences as organized efforts to understand them. Their major, though by no means only, concern has been with societies caught up in the throes of *historical change*. Sociology, in particular, as the newest of the social sciences, emerged, as we have seen, in response to the social transformations of modern history. The idea of *social structure*, Mills argues, is central to sociology but is nowadays no longer confined to that discipline. Because human institutions have become more closely interrelated and bound together in modern nation-states, social structure—the pattern of their interrelatedness—has to be taken into account by economists and political scientists, and even by anthropologists studying the changes going on in the underdeveloped world. The nation-state, Mills insists, has become the "prime unit" for the study of the most significant problems in the social sciences. This common focus reduces, therefore, the separateness of each discipline and makes "sociological imagination" a requirement for all of them.

Systematic reflection on man and his works, however, long antedates the birth of social science. What, then, is the relationship of sociology, and of social science in general, to older traditions and ways of thinking about human affairs? How do the aims and methods of sociology and social science resemble or differ from the aims and methods of the humanities and the arts? How is social science related to man's age-old search for the good and the beautiful? How is sociology related to efforts to imagine the good society and to projects for making it a reality?

Robert Redfield stresses the role of creative imagination in social science.

He points out that some of the greatest works of social science increase our understanding of man and society in ways that do not depend on their logical rigor nor rely on formal research methods. Such works possess an originality and freshness of vision similar to that of great works of literature, although in presenting generalized descriptions of actual rather than fictional persons and groups they are, unmistakably, contributions to social science. Redfield suggests that the depth and originality of the social scientist's insight into his own humanity and his experience as a participant in his own society are prerequisites for significant new generalizations in social science that go beyond the patient accumulation of facts. No formal course of scientific training can equip the social scientist with the kind of insight that leads to intellectual creativity. Redfield ascribes a dual nature to social science, one displaying aspects of both the humanities and the physical sciences. Important as it is to train the social scientist in technical methods of collecting and recording data, social science, he contends, is also an art that cannot entirely be taught but depends upon the reflective use the scientist makes of his direct experience as a man participating in the life of his society.

1

The Human Variety

C. WRIGHT MILLS

I

. . . What social science is properly about is the human variety, which consists of all the social worlds in which men have lived, are living, and might live. These worlds contain primitive communities that, so far as we know, have changed little in a thousand years; but also great power states that have, as it were, come suddenly into violent being. Byzantine and Europe, classical China and ancient Rome, the city of Los Angeles and the empire of ancient Peru—all the worlds men have known now lie before us, open to our scrutiny. Within these worlds there are open-

From *The Sociological Imagination* by C. Wright Mills. Copyright © 1959 by Oxford University Press, Inc. Reprinted by permission.

country settlements and pressure groups and boys' gangs and Navajo oil men; air forces pointed to demolish metropolitan areas a hundred miles wide; policemen on a corner; intimate circles and publics seated in a room; criminal syndicates; masses thronged one night at the crossroads and squares of the cities of the world; Hopi children and slave dealers in Arabia and German parties and Polish classes and Mennonite schools and the mentally deranged in Tibet and radio networks reaching around the world. Racial stocks and ethnic groups are jumbled up in movie houses and also segregated; married happily and also hating systematically; a thousand detailed occupations are seated in businesses and industries, in governments and localities, in near-continent-wide nations. A million little bargains are transacted every day, and everywhere there are more 'small groups' than anyone could ever count.

The human variety also includes the variety of individual human beings; these too the sociological imagination must grasp and understand. In this imagination an Indian Brahmin of 1850 stands alongside a pioneer farmer of Illinois; an eighteenth-century English gentleman alongside an Australian aboriginal, together with a Chinese peasant of one hundred years ago, a politician in Bolivia today, a feudal knight of France, an English suffragette on hunger strike in 1914, a Hollywood starlet, a Roman patrician. To write of 'man' is to write of all these men and women—also of Goethe, and of the girl next door.

The social scientist seeks to understand the human variety in an orderly way, but considering the range and depth of this variety, he might well be asked: Is this really possible? Is not the confusion of the social sciences an inevitable reflection of what their practitioners are trying to study? My answer is that perhaps the variety is not as 'disorderly' as the mere listing of a small part of it makes it seem; perhaps not even as disorderly as it is often made to seem by the courses of study offered in colleges and universities. Order as well as disorder is relative to viewpoint: to come to an orderly understanding of men and societies requires a set of viewpoints that are simple enough to make understanding possible, yet comprehensive enough to permit us to include in our views the range and depth of the human variety. The struggle for such viewpoints is the first and continuing struggle of social science.

Any viewpoint, of course, rests upon a set of questions, and the over-all questions of the social sciences . . . come readily to the mind that has firm hold of the orienting conception of social science as the study of biography, of history, and of the problems of their intersection within social structure. To study these problems, to realize the human variety, requires that our work be continuously and closely related to the level of historical reality—and to the meanings of this reality for individual men and women. Our aim is to define this reality and to discern these meanings; it is in terms of them that the problems of classic social science are formulated, and thus the issues and troubles these problems incorporate are confronted. It requires that we seek a fully comparative understanding of the social structures that have appeared and do now exist in world history. It requires that smaller-scale milieux be selected and studied in terms of larger-scale historical structures. It requires that we avoid the arbitrary specialization of academic departments, that we specialize our work variously according to topic and above all according to problem, and that in doing so we draw upon the perspectives and ideas, the materials and the methods, of any and all suitable studies of man as an historical actor.

Historically, social scientists have paid most attention to political and economic institutions, but military and kinship, religious and educational institutions have also been much studied. Such classification according to the objective functions institutions generally serve is deceptively simple, but still it is handy. If we understand how these institutional orders are related to one another, we understand the social structure of a society. For 'social structure,' as the conception is most commonly used, refers to just that—to the combination of institutions classified according to the functions each performs. As such, it is the most inclusive working unit with which social scientists deal. Their broadest aim, accordingly, is to understand each of the varieties of social structure, in its components and in its totality. The term 'social structure' itself is quite variously defined, and other terms are used for the conception, but if the distinction between milieu and structure is kept in mind, along with the notion of institution, no one will fail to recognize the idea of social structure when he comes upon it.

II

In our period, social structures are usually organized under a political state. In terms of power, and in many other interesting terms as well, the most inclusive unit of social structure is the nation-state. The nation-state is now the dominating form in world history and, as such, a major fact in the life of every man. The nation-state has split up and organized, in varying degree and manner, the 'civilizations' and continents of the world. The extent of its spread and the stages of its development are major clues to modern and now to world history. Within the nation-state, the political and military, cultural and economic means of decision and power are now organized; all the institutions and specific milieux in which most men live their public and private lives are now organized into one or the other of the nation-states.

Social scientists of course do not always study only national social structures. The point is that the nation-state is the frame within which they most often feel the need to formulate the problems of smaller and of larger units. Other 'units' are most readily understood as 'pre-national'—or as 'post-national.' For of course national units may 'belong' to one of the 'civilizations,' which usually means that their religious institutions are those of one or another of the 'world religions.' Such facts of 'civilization,' as well as many others, may suggest ways to compare the present-day variety of nation-states. But as used for example by writers like Arnold Toynbee, 'civilizations,' it seems to me, are much too sprawling and imprecise to be the prime units, the 'intelligible fields of study,' of the social sciences.

In choosing the national social structure as our generic working unit, we are adopting a suitable level of generality: one that enables us to avoid abandoning our problems and yet to include the structural forces obviously involved in many details and troubles of human conduct today. Moreover, the choice of national social structures enables us most readily to take up the major issues of public concern, for it is within and between the nation-states of the world that the effective means of power, and hence to a considerable extent of history-making, are now, for better or for worse, tightly organized.

It is of course true that not all nation-states are equal in their power to make history. Some are so small and dependent upon others that what happens within them can only be understood by studying The Great Power States. But that is merely another problem in the useful classification of our units—the nations—and in their necessarily comparative study. It is also true that all nation-states interact, and some clusters of them derive from similar contexts of tradition. But that is true of any sizable unit we might choose for social study. Moreover, especially since World War One, every nation-state capable of it has become increasingly self-sufficient.

Most economists and political scientists consider it obvious that their prime unit is the nation-state; even when they are concerned with 'the international economy' and 'international relations,' they must work closely in the terms of various and specific nation-states. The condition and the continuing practice of anthropologists are of course to study 'the whole' of a society or 'culture,' and in so far as they study modern societies they readily attempt, with varying success, to understand nations as wholes. But sociologists—or more exactly, research technicians—who do not have a very firm hold on the conception of social structure, often consider nations dubiously grand in scale. Apparently this is owing to a bias in favor of 'data collection' which can be less expensively indulged only in smaller-scale units. This means of course that their choice of units is not in accordance with what is needed for whatever problems they have chosen; instead both problem and unit are determined by their choice of method.

In a sense, this book as a whole is an argument against this bias. I think that when most social scientists come seriously to examine a significant problem, they find it most difficult to formulate in terms of any unit smaller than the nation-state. This is true for the study of stratification and of economic policy, of public opinion and the nature of political power, of work and leisure; even problems of municipal government cannot be adequately formulated without quite full reference to their national frame. The unit of the nation-state thus recommends itself by a good deal of empirical evidence available to anyone who is experienced in working on the problems of social science.

III

The idea of social structure, along with the contention that it is the generic unit of social science, is historically most closely associated with sociology, and sociologists have been its classical exponents. The traditional subject matter of both sociology and anthropology has been the total society; or, as it is called by anthropologists, 'the culture.' What is specifically 'sociological' in the study of any particular feature of a total society is the continual effort to relate that feature to others, in order to gain a conception of the whole. The sociological imagination, I have noted, is in considerable part a result of training in this kind of effort. But nowadays such a view and such practice is by no means confined to sociologists and anthropologists. What was once a promise in these disciplines has become at least a faltering practice, as well as an intention, in the social sciences generally.

Cultural anthropology, in its classic tradition and in its current developments, does not seem to me in any fundamental way distinguishable from sociological study. Once upon a time, when there were few or no surveys of contemporary societies, anthropologists had to collect materials about preliterate peoples in out-of-the-way places. Other social sciences—notably history, demography and political science—have from their beginnings depended upon documentary materials accumulated in literate societies. And this fact tended to separate the disciplines. But now 'empirical surveys' of various sorts are used in all the social sciences, in fact the technique has been most fully developed by psychologists and sociologists in connection with historical societies. In recent years, too, anthropologists have of course studied advanced communities and even nation-states, often at a considerable distance; in turn, sociologists and economists have studied 'the undeveloped peoples.' There is neither a distinction in method nor a boundary of subject matter that truly distinguishes anthropology from economics and sociology today.

Most economics and political science has been concerned with special institutional areas of social structure. About the 'economy' and about 'the state,' political scientists to a lesser extent, and economists to a greater, have developed 'classic theories' that have persisted for generations of scholars. They have, in short, built models, although the political scientists (along with the sociologists) have traditionally been less aware of their model building than the economists have been. Classical theory, of course, consists of making up conceptions and assumptions, from which deductions and generalizations are drawn; these in turn are compared with a variety of empirical propositions. In these tasks, conceptions and procedures and even questions are at least implicitly codified.

This may be all very well. However, for economics certainly and for political science and sociology in due course, two developments tend to make less relevant formal models of state and economy having neat, which is to say formal—and largely mutually exclusive —boundaries: (1) the economic and political development of the so-called underdeveloped areas, and (2) trends of twentieth-century forms of 'the political economy'—both totalitarian and formally democratic. The aftermath of World War Two has been at once erosive and fructifying for alert economic

theorists, in fact, for all social scientists worthy of the title.

A 'theory of prices' that is merely economic may be logically neat, but it cannot be empirically adequate. Such a theory demands consideration of the administration of business institutions and the role of decision-makers within and between them; it requires attention to the psychology of expectations about costs, in particular about wages; to the fixing of prices by small business cartels whose leaders must be understood, etc. In a similar way, to understand 'the rate of interest' often requires knowledge of the official and personal traffic between bankers and government officials as well as impersonal economic mechanics.

There is nothing for it, I think, but for each social scientist to join social science, and with it to go fully comparative—and that, I believe, is now a quite strong drift of interest. Comparative work, both theoretical and empirical, is the most promising line of development for social science today; and such work can best be done within a unified social science.

2

The Art of Social Science [1]

ROBERT REDFIELD

A dozen years ago I was a member of a committee of social scientists on social

Reprinted from *The American Journal of Sociology* 54 (November, 1948), pp. 181–190, by permission of the University of Chicago Press. Copyright 1948 by the University of Chicago Press. All rights reserved.
[1] A lecture delivered at the University of Chicago in May, 1948.

science method charged to appraise some outstanding published works of social science research. Our task was to find some good publications of social science research and then to discover in what their methodological virtue consisted. The first part of our task we passed on to the communities of social scientists themselves. We asked economists to name some outstanding work in their field, sociologists to pick a work in sociology, etc. We limited the choice to publications by living social scientists. Of the books or monographs that received the greatest number of nominations, three were then subjected to analysis and discussion. I participated in the study of the methodological virtues of *The Polish Peasant* by Thomas and Znaniecki and of Webb's *The Great Plains*. These were books nominated by sociologists and historians, respectively, as outstanding in merit.

A curious thing happened. Herbert Blumer, who analyzed *The Polish Peasant* for the committee, came to the conclusion that the method in that book was really unsuccessful because the general propositions set forth in the work could not be established by the particular facts adduced. The committee had to agree. Yet it remained with the impression that this was a very distinguished and important work. Webb's history of cultural transformation in the American West fared no better at the hands of the young historian who analyzed that work. He pointed out many undeniable failures of the author of *The Great Plains* to use and to interpret fully some of the evidence. And yet again a majority of the committee persisted in the impression that Webb's book was truly stimulating, original, and praiseworthy.

Of course one does not conclude from this experience that the failure of facts to support hypotheses, in whole or in part, is a virtue in social science or is to be recommended. No doubt these books would have been more highly praised had these defects been proved to be absent. But does not the experience suggest that there is something in social science which is good, perhaps essential, apart from success with formal method; that these works have virtues not wholly dependent on the

degree of success demonstrated in performing specified and formalized operations on restricted and precisely identified data?

I recall a comment I heard made by a distinguished social scientist whom I shall call A, about another distinguished social scientist whom I shall call B. A said of B: "He is very successful in spite of his method." Now, A was one who laid great stress on the obedience of the research worker to precise methods of operation with limited data, whereas B was much less so concerned. Yet A admired B, and the success he recognized in B was not worldly success but success in advancing our understanding and our control of man in society. Perhaps A felt that B's success was troubling to A's own views as to the importance of formal method. But A, a generous and able man, recognized something of virtue in B as a great student of man in society—a something other than methodological excellence.

What is that something? In attempting an answer here, I do not propose a separation between two ways of working in the scientific study of society. Nor do I deny that social science is dependent upon formal method. I seek rather to direct attention to an aspect of fruitful work in social science which is called for, in addition to formal method, if social science is to be most productive.

Let us here try to find out something about the nature of this non-formal aspect of social science through a consideration of three books about society that have long been recognized as important, influential, and meritorious: De Tocqueville's *Democracy in America*, Sumner's *Folkways*, and Veblen's *The Theory of the Leisure Class*. For from almost fifty to a hundred years these books have interested and have influenced many kinds of social scientists. Veblen and Sumner were economists, but the books they wrote are important for sociologists, anthropologists, historians, and other kinds of social scientists. De Tocqueville's book is a work interesting to political scientists as well as to historians of America, but it is quite as much a work in sociology, for De Tocqueville was concerned not so much in reporting what went on in the United States in 1830 as he was defining a sort of natural societal type: the democratic society, including in the type not merely its political institutions but also its moral, familial, and "cultural" institutions and attitudes, treated as a single whole.

None of these books tells very much about research method, in the sense of teaching special procedures of operation with certain kinds of data. There is nothing in any of them about kinship genealogies, or sampling, or guided interviews, or margins of error. There is nowhere in them any procedure, any kind of operation upon facts to reach conclusions which might not occur to any intelligent and generally educated person. Sumner made notes on the customs of exotic peoples as he read about them. Veblen's methods, as represented in *The Theory of the Leisure Class*, are no more formal than Sumner's. The factual substance of De Tocqueville's book is the record of his own observations as he traveled about America looking at what there was about him and talking to the people he met. If these books have merit, it is not by reason of any inventions or devices of method, for they exhibit none. Yet these are books which have for many years profoundly affected the course of social science and have contributed to our understanding of man in society. They might be even more important if they also made contributions to or through formal method, but, as they do not, something may be learned from them about that part of the study of society which is not formal method.

Perhaps these are not works of research. Perhaps for some "research" always means special procedures of operation which have to be learned or means analysis of some small set of facts or very limited problem. If this is your view of research, I shall not dispute it. Then the three books are not works of research. But what is there in them that is admired and that is valuable in the study of man in society that is not dependent upon formal method?

If these three classic books are not books in social science, what are they? They are surely not novels, or journalism, or yet belles-lettres. That they have qualities of literary style is true—and is not to be deplored—even Sumner's book impresses with the effective iteration of its terse, stark sentences. But the value of these books for the student of society lies not in any appeal they make to aesthetic sensibilities but for the illumination they throw upon man's nature or upon the nature of society. It is true that great novels do that too. But there are, of course, important differences between the books named, on the one hand, and, let us say, *War and Peace* and *The Remembrance of Things Past*, on the other. These last are works for social scientists to know about and to learn from, but they are not works of social science. They are not because neither Proust's book nor Tolstoi's is a generalized description of the nature of society stated at some remove from the personal experiences of the writer. De Tocqueville made his own observations, but he stated his results objectively in generalized and analytical terms making comparisons with other observations and conclusions easy. Tolstoi wrote about a real Russia during the real Napoleonic Wars, but his Pierres and Natashas are imagined, individual, personal, intimate, and ungeneralized. It is not difficult to distinguish the great analyses of society, as objectively studied and presented in generalized conclusions, from the works of personal record and of freely creative imagination.

Are the three books "objective" descriptions of society? In varying degree, but all three to some degree. Probably De Tocqueville, who of the three writers was least a professional social scientist, impresses one most with an air of severe detachment, of willingness to look at this social being, a democratic society, without blame or praise. De Tocqueville's work seems as objective as a social scientist might wish. Sumner, too, is describing, not evaluating, yet there is in the *Folkways* an undertone of patient scorn for the irrationality of man, for man's obedience to whatever folly his tradition may decree. Veblen seems the least objective. Below the forms of scientific analysis lies, urbanely and ironically disguised, the condemnation of a moralist. As a recent writer on Veblen has put it, he used "the realistic paraphernalia of scholarship" to attack the morality of capitalistic society.[2] Nevertheless, even Veblen's books presents a fresh description of a part of modern society, and the description is not that of a creative artist but of one who is responsible to facts studied and facts verifiable.

The three books are works which are not novels, which do not have much to say about formal procedures of research, and which, nevertheless, throw light upon man in society through the more or less objective presentation of generalized conclusions from the study of particular societies. In these respects they correspond with what is by at least some people called "scientific." What did the authors do that constitutes their contribution to the understanding of man in society?

It is surely not that these writers

[2] Daniel Aaron, "Thorstein Veblen—Moralist," *Antioch Review*, VII, No. 3 (Fall, 1947), 390.

have been proved to be invariably right. Indeed, in each case there are points in which in the later days they have been found wrong. Veblen's account overemphasizes competitiveness in terms of consumption and accepts a good deal of what was then current as to race and as to stages of social evolution which is now inacceptable today. Sumner's conception of the mores, immensely stimulating as it was, exaggerates the helplessness of men before tradition and is especially inadequate as a concept for understanding modern societies—as Myrdal has recently shown. And, although De Tocqueville's account of early American society is perceptive and revealing to a degree that is almost miraculous, there is certainly confusion in it between what is necessarily democratic and what is characteristic of the frontier and between what must be characteristic of any democracy and what happened to be in the Anglo-American tradition.

In three respects these books, which have nothing to teach about formal method, make great contributions to the understanding of man in society.

In the first place, each is an expression of some perception of human nature. In each case the writer has looked at people in a society, or in many societies, and has directly apprehended something about their ways of thinking and feeling which are characteristic of the human race under those particular circumstances. His central concern has not been some second- or third-hand index or sign of human nature, some check marks on a schedule or some numbered quantities of anything. He has looked at people with the vision of his own humanity.

Not all of what is called social science is concerned with human nature. The study of population is not concerned with it until matters of population policy are reached. Marginal analysis in economics is concerned with such a slender sliver of human nature, so artificially severed from the rest, that it, too, is unrepresentative of studies of human nature. And this is also of necessity true of much of the archeology of the North American Indian.

These last-mentioned kinds of investigation, worthy as they are, are the special or marginal cases that mark the outskirts of the study of man in society. The essential nature of man in society is his human nature and the expressions of that human nature in particular institutions. To find out the nature and significance of human nature there is no substitute for the human nature of the student himself. He must use his own humanity to understand humanity. To understand alien institutions, he must try to see in them the correspondences and the divergences they exhibit in relation to the institutions with which he is more closely familiar. To understand an alien culture, it is not, first of all, necessary to learn how to interview or how to make schedules for a house-to-house canvass, useful as these skills are. It is first needful to have experienced some culture—some culture which will serve as the touchstone in apprehending this new one.

One aspect of the great merit of the three works mentioned lies in the central attention directed by Sumner, Veblen, and De Tocqueville to the humanity of their subject matter and in the success each had in apprehending the particular facet of that humanity as it was shaped and conditioned by the surrounding circumstances. Sumner, looking especially at small, long-isolated societies or at the later little-changing societies derived from primitive conditions, saw the resulting creation, in each individual there born and reared, of motives and designs of life that were there, in the customs of that society, before him. He saw in human nature the extraordinary malleability of human nature and the precedence of custom over habit. Veblen looked freshly at the behavior of consumers, saw them as people who actually do buy and consume, in their families and their communities, and recognized theretofore insufficiently recognized aspects of human nature in society. De Tocqueville touched Americans in their age of self-confidence and in a great number of true perceptions saw what their behavior meant to them and why. Just compare his success in using his own humanity with imagination, and yet with detachment, with Mrs. Trollope's failure to achieve understanding of these same people.

It is at this point that the methods of the social sciences—now using "method" in its broadest sense to include all the ways of thinking and even feeling about subject matter—approach the methods of the creative artist. Like the novelist, the scientific student of society must project the sympathetic understanding which he has of people with motives, desires, and moral judgments into the subject he is treating. Neither the one nor the other can get along without this gift, this means of understanding. But whereas the novelist may let his imagination run freely, once it is stimulated by personal experience and reading, the scientific student must constantly return to the particular men, the particular societies, he has chosen to investigate, test his insights by these, and report these particular facts with such specificity that his successor may repeat the testing. In spite of this all-important difference, the territories of the humanities and of the scientific study of man in society are in part the same. The subject matter of both is, centrally, man as a human being. Human beings are not the subject matter of physics and chemistry. So it would be error to build a social science upon the image of physics or chemistry. Social science is neither the same as the humanities nor the same as the physical sciences. It is a way of learning about man in society which uses the precise procedures and the objectivity characteristic of physics as far as these will helpfully go in studying human beings but no further; and which uses, indispensably, that personal direct apprehension of the human qualities of behavior and of institutions which is shared by the novelist.

A second observation may be made about the three books chosen. Each brings forward significant generalizations. In the case of Veblen's book, the general conceptions that are known by the phrases "pecuniary emulation," "vicarious consumption," etc., are, like the concepts in *Folkways*, names for new insights into persistent and widely inclusive aspects of man's nature in society. In reading these books, we catch a glimpse of the eternal in the light of the ephemeral. We see ourselves as exemplifications of patterns in nature. Social science is concerned with uniformities. The uniformities are exaggerated; they transcend the particularity of real experience and historic event; they claim more than each fact by itself would allow; they say: "If it were really like this, this would be the pattern." De Tocqueville, too, offers such patterns that go beyond the particular facts. Indeed, the case of De Tocqueville is particularly plain in this connection, for so interested is he in presenting a system of coherent generalizations as to the necessary nature of democratic society that in many passages he makes no reference at all to what he saw in the United States but derives one generalization as to the democratic society he conceives from some other generalization already brought forward. He is not, therefore, to be rejected as a contributor to the scientific understanding of society, for these deductions are tied to generalizations that in turn rest upon many particular observations of many particular men and events. The concept, like the novel, is a work of creative imagination but a work more closely and publicly bound to particular facts of observation and record.

Like the apprehension of the humanly significant, the making of the generalization is a work of imagination. Sumner did not find out that there is such a thing as the mores by learning and applying some method of research. He discovered it by watching the people around him and by using the observations recorded by other men and then by making a leap of thought across many diversities to apprehend the degree of uniformity that deserves the term "mores." In the reaching of a significant generalization as to man in society there is an exercise of a gift of apprehension so personal and so subtly creative that it cannot be expected to result merely from application of some formal method of research.

The three books show thinkers about man in society who have had some new and generalized apprehension of human nature or of human institutions. They have succeeded in communicating this apprehension in such a way as to show it to be both important and true. It is true in the sense that there are facts accessible that support it. It is not, of course, all the truth, and it may be that some other apprehension will come to appear "more true," that is, even more illuminating, as applied to some set of circumstances.

There is another quality in the thinking and the creating of the three writers that deserves recognition by itself: the freshness and independence of viewpoint with which each looked at his subject matter. One feels, in reading any one of the three books, how the writer saw what he saw with his own eyes, as if the previous views of it were suspect, just because they were previous. One feels in the case of each writer a discontent with the way some aspect of man in society was then being regarded, a clear-headed wilfulness to take another look for himself. There is a disposition to make the thing looked at a true part of the viewer's own being, to go beyond obedience to the existing writings on the subject. De Tocqueville was dissatisfied with the views of democracy current in his time: the passionate condemnations or the equally passionate espousals. He would go to the country where the angel or the monster was actually in course of development, and he would, he resolved coolly, look for neither monster nor angel; he would look at what he should find, and grasp it, in its whole and natural condition, as one would look at a newly arrived class of animal. He could weigh the good and the bad, then, after he had come to understand the natural circumstances that would produce the creature. Sumner's book is in one way a reaffirmation of a viewpoint then current and in another way a reaction against it. As the folkways come about by no man's planning but through the accidental interactions of men and the competition of alternative solutions, they are consistent with that conception of unrestrained individualistic competition which Sumner supported in the economic sphere. On the other hand, the *Folkways* reads as a reaction against the Age of Reason. It seems to say that men do not, after all, solve their problems by rational calculation of utilities. Looked at anew, the ways of men appear not reasonable but unreasonable and determined by pre-existing customs and moral judgments which make the calculation of utilities seem absurd. From this point of view the book is an act of rebellion. An economist looks for himself at the whole human scene and says, too emphatically, no doubt, what needs to be said to correct the preceding vision. Something not so different could be

said about the fresh look that Veblen took.

It may be objected that the qualities in these three works are qualities one may expect to find only in an occasional book written by some unusual mind. These books have passed beyond social science, or they fall short of it; and the humbler toiler in the vineyard cannot expect to learn from them anything that would help him in tending the vines of his more limited hypotheses or in pressing the wine of his more restricted conclusions.

Yet all three of the qualities found in these works may be emulated by the student of any human aspect of man in society. It is not only in good major works that there is found that human sympathy which is needful in apprehending a human reality. The exercise of this capacity is demanded in every study of a community; it is exacted in every consideration of an institution in which men with motives and desires like our own fulfil the roles and offices that make it up; it is required in every interview. One may be taught how to pursue a course of questioning, how to map a neighborhood, or how to tabulate and treat statistically the votes cast in an election; but to know how to do these things is not to be assured of meaningful conclusions. Besides these skills, one needs also the ability to enter imaginatively, boldly, and, at the same time, self-critically into that little fraction of the human comedy with which one has become scientifically concerned. One must become a part of the human relations one studies, while holding one's self also a little to one side, so as to suspend judgment as to the worth of one's first insight. Then one looks at the scene again; perhaps, guided by something one has known or read of human beings in some comparable situation, in some other place or age, one may get a second insight that better withstands reexamination and the test of particular observations. This procedure, call it method, non-method, or what you will, is an essential part of most of social science, great and small.

As for the exercise of the ability to see the general in the particular, is this not also demanded of anyone who takes a scientific attitude toward anything in human nature or society? We are not freed from the obligation to look for what may be widely true by the narrowness, in time and space, of the facts before us. Surely Sumner did not wait to conceive of the mores until he had piled up those five hundred pages of examples. Malinowski provided a clearer understanding of the nature of myth, in its resemblance to and its difference from folk tale, from the view he had of the stories told and the ways they were told in a small community in the South Seas. Webb, a historian rather than one of those students of society who more easily announce generalizations thought to be widely applicable, does not, in his *The Great Plains*, announce any; but the value of the work lies for many in the fact that it is easily read as an exemplification of the tendency of institutions adjusted to one environment to undergo change when imported into a new and of the effects of changes in technology upon human relations. The social scientist is always called upon to use his imagination as to the general that may lie within the immediate particulars. The formal method may lead him to these generalizations; after he has added up the cases, or completed the tests, he may for the first time see some correspondences that suggest a generalization. But it happens at least as often that he sees the generalization long before the formal methods have been carried out; the exercise of the formal method may then test the worth of his insight. And a significant generalization may appear without formal

method. The conceptions of marginal utility in economics and of the marginal man in sociology perhaps illustrate the development of a concept, on the one hand, with close dependence upon formal method and, on the other, without such dependence. In the latter case Park was struck by resemblances in the conduct of particular men and women whom he met, American Negroes, mission-educated Orientals, and second-generation immigrants: humane insight, guided by scientific imagination, then created the concept.

The third quality of good social science in its less formal aspects is freshness of vision. It is the looking at what one is studying as if the world's comprehension of it depended solely on one's own look. In taking such a look, one does not ignore the views that other men have taken of the subject matter or of similar subject matter. But these earlier views are challenged. Maybe, one says, it is not as my teachers told me I should find it. I will look for myself. One has perhaps heard something about folk society. But at this particular society with which I am concerned I will look for myself. Perhaps there is no folk society there. Perhaps there is something else, much nearer the truth.

It is difficult for teachers who have expounded their own views of some aspect of man in society to teach their successors to take some other view of it. Perhaps it cannot be taught. Yet somehow each generation of social scientists must rear a following generation of rebels. Now rebellion is not well inculated in the teaching of formal procedure. Indeed, an exclusive emphasis on formal procedure may cause atrophy of the scientific imagination. To train a man to perform a technique may result in making him satisfied with mastery of the technique. Having learned so much about field procedure, or statistics, or the situations in which interviews are held and recorded, or the criticism of documents, the new social scientist may come to feel that he has accomplished all the learning he needs. He may rest content in proficiency. Proficiency is excellent, but it must be combined with an imaginative dissatisfaction. In little investigations as in large ones, the situation studied demands a whole look and a free look.

It is equally doubtful whether one can give instruction in the exercise of humane insight or in recognizing the general in the particular when the generality is not thrust upon the student by a marked statistical predominance. These are qualities of the social science investigator that perhaps depend upon the accidents of natural endowment. Humane insight is a gift. The concept is a work of creative imagination; apprehension is a gift. In stressing the necessity, in good social science, for the investigator to think and to speculate independently and freely, in emphasizing the reliance of good social science upon the personal and human qualities of the investigator, one seems to be talking not about a science but about an art and to be saying that social science is also an art. It is an art in that the social scientist creates imaginatively out of his own human qualities brought into connection with the facts before him. It is an art in degree much greater than that in which physics and chemistry are arts, for the student of the atom or of the element is not required, when he confronts his subject matter, to become a person among persons, a creature of tradition and attitude in a community that exists in tradition and in attitude. With half his being the social scientist approaches his subject matter with a detachment he shares with the physicist. With the other half he approaches it with a human sympathy which he shares with the novelist. And it is an

art to a greater degree than is physics or chemistry for the further reason that the relationships among the parts of a person or of a society are, as compared with physical relationships, much less susceptible of definitions, clear and machine precise. In spite of the great advances in formal method in social science, much of the understanding of persisting and general relationships depends upon a grasp that is intuitive and that is independent of or not fully dependent on some formal method. In advancing social science, we invent and practice techniques, and we also cultivate a humanistic art.

The nature of social science is double. In the circle of learning, its place adjoins the natural sciences, on the one hand, and the humanities, on the other. It is not a result of exceptional political ambition that political scientists and anthropologists are to be found included both in the Social Science Research Council and in the American Council of Learned Societies; it is a recognition of the double nature of social science. On the one hand, the student of society is called upon to apprehend the significant general characteristics of human beings with something of the same human insight which is practiced by a novelist or a dramatist. On the other hand, he is obliged to make his observations and his inferences as precise and as testable, and his generalizations as explicit and as compendent, as the examples of the natural sciences suggest and as his own different materials allow.

It is the example of the natural sciences which social scientists have on the whole striven to imitate. In the short history of social science its practitioners have turned their admiring gazes toward their neighbors on the scientific side. They have looked that way, perhaps, because the natural sciences were the current success. They have looked that way, surely, because when the students of human nature in society came to think of themselves as representing one or more disciplines, with professors and places in universities and in national councils, social science was not very scientific: it was speculative and imprecise. To achieve identity, it had to grow away from the making of personally conceived systems of abstract thought. It had to learn to build, a brick at a time, and to develop procedures that would make the building public and subject to testing.

But now the invention and the teaching of special procedures have received too exclusive an emphasis in the doing of social science and in the making of social scientists. In places the invention and the teaching of special procedures have gone ahead of the possibility of finding out anything very significant with their aid. It is certainly desirable to be precise, but it is quite as needful to be precise about something worth knowing. It is good to teach men and women who are to be social scientists how to use the instruments of observation and analysis that have been developed in their disciplines. But it is not good to neglect that other equally important side of social science.

To identify social science very closely with the physical sciences is to take one view of the education of social scientists: to think of that education chiefly in terms of formal method and formal knowledge of society already achieved and to be taught. Then programs for making social scientists will be made up of training in techniques and the opportunity to take part in some kind of research in which the procedures are already determined and the problems set by some established master. Then the holder of a fellowship will go to a school, where a way of working is well known and well fixed, and he will acquire the procedural competences taught at that school.

If this is all we do for young students of society, we are likely to have proficient technicians, but we are not likely to have great social scientists or to have many books written that are as illuminating and as influential as those by Sumner, Veblen, and De Tocqueville.

It would be well to give some attention to the humanistic aspect of social science. Part of the preparation of good social scientists is humanistic education. As what is called general education, or liberal education, is largely humanistic, it follows that the social scientist has two interests in liberal education. Like the physicist, like everybody else, the social scientist needs liberal education in his role as a citizen. But, in addition, he needs liberal humanistic education in his role as a social scientist.

The art of social science cannot be inculcated, but, like other arts, it can be encouraged to develop. The exercise of that art can be favored by humanistic education. If the social scientist is to apprehend, deeply and widely and correctly, persons and societies and cultures, then he needs experience, direct or vicarious, with persons, societies, and cultures. This experience is partly had through acquaintance with history, literature, biography, and ethnography. And if philosophy gives some experience in the art of formulating and in thinking about widely inclusive generalizations, then the social scientist needs acquaintance with philosophy. There is no longer any need to be fearful about philosophy. The time when young social science was struggling to make itself something different from philosophy is past. Now social science is something different. Now social scientists need to learn from philosophy, not to become philosophers, but to become better social scientists. The acquaintance with literature, biography, ethnography, and philosophy which is gained in that general education given in high schools and colleges is probably not rich enough or deep enough for some of those who are to become social scientists. The opportunities for advanced education given to some who appear to have exceptional gifts as students of man in society may well consist of the study of Chinese or East Indian culture, or of the novel in Western literature, or of the history of democracy.

The humanistic aspect of social science is the aspect of it that is today not well appreciated. Social science is essentially scientific in that its propositions describe, in general terms, natural phenomena; in that it returns again and again to special experience to verify and to modify these propositions. It tells what is, not what ought to be. It investigates nature. It strives for objectivity, accuracy, compendency. It employs hypotheses and formal evidence; it values negative cases; and, when it finds a hypothesis to be unsupported by the facts, it drops it for some other which is. But these are all aspects of social science so well known that it is tedious to list them again. What is less familiar, but equally true, is that to create the hypothesis, to reach the conclusion, to get, often, the very first real datum as to what are A's motives or what is the meaning of this odd custom or that too-familiar institution, requires on the part of one who studies persons and societies, and not rocks or proteins, a truly humanistic and freely imaginative insight into people, their conventions and interests and motives, and that this requirement in the social scientist calls for gifts and for a kind of education different from that required of any physicist and very similar to what is called for in a creative artist.

If this be seen, it may also be seen that the function of social science in our society is a double function. Social science is customarily explained and justified by reason of what social science contributes to the solution of particular problems that arise in the management of our society, as a help in getting particular things done. As social scientists we take satisfaction in the fact that today, as compared with thirty years ago, social scientists are employed because their employers think that their social science is applicable to some practical necessity. Some knowledge of techniques developed in social science may be used: to select taxicab drivers that are not likely to have accidents; to give vocational guidance; to discover why one business enterprise has labor troubles while a similar enterprise does not; to make more effective some governmental program carried into farming communities; to help the War Relocation Authority carry out its difficult task with Japanese-Americans.

All these contributions to efficiency and adjustment may be claimed with justice by social scientists. What is also to be claimed, and is less commonly stressed, is that social science contributes to that general understanding of the world around us which, as we say, "liberalizes," or "enriches." The relation of social science to humanistic learning is reciprocal. Social scientists need humanistic learning the better to be social scientists. And the understanding of society, personality, and human nature which is achieved by scientific methods returns to enrich that humanistic understanding without which none can become human and with which some few may become wise. Because its subject matter is humanity, the contribution of social science to general, liberal education is greater than is the contribution of those sciences with subject matter that is physical. In this respect also, creative artist and social scientist find themselves side by side. The artist may reveal something of universal human or social nature. So too may the social scientist. No one has ever applied, as a key to a lock, Sumner's *Folkways* or Tawney's *Religion and the Rise of Capitalism* or James's *The Varieties of Religious Experience*. These are not the works of social science that can be directly consulted and applied when a government office or a business concern has an immediate problem. But they are the books of lasting influence. Besides what influence they have upon those social scientists who come to work in the government office, or the business concern, in so far as they are read and understood and thought about by men and women who are not social scientists, or even as they are communicated indirectly by those who have read them to others, they are part of humanistic education, in the broad sense. Releasing us from our imprisonment in the particular, we are freed by seeing how we are exemplifications of the general. For how many young people has not Sumner's book, or Veblen's book, or some work by Freud, come as a swift widening of the doors of vision, truly a liberation, a seeing of one's self, perhaps for the first time, as sharing the experiences, the nature, of many other men and women? So I say that social science, as practiced, is something of an art and that, as its best works are communicated, it has something of the personal and social values of all the arts.

Part One

Basic Concepts and Perspectives of Sociology

INTRODUCTION

Much of contemporary social science developed in reaction against conclusions about the nature of man and society advanced by the first post-Darwinian thinkers. Darwin showed that man's bodily structure was continuous with that of subhuman species and had evolved in accordance with the same laws. A host of philosophers, psychologists, sociologists, and natural scientists concluded that if man is an animal like other animals, albeit a specially gifted one, then biological laws governing all other living things must also apply to human nature, history, and society. Accordingly, they espoused a variety of theories of biological determinism in which processes occurring in human societies were interpreted as reflections of similar processes occurring in the animal world.

The social Darwinists argued that human society itself was an arena of ruthless competition between individuals, groups, and entire peoples that conformed to the same principles of natural selection, or "survival of the fittest," that Darwin had seen as the explanation for the evolution of different species. The unilinear evolutionists maintained that human societies, like the various species, develop through a series of stages, from simple to more complex organization. The eugenics movement insisted that man's heredity determined his behavior and that criminal behavior, creativity, and character were the result of differing heredities. Racial theorists extended this assumption to the achievements of whole peoples, arguing that varying *group* heredities accounted for the diverse customs and institutions of mankind, just as the varying behavior of animal species reflected their different heredities. The school of instinct psychologists claimed that all human conduct was the manifestation of instincts that man had acquired long ago when he first emerged as a distinct species adapted to a primeval environment.

The assaults on all these ideas by twentieth-century social science—often inspired, as in the case of the doctrines of racial difference, by moral outrage over their social and political consequences—have recreated a view of the uniqueness of man almost as pronounced as that held by Darwin's original theological opponents, who believed that man was the specially created possessor of a soul and had little in common with his fellow living creatures. Recognizing that man's brain and nervous system are as much the products of biological evolution as the crab's shell or the bird's wing, social scientists have insisted that the learning capacity of the human brain has enabled man to dispense with inherited instincts as the dominant mode of adapting to his environment. Man's unique achievements stem from learning rather than from heredity. Conceptual thought and speech, made possible by a superior brain, have created a gulf between man and the rest of the animal world. Men are able to communicate what they have learned to their fellows and to later generations. In this way they create a variety of cultures, or collective ways of life, shared by different groups of men. Man and society both depend for growth and survival on the resourcefulness of cultural tradition, rather than on the "blind" process of natural selection and biological evolution. The historical cultures men have created are so diverse in origin and content and in the patterns of change they have undergone that they cannot be subsumed under any law of evolution that implies a sequence of fixed stages paralleling the stages of development through which the various living species have passed. In short, an emphasis on the *discontinuities* rather than the *continuities* between human life and the animal world has become characteristic of social thought in recent decades.

Attempts to define the essence of man, that is, what is uniquely human (the *differentia specifica* of man, as Aristotle put it), are very old, long antedating the controversy over Darwinism. The Greek philosophers called man the "rational animal" singling out *reason* as his distinctive gift. This emphasis on reason is reflected in the name given the human species: *Homo sapiens*, or man, the wise one. Speech too has long been regarded as a peculiarly human capacity, although it has usually been mistakenly treated as a mere consequence of man's prior ability to think and reason. Possession of conscience, a "sense of right and wrong," has also often been selected as defining the line between man and other animals. Some nineteenth-century thinkers saw man's ability to reshape his material environment with the aid of tools as his outstanding peculiarity and christened him *Homo faber:* man, the maker of things, a definition central to the Marxist tradition. William James considered self-consciousness, as opposed to mere consciousness, as a distinctively human mental attribute. Alfred Korzybski, the founder of semantics, has called man the "time-binding animal," the only organism who lives in simultaneous awareness of the past and the future as well as the present. Norman O. Brown characterizes man as the "neurotic animal" or the "repressed animal," the only creature who is so torn by emotional conflict that he almost literally drives himself mad.[1] A great many sociologists and anthropologists have considered man's creation and perpetuation of *culture,* a body of socially transmitted habits, beliefs, and sentiments, as the most important distinction between the human and the animal.

All these efforts to define the uniquely human contain a good deal of truth, nor are they mutually exclusive. Yet they are clearly partial in arbitrarily selecting a single feature of human conduct and failing to show how it is related to other traits that differentiate men and animals. In the present century trends within a number of intellectual disciplines, from metaphysics to experimental psychology and physical anthropology, have converged in pointing to the crucial significance of the human ability to create symbols as the source of most human behavior that is not duplicated by lower species. George Herbert Mead, an American

[1] Norman O. Brown, *Life Against Death* (Middletown, Conn.: Wesleyan University Press, 1970), pp. 3–10.

philosopher and social psychologist,[2] argued that mind, self, and society are all necessary consequences of man's possession of language, which is essentially a set of vocal symbols that name and represent the multitudinous aspects of lived experience. We have included a selection on the social origins of the self from his most influential book in Section B. The rationality so stressed by the early philosophers; man's selfhood, which enables him to get outside of his own skin and to respond to himself as an object; and his social nature, through which he relates himself to others in subtle and complex ways that have no counterparts in the animal world, all these, Mead insists, are results of symbolic communication. Man is, as Ernst Cassirer christened him in another selection reprinted here, the *animal symbolicum*—the symbolic animal.

In recent years there have been some signs in the social sciences of a renewed interest in man's animal nature. In part, this is no doubt attributable to general tendencies in contemporary history—the savagery of recent wars and revolutions, the increased preoccupation with sexuality as Victorian taboos are relaxed, and the primitivism and eulogy of the irrational in much modern art—that have made us more receptive to the idea that our animal heritage has by no means been transcended. In social thought, Freud has long been a partial counterinfluence to the belief that man's essence lies in his successful conquest of the limits his biology imposes on his behavior. In the biological sciences themselves, recent discoveries have modified older views of human evolution. New fossil finds of early human and hominoid forms, for example, have made obsolete the assumption that man's body evolved to the point where he became capable of symbolizing and of creating culture but then stopped evolving because his new cultural or "superorganic" mode of existence freed him from the pressures of natural selection. It now appears far more probable that skills in communicating, making and using tools, planning for the future, and living cooperatively in social groups gave their possessors adaptive advantages, with the result that the bodily structures supporting these skills were increasingly selected for survival. Upright posture, bipedalism, the development of the hand as a grasping organ, the specialization of the jaws and vocal cords for speech, a more complex brain, nonseasonal sexuality, greater infantile helplessness—all these organic traits that define man as a separate species can no longer be regarded simply as preconditions for culture and human social life, but they are themselves products of a process of natural selection that favored increasing reliance on culture. Man's cultural and social history, in other words, has shaped his biological history. These newer views of the relation between man's biological evolution and culture are summarized by Robert Endleman in our first selection.

If man's very culture-creating capacity is rooted in his body, in the kind of peculiar mammalian animal that he is, then it is unlikely that human nature is as variable or human society as malleable as social scientists have sometimes contended. Extreme versions of cultural relativism that regarded man as capable of creating an almost infinite variety of possible ways of life are less plausible today than several decades ago. The reaction against biological determinism in the social sciences has occasionally overshot its mark. It indeed succeeded in thoroughly refuting the extreme hereditarianism and the superficially be-

[2] The work of Mead that has most influenced sociologists is *Mind, Self and Society* (Chicago: University of Chicago Press, 1934).

guiling Darwinian analogies that dominated social thought from the middle of the nineteenth century until roughly the 1920's. But the critics of biological determinism did not address themselves to the issue of what limits man's biology sets to his historical variability; they were, perhaps inevitably, more concerned with asserting the reality of human variability against those who denied or minimized it. Because they have indisputably won their battle, today it is possible for social scientists to return to consideration of what is constant in human nature and universal in human society and what bearing man's animal heritage has on these.

Endleman discusses here the origins of language in the course of man's evolution as a species, while Cassirer traces the "slow and continuous process" of the growth of the individual mind's capacity to symbolize through speech. In addition to relating man's symbolizing capacities to the "Human Revolution" —the adoption by man's protohuman ancestors of a new hunting way of life on the savannahs of East Africa—Endleman also describes the emergence under these conditions of the basic human character structure identified by Freud. The sexual division of labor between male hunters and female child-raisers, the role of vocalization in play and in the mother-child relationship, the bearing of the long period of infantile dependence required for the development of a symbol and tool-making brain on adult psychosexual relations, the origins of repression in infantile helplessness and the emotionally overburdened tie to the parent are among the themes he develops. The interdependence between man's body and his psychic conflicts and their common origin in human evolution lead Endleman to question the utopian hopes of the Freudian Left, represented by Herbert Marcuse and Norman Brown, for the abolition of repression and the psychic liberation of mankind.[3]

Our readings in Section A deal with the biological and psychological origins of human nature and social life. While the authors are an anthropologisti-sociologist (Endleman) and a philosopher (Cassirer), they provide a general background to all of the social sciences. The readings in this section also introduce the student to the concept of culture, which is the generic term social scientists use to refer to everything men share as members of society as distinct from their biological heritage. Culture is man's social heritage and includes language, technology, the arts, and fundamental beliefs, as well as the patterns of social conduct with which sociologists are primarily concerned. The remaining sections in Part One deal with the basic concepts and approaches used by contemporary sociologists to describe and interpret the social world.

Sociology is a disciplined *perspective* on human social life. It is a way of examining the varied relations among people as we seek answers to questions that puzzle us about man and society. Some of these questions are of a *transhistorical* nature—that is, they are concerned with what all men and all societies have in common throughout time. Many of the questions to which we most urgently desire answers, however, are *historically specific*. They arise out of men's experiences living in particular historical epochs and types of

---

[3] See Brown, loc. cit.; and Herbert Marcuse, *Eros and Civilization* (Boston: Beacon Press, 1955). For a general discussion of the Freudian Left, see Paul A. Robinson, *The Freudian Left* (New York: Harper Colophon Books, 1969). One of the figures Robinson discusses is Géza Roheim, who is a major influence on Endleman and whose long out-of-print *The Origin and Function of Culture* has recently been reissued (Garden City, N.Y.: Doubleday Anchor Books, 1971).

society. We may want to know, for example, the origins of capitalism in modern Western history, the emerging pattern of race relations in twentieth-century America, the results of efforts to control population growth in countries where the death rate has rapidly declined, and the changing group interests that shape the programs of political parties.

The sociological perspective includes a set of *basic concepts* which sociologists employ in their inquiries. These concepts serve as lenses through which they examine the social world and try to understand it. The readings reprinted in Sections B, C, and D explain and illustrate the following basic concepts: *social action, social interaction, primary group, social norm, social role, social structure, institutions,* and *society.* All of these concepts are *universals;* they refer to features of social life found in all human societies.

In their universality they point to transhistorical aspects of social life. Several of them contain, in compressed form, an entire theory about some aspect of the nature of man and society. They represent, that is, an answer to some perennial question about human life. Thus, as we have previously seen, the concept of culture is a way of answering the ancient question "What is the *differentia specifica* of Man?" Similarly, the concept of social norm introduced in Section C is an assertion of the reality of man's moral nature, a denial that his behavior can be reduced to instinct, mechanical conditioning, rational calculation of self-interest, or the effects of coercion.

Although our basic concepts often imply answers to transhistorical questions about the general nature of man and society, they also are useful in answering specific historical questions about social life. We have called the basic concepts "lenses" through which the sociologist looks at social reality. To vary the metaphor, they are also the building blocks with which he constructs more elaborate conceptions of historically specific social phenomena, such as *bureaucracy, capitalism, mass society, class* and *caste,* or the *metropolitan community,* which are dealt with later in this book.

Concern with historically specific questions has always been a main focus of sociological inquiry because of the sociologist's inescapable involvement as man and citizen in the fate of his own country and era. We are all of us men embedded in history and our deepest curiosities and anxieties are often aroused by contemporary problems. Such a concern, however, in no sense condemns the sociologist to parochialism, to a narrow concentration on the here and now. For, as the work of Max Weber in particular shows, a full understanding of contemporary social life can only be achieved by comparing it and contrasting it with social life in other times and places. This is the meaning of the idea that the sociological perspective is *comparative.* As C. Wright Mills has said, the sociologist should "never think of describing an institution in twentieth-century America without trying to bear in mind similar institutions in other types of structures [societies] and periods." [4] Our sociological knowledge, therefore, is embodied both in transhistorical generalizations that are efforts to formulate timeless truths about man and society and in historically specific generalizations applicable only to life in particular changing societies. The sociologist, however, needs always to examine several societies even if his immediate aim is to define and isolate the unique features of one of them.

[4] C. Wright Mills, *The Sociological Imagination* (New York: Oxford University Press, Inc., 1959), p. 215.

The great French thinker Alexis de Tocqueville, who is not easily classifiable as a sociologist, a political scientist, or a historian, once wrote in reflecting on his classic *Democracy in America*:

In my work on America . . . though I seldom mentioned France, I did not write a page without thinking of her, and placing her as it were before me. And what I specifically tried to draw out, and to explain in the United States, was not the whole condition of that foreign society, but the points in which it differs from our own or resembled us. It is always by noting likenesses and contrasts that I succeeded in giving an interesting and accurate description of the New World. . . . I believe that this perpetual silent reference to France was a principal cause of the book's success.

This statement superbly summarizes the comparative approach to the study of human society that has become the hallmark of sociology. De Tocqueville regarded his comparative perspective as valuable because it illuminates both "likenesses *and* contrasts"—the similarities and the differences—between societies. The chief difference between de Tocqueville and the modern sociologist is that the latter substitutes for the former's "perpetual silent reference to France" a systematic, explicit comparative frame of reference. Our basic sociological concepts are an effort to build such a frame of reference. Let us review these concepts in detail.

Social action is behavior of individuals which is directed toward other people. *Social interaction* is two or more individuals responding to each other and mutually influencing one another's conduct.[5] Two pedestrians who collide accidentally while turning a street corner in opposite directions are not interacting socially, only physically. Two birds, however, who call to one another in the treetops are engaged in social interaction. Social interaction is the basic component of all the relationships, groups, and associations that constitute human society. Groups, associations, and societies are more or less complex patterns or networks of interactions among individuals. We have included as one of our readings a famous description of small, relatively undifferentiated, face-to-face groups—"primary groups" as he christened them—by the early twentieth-century American sociologist Charles Horton Cooley.

Sociologists are concerned with isolating and specifying the distinctive features of human social interaction. As we have seen, man's ability to create symbols, especially vocal symbols, of his experience is what chiefly distinguishes him from other animals. Symbolic communication, or symbolic interaction as some writers have called it, is the essence of human social behavior. Both W. J. H. Sprott and Peter Berger, in the readings presented here, describe the features of all human social interaction that depend on man's ability to communicate symbolically, and both acknowledge their indebtedness to the ideas of George Herbert Mead.[6]

Human social interaction both creates and is governed by *social norms*— rules or symbolized models of behavior present in the consciousness of men that guide and control their interactions. Social norms are an important part of the

---

[5] W. J. H. Sprott, in our first selection in Section B, does not distinguish between social action and social interaction, but uses the terms synonymously.

[6] An interesting attempt to arrive at a definition of the peculiar features of human social interaction which arrives at conclusions almost identical to those of the symbolic interactionists though starting from a quite different philosophical perspective is Jose Ortega y Gasset, *Man and People* (New York: W. W. Norton & Company, Inc., 1957), pp. 72–89.

culture men learn as members of a given society. Norms state the expectations people have of how others will behave toward them and toward one another. For example, we do not expect to be jostled in an unmannerly fashion when walking the streets, because we know that showing at least this minimal consideration for strangers is a widely accepted norm in American society. But our expectations are not merely predictions or anticipations of how others will act in the sense in which we expect the sun to rise in the East or material objects to behave in accordance with the laws of gravity. Our expectations of other people usually also amount to a *demand* that they be fulfilled. When the Admiral warns the sailors of the British fleet that "England expects every man to do his duty," or when a mother tells her children on their departure for school that she "expects" them to obey the teacher, it is clear that the Admiral and the mother are not merely voicing predictions about the behavior of the sailors and the children, but are trying to influence or control their behavior in advance.[7] Their admonitions clearly carry, at least implicitly, the suggestion that if the "expected" behavior is not forthcoming some penalty or *sanction* will be imposed upon the recalcitrant individual.

Norms are often classified according to the degree of severity, specificity, and certainty of the sanctions imposed if they are violated. *Laws* are norms that have been embodied in formal written statutes enforced by specially designated officials; the sanctions imposed on violators are decided upon by other specially designated officials or agencies such as judges, courts, and juries, or they may in some cases be themselves prescribed by statute. *Mores* are norms, the violation of which evokes a reaction of intense indignation and moral outrage from others, and the sanctions imposed are likely to be severe. *Custom* and *fashion* are norms which if not conformed to will be followed by milder and less certain sanctions such as ostracism and ridicule, which may nevertheless have psychologically devastating effects on the violator. The very complex relationship between norms—the detailed rules prescribed for behavior—and *values,* more general conceptions of what is good and desirable that may be invoked to justify particular norms, is explored by Judith Blake and Kingsley Davis in one of the readings in Section C.

Not all norms apply to every member of a group or society. Even in small informal groups and in primitive tribes, individuals differ in the parts they play in the total network of interactions among members. These different parts are what sociologists call *social roles.* Essentially, social roles are clusters of norms and expectations that apply to different classes of persons within a group or society. Thus in all societies somewhat different behavior is expected of men and women, the old and the young, and parents and children. Some differentiation of roles based on differences in sex, age, and kinship is a universal feature of human society. In the larger and more complex societies there is a much greater variety of roles—which is part of what we mean in describing them as complex societies. In the sphere of economic activities, the pattern of role differentiation is usually called the *division of labor.* Some examples of social roles in various known societies are *woman, father, adult, sorcerer, sage, beggar, nobleman, playboy, automobile salesman, physician, Catholic.* Obviously the

[7] This double sense in which we use the verb, *to expect,* is pointed out by Robert Cooley Angell, *Free Society and Moral Crisis* (Ann Arbor: University of Michigan Press, 1958), p. 34.

size of the categories of persons who fill these roles may vary from well over half the population in the case of *adult* to a single individual at any given time in the case of *head roles* in large organizations, such as the Pope of the Roman Catholic Church or the President of the United States. The norms and expectations that constitute a particular role may also govern one's interactions with only a few other people, as in the case of kinship roles, or with almost every person one encounters, as in the case of sex roles. Furthermore, the range of conduct prescribed by a role may be great, as for the roles of wife and priest, or a role may require little more than the occasional observance of a few simple rules, as in the case of customer or hotel guest.

The individual is likely to experience the demands and expectations of others most intensely in striving to fulfill the requirements of his social roles. Yet, as Peter Berger points out, he generally does not feel his role obligations as a coercive and tyrannical "power of society" limiting his freedom: often, "we *want* the parts that society has assigned to us." [8] Berger argues that our very sense of individual identity, our most intimate awareness of our self-hood, is shaped by the roles we play. That this shaping of self by role is rarely complete, however, is implied by Erving Goffman's concept of *role distance,* which he illustrates in the reading reprinted here with an account of the conduct of doctors and nurses during a surgical operation.

If the relation between the individual and society is illuminated by the concept of role, roles can also be examined in their mutual interrelationships. Roles are reciprocal in prescribing behavior toward persons in other roles whose behavior is similarly regulated. Thus one cannot describe the role of husband without at the same time describing the role of wife. The total pattern formed by a given arrangement of roles is a *social structure* or *social organization.* The study of such systems of linked roles differentiates sociology proper from social psychology, which is the study of the impact of social norms and roles on individual personality. Any recurring pattern of interaction among individuals playing different roles may be said to constitute a social structure. We may thus speak of the social structure of the American middle-class family, of a primitive tribe, of a ladies' bridge club, of Harvard University, and even of American society as a whole.

A *group* is a plurality of individuals in recurring interaction with one another, their interactions controlled by common norms and differentiated roles. The members of the group are at least to some degree aware of their membership and perceive the group as a coherent, relatively permanent entity. The group, in other words, possesses a common culture and a social structure and its members see it as a collectivity rather than merely as an aggregate of individuals. Cooley's "primary group" is the smallest and least structured but most universal type of group.

Those social structures specializing in such activities as economic production or the rearing of children that are found in nearly all societies are called institutions. Peter Berger and Thomas Luckmann show how institutions grow out of the routine interactions of people to the point where they are perceived as constraining external realities, even though their origins lie in the purposive activities of human beings. Peter Blau emphasizes this externality in describing

---

[8] Peter Berger, *Invitation to Sociology* (Garden City, N.Y.: Doubleday Anchor Books, 1963), p. 93.

institutions as "a historical reality that exists, at least in part, outside and independent of the human beings who make up societies." His qualification "at least in part" reduces the force of the assertion, but he presumably has in mind considerations such as those stressed by Berger and Luckmann that locate the origin of institutions in the activities of particular human beings and treat their perpetuation as the recurrent reproduction by other human beings of the original patterns of activity and interaction. Blau notes that it is through the transmission of institutional patterns from one generation to the next that the past survives into the present and continues to shape it. Society, thus, possesses an enduring structure even when, as Blau points out, there has been, after several generations, a complete turnover in its membership.

A society is simply the totality of the social relations and groups formed by a given population occupying a given territory. Where to draw the line between one society and another is largely a matter of convenience—for some purposes we may wish to speak of the United States as a single society, for others we may choose to speak of Western society, treating as a single entity the United States, Western (and even parts of Eastern) Europe, and overseas countries settled by Europeans. The nation-state is usually the largest social unit employed as a framework for analysis by sociologists studying contemporary societies.

Sociologists study social reality at all the levels of scope and complexity suggested by the basic concepts here reviewed. Some concentrate on primary groups and face-to-face interpersonal relations *within* much larger social units. Such studies are sometimes called "microsociology" to distinguish them from "macrosociology"—the study of large-scale social structures, major institutions, and their interrelations within whole societies. Sprott's account of his hypothetical pair of movie-going friends, many of Berger's illustrations of role theory, and Goffman's report on behavior in the operating room are examples of microsociological analysis. Parts Two and Three of this book emphasize readings that are macrosociological in character: the conception of industrial society as a whole, influencing the nature of all the individuals and groups within it, is the main organizing theme there. However, it should not be forgotten that such macrosociological units as nations, class systems, political economies, and large bureaucratic organizations are made up of microsociological interactions among concrete persons.

A Human Nature and Social Origins

3

Reflections on the Human Revolution

ROBERT ENDLEMAN

In a brilliant paper in the June 1964 issue of *Current Anthropology* a linguist and an archaeologist, Charles Hockett and Robert Ascher, present a new interpretation of what they call "The Human Revolution." [1] They attempt to trace the origins of man by drawing on linguistics as well as the usual paleontological, archaeological and geological reconstructions. What they have come up with is of extraordinary significance

From *The Psychoanalytic Review* (Summer 1966), pp. 169–188. Reprinted by permission.
[1] Charles F. Hockett and Robert Ascher. The Human Revolution. *Current Anthropology*, Vol. 5, No. 3, June 1964. pp. 135–147; with commentaries by Weston LaBarre, Frank B. Livingstone, G. G. Simpson and others, and replies by Hockett and Ascher, pp. 147–168.

for psychoanalysis and points to the need for a further elaboration of their theory in the light of a psychoanalytically-oriented anthropology. Hockett and Ascher themselves do not employ a psychoanalytic approach or refer to psychodynamic mechanisms, but the addition of these latter would fill out some of the lacunae and puzzles posed by their interpretation and I think the time is ripe for just such a development in anthropology. First let me summarize Hockett and Ascher's hypotheses:

1.

Tree-living primate ancestors of both the modern apes and man, living in the East African forests, faced an ecological crisis in the Miocene age (the geological period estimated at about 28 to 12 million years ago). Due to climatic changes, the forests receded and gave way to open grassy savanna, and in the competitive struggle for the declining forest territories, weaker bands of these "apes" ("protohominoids") were forced to the edges of the forest groves, and thence to migrate across open savanna in quest of other grove territory in which to continue their traditional arboreal and vegetarian existence. As such grove-to-grove treks became progressively greater so did the premium on these apes' developing in more fully bipedal mode of locomotion (possibly but only intermittently used by their ancestors). Hence we have the development of the characteristically human foot (the only important human bodily specialization). This bipedality and the related fully erect posture were adaptive not only for locomotion, but for two other signifi-can reasons: the value of being able to see predators over the savanna grasses and of being able to free the already prehensile hands for carrying weapons, first of defense against the existing larger animal predators, later of offense against other (especially large) animals, now *objects* of predation. As the forests continued to recede, these "failures" who were forced out had in time to accept the savannas as their necessary habitat, and therefore to adapt to it and the predation conditions in it or else! Occasional tool and weapon-carrying by the tree-ancestors and rela-tives now became a constant necessity and weapons of defense became weapons of offense as these "waifs", to survive in the new environment, became hunters themselves and changed from the vegetarian diet of the trees to the carnivorous or omnivorous diet of the new life. *Carrying* thus produced the "hunting revolution" and the "failures" of the forest struggle were on their way to evolving into men. Carrying of weapons and carrying of food frees the mouth and the teeth, essential for the

development of language. The hunting of larger animals, made possible by the carrying, first of *ad-hoc*, then of de-liberately manufactured weapons, in turn requires social cooperation and co-ordination. Hand-signaling is not feasi-ble if hands are carrying weapons or food or infants; visual attention mean-while is focused on the prey and or other hunters; therefore the most feasi-ble communication must be *auditory*. Hence selective survival chances go to those bands who further develop an already-existing primate system of vocal *calls* (something like that of the present-day gibbon).

Why should such a system of calls *need* to be further elaborated, in a di-rection that leads to language? Because social organization would necessarily have to become more complex under conditions of collective hunting of larger game animals, with its con-comitant of a larger range of food-*sharing*, and hence a wider range of "socialization" among the band mem-bers. It is assumed that these would have needed to move about in bands of some size (10–30 members), for singly or in very small groups they would have had very poor chances of surviving against larger and more power-ful predators better adapted to the savanna environment. It is also assumed that they would have transferred to the new environment habits of territoriality such primates tend to have in the trees: i.e., a safe "home-base" surrounded by a not-clearly bounded food-getting ter-ritory. Another factor: the adaptive de-velopment of fully erect posture (mean-ing that those who developed this feature had a better chance of surviving —and hence of passing erectness on to later generations—than those who did not) also brought about physical changes in the structure of the head, brain, face, jaws, and "organs of speech" that made distinctively human speech possible.

The development of true language

from an ape-type call system could have occurred like this: Calls are discrete vocal signals, each communicating the total Gestalt of a situation, e.g., "food here," "danger here," "I am here," etc. The first step toward language would be the *blending* of two different calls into a new composite, e.g. a new call indicating food *and* danger, using one constituent element of each of the old calls. While such blending must have occurred fortuitously thousands of times in the earlier tree life without being taken up and transmitted through the band, the new and socially more complex savanna life would put a premium upon the development of such innovations. Blending then institutes a process of *building* composite signals out of separate meaningful parts (linguists call this changing a *closed* system into an *open* one.) This opening up must have taken thousands of years, but once accomplished it is revolutionary, for new communication demands detailed conventions that cannot possibly be transmitted through the genes (presumably the main mechanism of earlier systems) and *must* be learned; therefore there is natural selection for greater learning capacity, hence of the bases in brain structure *for* such capacity. Opening up the system also involves *displacement*: that is, it makes possible something increasingly *necessary* in more complex social life: talking about *something* out of sight, in the past or future, or purely hypothetical or mythical. This is parallel to the elements of foresight and memory involved in carrying a weapon for which there is no *immediate* use, and each of these mental habits reinforces the other, and each is reciprocally related to the process of tool or weapon *manufacture*, as distinct from carrying sticks or stones only *used* as tools. During this process, probably taking hundreds of generations, the head-face-vocal-apparatus structure is changed to a form more like that of modern man, the use of such

blended-call pre-language increases the innervation of the vocal tract and enriches the cortical representation of that region. This sets the stage for the final development to language.

As "pre-language" (the system of multiple call-blend signals) develops, the number of different call-blends increases, until it reaches a point where it becomes difficult to distinguish some of them from others. Then by mutation, some individuals start to listen to, and to articulate, these call-Gestalten not as total units, but in terms of smaller constituent elements, discretely produced and heard, in varying arrangements, and the distinction between sound units ("phonological components" or "phonemes") and collections of sound units that have a minimum unit of meaning ("morphemes") is made. With this we have true language. If we take toolmaking and language as the criteria of humanity, then the ape-like ancestor has evolved into man.

As an aside, Hockett-Ascher mention another important by-product of man's erect posture: the change from a dorsal to a frontal position in coitus. Presumably the enlargement of the gluteus maximus produced by bipedal erectness made the old primate dorsal coital position awkward, and fostered the invention of the frontal position, almost unique to human beings. This position puts the adult male mate in a position to the adult female similar to that of the suckling infant, and can thereby enhance the diffusion and complexity of sexual feelings (a trend which probably had already begun with the nonseasonal year-round sexuality of advanced primates in tree life.) The importance of this phenomenon for the Oedipus complex is obvious.

Hockett and Ascher hypothesize that this whole evolutionary process—from the Miocene "waifs" to man—must have been *completed* by the beginning of the Pleistocene period (i.e., roughly a million years ago). That is, taking as "man" a generalized primate with one specialization (the human foot), with fully erect posture and bipedal gait, stereoscopic and color vision and very complex hand-eye-brain coordinations, a large complex brain, great learning capacity, the use and manufacture of tools, and language.

Weston LaBarre,[2] commenting on the Hockett-Ascher paper, notes that the shift to the frontal coital position must have a lot to do with the characteristically human development of *paternal feelings* toward offspring, the like of which we find in no other mammals, including our nearest primate relatives of today. He also sees another significance in the frontal position: a change in the role of the female in controlling the situation of sexual encounter. Whereas the primate female in dorsal position in effect controls the sexual situation, the human female in supine frontal position, if solitary, is vulnerable to any sexual encounter with the (usually) physically stronger male. This would help explain the development of institutions of male dominance, sexual possessiveness, familial protectiveness of the male toward the mate as well as the offspring, and also the necessity for sexual rules. Hunting males need social cooperation which unregulated sexuality would easily disrupt.

2.

Let us now consider some of the implications of this interpretation. First note that the last stage in the development from ape-like ancestor to man, as seen by Hockett and Ascher, is both a biological and a cultural process, and in a complex inter-causality involves all the elements that make us distinctively human: the use of hands to carry and use things like sticks and stones as tools

[2] *Current Anthropology*, Vol. 5, No. 3, June, 1964. pp. 147–150.

and weapons, then to *make* tools and weapons, with which man in turn *transforms* the environment rather than merely adapting to it; the freeing of the hands by the development of the specialized human foot; the transformation of man's ecological place dependent on both of these and the whole complex of hunting, its necessary social organization and the related social and sexual band relationships; the transformation and freeing of the face and mouth and head and brain; the development of more complex cortical processes; the increased duration and dependency of human infancy and the relation of this to the whole complex learning process; finally, the greater complexity of communication, culminating in the distinctively human phenomenon of language.

The implications of this postulated evolutionary process toward modern man ramify in all directions. Let us explore just a few.

First, the problems of human psychosexuality that are so central to psychoanalysis. The prolongation of infancy is made both *possible and necessary* by the evolutionary changes the authors are postulating: the great increase in the amount and variety of learning that can only be taught by other agents of the species (rather than transmitted through the genes), the greater complexity of band organization in the emerging hunting economy, the greater security-with-interdependency. This prolongation of infancy is one meaning of the phrase: "man is an infantilized ape." The other meaning is that man retains into adulthood traits that are infantile or embryonic in lower species, in particular the other higher primates (e.g., orthognathy, hairlessness, position of the foramen magnum, loss of pigmentation in skin, hair and eyes, the form of the pelvis, etc.). In the evolutionary progression from other mammals to primates to man, the duration of gestation increases, the typical number of offspring per birth declines, the period from birth to sexual maturity increases, and, even more dramatically, the period from birth to full adult growth increases. Further, the long pre-natal period and the protracted and helpless infancy are prerequisites for the ultimately high development of the nervous system and mental capacities. But alongside this infantilism, man's sexuality is precocious. The sexual pattern is present in infants before the gonadal hormone is produced in adequate quantities. The female ovum is practically fully developed at the early age of five. That is, the Soma lags far behind the Germa in man, so that within the frame of his general infantilism, his sexuality is relatively precocious.[3] With man's great reproductive economy, heightened further by the advancements of culture, his precocious and lifelong sexuality must therefore be seen as a kind of "surplus" or "discretionary" sexuality (to borrow concepts from economics), and, as LaBarre points out, very significantly for the social life of man. Freud, of course, taught us to see this close linkage of the social and the sexual, the simplified formulation of which is to say that *all* social ties are basically libidinal ties.

In this context, consider one of Hockett and Ascher's main points: The relative verticality of tree-living primates (in contrast with infra-primate land mammals) was further developed by the Miocene "rejects" into a more completely frontal approach to the world, by the development of totally upright posture and bipedal gait. This frontal

[3] For the development of this theme, drawing on the work of the anatomist L. Bolk, see Géza Róheim, *Psychoanalysis and Anthropology*, New York: International Universities Press, 1950, especially pages 400–404; and its further implications: Weston LaBarre, *The Human Animal*, Chicago: University of Chicago Press, 1954, throughout, but especially pp. 150–156, 304–310.

approach is further extended to the change of position in coitus. Now an implication of these changes is that all relationships, mate-to-mate as well as parent-to-child, are now face-to-face relationships, and this I think is an important determinant of what I would call man's peculiarly polymorphous *sexual sociality*. Infantilization means a much greater continuity, in man, of infantile (indeed, embryonic) processes and attachments throughout life, than in any infra-human mammals. This means a greater diffusion of sexual-social feeling throughout the range of inter-individual relationships, which is another way of referring to the poly-morphousness of infantile sexuality which persists (in the unconscious, if not overtly) throughout life. Add to this the convergence of mother-infant sexuality and mate-mate sexuality produced by the change to the frontal position in coitus, and we have the basis in evolution for the great extensiveness and displaceability of sexual-social ties that Freud taught us to recognize in man.

Róheim, in summarizing Bolk's evidence for the fetalization of man, argues that if a fetal quality becomes gradually permanent there must be an inhibitory factor that prevents the "normal" process of ontogenesis. Bolk assumes the cause must be endocrinological. In turn, such endocrine changes could come about through a change in *diet*. Now the transition from ape-like primate to man that the Hockett-Ascher reconstruction (in this respect in agreement with many other anthropological reconstructions) outlines, does in fact postulate a change of diet of major proportions: from the herbivorous one of the tree-dwellers, to the carnivorous one of land-living hunters. Here the pieces of the puzzle start to fit together. The diet change, of course, did not simply occur; it was a product of the whole complex of ecological, social and other body-structural changes, as Hockett and Ascher show.

The sexual-sociality of man, that is both infantile and precocious, is connected in turn with two other human phenomena: *language* and *play*. Hockett and Ascher's reconstruction of the possible line of development of language is ingenious, provocative, and internally consistent with the rest of their reconstruction of the "human revolution." But it is, I thing, incomplete. Language is an oral activity, most intensively developed in face-to-face contacts (in contrast with a call system, which operates primarily at a distance.) Perhaps then, the frontal coital position has as much to do with the development of language as the savanna hunting-organization. In turn, language is linked to the development of human sexuality through the phenomenon of *play*. Another way of talking about the persistence of man's infantile sexuality is to say that other animals grow up and *un*learn to play; *man never does*. Play is one of the more direct expressions of Eros. Since man's sexuality is both precocious and extravagantly out of line with reproductive necessities, the arena of play—as a channel for all this "surplus" sexuality—is greater and more complex in man than in other animals.

What are the connections between language and play? Hockett and Ascher make many references to play in their paper, but aside from noting that the introduction of pre-language into the new life of the apes-becoming-men, adds *verbal* to other types of play, they do not develop the connections. I do not think that a theory explaining the development from a call system to pre-language to language, *only* in terms of the *adaptive* value of the changes, is adequate. The assumption behind it (as of most anthropological "explanations" of cultural artifacts) is basically utilitarian. But what we know about Eros and play belies such assumptions.

Let us examine, instead, how play would be involved in the emergence of speech. First of all, innovations in vocalization (Hockett-Ascher refer to "generations of chattering") are as likely to come from play [4] as from such emergency situations as the need to communicate the simultaneous presence of food and danger. Play involves "playing around with" elements that are already given, trying them out in new combinations and sequences. Play may also involve body contact, as in fighting or sexual play (observable in nearly all mammals, and other animals as well), and one of the contexts for this is the mother-infant situation. In this situation the mother carries on a whole variety of vocalizations with the child. (Even in modern human mothers, there is still plenty of such phatic, pre-linguistic vocalization with the child, as part of a general context of play, relaxation and erotic exchange.) Such vocalizations must surely have been at least the *materials* for innovation, out of which language developed, alongside of (not instead of) a call system. (There is no good reason to suppose that one excludes the other.)

Speech has been defined by Róheim as "orality coming to terms with reality." And what situation is more oral than infancy? The progressive lengthening of infancy and heightening of dependency must have increased the significance of Eros and play in the mother-child situation and encouraged a greater variety of vocalization. Sim-

---

[4] Once when I was explaining the intricacies of a particular Australian kinship system to an anthropology class, one student, in great annoyance, blurted out: "Why should they have developed such a complicated system? I don't see what *use* it is! Surely they're not just playing games!" Since the utilitarian value of having 16 marriage-classes is by no means self-evident (in fact it is demonstrably anti-utilitarian in some ways) and taking a Freudian view of the "not" in the student's question, maybe he was on the right track.

ilarly, in the same period, there would be extensions of this into the spheres of inter-peer juvenile play and adult play, including the sexual relationship, which, now involving the frontal position, brings the mating pair into face-to-face relationship. The latter has two significances: greater *oral* contact, and greater vocal communication.

It is interesting that all of these play situations, involving direct person-to-person contacts, would use vocalizations at low volume and probably relatively low pitch. LaBarre comments (on the Hockett-Ascher paper, *loc. cit.* p. 149–50) that there is a puzzling difference between calls (e.g. gibbon calls, or a human female's or juvenile's "piercing" scream) and ordinary speech language; i.e. that the pitch of calls is in frequencies around 3000 cycles per second, near the *top* of the range for the human ear, and the range to which the human ear is most sensitive (i.e. calls of this pitch can be heard over much longer distances than lower-pitched calls of the same amplitude). By contrast, ordinary human speech is mainly in the range below 1000 c.p.s. Then LaBarre asks:

Whence the massive flatting of speech-frequencies in man? Or did speech not arise out of "closed" primate call-systems after all, but rather from the lower frequencies of feckless play-chatter, where speech has remained ever since? [*loc. cit.* p. 150]

Although LaBarre introduces this query by referring to "one *minor* linguistic problem" (my emphasis), the question is a critical one in reference to the Hockett-Ascher theory. It is of course not a question which can be answered with any certitude, given present evidence. But I would raise the further question: why the *either-or* in LaBarre's question? Why must language have developed exclusively either from a call system, or from "feckless play-chattering"? Since existing infra-

human primates show both, and since the whole Hockett-Ascher thesis about steps in the change toward language rests on the assumption of something like a gibbon's call system in our "proto-hominoid" ancestors, we are certainly as justified in assuming "feckless play-chatter" in those same putative ancestors.

Hockett and Ascher refer to "generations of chattering . . . increasing the innervation of the vocal tract" . . . etc. Now "chattering" is clearly not "calling." But it is the sort of thing youngsters (or adults for that matter) do at play. (Listen at any cocktail party.) Some of the chattering may be imitative of calls used in "serious" (i.e. instrumental) situations, just as much else in play is imitative of serious activities on the physical action plane. So play is one context of which a repertoire of signal-calls could be elaborated by innovations consisting of playful new combinations. But I think alongside of the process of elaboration of call signals, *another* set of innovations must have occurred, within the context of erotic-play-chattering.

Someone may object at this point: "How can you talk about juvenile play being at *low* volume? Haven't you ever heard a gang of kids playing outdoors?" There indeed we find elements of the call system at work (at play, rather). And we can argue that modifications of a call system might well have come about in *that* kind of play situation too, as well as in such "serious" situations as the food-and-danger example.

There are all kinds of pre-linguistic vocalizations: imitations of sounds heard in the environment (the "bow-wow" theory of language origins traces it to such vocalizations); emotive ejaculations evoked by intense feelings of any kind (the "pooh-pooh"—or better, the "ai-yai-yai!" theory); expiratory sounds made to the accompaniment of physical exertions (the "yo-he-ho" theory); exclamations in sing-song spontaneously made in exultation over a successful feat (the "ta-ra-ra-boom-te-day" theory); sounds made by infants sucking or chewing at the mother's breast (the "chew" theory)—to which could be added the whole repertory of non-linguistic sounds and exclamations animals at all like human beings make in carrying out any of the body processes (eating, eliminating, copulating, to name the classic triad, but also including scratching, rubbing, grooming the body, etc.) Sounds made in fighting should also be added to the list. *Any and all of these could have, in fact must have, contributed to the repertory of sounds in early proto-language.* Many of these types of sounds must have been important parts of the content of vocalizations in sub-human play. Play activities of a cortically increasingly complex animal would then allow innovative elaborations of such "raw material", expansion of the repertoire, and then the chance for playful recombinations of the elements. Add to such recombination or blending the process of conventionalization, and the animal is on the way to human language. (Conventionalization means that a particular sound comes to be conventionally associated with a particular referent; at first by the close affinity between the sound and the activity or thing referred to; but later, when such phatic elements are blended and recombined in ever-more-complex ways, the relationship between the sound-combination and the thing referred to becomes "purely conventional"—i.e., there is no longer any obvious connection, and the association of sound and referent has to be *learned*.)

Let us retrace some of these connections, then: Ape-like primates become more infantilized as they evolve into man. This heightens the significance of infantile sexuality. The adoption of the frontal coital position fosters the as-

similation of parent-infant sexuality with mate-mate sexuality. Constant non-seasonal mating abolishes the older mammal device of segregating mating from offspring-care activities. Heightened inter-individual dependency raises inter-individual empathy and communicability. Contexts of play are extended and elaborated, with the progressive juvenilization of the human animal. The range, number, and variety of vocalizations increases, and play (as well as certain "serious" emergency situations) increases the chances for innovations in the form of blendings and recombinations of elements. Playful innovations may come and go by the thousands, but the more complex conditions of social life start to put an evolutionary premium on (or select for) a more adequate communication system. Hence both a blending of call elements and a blending of phatic "chattering" elements take place, and through the imitativeness of play vocalization there is an interweaving of both processes.

The mother-infant situation—*not* typically a call situation— is important for language in yet another respect. Mammal teaching of the young is generally direct, behavioral, immediate in the situation involved (e.g. a cat teaching her kitten how to catch mice). As life for the proto-humans on the postulated Miocene savannas becomes more complex, socially and ecologically, there develops a need for more of the teaching to be *anticipatory* rather than contemporary with its uses, and more need to communicate *about* things, past, future, or potential. The various monistic theories of language origin are helpful in suggesting some ways in which early symbol-referent connections are made. However, we would still need something like the blending mechanism Hockett and Ascher postulate, before any purely ejaculatory, or exertion-respiratory, or onomatopoetic vocalizations, can reach the pre-linguistic level of call-blends, and thus provide the necessary displacement for anticipatory vocal-socialization. It seems reasonable then to postulate, alongside of Hockett-Ascher's call-blending, a similar blending of lower-frequency vocalizations of these latter types.

Psychodynamically, language means that symbol replaces object. We re-invest objects with libido by the meaning of words. But this implies the absence of *direct* cathexis with the objects. All this suggests a transformation of the animal's direct erotic relationship to the world, through a medium that holds out long-range potential for enormously greater mastery, but at this point stands *between* the animal (human being) and the object. Hence the magical quality of words. Language is bound up with repression, and can be regarded as one of those great compromise formations, at the cultural level, which permit much gratification of Eros while damming up other aspects.

A significant aspect of the linkage of language and repression is the phenomenon of negation. A call system may *imply* "Don't come near!" by a call signalling "Danger!" but by its nature, the call system communicates *positive* statements: "Here's food," "Here's danger" or "Here I am, over here!" etc., and not negative ones. However, the process of blending that Hockett and Ascher suggest starts a call system on the way to language, *introduces* the concept of negation. They suggest that if a call had elements ABCD and signified food; and another call with elements EFGH signified danger, a new situation including *both* food and danger might evoke a new call, that is a compromise between the two others, and consists of the elements ABGH. If this "caught on" and spread, there would now be *three* signals, *each* of them now having two units, AB with CD or GH and EF with GH. The implica-

tions of this are enormous, because *now* ABCD doesn't just mean "food", it means "food *and no danger."* Similarly, EFGH now means, not just "danger," but "danger *and no food."* Now it would become possible to have still a fourth signal: CDEF, meaning *"no* food and *no* danger." In other words, *the concept of negation has entered the signal system.* We can now raise the question: what are the preconditions for such conceptualization to occur, granted it *can* logically follow once a blend such as ABGH has occurred and then has been accepted and diffused throughout the community? Since the concept of negation does not appear in the unconscious, Freud argues [5] that it is tied up with the process of repression. Repression is the primal act of negation. At the same time, the *conscious* use of negation makes it possible to deal with the repressed material, so long as it is denied. Then the process that Hockett-Ascher describe, could be carried to its logical extension of "CD equals 'no danger' " *only* in an animal that has learned how to repress, that is, an animal that is human or close to human.

Norman Brown hypothesizes [6] that "formal logic and the law of contradiction are the rules whereby the mind submits to operate under general conditions of repression." Could not the hypothesis be extended to include all of language in general? In this view, language can arise only in an animal that has learned how to *repress.* What would have provoked the need to repress, in a proto-human animal? Very clearly, precisely the conditions we have been describing: a new challenging environment requiring more elaborate

[5] Sigmund Freud: On Negation. *Collected Papers,* Vol. 5, London: Hogarth Press, pp. 181–185.
[6] Norman O. Brown: *Life Against Death,* Middletown, Conn.: Wesleyan University Press, p. 321.

inter-individual dependency and co-operation, including the need to control intra-band aggression and sexuality, the developments in sexuality just described (which produce a conflict between parental and mate sexuality) combined with a heightening of libidinal attachments and their prolongation with the increasing infantilization of the human animal.

3.

Where does play fit in all this? I think the very difficulty we experience in seeing play elements or origins in "serious" customs or institutions, is a mark of that repression that is characteristic of the socialized man. One function of play is to evade such repression, with the excuse, "It's not serious, we don't mean it, we're just playing around, etc.," so that a portion of the repressed content can be expressed, usually disguised, but especially in some innocuous-looking form. Play is also the insurance that repression of unconscious forces is never quite complete (a totally repressed person cannot play at all, or enjoy others' play) so that some channels *are* open to reach those layers. Play is particularly the opportunity for creative forces of the unconscious. We can allow it, repressed human beings that we are, on the pretext that it is separate from things that "really" matter. All this suggests, then, that play is *antithetical* to the development of language, where language, built on repression, constitutes a formal system of constructs and categories that constrain and channelize the confrontation with "reality." Precisely so, and every language does constitute a certain arbitrary codification of reality that makes difficult, if not impossible, certain kinds of playful verbal elaborations or recombinations. Here poetry and myth attempt to come to the rescue—never entirely successfully—as preservers of pre-linguistic or non-linguistic play dealings with reality,

by verbal structures which defy the laws of logic, especially the law of contradiction, in ways analogous to the dream, that ever-renewed resource of the unconscious.

But I have argued earlier that play must have contributed, importantly, to the *origins of language*. Now we have a view of play which shows it as *antagonistic* to language. Both conditions, I would argue, are true, and they are connected: for play and language, just as myth and language, are in a dialectical relationship to each other, in a constant state of tension, language needing to formalize, i.e. constrain, repress and sublimate, the forces of play, yet still needing play for constant renewal and revitalization, and breaking through the rigidities of formalization, especially those involved in the process of negation and the linkage of language to the rules of formal logic. (As an aside, this is one reason that formally constructed artificial "universal" languages like Esperanto have been such dismal failures, for all their "reasonable" appeal; so too, the absurdities of language-translating machines.)

It seems entirely improbable that language, any more than other cultural creations, could have emerged *only* out of necessities (adaptiveness, etc.), and not also out of the arena of freedom whose epitome in activity is play. It is also improbable that anything so multifunctional as language could have come from only a single source. It may well have been "invented," as Hockett-Ascher argue, "only *once*" and then diffused (their arguments against the probability of parallel developments in different areas of the world, and later convergence, sound convincing), but this "invention" in a single population (a process which by their interpretation would require hundreds of generations) must very well have had a multiplicity of determinants (as all inventions, on close inspection, turn out to have). This would leave room for all of the factors that they indicate, and in addition *play* and its various ramifications, as I have attempted to show.

Let us return to the problems of psycho-sexuality, or sexual-sociality. Hockett-Ascher argue that in the emergence of a new ecological adaptation of the proto-hominoid ancestors to the savanna environment, vocal calls had to become elaborated because hands were occupied carrying weapons, tools, or food, while eyes were busy observing predators, objects of predation, and/or the other hunters. In my summary of their argument above, I had inadvertantly added ". . . hands carrying weapons, food, *or infants*" but on checking find that "*or infants*" does not appear in Hockett-Ascher's text. Thinking about this, we may say: with good reason. For what they describe are the circumstances of a group of *adult males* hunting large game, and adult males would not likely be carrying the infants. In other words, the elaboration of a closed to an open call system they relate to the *adult male activities of hunting*. This limitation makes it all the more imperative that we pay attention to the situation of adult females and offspring, in looking at the interrelated changes that our ancestors must have undergone during the period in question. Here we can refer again to my discussion of the mother-child situation, especially its elements of eroticism and play, as probable *additional* origins of the transformation toward language. Following Hockett-Ascher's type of reasoning: if the mother's hands are busy holding the infant, and her body busy giving it suck, her mouth and ears are free for other kinds of communication. However, the persistence to this day, of human mothers' babbling, cooing and gurgling and baby-talk to the child—in other words, pre-linguistic vocal communication—suggests that these phatic communications still have primacy for the adult female. By contrast, if *male*-interpersonal communications de-

veloped primarily out of the call system (i.e. *distance* rather than proximate communication) and with the development of the concept of negation through the blending process just described—with much less emphasis on direct body-contact phatic communication—perhaps we have here the roots of a very deep psychobiological sex difference, according to which the world of Logos has been universally, *predominantly* a male world, and the world of body-feeling predominantly a woman's world. (Granted, of course, that particular cultural configurations can accentuate or de-emphasize this difference.) The sheer physical dimorphism of human males and females, as LaBarre points out (*loc. cit.*), is surely attributable to selective adaptation to the sexual division of labor of the emergent hunting economy of the Miocene-Pliocene apes-becoming-men.

We must also consider, at this point, some further implications of the shift to the frontal position in intercourse, the universal (though not of course the exclusive) position used by human beings, and one which is almost a human monopoly. We have indicated that this shift promotes an assimilation, hence diffusion and confusion, of mother-child and male-female sexualities. Given human infantilization, and constant, precocious, ubiquitous and polymorphous human sexuality, this diffusion is bound to promote father-child, and *also* mother-child rivalries and animosities. For if to the female, the male in coitus is similar to a suckling child, *so*, in a sense, *is the female to the male*. For she, like a suckling infant, is receiving, through an erogenous body orifice, life-giving substances from a protuberance of the face-to-face partner's body.[7] (In fact it could be argued that, in this specific respect, *she* is more like a suck-

[7] Roger W. Wescott suggests this analogy, in his comments on the Hockett-Ascher paper. *Current Anthropology*, Vol 5, No. 3, June, 1964. p. 164.

ling infant than he is!) And of course psychoanalysis has had a lot to tell us about the re-arousal of unconscious infantile fantasy in the sexual activities of human adults. The Hockett-Ascher observations now give us some *evolutionary* understanding of these phenomena, and of their pan-human universality. This is not just mammalian behavior, but the behavior of a very special primate. The universality of the primary incest taboos (mother-son, father-daughter, brother-sister, and we might as well add, their homosexual coordinates), and of Oedipal phenomena (ignoring their minor variations with social structure) are also now understandable in a new evolutionary light.[8]

[8] There have been repeated attempts, in recent anthropology, to "disprove" the universality of these phenomena. Malinowski's famous case (*Sex and Repression*, 1927) against the existence of Oedipus Complex in the Trobriand Islands, has, however been adequately refuted by Ernest Jones, and more conclusively, by Geza Roheim (*Psychoanalysis and Anthropology*, 1950); and the noted royal cases (Egypt, Peru, Polynesia) are just that—*royal* exceptions. Even the great modern instance of a society *deliberately* trying to do away with Oedipal involvements by doing away with the nuclear family altogether—the Israeli Kibbutz—has succeeded in doing neither, as is quite clear from Melford Spiro's reports, *Kibbutz: Venture in Utopia* and *Children of the Kibbutz*, which show that the family, though bereft of economic-productive functions and residential territoriality, is still an emotionally-significant structure in the lives of parents (including toward each other) and of children; and that Oedipal feelings, though lacking the intensity they show in other Western societies, through lack of hostility-guilt feelings toward the father, nevertheless do appear. As for incest taboo, the whole collective is so much like a family to the children, that they *spontaneously* institute taboos against sexual relations or marriage with others they have grown up with on the Kibbutz. (See Yonina Talmon: "Mate Selection in Collective Settlements," *American Sociological Review*, Vol. 29, July, 1964. pp. 491–508.) For a fuller discussion of incest taboos and Oedipus complex generally, see R. Endleman: *Personality and So-*

We have here, then, another angle of vision on the phenomenon of *repression*, that special human problem. Repression is the mechanism that an infantilized human ape with a burgeoning polymorphous sexuality imposes upon himself, with the aid of the terrifying and nurturant giant lover-haters, the parents, to regulate the potential chaos of indiscriminate Eros. Language flows from, and helps consolidate this process. Play helps in the development of language, but also works against it and against repression, in the service of the polymorphous unconscious forces. Repression institutes the incest taboos and resolves the Oedipus Complex, while play, and its derivatives in poetry and myth, repeatedly break through these constrictions. Repression makes possible the whole complex of mastery on which man embarked by changing from dinner to diner on the Miocene African savannas, and the peculiarly crazy "rationality" by which he has constructed a whole world around himself, substituting his man-made environment (culture) and the constrictions of Logos, for instinct and the predation conditions of nature.

4. Epilogue

These reflections have an obvious relevance to the great problems raised by Freud in *Civilization and its Discontents*, by Herbert Marcuse in *Eros and Civilization* and by Norman O. Brown in *Life Against Death*. How is a non-repressive civilization possible? If language, that *sine qua non* of humanity, emerges out of the dialectic of repression and play, then what are the implications? If culture is rooted in the repressive transformations of polymorphous sexuality, the heritage of the

cial Life (Random House, 1967), which also includes an extensive chapter on the Kibbutz.

peculiar primate evolution of man, then what?

Brown and Marcuse explore the radical implications of Freud's breakthrough, in opposition to the gloomy pessimism of *Civilization and its Discontents*. But alongside their fervent plea for the *potentiality* of a non-repressive civilization, marked by liberation of Eros made possible by following psychoanalytical insights to their farther conclusions, their recital of the repressive, indeed *diseased*, bases of past and existing civilizations, is itself gloomy in the extreme—perhaps even more gloomy than Freud's own vision.

Pushing back behind history to the evolutionary origins of man (as is now more possible by such synthetic reconstructions as Hockett and Ascher's) seems, on the basis of the reflections I have suggested, to offer small comfort for any optimistic view such as Brown's or Marcuse's, but only to make more explicable and consistent their kind of interpretation of history, by rooting it in biological and cultural evolution. If Hockett and Ascher's interpretation, with the addenda I have suggested above, are basically correct, then this is the way man has been, from his emergence anywhere from a million to seven million years ago. Anthropologists seem in essential agreement that there has been no further *biological* evolution of man since *homo sapiens* emerged and then survived as the only remaining hominid species on this planet; that the emergence of *culture*, as the peculiar characteristic of man, abolishes the necessity for further biological evolution of the species.

The implications of this idea can be read, however, in several ways. One is to emphasize elements of fixity: i.e., that the peculiar historical circumstances of man's evolution from a tree-living primate to a ground-living savanna hunter, had set, once and for all, the peculiar bio-cultural problems of the species: i.e., infantilization, precocious and polymorphous sexuality, conflict-laden inter-individual intimacies and dependencies, communication necessities emerging in language, social control necessities favoring the process of repression, itself intimately tied to the development of language, and hence of the universal problems of culture. Freud, Marcuse, Brown—indeed, the whole corpus of critical reflections on our times—all document how we are still struggling with these same basic problems in the present desperate hour of civilization.

Another way to read the message of the end of biological evolution, however, is to emphasize its argument that *biological* evolution has stopped, has been rendered obsolete, because *cultural* evolution takes over. Man no longer (evolutionarily) adapts to the world, but instead proceeds to *transform* it. Earlier anthropological formulations of cultural evolution partook of the naive optimism of the Idea of Progress, later rejected as hopelessly out of touch with the desperate realities of the plight of man in "advanced" civilizations. Cultural evolutionism is today enjoying a revival in anthropology (partly in reaction against the anti-historical excesses of functionalist social anthropology), but in a greatly modified form, eschewing the grand simplicities of the 19th-century thinkers for more limited and more detailed regional reconstructions, and avoiding over-all progress formulations. However, cultural evolutionism of whatever stripe implies certain assumptions about the species nature of man, notably, for our concern, that man has the *potentiality* of transforming his own institutions. Hence no *particular civilization* has an ensured, inevitable holding power. Such a view is consistent with the faith of Brown and Marcuse that man *could* overcome the diseases of particular civilizations.

But then the question is: does the

potentiality to transform extend to the potentiality to conquer the disease of civilization *in general* (or to use the anthropologists' wider term, of *culture*, in general)? Brown and Marcuse are hopeful that it does, and draw upon their analyses of the *dialectical* interplay of repression and Eros to support such a faith. Their evidence, however, as already suggested, would appear to me to cast an enormous doubt on such possibilities, and to support instead the view that there is a great and tragic fixity to man's bio-cultural dilemmas, the evolutionary roots of which our present discussion has explored. What seems to me to be documented by their work, by Freud's, Roheim's, LaBarre's, and by the current anthropological evolutionary reconstructions, is the persistence in man's life of the same basic *conflicts* and *tensions*, never resolved, but re-expressed in changing transformations in different eras and cultures. *Plus ça change . . .*

That there *is* conflict and tension, rather than simple persistence of one set pattern or direction, can of course be read optimistically (*vide* Brown and Marcuse), that there *is* a chance for man really to liberate himself. Earlier cultural evolutionism (echoed in Freud's *Civilization and its Discontents*) assumed that man transformations of the world and civilization were necessarily the product of man's growing *intellectual* mastery—the forces that Brown brilliantly demonstrates as part of repressive culture, and more specifically, of anal-sadistic disease. May it not be possible, however, to have a new cultural evolutionism, in which the transforming mechanism in human potentiality is not intellectual mastery and its repression-based science and technology, but the forces of Eros and a science devoted to *its* cause, i.e., integrating the insights of the poets and mystics, along lines that Brown proposes? Hope springs eternal.

4

A Clue to the Nature of Man: The Symbol

ERNST CASSIRER

. . . No longer in a merely physical universe, man lives in a symbolic universe. Language, myth, art, and religion are parts of this universe. They are the varied threads which weave the symbolic net, the tangled web of human experience. All human progress in thought and experience refines upon and strengthens this net. No longer can man confront reality immediately; he cannot see it, as it were, face to face.

Physical reality seems to recede in proportion as man's symbolic activity advances. Instead of dealing with the things themselves man is in a sense constantly conversing with himself. He has so enveloped himself in linguistic forms, in artistic images, in mythical symbols or religious rites that he cannot see or know anything except by the interposition of this artificial medium. His situation is the same in the theoretical as in the practical sphere. Even here man does not live in a world of hard facts, or according to his immediate needs and desires. He lives rather in the midst of imaginary emotions, in hopes and fears, in illusions and disillusions, in his fantasies and dreams. "What disturbs and alarms man," said Epictetus, "are not the things, but his opinions and fancies about the things."

From the point of view at which we have just arrived we may correct and enlarge the classical definition of man. In spite of all the efforts of modern irrationalism this definition of man as an *animal rationale* has not lost its force. Rationality is indeed an inherent feature of all human activities. Mythology itself is not simply a crude mass of superstitions or gross delusions. It is not merely chaotic, for it possesses a systematic or conceptual form. But, on the other hand, it would be impossible to characterize the structure of myth as rational. Language has often been identified with reason, or with the very source of reason. But it is easy to see that this definition fails to cover the whole field. It is a *pars pro toto*; it offers us a part for the whole. For side by side with conceptual language there is an emotional language; side by side with logical or scientific language there is a language of poetic imagination. Primarily language does not express thoughts or ideas, but feelings and affections. And even a religion "within the limits of pure reason" as conceived and worked out by Kant is no more than a mere abstraction. It conveys only the ideal shape, only the shadow, of what a genuine and concrete religious life is. The great thinkers who have defined man as an *animal rationale* were not empiricists, nor did they ever intend to give an empirical account of human nature. By this definition they were expressing rather a fundamental moral imperative. Reason is a very inadequate term with which to comprehend the forms of man's cultural life in all their richness and variety. But all these forms are symbolic forms. Hence, instead of defining man

as an *animal rationale*, we should define him as an *animal symbolicum*. By so doing we can designate his specific difference, and we can understand the new way open to man—the way to civilization.

I

By our definition of man as an *animal symbolicum* we have arrived at our first point of departure for further investigations. But it now becomes imperative that we develop this definition somewhat in order to give it greater precision. That symbolic thought and symbolic behavior are among the most characteristic features of human life, and that the whole progress of human culture is based on these conditions, is undeniable. But are we entitled to consider them as the special endowment of man to the exclusion of all other organic beings? Is not symbolism a principle which we may trace back to a much deeper source, and which has a much broader range of applicability? If we answer this question in the negative we must, as it seems, confess our ignorance concerning many fundamental questions which have perennially occupied the center of attention in the philosophy of human culture. The question of the *origin* of language, of art, of religion becomes unanswerable, and we are left with human culture as a given fact which remains in a sense isolated and, therefore, unintelligible.

It is understandable that scientists have always refused to accept such a solution. They have made great efforts to connect the fact of symbolism with other well-known and more elementary facts. The problem has been felt to be of paramount importance, but unfortunately it has very rarely been approached with an entirely open mind. From the first it has been obscured and confused by other questions which belong to a quite different realm of discourse. Instead of giving us an unbiased description and analysis of the phenomena themselves the discussion of this problem has been converted into a metaphysical dispute. It has become the bone of contention between the different metaphysical systems: between idealism and materialism, spiritualism and naturalism. For all these systems the question of symbolism has become a crucial problem, on which the future shape of science and metaphysics has seemed to hinge.

With this aspect of the problem we are not concerned here, having set for ourselves a much more modest and concrete task. We shall attempt to describe the symbolic attitude of man in a more accurate manner in order to be able to contradistinguish it from other modes of symbolic behavior found throughout the animal kingdom. That animals do not always react to stimuli in a direct way, that they are capable of an indirect reaction, is evidently beyond question. The well-known experiments of Pavlov provide us with a rich body of empirical evidence concerning the so-called representative stimuli. In the case of the anthropoid apes a very interesting experimental study by Wolfe has shown the effectiveness of "token rewards." The animals learned to respond to tokens as substitute for food rewards in the same way in which they responded to food itself.[1] According to Wolfe the results of varied and protracted training experiments have demonstrated that symbolic processes occur in the behavior of anthropoid apes. Robert M. Yerkes, who describes these experiments in his latest book, draws from them an important general conclusion.

That they [symbolic processes] are relatively rare and difficult to observe is evident. One may fairly continue to question their existence, but I suspect that they presently will be identified as antecedents of human symbolic processes. Thus we leave this subject at a most exciting stage of development, when discoveries of moment seem imminent.[2]

It would be premature to make any predictions with regard to the future development of this problem. The field must be left open for future investigations. The interpretation of the experimental facts, on the other hand, always depends on certain fundamental concepts which have to be clarified before the empirical material can bear its fruit. Modern psychology and psychobiology take this fact into account. It seems to me highly significant that nowadays it is not the philosophers but the empirical observers and investigators who appear to be taking the leading roles in solving this problem. The latter tell us that after all the problem is not merely an empirical one but to a great degree a logical one. Georg Révész has recently published a series of articles in which he starts off with the proposition that the warmly debated question of so-called *animal language* cannot be solved on the basis of mere facts of animal psychology. Everyone who examines the different psychological theses and theories with an unbiased and critical mind must come at least to the conclusion that the problem cannot be cleared up by simply referring to forms of animal communication and to certain animal accomplishments which are gained by drill and training. All such accomplishments admit to the most contradictory interpretations. Hence it is necessary, first of all, to find a correct logical starting point, one which can lead us to a natural and sound interpretation

[1] J. B. Wolfe, "Effectiveness of Token-rewards for Chimpanzees," Comparative Psychology Monographs, 12, No. 5.

[2] Robert M. Yerkes, Chimpanzees. A Laboratory Colony (New Haven, Yale University Press, 1943), p. 189.

of the empirical facts. This starting point is the *definition of speech* (*die Begriffsbestimmung der Sprache*).[3] But instead of giving a ready-made definition of speech, it would be better perhaps to proceed along tentative lines. Speech is not a simple and uniform phenomenon. It consists of different elements which, both biologically and systematically, are not on the same level. We must try to find the order and interrelationships of the constituent elements; we must, as it were, distinguish the various geological strata of speech. The first and most fundamental stratum is evidently the language of the emotions. A great portion of all human utterance still belongs to this stratum. But there is a form of speech that shows us quite a different type. Here the word is by no means a mere interjection; it is not an involuntary expression of feeling, but a part of a sentence which has a definite syntactical and logical structure.[4] It is true that even in highly developed, in theoretical language the connection with the first element is not entirely broken off. Scarcely a sentence can be found—except perhaps the pure formal sentences of mathematics—without a certain affective or emotional tinge.[5] Analogies and parallels to emotional language may be found in abundance in the animal world. As regards chimpanzees Wolfgang Koehler states that they achieve a considerable degree of expression by means of gesture. Rage,

terror, despair, grief, pleading, desire, playfulness, and pleasure are readily expressed in this manner. Nevertheless one element, which is characteristic of and indispensable to all human language, is missing: we find no signs which have an objective reference or meaning. "It may be . taken as positively proved," say Koehler,

that their gamut of *phonetics* is entirely "subjective," and can only express emotions, never designate or describe objects. But they have so many phonetic elements which are also common to human languages, that their lack of articulate speech cannot be ascribed to *secondary* (gloss-labial) limitations. Their gestures too, of face and body like their expression in sound, never designate or "describe" objects (Bühler).[6]

II

Here we touch upon the crucial point in our whole problem. The difference between *propositional language* and *emotional language* is the real landmark between the human and the animal world. All the theories and observations concerning animal language are wide of the mark if they fail to recognize this fundamental difference.[7]

---

[3] G. Révész, "Die menschlichen Kommunikationsformen und die sogenannte Tiersprache," *Proceedings of the Netherlands Akademie van Wetenschappen*, XLIII (1940), Nos. 9, 10; XLIV (1941), No. 1.

[4] For the distinction between mere emotive utterances and "the normal type of communication of ideas that is speech," see the introductory remarks of Edward Sapir, *Language* (New York, Harcourt, Brace, 1921).

[5] For further details see Charles Bally, *Le langage et la vie* (Paris, 1936).

[6] Wolfgang Koehler, "Zur Psychologie des Schimpansen," *Psychologische Forschung*, I (1921), 27. Cf. the English ed., *The Mentality of Apes* (New York, Harcourt, Brace, 1925), App., p. 317.

[7] An early attempt to make a sharp distinction between propositional and emotional language was made in the field of the psychopathology of language. The English neurologist Jackson introduced the term "propositional language" in order to account for some very interesting pathological phenomena. He found that many patients suffering from aphasia had by no means lost the use of speech but that they could not employ their words in an objective, propositional sense. Jackson's distinction proved to be very fruitful. It has played an important part in the further development of the psychopathology of language. For details see Cassirer, *Philosophie der symbolischen Formen*, III, Chap. vi, 237–323.

In all the literature of the subject there does not seem to be a single conclusive proof of the fact that any animal ever made the decisive step from subjective to objective, from affective to propositional language. Koehler insists emphatically that speech is definitely beyond the powers of anthropoid apes. He maintains that the lack of this invaluable technical aid and the great limitation of those very important components of thought, the so-called images, constitute the causes which prevent animals from ever achieving even the least beginnings of cultural development.[8] The same conclusion has been reached by Révész. Speech, he asserts, is an anthropological concept which accordingly should be entirely discarded from the study of animal psychology. If we proceed from a clear and precise definition of speech, all the other forms of utterances, which we also find in animals, are automatically eliminated.[9] Yerkes, who has studied the problem with special interest, speaks in a more positive tone. He is convinced that even with respect to language and symbolism there exists a close relationship between man and the anthropoid apes. "This suggests," he writes, "that we may have happened upon an early phylogenetic stage in the evolution of symbolic process. There is abundant evidence that various other types of sign process than the symbolic are of frequent occurrence and function effectively in the chimpanzee." [10] Yet all this remains definitely prelinguistic. Even in the judgment of Yerkes all these functional expressions are exceedingly rudimentary, simple, and of limited usefulness by comparison with human cognitive processes.[11] The genetic question is not to be confused here with the analytical and phenomenological question. The logical analysis of human speech always leads us to an element of prime importance which has no parallel in the animal world. The general theory of evolution in no sense stands in the way of the acknowledgment of this fact. Even in the field of the phenomena of organic nature we have learned that evolution does not exclude a sort of original creation. The fact of sudden mutation and of emergent evolution has to be admitted. Modern biology no longer speaks of evolution in terms of earlier Darwinism; nor does it explain the causes of evolution in the same way. We may readily admit that the anthropoid apes, in the development of certain symbolic processes, have made a significant forward step. But again we must insist that they did not reach the threshold of the human world. They entered, as it were, a blind alley.

For the sake of a clear statement of the problem we must carefully distinguish between *signs* and *symbols*. That we find rather complex systems of signs and signals in animal behavior seems to be an ascertained fact. We may even say that some animals, especially domesticated animals, are extremely susceptible to signs.[12] A dog will react to the slightest changes in the behavior of his master; he will even distinguish the expressions of a human

[8] Koehler, *The Mentality of Apes*, p. 277.
[9] Révész, *op. cit.*, XLIII, Pt. II (1940), 33.
[10] Yerkes and Nissen, "Prelinguistic Sign Behavior in Chimpanzee," *Science*, LXXXIX, 587.
[11] Yerkes, *Chimpanzees*, p. 189.

[12] This susceptibility has, for instance, been proved in the famous case of "clever Hans" which a few decades ago created something of a sensation among psychobiologists. Clever Hans was a horse which appeared to possess an astounding intelligence. He could even master rather complicated arithmetical problems, extract cube roots, and so on, stamping on the ground as many times as the solution of the problem required. A special committee of psychologists and other scientists was called on to investigate the case. It soon became clear that the animal reacted to certain involuntary movements of its owner. When the owner was absent or did not understand the question, the horse could not answer it.

face or the modulations of a human voice.[13] But it is a far cry from these phenomena to an understanding of symbolic and human speech. The famous experiments of Pavlov prove only that animals can easily be trained to react not merely to direct stimuli but to all sorts of mediate or representative stimuli. A bell, for example, may become a "sign for dinner," and an animal may be trained not to touch its food when this sign is absent. But from this we learn only that the experimenter, in this case, has succeeded in changing the food-situation of the animal. He has complicated this situation by voluntarily introducing into it a new element. All the phenomena which are commonly described as conditioned reflexes are not merely very far from but even opposed to the essential character of human symbolic thought. Symbols— in the proper sense of this term—cannot be reduced to mere signals. Signals and symbols belong to two different universes of discourse: a signal is a

part of the physical world of being; a symbol is a part of the human world of meaning. Signals are "operators"; symbols are "designators."[14] Signals, even when understood and used as such, have nevertheless a sort of physical or substantial being; symbols have only a functional value.

Bearing this distinction in mind, we can find an approach to one of the most controverted problems. The question of the *intelligence of animals* has always been one of the greatest puzzles of anthropological philsophy. Tremendous efforts, both of thought and observation, have been expended on answers to this question. But the ambiguity and vagueness of the very term "intelligence" has always stood in the way of a clear solution. How can we hope to answer a question whose import we do not understand? Metaphysicians and scientists, naturalists and theologians have used the word intelligence in varying and contradictory senses. Some psychologists and psychobiologists have flatly refused to speak of the intelligence of animals. In all animal behavior they saw only the play of a certain automatism. This thesis had behind it the authority of Descartes; yet it has been reasserted in modern psychology. "The animal," says E. L. Thorndike in his work on animal intelligence, "does not think one is like the other, nor does it, as is so often said, mistake one for the other. It does not think *about* it at all; it just thinks *it* . . . The idea that animals react to a particular and absolutely defined and realized sense-impression, and that a similar reaction to a sense-impression which varies from the first proves an association by similarity, is a myth." [15] Later and more exact ob-

[13] To illustrate this point I should like to mention another very revealing example. The psychologist, Dr. Pfungst, who had developed some new and interesting methods for the study of animal behavior, once told me that he had received a letter from a major about a curious problem. The major had a dog which accompanied him on his walks. Whenever the master got ready to go out the animal showed signs of great joy and excitement. But one day the major decided to try a little experiment. Pretending to go out, he put on his hat, took his cane, and made the customary preparations—without, however, any intention of going for a walk. To his great surprise the dog was not in the least deceived; he remained quietly in his corner. After a brief period of observation Dr. Pfungst was able to solve the mystery. In the major's room there was a desk with a drawer which contained some valuable and important documents. The major had formed the habit of rattling this drawer before leaving the house in order to make sure that it was locked. He did not do so the day he did not intend to go out. But for the dog this had become a signal, a necessary element of the walk-situation. Without this signal the dog did not react.

[14] For the distinction between operators and designators see Charles Morris, "The Foundation of the Theory of Signs," *Encyclopedia of the Unified Sciences* (1938).
[15] Edward L. Thorndike, *Animal Intelligence* (New York, Macmillan, 1911), pp. 119 ff.

servations led to a different conclusion.
In the case of the higher animals it became clear that they were able to solve
rather difficult problems and that these
solutions were not brought about in a
merely mechanical way, by trial and
error. As Koehler points out, the most
striking difference exists between a
mere chance solution and a genuine
solution, so that the one can easily be
distinguished from the other. That at
least some of the reactions of the higher
animals are not merely a product of
chance but guided by insight appears
to be incontestable.[16] If by intelligence
we understand either adjustment to the
immediate environment or adaptive
modification of environment, we must
certainly ascribe to animals a comparatively highly developed intelligence. It
must also be conceded that not all animal actions are governed by the presence of an immediate stimulus. The
animal is capable of all sorts of detours
in its reactions. It may learn not only
to use implements but even to invent
tools for its purposes. Hence some
psychobiologists do not hesitate to
speak of a creative or constructive imagination in animals.[17] But neither this
intelligence nor this imagination is of
the specifically human type. In short,
we may say that the animal possesses
a practical imagination and intelligence
whereas man alone has developed a
new form: *a symbolic imagination and
intelligence.*

Moreover, in the mental development of the individual mind the transition from one form to the other—from
a merely practical attitude to a symbolic attitude—is evident. But here this
step is the final result of a slow and
continuous process. By the usual methods of psychological observation it is
not easy to distinguish the individual

stages of this complicated process.
There is, however, another way to obtain full insight into the general character and paramount importance of
this transition. Nature itself has here,
so to speak, made an experiment capable of throwing unexpected light upon
the point in question. We have the
classical cases of Laura Bridgman and
Helen Keller, two blind deaf-mute children, who by means of special methods
learned to speak. Although both cases
are well known and have often been
treated in psychological literature,[18] I
must nevertheless remind the reader of
them once more because they contain
perhaps the best illustration of the general problem with which we are here
concerned. Mrs. Sullivan, the teacher
of Helen Keller, has recorded the exact
date on which the child really began to
understand the meaning and function
of human language. I quote her own
words:

I must write you a line this morning because something very important has happened. Helen has taken the second great
step in her education. She has learned
that *everything has a name, and that the
manual alphabet is the key to everything
she wants to know.*

. . . This morning, while she was washing, she wanted to know the name for
"water." When she wants to know the
name of anything, she points to it and
pats my hand. I spelled "w-a-t-e-r" and
thought no more about it until after
breakfast. . . . [Later on] we went out
to the pump house, and I made Helen
hold her mug under the spout while I
pumped. As the cold water gushed forth,
filling the mug, I spelled "w-a-t-e-r" in
Helen's free hand. The word coming so
close upon the sensation of cold water

[16] See Koehler, *op. cit.*, chap. vii, " 'Chance'
and 'Imitation.' "
[17] See R. M. and A. W. Yerkes, *The Great
Apes* (New Haven, Yale University Press,
1929), pp. 368 ff., 520 ff.

[18] For Laura Bridgman see Maud Howe and
Florence Howe Hall, *Laura Bridgman* (Bos-
ton, 1903); Mary Swift Lamson, *Life and
Education of Laura Dewey Bridgman* (Bos-
ton, 1881); Wilhelm Jerusalem, *Laura
Bridgman, Erziehung einer Taubstumm-
Blinden* (Berlin, 1905).

rushing over her hand seemed to startle her. She dropped the mug and stood as one transfixed. A new light came into her face. She spelled "water" several times. Then she dropped on the ground and asked for its name and pointed to the pump and the trellis and suddenly turning round she asked for my name. I spelled "teacher." All the way back to the house she was highly excited, and learned the name of every object she touched, so that in a few hours she had added thirty new words to her vocabulary. The next morning she got up like a radiant fairy. She has flitted from object to object, asking the name of everything and kissing me for very gladness. . . . Everything must have a name now. Wherever we go, she asks eagerly for the names of things she has not learned at home. She is anxious for her friends to spell, and eager to teach the letters to everyone she meets. She drops the signs and pantomime she used before, as soon as she has words to supply their place, and the acquirement of a new word affords her the liveliest pleasure. And we notice that her face grows more expressive each day.[19]

The decisive step leading from the use of signs and pantomime to the use of words, that is, of symbols, could scarcely be described in a more striking manner. What was the child's real discovery at this moment? Helen Keller had previously learned to combine a certain thing or event with a certain sign of the manual alphabet. A fixed association had been established between these things and certain tactile impressions. But a series of such associations, even if they are repeated and amplified, still does not imply an understanding of what human speech is and means. In order to arrive at such an understanding the child had to make a new and much more significant discovery. It had to understand that *every-thing has a name*—that the symbolic

function is not restricted to particular cases but is a principle of *universal* applicability which encompasses the whole field of human thought. In the case of Helen Keller this discovery came as a sudden shock. She was a girl seven years of age who, with the exception of defects in the use of certain sense organs, was in an excellent state of health and possessed of a highly developed mind. By the neglect of her education she had been very much retarded. Then, suddenly, the crucial development takes place. It works like an intellectual revolution. The child begins to see the world in a new light. It has learned the use of words not merely as mechanical signs or signals but as an entirely new instrument of thought. A new horizon is opened up, and henceforth the child will roam at will in this incomparably wider and freer area.

The same can be shown in the case of Laura Bridgman, though hers is a less spectacular story. Both in mental ability and in intellectual development Laura Bridgman was greatly inferior to Helen Keller. Her life and education do not contain the same dramatic elements we find in Helen Keller. Yet in both cases the same typical elements are present. After Laura Bridgman had learned the use of the finger-alphabet she, too, suddenly reached the point at which she began to understand the symbolism of human speech. In this respect we find a surprising parallelism between the two cases. "I shall never forget," write Miss Drew, one of the first teachers of Laura Bridgman, "the first meal taken after she appreciated the use of the finger-alphabet. Every article that she touched must have a name; and I was obliged to call some one to help me wait upon the other children, while she kept me busy in spelling the new words."[20]

[19] See Helen Keller, *The Story of My Life* (New York, Doubleday, Page & Co., 1902, 1903), Supplementary Account of Helen Keller's Life and Education, pp. 315 ff.

[20] See Mary Swift Lamson, *Life and Education of Laura Dewey Bridgman, the Deaf, Dumb, and Blind Girl* (Boston, Houghton, Mifflin Co., 1881), pp. 7 f.

III

The principle of symbolism, with its universality, validity, and general applicability, is the magic word, the Open Sesame! giving access to the specifically human world, to the world of human culture. Once man is in possession of this magic key further progress is assured. Such progress is evidently not obstructed or made impossible by any lack in the sense material. The case of Helen Keller, who reached a very high degree of mental development and intellectual culture, shows us clearly and irrefutably that a human being in the construction of his human world is not dependent upon the quality of his sense material. If the theories of sensationalism were right, if every idea were nothing but a faint copy of an original sense impression, then the condition of a blind, deaf, and dumb child would indeed be desperate. For it would be deprived of the very sources of human knowledge; it would be, as it were, an exile from reality. But if we study Helen Keller's autobiography we are at once aware that this is untrue, and at the same time we understand why it is untrue. Human culture derives its specific character and its intellectual and moral values, not from the material of which it consists, but from its form, its architectural structure. And this form may be expressed in any sense material. Vocal language has a very great technical advantage over tactile language; but the technical defects of the latter do not destroy its essential use. The free development of symbolic thought and symbolic expression is not obstructed by the use of tactile signs in the place of vocal ones. If the child has succeeded in grasping the meaning of human language, it does not matter in which particular material this meaning is accessible to it. As the case of Helen Keller proves, man can construct his symbolic world out of the poorest and scantiest materials. The thing of vital importance is not the individual bricks and stones but their general *function* as architectural form. In the realm of speech it is their general symbolic function which vivifies the material signs and "makes them speak." Without this vivifying principle the human world would indeed remain deaf and mute. With this principle, even the world of a deaf, dumb, and blind child can become incomparably broader and richer than the world of the most highly developed animal.

Universal applicability, owing to the fact that everything has a name, is one of the greatest prerogatives of human symbolism. But it is not the only one. There is still another characteristic of symbols which accompanies and complements this one, and forms its necessary correlate. A symbol is not only universal but extremely variable. I can express the same meaning in various languages; and even within the limits of a single language a certain thought or idea may be expressed in quite different terms. A sign or signal is related to the thing to which it refers in a fixed and unique way. Any one concrete and individual sign refers to a certain individual thing. In Pavlov's experiments the dogs could easily be trained to reach for food only upon being given special signs; they would not eat until they heard a particular sound which could be chosen at the discretion of the experimenter. But this bears no analogy, as it has often been interpreted, to human symbolism; on the contrary, it is in opposition to symbolism. A genuine human symbol is characterized not by its uniformity but by its versatility. It is not rigid or inflexible but mobile. It is true that the full *awareness* of this mobility seems to be a rather late achievement in man's intellectual and cultural development. In primitive mentality this awareness is very seldom attained. Here the symbol is still regarded as a property of the thing like other physical properties. In mythical thought the name of a god is an integral part of the nature of the god. If I do not call the god by his right name, then the spell or prayer becomes ineffective. The same holds good for symbolic actions. A religious rite, a sacrifice, must always be performed in the same invariable way and in the same order if it is to have its effect. [21] Children are often greatly confused when they first learn that not every name of an object is a "proper name," that the same thing may have quite different names in different languages. They tend to think that a thing "is" what it is called. But this is only a first step. Every normal child will learn very soon that it can use various symbols to express the same wish or thought. For this variability and mobility there is apparently no parallel in the animal world. [22] Long before Laura Bridgman had learned to speak, she had developed a very curious mode of expression, a language of her own. This language did not consist of articulated sounds but only of various noises, which are described as "emotional noises." She was in the habit of uttering these sounds in the presence of certain persons. Thus they become entirely individualized; every person in her environment was greeted by a special noise. "Whenever she met unexpectedly an acquaintance," writes Dr. Lieber, "I found that she repeatedly uttered the word for that person before she began to speak. It was the utterance of pleasurable recognition." [23] But when by means of the finger alphabet the child had grasped the meaning of human language the case was altered. Now the sound really became a name: and this name was not bound to an in-

dividual person but could be changed if the circumstances seemed to require it. One day, for instance, Laura Bridgman had a letter from her former teacher, Miss Drew, who, in the meantime, by her marriage had become a Mrs. Morton. In this letter she was invited to visit her teacher. This gave her great pleasure, but she found fault with Miss Drew because she had signed the letter with her old name instead of using the name of her husband. She even said that now she must find another noise for her teacher, as the one for Drew must not be the same as that for Morton.[24] It is clear that the former "noises" have here undergone an important and very interesting change in meaning. They are no longer special utterances, inseparable from a particular concrete situation. They have become abstract names. For the new name invented by the child did not designate a new individual but the same individual in a new relationship.

IV

Another important aspect of our general problem now emerges—the problem of the *dependence of relational thought upon symbolic thought*. Without a complex system of symbols relational thought cannot arise at all, much less reach its full development. It would not be correct to say that the mere *awareness* of relations presupposes an intellectual act, an act of logical or abstract thought. Such an awareness is necessary even in elementary acts of perception. The sensationalist theories used to describe perception as a mosaic or simple sense data. Thinkers of this persuasion constantly overlooked the fact that sensation itself is by no means a mere struggle or bundle of isolated impressions. Modern Gestalt psychology has corrected this view. It has shown that the very simplest perceptual processes imply fundamental structural

[21] For further details see Cassirer, *Sprache und Mythos* (Leipzig, 1925).
[22] For this problem see W. M. Urban, *Language and Reality*, Pt. I, iii, 95 ff.
[23] See Francis Lieber, "A Paper on the Vocal Sounds of Laura Bridgman," *Smithsonian Contributions to Knowledge*, II, Art. 2, p. 27.

[24] See Mary Swift Lamson, *op. cit.*, p. 84.

elements, certain patterns or configurations. This principle holds both for the human and the animal world. Even in comparatively low stages of animal life the presence of these structural elements—especially of spatial and optical structures—has been experimentally proved.[25] The mere awareness of relations cannot, therefore, be regarded as a specific feature of human consciousness. We do find, however, in man a special type of relational thought which has no parallel in the animal world. In man an ability to isolate relations—to consider them in their abstract meaning—has developed. In order to grasp this meaning man is no longer dependent upon concrete sense data, upon visual, auditory, tactile, kinesthetic data. He considers these relations "in themselves"—αὐτὸ καθ' αὐτό, as Plato said. Geometry is the classic example of this turning point in man's intellectual life. Even in elementary geometry we are not bound to the apprehension of concrete individual figures. We are not concerned with physical things or perceptual objects, for we are studying universal spatial relations for whose expression we have an adequate symbolism. Without the preliminary step of human language such an achievement would not be possible. In all the tests which have been made of the processes of abstraction or generalization in animals, this point has become evident. Koehler succeeded in showing the ability of chimpanzees to respond to the *relation* between two or more objects instead of to a particular object. Confronted by two food-containing boxes, the chimpanzee by reason of previous general training would constantly choose the larger—even though

the particular object might in a previous experiment have been rejected as the smaller of the pair. Similar capacity to respond to the nearer object, the brighter, the bluer, rather than to a particular box was demonstrated. Koehler's results were confirmed and extended by later experiments. It could be shown that the higher animals are capable of what has been called the "isolation of perceptual factors." They have the potentiality for singling out a particular perceptual quality of the experimental situation and reacting accordingly. In this sense animals are able to abstract color from size and shape or shape from size and color. In some experiments made by Mrs. Kohts a chimpanzee was able to select from a collection of objects varying extremely in visual qualities those which had some one quality in common; it could, for instance, pick out all objects of a given color and place them in a receiving box. These examples seem to prove that the higher animals are capable of that process which Hume in his theory of knowledge terms making a *"distinction of reason."* [26] But all the experimenters engaged in these investigations have also emphasized the rarity, the rudimentariness, and the imperfection of these processes. Even after they have learned to single out a particular quality and to reach toward this, animals are liable to all sorts of curious mistakes.[27] If there are certain traces of a *distinctio rationis* in the animal world, they are, as it were, nipped in the bud. They cannot develop because they do not possess that invaluable and indeed indispensable aid of human speech, of a system of symbols. . . .

[25] See Wolfgang Koehler, "Optische Untersuchungen am Schimpansen und am Haushuhn; Nachweis einfacher Strukturfunktionen beim Schimpansen und beim Haushuhn," *Abhandlungen der Berliner Akademie der Wissenschaften* (1915, 1918).

[26] Hume's theory of the "distinction of reason" is explained in his *Treatise of Human Nature*, Pt. I, sec. 7 (London, Green and Grosse, 1874), I, 332 ff.

[27] Examples are given by Yerkes in *Chimpanzees*, pp. 103 ff.

B Social Action and the Development of the Self

5

The Nature of Social Action

W. J. H. SPROTT

. . . If it is true that the natural sciences are, as it were, an elaboration of the day-to-day practical rules that everyone has to learn in order to cope with his physical environment, it is indeed the case that psychology and the social sciences are an elaboration of the day-to-day practical rules we have to apply in dealing with one another. It is true, of course, that while the non-specialists are applying such a general corpus of knowledge as has become common property the specialist in the natural sciences investigates new problems; and he makes discoveries which are surprising to his fellow men. And

From *Science and Social Action* by W. J. H. Sprott. Copyright © by C. A. Watts & Co. Ltd. Used by permission.

this is what makes it sound odd to say that his work is an "elaboration of day-to-day practical rules." I use the expression to link up the "pure" scientist with action. The surprises are due to the fact that the scientific discoverer in the field of the natural sciences is either handling old materials in a new way, or handling new materials altogether. He is enlarging the world in which we live and extending the scope of our action, much as the early explorers extended the world in which we live by discovering places previously unknown, and much as—in a microscopic region —the cook who discovers that the best way to cook brussels sprouts is to plunge them for five minutes into boiling water, is extending her culinary sphere and those of her friends to whom she reveals her secret.

Now with psychology and sociology all this seems to me to be different. If we say, very rightly, that psychology is the study of human behaviour, and sociology the study of social behaviour and its accompaniments, surely it is absurd to suggest that no one studied human beings and groups of human beings before Wundt and Comte. . . . Surely man was studying woman from the very beginning in the Garden of Eden. And as to social psychology, it was applied with some effect by the serpent. Social science was applied in action by the first administrator. Man has been studying man, and men have administered their fellows, ever since men emerged and lived in groups large enough to call for the concept of "society." And this has gone on down the ages. No wonder the self-conscious and explicit study of men and society brings with it so few surprises. Even psychoanalysis is really an elaboration of what was already known: namely that certain people give bona fide reasons for doing things—reasons which other people know to be false. Let me hasten to say that I am not minimizing the importance of this. All I am saying is that psychology and sociology are quite obviously elaborations of ideas which we inevitably get from our everyday social intercourse with other people like ourselves. Unlike the fields of natural science, we are not coming across new materials, new places, new techniques—or very rarely; we are ever defining our concepts about the same old thing. It is this that depresses many modern psychologists. They want something new, something startling. And where do they look? To physiology, of course. There they can find new physical materials, such as endocrine secretions, which influence human behaviour in unexpected ways. They study the physiology of conditioning and try

to reduce it to a system. They handle the body in new ways, giving it electric shocks, pumping in insulin, or severing brain-fibres by pre-frontal leucotomy; and the results are startling indeed. But psychology, in the sense that we usually understand it—the study of men's behaviour in terms of conscious and unconscious motives—does not spring from the study of their nervous systems; it springs from the inevitabilities of social action, and so, I shall suggest, does sociology. . . .

Let us now look more closely into the concept of social action. My first point is that all social action involves mutual adaptation. The conduct of A is determined by A's expectation of B's response, and B's response is determined by B's interpretation of A's conduct and the expectation he attributes to him, and also by his expectation of A's counter-response, and so on. This, as George Mead has pointed out, is true of the intercourse of animals below human level. The sexual, playful, and quarrelsome interaction of dogs and cats and birds all involve such mutual adaptation. So does the intercourse between humans and such domestic animals as interact with them. These range from such creatures as one can, as they say, "make pets of" to such creatures as one cannot because their interaction is limited to the mere approach to food and retreat from contact. With human beings the same "pet" level is found between mother and her infant child. With human beings, however, something else is present. At some point in the evolutionary series creatures emerged whose gestures became not merely significant in the sense of eliciting appropriate responses, but significant to themselves—the point at which a gesture is awarefully directed to the eliciting of a response. How this came about we do not know. To say that the forebrain became bigger does not help us until we know what goes on inside it.

It may be that something like what George Mead suggested took place: that the turning point was the incipient adumbration in the actor of the response of the other, so that he, the actor, takes the role of the other in himself, thus paving the way for a contrast between his own "other" response, the *real* response of the other, and between both and his own spontaneous spring of activity. It may be that language, with its peculiar characteristics of being uttered and heard—both action and self-stimulus—by the actor, played a significant part in the development of man as such. We cannot go back and look. We can say that such feral men as have come to our notice—children brought up by animals or neglected by men—are scarcely human at all; but as for our own remote prehuman ancestry, we can but speculate. One thing seems to be plausible, and that is that only through social interaction at a level at which the awareful eliciting of counter-responses becomes possible do men become men, aware of themselves as separate beings having meaning intercourse with one another.

And what happens then? I think one can get some insight into this by examining one or two trivial and very familiar experiences—so trivial that I feel somewhat apologetic about bringing them to your attention.

Imagine two friends who have been so related for some time. The actions of each when they are together are mutually adapted. After a while each can, as we say, "count upon" the other. In fact it is not merely that A can guess what B will do, as a psychiatrist can guess at the likely response of his patient, and it is not merely that B can guess what A will do, as, indeed, the patient may guess at the likely conduct of the psychiatrist. There is more to it than that. A knows that B knows what A is likely to do, and B knows what A expects B to expect. Something which one can call a mutually accepted system of expectations gets established. Each knows the other's little ways, and knows that the other knows his. There may, indeed, be unspoken secrets which each keeps from the other. Each has his own perspective in the duality; but for the relationship to persist there must be a mutual system controlling the conduct of both. The importance of this may indeed be realized when one reflects upon the common complaint you hear people make about some acquaintance: "Of course," they say, "you can't really make friends with him because he's so incalculable; you don't know what he's going to do next." Without a mutually accepted framework of behaviour no persistent social intercourse is possible. I would even extend this notion to hostility, though here there are complications. One enemy may destroy the other, and the relationship is at an end in default of one of the relata. The enemies may part and hate at a distance, and in some sense the relationship is at an end. They may, however, persist together or near at hand, and then, as we all know, for the mutual hate to be kept up, a mutually accepted system of not speaking or passing nasty remarks, or reciprocal head-tossing must be preserved. That, surely, is one of the reasons why a soft answer turneth away wrath. That is why it takes two to make a quarrel.

Corresponding to the overt mutual adjustments and registering their consistency over a period we can conveniently endow the interacting parties with "frames of reference." This intervening variable we can build into that other construct: "personality," in terms of which we explain the total behaviour of each. By saying that persistent social intercourse engenders frames of reference I mean that each participant views and thinks of the other in terms of those expectations which he has acquired in the course of their friendship. Each will, as we say, "understand" the other, interpreting his gestures and his speech in terms of the mutual scheme which has become established.

And even this trivial example can be carried a little further. The two parties may, of course, interact to their mutual satisfaction without either of them mentioning the matter either to the other or to himself. On the other hand, they may, when perhaps the expectations of one are falsified: "I never expected you to do such a thing" one might say; then what I have called the scheme of accepted values may become symbolized as "our friendship." Doubtless the symbol will be slightly different in one from what it is in the other; but there must be common constituents, otherwise neither will be intelligible to the other. Again, it might be that one of them wants to do something which will cause pain to the other, something indeed which conflicts with their mutual system. Then he may say to himself: "I really ought not," or even, "I really *cannot* do this or that. It would ruin our friendship." Suppose, for instance, it is their wont to go to the pictures every Saturday night. Suppose A has an enticing invitation for one Saturday night. Will there not be a conflict in A's mind? And, indeed, supposing both A and B receive an invitation for a Saturday night. Is it a gross exaggeration to suggest that they may say to one another: "Well, of course it means giving up *our* Saturday night's pictures"? Something has been ever so slightly outraged. What, surely, has happened is that this day-to-day mutual scheme of inter-responses has become externalized and now stands out against them coercively. We are at once reminded of Durkheim's [1] definition of a

social fact: "Un fait social se reconnaît au pouvoir de coercition externe qu'il exerce ou est susceptible d'exercer sur les individus; et la présence de ce pouvoir se reconnait a son tour soit à l'existance de quelque sanction determinée, soit à la résistance que le fait oppose à toute entreprise individuelle qui tend à lui faire violence." [2]

This going to the pictures on a Saturday night is, when we come to think of it, an institution of our society of two. It would be "wrong" of A to act in disaccord with its rules in despite of B, and even slightly "wrong" of A and B to alter it. And this, not only because of a cultural standard of "friendship," —though of course any example I take will in fact bring this wider context in —but, I suggest, mainly because their relationship cannot continue without such mutually accepted norms. Certainly there are variations in the range of permissible behaviour when you compare two pairs of friends—as there are when you compare two societies on a larger scale—but some regulation there must be for any social relationship to persist.

What I am trying to suggest to you is that social institutions, law, and morality are the necessary products of all persistent social intercourse. Embryonically they are there even at the pre-human level, but their symbolization in language makes a vital difference. Without language I do not see how they could achieve the external validity they do achieve.

This becomes even clearer if we take a group larger than a pair. Imagine four people setting up house together:

[1] *Règles de la Méthode Sociologique* (Presses Universitaires, 1947 edition), p. 11.

[2] A social fact may be recognized by the coercive pressure which it brings to bear on the individual from outside; and the presence of this pressure can be detected either by the existence of some determinate sanction, or by the resistance which is set up against any attempt by the individual to violate the social fact.

it might be four students. Again mutual adaptation of each to each, and each, in a sense, to all, is essential. They cannot, we will suppose, all sit on the same chair; they cannot all get into the bath at the same time. Problems arise, and a mutually acceptable solution must be found. The seating arrangements, the bath rota, the rules for washing up, and the times for meals will become established institutions; and any new-comer will find himself confronted with an order—let us say, "a culture"—not of his devising, external and coercive, to which he has to submit. The order will be felt to be "right"; that accommodation of conflicting interests, which we call "justice," will be achieved. I mentioned the new-comer, who is confronted with a pattern of interaction. How is it conveyed to him? He might, of course, painstakingly watch and note the interlocking conduct, and form in his mind a patterned construct to represent it. More likely, of course, he will be told by the participants. "This," they might say, "is our way of life." It will have been symbolized.

And now increase this number. Let us suppose that the scheme is a success and that more students want to join. The group moves to larger quarters. They no longer, perhaps, consist of intimate friends, but acquaintances who have to be initiated. Mutual adjustment on a purely spontaneous basis becomes less reliable. The bath rota, the meal times, and so forth must be more strictly adhered to. Rules may even be written down on a sheet of paper and pinned up in the hall. Now let us suppose that in the early days each of our four friends took turns with the catering; there would not be much to do for four. But increased numbers, increased household expenses, increased responsibility for a larger establishment, present difficulties. One of their number might be specially

good at dealing with them, perhaps the one who suggested the scheme in the first place—the leader or the eldest. Here the staging of my example in student circles becomes a little unrealistic, but I will ask you to bear with me, because the unrealism is really unimportant for my purpose. Let us suppose that this skilful organizer takes on the organizing as a whole-time job. To keep him contributions must be made, perhaps larger numbers still might be needed. The group incorporates anyone who wishes to join. A room is set aside for the organizer, now called the Warden. Note what has happened. The spontaneously interacting group of people who have precipitated their own norms in the course of living together has grown into an "enterprise"—a going concern. Organization brings with it its stratification; a hierarchy is in the offing. Administration has begun. A post, a social position with its appropriate role, has been created. A *new form of social action has come into being*. And look into the future. Generations of members have passed through the group. Wardens have come and gone, each judged not by his charm but by his efficiency. The group is enlarged still further, and along come an accountant, a secretary, a matron, and a staff of waiters. There are so many in the community that the Warden, who now sits upon a dais, cannot know them all. They are just anonymous students, mere names upon alphabetical lists, allotted rooms in order of application. The group has a name, a badge, a tie and a yell. The picture of the founder hangs in a prominent place in the refectory. To go further would be frivolous. We might even imagine that when servants are in short supply, our establishment might capture the smaller hostel next door, incorporate it, and reduce its inhabitants to servitude.

Now I suggest that here we have, in

an example not so fictitious as to be quite absurd, something very like what I think Hegel and Engels had in mind when they spoke of increase in quantity often leading to a change in quality. The impersonal world of administration produces frames of reference different from those which are developed in purely personal intercourse. They are explicitly symbolized and are applied to a different kind of content. The administrator's frame of reference, when he is playing his role, is not of such a kind as is brought into action when he thinks of: "My friendship with dear old George, who is so charming even when he does get het up, though of course he only does it in order to tease me." It is not like that at all. Whether he thinks in pictures or words or both, he thinks of a larger scheme with a name attached to it—the hostel, the business, the county, the city, the country, the party. He thinks in terms of individuals occupying certain positions in the concern which, as position, are relatively permanent. He thinks of the occupants as functionaries rather than as personalities, though of course he recognizes their personalities as making them good or bad role-players. And beside the functionaries, whom he might possibly name, there are the anonymous many who are administered for his own benefit, for the benefit of someone else, or for their own benefit. Here language is essential to the working of the scheme. Communications must run backward and forward, couched in terms which are intelligible to the intercommunicants. This means that the frame of reference of all involved, the key men and the masses, must have common elements. They too must think in terms of the hostel, the business, the county, the city, the country, the party, or whatever type of concern they, as we say, belong to. In fact I would say that "belonging," in anything more than a purely classifica-

tory sense, positively *means* thinking in such terms.

But thinking in terms of the concern is by no means the whole story. In the first place, each member will see it from his own point of view; but their points of view must contain common elements for communication to be possible. The student thinks of himself as a student at Birmingham University, the lecturer as a lecturer at Birmingham University, the lab-steward as lab-steward at Birmingham University, and so on. They all mean something the same by "Birmingham University." Secondly, each will have an attitude towards the concern. He may identify himself with it and act with enthusiasm in terms of its regulations and in terms of his notion of the accepted ethos; he may dissociate himself from the concern, merely keeping the rules in order to avoid the consequences of breaking them; or he may be indifferent to the concern but keep the rules because life is simpler that way; or break them when he thinks he can get away with it. But whichever he does, he must have somewhat the same notion of the concern and its rules as his fellow members. The future history of the concern will of course in part depend on the proportions of those who identify themselves with it as compared with those who dissociate themselves from it, and the intensity of their feelings, which, in turn, will be largely dependent on their conscious or unconscious interests.

Now all the time we must remember that within the concern, whatever it may be, there is always personal intercourse going on, with its mutual adjustments, its private codes of behaviour, its crises, and their resolutions. The administrator has his wife, his daughter, his cronies, and his carpet slippers. Indeed, one of the administrated, meeting him *en pantouffles*, may say afterwards: "the old man was really quite human"—a significant phrase. And yet, again, these private affairs occur upon a public stage. Thus we must fuse or combine our frames of reference. Every man is both a "private person" and a "public personage"—using the latter phrase in no status-conferring sense. He is in love with, devoted to, or indifferent to, the woman with whom he shares his leisure hours; at the same time he is her husband, her fiancé, or her lover. One evening he is with his intimates, but has to leave them to take the chair at a meeting. He is having dinner with his friend Tom and is called away to a patient.

And so we might go on, but we must beware of imputing the analytical world view of the social scientist to the subjects of his study without qualification. A man's conduct is less awarefully governed than we are apt to imagine. It is ridiculous to suppose that a person says to himself: "Now I am a private person, now I am a civil servant, foreign secretary, dustman," or whatever position he may occupy. The analytic view is seen through the frame of reference of the sociologist. Nevertheless we can say that every man and woman is brought up to develop a kind of double world in which he or she lives: a world of immediacies set in a context of remoter relationships, institutions, beliefs, and concerns. . . . A man works beside Fred, a decent sort of chap even if he is a bit of a boozer; his face-to-face intercourse with Fred takes place in a context of the firm who employs them, and that is situated in a city, and the city in a country which has relations with other countries in the world. Sometimes the man thinks in terms of Fred's Freddishness, if I may be allowed the expression, sometimes in terms of "the country." He has learnt to handle Fred partly by past experience with other people, and partly by trial and error with Fred himself; he has learnt to think in terms of the firm and the country because these

concepts have been conveyed to him in language. In the latter case there is no direct contact because in some sense the firm and the country exist only in virtue of the agreed conventions of the people he meets and of multitudes of other people whom he does not meet. Of course there has to be a material substratum for it all; there have to be other human beings able to do things with their hands and with machines; there have to be materials to mould into the desired shapes; there have to be buildings in which this is done. Without all this the notion of "the firm" will not come into existence. All the same, the accumulation of these articles in one place is the result of social action. Our worker does not merely mean by "the firm" these physical things: he means the whole concern with its positions of manager and foreman, its profit-making, its clocking-in system, and so on, within which the men, machine and building have their meaning.

Now not all of the world-views I have been discussing are of equal importance to the sociologist. There are some which more closely approximate to the one he is trying to formulate. The world of the peasant may be limited by the boundaries of his village with a vague penumbra behind his religion and the fruits of his labour, a vague notion of distant co-believers and tax-collectors. He is more concerned with day-to-day personal contacts. The administrator, as we have seen, has a different and wider view. He thinks in terms of countries, of cities, of economic problems. He, indeed, has the sociological view. The sociologist, I suggest, is the specialist who tries to elaborate and make precise the administrative world-picture.

I have put the whole matter in this way because I want to make two points. In the first place, just as the first man who moulded metal was the first metallurgist, so the first person who aware-fully considered the character of the person he was dealing with was the first psychologist; and the first administrator, whether chief or warrior, who thought in terms of the tribe, the clan, or the army, was the first sociologist. Metallurgy, psychology, and sociology as scientific disciplines arise when thought about these things becomes too complicated for the practical man. In the second place, the emergence of psychology and sociology is a natural development from the necessities of social action when performed by creatures capable of reflection and symbolic registration.

We cannot penetrate the night of time. We can, I think, plausibly assume that something like this happened. In the beginning was the word. Our ancestors at some point or other began to use words meaningfully and not as mere emotive utterances. They were then capable of symbolizing the rules according to which their social action was conducted, and handed on these rules to their children. Then, when technology enabled large numbers to keep together, a more complicated régime was necessary to ensure their efficient co-operation, and this means social action at the administrative level, with the appropriate conceptual superstructure. Once this is established and gets verbalized, then the ball is set rolling from those distant ages down to our own times. The whole apparatus of sociological analysis is there from the start: law, morality, beliefs, society, technology, economics, politics, the in-group, the out-group, the face-to-face group, the indirectly-related group, the system of positions and accompanying roles, and moreover, even the embryonic concept of status, whereby some are accepted as higher than others.

It will, I dare say, be objected that I have concentrated too much on human beings interacting with one another and that I have left their material conditions out of account. This is only because one cannot say everything at once. Of course the development of societies depends on material conditions, the appraisal of them as valuable or indifferent, and the presence or absence of things to appraise. And each generation is brought up to apprehend the significance of the physical environment as understood by the technological standards of its parents. Their own efforts will change the world both materially and evaluatively for their progeny, often in ways which they did not expect and the stage is set for another act.

In stressing the vital importance of men's *ideas* of the groups to which they belong, I may be accused of treating the whole subject too mentalistically; I may be accused of idealism, in some of the many senses of that term of abuse. But surely mental talk is the only talk we can use. Picture a little boy in a forest; along the path comes a man; the lad peeps out to see who is coming so that he can prepare himself for appropriate behaviour. It might be his maternal uncle, it might be a relation with whom it is incumbent upon him to joke or tell dirty stories, it might be the chief. The boy will recognize the on-comer and act accordingly. "He knows who it is, he has learnt how to behave, he believes that certain conduct is right and certain conduct is wrong," we say. And will any physiological story about the intruder be more helpful? X-ray him, subject him to electroencephalography, dissect him, tell us all you can about his physical make-up, and now tell us whether he really was the boy's maternal uncle or not. And the boy himself? Look into his fore-brain for traces and you will have to interpret your findings in terms of the boy's actual conduct. It may, of course, well be that in the future we shall be able to peer into the nervous system of such a little boy and say, *before* he acts: "See, that neural explosion is the maternal-uncle index; now he will be neurally caused to do so and so." But such predictive powers lie in the future. We can make our little curtsy to some useless but fashionable form of materialism and say what is doubtless true: "It all depends on our brains." Then we must pass on to talk in terms which are intelligible.

Again I may be accused of psychologism—of saying that we can understand and interpret social events by direct reference to human intentions. I am saying no such thing. Human intentions are certainly basic to social happenings, but the social happenings themselves are frequently—more often than not—unintended. Each of our two friends had intentions, but they did not intend to precipitate the coercive social fact of friendship. We intend to reap where we have sown, but we did not intend to make a dust-bowl. Men and women intend to have fewer children, they do not intend to alter the age-structure of the population. Once an agreed structure is established with its appropriate frames-of-reference, as a resultant of the interaction of individuals, whether the structure be tribalism, the slave state, feudalism, capitalism, or communism, individuals privately intend to do this or that within whatever context they may be operating. The result of the totality of their private intentions—desires for money, prestige, sexual intercourse, or the satisfaction of curiosity—will be the perpetuation, the alteration, the transformation, or the destruction of the social pattern. But the result cannot be attributed to the individual wishes of any one of them, save perhaps to a very few in key positions.

I have suggested, then, that social action takes place between persons who agree among themselves that they hold certain positions in a social structure. As participants in that structure they have been brought up to entertain certain beliefs. And they and their fellow participants are confronted by certain physical opportunities and hazards, including among them the number of participants there are.

Thus we have four aspects of social action to study: interaction itself; the social constructs within which it is performed; the beliefs which it produces and which in turn guide it; and the physical and demographic environment in which it takes place. . . .

6

The Development of the Self in Social Interaction

GEORGE HERBERT MEAD

In our statement of the development of intelligence we have already suggested that the language process is essential for

Reprinted from *Mind, Self and Society* by George Herbert Mead by permission of The University of Chicago Press. Copyright © 1934 by The University of Chicago Press.

the development of the self. The self has a character which is different from that of the physiological organism proper. The self is something which has a development; it is not initially there, at birth, but arises in the process of social experience and activity, that is, develops in the given individual as a result of his relations to that process as a whole and to other individuals within that process.

. . . .

It is the characteristic of the self as an object to itself that I want to bring out. This characteristic is represented in the word "self," which is a reflexive, and indicates that which can be both subject and object. This type of object is essentially different from other objects, and in the past it has been distinguished as conscious, a term which indicates an experience with, an experience of, one's self. It was assumed that consciousness in some way carried this capacity of being an object to itself. In giving a behavioristic statement of consciousness we have to look for some sort of experience in which the physical organism can become an object to itself.[1]

When one is running to get away from someone who is chasing him, he is entirely occupied in this action, and his experience may be swallowed up in the objects about him, so that he has, at the time being, no consciousness of self at all. We must be, of course, very completely occupied to have that take place, but we can, I think, recognize that sort of a possible experience in which the self does not enter. We can, perhaps, get some light on that situation through those experiences in which in very intense action there appear in the experience of the individual, back of this intense action, memories and anticipations. Tolstoi as an officer in

the war gives an account of having pictures of his past experience in the midst of his most intense action. There are also pictures that flash into a person's mind when he is drowning. In such instances there is a contrast between an experience that is absolutely wound up in outside activity in which the self as an object does not enter, and an activity of memory and imagination in which the self is the principal object. The self is then entirely distinguishable from an organism that is surrounded by things and acts with reference to things, including parts of its own body. These latter may be objects like other objects, but they are just objects out there in the field, and they do not involve a self that is an object to the organism. This is, I think, frequently overlooked. It is that fact which makes our anthropomorphic reconstructions of animal life so fallacious. How can an individual get outside himself (experientially) in such a way as to become an object to himself? This is the essential psychological problem of selfhood or of self-consciousness; and its solution is to be found by referring to the process of social conduct or activity in which the given person or individual is implicated. The apparatus of reason would not be complete unless it swept itself into its own analysis of the field of experience; or unless the individual brought himself into the same experiential field as that of the other individual selves in relation to whom he acts in any given social situation. Reason cannot become impersonal unless it takes an objective, non-affective attitude toward itself; otherwise we have just consciousness, not *self*-consciousness. And it is necessary to rational conduct that the individual should thus take an objective, impersonal attitude toward himself, that he should become an object to himself. For the individual organism is obviously an essential and important

[1] Man's behavior is such in his social group that he is able to become an object to himself, a fact which constitutes him a more advanced product of evolutionary development than are the lower animals. Fundamentally it is this social fact—and not his alleged possession of a soul or mind with which he, as an individual, has been mysteriously and supernaturally endowed, and with which the lower animals have not been endowed—that differentiates him from them.

fact or constituent element of the empirical situation in which it acts; and without taking objective account of itself as such, it cannot act intelligently, or rationally.

The individual experiences himself as such, not directly, but only indirectly, from the particular standpoints of other individual members of the same social group, or from the generalized standpoint of the social group as a whole to which he belongs. For he enters his own experience as a self or individual, not directly or immediately, not by becoming a subject to himself, but only in so far as he first becomes an object to himself just as other individuals are objects to him or in his experience; and he becomes an object to himself only by taking the attitudes of other individuals toward himself within a social environment or context of experience and behavior in which both he and they are involved.

The importance of what we term "communication" lies in the fact that it provides a form of behavior in which the organism or the individual may become an object to himself. It is that sort of communication which we have been discussing—not communication in the sense of the cluck of the hen to the chickens, or the bark of a wolf to the pack, or the lowing of a cow, but communication in the sense of significant symbols, communication which is directed not only to others but also to the individual himself. So far as that type of communication is a part of behavior it at least introduces a self. Of course, one may hear without listening; one may see things that he does not realize; do things that he is not really aware of. But it is where one does respond to that which he addresses to another and where that response of his own becomes a part of his conduct, where he not only hears himself but responds to himself, talks and replies to himself as truly as the other person

replies to him, that we have behavior in which the individuals become objects to themselves.

. . . .

The self, as that which can be an object to itself, is essentially a social structure, and it arises in social experience. After a self has arisen, it in a certain sense provides for itself its social experiences, and so we can conceive of an absolutely solitary self. But it is impossible to conceive of a self arising outside of social experience. When it has arisen we can think of a person in solitary confinement for the rest of his life, but who still has himself as a companion, and is able to think and to converse with himself as he had communicated with others. That process to which I have just referred, of responding to one's self as another responds to it, taking part in one's own conversation with others, being aware of what one is saying and using that awareness of what one is saying to determine what one is going to say thereafter—that is a process with which we are all familiar. We are continually following up our own address to other persons by an understanding of what we are saying, and using that understanding in the direction of our continued speech. We are finding out what we are going to say, what we are going to do, by saying and doing, and in the process we are continually controlling the process itself. In the conversation of gestures what we say calls out a certain response in another and that in turn changes our own action, so that we shift from what we started to do because of the reply the other makes. The conversation of gestures is the beginning of communication. The individual comes to carry on a conversation of gestures with himself. He says something, and that calls out a certain reply in himself which makes him change what he was going to say. One starts to say something, we will presume an unpleasant something, but when he starts to say it he realizes it is cruel. The effect on himself of what he is saying checks him; there is here a conversation of gestures between the individual and himself. We mean by significant speech that the action is one that affects the individual himself, and that the effect upon the individual himself is part of the intelligent carrying-out of the conversation with others. Now we, so to speak, amputate that social phase and dispense with it for the time being, so that one is talking to one's self as one would talk to another person.

This process of abstraction cannot be carried on indefinitely. One inevitably seeks an audience, has to pour himself out to somebody. In reflective intelligence one thinks to act, and to act solely so that this action remains a part of a social process. Thinking becomes preparatory to social action. The very process of thinking is, of course, simply an inner conversation that goes on, but it is a conversation of gestures which in its completion implies the expression of that which one thinks to an audience. One separates the significance of what he is saying to others from the actual speech and gets it ready before saying it. He thinks it out, and perhaps writes it in the form of a book; but it is still a part of social intercourse in which one is addressing other persons and at the same time addressing one's self, and in which one controls the address to other persons by the response made to one's own gesture. That the person should be responding to himself is necessary to the self, and it is this sort of social conduct which provides behavior within which that self appears. I know of no other form of behavior than the linguistic in which the individual is an object to himself, and, so far as I can see, the individual is not a self in the reflexive sense unless he is an object to himself. It is this fact that gives a critical importance to communication, since this is a type of be-

havior in which the individual does so respond to himself.

We realize in everyday conduct and experience that an individual does not mean a great deal of what he is doing and saying. We frequently say that such an individual is not himself. We come away from an interview with a realization that we have left out important things, that there are parts of the self that did not get into what was said. What determines the amount of the self that gets into communication is the social experience itself. Of course, a good deal of the self does not need to get expression. We carry on a whole series of different relationships to different people. We are one thing to one man and another thing to another. There are parts of the self which exist only for the self in relationship to itself. We divide ourselves up in all sorts of different selves with reference to our acquaintances. We discuss politics with one and religion with another. There are all sorts of different selves answering to all sorts of different social reactions. It is the social process itself that is responsible for the appearance of the self; it is not there as a self apart from this type of experience.

A multiple personality is in a certain sense normal, as I have just pointed out. There is usually an organization of the whole self with reference to the community to which we belong, and the situation in which we find ourselves. What the society is, whether we are living with people of the present, people of our own imaginations, people of the past, varies, of course, with different individuals. Normally, within the sort of community as a whole to which we belong, there is a unified self, but that may be broken up.

. . . .

The unity and structure of the complete self reflects the unity and structure of the social process as a whole; and each of the elementary selves of which it is composed reflects the unity and structure of one of the various aspects of that process in which the individual is implicated. In other words, the various elementary selves which constitute, or are organized into, a complete self are the various aspects of the structure of that complete self answering to the various aspects of the structure of the social process as a whole; the structure of the complete self is thus a reflection of the complete social process. The organization and unification of a social group is identical with the organization and unification of any one of the selves arising within the social process in which that group is engaged, or which it is carrying on.

The phenomenon of dissociation of personality is caused by a breaking up of the complete, unitary self into the component selves of which it is composed, and which respectively correspond to different aspects of the social process in which the person is involved, and within which his complete or unitary self has arisen; these aspects being the different social groups to which he belongs within that process.

.   .   .   .

We find in children . . . imaginary companions which a good many children produce in their own experience. They organize in this way the responses which they call out in other persons and call out also in themselves. Of course, this playing with an imaginary companion is only a peculiarly interesting phase of ordinary play. Play in this sense, especially the stage which precedes the organized games, is a play at something. A child plays at being a mother, at being a teacher, at being a policeman; that is, it is taking different rôles, as we say. We have something that suggests this in what we call the play of animals: a cat will play with her kittens, and dogs play with each other. Two dogs playing with each other will attack and defend, in a process which if carried through would amount to an actual fight. There is a combination of responses which checks the depth of the bite. But we do not have in such a situation the dogs taking a definite rôle in the sense that a child deliberately takes the rôle of another. This tendency on the part of the children is what we are working with in the kindergarten where the rôles which the children assume are made the basis for training. When a child does assume a rôle he has in himself the stimuli which call out that particular response or group of responses. He may, of course, run away when he is chased, as the dog does, or he may turn around and strike back just as the dog does in his play. But that is not the same as playing at something. Children get together to "play Indian." This means that the child has a certain set of stimuli which call out in itself the responses that they would call out in others, and which answer to an Indian. In the play period the child utilizes his own responses to these stimuli which he makes use of in building a self. The response which he has a tendency to make to these stimuli organizes them. He plays that he is, for instance, offering himself something, and he buys it; he gives a letter to himself and takes it away; he addresses himself as a parent, as a teacher; he arrests himself as a policeman. He has a set of stimuli which call out in himself the sort of responses they call out in others. He takes this group of responses and organizes them into a certain whole. Such is the simplest form of being another to one's self. It involves a temporal situation. The child says something in one character and responds in another character, and then his responding in another character is a stimulus to himself in the first character, and so the conversation goes on. A certain organized structure arises in him and in his other which replies to it, and these carry on the conversation of gestures between themselves.

If we contrast play with the situation in an organized game, we note the essential difference that the child who plays in a game must be ready to take the attitude of everyone else involved in that game, and that these different rôles must have a definite relationship to each other. Taking a very simple game such as hide-and-seek, everyone with the exception of the one who is hiding is a person who is hunting. A child does not require more than the person who is hunted and the one who is hunting. If a child is playing in the first sense he just goes on playing, but there is no basic organization gained. In that early stage he passes from one rôle to another just as a whim takes him. But in a game where a number of individuals are involved, then the child taking one rôle must be ready to take the rôle of everyone else. If he gets in a baseball nine he must have the responses of each position involved in his own position. He must know what everyone else is going to do in order to carry out his own play. He has to take all of these rôles. They do not all have to be present in consciousness at the same time, but at some moments he has to have three or four individuals present in his own attitude, such as the one who is going to throw the ball, the one who is going to catch it, and so on. These responses must be, in some degree, present in his own make-up. In the game, then, there is a set of responses of such others so organized that the attitude of one calls out the appropriate attitudes of the other.

This organization is put in the form of the rules of the game. Children take a great interest in rules. They make rules on the spot in order to help themselves out of difficulties. Part of the enjoyment of the game is to get these rules. Now, the rules are the set of responses which a particular attitude calls out. You can demand a certain response in others if you take a certain attitude. These responses are all in yourself as well. There you get an organized set of such responses as that to

which I have referred, which is something more elaborate than the rôles found in play. Here there is just a set of responses that follow on each other indefinitely. At such a stage we speak of a child as not yet having a fully developed self. The child responds in a fairly intelligent fashion to the immediate stimuli that come to him, but they are not organized. He does not organize his life as we would like to have him do, namely, as a whole. There is just a set of responses of the type of play. The child reacts to a certain stimulus, and the reaction is in himself that is called out in others, but he is not a whole self. In his game he has to have an organization of these rôles; otherwise he cannot play the game. The game represents the passage in the life of the child from taking the rôle of others in play to the organized part that is essential to self-consciousness in the full sense of the term.

We were speaking of the social conditions under which the self arises as an object. In addition to language we found two illustrations, one in play and the other in the game, and I wish to summarize and expand my account on these points. I have spoken of these from the point of view of children. We can, of course, refer also to the attitudes of more primitive people out of which our civilization has arisen. A striking illustration of play as distinct from the game is found in the myths and various of the plays which primitive people carry out, especially in religious pageants. The pure play attitude which we find in the case of little children may not be found here, since the participants are adults, and undoubtedly the relationship of these play processes to that which they interpret is more or less in the minds of even the most primitive people. In the process of interpretation of such rituals, there is an organization of play which perhaps might be compared to that which is taking place in the kindergarten in dealing with the plays of little children, where these are made into a set that will have a definite structure or relationship. At least something of the same sort is found in the play of primitive people. This type of activity belongs, of course, not to the everyday life of the people in their dealing with the objects about them— there we have a more or less definitely developed self-consciousness—but in their attitudes toward the forces about them, the nature upon which they depend; in their attitude toward this nature which is vague and uncertain, there we have a much more primitive response; and that response finds its expression in taking the rôle of the other, playing at the expression of their gods and their heroes, going through certain rites which are the representation of what these individuals are supposed to be doing. The process is one which develops, to be sure, into a more or less definite technique and is controlled; and yet we can say that it has arisen out of situations similar to those in which little children play at being a parent, at being a teacher—vague personalities that are about them and which affect them and on which they depend. These are personalities which they take, rôles they play, and in so far control the development of their own personality. This outcome is just what the kindergarten works toward. It takes the characters of these various vague beings and gets them into such an organized social relationship to each other that they build up the character of the little child.[2] The very introduction of organization from outside supposes a lack of organization at this period in the child's experience. Over against such a situation of the little child and primitive people, we have the game as such.

The fundamental difference between the game and play is that in the latter

the child must have the attitude of all the others involved in that game. The attitudes of the other players which the participant assumes organize into a sort of unit, and it is that organization which controls the response of the individual. The illustration used was of a person playing baseball. Each one of his own acts is determined by his assumption of the action of the others who are playing the game. What he does is controlled by his being everyone else on that team, at least in so far as those attitudes affect his own particular response. We get then an "other" which is an organization of the attitudes of those involved in the same process.

The organized community or social group which gives to the individual his unity of self may be called "the generalized other." The attitude of the generalized other is the attitude of the whole community.[3] Thus, for example, in the case of such a social group as a

[2] ["The Relation of Play to Education," *University of Chicago Record*, I (1896–97), 140 ff.]

[3] It is possible for inanimate objects, no less than for other human organisms, to form parts of the generalized and organized—the completely socialized—other for any given human individual, in so far as he responds to such objects socially or in a social fashion (by means of the mechanism of thought, the internalized conversation of gestures). Any thing—any object or set of objects, whether animate or inanimate, human or animal, or merely physical—toward which he acts, or to which he responds, socially, is an element in what for him is the generalized other; by taking the attitudes of which toward himself he becomes conscious of himself as an object or individual, and thus develops a self or personality. Thus, for example, the cult, in its primitive form, is merely the social embodiment of the relation between the given social group or community and its physical environment—an organized social means, adopted by the individual members of that group or community, of entering into social relations with that environment, or (in a sense) of carrying on conversations with it; and in this way that environment becomes part of the total generalized other for each of the individual members of the given social group or community.

ball team, the team is the generalized other in so far as it enters—as an organized process or social activity—into the experience of any one of the individual members of it.

If the given human individual is to develop a self in the fullest sense, it is not sufficient for him merely to take the attitudes of other human individuals toward himself and toward one another within the human social process, and to bring that social process as a whole into his individual experience merely in these terms: he must also, in the same way that he takes the attitudes of other individuals toward himself and toward one another, take their attitudes toward the various phases or aspects of the common social activity or set of social undertakings in which, as members of an organized society or social group, they are all engaged; and he must then, by generalizing these individual attitudes of that organized society or social group itself, as a whole, act toward different social projects which at any given time it is carrying out, or toward the various larger phases of the general social process which constitutes its life and of which these projects are specific manifestations. This getting of the broad activities of any given social whole or organized society as such within the experiential field of any one of the individuals involved or included in that whole is, in other words, the essential basis and prerequisite of the fullest development of that individual's self: only in so far as he takes the attitudes of the organized social group to which he belongs toward the organized, co-operative social activity or set of such activities in which that group as such is engaged, does he develop a complete self or possess the sort of complete self he has developed. And on the other hand, the complex co-operative processes and activities and institutional functionings of organized human society are also possible only in so far as every individual involved in them or belonging to that

society can take the general attitudes of all other such individuals with reference to these processes and activities and institutional functionings, and to the organized social whole of experiential relations and interactions thereby constituted—and can direct his own behavior accordingly.

It is in the form of the generalized other that the social process influences the behavior of the individuals involved in it and carrying it on, i.e., that the community exercises control over the conduct of its individual members; for it is in this form that the social process or community enters as a determining factor into the individual's thinking. In abstract thought the individual takes the attitude of the generalized other [4] toward himself, without reference to its expression in any particular other individuals; and in concrete thought he takes that attitude in so far as it is expressed in the attitudes toward his behavior of those other individuals with whom he is involved in the given social situation or act. But only by taking the attitude of the generalized other toward himself, in one or another of these ways, can he think at all; for only thus can thinking—or the internalized conversation of gestures which constitutes thinking—occur. And only through the taking by individuals of the attitude or attitudes of the generalized other toward themselves is the existence of a universe of discourse, as that system of common or social meanings which thinking presupposes at its context, rendered possible.

.   .   .   .

What goes to make up the organized self is the organization of the attitudes

---

[4] We have said that the internal conversation of the individual with himself in terms of words or significant gestures . . . is carried on by the individual from the standpoint of the "generalized other." And the more abstract that conversation is, the more abstract thinking happens to be, the further removed is the generalized other from any connection with particular individuals . . .

which are common to the group. A person is a personality because he belongs to a community, because he takes over the institutions of that community into his own conduct. He takes its language as a medium by which he gets his personality, and then through a process of taking the different rôles that all the others furnish he comes to get the attitude of the members of the community. Such, in a certain sense, is the structure of a man's personality. There are certain common responses which each individual has toward certain common things, and in so far as those common responses are awakened in the individual when he is affecting other persons he arouses his own self. The structure, then, on which the self is built is this response which is common to all, for one has to be a member of a community to be a self. Such responses are abstract attitudes, but they constitute just what we term a man's character. They give him what we term his principles, the acknowledged attitudes of all members of the community toward what are the values of that community. He is putting himself in the place of the generalized other, which represents the organized responses of all the members of the group. It is that which guides conduct controlled by principles, and a person who has such an organized group of responses is a man whom we say has character, in the moral sense.

. . . .

I have so far emphasized what I have called the structures upon which the self is constructed, the framework of the self, as it were. Of course we are not only what is common to all: each one of the selves is different from everyone else; but there has to be such a common structure as I have sketched in order that we may be members of a community at all. We cannot be ourselves unless we are also members in whom there is a community of attitudes which control the attitudes of all. We can-

not have rights unless we have common attitudes. That which we have acquired as self-conscious persons makes us such members of society and gives us selves. Selves can only exist in definite relationships to other selves. No hard-and-fast line can be drawn between our own selves and the selves of others, since our own selves exist and enter as such into our experience only in so far as the selves of others exist and enter as such into our experience also. The individual possesses a self only in relation to the selves of the other members of his social group; and the structure of his self expresses or reflects the general behavior pattern of this social group to which he belongs, just as does the structure of the self of every other individual belonging to this social group.

. . . .

There is one other matter which I wish briefly to refer to now. The only way in which we can react against the disapproval of the entire community is by setting up a higher sort of community which in a certain sense outvotes the one we find. A person may reach a point of going against the whole world about him; he may stand out by himself over against it. But to do that he has to speak with the voice of reason to himself. He has to comprehend the voices of the past and of the future. That is the only way in which the self can get a voice which is more than the voice of the community. As a rule we assume that this general voice of the community is identical with the larger community of the past and the future; we assume that an organized custom represents what we call morality. The things one cannot do are those which everybody would condemn. If we take the attitude of the community over against our own responses, that is a true statement, but we must not forget this other capacity, that of replying to the community and insisting on the gesture of the community changing. We can reform the order of things;

we can insist on making the community standards better standards. We are not simply bound by the community. We are engaged in a conversation in which what we say is listened to by the community and its response is one which is affected by what we have to say. This is especially true in critical situations. A man rises up and defends himself for what he does; he has his "day in court"; he can present his views. He can perhaps change the attitude of the community toward himself. The process of conversation is one in which the individual has not only the right but the duty of talking to the community of which he is a part, and bringing about those changes which take place through the interaction of individuals. That is the way, of course, in which society gets ahead, by just such interactions as those in which some person thinks a thing out. We are continually changing our social system in some respects, and we are able to do that intelligently because we can think. . . .

7

Primary Groups

CHARLES HORTON COOLEY

By primary groups I mean those characterized by intimate face-to-face association and coöperation. They are primary in several senses, but chiefly in that they are fundamental in forming the social nature and ideals of the individual. The result of intimate association, psychologically, is a certain fusion of individualities in a common whole, so that one's very self, for many purposes at least, is the common life and purpose of the group. Perhaps the simplest way of describing this wholeness is by saying that it is a "we"; it involves the sort of sympathy and mutual identification for which "we" is the natural expression. One lives in the feeling of the whole and finds the chief aims of his will in that feeling.

It is not to be supposed that the unity of the primary group is one of mere harmony and love. It is always a differentiated and usually a competitive unity, admitting of self-assertion and various appropriative passions; but these passions are socialized by sympathy, and come, or tend to come, under the discipline of a common spirit. The individual will be ambitious, but the chief object of his ambition will be some desired place in the thought of the others, and he will feel allegiance to common standards of service and fair play. So the boy will dispute with his fellows a place on the team, but above such disputes will place the common glory of his class and school.

The most important spheres of this intimate association and coöperation—though by no means the only ones—are the family, the play-group of children, and the neighborhood or community group of elders. These are practically universal, belonging to all times and all stages of development;

"Primary Groups" is reprinted by permission of Charles Scribner's Sons from *Social Organization* by Charles Horton Cooley. Copyright 1909 Charles Scribner's Sons; renewal copyright 1937 Elsie Jones Cooley.

and are accordingly a chief basis of what is universal in human nature and human ideals. The best comparative studies of the family, such as those of Westermarck [1] or Howard,[2] show it to us as not only a universal institution, but as more alike the world over than the exaggeration of exceptional customs by an earlier school had led us to suppose. Nor can any one doubt the general prevalence of play-groups among children or of informal assemblies of various kinds among their elders. Such association is clearly the nursery of human nature in the world about us, and there is no apparent reason to suppose that the case has anywhere or at any time been essentially different.

As regards play, I might, were it not a matter of common observation, multiply illustrations of the universality and spontaneity of the group discussion and coöperation to which it gives rise. The general fact is that children, especially boys after about their twelfth year, live in fellowships in which their sympathy, ambition and honor are engaged even more, often, than they are in the family. Most of us can recall examples of the endurance by boys of injustice and even cruelty, rather than appeal from their fellows to parents or teachers—as, for instance, in the hazing so prevalent at schools, and so difficult, for this very reason, to suppress. And how elaborate the discussion, how cogent the public opinion, how hot the ambitions in these fellowships.

Nor is this facility of juvenile association, as is sometimes supposed, a trait peculiar to English and American boys; since experience among our immigrant population seems to show that the offspring of the more restrictive civilizations of the continent of Europe form self-governing play-groups with almost equal readiness. Thus Miss Jane Addams, after pointing out that the

"gang" is almost universal, speaks of the interminable discussion which every detail of the gang's activity receives, remarking that "in these social folkmotes, so to speak, the young citizen learns to act upon his own determination." [3]

Of the neighborhood group it may be said, in general, that from the time men formed permanent settlements upon the land, down, at least, to the rise of modern industrial cities, it has played a main part of the primary, heart-to-heart life of the people. Among our Teutonic forefathers the village community was apparently the chief sphere of sympathy and mutual aid for the commons all through the "dark" and middle ages, and for many purposes it remains so in rural districts at the present day. In some countries we still find it with all its ancient vitality, notably in Russia, where the mir, or self-governing village group, is the main theatre of life, along with the family, for perhaps fifty millions of peasants.

In our own life the intimacy of the neighborhood has been broken up by the growth of an intricate mesh of wider contacts which leaves us strangers to people who live in the same house. And even in the country the same principle is at work, though less obviously, diminishing our economic and spiritual community with our neighbors. How far this change is a healthy development, and how far a disease, is perhaps still uncertain.

Besides these almost universal kinds of primary association, there are many others whose form depends upon the particular state of civilization; the only essential thing, as I have said, being a certain intimacy and fusion of personalities. In our own society, being little bound by place, people easily form clubs, fraternal societies and the like, based on congeniality, which may give rise to real intimacy. Many such

[1] *The History of Human Marriage.*
[2] *A History of Matrimonial Institutions.*
[3] *Newer Ideals of Peace*, 177.

relations are formed at school and college, and among men and women brought together in the first instance by their occupations—as workmen in the same trade, or the like. Where there is a little common interest and activity, kindness grows like weeds by the roadside.

But the fact that the family and neighborhood groups are ascendant in the open and plastic time of childhood makes them even now incomparably more influential than all the rest.

Primary groups are primary in the sense that they give the individual his earliest and completest experience of social unity, and also in the sense that they do not change in the same degree as more elaborate relations, but form a comparatively permanent source out of which the latter are ever springing. Of course they are not independent of the larger society, but to some extent reflect its spirit; as the German family and the German school bear somewhat distinctly the print of German militarism. But this, after all, is like the tide setting back into creeks, and does not commonly go very far. Among the German, and still more among the Russian, peasantry are found habits of free cooperation and discussion almost uninfluenced by the character of the state; and it is a familiar and well-supported view that the village commune, self-governing as regards local affairs and habituated to discussion, is a very widespread institution in settled communities, and the continuator of a similar autonomy previously existing in the clan. "It is man who makes monarchies and establishes republics, but the commune seems to come directly from the hand of God." [4]

In our own cities the crowded tenements and the general economic and social confusion have sorely wounded the family and the neighborhood, but

[4] De Tocqueville, *Democracy in America*, vol. i, chap. 5.

it is remarkable, in view of these conditions, what vitality they show; and there is nothing upon which the conscience of the time is more determined than upon restoring them to health.

These groups, then, are springs of life, not only for the individual but for social institutions. They are only in part moulded by special traditions, and, in larger degree, express a universal nature. The religion or government of other civilizations may seem alien to us, but the children or the family group wear the common life, and with them we can always make ourselves at home.

By human nature, I suppose, we may understand those sentiments and impulses that are human in being superior to those of lower animals, and also in the sense that they belong to mankind at large, and not to any particular race or time. It means, particularly, sympathy and the innumerable sentiments into which sympathy enters, such as love, resentment, ambition, vanity, hero-worship, and the feeling of social right and wrong.

Human nature in this sense is justly regarded as a comparatively permanent element in society. Always and everywhere men seek honor and dread ridicule, defer to public opinion, cherish their goods and their children, and admire courage, generosity, and success. It is always safe to assume that people are and have been human. . . .

There is no better proof of this generic likeness of human nature than in the ease and joy with which the modern man makes himself at home in literature depicting the most remote and varied phases of life—in Homer, in the Nibelung tales, in the Hebrew Scriptures, in the legends of the American Indians, in stories of frontier life, of soldiers and sailors, of criminals and tramps, and so on. The more penetratingly any phase of human life is studied the more an essential likeness to ourselves is revealed.

To return to primary groups: the view here maintained is that human nature is not something existing separately in the individual, but a *group-nature or primary phase of society*, a relatively simple and general condition of the social mind. It is something more, on the one hand, than the mere instinct that is born in us—though that enters into it—and something less, on the other, than the more elaborate development of ideas and sentiments that makes up institutions. It is the nature which is developed and expressed in those simple, face-to-face groups that are somewhat alike in all societies; groups of the family, the playground, and the neighborhood. In the essential similarity of these is to be found the basis, in experience, for similar ideas and sentiments in the human mind. In these, everywhere, human nature comes into existence. Man does not have it at birth; he cannot acquire it except through fellowship, and it decays in isolation.

If this view does not recommend itself to common-sense I do not know that elaboration will be of much avail. It simply means the application at this point of the idea that society and individuals are inseparable phases of a common whole, so that wherever we find an individual fact we may look for a social fact to go with it. If there is a universal nature in persons there must be something universal in association to correspond to it.

What else can human nature be than a trait of primary groups? Surely not an attribute of the separate individual—supposing there were any such thing—since its typical characteristics, such as affection, ambition, vanity, and resentment, are inconceivable apart from society. If it belongs, then, to man in association, what kind or degree of association is required to develop it? Evidently nothing elaborate, because elaborate phases of society are transient and diverse, while human nature is comparatively stable and universal. In short the family and neighborhood life is essential to its genesis and nothing more is.

Here as everywhere in the study of society we must learn to see mankind in psychical wholes, rather than in artificial separation. We must see and feel the communal life of family and local groups as immediate facts, not as combinations of something else. And perhaps we shall do this best by recalling our own experience and extending it through sympathetic observation. What, in our life, is the family and the fellowship; what do we know of the we-feeling? Thought of this kind may help us to get a concrete perception of that primary group-nature of which everything social is the outgrowth.

C Roles, Norms, and Values in Social Life

8

Social Roles: Society in Man

PETER L. BERGER

. . . Role theory has been almost entirely an American intellectual development. Some of its germinal insights go back to William James, while its direct parents are two other American thinkers, Charles Cooley and George Herbert Mead. It cannot be our purpose here to give a historical introduction to this quite fascinating portion of intellectual history. Rather than try this even in outline, we shall start more systematically by beginning our consideration of the import of role theory with another look at Thomas' concept of the definition of the situation.

From *Invitation to Sociology* by Peter L. Berger. Copyright © 1963 by Peter L. Berger. Reprinted by permission of Doubleday & Company, Inc. and Penguin Books, Ltd.

The reader will recall Thomas' understanding of the social situation as a sort of reality agreed upon *ad hoc* by those who participate in it, or, more exactly, those who do the defining of the situation. From the viewpoint of the individual participant this means that each situation he enters confronts him with specific expectations and demands of him specific responses to these expectations. As we have already seen, powerful pressures exist in just about any social situation to ensure that the proper responses are indeed forthcoming. Society can exist by virtue of the fact that most of the time most people's definitions of the most important situations at least coincide approximately. The motives of the publisher and writer of these lines may be rather different, but the ways the two define the situation in which this book is being produced are sufficiently similar for the joint venture to be possible. In similar fashion there may be quite divergent interests present in a classroom of students, some of them having little connection with the educational activity that is supposedly going on, but in most cases these interests (say, that one student came to study the subject being taught, while another simply registers for every course taken by a certain redhead he is pursuing) can coexist in the situation without destroying it. In other words, there is a certain amount of leeway in the extent to which response must meet expectation for a situation to remain sociologically viable. Of course, if the definitions of the situation are too widely discrepant, some form of social conflict or disorganization will inevitably result—say, if some students interpret the classroom meeting as a party, or if an author has no intention of producing a book but is using his contract with one publisher to put pressure on another.

While an average individual meets up with very different expectations in different areas of his life in society, the situations that produce these expectations fall into certain clusters. A student may take two courses from two different professors in two different departments, with considerable variations in the expectations met with in the two situations (say, as between formality or informality in the relations between professor and students). Nevertheless, the situations will be sufficiently similar to each other and to other classroom situations previously experienced to enable the student to carry into both situations essentially the same overall response. In other words, in both cases, with but a few modifications, he will be able to *play the role* of student. A role, then, may be defined as a typified response to a typified expectation. So-

ciety has predefined the fundamental typology. To use the language of the theater, from which the concept of role is derived, we can say that society provides the script for all the *dramatis personae*. The individual actors, therefore, need but slip into the roles already assigned to them before the curtain goes up. As long as they play their roles as provided for in this script, the social play can proceed as planned.

The role provides the pattern according to which the individual is to act in the particular situation. Roles, in society as in the theater, will vary in the exactness with which they lay down instructions for the actor. Taking occupational roles for an instance, a fairly minimal pattern goes into the role of garbage collector, while physicians or clergymen or officers have to acquire all kinds of distinctive mannerisms, speech and motor habits, such as military bearing, sanctimonious diction or bedside cheer. It would, however, be missing an essential aspect of the role if one regarded it merely as a regulatory pattern for externally visible actions. One feels more ardent by kissing, more humble by kneeling and more angry by shaking one's fist. That is, the kiss not only expresses ardor but manufactures it. Roles carry with them both certain actions and the emotions and attitudes that belong to these actions. The professor putting on an act that pretends to wisdom comes to feel wise. The preacher finds himself believing what he preaches. The soldier discovers martial stirrings in his breast as he puts on his uniform. In each case, while the emotion or attitude may have been present before the role was taken on, the latter inevitably strengthens what was there before. In many instances there is every reason to suppose that nothing at all anteceded the playing of the role in the actor's consciousness. In other words, one becomes wise by being appointed a professor, believing by engaging in activities that presuppose belief, and ready for battle by marching in formation.

Let us take an example. A man recently commissioned as an officer, especially if he came up through the ranks, will at first be at least slightly embarrassed by the salutes he now receives from the enlisted men he meets on his way. Probably he will respond to them in a friendly, almost apologetic manner. The new insignia on his uniform are at that point still something that he has merely put on, almost like a disguise. Indeed, the new officer may even tell himself and others that underneath he is still the same person, that he simply has new responsibilities (among which, en passant, is the duty to accept the salutes of enlisted men). This attitude is not likely to last very long. In order to carry out his new role of officer, our man must maintain a certain bearing. This bearing has quite definite implications. Despite all the double-talk in this area that is customary in so-called democratic armies, such as the American one, one of the fundamental implications is that an officer is a superior somebody, entitled to obedience and respect on the basis of this superiority. Every military salute given by an inferior in rank is an act of obeisance, received as a matter of course by the one who returns it. Thus, with every salute given and accepted (along, of course, with a hundred other ceremonial acts that enhance his new status) our man is fortified in his new bearing—and in its, as it were, ontological presuppositions. He not only acts like an officer, he feels like one. Gone are the embarrassment, the apologetic attitude, the I'm-just-another-guy-really grin. If on some occasion an enlisted man should fail to salute with the appropriate amount of enthusiasm or even commit the unthinkable act of failing to salute at all, our officer is not merely going to punish a violation of

military regulations. He will be driven with every fiber of his being to redress an offense against the appointed order of his cosmos.

It is important to stress in this illustration that only very rarely is such a process deliberate or based on reflection. Our man has not sat down and figured out all the things that ought to go into his new role, including the things that he ought to feel and believe. The strength of the process comes precisely from its unconscious, unreflecting character. He has become an officer almost as effortlessly as he grew into a person with blue eyes, brown hair and a height of six feet. Nor would it be correct to say that our man must be rather stupid and quite an exception among his comrades. On the contrary, the exception is the man who reflects on his roles and his role changes (a type, by the way, who would probably make a poor officer). Even very intelligent people, who faced with doubt about their roles in society, will involve themselves even more in the doubted activity rather than withdraw into reflection. The theologian who doubts his faith will pray more and increase his church attendance, the businessman beset by qualms about his rat-race activities starts going to the office on Sundays too, and the terrorist who suffers from nightmares volunteers for nocturnal executions. And, of course, they are perfectly correct in this course of action. Each role has its inner discipline, what Catholic monastics would call its "formation." The role forms, shapes, patterns both action and actor. It is very difficult to pretend in this world. Normally, one becomes what one plays at.

Every role in society has attached to it a certain identity. As we have seen, some of these identities are trivial and temporary ones, as in some occupations that demand little modification in the being of their practitioners. It is not difficult to change from garbage collector to night watchman. It is considerably more difficult to change from clergyman to officer. It is very, very difficult to change from Negro to white. And it is almost impossible to change from man to woman. These differences in the case of role changing ought not to blind us to the fact that even identities that we consider to be our essential selves have been socially assigned. Just as there are racial roles to be acquired and identified with, so there are sexual roles. To say "I am a man" is just as much a proclamation of role as to say "I am a colonel in the U.S. Army." We are well aware of the fact that one is born a male, while not even the most humorless martinet imagines himself to have been born with a golden eagle sitting on his umbilical cord. But to be biologically male is a far cry from the specific, socially defined (and, of course, socially relative) role that goes with the statement "I am a man." A male child does not have to learn to have an erection. But he must learn to be aggressive, to have ambitions, to compete with others, and to be suspicious of too much gentleness in himself. The male role in our society, however, requires all these things that one must learn, as does a male identity. To have an erection is not enough—if it were, regiments of psychotherapists would be out of work.

This significance of role theory could be summarized by saying that, in a sociological perspective, identity is socially bestowed, socially sustained and socially transformed. The example of the man in process of becoming an officer may suffice to illustrate the way in which identities are bestowed in adult life. However, even roles that are much more fundamentally part of what psychologists would call our personality than those associated with a particular adult activity are bestowed in very similar manner through a social process.

This has been demonstrated over and over again in studies of so-called socialization—the process by which a child learns to be a participant member of society.

Probably the most penetrating theoretical account of this process is the one given by Mead, in which the genesis of the self is interpreted as being one and the same event as the discovery of society. The child finds out who he is as he learns what society is. He learns to play roles properly belonging to him by learning, as Mead puts it, "to take the role of the other"—which, incidentally, is the crucial sociopsychological function of play, in which children masquerade with a variety of social roles and in doing so discover the significance of those being assigned to them. All this learning occurs, and can only occur, in interaction with other human beings, be it the parents or whoever else raises the child. The child first takes on roles *vis-à-vis* what Mead calls his "significant others," that is, those persons who deal with him intimately and whose attitudes are decisive for the formation of his conception of himself. Later, the child learns that the roles he plays are not only relevant to this intimate circle, but relate to the expectations directed toward him by society at large. This higher level of abstraction in the social response Mead calls the discovery of the "generalized other." That is, not only the child's mother expects him to be good, clean and truthful, society in general does so as well. Only when this general conception of society emerges is the child capable of forming a clear conception of himself. "Self" and "society," in the child's experience, are the two sides of the same coin.

In other words, identity is not something "given," but is bestowed in acts of social recognition. We become that as which we are addressed. The same idea is expressed in Cooley's well-known description of the self as a reflection in a looking glass. This does not mean, of course, that there are not certain characteristics an individual is born with, that are carried by his genetic heritage regardless of the social environment in which the latter will have to unfold itself. Our knowledge of man's biology does not as yet allow us a very clear picture of the extent to which this may be true. We do know, however, that the room for social formation within those genetic limits is very large indeed. Even with the biological questions left largely unsettled, we can say that to be human is to be recognized as human, just as to be a certain kind of man is to be recognized as such. The child deprived of human affection and attention becomes dehumanized. The child who is given respect comes to respect himself. A little boy considered to be a *schlemiel* becomes one, just as a grown-up treated as an awe-inspiring young god of war begins to think of himself and act as is appropriate to such a figure—and, indeed, merges his identity with one he is presented with in these expectations.

Identities are socially bestowed. They must also be socially sustained, and fairly steadily so. One cannot be human all by oneself and, apparently, one cannot hold on to any particular identity all by oneself. The self-image of the officer as an officer can be maintained only in a social context in which others are willing to recognize him in this identity. If this recognition is suddenly withdrawn, it usually does not take very long before the self-image collapses.

Cases of radical withdrawal of recognition by society can tell us much about the social character of identity. For example, a man turned overnight from a free citizen into a convict finds himself subjected at once to a massive assault on his previous conception of himself. He may try desperately to hold

on to the latter, but in the absence of others in his immediate environment confirming his old identity he will find it almost impossible to maintain it within his own consciousness. With frightening speed he will discover that he is acting as a convict is supposed to, and feeling all the things that a convict is expected to feel. It would be a misleading perspective on this process to look upon it simply as one of the disintegration of personality. A more accurate way of seeing the phenomenon is as a reintegration of personality, no different in its sociopsychological dynamics from the process in which the old identity was integrated. It used to be that our man was treated by all the important people around him as responsible, dignified, considerate and aesthetically fastidious. Consequently he was able to be all these things. Now the walls of the prison separate him from those whose recognition sustained him in the exhibition of these traits. Instead he is now surrounded by people who treat him as irresponsible, swinish in behavior, only out for his own interests and careless of his appearance unless forced to take care by constant supervision. The new expectations are typified in the convict role that responds to them just as the old ones were integrated into a different pattern of conduct. In both cases, identity comes with conduct and conduct occurs in response to a specific social situation.

Extreme cases in which an individual is radically stripped of his old identity simply illustrate more sharply processes that occur in ordinary life. We live our everyday lives within a complex web of recognitions and nonrecognitions. We work better when we are given encouragement by our superiors. We find it hard to be anything but clumsy in a gathering where we know people have an image of us as awkward. We become wits when people expect us to be funny, and interesting characters when we know that such a reputation has preceded us. Intelligence, humor, manual skills, religious devotion and even sexual potency respond with equal alacrity to the expectations of others. This makes understandable the previously mentioned process by which individuals choose their associates in such a way that the latter sustain their self-interpretations. To put this succinctly, every act of social affiliation entails a choice of identity. Conversely every identity requires specific social affiliations for its survival. Birds of the same feather flock together not as a luxury but out of necessity. The intellectual becomes a slob after he is kidnapped by the army. The theological student progressively loses his sense of humor as he approaches ordination. The worker who breaks all norms finds that he breaks even more after he has been given a medal by management. The young man with anxieties about his virility becomes hell-on-wheels in bed when he finds a girl who sees him as an avatar of Don Giovanni. . . .

Such sociological perspective on the character of identity gives us a deeper understanding of the human meaning of prejudice. As a result, we obtain the chilling perception that the prejudging not only concerns the victim's external fate at the hands of his oppressors, but also his consciousness as it is shaped by their expectations. The most terrible thing that prejudice can do to a human being is to make him tend to become what the prejudiced image of him says that he is. The Jew in an anti-Semitic milieu must struggle hard not to become more and more like the anti-Semitic stereotype, as must the Negro in a racist situation. Significantly, this struggle will only have a chance of success when, the individual is protected from succumbing to the prejudiced program for his personality by what we could call the counterrecognition of those within his immediate community.

The Gentile world might recognize him as but another despicable Jew of no consequence, and treat him accordingly, but this nonrecognition of his worth may be balanced by the counter-recognition of him within the Jewish community itself as, say, the greatest Talmudic scholar in Latvia.

In view of the sociopsychological dynamics of this deadly game of recognitions, it should not surprise us that the problem of "Jewish identity" arose only among modern Western Jews when assimilation into the surrounding Gentile society had begun to weaken the power of the Jewish community itself to bestow alternate identities on its members as against the identities assigned to them by anti-Semitism. As an individual is forced to gaze at himself in a mirror so constructed as to let him see a leering monster, he must frantically search for other men with other mirrors, unless he is to forget that he ever had another face. To put this a little differently, human dignity is a matter of social permission.

The same relationship between society and identity can be seen in cases where, for one reason or another, an individual's identity is drastically changed. The transformation of identity, just as its genesis and its maintenance, is a social process. We have already indicated the way in which any reinterpretation of the past, any "alternation" from one self-image to another, requires the presence of a group that conspires to bring about the metamorphosis. What anthropologists call a rite of passage involves the repudiation of an old identity (say, that of being a child) and the initiation into a new one (such as that of adult). Modern societies have milder rites of passage, as in the institution of the engagement, by which the individual is gently led by a general conspiracy of all concerned over the threshold between bachelor freedom and the captivity of marriage.

If it were not for this institution, many more would panic at the last moment before the enormity of what they are about to undertake.

We have also seen how "alternation" operates to change identities in such highly structured situations as religious training or psychoanalysis. Again taking the latter as a timely illustration, it involves an intensive social situation in which the individual is led to repudiate his past conception of himself and to take on a new identity, the one that has been programmed for him in the psychoanalytic ideology. What psychoanalysts call "transference," the intense social relationship between analyst and analysand, is essentially the creation of an artificial social milieu within which the alchemy of transformation can occur, that is, within which this alchemy can become plausible to the individual. The longer the relationship lasts and the more intensive it becomes, the more committed does the individual become to his new identity. Finally, when he is "cured," this new identity has indeed become what he is. It will not do, therefore, to dismiss with a Marxist guffaw the psychoanalyst's claim that his treatment is more effective if the patient sees him frequently, does so over a long time and pays a considerable fee. While it is obviously in the analyst's economic interest to hold to this position, it is quite plausible sociologically that the position is factually correct. What is actually "done" in psychoanalysis is that a new identity is constructed. The individual's commitment to this new identity will obviously increase the more intensively, the longer and the more painfully he invests in its manufacture. Certainly his capacity to reject the whole business as a fake has become rather minimal after an investment of several years of his life and thousands of dollars of hard-earned cash.

The same kind of "alchemistic" environment is established in situations of "group therapy." The recent popularity of the latter in American psychiatry can again not be interpreted simply as an economic rationalization. It has its sociological basis in the perfectly correct understanding that group pressures work effectively to make the individual accept the new mirror-image that is being presented to him. Erving Goffman, a contemporary sociologist, has given us a vivid description of how these pressures work in the context of a mental hospital, with the patients finally "selling out" to the psychiatric interpretation of their existence that is the common frame of reference of the "therapeutic" group.

The same process occurs whenever an entire group of individuals is to be "broken" and made to accept a new definition of themselves. It happens in basic training for draftees in the army; much more intensively in the training of personnel for a permanent career in the army, as at military academies. It happens in the indoctrination and "formation" program of cadres for totalitarian organizations, such as the Nazi SS or the Communist Party elite. It has happened for many centuries in monastic novitiates. It has recently been applied to the point of scientific precision in the "brainwashing" techniques employed against prisoners of totalitarian secret-police organizations. The violence of such procedures, as compared with the more routine initiations of society, is to be explained sociologically in terms of the radical degree of transformation of identity that is sought and the functional necessity in these cases that commitment to the transformed identity be foolproof against new "alternations."

Role theory, when pursued to its logical conclusions, does far more than provide us with a convenient shorthand for the description of various social activities. It gives us a sociological anthropology, that is, a view of man based on his existence in society. This view tells us that man plays dramatic parts in the grand play of society, and that, speaking sociologically, he *is* the masks that he must wear to do so. The human person also appears now in a dramatic context, true to its theatrical etymology (*persona*, the technical term given to the actors' masks in classical theater). The person is perceived as a repertoire of roles, each one properly equipped with a certain identity. The range of an individual person can be measured by the number of roles he is capable of playing. The person's biography now appears to us as an uninterrupted sequence of stage performances, played to different audiences, sometimes involving drastic changes of costume, always demanding that the actor *be* what he is playing.

Such a sociological view of personality is far more radical in its challenge to the way that we commonly think of ourselves than most psychological theories. It challenges radically one of the fondest presuppositions about the self —its continuity. Looked at sociologically, the self is no longer a solid, given entity that moves from one situation to another. It is rather a process, continuously created and re-created in each social situation that one enters, held together by the slender thread of memory. How slender this thread is, we have seen in our discussion of the reinterpretation of the past. Nor is it possible within this framework of understanding to take refuge in the unconscious as containing the "real" contents of the self, because the presumed unconscious self is just as subject to social production as is the so-called conscious one, as we have seen. In other words, man is not *also* a social being, but he is social in every aspect of his being that is open to empirical investigation. Still speaking sociologically, then, if one wants to ask who an

individual "really" is in this kaleidoscope of roles and identities, one can answer only by enumerating the situations in which he is one thing and those in which he is another.

Now, it is clear that such transformations cannot occur *ad infinitum* and that some are easier than others. An individual becomes so habituated to certain identities that, even when his social situation changes, he has difficulty keeping up with the expectations newly directed toward him. The difficulties that healthy and previously highly active individuals have when they are forced to retire from their occupation show this very clearly. The transformability of the self depends not *only* on its social context, but also on the degree of its habituation to previous identities and perhaps also on certain genetically given traits. While these modifications in our model are necessary to avoid a radicalization of our position, they do not detract appreciably from the discontinuity of the self as revealed by sociological analysis.

If this not very edifying anthropological model is reminiscent of any other, it would be of that employed in early Buddhist psychology in India, in which the self was compared to a long row of candles, each of which lights the wick of its neighbor and is extinguished in that moment. The Buddhist psychologists used this picture to decry the Hindu notion of the transmigration of the soul, meaning to say thereby that there is no entity that passes from one candle to another. But the same picture fits our present anthropological model quite well.

One might obtain the impression from all of this that there is really no essential difference between most people and those afflicted with what psychiatry calls "multiple personality." If someone wanted to harp on the word "essential" here, the sociologist might agree with the statement. The actual difference, however, is that for "normal" people (that is, those so recognized by their society) there are strong pressures toward consistency in the various roles they play and the identities that go with these roles. These pressures are both external and internal. Externally the others with whom one must play one's social games, and on whose recognition one's own parts depend, demand that one present at least a relatively consistent picture to the world. A certain degree of role discrepancy may be permitted, but if certain tolerance limits are passed society will withdraw its recognition of the individual in question, defining him as a moral or psychological aberration. Thus society will allow an individual to be an emperor at work and a serf at home, but it will not permit him to impersonate a police officer or to wear the costume assigned to the other sex. In order to stay within the limits set to his masquerades, the individual may have to resort to complicated maneuvers to make sure that one role remains segregated from the other. The imperial role in the office is endangered by the appearance of one's wife at a director's meeting, or one's role in one circle as an accomplished *raconteur* is threatened by the intrusion of someone from that other circle in which one has been typed as the fellow who never opens his mouth without putting his foot into it. Such role segregation is increasingly possible in our contemporary urban civilization, with its anonymity and its means of rapid transportation, although even here there is a danger that people with contradictory images of oneself may suddenly bump into each other and endanger one's whole stage management. Wife and secretary might meet for coffee, and between them reduce both home-self and office-self to a pitiable shambles. At that point, for sure, one will require a psychotherapist to put a new Humpty Dumpty together again.

There are also internal pressures toward consistency, possibly based on very profound psychological needs to perceive oneself as a totality. Even the contemporary urban masquerader, who plays mutually irreconcilable roles in different areas of his life, may feel internal tensions though he can successfully control external ones by carefully segregating his several *mises en scène* from each other. To avoid such anxieties people commonly segregate their consciousness as well as their conduct. By this we do not mean that they "repress" their discrepant identities into some "unconscious," for within our model we have every reason to be suspicious of such concepts. We rather mean that they focus their attention only on that particular identity that, so to speak, they require at the moment. Other identities are forgotten for the duration of this particular act. The way in which socially disapproved sexual acts or morally questionable acts of any kind are segregated in consciousness may serve to illustrate this process. The man who engages in, say, homosexual masochism has a carefully constructed identity set aside for just these occasions. When any given occasion is over, he checks that identity again at the gate, so to speak, and returns home as affectionate father, responsible husband, perhaps even ardent lover of his wife. In the same way, the judge who sentences a man to death segregates the identity in which he does this from the rest of his consciousness, in which he is a kindly, tolerant and sensitive human being. The Nazi concentration-camp commander who writes sentimental letters to his children is but an extreme case of something that occurs all the time.

It would be a complete misunderstanding of what has just been said if the reader now thought that we are presenting a picture of society in which everybody schemes, plots and deliberately puts on disguises to fool his fellow men. On the contrary, role-playing and identity-building processes are generally unreflected and unplanned, almost automatic. The psychological needs for consistency of self-image just mentioned ensure this. Deliberate deception requires a degree of psychological self-control that few people are capable of. That is why insincerity is rather a rare phenomenon. Most people are sincere, because this is the easiest course to take psychologically. That is, they believe in their own act, conveniently forget the act that preceded it, and happily go through life in the conviction of being responsible in all its demands. Sincerity is the consciousness of the man who is taken in by his own act. Or as it has been put by David Riesman, the sincere man is the one who believes in his own propaganda. In view of the socio-psychological dynamics just discussed, it is much more likely that the Nazi murderers are sincere in their self-portrayals as having been bureaucrats faced with certain unpleasant exigencies that actually were distasteful to them than to assume that they say this only in order to gain sympathy from their judges. Their humane remorse is probably just as sincere as their erstwhile cruelty. As the Austrian novelist Robert Musil has put it, in every murderer's heart there is a spot in which he is eternally innocent. The seasons of life follow one another, and one must change one's face as one changes one's clothes. At the moment we are not concerned with the psychological difficulties or the ethical import of such "lack of character." We only want to stress that it is the customary procedure.

To tie up what has just been said about role theory with what was said in the preceding chapter about control systems we refer to what Hans Gerth and C. Wright Mills have called "person selection." Every social structure selects those persons that it needs for its functioning and eliminates in one way or another those that do not fit. If no persons are available to be selected, they will have to be invented—or rather, they will be produced in accordance with the required specifications. In this way, through its mechanisms of socialization and "formation," society manufactures the personnel it requies to keep going. The sociologist stands on its head the commonsense idea that certain institutions arise because there are certain persons around. On the contrary, fierce warriors appear because there are armies to be sent out, pious men because there are churches to be built, scholars because there are universities to be staffed, and murderers because there are killings to be performed. It is not correct to say that each society gets the men it deserves. Rather, each society produces the men it needs. We can derive some comfort from the fact that this production process sometimes runs into technical difficulties. We shall see later that it can also be sabotaged. For the moment, however, we can see that role theory and its concomitant perceptions add an important dimension to our sociological perspective on human existence.

9

Norms, Values, and Sanctions

JUDITH BLAKE AND KINGSLEY DAVIS

The meaning of "norm" in everyday usage is ambiguous. It often refers to a statistical regularity, as when we say that one's temperature is "normal" or that a man who has been sick has resumed his "normal" activities. On the other hand, it may indicate an accepted standard or model, as in the phrase "set the norm" or "conform to ethical norms." In sociology the same ambiguity is found, although ostensibly, at least, when a formal definition is given, the second meaning is stipulated. Thus the term is presumably employed . . . to designate any standard or rule that states what human beings should or should not think, say, or do under given circumstances.

In this strict sociological usage, the most important element is the *should*, for it clearly implies two important propositions: first, that actual behavior *may* differ from the norm; second, that it *will* differ from the norm unless some effort or force is exerted to bring about conformity. The sociological use of the term generally assumes, without always saying so, that norms are shared to some extent. A purely private, or individual, view of what people should do or think is a norm, but unless it is shared by others, it has no social significance.

Anything in society which pertains to norms, including statements concerning their nature, rationalizations justifying them, and reactions to their violation, may be designated by the adjective "normative." Employed in this way, the word is seen to refer to an entire aspect of human society. It also refers to an element in individual behavior, as when we say that someone's actions are influenced by "normative" factors.

Construed in this way, the normative aspect of human society and human behavior is broad in coverage but conceptually distinct. It embraces, for example, the notion of "values," which are the goals or principles in terms of which specific norms are claimed to be desirable. For example, the rule that political officials should be elected is justified, or "explained," by saying that popular election is necessary if "democracy" is to be realized. The rule itself is the norm, but the value, democracy, is part of the normative reasoning. Disembodied values—i.e., values without any norms through which they can be collectively achieved—are, like purely private norms, sociologically irrelevant.

The "normative" further embraces the inner and outer compulsions (generally called "sanctions") which tend to enforce conformity. A banker who embezzles funds must contend, even when he is successful, with the efforts of others to catch him and with his own ideas of the potential dangers if he is caught. His behavior is therefore "normatively oriented," not so much because of the sheer rule prohibiting embezzlement as because of the sanctions against violation of the rule.

Judith Blake and Kingsley Davis, "Norms, Values and Sanctions," in Robert E. L. Faris (Ed.), *Handbook of Modern Sociology,* © 1964 by Rand McNally & Company, Chicago, pp. 456–66.

Why the Normative Plays a Crucial Role in Sociology

The reason that sociology has given a great deal of attention to norms is clear.

Human society, as distinct from insect and animal societies, is in part organized, and made possible by rules of behavior. By contrast, the intricate interactions of an ant colony or a beehive, like those of a prairie dog village, are governed mainly by instinctive reactions to natural and social stimuli. Such interactions may involve learning to some degree, but this learning, if it occurs, is mainly a matter of habituation to (hence remembrance of) particular environmental stimuli, to which a stereotyped response becomes affixed. In human groups, on the other hand, instinctive responses are channeled or even repressed by the enforcement of behavioral rules that are transmitted by symbolic communication. These rules differ in character from one group to another, and thus help to account for differences in behavior among human societies. For insects and animals, however, behavior tends to be nearly identical from one group to another within the same species, varying only with external conditions. Obviously, then, if the structure of human societies is to be understood, if human behavior is to be adequately explained, the normative aspect must be dealt with. A biologist, habituated to viewing behavior as a function of a physical organism reacting to physical stimuli presented by the environment and other organisms, is apt to bring the same outlook to his analysis of human conduct. If he does so in the concrete sense of offering a complete explanation of some social phenomenon, he is "biologizing" human society. This fallacy is no less bizarre than the opposite—namely, an explanation of some aspect of insect or animal society in terms of presumed norms governing behavior.

Not only does the role of norms account for the difference between human sociology and biology, but it helps account for the division of labor between sociology and economics. In general, economics assumes a normative framework in terms of which the process of production and exchange takes place. Sociology, on the other hand, in trying to understand the way the entire society works (not merely its economic system) has to deal with the norms themselves. For instance, a popular economics textbook points out that in the United States the distribution of income is influenced by the fact that women and Negroes are kept out of certain good jobs and are sometimes paid less for the same job (Samuelson, 1961). If this fact were due to differences in capacity between the races or the sexes, it would come under the economic system of explanation, because the "human resources" available to enter into production would be different. But, finding that "there are numerous jobs which either sex or race can do equally well," the author attributes the discrimination to "prejudice" (pp. 126–127). As an economist he is not obliged to explain why this prejudice occurs (the word is not even in the index), although, as he says, it affects something he is concerned with, the distribution of income. He takes the prejudice for granted, whereas the sociologist must explain its existence by accounting for the norms governing differential hiring and pay. One way in which he does this is by examining nonoccupational roles. The norms governing women's participation in the labor force certainly have something to do with their particular role within the family.

If it be granted that social norms affect behavior, then the totality of norms, or at least the totality of major norms, within a society can be expected to have some consistency, or order.   Otherwise, the social system would not approximate a "system," and the society would tend to fall to pieces and be absorbed by another one which was orderly. It follows that an important aspect of the study of social organization is the study of the "normative order."

Values and Norms

So far we have tried to distinguish the normative factor in behavior and to assess the reasons for its importance to sociology. Let us now admit that this "factor" is quite diverse in character and try to distinguish some of its elements or parts.

Probably the greatest single distinction within the normative realm is that between something variously called values, sentiments, themes, or ethical principles, on the one hand, and the specific rules of conduct, thought, and speech on the other. The line between the two is always fuzzy (Is the doctrine of freedom of the press, for example, a norm or a value?), but the attempt to separate them has been made again and again in sociological and philosophical thought. Apparently the reasons for this effort have varied, but two seem to stand out. Investigators have felt it necessary to probe beyond external behavior to the motives that impel behavior. In addition, since subjective phenomena seem bewildering in the number and variety of their expressions, observers have felt it must be possible to reduce them to a few recurrent, underlying principles, or perhaps "real motives." In any case, the task of finding these subjective forces or entities has been complicated by the fact that human beings not only act but give reasons for their actions. An observer must therefore decide whether to accept the reason given or to judge that, through ignorance or deception, it is not the real one. Not only do persons give private reasons, but there are official versions of what are the proper reasons for given kinds of conduct.

An early attempt to separate the essential values from the kaleidoscope of external manifestations was made by Vilfredo Pareto. In his general treatise on sociology (1935) he not only distinguished basic subjective factors but sought to use them in the analysis of social structure and social change. Underlying the countless rules and rites, verbal arguments and rationalizations (or "derivations"), he thought he could distill a few recurrent motives, or themes, which he called "residues," and which he thought responded to corresponding sentiments. The social system was, for him, a "social equilibrium" consisting of these sentiments acting as forces, and "social dynamics" was, in large part, a matter of the "circulation of the elite" in which differential strength of the various sentiments among the social classes was the main explanatory principle (pp. 509–519, 885–1120, 1740–1929).

Pareto was a student of advanced societies and therefore had to deal with the limitless sophistries of thought which came from the mouths and pens of priests, philosophers, statesmen, scholars, journalists, scientists, and other literate specialists and pleaders. He had to deal with conflicts and differences of opinion. For this reason he had particularly to wrestle with the problem of how to cope with the verbal arguments and explanations in getting to the actual motives hidden behind them. For William Graham Sumner, on the other hand, the problem was somewhat different. This great student of the norms drew his materials mostly from reports about primitive tribes. He therefore was required to pay little or no attention to written expressions of human thought as objects of study and did not need to consider seriously the supernatural and magical explanations that primitive people gave for their norms. In contrast to Pareto, therefore, he barely recognized anything like general principles or abstract values, and when he did, he saw them as consequences rather than determinants of the norms themselves, which he called folkways and mores.

All are forced to conform, and the folkways dominate social life. They seem true and right, and arise into mores as the norm of welfare. Thence are produced faiths, ideas, doctrines, religions, and philosophies, according to the stage of civilization and the fashion of reflection and generalization (Sumner, 1906, p. 38).

Both Pareto and Sumner refused to take the explanations people give for their norms or their conduct at face value. But Pareto sought to find behind the explanations a few basic motives or sentiments, while Sumner emphasized the norms themselves, simply regarding the verbal expressions of people as part of the normative system.

It seems that in general the literature dealing with norms has followed both men in certain respects, regardless of whether or not it was actually influenced directly by them. There has been a tendency to draw materials and inspiration, as Sumner did, from studies of preliterate villagers. Hence conflict, deviation, and the complexity of verbal statement and argument have been minimized. This line of treatment has of course been prominent among the social anthropologists, but it has been present too in the work of Talcott Parsons and some of his students. Due to the emphasis on *different* societies in anthropological thought, the search for values tended to take a new turn. It became a search for the particular underlying values, cultural themes, or ethos of each particular society. This development raised in turn the question of whether the values of one society had any relation to the values of another. In other words, is cultural relativity absolute, or is there a single set of values of which those of different societies are simply variant expressions? Pareto had made it clear that he regarded the sentiments as having "social utility"; Sumner thought that the folkways and mores were adaptive, keeping the society in touch with reality and contributing to its survival. Presumably, in anthropological and sociological thought since Emile Durkheim and Bronislaw Malinowski, the values must have a *function* in society; but the question is obscure because, for many social scientists at least, what is taken as a value may be disfunctional, and what is functional may not be valued. . . .

There is, of course, a distinction to be made between the standards involved in judgments, on the one hand, and the application of those standards in specific judgments, on the other. Thus, in regard to social behavior, it is one thing to say that parents prefer sons to daughters, and quite another to say that parents feel they should treat their daughters in a certain way under given circumstances. Presumably, a preference for sons is a value, but it says nothing concrete concerning parental conduct and it has no sanctions. A norm, on the other hand, says that a given line of conduct must, or should, be followed. Thus a preference for sons in the United States does not mean that female infanticide is permitted or that boys are given more clothes. What, then, is the utility of the distinction between values and norms?

Whatever the utility may be, it surely is not that of designating cause and effect. Presumably a norm "exemplifies" a value, but this does not mean that the norm is *caused* by the value it exemplifies, or that the value is the motive and the norm simply the expression of this motive with respect to behavior. Such a mode of explanation is extremely tempting, not only because it is the way people think anyway— that is, the individual always has a reason for doing whatever he does— but also because it gives an unfailing mode of explaining norms and behavior. The flaw, however, lies in the question of logic and evidence. Can we accept as true people's verbal description of their values? These may be nothing more than a rationalization of the norms—as when, for instance, someone justifies the exclusion of married women from jobs on the ground that a woman's place is in the home. Can we adopt some indirect technique of getting verbal statements of values, thus deceiving the subject into revealing what he would not reveal if he knew our purpose? Such a technique still makes the assumption that the values are consciously held and are rationally connected with norms and conduct—an old-fashioned view controverted by voluminous evidence. Can we then take people's statements and *reinterpret* them to get at "underlying" values? Yes, provided we wish to make the questionable assumption that verbal statements inevitably reflect real values, and provided we admit that the process of symbolic reinterpretation in itself has no empirical controls and consequently may differ radically from one observer to another.

In practice, we tend to find the best evidence of values in the norms themselves. If people manifest a dislike of cheating in examinations, of dishonest advertising in business, and of unnecessary roughness in sports, we infer something like a value of "fair competition." Such a process of reasoning may help us to insert the motivational linkages and thus integrate a body of diverse information. At bottom, however, it is a classification. Its usefulness does not extend to causal explanation, because the inferred value comes only from the specific norms themselves and hence cannot be used as an explanation of those norms. In other words, unless we have evidence independent of the norms themselves, we cannot logically derive norms from values. Independent evidence, if obtainable, may show that the so-called values are nonexistent, that they are consequences of the norms, or that they derive from a third factor which is also responsible for the norms.

It is the norms, not the values, that have the pressure of reality upon them. It is the norms that are enforced by sanctions, that are subject to the necessity of action and the agony of decision. It is therefore the norms that represent the cutting edge of social control. In this regard Sumner seems to have been more correct than some of his successors, for he emphasized the importance of the folkways and mores in understanding society rather than the vague, slippery ideologies, rationalizations, and generalizations people use in justifying their observance or nonobservance of norms.

A more satisfactory use of "values" in sociological analysis is to abandon them as causal agents and to recognize them frankly as sheer constructs by which we attempt to fill in the subjective linkages in the analysis of social causation. For example, the movement of peasants to cities during the process of industrialization is not "explained" by saying that they prefer the bright lights of the city to the drab monotony of the village. Only when the evolving economic and social situation in both the village and the city are taken into account can we begin to explain this recurrent major social phenomenon. It helps us understand the process, however, if we can get some inkling of how the peasant's feelings and thoughts take shape in view of these conditions; and so we try to put together a model of his mental reactions and test it out against various kinds of empirical evidence, including his verbal statements.

The Fallacy of Normative Determinism

We raise the question of causation with respect to values and norms because we believe that conceptual distinctions unrelated to empirical investigation are empty exercises. For the same reason, we wish to push on to the wider question of normative causation in general, apart from the distinction between values and norms. In doing so, we come to one of the most confused and at the same time basic issues in sociology and social anthropology. No one can doubt that norms exercise *some* influence on behavior, but the question of *how much* influence they exercise is highly debatable. At times, sociologists and social anthropologists have seemed to adopt an extreme view by treating the normative system as the sole object of analysis or as the sole determinant of social phenomena. This has usually been done by implicit assumption and careless overstatement rather than by deliberate doctrine, and it has been camouflaged at times by a seemingly broader position of cultural determinism. At any rate, it is a position that affords a good point of departure in analyzing the interrelation between norms and other factors in behavior.

At its most naive level, normative determinism takes the fact that norms *are meant* to control behavior as the basis for assuming that they *do* control it. The only task of social science is then to discover the particular norms in any given society. By this reasoning, nearly all social scientists in Latin America are trained in the law rather than in statistics and social research. The law, being the crystallization of the normative order, is assumed to be what one needs to know. At a more sophisticated level, the assumption is made that the independent variable consists in "cultural configurations," "basic value-orientations," or "the institutional system," which determines everything else in a society. This has a doctrinal side—e.g., in statements about the nature of man—as well as a methodological side. An anthropologist states with approval that national character studies assume that

each member of a society is systematically representative of the cultural pattern of that society, so that the treatment accorded infant or immigrant, pupils or employees or rulers, is indicative of the culturally regular character-forming methods of that society (Mead, 1953, p. 643).

C. Kluckhohn expresses a common dictum when he says that the constants in human life from one society to another "arise out of the biological nature of the species" and its fixed environment, whereas the variations arise from culture. Each culture, he says, has a "grammar." "The function of linguistic grammar is to control the freedom of words so that there is no needless congestion of the communication traffic. The grammar of culture, in general, likewise makes for orderliness" (1959, pp. 273–274).

According to this view, the avenue to understanding actual societies is to understand their cultures. The term culture has a bewildering and altogether too convenient variety of definitions. Sometimes it is used so broadly as to cover all material products of man, all social behavior, all ideas and goals. Used in this way, it includes society itself, and therefore the cultural determinism of social phenomena becomes a tautology. Frequently, however, the term culture is used primarily in the sense of a normative system. In this case we get what may be called a "blueprint theory" of society, namely, that there is a set of "culture-patterns" which are, so to speak, laid down in advance and followed by the members of the society. The determinism implicit in this view is indicated by such phrases as "handed down," "shaped by his culture," "ultimate values," "culture-bound," "way of life," and others.

The way of life that is *handed down* as the social heritage of every people does more than *supply* a set of skills for making a living and a *set of blueprints* for human relations. Each different way of life *makes its own assumptions* about the ends and purposes of human existence . . . (Italics supplied) (C. Kluckhohn, 1959, p. 247).

Similarly, Parsons and his followers have placed heavy emphasis on value-orientations as the key to sociological analysis. In the hands of some, this emphasis gets translated into dogma; for example, "Values determine the choices men make, and the ends they live by" (Stein and Cloward, 1958, p. 263).

Under the assumption of the supremacy of the norms and "dominant" value-orientations, the chief research method of the social disciplines becomes that of questioning informants. The investigator asks a member of the society what people are *supposed* to do, and hence the normative pattern will emerge. The informant necessarily knows the "culture," because he lives it and is determined by it.

Any member of a group, provided that his position within that group is specified, is a perfect sample of the group-wide pattern on which he is acting as an informant (Mead, 1953, p. 648).

Furthermore, with this reliance on norms and values as determinants of social phenomena, peculiar importance is naturally given to "socialization," normally interpreted to mean the acquisition, or "internalization," of the norms. According to Parsons:

There is reason to believe that, among the learned elements of personality in certain respects the stablest and most enduring are the major value-orientation patterns and there is much evidence that these are "laid down" in childhood and are not on a large scale subject to drastic alteration during adult life. There is good reason to treat these patterns of value-orientation, as analyzed in terms of pattern variable combinations, as the core of what is sometimes called "basic personality structure" . . . (1951, p. 208).

Most of the sociologists and anthropologists who stress culture, culture patterns, norms, value-attitudes, and such concepts would deny that they are determinists. They would say they are abstracting—treating behavior *as if* it were determined by the normative system. In practice, however, the emphasis on values and norms leads, as critics have been quick to point out, to deficiencies in the scientific understanding of real societies. The gravest deficiency arises, ironically, in the failure to deal adequately with norms themselves. As long as the cultural configurations, basic value-attitudes, prevailing mores, or what not are taken as the starting point and principal determinant, they have the status of unanalyzed assumptions. The very questions that would enable us to understand the norms tend not to be asked, and certain facts about society become difficult, if not impossible, to comprehend. For instance, an assumption of normative primacy renders it difficult to explain deviancy and crime, although the real world plainly exhibits a great deal of normative violation. If one is to understand deviancy, one must ask why societies frequently reward violation more heavily than conformity to the norms; why legitimate authority is one of the most widespread bases of illegitimate power; why ego and alter so frequently disagree on norms applicable to their relationship; why any action, no matter how atrocious, can be justified in terms of the verbal formulas in which norms and values are couched. Furthermore, the origin and appearance of new norms and their constant change—again facts of social existence—become incomprehensible under an assumption of normative sovereignty. . . .

Presumably if one's interpretation is in terms of norms rather than values, one is on firmer ground. Yet the difficulty of proving the existence of the norm is great. As a consequence, there is a tendency to take regularities in behavior as the evidence of the norm. When this is done, to explain the behavior in terms of the norm is a redundancy. Seen in this light, statements such as the following are also redundant: "Knowledge of a culture makes it possible to predict a good many of the actions of any person who shares that culture" (C. Kluckhohn, 1949, p. 38). Why not simply say, "Knowledge of behavior in a society makes it possible to predict behavior in that society"? Of course, if norms are taken to be regularities of behavior, they have no analytical significance at all; they are then merely another name for behavior itself, and cannot contribute to an understanding of behavior.

Types of Norms

The blueprint theory of society does not fit the facts of social existence. Societies as we know them are highly active and dynamic, filled with conflict, striving, deceit, cunning. Behavior in a given situation tends to be closely related to that situation, to be strongly affected by individual interests, to be unpredictable from a knowledge of the norms alone. Far from being fully determinant, the norms themselves tend to be a product of the constant interaction involving the interplay of interests, changing conditions, power, dominance, force, fraud, ignorance, and knowledge.

Furthermore it is surprising how simplified the view of culture and of the normative system tends to be in the hands of many who emphasize their role. To show this, let us attempt a brief listing of the variegated aspects of the norms—aspects seldom all dealt with in the social science literature. . . .

1. Content
   a. Societal requirement involved.

(Norms ordinarily concern some functional requirement such as reproduction, division of labor, allocation of power. Norms clustered around a given functional requirement are often collectively designated as "institutions.")
   b. Whether the norm relates to a goal or to the means.
   c. How the norm is stated—whether put negatively (should not) or positively (should).
2. Types of Sanctions
   a. Maximum or minimum.
   b. Reward or punishment.
      Repressive or restitutive (in the case of punishment).
   c. Specific or diffuse (may be both).
3. Acceptance of the Norm
   a. Extent of acceptance (accepted as obligatory by virtually everyone or accepted as obligatory by only certain groups, such as certain ethnic groups).
   b. Degree of acceptance (felt to be mildly obligatory or felt to be mandatory).
4. Mode of Transmission
   a. Primary socialization.
   b. Secondary socialization.
5. Source of Imputed Authority for the Norm
   a. Tradition.
   b. Law.
   c. A nonempirical or supernatural agency ("natural law," God, some member of a pantheon, ghosts, etc.).
   d. Public opinion.
6. Extent of Application of the Norm
   a. To which statuses does the norm apply? (The reader will note that the extent of application of a norm is different from the extent of its acceptance. A norm which applies only to the occupant of a particular status may nonetheless be accepted by everyone as the proper conduct for that status. Example: Everyone thinks a

judge should be fair and impartial.)

b. To what groups does the norm apply?

7. Mode of Origination
   a. Formal enactment.
   b. Informal, traditional, accretion.

8. Formal Properties of the Statement of the Norm
   a. Explicit (a body of law, regulations, codes).
   b. Implicit ("gentlemen's agreements," rarely verbalized but understood ways of behaving and thinking).
   c. Vague, diffuse statement.
   d. Specific, detailed statement.
   e. Rigid (requires exact conformity).
   f. Flexible (latitude in the precision with which the normative demand must be met).

Clearly, these ways in which social norms can vary are interrelated. For example, a norm that is stated positively is, in effect, stated in terms of some *reward* for compliance, whereas a negative normative statement implies punishment. Moreover, maximum sanctions—either rewards or punishments —typically imply that the norm involved is widely accepted (in the society, or group, or organization under consideration) and that strong sentiments support it. A norm of this type will also very likely be one that individuals have learned early in life at a time (the period of "primary socialization") when they must accept social rules in a more unreflective fashion than later. Further, norms carrying maximum sanctions are usually felt by people to be inherently right (natural) rather than simply legitimated by reference to law, tradition, or public opinion. Also, for maximum sanctions actually to be applied, the norm must definitely specify the relevant status. For instance, even a so-called universal

in the United States such as the norm against killing another human being has so many legitimized exceptions that these must be clearly specified before sanctions can be brought to bear.

Sanctions

People not only conform to rules themselves but, by means of their sanctioning of others' behavior, motivate others to conform also. In most cases sanctions are informal—an approving or contemptuous glance, an encouraging or derisive laugh, a sympathetic or embarrassed silence. Such seemingly trivial but pervasive sanctions enable human beings to control informally a share of their own actions and reactions and the actions and reactions of others. However, it is also true that behavior is frequently controlled by formal sanctions as well—by a medal or a jail, an honorary dinner or an electric chair, a parade or a court-martial. In the ordinary course of our lives, we tend to be more aware of the explicitly sanctioning nature of formal than of informal rewards and punishments. Indeed, the relatively unruffled fashion in which informal sanctions operate constitutes one of their most important societal functions—they control behavior in a relatively painless manner before more formal measures are necessary.

Yet every viable society must develop supports to help individuals *resist* this type of informal pressure as well as to help them conform to it, for such pressures never are so finely geared to changing situations that it is socially advantageous for individuals always to respond with gusto to sanctions of this type. To be sure, the system is partially self-corrective in that what is negatively sanctioned by one individual may be highly rewarded by another. But this capacity for self-correction is limited, because individuals deal with one another in terms of social roles which, by definition, tend to be highly standardized sets of expectations. Hence, one of the problems that every society faces constantly is that of assuring itself role flexibility in the face of changing conditions.

Since so many sanctions are informal and applied continuously in the course of daily living, we are all in effect constantly "administering" the normative order. There must accordingly be mechanisms to keep individuals *cognitively* primed or "briefed" about the norms (what the norms are, to whom they apply, in what situations, etc.) and, in addition, to keep people *emotionally* primed respecting the *legitimacy* of norms. By and large people must feel that behavior they are punishing or rewarding (either in themselves or others) is at least roughly the same as other people would punish or reward in similar situations. Yet, like any other set of rules, social norms are only approximations of how people should act. In specific situations, individuals must take many things into account, and, in particular, they are faced with the difficulty that adherence to the letter of a norm (or to the formal content of a number of different norms) may place them or others in situations having no apparent legitimacy at all. The result is that much of our lives is spent in seeking out the legitimacy of various courses of action and thereby inevitably redefining the legitimacy of specific norms—an example of how the effort at conformity with social rules provides a dynamic source of social change.

A significant share of orderly conduct is, however, a result of assessing the consequences for nonconformity rather than a result of the "internalization" of the norms as just discussed. In fact, individuals' internalization of norms is doubtless differentiated and segmental in most societies. Individuals are emotionally committed to some norms and others they merely conform to, if they conform at all, out of calculation and rational assessment. Such a criss-crossing of commitment and objectivity toward norms gives societies another source of change and of stability. There are some people who regard certain rules as "outdated" and "unjust" and make efforts to change the rules, and there are people who, feeling that the same rules are adequate and legitimate, resist this change. Because of this criss-crossing, many societies can undergo remarkable social transformations, all the while retaining an adequate degree of social control.

Much of modern sociological thinking has strongly emphasized the internalization of role expectations as the prime mover in social control, to the extent that the importance of calculation with respect to sanctions tends to be overlooked except as a last resort. Yet, we must never forget that social rules require doing what would ordinarily not be done if the rules did not exist. Since these rules therefore, by definition, have such a high nuisance value for human beings, it seems inconceivable that most people do not calculate extensively. . . .

References

KLUCKHOHN, C. *Mirror for man.* New York: McGraw, 1949.

KLUCKHOHN, C. Common humanity and diverse cultures. In D. Lerner (ed.), *The human meaning of the social sciences.* New York: Meridian Books, 1959, pp. 245–284.

MEAD, MARGARET. National character. In A. L. Kroeber (ed.), *Anthropology today.* Chicago: Univer. of Chicago Press, 1953, pp. 642–667.

PARETO, V. *General treatise on sociology.* (Mistrans. as *The mind and society.*) New York: Harcourt, 1935.

PARSONS, T. *The social system.* Glencoe, Ill.: Free Press, 1951.

SAMUELSON, P. A. *Economics: An introductory analysis.* (5th ed.) New York: McGraw, 1961.

STEIN, H., and CLOWARD, R. A. *Social perspectives on behavior.* Glencoe, Ill.: Free Press, 1958.

SUMNER, W. G. *Folkways.* Boston: Ginn, 1906.

10

The Operating Room: A Study in Role Distance

ERVING GOFFMAN

Surgery As an Activity System

I have suggested some cases where the scene of activity generates for the individual a self which he is apparently loath to accept openly for himself, since his conduct suggests that some disaffiliation exists between himself and his role. But a peek into some odd corner of social life provides no basis, perhaps, for generalizing about social life. As a test, then, of the notion of role distance (and role), let us take a scene in which activity generates a self for the individual that appears to be a most likely one for self-attachment. Let us take, for example, the activity system sustained during a surgical operation. The components consist of verbal and physical acts and the changing states of the organism undergoing the operation. Here, if anywhere in our society, we should find performers flushed with a feeling of the weight and dignity of their action. A Hollywood ideal is involved: the white-coated chief surgeon strides into the operating theater after the patient has been anesthetized and opened by assistants. A place is automatically made for him.

From *Encounters* by Erving Goffman, copyright © 1961 by The Bobbs-Merrill Company, Inc., reprinted by permission of the publishers.

He grunts a few abbreviated preliminaries, then deftly, almost silently, gets to work, serious, grim, competently living up to the image he and his team have of him, yet in a context where momentary failure to exhibit competence might permanently jeopardize the relation he is allowed to have to his role. Once the critical phase of the operation is quite over, he steps back and, with a special compound of tiredness, strength, and disdain, rips off his gloves; he thus contaminates himself and abdicates his role, but at a time when his own labors put the others in a position to "close up." While he may be a father, a husband, or a baseball fan at home, he is here one and only one thing, a surgeon, and being a surgeon provides a fully rounded impression of the man. If the role perspective works, then, surely it works here, for in our society the surgeon, if anyone, is allowed and obliged to put himself into his work and gets a self out of it. . . .[1]

If we start with the situation of the

[1] Much the same conceit has already been employed by Temple Burling in *Essays on Human Aspects of Administration,* Bulletin 25 (August 1953) of the New York State School of Industrial and Labor Relations, Cornell University, pp. 9–10. The fullest published accounts of conduct in the operating room that I know of are to be found

lesser medical personnel,[2] the intern and the junior resident, the test will not be fair, for here, apparently, is a situation much like the ones previously mentioned. The tasks these juniors are given to do—such as passing hemostats, holding retractors, cutting small tied-off veins, swabbing the operating area before the operation, and perhaps suturing or closing at the end—are not large enough to support much of a surgical role. Furthermore, the junior person may find that he performs even these lowly tasks inadequately, and that the scrub nurse as well as the chief surgeon tells him so. And when the drama is over and the star performer has dropped his gloves and gown and walked out, the nurses may underline the intern's marginal position by lightly demanding his help in moving the body from the fixed table to the movable one, while automatically granting him a taste of the atmosphere they maintain when real doctors are absent. As for the intern himself, surgery is very likely *not* to be his chosen specialty; the three-month internship is a course requirement and he will shortly see the last of it. The intern may confirm all this ambivalence to his work on oc-

casions away from the surgery floor, when he scathingly describes surgery as a plumber's craft exercised by mechanics who are told what to look for by internists.

The surgical junior, especially the intern, has, then, a humbling position during surgery. Whether as a protection against this condition or not, the medical juniors I observed, like over-age merry-go-round riders, analysands, and carnival pitchmen, were not prepared to embrace their role fully; elaborate displays of role distance occurred.[3] A careful, bemused look on the face is sometimes found, implying, "This is not the real me." Sometimes the individual will allow himself to go "away," dropping off into a brown study that removes him from the continuity of events, increases the likelihood that his next contributory act will not quite fit into the flow of action, and effectively gives the appearance of occupational disaffection; brought back into play, he may be careful to evince little sign of chagrin. He may rest himself by leaning on the patient or by putting a foot on an inverted bucket but in a manner too contrived to allow the others to feel it is a matter of mere resting. Interestingly enough, he sometimes takes on the function of the jester, endangering his reputation with antics that temporarily place him in a doubtful and special position, yet through this providing the others present with a reminder of less exalted worlds:

in T. Burling, E. Lentz and R. Wilson, *The Give and Take in Hospitals* (New York: Putnam, 1956), Chap. 17, pp. 260–283, and R. Wilson, "Teamwork in the Operating Room," *Human Organization*, 12 (1954), pp. 9–14.
[2] My own material on interaction during surgery, from which all staff practices and verbal responses cited in this page are drawn, derives from brief observations to the medical building of a mental hospital and the operating rooms of a surburban community hospital. Not deriving from the most formal hospitals, these data load the facts a little in my favor.

I am grateful to Dr. Otis R. Farley, and his staff in the Medical and Surgical Branch of St. Elizabeth's Hospital, Washington, D.C., and to John F. Wight, Administrative Director, and Lenore Jones, Head Surgical Nurse, of Herrick Memorial Hospital, Berkeley, California, for full research freedom and great courtesy.

CHIEF SURGEON JONES (*in this case a senior resident*): A small Richardson please.

SCRUB NURSE: Don't have one.

DR. JONES: O.K., then give me an Army and Navy.

[3] Some of the interns I observed had plans to take a psychiatric residency and, apparently because of this, were doing their stint of surgical internship in the medical building of a mental hospital; they therefore had wider institutional support for their lack of interest in physical techniques.

SCRUB NURSE: It looks like we don't have one.

DR. JONES (*lightly joking*): No Army or Navy man here.

INTERN (*dryly*): No one in the armed forces, but Dr. Jones here is in the Boy Scouts.

SCRUB NURSE: Will there be more than three [sutures] more? We're running out of sutures.

CHIEF SURGEON: I don't know.

INTERN: We can finish up with Scotch tape.

INTERN (*looking for towel clamps around body*): Where in the world . . . . ?

SCRUB NURSE: Underneath the towel.

(*Intern turns to the nurse and in slow measure makes a full cold bow to her.*)

SCRUB NURSE (*to intern*): Watch it, you're close to my table! [A *Mayo stand containing instruments whose asepsis she must guard and guarantee.*] (*Intern performs a mock gasp and clownishly draws back.*)

As I have suggested, just as we cannot use a child over four riding a merry-go-round as an exhibition of how to embrace an activity role, so also we cannot use the junior medical people on a surgical team. But surely the chief surgeon, at least, will demonstrate the embracing of a role. What we find, of course, is that even this central figure expresses considerable role distance.

Some examples may be cited. One can be found in medical etiquette. This body of custom requires that the surgeon, on leaving the operation, turn and thank his assistant, his anesthetist, and ordinarily his nurses as well. Where a team has worked together for a long time and where the members are of the same age-grade, the surgeon may guy this act, issuing the thanks in what he expects will be taken as an ironical and farcical tone of voice: "Miss Westly, you've done a simply wonderful job here." Similarly, there is a formal rule that in preparing a

requested injection the nurse show the shelved vial to the surgeon before its sealed top is cracked off so that he can check its named contents and thereby take the responsibility on himself. If the surgeons are very busy at the time, this checking may be requested but not given. At other times, however, the checking may be guyed.

CIRCULATING NURSE: Dr. James, would you check this?

DR. JAMES (*in a loud ministerial voice, reading the label*): Three cubic centimeters of heparin at ten-milligram strength, put up by Invenex and held by Nurse Jackson at a forty-five-degree angle. That is right, Nurse Jackson.

Instead of employing technical terms at all times, he may tease the nurses by using homey appelations: "Give me the small knife, we'll get in just below the belly button"; and he may call the electric cauterizer by the apt name of "sizzler," ordering the assistant surgeon to "sizzle here, and here." Similarly, when a nurse allows her non-sterile undergown to be exposed a little, a surgeon may say in a pontifical and formal tone, "Nurse Brown, can I call your attention to the anterior portion of your gown. It is exposing you. I trust you will correct this condition," thereby instituting social control, reference to the nurse's non-nursing attributes, and satire of the profession, all with one stroke. So, too, returning to the operating room with a question, "Dr. Williams?" may be answered by a phrase of self-satirization: "In person," or, "This is Dr. Williams." And a well-qualified surgeon, in taking the situated role of assistant surgeon for the duration of a particular operation, may tell the nurses, when they have been informed by the chief surgeon that two electric cauterizers will be employed, "I'm going to get one too, just like the big doctors, that's what I like to hear." A chief surgeon, then, may certainly express role distance. Why he does so, and with what effect, are clearly additional questions, and ought to be considered.

The Functions of Role Distance for Surgery

I have suggested that in surgery, in a room that pridefully keeps out germs and gives equal medical treatment to bodies of different socio-economic status, there is no pretense at expressional asepsis. Role distance is routinely expressed.

But why should the individual be disinclined to embrace his role self? The situation of the junior medical man suggests that defensive activity is at work. We cannot say, however, that role distance protects the individual's ego, self-esteem, personality, or integrity from the implications of the situation without introducing constructs which have no place in a strictly sustained role perspective. We must find a way, then, of getting the ego back into society.

We can begin to do this by noting that when the individual withdraws from a situated self he does not draw into some psychological world that he creates himself but rather acts in the name of some other socially created identity. The liberty he takes in regard to a situated self is taken because of other, equally social, constraints. A first example of this is provided us when we try to obtain a systematic view of the functions performed by role distance in surgery, for immediately we see a paradoxical fact: one of the concerns that prevents the individual from fully accepting his situated self is his commitment to the situated activity system itself. We see this when we shift our point of view from the individual to the situated system and look at the functions that role distance serves for it. We find that certain maneuvers which act to integrate the system require for their execution individuals

who do not fully embrace their situated selves. System-irrelevant roles can thus themselves be exploited for the system as a whole. In other words, one of the claims upon himself that the individual must balance against all others is the claim created by the over-all "needs" [4] of the situated activity system itself, apart from his particular role in it.

An illustration of these contingencies is provided by the chief surgeon. Like those in many other occupational positions, the chief surgeon finds that he has the obligation to direct and manage a particular activity system, in this case a surgical operation. He is obliged to see that the operation is effectively carried through, regardless of what this may sometimes express about himself.

Now for the surgical team to function usefully, each member, as already suggested, must sustain his capacity as a communicator, an individual capable of giving and receiving verbal communications and their substitutes. And, as in other activity systems, each member must be able to execute physical actions requiring some coolness and self-command. Anything that threatens either this verbal or physical poise threatens the participant's capacity to contribute, and hence the activity system itself. Each individual member of the surgical team must be in command of himself, and where he is not able to handle himself, others, especially the chief surgeon, must help him do it.

In order to ensure that the members of his team keep their heads during the operation, the chief surgeon finds himself under pressure to modulate his own demands and his own expectations of what is due him. If he exercises his situated rights openly to criticize incompetent conduct, the surgeon may only further weaken the defaulter's

[4] In the sense used by Philip Selznick in "Foundations of the Theory of Organization," *American Sociological Review*, 13 (1948), pp. 29–30.

self-command and further endanger the particular operation. In short, the chief surgeon is likely to find himself with the situated role function of anxiety management [5] and may find that he must draw on his own dignity, on what is owed his station, in order to fulfil this function. A kind of bargaining or bribery [6] occurs, whereby the surgeon receives a guarantee of equability from his team in return for being "a nice guy"—someone who does not press his rightful claims too far. Of course, the surgeon may save his dignity and lose the operation, but he is under pressure not to do so.

Given the conflict between correcting a subordinate and helping him maintain his poise, it is understandable that surgeons will employ joking means of negative sanction, so that it is difficult to determine whether the joke is a cover for the sanction, or the sanction a cover for the joke. In either case, some distance from usual surgical decorum is required:

(Intern holds retractor at wrong end of incision and goes "away," being uninterested in the operation.)
CHIEF SURGEON (in mock English accent): You don't have to hold that up there, old chap, perhaps down here. Going to sleep, old boy?
CHIEF SURGEON (on being accidentally stabbed in the finger by the assistant surgeon, who is using the electric scalpel): If I get syphalis [sic] I'll know where I got it from, and I'll have witnesses.

If some of these jokes seem weak and unnecessary, we must appreciate that to let a small error of conduct go by with-

out comment has its own dangers, apart from what this laxness might mean for staff training. In the presence of a mistake, staff members can ready themselves for the occurrence of a corrective sanction, and unless something pertinent is said, this readiness may act as an anxiety-producing distraction. The immediate expression of a joking sanction, however labored, grounds this sort of tension.

Just as a negative sanction may be toned down to prevent the offender from acting still more disruptively, so also direct commands may be softened into requests even though the surgeon's general occupational status and particular situated role empower him to command. Where he has a right to issue a peremptory order for an instrument, he may instead employ courtesies: "Let's have another Richardson," "Could I have a larger retractor." Instead of flaring up when no suitable ready-made instrument is available, he may choose to express a boyish mechanical ingenuity, constructing on the spot a make-do instrument.

I am suggesting that he who would effectively direct an operation at times may have to employ a touch so light as to embarrass the dark dignities of his position. In fact, we can expect that the more that is demanded from a subordinate in the way of delicacy, skill, and pure concentration, the more informal and friendly the superordinate is likely to become. If one person is to participate in a task as if he were an extension of another participant, opening himself up to the rapid and delicate feedback control that an individual ordinarily obtains only of and for himself, then, apparently, he must be favorably disposed to the person in command, for such cooperativeness is much easier to win than to exact.

I would like to note here that the chief surgeon may feel obliged to introduce distractions as well as to dispel them. When the spontaneous engage-

[5] This role function is one which the M.D. anesthetist often performs, or tries to perform, sometimes apparently quite intentionally, as a filler for a position that might otherwise not have enough weight for the person who fills it.
[6] The notion of "role bargain" is usefully developed in W. J. Goode, "A Theory of Role Strain," *American Sociological Review*, 25 (1960), pp. 483–496.

ment of the participants in the task activity itself seems likely to tax them too much, the chief surgeon may distract them, for example, by joking. This is just the reverse of the process previously described. Thus, at a point of high tenseness, when a large renal tumor has been completely exposed and was ready to be pierced by a draining needle, a chief surgeon lightly warned before he pierced: "Now don't get too close." Another instance of this easing process is found in the fact that the others often seem to look to the chief surgeon to mark the end of a critical phase of action and the beginning of a less critical phase, one that can be used for a general letdown in the sustained concentration of attention and effort. In order to set the tone for these functionally useful relaxations, at the end of a phase of action, the surgeon may stretch himself in a gawky, exaggerated, and clownish way and utter a supportive informality such as "okey-dokey" or "th-ar sh' be." Before the critical phase is begun, and after it has been terminated, he may engage others present in talk about last night's party, the recent ball game, or good places to fish.[7] And when the patient is being closed up and the critical work is quite over, the chief surgeon may

[7] Under strictest possible procedure, no talking would be tolerated except when technically necessary, since germs can apparently be spread through masks in this way. My own experience was in relatively informal hospitals where irrelevant talk and byplays did occur. Burling and Wilson report a similar experience. Presumably the medical traditions of different regions differ in this regard, as suggested by Eugene de Savitsch, *In Search of Complications* (New York: Simon and Schuster, 1940), pp. 374–375: "In a clinic or operating room almost anywhere in the world all would be silence, soft lights, and sustained tension. In France everybody chatters away as merrily as in a cafe. While a brain tumor, for instance, is removed, the surgeon, his assistants, and the audience—if any—argue over the merits of the present cabinet, disclose the shortcomings of their wives, and exchange advice about stocks and bonds."

initiate and tolerate joking with nurses, bantering with them about their lack of proficiency or about the operation not being nearly over. If no male nurse is present to lift the patient from the operating table to the trolley, the chief surgeon, if he is still in the operating room, may gallantly brush aside the efforts of one of the nurses and insist on lifting the heaviest part of the patient, the middle, himself, acting now in the capacity of a protective male, not a medical person.

Just as the chief surgeon may mark the point where attentiveness may be usefully relaxed, so he, and sometimes others on the team, will put brackets around the central task activity with the result that the level of concern required for it will not be demanded of the team before matters actually get under way and after they have ended. This is nicely shown not merely in the ritual of tearing off one's gloves and immediately leaving the operating room, by which the chief surgeon tells the team that teacher is no longer checking up on them and they can relax, but also in the way in which the body is handled. During the operation, the body of the patient is the rightful focus of a great deal of respectful sustained consideration, technically based, especially in connection with the maintenance of asepsis, blood levels, and respiration. It is as if the body were a sacred object, regardless of the socioeconomic character of its possessor, but in this case the consideration given is rational as well as ritual. As might be expected, then, before and after the operation proper there can be observed minor acts of desacralization, whereby the patient is reduced to more nearly profane status. At the beginning of the task the surgeon may beat a tattoo on the leg of the anesthetized patient, and at the end he may irreverently pat the patient on the bottom, commenting that he is now better than new. The surgeon is not alone in this activity. While scrubbing the anesthetized patient, the nurse may lift up a foot by the toe and speak to it: "You're not sterile, are you?" In moving the now groggy patient from the operating table to the trolley for the trip to the recovery room, the anesthetist, taking charge of this relatively unskilled physical action, may obtain concerted effort from the other persons helping him by saying: "Ready, aim, fire." Similarly, in moving an anesthetized patient on his side for a thoracotomy, the anesthetist may say: "O.K., kids, are we ready to play flip flop? Ready? O.K."

In addition to maintaining the capacities and poise of other members of the team, the chief surgeon has, of course, an obligation to maintain his own. Moreover, he must be concerned not only with sustaining his own mobilization of personal resources, but also with the anxious attention that other members of the team might give to this. If they feel he is about to lose his temper, or that he has lost his skill, they themselves can become extremely uneasy and inefficient. Thus, when the surgeon runs into trouble that could cause his teammates a distracting and suppressed concern over how he might react to his trouble, we find him engaging in quite standard strategies of tension management, sometimes concealing his own real concerns to do so. He alludes openly to the incident in such a way as to rob it of its capacity to distract the team. When he drops an instrument, he may respond unseriously to his own action by a word such as "oopsadaisy." If he must give an order to one of his assistants which might leave the others not knowing if he were angry or not, he may deliver it in a false English accent, in adolescent slang, or in some other insulating way. Unable to find the right spot for a lumbar puncture, he may, after three tries, shake his head a little, as if to suggest that he, as a person sensitive to ideal standards, is still sensitive to them and

yet in quiet control of himself, in short, that the implied discrediting of him has not made him lose poise.

Since the chief surgeon's own self-control is crucial in the operation, and since a question concerning it could have such a disquieting effect upon the other members of the team, he may feel obliged to demonstrate that he is in possession of himself, not merely at times of crisis and trouble, but even at times when he would otherwise be silent and so be providing no information one way or the other about his state of mind. Thus, when puzzled about what to do, he may ruminate half out loud, ingenuously allowing others present a close glimpse of his thoughts. During quite delicate tasks, he may softly sing incongruous undignified tunes such as "He flies through the air with the greatest of ease." In clamping hemostats, he may let them go from his fingers, flipping them back upon the patient's body in a neat row with the verve and control that parking attendants manifest while parking cars, or merry-go-round managers display in collecting tickets while moving around on the turning platform.

What we have here is a kind of "externalization" of such feelings and thoughts as are likely to give security and confidence to the other members of the team. This externalization, as well as the constant cutting back of any distractive concern that might have arisen for the team in the course of action, also provides a constant stimulus to team members' attentiveness and task engagement, in both ways helping to hold them to the task as usable participants. Some surgeons, in fact, maintain something of a running line of patter during the operation, suggesting that whenever there is teamwork, someone is likely to have the role function of "talking it up."

We see that the chief surgeon is something of a host to persons at his party, as well as the director of his operating team. He is under pressure (however he responds to this pressure) to make sure that those at his table feel good about what is happening so that whatever their capacities they can better exploit them. And to do this morale-maintaining job, at least in America, the surgeon makes use of and draws upon activities not expected of one in his dignified position. When he himself does not perform the clown function, he may encourage someone else, such as the intern or circulating nurse, to take on the job.

In discussing the special responsibilities of the chief surgeon and his frequent need to draw on informality in order to meet these responsibilities, it was implied that the superordinate present may have some special reasons for exhibiting role distance. A further comment should be added concerning the relation between role distance and social ranking.

It seems characteristic of the formalities of a role that adherence to them must be allowed and confirmed by the others involved in the situation; this is one of the basic things we mean by the notion that something is formal and official. Adherence to formalities seems to guarantee the status quo of authority and social distance; under the guidance of this style, one can be assured that the others will not be able to move in on one. Reversing the role point of view, we can see that adherence to the formalities one owes to others can be a relatively protective matter, guaranteeing that one's conduct will have to be accepted by the others, and, often, that it will not be difficult to dissociate one's purely covert personal attachments from one's role projection. Finally, it should be added that in general we assume that it is to the advantage of the subordinate to decrease distance from the superordinate and to the advantage of the latter to sustain or increase it.

From these considerations it should be apparent that the exercise of role distance will take on quite different meanings, depending on the relative rank of the individual who exercises it. Should a subordinate exercise role distance, this is likely to be seen as a sign of his refusal to keep his place (thereby moving toward greater intimacy with the superordinate, which the latter is likely to disapprove), or as rejection of authority,[8] or as evidence of low morale. On the other hand, the manifestations of role distance on the part of the superordinate is likely to express a willingness to relax the status quo, and this the subordinate is likely to approve because of its potential profitability for him. In the main, therefore, the expression of role distance is likely to be the prerogative of the superodinate in an interaction. In fact, since informality on the part of the inferior is so suspect, a tacit division of labor may arise, whereby the inferior contributes respect for the status quo on behalf of both parties, while the superior contributes a glaze of sociability that all can enjoy. Charm and colorful little informalities are thus usually the prerogatives of those in higher office, leading us mistakenly to assume that an individual's social graces helped him to his high position, instead of what is perhaps more likely, that the graces become possible for anyone who attains the office.[9] Hence, it is the sur-

[8] For example, I know of a nurse who was transferred from an experimental surgery team, in part because she enacted simulated yawns, meant to be humorous, during the ticklish part of a delicate surgical technique, thereby showing role distance above her station.

[9] An empirical illustration of this is presented in an excellent paper by Rose Coser in which she demonstrates the special joking prerogatives of senior psychiatrists during ward meetings; see her "Laughter Among Colleagues," Psychiatry, 23 (1960), pp. 81–95. For further illustrations of role distance on the part of superordinates, see Ralph Turner, "The Navy Disbursing Officer as a Bureaucrat," American Sociological Review, 12 (1947), pp. 342–348.

geon, not the surgical nurse, who injects irony into medical etiquette. All of this, it may be added, fits other things we know about relations between unequals. It is the ship's captain who has a right to enter the territory of the ordinary seamen, the "fo'c'sle," not they to enter his. An officer has a right to penetrate the private life of a soldier serving under him, whereas the private does not have a similar right. In this connection, one student has been led to speak of the social distance between two individuals as being of different extent depending from whose place one starts.[10]

But, of course, subordinates can exercise much role distance, and not merely through grumbling. By sacrificing the seriousness of their claim to being treated as full-fledged persons, they can exercise liberties not given to social adults.

We can now see that with the chief surgeon on one side and the intern on the other there appears to be a standard distribution of role-distance rights and role-distance tendencies. The intern may sacrifice his character as a full and serious person, becoming, thereby, a half-child in the system, in return for which he is allowed to offend medical role requirements with impunity. The person with dominating status can also offend with impunity because his position gives others present a special reason for accepting the offense.

I would like to add that although the person who manifests much role distance may, in fact, be alienated from the role, still, the opposite can well be true: in some cases only those who feel secure in their attachment may be able to chance the expression of distance. And, in fact, in spite of interns, it appears that conformity to the prescriptive aspects of role often occurs most thoroughly at the neophyte level, when

the individual must prove his competence, sincerity, and awareness of his place, leaving the showing of distance from a role to a time when he is firmly "validated" in that role.

Another peculiarity should be mentioned. To express role-irrelevant idiosyncrasies of behavior is to expose oneself to the situation, making more of oneself available in it than is required by one's role. The executive's family picture on his desk, telling us that he is not to be considered entirely apart from his loved ones, also tells us, in a way, that they are in this occupation with him, and that they might understand his having to work late or open up his house to politically wise sociability.

The differing bases of role distance displayed by the chief surgeon and by the intern imply a division of labor or role differentiation. The nursing personnel exhibit a similar kind of differentiation among themselves: the division of labor and responsibility between the scrub nurse and the circulating nurse is associated with a difference in manifestation of role distance. The scrub nurse, in addition to her continued task obligation during the operation, may feel obliged to maintain the role function of standard-maintainer, policing the aseptic character of the order that is maintained, as well as keeping a Management's eye on the skills of the physicians. Any withdrawal of herself into the role of female might, therefore, jeopardize the situated system. The circulating nurse, on the other hand, has no such responsibilities, and, apparently, these sexual considerations can be displaced onto her. Further, not needing to be "in" the operation as must the scrub nurse, she can withdraw into herself, or into a conversation with the anesthetist or the nurses in the adjacent operating room, without jeopardizing matters. To place her in a female capacity does not reduce manpower. It is not surprising, therefore,

[10] Donald MacRae, "Class Relationships and Ideology," *The Sociological Review*, n.s., 6 (1958), pp. 263–264.

that the circulating nurse, in addition to the intern, is allowed to be flighty—to act without character.

The division of role-function labor that I have described has a characteristic subtlety that should be mentioned again in conclusion. A person with a specialized task not only performs a service needed by the system but also provides a way of being, a selfhood, with which others in the system can identify, thus allowing them to sustain an image of themselves that would disrupt matters if sustained other than vicariously. The "good guy" informality of the chief surgeon can give his subordinates a feeling that they are not the sort to tolerate strict subordination, that in fact the surgeon must see this and has adjusted himself correspondingly, yet this is, of course, a vicarious rebelliousness carried out principally by the very agency against which one would ordinarily rebel. In the same way, the circulating nurse can establish the principle of female sexuality in which the surgical nurse can see her own reflection, even while the surgeon is calling her by a masculine last-name term of address and receiving a man-sized work contribution from her.

Some final points may now be mentioned concerning the function of role distance, now not merely in surgery but in situated systems in general.

First, by not demanding the full rights of his position, the individual finds that he is not completely committed to a particular standard of achievement; should an unanticipated discrediting of his capacity occur, he will not have committed himself and the others to a hopelessly compromised position. Second, it appears that social situations as such retain some weight and reality in their own right by drawing on role distance—on the margin of reservation the individual has placed between himself and his situated role.

An interesting confirmation of the functional significance of role distance in situated activity systems is to be had by examining situations where roles are played *at*.

There seems to be a little difficulty in getting stage actors to portray a character who is inflated with pomposity or bursting with emotion, and directors often have to restrain members of the cast from acting too broadly. The actor is apparently pleased to express before a large audience a lack of reservation which he would probably blush to express off the stage. However, this willingness to embrace a staged role is understandable. Since the actor's performed character is not his real one, he feels no need to safeguard himself by hedging his taken stand. Since the staged drama is not a real one, over-involvement will simply constitute the following of a script, not a threat to one's capacity to follow it. An acted lack of poise has none of the dysfunctions of real flustering.

More significant, there is the fact that in prisons and mental hospitals, where some inmates may constantly sustain a heroic edifice of withdrawal, uncooperativeness, insolence, and combativeness, the same inmates may be quite ready to engage in theatricals in which they enact excellent portraits of civil, sane, and compliant characters. But this very remarkable turnabout is understandable too. Since the staged circumstances of the portrayed character are not the inmate's real ones, he has no need (in the character's name) to exhibit distance from them, unless, of course, the script calls for it.

D Institutionalization of Social Action

11

Creating Social Institutions

PETER L. BERGER AND THOMAS LUCKMANN

All human activity is subject to habitualization. Any action that is repeated
frequently becomes cast into a pattern,
which can then be reproduced with an
economy of effort and which, *ipso facto*,
is apprehended by its performer *as* that
pattern. Habitualization further implies
that the action in question may be
performed again in the future in the
same manner and with the same economical effort. This is true of non-
social as well as of social activity. Even
the solitary individual on the proverbial
desert island habitualizes his activity.
When he wakes up in the morning and
resumes his attempts to construct a

From *The Social Construction of Reality*,
copyright © 1966 by Peter L. Berger and
Thomas Luckmann. Reprinted by permission of Doubleday & Company, Inc.

canoe out of matchsticks, he may mum-
ble to himself, "There I go again," as
he starts on step one of an operating
procedure consisting of, say, ten steps.
In other words, even solitary man has
at least the company of his operating
procedures.

Habitualized actions, of course, retain their meaningful character for the
individual although the meanings involved become embedded as routines in
his general stock of knowledge, taken
for granted by him and at hand for
his projects into the future. Habitualization carries with it the important
psychological gain that choices are
narrowed. While in theory there may be
a hundred ways to go about the project
of building a canoe out of matchsticks,
habitualization narrows these down to

one. This frees the individual from the burden of "all those decisions," providing a psychological relief that has its basis in man's undirected instinctual structure. Habitualization provides the direction and the specialization of activity that is lacking in man's biological equipment, thus relieving the accumulation of tensions that result from undirected drives. And by providing a stable background in which human activity may proceed with a minimum of decision-making most of the time, it frees energy for such decisions as may be necessary on certain occasions. In other words, the background of habitualized activity opens up a foreground for deliberation and innovation.

In terms of the meanings bestowed by man upon his activity, habitualization makes it unnecessary for each situation to be defined anew, step by step. A large variety of situations may be subsumed under its predefinitions. The activity to be undertaken in these situations can then be anticipated. Even alternatives of conduct can be assigned standard weights.

These processes of habitualization precede any institutionalization, indeed can be made to apply to a hypothetical solitary individual detached from any social interaction. The fact that even such a solitary individual, assuming that he has been formed as a self (as we would have to assume in the case of our matchstick-canoe builder), will habitualize his activity in accordance with biographical experience of a world of social institutions preceding his solitude need not concern us at the moment. Empirically, the more important part of the habitualization of human activity is coextensive with the latter's institutionalization. The question then becomes how do institutions arise.

Institutionalization occurs whenever there is a reciprocal typification of habitualized actions by types of actors.

Put differently, any such typification is an institution. What must be stressed is the reciprocity of institutional typifications and the typicality of not only the actions but also the actors in institutions. The typifications of habitualized actions that constitute institutions are always shared ones. They are *available* to all the members of the particular social group in question, and the institution itself typifies individual actors as well as individual actions. The institution posits that actions of type X will be performed by actors of type X. For example, the institution of the law posits that heads shall be chopped off in specific ways under specific circumstances, and that specific types of individuals shall do the chopping (executioners, say, or members of an impure caste, or virgins under a certain age, or those who have been designated by an oracle).

Institutions further imply historicity and control. Reciprocal typifications of actions are built up in the course of a shared history. They cannot be created instantaneously. Institutions always have a history, of which they are the products. It is impossible to understand an institution adequately without an understanding of the historical process in which it was produced. Institutions also, by the very fact of their existence, control human conduct by setting up predefined patterns of conduct, which channel it in one direction as against the many other directions that would theoretically be possible. It is important to stress that this controlling character is inherent in institutionalization as such, prior to or apart from any mechanisms of sanctions specifically set up to support an institution. These mechanisms (the sum of which constitute what is generally called a system of social control) do, of course, exist in many institutions and in all the agglomerations of institutions that we call societies. Their controlling efficacy, however, is of a secondary or supplementary kind. As we shall see again later, the primary social control is given in the existence of an institution as such. To say that a segment of human activity has been institutionalized is already to say that this segment of human activity has been subsumed under social control. Additional control mechanisms are required only insofar as the processes of institutionalization are less than completely successful. Thus, for instance, the law may provide that anyone who breaks the incest taboo will have his head chopped off. This provision may be necessary because there have been cases when individuals offended against the taboo. It is unlikely that this sanction will have to be invoked continuously (unless the institution delineated by the incest taboo is itself in the course of disintegration, a special case that we need not elaborate here). It makes little sense, therefore, to say that human sexuality is socially controlled by beheading certain individuals. Rather, human sexuality is socially controlled by its institutionalization in the course of the particular history in question. One may add, of course, that the incest taboo itself is nothing but the negative side of an assemblage of typifications, which define in the first place which sexual conduct is incestuous and which is not.

In actual experience institutions generally manifest themselves in collectivities containing considerable numbers of people. It is theoretically important, however, to emphasize that the institutionalizing process of reciprocal typification would occur even if two individuals began to interact *de novo*. Institutionalization is incipient in every social situation continuing in time. Let us assume that two persons from entirely different social worlds begin to interact. By saying "persons" we presuppose that the two individuals have formed selves, something that could, of course, have

occurred only in a social process. We are thus for the moment excluding the cases of Adam and Eve, or of two "feral" children meeting in a clearing of a primeval jungle. But we are assuming that the two individuals arrive at their meeting place from social worlds that have been historically produced in segregation from each other, and that the interaction therefore takes place in a situation that has not been institutionally defined for either of the participants. It may be possible to imagine a Man Friday joining our matchstick-canoe builder on his desert island, and to imagine the former as a Papuan and the latter as an American. In that case, however, it is likely that the American will have read or at least have heard about the story of Robinson Crusoe, which will introduce a measure of pre-definition of the situation at least for him. Let us, then, simply call our two persons A and B.

As A and B interact, in whatever manner, typifications will be produced quite quickly. A watches B perform. He attributes motives to B's actions and, seeing the actions recur, typifies the motives as recurrent. As B goes on performing, A is soon able to say to himself, "Aha, there he goes again." At the same time, A may assume that B is doing the same thing with regard to him. From the beginning, both A and B assume this reciprocity of typification. In the course of their interaction these typifications will be expressed in specific patterns of conduct. That is, A and B will begin to play roles *vis-à-vis* each other. This will occur even if each continues to perform actions different from those of the other. The possibility of taking the role of the other will appear with regard to the same actions performed by both. That is, A will inwardly appropriate B's reiterated roles and make them the models for his own role-playing. For example, B's role in the activity of preparing food is not only typified as such by A, but enters as a constitutive element into A's own food-preparation role. Thus a collection of reciprocally typified actions will emerge, habitualized for each in roles, some of which will be performed separately and some in common. While this reciprocal typification is not yet institutionalization (since, there only being two individuals, there is no possibility of a typology of actors), it is clear that institutionalization is already present *in nucleo*.

At this stage one may ask what gains accrue to the two individuals from this development. The most important gain is that each will be able to predict the other's actions. Concomitantly, the interaction of both becomes predictable. The "There he goes again" becomes a "There *we* go again." This relieves both individuals of a considerable amount of tension. They save time and effort, not only in whatever external tasks they might be engaged in separately or jointly, but in terms of their respective psychological economies. Their life together is now defined by a widening sphere of taken-for-granted routines. Many actions are possible on a low level of attention. Each action of one is no longer a source of astonishment and potential danger to the other. Instead, much of what goes on takes on the triviality of what, to both, will be everyday life. This means that the two individuals are constructing a background, in the sense discussed before, which will serve to stabilize both their separate actions and their interaction. The construction of this background of routine in turn makes possible a division of labor between them, opening the way for innovations, which demand a higher level of attention. The division of labor and the innovations will lead to new habitualizations, further widening the background common to both individuals. In other words, a social world will be in process of construction, containing within it the roots of an expanding institutional order.

Generally, all actions repeated once or more tend to be habitualized to some degree, just as all actions observed by another necessarily involve some typification on his part. However, for the kind of reciprocal typification just described to occur there must be a continuing social situation in which the habitualized actions of two or more individuals interlock. Which actions are likely to be reciprocally typified in this manner?

The general answer is, those actions that are relevant to both A and B within their common situation. The areas likely to be relevant in this way will, of course, vary in different situations. Some will be those facing A and B in terms of their previous biographies, others may be the result of the natural, presocial circumstances of the situation. What will in all cases have to be habitualized is the communication process between A and B. Labor, sexuality and territoriality are other likely foci of typification and habitualization. In these various areas the situation of A and B is paradigmatic of the institutionalization occurring in larger societies.

Let us push our paradigm one step further and imagine that A and B have children. At this point the situation changes qualitatively. The appearance of a third party changes the character of the ongoing social interaction between A and B, and it will change even further as additional individuals continue to be added. The institutional world, which existed *in statu nascendi* in the original situation of A and B, is now passed on to others. In this process institutionalization perfects itself. The habitualizations and typifications undertaken in the common life of A and B, formations that until this point still had the quality of *ad hoc* conceptions of two individuals, now become historical institutions. With the acquisition of historicity, these formations also acquire another crucial quality, or, more accurately, perfect a quality that was incipient as soon as A and B began the reciprocal typification of their conduct: this quality is objectivity. This means that the institutions that have now been crystallized (for instance, the institution of paternity as it is encountered by the children) are experienced as existing over and beyond the individuals who "happen to" embody them at the moment. In other words, the institutions are now experienced as possessing a reality of their own, a reality that confronts the individual as an external and coercive fact.

As long as the nascent institutions are constructed and maintained only in the interaction of A and B, their objectivity remains tenuous, easily changeable, almost playful, even while they attain a measure of objectivity by the mere fact of their formation. To put this a little differently, the routinized background of A's and B's activity remains fairly accessible to deliberate intervention by A and B. Although the routines, once established, carry within them a tendency to persist, the possibility of changing them or even abolishing them remains at hand in consciousness. A and B alone are responsible for having constructed this world. A and B remain capable of changing or abolishing it. What is more, since they themselves have shaped this world in the course of a shared biography which they can remember, the world thus shaped appears fully transparent to them. They understand the world that they themselves have made. All this changes in the process of transmission to the new generation. The objectivity of the institutional world "thickens" and "hardens," not only for the children, but (by a mirror effect) for the parents as well. The "There we go again" now becomes "This is how these things are done." A world so regarded attains a firmness in consciousness; it becomes real in an ever more massive way and it can no longer be changed so readily. For the children, especially in the early phase of their socialization into it, it becomes *the* world. For the parents, it loses its playful quality and becomes "serious." For the children, the parentally transmitted world is not fully transparent. Since they had no part in shaping it, it confronts them as a given reality that, like nature, is opaque in places at least.

Only at this point does it become possible to speak of a social world at all, in the sense of a comprehensive and given reality confronting the individual in a manner analogous to the reality of the natural world. Only in this way, *as* an objective world, can the social formations be transmitted to a new generation. In the early phases of socialization the child is quite incapable of distinguishing between the objectivity of natural phenomena and the objectivity of the social formations. To take the most important item of socialization, language appears to the child as inherent in the nature of things, and he cannot grasp the notion of its conventionality. A thing *is* what it is called, and it could not be called anything else. All institutions appear in the same way, as given, unalterable and self-evident. Even in our empirically unlikely example of parents having constructed an institutional world *de novo*, the objectivity of this world would be increased for them by the socialization of their children, because the objectivity experienced by the children would reflect back upon their own experience of this world. Empirically, of course, the institutional world transmitted by most parents already has the character of historical and objective reality. The process of transmission simply strengthens the parents' sense of reality, if only because, to put it crudely, if one says,

"This is how these things are done," often enough one believes it oneself.

An institutional world, then, is experienced as an objective reality. It has a history that antedates the individual's birth and is not accessible to his biographical recollection. It was there before he was born, and it will be there after his death. This history itself, as the tradition of the existing institutions, has the character of objectivity. The individual's biography is apprehended as an episode located within the objective history of the society. The institutions, as historical and objective facticities, confront the individual as undeniable facts. The institutions are *there*, external to him, persistent in their reality, whether he likes it or not. He cannot wish them away. They resist his attempts to change or evade them. They have coercive power over him, both in themselves, by the sheer force of their facticity, and through the control mechanisms that are usually attached to the most important of them. The objective reality of institutions is not diminished if the individual does not understand their purpose or their mode of operation. He may experience large sectors of the social world as incomprehensible, perhaps oppressive in their opaqueness, but real nonetheless. Since institutions exist as external reality, the individual cannot understand them by introspection. He must "go out" and learn about them, just as he must to learn about nature. This remains true even though the social world, as a humanly produced reality, is potentially understandable in a way not possible in the case of the natural world.

It is important to keep in mind that the objectivity of the institutional world, however massive it may appear to the individual, is a humanly produced, constructed objectivity. The process by which the externalized products of human activity attain the character of objectivity is objectivation. The institutional world is objectivated human activity, and so is every single institution. In other words, despite the objectivity that marks the social world in human experience, it does not thereby acquire an ontological status apart from the human activity that produced it. The paradox that man is capable of producing a world that he then experiences as something other than a human product will concern us later on. At the moment, it is important to emphasize that the relationship between man, the producer, and the social world, his product, is and remains a dialectical one. That is, man (not, of course, in isolation but in his collectivities) and his social world interact with each other. The product acts back upon the producer. Externalization and objectivation are moments in a continuing dialectical process. The third moment in this process, which is internalization (by which the objectivated social world is retrojected into consciousness in the course of socialization), will occupy us in considerable detail later on. It is already possible, however, to see the fundamental relationship of these three dialectical moments in social reality. Each of them corresponds to an essential characterization of the social world. *Society is a human product. Society is an objective reality. Man is a social product.* It may also already be evident that an analysis of the social world that leaves out any one of these three moments will be distortive. One may further add that only with the transmission of the social world to a new generation (that is, internalization as effectuated in socialization) does the fundamental social dialectic appear in its totality. To repeat, only with the appearance of a new generation can one properly speak of a social world.

At the same point, the institutional world requires legitimation, that is, ways by which it can be "explained" and justified. This is not because it appears less real. As we have seen, the reality of the social world gains in massivity in the course of its transmission. This reality, however, is a historical one, which comes to the new generation as a tradition rather than as a biographical memory. In our paradigmatic example, A and B, the original creators of the social world, can always reconstruct the circumstances under which their world and any part of it was established. That is, they can arrive at the meaning of an institution by exercising their powers of recollection. A's and B's children are in an altogether different situation. Their knowledge of the institutional history is by way of "hearsay." The original meaning of the institutions is inaccessible to them in terms of memory. It, therefore, becomes necessary to interpret this meaning to them in various legitimating formulas. These will have to be consistent and comprehensive in terms of the institutional order, if they are to carry conviction to the new generation. The same story, so to speak, must be told to all the children. It follows that the expanding institutional order develops a corresponding canopy of legitimations, stretching over it a protective cover of both cognitive and normative interpretation. These legitimations are learned by the new generation during the same process that socializes them into the institutional order. This, again, will occupy us in greater detail further on.

The development of specific mechanisms of social controls also becomes necessary with the historicization and objectivation of institutions. Deviance from the institutionally "programmed" courses of action becomes likely once the institutions have become realities divorced from their original relevance in the concrete social processes from which they arose. To put this more simply, it is more likely that one will

deviate from programs set up for one by others than from programs that one has helped establish oneself. The new generation posits a problem of compliance, and its socialization into the institutional order requires the establishment of sanctions. The institutions must and do claim authority over the individual, independently of the subjective meanings he may attach to any particular situation. The priority of the institutional definitions of situations must be consistently maintained over individual temptations at redefinition. The children must be "taught to behave" and, once taught, must be "kept in line." So, of course, must the adults. The more conduct is institutionalized, the more predictable and thus the more controlled it becomes. If socialization into the institutions has been effective, outright coercive measures can be applied economically and selectively. Most of the time, conduct will occur "spontaneously" within the institutionally set channels. The more, on the level of meaning, conduct is taken for granted, the more possible alternatives to the institutional "programs" will recede, and the more predictable and controlled conduct will be.

In principle, institutionalization may take place in any area of collectively relevant conduct. In actual fact, sets of institutionalization processes take place concurrently. There is no *a priori* reason for assuming that these processes will necessarily "hang together" functionally, let alone as a logically consistent system. To return once more to our paradigmatic example, slightly changing the fictitious situation, let us assume this time, not a budding family of parents and children, but a piquant triangle of a male A, a bisexual female B, and a Lesbian C. We need not belabor the point that the sexual relevances of these three individuals will not coincide. Relevance A-B is not shared by C. The habitualizations engendered as a result of relevance A-B need bear no relationship to those engendered by relevances B-C and C-A. There is, after all, no reason why two processes of erotic habitualization, one heterosexual and one Lesbian, cannot take place side by side without functionally integrating with each other or with a third habitualization based on a shared interest in, say, the growing of flowers (or whatever other enterprise might be jointly relevant to an active heterosexual male and an active Lesbian). In other words, three processes of habitualization or incipient institutionalization may occur without their being functionally or logically integrated as social phenomena. The same reasoning holds if A, B and C are posited as collectivities rather than individuals, regardless of what content their relevances might have. Also, functional or logical integration cannot be assumed *a priori* when habitualization or institutionalization processes are limited to the same individuals or collectivities, rather than to the discrete ones assumed in our example.

Nevertheless, the empirical fact remains that institutions do tend to "hang together." If this phenomenon is not to be taken for granted, it must be explained. How can this be done? First, one may argue that *some* relevances will be common to all members of a collectivity. On the other hand, many areas of conduct will be relevant only to certain types. The latter involves an incipient differentiation, at least in the way in which these types are assigned some relatively stable meaning. This assignment may be based on presocial differences, such as sex, or on differences brought about in the course of social interaction, such as those engendered by the division of labor. For example, only women may be concerned with fertility magic and only hunters may engage in cave painting. Or, only the old men may perform the rain

ceremonial and only weapon makers may sleep with their maternal cousins. In terms of their external social functionality, these several areas of conduct need not be integrated into *one* cohesive system. They can continue to coexist on the basis of segregated performances. But while performances can be segregated, meanings tend toward at least minimal consistency. As the individual reflects about the successive moments of his experience, he tries to fit their meanings into a consistent biographical framework. This tendency increases as the individual shares with others his meanings and their biographical integration. It is possible that this tendency to integrate meanings is based on a psychological need, which may in turn be physiologically grounded (that is, that there may be a built-in "need" for cohesion in the psychophysiological constitution of man). Our argument, however, does not rest on such anthropological assumptions, but rather on the analysis of meaningful reciprocity in processes of institutionalization.

It follows that great care is required in any statements one makes about the "logic" of institutions. The logic does not reside in the institutions and their external functionalities, but in the way these are treated in reflection about them. Put differently, reflective consciousness superimposes the quality of logic on the institutional order.

Language provides the fundamental superimposition of logic on the objectivated social world. The edifice of legitimations is built upon language and uses language as its principal instrumentality. The "logic" thus attributed to the institutional order is part of the socially available stock of knowledge and taken for granted as such. Since the well-socialized individual "knows" that his social world is a consistent whole, he will be constrained to explain both its functioning and malfunctioning in terms of this "knowledge." It is very easy, as a result, for the observer of any society to assume that its institutions do indeed function and integrate as they are "supposed to."

De facto, then, institutions *are* integrated. But their integration is not a functional imperative for the social processes that produce them; it is rather brought about in a derivative fashion. Individuals perform discrete institutionalized actions within the context of their biography. This biography is a reflected-upon whole in which the discrete actions are thought of not as isolated events, but as related parts in a subjectively meaningful universe whose meanings are not specific to the individual, but socially articulated and shared. Only by way of this detour of socially shared universes of meaning do we arrive at the need for institutional integration.

This has far-reaching implications for any analysis of social phenomena. If the integration of an institutional order can be understood only in terms of the "knowledge" that its members have of it, it follows that the analysis of such "knowledge" will be essential for an analysis of the institutional order in question. It is important to stress that this does not exclusively or even primarily involve a preoccupation with complex theoretical systems serving as legitimations for the institutional order. Theories also have to be taken into account, of course. But theoretical knowledge is only a small and by no means the most important part of what passes for knowledge in a society. Theoretically sophisticated legitimations appear at particular moments of an institutional history. The primary knowledge about the institutional order is knowledge on the pretheoretical level. It is the sum total of "what everybody knows" about a social world, an assemblage of maxims, morals, proverbial nuggets of wisdom, values and be-

liefs, myths, and so forth, the theoretical integration of which requires considerable intellectual fortitude in itself, as the long line of heroic integrators from Homer to the latest sociological system-builders testifies. On the pretheoretical level, however, every institution has a body of transmitted recipe knowledge, that is, knowledge that supplies the institutionally appropriate rules of conduct.

Such knowledge constitutes the motivating dynamics of institutionalized conduct. It defines the institutionalized areas of conduct and designates all situations falling within them. It defines and constructs the roles to be played in the context of the institutions in question. *Ipso facto*, it controls and predicts all such conduct. Since this knowledge is socially objectivated *as* knowledge, that is, as a body of generally valid truths about reality, any radical deviance from the institutional order appears as a departure from reality. Such deviance may be designated as moral depravity, mental disease, or just plain ignorance. While these fine distinctions will have obvious consequences for the treatment of the deviant, they all share an inferior cognitive status within the particular social world. In this way, the particular social world becomes the world *tout court*. What is taken for granted as knowledge in the society comes to be coextensive with the knowable, or at any rate provides the framework within which anything not yet known will come to be known in the future. This is the knowledge that is learned in the course of socialization and that mediates the internalization within individual consciousness of the objectivated structures of the social world. Knowledge, in this sense, is at the heart of the fundamental dialectic of society. It "programs" the channels in which externalization produces an objective world. It objectifies this world through language and the cognitive apparatus based on language, that is, it orders it into objects to be apprehended as reality. It is internalized again *as* objectively valid truth in the course of socialization. Knowledge about society is thus a *realization* in the double sense of the word, in the sense of apprehending the objectivated social reality, and in the sense of ongoingly producing this reality.

For example, in the course of the division of labor a body of knowledge is developed that refers to the particular activities involved. In its linguistic basis, this knowledge is already indispensable to the institutional "programming" of these economic activities. There will be, say, a vocabulary designating the various modes of hunting, the weapons to be employed, the animals that serve as prey, and so on. There will further be a collection of recipes that must be learned if one is to hunt correctly. This knowledge serves as a channeling, controlling force in itself, an indispensable ingredient of the institutionalization of this area of conduct. As the institution of hunting is crystallized and persists in time, the same body of knowledge serves as an objective (and, incidentally, empirically verifiable) description of it. A whole segment of the social world is objectified by this knowledge. There will be an objective "science" of hunt-

ing, corresponding to the objective reality of the hunting economy. The point need not be belabored that here "empirical verification" and "science" are not understood in the sense of modern scientific canons, but rather in the sense of knowledge that may be borne out in experience and that can subsequently become systematically organized as a body of knowledge.

Again, the same body of knowledge is transmitted to the next generation. It is learned as objective truth in the course of socialization and thus internalized as subjective reality. This reality in turn has power to shape the individual. It will produce a specific type of person, namely the hunter, whose identity and biography *as* a hunter have meaning only in a universe constituted by the aforementioned body of knowledge as a whole (say, in a hunters' society) or in part (say, in our own society, in which hunters come together in a subuniverse of their own). In other words, no part of the institutionalization of hunting can exist without the particular knowledge that has been socially produced and objectivated with reference to this activity. To hunt and to be a hunter implies existence in a social world defined and controlled by this body of knowledge. *Mutatis mutandis*, the same applies to any area of institutionalized conduct.

12

The Perpetuation of Social Institutions

PETER M. BLAU

. . . Legitimate organizations are faced with the problem of their perpetuation through time. To be sure, all populations, animal as well as human, reproduce themselves, and no special arrangements are necessary to assure the survival of the species for many generations. The survival of a legitimate social order beyond the life span of individuals, however, does require special institutions. The basic cultural values and beliefs that are sacred or virtually sacred to people make them eager to preserve these ideas and ideals for future generations. The investments made in the organized patterns of social life that are legitimated by these values and embody them, and in the knowledge and technology that further the common welfare, make men interested in preserving those too. Formalized arrangements are instituted perpetuating the legitimate order and the social values that sustain it through time by making them independent of individual human beings. The organized community survives total turnover of its membership, often for many generations. . . . What persists are the principles governing social relations and patterns of conduct, and the reason for their persistence is that they have become institutionalized.

Institutionalization involves formalized procedures that perpetuate organizing principles of social life from generation to generation. Establishing a formal procedure requires an investment of resources, and it preserves and rigidifies patterns of social conduct and relations. Merely making explicit a

course of action that has become customary entails effort and stabilizes it. Setting up rules to be consistently followed involves further costs and crystalizes the pattern of action further. The members of organizations sometimes operate under the guidance of superiors and on the basis of precedent without having written procedures to follow. Ascertaining the principles underlying their decisions and producing an official manual of procedures is a difficult task necessitating major investments, which are made in the hope of the future benefits resulting from having such formalized procedures. The explicitly formulated set of procedures, which are expected to govern the decisions of all members of the organization, and which can be readily taught to newcomers, are manifest in a pattern of actions and social interactions that are independent of the specific individuals who carry them out. Formalized rules make an organized pattern of social relations and conduct independent of particular human beings, which is the first requirement of a social institution. Other requirements of institutionalization are that the rules of conduct be legitimated by traditional values and enforced by powerful groups, thereby being made resistant against ready change.

There is a great diversity of social institutions. Examples are the dogma and ritual of a church, the form of government of a country, its laws and courts, the stock exchange that coordinates complex economic transactions, and monogamous marriage. What they all have in common is that legitimating values and formalized procedures perpetuate an organized pattern of social associations. The values that identify men in a society, and the dominant groups in particular, with their institutions and the advantages they derive from them make them interested in preserving these institutions for posterity. Sacred values are more important for the survival of some institutions, such as a church; material advantages are more important for the survival of others, such as a stock exchange; but all are legitimated by some common values. Two complementary social mechanisms preserve the institutions of men though they themselves die, external social arrangements that are historically transmitted and internalized social values that are transmitted in the process of socialization.

Social institutions constitute a historical reality that exists, at least in part, outside and independent of the human beings who make up societies. This historical reality is transmitted through oral traditions in nonliterate societies, but in literate societies it is primarily transmitted through written documents that embody the basic formalized values and norms of the communal life of men—their constitutions and their laws, their bibles and their commandments. To be sure, it is not the parchment or paper on which these documents are written that is of significance but the principles of human conduct they contain. The fact that these principles are written down, however, is of significance, since it assures their survival in fixed form and symbolizes the historical persistence of institutionalized principles of social life, independent of the specific human beings in whom these principles express themselves at any particular time.[1] Although these historical documents must continue to be believed by people to

govern social life, they do exert an influence of their own, as Durkheim has noted in his discussion of *written* dogmas and laws:

However well digested, they would of course remain dead letters if there were no one to conceive their significance and put them into practice. But though they are not self-sufficient, they are none the less in their own way factors of social activity. They have a manner of action of their own. Juridical relations are widely different depending on whether or not the law is written. Where there is a constituted code, jurisprudence is more regular but less flexible. . . . The material forms it assumes are thus not merely ineffective verbal combinations but active realities, since they produce effects which would not occur without their existence. They are not only external to individual consciousness, but this very externality establishes their specific qualities.[2]

Complementary to the historical transmission of the external forms of social institutions is the transmission of the basic cultural values and norms in the process of socialization that give these forms flesh and blood and continuing life, as it were. In the course of rearing their children, people inculcate in them their most profound values and beliefs, often without explicit intent. The dominant values and norms shared by the members of a society or its segments are, therefore, transmitted to succeeding generations. While the rebellion of children against their parents and, especially, the deprivations produced by political oppression or economic exploitation sometimes lead to the rejection of traditional values, only selected political or economic values are usually rejected. The major part of the cultural heritage tends to persist, even in periods of revolutionary transformations. In any case, the process of socialization results in many of the legitimating values of organized community

[1] The great importance rituals assume in nonliterate societies, compared to their lesser importance in modern societies, may be the result of a greater need for rituals to perpetuate institutionalized practices in the absence of written codes for doing so.

[2] Durkheim, *Suicide*, New York: Free Press, 1951, pp. 314–315.

life being passed on to future generations, and these are the institutionalized values that sustain and invigorate the external forms of institutions, which without them would be dead skeletons.

A third factor that supplements the other two in sustaining institutions is that they are rooted in the power structure. The cultural values and social arrangements that become institutionalized are those with which the dominant groups in the society are strongly identified, since these groups have the power to make their convictions prevail and to enforce the relevant social norms. Freedom of speech is institutionalized in a society, for example, if powerful groups value and defend it, even if the majority should care little about it or possibly deprecate it; when the powerful are no longer concerned with maintaining free speech its survival as an institution is imperiled. An institution exerts external constraints on succeeding generations in large part because, and as long as, powerful groups that can enforce institutional demands continue to be interested in its preservation. Powerful men and their wives are more likely than others to inculcate traditional values in their children in the process of socialization, inasmuch as the institutional structure embodying these values is the one on which their dominant position rests. Socialization, however, is not confined to childhood but occurs also later in life, notably when individuals join new groups, and members of lower strata who move up into dominant positions tend to be socialized by the established persons there to acquire a proper concern with traditional values and institutions. In brief, institutionalized patterns are typically those with which the dominant groups in a society are most identified, and these groups are the instruments of their historical perpetuation by enforcing the demands necessary for this purpose.[3]

Three conditions, therefore, must be met for aspects of social structures to become institutionalized, that is, to be perpetuated from one generation to the next. Patterns of organized community life must become formalized and part of the historical conditions that persist through time, the social values that legitimate these patterns must be transmitted in the process of socialization, and the society's dominant groups must be especially interested in the survival of these patterns. The historical forms without continued acceptance of the legitimating values become empty shells, and cultural values without institutional forms are ideals yet to be realized; both are required to maintain institutions, and so is their support by powerful groups. These factors can be illustrated with our political institutions. On the one hand, our Congressional form of government, the U.S. Constitution and laws, the various branches of government, and the election machinery, are formalized procedures embodied in documents and manifest in many organizations and agencies that persist as part of the historical reality, independent of the particular incumbents of the various offices. On the other hand, democratic and patriotic values, respect for the law and the mores that support it, as well as related values and norms, are transmitted to children in their homes and schools. Americans are born into a historical situation in which certain political forms exist, and they acquire, in their youth, values and norms that legitimate these institutional forms. The foundations of the authority of the law and of political authority are the historical traditions in which they are

[3] I am indebted to Arthur L. Stinchcombe for calling my attention to these points in a private communication.

grounded and the pertinent normative orientations that the members of our society have internalized in the course of socialization as part of their basic personality. The support of the nation's dominant groups, moveover, has sustained the American form of government and legal institutions even in periods when large-scale immigration filled the country with people from other traditions and with different orientations. Institutional constraints generally derive their distinctive force from the combination of being buttressed by the power structure and having twofold historical roots, in the traditions of society and in the childhood socialization experiences of its individual members.

Institutions reflect the historical dimension in social life, the impact of the past on the present. The relationship between institutions and social structure is in some ways parallel to that between social structure and human conduct. Institutions are those aspects of the social structure that persist for long periods of time, and the social structure consists of those patterns of conduct that prevail throughout a collectivity. Yet institutions exert traditional constraints on the social structure that exists at any one time, just as the social structure exerts external constraints on the behavior of individuals. Thus the values and norms shared by most members of a collectivity constitute external structural constraints for each one of them to which he must adapt. Similarly, the traditional values and their external institutional forms constitute a historical framework to which the social structure at any one time must adapt. Men collectively can change the social structure that restrains them, however, and communities in the course of time can change the institutions that confine their social life. In short, institutions impose his-

torical limits on the social structure which in turn exerts structural constraints on individual conduct.

The typology of social values as mediators of social transactions presented in the preceding section can be employed to classify social institutions. First, integrative institutions perpetuate particularistic values, maintain social solidarity, and preserve the distinctive character and identity of the social structure that differentiates it from others. The core of this institutional complex is the kinship system, which assures every member of the society an integrated position in a network of cohesive social relations and socioemotional support on the basis of ascribed qualities, and which preserves the distinctive social structure by transmitting cultural values and norms to succeeding generations as well as by reproducing the population biologically. Mate selection in accordance with the incest taboo recurrently establishes new particularistic ties of kinship allegiance between subgroups previously separated by these particularistic boundaries. Religious institutions constitute the second main component of this complex, since moral dogmas and hallowed symbols are fundamental elements of particularism and sacred ceremonies and rituals greatly strengthen commitment to the particularistic values they represent. Inasmuch as most religious bodies in the modern world cut across national boundaries, the common traditions and allegiances they create do too, and separate patriotic doctrines, symbols, and ceremonies—the Declaration of Independence, the Stars and Stripes, Fourth-of-July celebrations—develop to bolster national traditions, solidarity, and loyalty.

A second major type of institution functions to preserve the social arrangements that have been developed for the production and distribution of needed social facilities, contributions, and rewards of various kinds. This type includes, of course, the economic institutions in a society, but it also includes other institutions that are governed by universalistic standards of instrumental value. It encompasses educational institutions, through which technological skills and instrumental knowledge are transmitted to future generations, and which, in their higher branches, simultaneously serve the function of advancing knowledge through research. The stratification system too is part of this institutional complex, insofar as it entails an incentive system for recruiting and channeling men into occupations where they furnish diverse services. It is important in this connection to distinguish two aspects of social stratification.[4] On one hand, the stratification system consists of a hierarchy of social positions, not the persons who occupy them, that yield differential rewards. On the other hand, the class structure consists of actual collectivities of individuals, not abstract positions, who differ in wealth, power, and prestige. The stratification system is an institution, while class structure is not. Although not an institution, the class structure is instrumental in fortifying other institutions, as noted above, and important elements of it typically persist from generation to generation, just as institutions do, because wealth and consequently some aspects of class position can be inherited. The resulting rigidities in the class structure impede the function of the stratification system as a mechanism for distributing human resources, since hereditary status rewards are not effective incentives for achievement.

A third main set of institutions serves to perpetuate the authority and organization necessary to mobilize resources and coordinate collective effort in the pursuit of social objectives. The prototype is the lasting political organization of a society, including not only its form of government and various specific political institutions, such as the legislature, but also such corollary institutions as the judiciary that maintains law and order, the military establishment that protects national security and strength, and the administrative agencies that implement the decisions of the government. To this set of institutions belong also the formal organizations that have become established outside the political arena in a society—like business concerns, unions, and professional associations—and notably the enduring principles of management and administration in terms of which they are governed. Private as well as public organizations are the instruments through which a community attains its social objectives, such as a higher standard of living, and their internal structure corresponds to the executive segment of a political system. Persisting organizations, therefore, are analytically part of the complex of political institutions.[5]

The cultural heritage of a society, finally, contains what may be called a "counterinstitutional component," consisting of those basic values and ideals that have not been realized and have not found expression in explicit institutional forms, and which are the ultimate source of social change. The conflict between these as yet unrealized, but culturally legitimated, ideals and the actual conditions of social existence is

[4] See Walter Buckley, "Social Stratification and the Functional Theory of Social Differentiation," *American Sociological Review*, 23 (1958), 369–375, and Kingsley Davis, "The Abominable Heresy," *American Sociological Review*, 24 (1959), 82–83.

[5] See Parsons, *Structure and Process in Modern Societies*, New York: Free Press, 1960, pp. 41–44.

at the base of social opposition to existing institutions. For this conflict to become activated typically requires that the diffuse discontent become focused in an opposition ideology. Although some opposition movements formulate revolutionary ideologies that reject many basic values and advocate the complete overthrow of many institutional arrangements, they do so within the framework of some of the ideals and ultimate objectives legitimated by the prevailing culture. Even the most radical revolutionary ideologies are not independent of and receive some legitimation from traditional social values. The very cultural values that legitimate existing institutions contain the seeds of their potential destruction, because the idealized expectations these values raise in the minds of men in order to justify the existing social order cannot be fully met by it and thus may serve as justification, if need be, for opposition to it.[6]

[6] The schema presented reveals some parallels to Parsons' schema of four functional imperatives—adaptation, goal gratification, integration, and latency—but there are also some fundamental differences; see Parsons and Neil J. Smelser, *Economy and Society*, New York: Free Press, 1956, pp. 16–28 and *passim*.

Part Two

Industrial Society and the Origins of Sociology

INTRODUCTION

Sociology was founded by a number of thinkers who lived through the last great transformation of Western European life, the change from agrarian society to modern industrial capitalism, which took place approximately between the years of 1780 and 1850. E. J. Hobsbawm has called this period the age of the "dual revolution." [1] During this time the industrial revolution took place in England and industrial capitalism gradually spread from there to the Continent, replacing preindustrial economies. The French Revolution of 1789 destroyed the old political regime of the monarchy and the nobility and replaced it with the first modern republican form of national government, and the idea of the modern democratic nation-state was carried over much of the rest of Europe by the conquering Republican armies of Napoleon.

The first sociologists—Henri Comte de Saint-Simon and Auguste Comte in France; Herbert Spencer in England; and Karl Marx, the German who wrote his early works in Paris and his later studies in London—all lived through some part of this period of upheaval and revolution which brought about a total transformation of social life for Western man. The forms of this new society—commercial capitalism, the new machine technology, the large industrial city, and the modern nation-state, with its elected representative government—gradually spread from France and England to central and southern Europe, southern Scandinavia, and across the Atlantic to North America. The "second generation" of classical sociologists, including Emile Durkheim in France; Max Weber, Ferdinand Toennies, and Georg Simmel in Germany; and William Graham Sumner in the United States, experienced the later effects of these new social forces and analyzed their development and consequences for the lives of their contemporaries. These men were deeply and personally concerned with the problems the new social forms created for living what they considered a decent human life. Most of them viewed the scientific analysis of social life as a way of providing men with the knowledge necessary to improve their collective life. [2]

[1] E. J. Hobsbawm, *The Age of Revolution, 1789–1848* (New York: World Publishing Company, 1962).
[2] Herbert Spencer and William Graham Sumner must be excepted from this concern. As strict social Darwinists, they felt men should not presume to interfere with the natural and necessary course of the development of society or social evolution.

Emile Durkheim's description of the life and work of Saint-Simon, whom he considers the first man to engage in systematic sociological analysis, shows all these aspects of classical sociology. Saint-Simon himself lived through the French Revolution and was transformed by it from a feudal nobleman to first a capitalist entrepreneur and then a student of the new society, known then as a "social philosopher." Saint-Simon's "philosophies," however, as Durkheim makes clear, were astute analyses of the social forces developing in European feudal society which eventually brought about the demise of that society and the rise of modern urban-industrial society. There were two main forces that Saint-Simon believed responsible for undermining and eventually destroying the old order in Europe. One of these was the free villages, communities which bought their political freedom from the feudal nobility and the medieval clergy and established themselves as centers of trade and handicraft manufacturing. Second, there were the physical and biological sciences, brought to Europe by the conquering Arabs at the apex of Islamic civilization and left in Europe after the waning of Saracen influence. The old society, he said, contained within it the seeds of the new, in the form of commerce and science, and therefore the seeds of its own destruction. Following the analytic history in which Saint-Simon explains how these forces helped bring about the transformation from feudal to modern society, Durkheim shows that he was concerned over the apparent instability of the new society and the problems this created for people living in this time of transition. Saint-Simon tried to discover the sources of this instability and thought he found some of them in the fact that lawyers, a group of functionaries developed in agrarian society to mediate the interests of the nobility and those of the rising commercial and industrial groups, dominated the postrevolutionary government of France. The new society, Saint-Simon said, was predominantly an industrial society, one in which the principal activity was production. As such, it could only be run effectively by those engaged in this activity—those he called the "industrials," meaning all those who carried on economically, and intellectually, productive activities. Saint-Simon's later works, Durkheim points out, contained the outlines of the industrially based organization of society which he felt had to replace the old political order before stability could be restored to European society.

Karl Marx spent his lifetime studying the new society of industrial capitalism, first in Germany, then in France, and finally in England, where he spent most of his working life and where he wrote his monumental three-volume study *Capital* There is only one small passage in all the volumes he produced, many of them with the help of his friend Friedrich Engels, in which Marx gives a formal statement of his theory of social structure and change. In this, a passage from *A Contribution to the Critique of Political Economy,* which is reprinted in this section, Marx presents the classic statement of the materialist theory of social structure and historical change. This is what might be called an "architectural" theory of the social structure in which all the institutions and activities of the society, such as the family, religion, politics, science, and philosophy, are seen to be built upon the foundation of the society's economy by the basic groups, social classes, which develop from the economy. The economy is seen as the "basic" institution in that it connects the society with its natural environment through the sustenance-producing activities of the group. The economy includes the technology available to the group and the division of labor, through which different people specialize in different aspects of the economic activities. Out of this division of labor develops the class system, which Marx sees as always containing two major classes—the owners of the means of economic production, such as land and tools, and the people who actually carry on the labor of economic production—the slaves in ancient society, the serfs in feudal society, and the wage laborers of capitalist society. It is out of this basic social structure, the class system, that all the other institutions of society develop, including the kinship system, the political system, and organized religion. All of society, then, reflects the basic class division, and Marx maintains that the important institutions, such as government and law, are controlled by the owning class, which becomes then the "ruling class," because the government represents their interests whenever they are opposed to those of the other classes. Social change occurs, in this theory, when changes in the economy and the technology lead to the development of a new division of labor, which gives birth to new social classes which become powerful and eventually challenge the ruling class for control of society, overthrow it, and establish themselves as the ruling class.

Marx and Engels, in the excerpt from *The Communist Manifesto* reprinted in this section, provide an example of this process in their analysis of how the bourgeoisie, or the commercial and manufacturing middle class, rose to power and created modern capitalist society. The bourgeoisie came into being with the development of trade and industry in the Middle Ages; eventually became strong enough, in numbers, money, and power, to challenge the political control of the nobility, clergy, and the monarchy; and eventually overthrew these ruling classes, establishing the new society of industrial capitalism. They became the ruling class and the economy which they represented, that of modern industry, became the dominant economic system of Western European countries. At the time Marx and Engels were writing, the middle of the nineteenth century, conditions of life for the urban factory workers in the industrial countries were probably at their worst. Open rebellions had been staged by hungry, overworked, and underpaid workers in the major industrial cities of England and France. Marx and Engels felt these uprisings were the beginning of the next revolutionary movement in history, one in which the proletariat, or working class, of the industrial countries would organize themselves, overthrow the bourgeois governments, and take control of these societies. They felt this would be a kind of "end of history," because the proletariat in capitalist society were the last exploited, underdog social class, and the society which they would create would be a classless society which would no longer breed exploitation and revolutionary change.

Max Weber, looking back on the origins of capitalism from the perspective of a century and a half, discerned another social force which had developed in the preindustrial society of Europe and which he felt had helped to create the society of modern industrial capitalism. This force was ascetic Protestantism, as preached and practiced by John Calvin, Martin Luther, and their followers. Weber was convinced that the modern European merchant and manufacturer was a unique kind of person in world history, and that ascetic Protestantism was responsible for some of the economically crucial character traits of this "new" man. Middle-class Protestants from the mid-fifteenth century on were relatively free men; they were generally engaged in individual business enterprises, they were not tied by bonds of slavery or serfdom to any master, and, of course, they did not owe allegiance to the Pope and the hierarchy of the Roman Catholic Church, as did all other Europeans except the Jews. However, Weber points out, they created for themselves a bondage of another kind, that of the strict moral codes of early Protestant doctrines. This new moral code, or "Protestant ethic," as Weber calls it, had a great deal to do with the development of what he calls the spirit of modern capitalism. In the excerpt included here from Weber's book on this subject, he points out that the early Protestant (and he stresses these as characteristics of *early* Protestants, not necessarily Protestants of today, and not necessarily found *only* among Protestants today) believed that a lifetime of hard work in an occupation to which a person was "called" was the kind of behavior most pleasing to God. Protestants came to believe, Weber says, that success in worldly business endeavors was a sign that a man was looked upon with favor by God and would probably go to heaven after he died. At the same time, the Protestant was strictly forbidden to live in luxury or to make ostentatious display of material wealth. This meant, Weber says, that the Protestant capitalist, as distinct from capitalists who had appeared at previous times in world history, could not spend his profits on consumption for himself and his family. He was supposed to live austerely, or at least plainly, for too much comfort, it was be-lieved, might make him slothful. The combined forces of the drive toward profit making as a sign of God's favor and the ban on spending for personal consump-tion beyond life's necessities led the Protestant capitalist to reinvest his profits. This reinvestment of profits in the business meant, of course, the expansion of the business and led to a cycle of economic growth which eventually made capitalism the dominant form of economic activity in Europe and created the large capital investments required in modern industrial economies. Protestantism even had a hand in providing labor for the business and industry of the capital-ists, Weber feels, because Protestants who were not businessmen were enjoined by their ethic to work hard and diligently whatever their occupation. Protestant belief thus contributed to the creation of the disciplined industrial labor force needed for the modern economy.

The classical sociologists, as we have just seen, were interested in discovering how the modern world had come into being. They observed their societies to discover their dominant characteristics—industrial technology, capitalist market economies, large industrial cities, and republican nation-states. Then they asked, "How did these arise?"—a question which led them into analytic history and comparative sociology. These same sociologists also asked another question, of equal importance in their own minds, which was, "What does it mean for the individual person to have to live in such a society?"

Karl Marx developed the idea of alienation in his early writings, while he was still living in Paris, to describe the consequences for the individual of life under industrial capitalism. In this society, Marx said, the workers in industry, who are a majority of the population, are "separated" from the product of their labor because they do not own it. Rather, the capitalist who owns the factory and buys their labor owns (or "expropriates," to use Marx's stronger term) what they produce, the product of their labor. Under capitalism, then, man is alien-ated from the product of his labor. But if this is true, man is also alienated from his work as an activity, because it does not bring him anything which is his, says Marx. One of Marx's basic philosophic assumptions, which he shares with many of the thinkers of his day and of our own day, is that work is man's basic self-defining activity: man *is Homo faber,* the animal that produces the means of his own livelihood. To remove intrinsic meaning from man's work, Marx believed, is to remove the keystone of meaning from his life. When work be-comes meaningless, life becomes meaningless, and Marx felt that almost all work becomes meaningless in the economy of industrial capitalism. This concept of alienation has recently gained new popularity in industrial societies, both capitalist and socialist. It has, it would seem, a wider relevance than Marx himself gave it. It appears that the minute division of labor and the great size of industrial bureaucracies in all modern societies make it difficult for individuals to find meaning in their work. Psychologists, philosophers, and sociologists in such diverse modern nations as Poland, France, Yugoslavia, and the United States are studying this problem in its contemporary form: How modern industrial societies can be organized so that meaningful, self-defining, creative activities are available to individuals.

Modern societies have been referred to by sociologists as urban-industrial societies because they regard urbanism and industrialism as the defining characteristics of these societies. The early German sociologist Ferdinand Toennies observed the decline of peasant villages and the rise of cities and described this transition in his book *Gemeinschaft und Gesellschaft (Community and Society),* one of the classic sociological studies.[3] Georg Simmel, another German, outlined some of the consequences of urban life for the individual in his famous essay included here. The city dweller, Simmel says, is bombarded daily by a great multitude of stimuli, or sensory perceptions. The human psyche cannot, Simmel thinks, respond to all the sensory stimuli of the urban environment, so the urbanite must develop protective mechanisms. These involve a highly selective intellectual apparatus for deciding which stimuli call for a response and which do not, accompanied by a detached, blasé attitude toward the world. A major part of the "psychic stimulation" of the urban environment is, of course, provided by the great numbers of people with whom the city dweller comes briefly into contact. Under such conditions, Simmel contends, people soon become callous toward others, for it is just not possible to respond in a warm and friendly way to such large numbers of people or to be concerned about them in any genuine way. In fact, Simmel argues that this callousness actually masks a latent hostility toward other people which urban life produces in individuals. At the same time, Simmel points out, the city makes possible freedom which people cannot find in small communities where everyone knows everyone else and everyone else's business. The privacy and freedom of action found in the city provide the person with greater chances to develop his individuality.

Emile Durkheim's study *Suicide,* from which an extract is reprinted here, is an acknowledged landmark of sociological research. In it Durkheim conceptualizes the act of killing oneself in sociological terms as the act of leaving society. Studying statistics from a great number of European countries over the last half of the nineteenth century, he finds that the rate of suicide increases with the advance of urban-industrial civilization. Durkheim came to feel that the new social order of modern industrial capitalism was creating a situation in which more and more people were choosing to kill themselves rather than live in their societies. Durkheim was much disturbed by a trend toward what he called *anomie,* a state in which group norms no longer provide effective limits to individual aspirations and actions, and which he thought responsible for the increased rates of self-destruction in the new society. He discovered in the course of his investigations that strong ties to social groups tended to "protect" people against self-destruction; the more groups a person was a member of, and the more com-

---

[3] Ferdinand Toennies, *Community and Society,* translated and edited by Charles P. Loomis (East Lansing: The Michigan State University Press, 1957).

pletely the group norms controlled his behavior, the less likely he was to leave the group by killing himself. Now the transition to the society of industrial capitalism, Durkheim pointed out, involved both the destruction of old social groups, such as the small peasant villages which people were leaving for the new industrial cities, and the loosening of the social ties of such surviving groups as the family and the church. By a loosening of social ties Durkheim usually means a decrease in the extent to which group norms control individual behavior. Under such anomic conditions, old norms, which had effectively limited human action and aspiration in the preindustrial world, no longer provided such limitations in the modern world, Durkheim thought, and the modern society had not as yet developed a new set of norms to guide individual behavior. Modern man, as a result, may have relatively limitless aspirations and when he cannot fulfill these may not feel effective group prohibitions of suicide as a response to his frustrations. Durkheim said anomie, or normlessness, was one of the dangerous characteristics of the modern world, and today statistics still show that the highest rates of suicide and other means of escape from social life, such as alcoholism, drug addiction, and psychosis, are found in the most advanced industrial countries.[4]

Science, one of the forces responsible for the creation of modern society, has often been looked to as a source of norms and values by which man can organize his world and live in the new society. Max Weber, in the last selection in this section, holds that this is a mistaken hope. Science, he maintains, cannot provide man with a new set of values by which to live in the new society. Science can supply knowledge of the world, and man can use this knowledge to predict the probable outcomes of actions he contemplates, but science cannot decide which actions are good and which are bad, or which should be taken and which should be avoided. Science, Weber avers, is the most effective method yet developed by man for understanding the world, both the physical and the social world, but it is not a source of morality. Science provides information with which man may implement his purposes, but these purposes arise from systems of values and beliefs outside the realm of science. Weber agrees with the Russian novelist Tolstoy that science cannot tell us how to live. He disagrees with Tolstoy, however, in the conclusion that science is therefore useless. With scientific knowledge of the world, Weber says, man can foresee some of the consequences of choosing one kind of action over another and can discover the most efficient means for carrying out the action he has decided upon. Weber sees very serious consequences in the fact that the modern way of knowing the world does not provide man with guidance for living in the world. The modern world is "disenchanted," Weber says, meaning that rational science has replaced metaphysical speculation, religious dogma, and magical thinking as the chief way of knowing the world. Organized religion, Weber thought, has lost its power to define ultimate goals and appropriate means for attaining them in the contemporary world of the twentieth century. Contemporary man, Weber believes, must find new ways of giving purpose and meaning to his life.

---

[4] An extremely interesting and very controversial study of modern society along these lines and a prescription for its reorganization to eliminate these problems is found in the book by Erich Fromm, *The Sane Society* (New York: Holt, Rinehart, & Winston, Inc. 1955).

A Theories of the Origins of Industrial Capitalism

13

Saint-Simon on the Origins of Industrial Society and Scientific Sociology

EMILE DURKHEIM

The Origins of Sociology in the Life and Work of Saint-Simon

[The system of Saint-Simon] had a success without equal in the history of the century. . . . Its author is so misunderstood and, besides, has so original a character that it warrants our pausing. Before studying the doctrine let us look at the man.

Claude Henri de Rouvroy, Count of Saint-Simon, was born on the 17th of October, 1750. He belonged to the fam-

From Emile Durkheim, *Socialism and Saint-Simon*. Edited and with an Introduction by Alvin W. Gouldner. Translated by Charlotte Sattler. Copyright © 1958 by The Antioch Press. Reprinted by permission of The Antioch Press.

ily of the author of the *Mémoires* [of the Court of Louis XIV], though of another branch. From infancy he evidenced rare energy and independence of character. At thirteen he refused to take his first communion. For this reason he was imprisoned in Saint-Lazare from which he escaped. Bitten by a mad dog, he himself cauterized the wound with a burning coal. One day when a coachman, in order to pass, was about to interrupt his play, he lay down on the ground in front of the moving carriage. Struck by the extraordinary nature of their child, his parents hurried his education—about which he later complained. "I was weighed down with teachers," said he, "without being left time to reflect on what they were teaching me." However, at an early age he made the acquaintance of d'Alembert who exerted considerable influence—and this undoubtedly is one of the causes which contributed to the development of his scientific mind. This is also, without doubt, the source of his plan—which his school inherited—to write the Encyclopedia of the eighteenth century in order to harmonize it with the new state of science.

He played successively, in the course of his life, the most diverse roles. To conform to the tradition of his family, he first tried an army career. A captain at the time when war [of national independence, 1776] broke out in America, he followed one of his relatives who was in command of the expeditionary force and took part in the war as a staff officer. In the battle of Saintes he was wounded and made prisoner. But on his return to France after peace was concluded, the *ennui* of garrison life became unbearable and he resolved to leave the army.

In the midst of all this the [French] Revolution broke out. He accepted it with enthusiasm but refused to play a role in it, believing that while the battle of parties lasted, former noblemen should keep their distance from public affairs. Still, he was not satisfied to stand by as an inactive witness or passive observer of the events that were unfolding and entered the revolutionary movement through another door. The former soldier made himself a business man and purchaser of national property. In this he was associated with a Prussian, the Count of Redern, who for this purpose placed at his disposal a sum of 500,000 francs. The undertaking which Saint-Simon was to direct alone succeeded beyond all expectations. However, in spite of the proof he thus gave of his confidence in the final triumph of the Revolution, he ended by becoming suspect. Ordered arrested, he was imprisoned at Saint-Pélgie, then at Luxembourg, under the name of Jacques Bonhomme, which he had adopted for his business transactions. The 9th of Thermidor [general amnesty] happily came to deliver him. . . .

Then began the third phase in the life of Saint-Simon. The speculator was transformed into a grand lordly friend of luxury and learning. In his magnificent mansion on the Rue de Chabanais he held open house, but it was almost exclusively with artists and especially scholars that he surrounded himself Monge and Lagrange were his principal companions. At the same time he helped very generously—and even more discretely—all young men of promise who were referred to him. Poisson and Dupuytren stayed with him a long time. He sought out these contacts in order to educate himself. He even went so far as to become a student again, and set up residence beside the École Polytechnique where he took courses. Then he moved—again for the same reason—near the École de Médecine. He even assumed the expenses of numerous experiments. I will not discuss his marriage which ended in amicable divorce at the end of a year, as it was an event without significance in his life.

But Saint-Simon's fortune was much too modest for this life of Maecenus to last. We can be sure that in 1797 he only possessed 144,000 livres. He lost his fortune knowingly, and by 1805 nothing was left. Then begins the last period of his life, when he produced all his works. But although productive, life did not cease being hard on this unfortunate thinker who more than once found himself with nothing to eat.

He sought a position, and through the intervention of the Comte de Ségur was named copyist to Mont-de-Pitié, with a stipend of a thousand francs a year. As duties occupied his whole day he was obliged to use his nights to pursue the personal works he had just begun. His health was in a deplorable state (he coughed blood) when chance placed in his path a man (Diard) who had formerly been in his service and who had become wealthy. This good man took him in and Saint-Simon was the guest of his former servant for four years, until 1810. It was at that time that he published his first great work: the *Introduction aux travaux scientifiques du XIXe siècle.* But Diard died, and living again presented difficulties for Saint-Simon. However, in 1814 he seems to have escaped them for a time, although it is not known just how. It is then that he successively had as secretaries Augustin Thierry and Auguste Comte. In 1817 his financial condition even permitted him to give the latter 300 francs a month. Some works he published at this time enjoyed great success and brought him important subscriptions for later works that he had in preparation. Among the subscribers are the names Vital Roux, Perior, de Broglie, La Fayette, La Rochefoucauld, etc. But the daring nature of the author's ideas ended by frightening them. For one thing, Saint-Simon led a very irregular life. He was always extravagant, and poverty began once more. At times during this period, he was tormented by hunger and could not always find—even among those he had previously helped—the assistance he might have expected. Dupuytren, who he had come across, offered him a hundred sous. Crushed, the philosopher surrendered to despair and on the 9th of March, 1823, shot himself. He lost an eye but his brain remained uninjured, and after 15 days the patient was better. This period of discouragement over, he returned to his work, and this time fortune was good to him. A small group of fervent disciples gathered around and maintained him until death, which occurred on the 19th of May, 1825. He died surrounded by friends, conversing with them about work undertaken in common, and about his next triumph.

It was, as one can see, a singularly unstable life. Nevertheless it was far from lacking in unity. What set its course from the first was the very character of Saint-Simon, which reappears —the same—in all the roles he successively played. What dominated him above all was a horror of everything common and vulgar and a passion for the great and new. From early infancy he had given indications of this. His faith in himself and the grandeur of his destiny were never belied. From the time he was fifteen his valet would awaken him every morning with the words: "Wake up, monsieur le comte, you have great things to do." Later, he related that he had a dream of Charlemagne, from whom his family claimed descent, and the great emperor said to him, "My son, your successes as a philosopher will equal mine as a soldier and statesman." Dedicating one of his books to a nephew, he wrote him, "My intention in dedicating my work to you is to urge you on to nobleness. It is an obligation for you to do great things." It is this passion that explains the lack of moderation he practiced in life, his wastefulness, and his debauchery, which did him the greatest harm in the eyes of his contemporaries. "I have made every effort," he wrote in another letter, "to excite you, that is to say, to make you mad—for madness, my dear Victor, is nothing but extreme ardor, and enhanced ardor, is indispensable for accomplishing great things. One does not enter the temple of glory except that he has escaped from the Petites-Maison." . . . Indeed, he exerted considerable influence on the most distinguished minds of his day: Poisson, Halévy, Olinde Rodrigues, Rouget de Lisle, and finally and above all, Auguste Comte, who owed him much more than he acknowledged.

But his career did not have a merely formal unity, due to the very personal mark his character placed on everything he did. Actually, in everything he undertook he pursued only one and the same end. . . . [he] was a man of a single idea. . . . To reorganize European societies by giving them science and industry as bases—that was the objective he never lost sight of. From the time of the American campaign it was on this that he reflected. At that time he was writing his father, "If I were in a calmer situation I would clarify my thoughts. They are still raw, but I have a clear expectation that after they have matured I should find myself in a condition to do a scientific work useful to humanity—which is the principal aim I am setting for my life." It is under the influence of this idea that he devoted himself both to scientific works and large economic enterprises. For his speculations on national possessions were not the only ones. In America he suggested to the viceroy of Mexico, a canal between the two oceans. He offered to build a canal from Madrid to the sea for the Spanish Government. Later he dreamed of a gigantic bank whose revenue would serve to execute useful works for humanity. . . . In any case, there is no doubt that the last part of his life . . . realizes an idea which is that of his life's work. . . .

To add a science to the list of sciences is always a very laborious operation, but more productive than the annexation of a new continent to old continents. And it is at once much more fruitful when the science has man for its object. It almost had to do violence to the human spirit and to triumph over the keenest resistance to make it understood that in order to act upon things it was first necessary to put them on trial [that is, to study them systematically and objectively]. The resistance has been particularly stubborn when the material to be examined was ourselves, due to our tendency to place ourselves outside of things, to demand a place apart in the universe.

Saint-Simon was the first who resolutely freed himself from these prejudices. Although he may have had precursors, never had it been so clearly asserted that man and society could not be directed in their conduct unless one began by making them objects of science and further that this science could not rest on any other principles than do the sciences of nature. And this new science—he not only laid out its design but attempted to realize it in part. We can see here all that Auguste Comte, and consequently all that the thinkers of the nineteenth century, owe him. In him we encounter the seeds already developed of all the ideas which have fed the thinking of our time. We [find] in it positivist philosophy, positivist sociology. We will see that we will also find socialism in it. . . .

. . . Human sciences [according to Saint-Simon] have to be constructed in imitation of the other natural sciences, for man is only one part of nature. There are not two words in the world, one which depends on scientific observation, and the other which escapes it. The universe is one, and the same method must serve to explore it in all of its parts. Man and the universe, says Saint-Simon, are like a mechanism on two scales—the first is a reduction of the second but does not differ from it in nature. Man is related to the universe like "a watch enclosed within a great clock from which it receives movement." Since it is demonstrated that the positive method alone allows us to know the inorganic world, it follows that it alone is suited to the human world, also. The tendency of the human spirit since the fifteenth century "is to base all its reasoning on observed and examined facts. Already it has reorganized astronomy, physics and chemistry on this positive basis. . . . One concludes necessarily that physiology, of which the science of man is part, will be treated by the method adopted for the other physical sciences." . . . "The domain of physiology viewed as a whole is generally composed of all facts relating to organic beings." . . . Physiology consists of two parts: one which deals with individual organs, the other with social organs. "Physiology is not only the science which, addressing itself to our organs one by one, experiments on each of them . . . to better determine the spheres of activity. . . . It does not consist only in this comparative knowledge which draws from the study of plants and animals valuable ideas on the functions of the parts we possess in common with these different classes of organic beings." In addition to this special physiology there is another, a general physiology which, "rich in all the facts discovered through valuable pieces of work undertaken in these different directions, addresses itself to considerations of a higher order. It towers above individuals, looking upon them merely as organs of the social body, whose organic functions it must examine, just as specialized physiology studies those of individuals." . . . "Society is not at all a simple conglomeration of living beings whose actions have no other cause but the arbitrariness of individual wills, nor other result than ephemeral or unimportant accidents. On the contrary, society is above all a veritable organized machine, all of whose parts contribute in a different way to the movement of the whole. The gathering of men constitutes a veritable being whose existence is more or less certain or precarious according to whether its organs acquit themselves more or less regularly of the functions entrusted to them." This is the social organism.

This general and social physiology naturally embraces morality and politics which consequently must themselves become positive sciences. Once physiology is advanced, says Saint-Simon, "politics will become a science of observation, and political questions handled by those who would have studied the positive science of man by the same method and in the same way that today one treats those relating to other phenomena." And it is only when politics are dealt with in this manner, and when, as a result, it can be taught in schools like other sciences, that the European crisis can be resolved.

But this *sui generis* thing—the object of this new science—what is the proper perspective for it to be viewed in order to study it? Today it is generally acknowledged that to have as complete as possible knowledge of it, it must be considered successively from two different aspects. One can consider human societies at a determinate and fixed moment in their evolution and then examine how, in this phase, their different parts act and react on each other —in a word, how they contribute to the collective life. Or else, instead of fixing and immobilizing them artificially in one moment of time, one can follow them through the successive stages they have travelled in the course of history, and then propose to find how each stage has contributed to determine the one that followed. In the first case one attempts to determine the law of social organization at such and such a phase of historic development, while in the other, one inquires about the law according to which these different phases have succeeded each other, what is the order of succession and what accounts for this order—in other words, what is the law of progress. In the eyes of Saint-Simon the second point of view is the more important. . . .

In fact, according to him, the law of progress dominates us with an absolute necessity. We submit to it—we do not make it. We are its instruments—not its authors. "The supreme law of progress of the human spirit carries along and dominates everything; men are but its instruments. Although this force derives from us, it is no more in our power to withhold ourselves from its influence, or master its action, than to change at will the primary impulse which makes our planet revolve around the sun. All we can do is to obey this law by accounting for the course it directs, instead of being blindly pushed by it; and, incidentally, it is precisely in this that the great philosophic development reserved for the present era will consist." . . .

So we see both how the problem of social physiology is posed and by what method it must be resolved. Since the progress of human societies is subjected to a necessary law, the primary aim of science is to find this law. And once discovered, it will itself indicate the direction progress must follow. To discover the order in which humanity developed in the past, in order to determine what this development should become—that is the urgent question, *par excellence*, which imposes itself on a thinker. In this way politics can be treated scientifically. "The future consists of the last items of a series of which the first composed the past. When one has properly examined the first terms of a series, it is easy to postulate those following. Thus, from the past, deeply observed, one can with ease deduce the future." The fault of statesmen, usually, is to have their eyes fixed on the present. And thus they expose themselves to inevitable errors. For how, if one limits oneself to the consideration of so brief a period, distinguish "the remains of a past which was disappearing and the seeds of a future which is arising?" It is only by observing series of broadly extended facts, as a result of searching deeply

into the past, that one can disentangle among the various elements of the present those large with future from those which are no more than monuments of a past that has outlived itself. Since it will be easy to establish that the former belong to an ascending series and the latter to a regressive one, it will be relatively simple to make a selection and to orient progress. . . .

Sociological Analysis of the Rise of Industrial Society

. . . We find the new science limited to a single and unique problem [the origins and development of industrial society] whose interest is more practical than speculative. But at least Saint-Simon undertakes to treat it according to the scientific and positive method whose fundamental rules we saw him formulate earlier. It is not a question of inventing a new system, created out of many pieces—as do utopians of the eighteenth century and other periods—but merely of discovering by observation what is in process of being worked out [in the new society-in-the-making]. "One does not create a system of social organization. One perceives the new chain of ideas and interests which has been formed, and points it out—that is all." . . . All one can do is to be aware of the direction the development is taking; next, to distinguish, among the elements of which the present is made up, those which are developing more and more—and developing more completely—and those which more and more are ceasing to be; finally, to recognize the future behind the survivals of the past which conceal it. To do these things, it is necessary to study the growth of our societies since they were definitively established. According to our author, it is in the Middle Ages—the eleventh and twelfth centuries—that they were formed with all their essential characteristics. That epoch is consequently "the most suitable point of departure" for "that philosophic observation of the past" which alone can enlighten the future. Let us see what societies were like at that time and how they evolved since.

What gave them an organized character when, toward the tenth century, they began to free themselves from the chaos produced by barbarian invasions, was that the social system revolved completely around two centers of gravity, distinct but closely associated. On the one hand, there were the chiefs of the army, who constituted what is since called feudalism, and to whom all of secular society was closely subjected. All property, real and personal, was in their hands, and workers —individually and collectively—were dependent upon them. On the other hand, there were the clergy, who controlled the spiritual direction of society, generally and specifically. Their doctrines and decisions served as guides to opinion; but what overwhelmingly established their authority was their absolute mastery over general and particular education. In other words, the entire economic life of society depended on the lords, and all intellectual life on the priests. The first ruled supremely over productive operations, the second over consciences. Thus all collective functions were strictly subjected either to military power or religious authority, and this double subjugation consituted the social organization [of feudalism]. . . . War was then chronic . . . consequently it was natural that only those capable of directing it were invested with the highest degree of authority and respect. Likewise, as the clergy was the only group which then possessed learning, it was out of real necessity that it exercised an absolute power over minds. Thus this two-pronged supremacy was based on the nature of things. It corresponded to a social superiority of these two classes which was real and which it merely expressed.

This is the origin. Let us now see what this organization became in the course of history.

It is a general rule that the apogee of a social system coincides with the beginning of its decadence. In the eleventh century, spiritual and temporal powers were definitively established; never was the authority of clergy and lords more undisputed. But coming into existence at that very moment were two new social forces. . . . These two forces were the free commune and exact science.

What had accounted for the strength of feudal organization was the subjugation of the industrial class by what then took its place, the military class. . . . All economic life was subordinated to the interests of war and warriors. But with the twelfth century began the great movement of the emancipation of the commune. Villages, by payment of silver, were freeing themselves from seigneurial tutelage. And they were totally composed of artisans and merchants. A whole segment of the economic structure thus found itself detached from the others who until then were forcing their control on it. . . . Liberated industry was going to be able freely to realize its own nature, to propose for itself purely industrial ends, which not only differed from but contradicted those the [feudal] system had forced upon it. A new force, *sui generis*, had entered the heart of the social body, and as by nature and origin it was foreign to the old organization— and could only disturb it—it was inevitable that its very presence would disconcert the latter's functioning and would develop only by destroying it.

At the same time the exact sciences were imported into Europe by the Arabs. The schools they founded in their conquered parts of Europe were quickly imitated elsewhere. Similar establishments arose in all occidental Europe, "observatories, dissection rooms, study rooms for natural history were set up in Italy, France, England, Germany. As early as the thirteenth century, Bacon was brilliantly cultivating the physical sciences." Gradually, in opposition to the clergy, a new body was forming, which like the preceding one aimed at directing the intellectual life of society. These were the scholars who, in their relation to the clerical class were in exactly the same situation as were the enfranchised communes—that is, the corporation of artisans and merchants —vis-à-vis feudalism. Thus two seeds of destruction were introduced into the theological-feudal system, and in fact from that moment the two forces which were the source of its strength began to grow weaker. . . .

Nevertheless, . . . it is only in the sixteenth century that the forces antagonistic to the old system found themselves strong enough to come into the open, in such a way that the results could be perceived by anyone. At first these forces were directed against theological rule; Luther and his co-reformers upset pontifical authority as a power in Europe. At the same time in a general way they undermined theological authority "by destroying the principle of blind faith, by replacing it with the right of examination which—restrained at first within quite narrow limits—was to inevitably increase . . . and finally to embrace an indefinite area." This two-fold change operated not only among the peoples converted to Protestantism, but even among those who remained Catholic. For once the principle was established, it extended well beyond the countries where it had first been proclaimed. As a result, the bond which tied individual consciences to ecclesiastical power—although not shattered—was loosened, and the moral unity of the social system definitely unsettled.

The entire sixteenth century was seized by this great intellectual revolu-tion. But it was at its close that the struggle—began against spiritual power —proceeded against temporal power. It took place at almost the same time in France and in England. In both countries it was led by the common people, with one of the two branches of temporal power as leader. With the English, feudalism placed 'itself at their head to combat royal authority; in France royalty made itself their ally against feudal strength. Actually the coalition—in both peoples—had begun as early as the enfranchisement of the lower class, but it is only in the seventeenth century that the domestic rearrangements on both sides of the channel came into the open and battle was joined in broad daylight. Here Richelieu, then Louis XIV shattered seigneurial power; there [England], the Revolution of 1688 broke out, limiting royal authority as much as was possible without overturning the old organization. The final result of these events was a weakening of the military system in its entirety. It was weakened, first because it lost unity due to a schism between the two elements of which it was formed —and a system cannot be disunited without being enfeebled—and then because one of these elements departed from battle crushed. Therefore, although at this time feudalism—at least in France—seemed to burn with a strong flame, in reality these magnificent external appearances concealed a state of internal deterioration which events of the following century soon made clear. . . .

But at the same time that this regressive process was developing, another was occurring in reverse direction with no less significance. Industrial and scientific forces, once formed, did not manifest themselves exclusively by destructive effects, that is, by overthrowing the old social order. They gave rise to another. They did not limit themselves to detaching consciences and individual wills from the centers which until then, by providing a similar direction, had made a single body of them. But to the degree they acquired more energy, they themselves became foci of common action and centers of organization. Around them gradually formed the social elements which the old forces—more and more powerless to keep them subordinate—were allowing to escape. Under these new influences, a new social system was slowly arising in the bosom of the old, which was disintegrating.

As long as arts and crafts had been narrowly subordinated to theological and military authority, having to serve as instruments for ends which were not their own, they had been impeded in their progress. But as soon as they began to be free—thanks to the liberation of the common people [these free villagers engaged in commerce and industry]—they took flight and developed so quickly that they soon became a social force to be reckoned with. Little by little all society fell into dependence upon them, because nothing was any longer possible without them. Military force itself was subjected to them, once war became a complex and costly thing, once it demanded not merely native courage and a certain disposition of character, but money, machines, arms. More and more, improvements in industry, the inventions of science, and finally wealth, were proving more vital to success in arms than innate bravery. But when a class acquires greater importance and respect, when the functions it fulfills become more essential, it is inevitable for it to wield greater influence on the direction of society and increased political authority. This in fact is what occurred. Little by little one sees representatives of industry admitted to governmental councils, playing a greater and greater part, and as a result having a larger share in determining the general course of society. It

is especially in England that this phenomenon manifests itself. Gradually the common people—in other words, the classes which fulfill only economic functions—obtain first a consultative voice in the tax vote, then a deliberative voice, then the exclusive right to vote on budget. They substitute themselves for the old temporal power in one of its most important functions, and are able henceforth to act in conformity with their own interest in the direction of society; they modify its orientation, since they have altogether different ends than the military classes [feudal nobility]. In other words, the social system begins to revolve about a new center.

This is not all. One of the essential prerogatives of feudal power consisted in administering justice. Seigneurial justice was one of the essential characteristics of feudal organization. But once the villages were freed, one of the rights considered most important to achieve was the administration of justice. "From then on municipal [courts] were formed and entrusted with this care. Its members were designated by the citizens and for a limited term." . . . The appearance of these tribunals is an important event in the process of organization we are tracing. From this moment, in fact, the industrial class had a judiciary organ which was its own, in harmony with its special nature, and which contributed to complete the system which was in process of formation. . . .

Just as with industry, science, as it grew, developed an organization appropriate to its own character, and very different, consequently, from that permitted by theological authority. Scholars became esteemed personages whom royalty more and more made a habit of consulting. It is as a result of these repeated consultations that great scientific bodies were gradually established at the pinnacle of the system. These are the academies. Thereafter there arose all kinds "of special schools for science where the influence of theology and metaphysics were, so to speak, nil." "A larger and larger mass of scientific ideas entered ordinary education at the same time that religious doctrines gradually lost influence." Finally, just as with industry, this early organization did not remain confined to the higher levels of society, but extended to the mass of people. With respect to the body of scholars, they were in a state of subordination analogous to their former position vis-à-vis the body ecclesiastic. "The people, organized industrially, soon perceived that their usual works of art and craft were not at all in rapport with their theological ideas . . . and wherever they could be in contact with savants they lost the habit of consulting priests, and acquired the custom of placing themselves in touch with those who possessed positive [empirical, objective, scientific] knowledge." And since they found themselves benefitted by the counsel given them, they ended by according "the unanimous opinion of the scholars the same degree of confidence that in the Middle Ages they accorded the decisions of spiritual power. It is by a kind of faith of a new type that they successively accepted the movement of the earth, modern astronomical theory, the circulation of the blood, the identity of lightning and of electricity, etc., etc." "So it is proven," concludes Saint-Simon "that people have become spontaneously confident in and subordinate to their leaders in the fields of science, just as they are temporally with regard to their industrial leaders. I have, consequently, the right to conclude that confidence as well as social rankings are developed within the new system."

The results of this double evolution can be summarized as follows: In the measure that the ancient social system gave way, another was formed in the very bosom of the first. The old society contained within itself a new society, in process of formation and every day acquiring more strength and consistency. But these two organizations are necessarily antagonistic to each other. They result from opposing forces and aim at contradictory ends. One is essentially aggressive, war-like, the other essentially peaceful. The one sees in other peoples enemies to destroy; the other tends to view them as collaborators in a common [economic] undertaking. One has conquest for its aim, the other, production. Similarly, in spiritual affairs the first calls on faith and imposes beliefs which it puts beyond discussion. The second calls on reason and even trust—it requires a type of intellectual subordination which is essential to rationality, a commitment to further exploration and testing. Thus these two societies could not coexist without contradicting each other. . . .

Such was the situation on the eve of the Revolution, and out of it the Revolution was born. "This tremendous crisis did not at all have its origin in this or that isolated fact. . . . It operated as an overturning of the political system for the single reason that the state of society to which the ancient order corresponded had totally changed in nature. A civil and moral revolution which had gradually developed for more than six centuries engendered and necessitated a political revolution. . . . If one insists on attributing the French Revolution to one source, it must be dated from the day the liberation of the communes and the cultivation of exact sciences in western Europe began." . . .

But on the land thus cleared, the Revolution built nothing new. It asserted that one was no longer obliged to accept the old beliefs but did not attempt to elaborate a new body of rational beliefs that all minds could accept. It destroyed the foundations on which political authority rested but failed to establish others of any stability. It proclaimed that political power was not to belong to those who had monopolized it until then, but did not assign it to any definite organ. . . . [and] the absence of organization from which industrial society suffered became far more perceptible once all that remained of the old had disappeared. The weak cohesion of this dawning society became a much graver social peril once the old social bonds were completely destroyed. . . . It is certainly from this that there stemmed a kind of uncertainty, an exasperated anguish, which is characteristic of the revolutionary epoch. . . .

But why had [the Revolution] stopped midway? What prevented it from ending in positive results? The explanation Saint-Simon gives deserves consideration.

It is in the nature of man, he says, to be unable to pass without intermediary from one doctrine to another, from one social system to a differing system. That is why the authority of science and industry would never have been able to replace that of clergy and feudalism unless—when the first began to arise and the second weaken—there had not constituted itself between the two "a temporal and spiritual power of an intermediary kind, illegitimate, transitory, whose unique role was to direct the transition from one social system to another." Thus between the feudal body and the industrial body appeared the class of lawyers. Lawyers, just as workers, had been at first merely agents of the lords. But gradually they formed a distinct class, whose autonomy kept growing, whose action, consequently, opposed feudal action and modified it "by the establishment of jurisprudence, which had merely been an organized system of barriers opposed to the exercise of force." An equity was then established which was not purely feudal, and military power found itself

subject to limitations and rules drawn in the interest of commercial men—for these latter necessarily profited from any restriction brought against the antagonistic power they fought. In the spiritual realm similarly, metaphysicians—rising from the very heart of theology—wedged themselves between positive science and clergy, inspired at once with the spirit of both. And without ceasing to base their reasoning on religious foundations, they nevertheless modified theological influence by establishing the right of examination in matters of law and morality.

These are the two intermediate and fused forces which occupied the political stage almost exclusively until the Revolution, because by their composite and ambiguous nature they corresponded better than all others to the equally ambiguous state of civilization. Without doubt they thus rendered the greatest services and contributed in large measure to the final liberation of science and industry. Thanks to one, the working world escaped feudal tribunals. Thanks to the other, the idea took hold more and more that society could maintain itself without individual consciences being subordinated to theological doctrines. Their authority was so great when the Revolution broke out that quite naturally people took direction from them. Manufacturers and scholars believed they could do no better than blindly entrust their cause to them. Thus the men of law and the metaphysically-trained almost exclusively composed the revolutionary assemblies and inspired their actions. . . . But if these lawyers and metaphysicians were admirably prepared and organized to lead this revolutionary work to its final goal, they possessed nothing of what was required to erect a new system. For, although they did not understand this, it was from the past, from the old order of things, that they inherited the whole groundwork of their doctrines.

How could jurists bring themselves to a conception of a social order different from the one they had just destroyed, since "their political opinions are inevitably deduced, for the most part, from Roman law, from the ordinances of our kings, from feudal customs—in a word, from all the legislation which preceded the "Revolution." How could metaphysicians—the entire philosophic school of the eighteenth century—establish a system of ideas and beliefs in harmony with a particular social condition when, under the influence of the theologic spirit which continued to animate them, they were aspiring in all practical questions to absolute solutions, independent of any consideration of time and place, any historic condition? The effective role of both was therefore reduced to merely destroying. "When they wished to go further, they were thrust into the absolute question of the best government imaginable, and—always controlled by the same habits— treated it as a question of jurisprudence and metaphysics. For the theory of the rights of man—which has always been the foundation of their work in general politics—is nothing other than an application of high metaphysics to high jurisprudence." . . .

Even as they stand, Saint-Simon's observations are noteworthy. But they represent still another significant point in the history of ideas. If, in fact, one relates them to what was previously said, one arrives at the conclusion that according to Saint-Simon, European societies have passed successively through three social systems; the theological or feudal, the metaphysical or juridical, and the positive. We recognize in this formula the famous law of three stages which Comte was to make the foundation of his doctrine. However, it is of Saint-Simonian origin. . . .

It would take too long to point out all the fertile ideas contained in this broad tableau of our historic develop-

ment. It is Saint-Simon who was the first, before Guizot, to understand the full social significance of the communal movement and the ties which bound it to the Revolution and to current problems. He was also the first to judge the work of the Revolution with the impartiality of history, without condemning it in general—as did the defenders of the old regime—and without systematically extolling it—as did the liberals of his time—and on this point again Comte was his heir. On the whole, one must admire his complete absence of all prejudice, and the feeling for historic continuity he discovered in the role of every period—even the most discredited, like the Middle Ages—in the uninterrupted course of transformations which bind the society of the tenth century to contemporary times.

Saint-Simon's Proposed Organization of the Industrial System

Let us now return to the practical question noted in this historical analysis. Granted that our present societies contain in them two different, and even contradictory, social systems—one which is becoming weaker and weaker, the other emerging more and more— how can the crisis resulting from their antagonism be solved? . . .

It is neither possible nor useful to restore the old system in its entirety. But on the other hand we know that every eclectic combination is contradictory and incoherent, that a social organization cannot be regarded as stable except as it is entirely homogeneous. In other words, society must be based on only one of the two conflicting principles, and the other be excluded. It follows that modern societies will be definitely in equilibrium only when organized on a purely industrial basis. . . .

The most vital trait of this . . . organization is that its goal, and its exclusive goal, is to increase the control of man over things. "To concern itself only in acting on nature, in order to modify it as advantageously as possible for humankind," has been the unique task of the communes since their enfranchisement—that is, of the new society in process of formation. Instead of seeking to extend the national domain, instead of diverting the attention of men from worldly wealth, it addressed itself, on the contrary, to peacefully increasing their well-being through the development of arts, science and industry. It has had as its unique function the production of useful things for our worldly existence. Consequently, since all reform consists of extending to all of society what until now has been so only for a portion of it, the crisis will only be resolved when all social life converges toward this same goal, to the exclusion of every other. The only normal form that collective activity can take henceforth, is the industrial form. Society will be fully in harmony with itself only when it is totally industrialized. "The production of useful things is the only reasonable and positive end that political societies can set themselves." . . .

From this principle flows a significant conclusion. It is that "the producers of useful things—being the only useful people in society—are the only ones who should cooperate to regulate its course." It is therefore to them and them alone that law-making belongs. It is in their hands that all political power should be deposited. Since, hypothetically, the whole fabric of social life would be made up of industrial relationships, is it not obvious that only men of industry are in a position to direct it? The vital rationale consists of two stages: 1. Since in this system there is nothing more socially central than economic activity, the regulating organ of social functions should preside over the economic activity of society. There is no longer place for a central

organ with a differing objective since there is no longer other material in the common life; 2. This organ must necessarily be of the same nature as those which it is charged with regulating—that is to say, it must be composed exclusively of representatives of industrial life.

But what is understood by "industrial life?" . . . There are, says Saint-Simon, two major groups: one consists of the immense majority of the nation—that is to say, all workers—and which Saint-Simon calls national and industrial; and the other, which he labels anti-national, because it is like a parasitic body whose presence only interrupts the play of social functions. In the latter are included noblemen . . . and "owners living like nobles, that is to say, doing nothing." . . . But it is important to note that it is not all capitalists who are placed beyond the pale of regular society, but only those who live on unearned income. As for those who themselves make their wealth productive, who enrich it with their toil—they are industrials. Consequently, industrial society comprises all those who actively participate in the economic life, whether they are owners or not. The fact of possessing does not provide access to it but does not preclude them from it. . . .

But if [some] owners are not to be considered producers, it is not the same with scholars, who are the indispensable auxiliaries of industry. "The social body," says Saint-Simon, "consists of two great families: that of intellectuals, or industrials of theory, and that of immediate producers, or scholars of application." Consequently they too have the right to be represented in the managing organs of society, and this representation is actually indispensable since industry cannot do without the knowledge of science. It is necessary therefore that the supreme council of industry be assisted by a supreme council of the

learned. However, the two organs—
though united—must be distinct, for
the two functions—theory on one side
and practice on the other—are too different to be fused. . . . Thinkers must
be able to speculate with complete independence and without servilely ca-
pitulating to the needs of practice; but
it is essential that the practical men
decide finally on all that concerns execution. Moreover the two organs should
not be placed on the same footing;
there must exist between them a certain
hierarchy. It is to the industrials that
the principal role should belong, for it
is on them that the existence of the
thinkers depends. "Scholars render very
important services to the industrial
class, but receive services from it that
are much more important. They receive
existence. . . . The industrial class is
the fundamental class, the providing
class of society." The learned form but

"a secondary class." Between the two,
finally, are the artists, whose position in
the system is less clearly fixed. Occasionally Saint-Simon seems to treat them as
a class apart, represented by a special
organ in the managing centers of society; at other times they disappear into
the industrial class.

In summary, granted that social
functions can be only secular or spiritual—that is, turned towards thought
or towards action—that in the present
state of civilization the only rational
form of the temporal is industry and of
the spiritual, science, Saint-Simon concludes: 1. That normal society should
consist only of producers and scholars;
2. That as a consequence it should be
subordinated to directing organs composed of similar elements, with a certain preeminence of the first over the
second. This is the fundamental principle of the new system. . . .

14

Class Struggle and the Change from Feudalism to Capitalism

KARL MARX AND FRIEDRICH ENGELS

Theory of Social Structure and Change *

I was led by my studies to the conclusion that legal relations as well as
forms of state could be neither understood by themselves nor explained by
the so-called general progress of the
human mind, but that they are rooted
in the material conditions of life, which
are summed up by Hegel after the fash-

* From Karl Marx, *A Contribution to the
Critique of Political Economy*, Preface. First
published in 1859.

ion of the English and French of the
eighteenth century under the name
"civil society"; the anatomy of that civil
society is to be sought in political economy. The study of the latter, which I
had taken up in Paris, I continued at
Brussels, whither I immigrated on account of an order of expulsion issued by
Mr. Guizot.

The general conclusion at which I
arrived and which, once reached, continued to serve as the leading thread in
my studies may be briefly summed up
as follows: In the social production

which men carry on they enter into definite relations that are indispensable and independent of their will; these relations of production correspond to a definite stage of development of their material powers of production. The sum total of these relations of production constitutes the economic structure of society—the real foundation, on which rise legal and political superstructures and to which correspond definite forms of social consciousness. The mode of production in material life determines the general character of the social, political, and spiritual processes of life. It is not the consciousness of men that determines their existence, but, on the contrary, their social existence determines their consciousness. At a certain stage of their development the material forces of production in society come into conflict with the existing relations of production, or—what is but a legal expression for the same thing—with the property relations within which they had been at work before. From forms of development of the forces of production these relations turn into their fetters. Then comes the period of social revolution. With the change of the economic foundation the entire immense superstructure is more or less rapidly transformed. In considering such transformations the distinction should always be made between the material transformation of the economic conditions of production, which can be determined with the precision of natural science, and the legal, political, religious, aesthetic, or philosophic—in short, ideological—forms in which men become conscious of this conflict and fight it out. Just as our opinion of an individual is not based on what he thinks of himself, so can we not judge such a period of transformation by its own consciousness; on the contrary, this consciousness must rather be explained from the contradictions of material life, from the existing conflict between the social

forces of production and the relations of production. No social order ever disappears before all the productive forces for which there is room in it have been developed, and new, higher relations of production never appear before the material conditions of their existence have matured in the womb of the old society. Therefore mankind always takes up only such problems as it can solve, since, looking at the matter more closely, we will always find that the problem itself arises only when the material conditions necessary for its solution already exist or are at least in the process of formation. In broad outlines we can designate the Asiatic, the ancient, the feudal, and the modern bourgeois methods of production as so many epochs in the progress of the economic formation of society. The bourgeois relations of production are the last antagonistic form of the social process of production —antagonistic not in the sense of individual antagonism, but of one arising from conditions surrounding the life of individuals in society; at the same time the productive forces developing in the womb of bourgeois society create the material conditions for the solution of that antagonism. This social formation constitutes, therefore, the closing chapter of the prehistoric stage of human society.

Class Conflict and Industrial Capitalism †

The history of all hitherto existing society is the history of class struggles.

Free man and slave, patrician and plebeian, lord and serf, guild master and journeyman, in a word, oppressor and oppressed, stood in constant opposition to one another, carried on an uninterrupted, now hidden, now open fight, a fight that each time ended either in a

† From Karl Marx and Friedrich Engels, *The Communist Manifesto*, Part I. First published in 1848.

Ecological expansion: E

revolutionary reconstitution of society at large or in the common ruin of the contending classes.

In the earlier epochs of history we find almost everywhere a complicated arrangement of society into various orders, a manifold gradation of social rank. In ancient Rome we have patricians, knights, plebeians, slaves; in the Middle Ages, feudal lords, vassals, guild masters, journeymen, apprentices, serfs; in almost all of these classes, again, subordinate gradations.

The modern bourgeois society that has sprouted from the ruins of feudal society has not done away with class antagonisms. It has but established new classes, new conditions of oppression, new forms of struggle in place of the old ones.

Our epoch, the epoch of the bourgeoisie, possesses, however, this distinctive feature: it has simplified the class antagonisms. Society as a whole is more and more splitting up into two great hostile camps, into two great classes directly facing each other: bourgeoisie and proletariat.[1]

From the serfs of the Middle Ages sprang the chartered burghers of the earliest towns. From these burgesses the first elements of the bourgeoisie were developed.

The discovery of America, the rounding of the Cape opened up fresh ground for the rising bourgeoisie. The East Indian and Chinese markets, the colonization of America, trade with the colonies, the increase in the means of exchange and in commodities generally, gave to commerce, to navigation, to industry an impulse never before known, and thereby, to the revolutionary ele-

ment in the tottering feudal society, a rapid development.

The feudal system of industry, under which industrial production was monopolized by closed guilds, now no longer sufficed for the growing wants of the new markets. The manufacturing system took its place. The guild masters were pushed on one side by the manufacturing middle class; division of labor between the different corporate guilds vanished in the face of division of labor in each single workshop.

Meantime the markets kept ever growing, the demand ever rising. Even manufacture no longer sufficed. Thereupon steam and machinery revolutionized industrial production. The place of manufacture was taken by the giant, modern industry, the place of the industrial middle class by industrial millionaires, the leaders of whole industrial armies, the modern bourgeois.

Modern industry has established the world market, for which the discovery of America paved the way. This market has given an immense development to commerce, to navigation, to communication by land. This development has, in its turn, reacted on the extension of industry; and in proportion as industry, commerce, navigation, railways extended, in the same proportion the bourgeoisie developed, increased its capital, and pushed into the background every class handed down from the Middle Ages.

We see, therefore, how the modern bourgeoisie is itself the product of a long course of development, of a series of revolutions in the modes of production and of exchange.

Each step in the development of the bourgeoisie was accompanied by a corresponding political advance of that class. An oppressed class under the sway of the feudal nobility, an armed and self-governing association in the medieval commune; here independent urban republic (as in Italy and Ger-

---

[1] By "bourgeoisie" is meant the class of modern capitalists, owners of the means of social production and employers of wage labor. By proletariat, the class of modern wage laborers who, having no means of production of their own, are reduced to selling their labor power in order to live.

many), there taxable "third estate" of the monarchy (as in France), afterwards, in the period of manufacture proper, serving either the semi-feudal or the absolute monarchy as a counterpoise against the nobility, and, in fact, cornerstone of the great monarchies in general, the bourgeoisie has at last, since the establishment of modern industry and of the world market, conquered for itself, in the modern representative state, exclusive political sway. The executive of the modern state is but a committee for managing the common affairs of the whole bourgeoisie.

The bourgeoisie, historically, has played a most revolutionary part.

The bourgeoisie, wherever it has got the upper hand, has put an end to all feudal, patriarchal, idyllic relations. It has pitilessly torn asunder the motley feudal ties that bound man to his "natural superiors," and has left remaining no other nexus between man and man than naked self-interest, than callous "cash payment." It has drowned the most heavenly ecstasies of religious fervor, of chivalrous enthusiasm, of Philistine sentimentalism in the icy water of egotistical calculation. It has resolved personal worth into exchange value and, in place of the numberless indefeasible chartered freedoms, has set up that single, unconscionable freedom—free trade. In one word, for exploitation, veiled by religious and political illusions, it has substituted naked, shameless, direct, brutal exploitation.

The bourgeoisie has stripped of its halo every occupation hitherto honored and looked up to with reverent awe. It has converted the physician, the lawyer, the priest, the poet, the man of science into its paid wage laborers.

The bourgeoisie has torn away from the family its sentimental veil, and has reduced the family relation to a mere money relation.

The bourgeoisie has disclosed how it came to pass that the brutal display of vigor in the Middle Ages, which reactionists so much admire, found its fitting complement in the most slothful indolence. It has been the first to show what man's activity can bring about. It has accomplished wonders far surpassing Egyptian pyramids, Roman aqueducts, and Gothic cathedrals; it has conducted expeditions that put in the shade all former exoduses of nations and crusades.

The bourgeoisie cannot exist without constantly revolutionizing the instruments of production, and thereby the relations of production, and with them the whole relations of society. Conservation of the old modes of production in unaltered form was, on the contrary, the first condition of existence for all earlier industrial classes. Constant revolutionizing of production, uninterrupted disturbance of all social conditions, everlasting uncertainty and agitation distinguish the bourgeois epoch from all earlier ones. All fixed, fast-frozen relations, with their train of ancient and venerable prejudices and opinions, are swept away, all new-formed ones become antiquated before they can ossify. All that is solid melts into air, all that is holy is profaned, and man is at last compelled to face with sober senses his real conditions of life and his relations with his kind.

The need of a constantly expanding market for its products chases the bourgeoisie over the whole surface of the globe. It must nestle everywhere, settle everywhere, establish connections everywhere.

The bourgeoisie has through its exploitation of the world market given a cosmopolitan character to production and consumption in every country. To the great chargrin of reactionists, it has drawn from under the feet of industry the national ground on which it stood. All old-established national industries have been destroyed or are daily being destroyed. They are dislodged by new

*T (3)
re futuristic attitude toward social change*

*T (.)
re ideas + tools*

industries, whose introduction becomes a life and death question for all civilized nations, by industries that no longer work up indigenous raw material, but raw material drawn from the remotest zones; industries whose products are consumed not only at home, but in every quarter of the globe. In place of the old wants, satisfied by the productions of the country, we find new wants, requiring for their satisfaction the products of distant lands and climes. In place of the old local and national seclusion and self-sufficiency we have intercourse in every direction, universal interdependence of nations. And as in material, so also in intellectual production. The intellectual creations of individual nations become common property. National one-sidedness and narrow-mindedness become more and more impossible, and from the numerous national and local literatures there arises a world literature.

The bourgeoisie, by the rapid improvement of all instruments of production, by the immensely facilitated means of communication, draws all, even the most barbarian, nations into civilization. The cheap prices of its commodities are the heavy artillery with which it batters down all Chinese walls, with which it forces the barbarians' intensely obstinate hatred of foreigners to capitulate. It compels all nations, on pain of extinction, to adopt the bourgeois mode of production; it compels them to introduce what it calls civilization into their midst, i.e., to become bourgeois themselves. In one word, it creates a world after its own image.

The bourgeoisie has subjected the country to the rule of the towns. It has created enormous cities, has greatly increased the urban population as compared with the rural, and has thus rescued a considerable part of the population from the idiocy of rural life. Just as it has made the country dependent on the towns, so it has made barbarian and semi-barbarian countries dependent on the civilized ones, nations of peasants on nations of bourgeois, the East on the West.

The bourgeoisie keeps more and more doing away with the scattered state of the population, of the means of production, and of property. It has agglomerated population, centralized means of production, and has concentrated property in a few hands. The necessary consequence of this was political centralization. Independent, or but loosely connected provinces, with separate interests, laws, governments and systems of taxation, became lumped together into one nation, with one government, one code of laws, one national class interest, one frontier, and one customs tariff.

The bourgeoisie, during its rule of scarce one hundred years, has created more massive and more colossal productive forces than have all preceding generations together. Subjection of nature's forces to man, machinery, application of chemistry to industry and agriculture, steam navigation, railways, electric telegraphs, clearing of whole continents for cultivation, canalization of rivers, whole populations conjured out of the ground—what earlier century had even a presentiment that such productive forces slumbered in the lap of social labor?

We see then: the means of production and of exchange, on whose foundation the bourgeoisie built itself up, were generated in feudal society. At a certain stage in the development of these means of production and of exchange, the conditions under which feudal society produced and exchanged, the feudal organization of agriculture and manufacturing industry, in one word, the feudal relations of property, became no longer compatible with the already developed productive forces; they became so many fetters. They had to be burst asunder; they were burst asunder.

Into their place stepped free competition, accompanied by a social and political constitution adapted to it, and by the economic and political sway of the bourgeois class.

A similar movement is going on before our own eyes. Modern bourgeois society with its relations of production, of exchange, and of property, a society that has conjured up such gigantic means of production and of exchange, is like the sorcerer who is no longer able to control the powers of the nether world whom he has called up by his spells. For many a decade past, the history of industry and commerce is but the history of the revolt of modern productive forces against modern conditions of production, against the property relations that are the conditions for the existence of the bourgeoisie and of its rule. It is enough to mention the commercial crises that by their periodic return put on its trial, each time more threateningly, the existence of the entire bourgeois society. In these crises a great part not only of the existing products but also of the previously created productive forces are periodically destroyed. In these crises there breaks out an epidemic that in all earlier epochs would have seemed an absurdity—the epidemic of overproduction. Society suddenly finds itself put back into a state of momentary barbarism; it appears as if a famine, a universal war of devastation had cut off the supply of every means of subsistence; industry and commerce seem to be destroyed; and why? Because there is too much civilization, too much means of subsistence, too much industry, too much commerce. The productive forces at the disposal of society no longer tend to further the development of the conditions of bourgeois property; on the contrary, they have become too powerful for these conditions, by which they are fettered, and as soon as they overcome these fetters they bring disorder into the whole of bourgeois society, endanger the existence of bourgeois property. The conditions of bourgeois society are too narrow to comprise the wealth created by them. And how does the bourgeoisie get over these crises? On the one hand, by enforced destruction of a mass of productive forces; on the other, by the conquest of new markets, and by the more thorough exploitation of the old ones. That is to say, by paving the way for more extensive and more destructive crises, and by diminishing the means whereby crises are prevented.

The weapons with which the bourgeoisie felled feudalism to the ground are now turned against the bourgeoisie itself.

But not only has the bourgeoisie forged the weapons that bring death to itself; it has also called into existence the men who are to wield those weapons—the modern working class—the proletarians.

In proportion as the bourgeoisie, i.e., capital, is developed, in the same proportion is the proletariat, the modern working class, developed—a class of laborers, who live only so long as they find work, and who find work only so long as their labor increases capital. These laborers, who must sell themselves piecemeal, are a commodity, like every other article of commerce, and are consequently exposed to all the vicissitudes of competition, to all the fluctuations of the market.

Owing to the extensive use of machinery and to division of labor, the work of the proletarians has lost all individual character and, consequently, all charm for the workman. He becomes an appendage of the machine, and it is only the simplest, most monotonous, and most easily acquired knack that is required of him. Hence the cost of production of a workman is restricted, almost entirely, to the means of subsistence that he requires for his maintenance and for the propagation of his race. But the price of a commodity, and therefore also of labor, is equal to its cost of production. In proportion, therefore, as the repulsiveness of the work increases, the wage decreases. Nay, more, in proportion as the use of machinery and division of labor increases, in the same proportion the burden of toil also increases, whether by prolongation of the working hours, by increase of the work exacted in a given time, or by increased speed of the machinery, etc.

. Modern industry has converted the little workshop of the patriarchal master into the great factory of the industrial capitalist. Masses of laborers, crowded into the factory, are organized like soldiers. As privates of the industrial army they are placed under the command of a perfect hierarchy of officers and sergeants. Not only are they slaves of the bourgeois class, and of the bourgeois state; they are daily and hourly enslaved by the machine, by the overlooker, and, above all, by the individual bourgeois manufacturer himself. The more openly this despotism proclaims gain to be its end and aim, the more petty, the more hateful, and the more embittering it is.

The less the skill and exertion of strength implied in manual labor, in other words, the more modern industry becomes developed, the more is the labor of men superseded by that of women. Differences of age and sex have no longer any distinctive social validity for the working class. All are instruments of labor, more or less expensive to use, according to their age and sex.

No sooner is the exploitation of the laborer by the manufacturer over, to the extent that he receives his wages in cash, than he is set upon by the other portions of the bourgeoisie, the landlord, the shopkeeper, the pawnbroker, etc.

The lower strata of the middle class —the small trades-people, shopkeepers, and retired tradesmen generally, the handicraftsmen and peasants—all these sink gradually into the proletariat, partly because their diminutive capital does not suffice for the scale on which modern industry is carried on, and is swamped in the competition with the large capitalists, partly because their specialized skill is rendered worthless by new methods of production. Thus the proletariat is recruited from all classes of the population.

The proletariat goes through various stages of development. With its birth begins its struggle with the bourgeoisie. At first the contest is carried on by individual laborers, then by the workpeople of a factory, then by the operatives of one trade, in one locality, against the individual bourgeois who directly exploits them. They direct their attacks not against the bourgeois conditions of production, but against the instruments of production themselves; they destroy imported wares that compete with their labor, they smash to pieces machinery, they set factories ablaze, they seek to restore by force the vanished status of the workman of the Middle Ages.

At this stage the laborers still form an incoherent mass scattered over the whole country and broken up by their mutual competition. If anywhere they unite to form more compact bodies, this is not yet the consequence of their own active union, but of the union of the bourgeoisie, which class, in order to attain its own political ends, is compelled to set the whole proletariat in motion, and is moreover yet, for a time, able to do so. At this stage, therefore, the proletarians do not fight their enemies, but the enemies of their enemies, the non-industrial bourgeois, the petty bourgeoisie. Thus the whole historical movement is concentrated in the hands of the bourgeoisie; every victory so obtained is a victory for the bourgeoisie.

But with the development of industry

the proletariat not only increases in number; it becomes concentrated in greater masses, its strength grows, and it feels that strength more. The various interests and conditions of life within the ranks of the proletariat are more and more equalized, in proportion as machinery obliterates all distinctions of labor and nearly everywhere reduces wages to the same low level. The growing competition among the bourgeois and the resulting commercial crises make the wages of the workers ever more fluctuating. The unceasing improvement of machinery, ever more rapidly developing, makes their livelihood more and more precarious; the collisions between individual workmen and individual bourgeois take more and more the character of collisions between two classes. Thereupon the workers begin to form combinations (trade unions) against the bourgeois; they club together in order to keep up the rate of wages; they found permanent associations in order to make provision beforehand for these occasional revolts. Here and there the contest breaks out into riots.

Now and then the workers are victorious, but only for a time. The real fruit of their battles lies not in the immediate result, but in the ever expanding union of the workers. This union is helped on by the improved means of communication that are created by modern industry and that place the workers of different localities in contact with one another. It was just this contact that was needed to centralize the numerous local struggles, all of the same character, into one national struggle between classes. But every class struggle is a political struggle. And that union, to attain which the burghers of the Middle Ages, with their miserable highways, required centuries, the modern proletarians, thanks to railways, achieve in a few years.

This organization of the proletarians into a class, and consequently into a political party, is continually being upset again by the competition between the workers themselves. But it ever rises up again, stronger, firmer, mightier. It compels legislative recognition of particular interests of the workers by taking advantage of the divisions among the bourgeoisie itself. Thus the ten-hour bill in England was carried.

Altogether collisions between the classes of the old society further, in many ways, the course of development of the proletariat. The bourgeoisie finds itself involved in a constant battle. At first with the aristocracy; later on, with those portions of the bourgeoisie itself whose interests have become antagonistic to the progress of industry; at all times, with the bourgeoisie of foreign countries. In all these battles it sees itself compelled to appeal to the proletariat, to ask for its help, and thus to drag it into the political arena. The bourgeoisie itself, therefore, supplies the proletariat with its own elements of political and general education: in other words, it furnishes the proletariat with weapons for fighting the bourgeoisie.

Further, as we have already seen, entire sections of the ruling classes are, by the advance of industry, precipitated into the proletariat, or are at least threatened in their conditions of existence. These also supply the proletariat with fresh elements of enlightenment and progress.

Finally, in times when the class struggle nears the decisive hour, the process of dissolution going on within the ruling class, in fact within the whole range of old society, assumes such a violent, glaring character that a small section of the ruling class cuts itself adrift and joins the revolutionary class, the class that holds the future in its hands. Just as, therefore, at an earlier period, a section of the nobility went over to the bourgeoisie, so now a portion of the bourgeoisie goes over to the proletariat, and in particular a portion of the bourgeois ideologists, who have raised themselves to the level of comprehending theoretically the historical movement as a whole.

Of all the classes that stand face to face with the bourgeoisie today, the proletariat alone is a really revolutionary class. The other classes decay and finally disappear in the face of modern industry; the proletariat is its special and essential product.

The lower-middle class, the small manufacturer, the shopkeeper, the artisan, the peasant, all these fight against the bourgeoisie, to save from extinction their existence as fractions of the middle class. They are therefore not revolutionary, but conservative. Nay, more, they are reactionary, for they try to roll back the wheel of history. If by chance they are revolutionary they are so only in view of their impending transfer into the proletariat; they thus defend not their present but their future interests, they desert their own standpoint to place themselves at that of the proletariat.

The "dangerous class," the social scum, that passively rotting mass thrown off by the lowest layers of old society, may, here and there, be swept into the movement by a proletarian revolution; its conditions of life, however, prepare it far more for the part of a bribed tool of reactionary intrigue.

In the conditions of the proletariat those of old society at large are already virtually swamped. The proletarian is without property; his relation to his wife and children has no longer anything in common with the bourgeois family relations; modern industrial labor, modern subjection to capital, the same in England as in France, in America as in Germany, has stripped him of every trace of national character. Law, morality, religion are to him so many bourgeois prejudices, behind which lurk in ambush just as many bourgeois interests.

All the preceding classes that got the upper hand sought to fortify their already acquired status by subjecting society at large to their conditions of appropriation. The proletarians cannot become masters of their productive forces of society, except by abolishing their own previous mode of appropriation, and thereby also every other previous mode of appropriation. They have nothing of their own to secure and to fortify; their mission is to destroy all previous securities for, and insurances of, individual property.

All previous historical movements were movements of minorities, or in the interest of minorities. The proletarian movement is the self-conscious, independent movement of the immense majority, in the interests of the immense majority. The proletariat, the lowest stratum of our present society, cannot stir, cannot raise itself up, without the whole superincumbent strata of official society being sprung into the air.

Though not in substance, yet in form, the struggle of the proletariat with the bourgeoisie is at first a national struggle. The proletariat of each country must, of course, first of all settle matters with its own bourgeoisie.

In depicting the most general phases of the development of the proletariat, we traced the more or less veiled civil war, raging within existing society, up to the point where that war breaks out into open revolution, and where the violent overthrow of the bourgeoisie lays the foundation for the sway of the proletariat.

Hitherto every form of society has been based, as we have already seen, on the antagonism of oppressing and oppressed classes. But in order to oppress a class certain conditions must be assured to it under which it can, at least, continue its slavish existence. The serf, in the period of serfdom, raised himself to membership in the commune, just as the petty bourgeois, under the yoke of feudal absolutism, managed to develop into a bourgeois. The modern laborer, on the contrary, instead of rising with the progress of industry, sinks deeper and deeper below the conditions of existence of his own class. He becomes a pauper, and pauperism develops more rapidly than population and wealth. And here it becomes evident that the bourgeoisie is unfit any longer to be the ruling class in society, and to impose its conditions of existence upon society as an overriding law. It is unfit to rule because it is incompetent to assure an existence to its slave within his slavery, because it cannot help letting him sink into such a state that it has to feed him instead of being fed by him. Society can no longer live under this bourgeoisie: in other words, its existence is no longer compatible with society.

The essential condition for the existence, and for the sway of the bourgeois class, is the formation and augmentation of capital; the condition for capital is wage labor. Wage labor rests exclusively on competition between the laborers. The advance of industry, whose involuntary promoter is the bourgeoisie, replaces the isolation of the laborers, due to competition, by their revolutionary combination, due to association. The development of modern industry, therefore, cuts from under its feet the very foundation on which the bourgeoisie produces and appropriates products. What the bourgeoisie, therefore, produces, above all, is its own gravediggers. Its fall and the victory of the proletariat are equally inevitable.

15

Protestantism and the Rise of Modern Capitalism

MAX WEBER

The Uniqueness of Modern Capitalism

A product of modern European civilization, studying any problem of universal history, is bound to ask himself to what combination of circumstances the fact should be attributed that in Western civilization, and in Western civilization only, cultural phenomena have appeared which (as we like to

think) lie in a line of development having *universal* significance and value. . . .

. . . The Occident has developed capitalism both to a quantitative extent, and (carrying this quantitative development) in types, forms, and directions which have never existed elsewhere. All over the world there have been merchants, wholesale and retail, local and engaged in foreign trade. Loans of all kinds have been made, and there have been banks with the most various functions, at least comparable to ours of, say, the sixteenth century. . . . Whenever money finances of public bodies have existed, money-lenders have appeared, as in Babylon, Hellas, India, China, Rome. They have financed wars and piracy, contracts and building operations of all sorts. In overseas policy they have functioned as colonial entrepreneurs, as planters with slaves, or directly or indirectly forced labour, and have farmed domains, offices, and, above all, taxes. They have financed party leaders in elections and *condottieri* in civil wars. And, finally, they have been speculators in chances for pecuniary gain of all kinds. This kind of entrepreneur, the capitalistic adventurer, has existed everywhere. With the exception of trade and credit and banking transactions, their activities were predominantly of an irrational and speculative character, or directed to acquisition by force, above all the acquistion of booty, whether directly in war or in the form of continuous fiscal booty by exploitation of subjects.

The capitalism of promoters, large-scale speculators, concession hunters, and much modern financial capitalism even in peace time, but, above all, the capitalism especially concerned with exploiting wars, bears this stamp even in modern Western countries, and some, but only some, parts of large-scale international trade are closely related to it, to-day as always.

But in modern times the Occident has developed, in addition to this, a very different form of capitalism which has appeared nowhere else: the rational capitalistic organization of (formally) free labour. . . . Real domestic industries with free labour have definitely been proved to have existed in only a few isolated cases outside the Occident. . . .

Rational industrial organization, attuned to a regular market, and neither to political nor irrationally speculative opportunities for profit, is not, however, the only peculiarity of Western capitalism. The modern rational organ-

ization of the capitalistic enterprise would not have been possible without two other important factors in its development: the separation of business from the household, which completely dominates modern economic life, and closely connected with it, rational book-keeping. A spatial separation of places of work from those of residence exists elsewhere, as in the Oriental bazaar and in the *ergasteria* of other cultures. The development of capitalistic associations with their own accounts is also found in the Far East, the Near East, and in antiquity. But compared to the modern independence of business enterprises, those are only small beginnings. The reason for this was particularly that the indispensable requisites for this independence, our rational business book-keeping and our legal separation of corporate from personal property, were entirely lacking, or had only begun to develop. The tendency everywhere else was for acquisitive enterprises to arise as parts of a royal or manorial *household* (of the *oikos*), which is, as Rodbertus has perceived, with all its superficial similarity, a fundamentally different, even opposite, development.

However, all these peculiarities of Western capitalism have derived their significance in the last analysis only from their association with the capitalistic organization of labour. Even what is generally called commercialization, the development of negotiable securities and the rationalization of speculation, the exchanges, etc., is connected with it. For without the rational capitalistic organization of labour, all this, so far as it was possible at all, would have nothing like the same significance, above all for the social structure and all the specific problems of the modern Occident connected with it. Exact calculation—the basis of everything else —is only possible on a basis of free labour. . . .

Hence in a universal history of culture the central problem for us is . . . the origin of this sober bourgeois capitalism with its rational organization of free labour. Or in terms of cultural history, the problem is that of the origin of the Western bourgeois class and of its peculiarities. . . .

Now the peculiar modern Western form of capitalism has been, at first sight, strongly influenced by the development of technical possibilities. Its rationality is to-day essentially dependent on the calculability of the most important technical factors. But this means fundamentally that it is dependent on the peculiarities of modern science, especially the natural sciences based on mathematics and exact and rational experiment. On the other hand, the development of these sciences and of the technique resting upon them now receives important stimulation from these capitalistic interests in its practical economic application. It is true that the origin of Western science cannot be attributed to such interests. Calculation, even with decimals, and algebra have been carried on in India, where the decimal system was invented. But it was only made use of by developing capitalism in the West, while in India it led to no modern arithmetic or book-keeping. Neither was the origin of mathematics and mechanics determined by capitalistic interests. But the *technical* utilization of scientific knowledge, so important for the living conditions of the mass of people, was certainly encouraged by economic considerations, which were extremely favourable to it in the Occident. But this encouragement was derived from the peculiarities of the social structure of the Occident. We must hence ask, from *what* parts of that structure was it derived, since not all of them have been of equal importance?

Among those of undoubted importance are the rational structures of law and of administration. For modern rational capitalism has need, not only of the technical means of production, but of a calculable legal system and of administration in terms of formal rules. Without it adventurous and speculative trading capitalism and all sorts of politically determined capitalisms are possible, but no rational enterprise under individual initiative, with fixed capital and certainty of calculations. Such a legal system and such administration have been available for economic activity in a comparative state of legal and formalistic perfection only in the Occident. We must hence inquire where that law came from. Among other circumstances, capitalistic interests have in turn undoubtedly also helped, but by no means alone nor even principally, to prepare the way for the predominance in law and administration of a class of jurists specially trained in rational law. But these interests did not themselves create that law. Quite different forces were at work in this development. And why did not the capitalistic interests do the same in China or India? Why did not the scientific, the artistic, the political, or the economic development there enter upon that path or rationalization which is peculiar to the Occident?

For in all the above cases it is a question of the specific and peculiar rationalism of Western culture. Now by this term very different things may be understood, as the following discussion will repeatedly show. There is, for example, rationalization of mystical contemplation, that is of an attitude which, viewed from other departments of life, is especially irrational, just as much as there are rationalizations of economic life, of technique, of scientific research, of military training, of law and administration. Furthermore, each one of these fields may be rationalized in terms of very different ultimate values and ends, and what is rational from one point of view may well be irrational from another. Hence rationalizations of the most varied character have existed in various departments of life and in all areas of culture. To characterize their differences from the view-point of cultural history it is necessary to know what departments are rationalized, and in what direction. It is hence our first concern to work out and to explain genetically the special peculiarity of Occidental rationalism, and within this field that of the modern Occidental form. Every attempt at explanation must, recognizing the fundamental importance of the economic factor, above all take account of the economic conditions. But at the same time the opposite correlation must not be left out of consideration. For though the development of economic rationalism is partly dependent on rational technology and law, it is at the same time determined by the ability and disposition of men to adopt certain types of practical rational conduct. When these types have been obstructed by spiritual obstacles, the development of rational economic conduct has also met serious inner resistance. The magical and religious forces, and the ethical ideas of duty based upon them, have in the past always been among the most important formative influences on conduct. In the studies collected here we shall be concerned with . . . the influence of certain religious ideas on the development of an economic spirit, or the *ethos* of an economic system. In this case we are dealing with the connection of the spirit of modern economic life with the rational ethics of ascetic Protestantism. . . .

Protestantism and Modern Capitalism

In order to understand the connection between the fundamental religious ideas of ascetic Protestantism and its maxims for everyday economic conduct, it is necessary to examine with especial care such writings as have evidently been derived from ministerial practice. For a time in which the beyond meant everything, when the social position of the Christian depended upon his admission to the communion, the clergyman, through his ministry, Church discipline, and preaching, exercised an influence (as a glance at collections of *consilia, casus conscientiæ*, etc., shows) which we modern men are entirely unable to picture. In such a time the religious forces which express themselves through such channels are the decisive influences in the formation of national character. . . .

Since that side of English Puritanism which was derived from Calvinism gives the most consistent religious basis for the idea of the calling, we shall, . . . place one of its representatives at the centre of the discussion. Richard Baxter stands out above many other writers on Puritan ethics, both because of his eminently practical and realistic attitude, and, at the same time, because of the universal recognition accorded to his works, which have gone through many new editions and translations. He was a Presbyterian and an apologist of the Westminster Synod, but at the same time, like so many of the best spirits of his time, gradually grew away from the dogmas of pure Calvinism. At heart he opposed Cromwell's usurpation as he would any revolution. He was unfavourable to the sects and the fanatical enthusiasm of the saints, but was very broad-minded about external peculiarities and objective towards his opponents. He sought his field of labour most especially in the practical promotion of the moral life through the Church. In the pursuit of this end, as one of the most successful ministers known to history, he placed his services at the disposal of the Parliamentary Government, of Cromwell, and of the Restoration, until he retired from office under the last, before St. Bartholomew's day. His *Christian Directory* is the most complete compendium of Puritan ethics, and is continually adjusted to the practical experiences of his own ministerial activity. In comparison we shall make use of Spener's *Theologische Bedenken*, as representative of German Pietism, Barclay's *Apology* for the Quakers, and some other representatives of ascetic ethics, which, however, in the interest of space, will be limited as far as possible.

Now, in glancing at Baxter's *Saint's Everlasting Rest*, or his *Christian Directory*, or similar works of others, one is struck at first glance by the emphasis placed, in the discussion of wealth and its acquisition, on the ebionitic elements of the New Testament. Wealth as such is a great danger; its temptations never end, and its pursuit is not only senseless as compared with the dominating importance of the Kingdom of God, but it is morally suspect. Here asceticism seems to have turned much more sharply against the acquisition of earthly goods than it did in Calvin, who saw no hindrance to the effectiveness of the clergy in their wealth, but rather a thoroughly desirable enhancement of their prestige. Hence he permitted them to employ their means profitably. Examples of the condemnation of the pursuit of money and goods may be gathered without end from Puritan writings, and may be contrasted with the late mediæval ethical literature, which was much more open-minded on this point.

Moreover, these doubts were meant with perfect seriousness; only it is necessary to examine them somewhat more closely in order to understand their true ethical significance and implications. The real moral objection is to relaxation in the security of possession, the enjoyment of wealth with the consequence of idleness and the temptations of the flesh, above all of distraction from the pursuit of a righteous life. In fact, it is only because possession involves this danger of relaxation that it is objectionable at all. For the saints' everlasting rest is in the next world; on earth man must, to be certain of his state of grace, "do the works of him who sent him, as long as it is yet day." Not leisure and enjoyment, but only activity serves to increase the glory of God, according to the definite manifestations of His will.

Waste of time is thus the first and in principle the deadliest of sins. The span of human life is infinitely short and precious to make sure of one's own election. Loss of time through sociability, idle talk, luxury, even more sleep than is necessary for health, six to at most eight hours, is worthy of absolute moral condemnation. It does not yet hold, with Franklin, that time is money, but the proposition is true in a certain spiritual sense. It is infinitely valuable because every hour lost is lost to labour for the glory of God. Thus inactive contemplation is also valueless, or even directly reprehensible if it is at the expense of one's daily work. For it is less pleasing to God than the active performance of His will in a calling. Besides, Sunday is provided for that, and, according to Baxter, it is always those who are not diligent in their callings who have no time for God when the occasion demands it.

Accordingly, Baxter's principal work is dominated by the continually repeated, often almost passionate preaching of hard, continuous bodily or mental labour. It is due to a combination of two different motives. Labour is, on the one hand, an approved ascetic technique, as it always has been in the Western Church, in sharp contrast not only to the Orient but to almost all monastic rules the world over. It is in particular the specific defence against all those temptations which Puritanism united under the name of the unclean life, whose rôle for it was by no means small. The sexual asceticism of Puritanism differs only in degree, not in fundamental principle, from that of monasticism; and on account of the Puritan conception of marriage, its practical influence is more far-reaching than that of the latter. For sexual intercourse is permitted, even within marriage, only as the means willed by God for the increase of His glory according to the commandment, "Be fruitful and multiply." Along with a moderate vegetable diet and cold baths, the same prescription is given for all sexual temptations as is used against religious doubts and a sense of moral unworthiness: "Work hard in your calling." But the most important thing was that even beyond that labour came to be considered in itself the end of life, ordained as such by God. St. Paul's "He who will not work shall not eat" holds unconditionally for everyone. Unwillingness to work is symptomatic of the lack of grace.

Here the difference from the mediæval view-point becomes quite evident. Thomas Aquinas also gave an interpretation of that statement of St. Paul. But for him labour is only necessary *naturali ratione* for the maintenance of individual and community. Where this end is achieved, the precept ceases to have any meaning. Moreover, it holds only for the race, not for every individual. It does not apply to anyone who can live without labour on his possessions, and of course contemplation, as a spiritual form of action in the Kingdom of God, takes precedence over the commandment in its literal sense. Moreover, for the popular theology of the time, the highest form of monastic productivity lay in the increase of the *Thesaurus ecclesiæ* through prayer and chant.

Now only do these exceptions to the duty to labour naturally no longer hold for Baxter, but he holds most emphatically that wealth does not exempt anyone from the unconditional command. Even the wealthy shall not eat without working, for even though they do not need to labour to support their own needs, there is God's commandment which they, like the poor, must obey. For everyone without exception God's Providence has prepared a calling, which he should profess and in which he should labour. And this calling is not, as it was for the Lutheran, a fate to which he must submit and which he must make the best of, but God's commandment to the individual to work for the divine glory. This seemingly subtle difference had far-reaching psychological consequences, and became connected with a further development of the providential interpretation of the economic order which had begun in scholasticism.

The phenomenon of the division of labour and occupations in society had, among others, been interpreted by Thomas Aquinas, to whom we may most conveniently refer, as a direct consequence of the divine scheme of things. But the places assigned to each man in this cosmos follow *ex causis naturalibus* and are fortuitous (contingent in the Scholastic terminology). The differentiation of men into the classes and occupations established through historical development became for Luther, as we have seen, a direct result of the divine will. The perseverance of the individual in the place and within the limits which God had assigned to him was a religious duty. This was the more certainly the consequence since the relations of Lutheranism to the world were in general uncertain from the beginning and remained so. Ethical principles for the reform of the world could not be found in Luther's realm of ideas; in fact it never quite freed itself from Pauline indifference. Hence the world had to be accepted as it was, and this alone could be made a religious duty.

But in the Puritan view, the providential character of the play of private economic interests takes on a somewhat different emphasis. True to the Puritan tendency to pragmatic interpretations, the providential purpose of the division of labour is to be known by its fruits. On this point Baxter expresses himself in terms which more than once directly recall Adam Smith's well-known apotheosis of the division of labour. The specialization of occupations leads, since it makes the development of skill possible, to a quantitative and qualitative improvement in production, and thus serves the common good, which is identical with the good of the greatest possible number. So far, the motivation is purely utilitarian, and is closely related to the customary view-point of much of the secular literature of the time.

But the characteristic Puritan element appears when Baxter sets at the head of his discussion the statement that "outside of a well-marked calling the accomplishments of a man are only casual and irregular, and he spends more time in idleness than at work," and when he concludes it as follows: "and he [the specialized worker] will carry out his work in order while another remains in constant confusion, and his business knows neither time nor place . . . therefore is a certain calling the best for everyone." Irregular work, which the ordinary labourer is often forced to accept, is often unavoidable, but always an unwelcome state of transition. A man without a calling thus lacks the systematic, methodical character which is, as we have seen, demanded by worldly asceticism.

The Quaker ethic also holds that a man's life in his calling is an exercise in ascetic virtue, a proof of his state of grace through his conscientiousness, which is expressed in the care and method with which he pursues his calling. What God demands is not labour in itself, but rational labour in a call-

ing. In the Puritan concept of the calling the emphasis is always placed on this methodical character of worldly asceticism, not, as with Luther, on the acceptance of the lot which God has irretrievably assigned to man. . . .

Hence the question whether anyone may combine several callings is answered in the affirmative, if it is useful for the common good or one's own, and not injurious to anyone, and if it does not lead to unfaithfulness in one of the callings. Even a change of calling is by no means regarded as objectionable, if it is not thoughtless and is made for the purpose of pursuing a calling more pleasing to God, which means, on general principles, one more useful.

It is true that the usefulness of a calling, and thus its favour in the sight of God, is measured primarily in moral terms, and thus in terms of the importance of the goods produced in it for the community. But a further, and, above all, in practice the most important, criterion is found in private profitableness. For if that God, whose hand the Puritan sees in all the occurrences of life, shows one of His elect a chance of profit, he must do it with a purpose. Hence the faithful Christian must follow the call by taking advantage of the opportunity. "If God show you a way in which you may lawfully get more than in another way (without wrong to your soul or to any other), if you refuse this, and choose the less gainful way, you cross one of the ends of your calling, and you refuse to be God's steward, and to accept His gifts and use them for Him when He requireth it: you may labour to be rich for God, though not for the flesh and sin."

Wealth is thus bad ethically only in so far as it is a temptation to idleness and sinful enjoyment of life, and its acquisition is bad only when it is with the purpose of later living merrily and without care. But as a performance of duty in a calling it is not only morally permissible, but actually enjoined. The parable of the servant who was rejected because he did not increase the talent which was entrusted to him seemed to say so directly. To wish to be poor was, it was often argued, the same as wishing to be unhealthy; it is objectionable as a glorification of works and derogatory to the glory of God. Especially begging, on the part of one able to work, is not only the sin of slothfulness, but a violation of the duty of brotherly love according to the Apostle's own word.

The emphasis on the ascetic importance of a fixed calling provided an ethical justification of the modern specialized division of labour. In a similar way the providential interpretation of profit-making justified the activities of the business man. The superior indulgence of the *seigneur* and the parvenu ostentation of the *nouveau riche* are equally detestable to asceticism. But, on the other hand, it has the highest ethical appreciation of the sober, middle-class, self-made man. "God blesseth His trade" is a stock remark about those good men who had successfully followed the divine hints. The whole power of the God of the Old Testament, who rewards His people for their obedience in this life, necessarily exercised a similar influence on the Puritan who, following Baxter's advice, compared his own state of grace with that of the heroes of the Bible, and in the process interpreted the statements of the Scriptures as the articles of a book of statutes. . . .

In addition to the relationships already pointed out, it is important for the general inner attitude of the Puritans, above all, that the belief that they were God's chosen people saw in them a great renaissance. Even the kindly Baxter thanked God that he was born in England, and thus in the true Church, and nowhere else. This thankfulness for one's own perfection by the grace of God penetrated the attitude toward life of the Puritan middle class, and played its part in developing that formalistic, hard, correct character which was peculiar to the men of that heroic age of capitalism.

Let us now try to clarify the points in which the Puritan idea of the calling and the premium it placed upon ascetic conduct was bound directly to influence the development of a capitalistic way of life. As we have seen, this asceticism turned with all its force against one thing: the spontaneous enjoyment of life and all it had to offer. This is perhaps most characteristically brought out in the struggle over the *Book of Sports* which James I and Charles I made into law expressly as a means of counteracting Puritanism, and which the latter ordered to be read from all the pulpits. The fanatical opposition of the Puritans to the ordinances of the King, permitting certain popular amusements on Sunday outside of Church hours by law, was not only explained by the disturbance of the Sabbath rest, but also by resentment against the intentional diversion from the ordered life of the saint, which it caused. And, on his side, the King's threats of severe punishment for every attack on the legality of those sports were motivated by his purpose of breaking the anti-authoritarian ascetic tendency of Puritanism, which was so dangerous to the State. The feudal and monarchical forces protected the pleasure seekers against the rising middle-class morality and the anti-authoritarian ascetic conventicles, just as to-day capitalistic society tends to protect those willing to work against the class morality of the proletariat and the anti-authoritarian trade union.

As against this the Puritans upheld their decisive characteristic, the principle of ascetic conduct. For otherwise the Puritan aversion to sport, even for the Quakers, was by no means simply one of principle. Sport was accepted if it served a rational purpose, that of recreation necessary for physical efficiency. But as a means for the spontaneous expression of undisciplined impulses, it was under suspicion; and in so far as it became purely a means of enjoyment, or awakened pride, raw instincts or the irrational gambling instinct, it was of course strictly condemned. Impulsive enjoyment of life, which leads away both from work in a calling and from religion, was as such the enemy of rational asceticism, whether in the form of seigneurial sports, or the enjoyment of the dance-hall or the public-house of the common man. . . .

Its attitude was thus suspicious and often hostile to the aspects of culture without any immediate religious value. It is not, however, true that the ideals of Puritanism implied a solemn, narrow-minded contempt of culture. Quite the contrary is the case at least for science, with the exception of the hatred of Scholasticism. Moreover, the great men of the Puritan movement were thoroughly steeped in the culture of the Renaissance. The sermons of the Presbyterian divines abound with classical allusions, and even the Radicals, although they objected to it, were not ashamed to display that kind of learning in theological polemics. Perhaps no country was ever so full of graduates as New England in the first generation of its existence. The satire of their opponents, such as, for instance, Butler's *Hudibras*, also attacks primarily the pendantry and highly trained dialectics of the Puritans. This is partially due to the religious valuation of knowledge which followed from their attitude to the Catholic *fides implicita*.

But the situation is quite different when one looks at non-scientific literature, and especially the fine arts. Here asceticism descended like a frost on

the life of "Merrie old England." And not only worldly merriment felt its effect. The Puritan's ferocious hatred of everything which smacked of superstition, of all survivals of magical or sacramental salvation, applied to the Christmas festivities and the May Pole and all spontaneous religious art. . . .

The theatre was obnoxious to the Puritans, and with the strict exclusion of the erotic and of nudity from the realm of toleration, a radical view of either literature or art could not exist. The conceptions of idle talk, of superfluities, and of vain ostentation, all designations of an irrational attitude without objective purpose, thus not ascetic, and especially not serving the glory of God, but of man, were always at hand to serve in deciding in favour of sober utility as against any artistic tendencies. This was especially true in the case of decoration of the person, for instance clothing. That powerful tendency toward uniformity of life, which to-day so immensely aids the capitalistic interest in the standardization of production, had its ideal foundations in the repudiation of all idolatry of the flesh. . . .

Although we cannot here enter upon a discussion of the influence of Puritanism in all these directions, we should call attention to the fact that the toleration of pleasure in cultural goods, which contributed to purely æsthetic or athletic enjoyment, certainly always ran up against one characteristic limitation: they must not cost anything. Man is only a trustee of the goods which have come to him through God's grace. He must, like the servant in the parable, give an account of every penny entrusted to him, and it is at least hazardous to spend any of it for a purpose which does not serve the glory of God but only one's own enjoyment. What person, who keeps his eyes open, has not met representatives of this view-point even in the present?

The idea of a man's duty to his possessions, to which he subordinates himself
as an obedient steward, or even as an
acquisitive machine, bears with chilling
weight on his life. The greater the possessions the heavier, if the ascetic attitude toward life stands the test, the
feeling of responsibility for them, for
holding them undiminished for the
glory of God and increasing them by
restless effort. . . .

This worldly Protestant asceticism,
as we may recapitulate up to this point,
acted powerfully against the spontaneous enjoyment of possessions; it restricted consumption, especially of
luxuries. On the other hand, it had the
psychological effect of freeing the acquisition of goods from the inhibitions
of traditionalistic ethics. It broke the
bonds of the impulse of acquisition in
that it not only legalized it, but (in the
sense discussed) looked upon it as directly willed by God. The campaign
against the temptations of the flesh, and
the dependence on external things, was,
as besides the Puritans the great
Quaker apologist Barclay expressly
says, not a struggle against the rational
acquistion, but against the irrational
use of wealth.

But this irrational use was exemplified in the outward forms of luxury
which their code condemned as idolatry
of the flesh, however natural they had
appeared to the feudal mind. On the
other hand, they approved the rational
and utilitarian uses of wealth which
were willed by God for the needs of the
individual and the community. They
did not wish to impose mortification
on the man of wealth, but the use of
his means for necessary and practical
things. The idea of comfort characteristically limits the extent of ethically
permissible expenditures. It is naturally
no accident that the development of a
manner of living consistent with that
idea may be observed earliest and most
clearly among the most consistent rep-

resentatives of this whole attitude toward life. Over against the glitter and
ostentation of feudal magnificence,
which, resting on an unsound economic
basis, prefers a sordid elegance to a
sober simplicity, they set the clean and
solid comfort of the middle-class home
as an ideal.

On the side of the production of
private wealth, asceticism condemned
both dishonesty and impulsive avarice.
What was condemned as covetousness,
Mammonism, etc., was the pursuit of
riches for their own sake. For wealth
in itself was a temptation. But here
asceticism was the power "which ever
seeks the good but ever creates evil";
what was evil in its sense was possession and its temptations. For, in conformity with the Old Testament and in
analogy to the ethical valuation of good
works, asceticism looked upon the pursuit of wealth as an end in itself as
highly reprehensible; but the attainment of it as a fruit of labour in a
calling was a sign of God's blessing.
And even more important: the religious
valuation of restless, continuous, systematic work in a worldly calling, as
the highest means to asceticism, and at
the same time the surest and most evident proof of rebirth and genuine faith,
must have been the most powerful conceivable lever for the expansion of that
attitude toward life which we have here
called the spirit of capitalism.

When the limitation of consumption
is combined with this release of acquisitive activity, the inevitable practical
result is obvious: accumulation of capital through ascetic compulsion to save.
The restraints which were imposed
upon the consumption of wealth naturally served to increase it by making
possible the productive investment of
capital. How strong this influence was
is not, unfortunately, susceptible of
exact statistical demonstration. In New
England the connection is so evident
that it did not escape the eye of so

discerning a historian as Doyle. But also in Holland, which was really only dominated by strict Calvinism for seven years, the greater simplicity of life in the more seriously religious circles, in combination with great wealth, led to an excessive propensity to accumulation. . . .

As far as the influence of the Puritan outlook extended, under all circumstances—and this is, of course, much more important than the mere encouragement of capital accumulation—it favoured the development of a rational bourgeois economic life; it was the most important, and above all the only consistent influence in the development of that life. It stood at the cradle of the modern economic man.

To be sure, these Puritanical ideals tended to give way under excessive pressure from the temptations of wealth, as the Puritans themselves knew very well. With great regularity we find the most genuine adherents of Puritanism among the classes which were rising from the lowly status, the small bourgeois and farmers, while the *beati possidentes*, even among Quakers, are often found tending to repudiate the old ideals. It was the same fate which again and again befell the predecessor of this worldly asceticism, the monastic asceticism of the Middle Ages. In the latter case, when rational economic activity had worked out its full effects by strict regulation of conduct and limitation of consumption, the wealth accumulated either succumbed directly to the nobility, as in the time before the Reformation, or monastic discipline threatened to break down, and one of the numerous reformations became necessary.

In fact the whole history of monasticism is in a certain sense the history of a continual struggle with the problem of the secularizing influence of wealth. The same is true on a grand scale of the worldly asceticism of Puritanism.

The great revival of Methodism, which preceded the expansion of English industry toward the end of the eighteenth century, may well be compared with such a monastic reform. We may hence quote here a passage from John Wesley himself which might well serve as a motto for everything which has been said above. For it shows that the leaders of these ascetic movements understood the seemingly paradoxical relationships which we have here analysed perfectly well, and in the same sense that we have given them. He wrote:

I fear, wherever riches have increased, the essence of religion has decreased in the same proportion. Therefore I do not see how it is possible, in the nature of things, for any revival of true religion to continue long. For religion must necessarily produce both industry and frugality, and these cannot but produce riches. But as riches increase, so will pride, anger, and love of the world in all its branches. How then is it possible that Methodism, that is, a religion of the heart, though it flourishes now as a green bay tree, should continue in this state? For the Methodists in every place grow diligent and frugal; consequently they increase in goods. Hence they proportionately increase in pride, in anger, in the desire of the flesh, the desire of the eyes, and the pride of life. So, although the form of religion remains, the spirit is swiftly vanishing away. Is there no way to prevent this—this continual decay of pure religion? We ought not to prevent people from being diligent and frugal; *we must exhort all Christians to gain all they can, and to save all they can; that is, in effect, to grow rich.* . . .

What the great religious epoch of the seventeenth century bequeathed to its utilitarian successor was, . . . above all an amazingly good, we may even say a pharisaically good, conscience in the acquisition of money, so long as it took place legally. . . .

A specifically bourgeois economic ethic had grown up. With the consciousness of standing in the fullness of God's grace and being visibly blessed by Him, the bourgeois business man, as long as he remained within the bounds of formal correctness, as long as his moral conduct was spotless and the use to which he put his wealth was not objectionable, could follow his pecuniary interests as he would and feel that he was fulfilling a duty in doing so. The power of religious asceticism provided him in addition with sober, conscientious, and unusually industrious workmen, who clung to their work as to a life purpose willed by God.

Finally, it gave him the comforting assurance that the unequal distribution of the goods of this world was a special dispensation of Divine Providence, which in these differences, as in particular grace, pursued secret ends unknown to men. Calvin himself had made the much-quoted statement that only when the people, i.e. the mass of labourers and craftsmen, were poor did they remain obedient to God. In the Netherlands (Pieter de la Court and others), that had been secularized to the effect that the mass of men only labour when necessity forces them to do so. This formulation of a leading idea of capitalistic economy later entered into the current theories of the productivity of low wages. Here also, with the dying out of the religious root, the utilitarian interpretation crept in unnoticed, in the line of development which we have again and again observed. . . .

Now naturally the whole ascetic literature of almost all denominations is saturated with the idea that faithful labour, even at low wages, on the part of those whom life offers no other opportunities, is highly pleasing to God. In this respect Protestant Asceticism added in itself nothing new. But it not only deepened this idea most powerfully, it also created the force which was alone decisive for its effectiveness: the psychological sanction of it through the conception of this labour as a calling, as the best, often in the last analy-

sis the only means of attaining certainty of grace. And on the other hand it legalized the exploitation of this specific willingness to work, in that it also interpreted the employer's business activity as a calling. It is obvious how powerfully the exclusive search for the Kingdom of God only through the fulfilment of duty in the calling, and the strict asceticism which Church discipline naturally imposed, especially on the propertyless classes, was bound to affect the productivity of labour in the capitalistic sense of the word. The treatment of labour as a calling became as characteristic of the modern worker as the corresponding attitude toward acquisition of the business man. It was a perception of this situation, new at his time, which caused so able an observer as Sir William Petty to attribute the economic power of Holland in the seventeenth century to the fact that the very numerous dissenters in that country (Calvinists and Baptists) "are for the most part thinking, sober men, and such as believe that Labour and Industry is their duty towards God." . . .

One of the fundamental elements of the spirit of modern capitalism, and not only of that but of all modern culture: rational conduct on the basis of the idea of the calling, was born—that is what this discussion has sought to demonstrate—from the spirit of Christian asceticism. . . .

The Puritan wanted to work in a calling; we are forced to do so. For when asceticism was carried out of monastic cells into everyday life, and began to dominate worldly morality, it did its part in building the tremendous cosmos of the modern economic order. This order is now bound to the technical and economic conditions of machine production which to-day determine the lives of all the individuals who are born into this mechanism, not only those directly concerned with economic acquisition, with irresistible force. Perhaps it will so determine them until the last ton of fossilized coal is burnt. In Baxter's view the care for external goods should only lie on the shoulders of the "saint like a light cloak, which can be thrown aside at any moment." But fate decreed that the cloak should become an iron cage.

Since asceticism undertook to remodel the world and to work out its ideals in the world, material goods have gained an increasing and finally an inexorable power over the lives of men as at no previous period in history. Today the spirit of religious asceticism—whether finally, who knows?—has escaped from the cage. But victorious capitalism, since it rests on mechanical foundations, needs its support no longer. The rosy blush of its laughing heir, the Enlightenment, seems also to be irretrievably fading, and the idea of duty in one's calling prowls about in our lives like the ghost of dead religious beliefs. Where the fulfilment of the calling cannot directly be related to the highest spiritual and cultural values, or when, on the other hand, it need not be felt simply as economic compulsion, the individual generally abandons the attempt to justify it at all. In the field of its highest development, in the United States, the pursuit of wealth, stripped of its religious and ethical meaning, tends to become associated with purely mundane passions, which often actually give it the character of sport.

No one knows who will live in this cage in the future, or whether at the end of this tremendous development entirely new prophets will arise, or there will be a great rebirth of old ideas and ideals, or, if neither, mechanized petrification, embellished with a sort of convulsive self-importance. For of the last stage of this cultural development, it might well be truly said: "Specialists without spirit, sensualists without heart; this nullity imagines that it has attained a level of civilization never before achieved."

But this bring us to the world of judgments of value and of faith, with which this purely historical discussion need not be burdened. The next task would be rather to show the significance of ascetic rationalism, which has only been touched in the foregoing sketch, for the content of practical social ethics, thus for the types or organization and the functions of social groups from the conventicle to the State. Then its relations to humanistic rationalism, its ideals of life and cultural influence; further to the development of philosophical and scientific empiricism, to technical development and to spiritual ideals would have to be analysed. Then its historical development from the mediæval beginnings of worldly asceticism to its dissolution into pure utilitarianism would have to be traced out through all the areas of ascetic religion. Only then could the quantitative cultural significance of ascetic Protestantism in its relation to the other plastic elements of modern culture be estimated.

Here we have only attempted to trace the fact and the direction of its influence to their motives in one, though a very important point. But it would also further be necessary to investigate how Protestant Asceticism was in turn influenced in its development and its character by the totality of social conditions, especially economic. The modern man is in general, even with the best will, unable to give religious ideas a significance for culture and national character which they deserve. But it is, of course, not my aim to substitute for a one-sided materialistic an equally one-sided spiritualistic causal interpretation of culture and of history. Each is equally possible, but each, if it does not serve as the preparation, but as the conclusion of an investigation, accomplishes equally little in the interest of historical truth.

B Theories of the Human Consequences of the Industrial Transformation

16
Alienated Labour

KARL MARX

. . . Thus we have now to grasp the real connexion between this whole system of alienation—private property, acquisitiveness, the separation of labour, capital and land, exchange and competition, value and the devaluation of man, monopoly and competition—and the system of *money*.

Let us not begin our explanation, as does the economist, from a legendary primordial condition. Such a primordial condition does not explain anything; it merely removes the question into a grey and nebulous distance. It asserts as a fact or event what it should deduce, namely, the necessary relation between two things; for example, between the

From *Karl Marx: Early Writings* translated and edited by T. B. Bottomore (London, 1963, C. A. Watts). Reprinted by permission of the publishers.

division of labour and exchange. In the same way theology explains the origin of evil by the fall of man; that is, it asserts as a historical fact what it should explain.

We shall begin from a *contemporary* economic fact. The worker becomes poorer the more wealth he produces and the more his production increases in power and extent. The worker becomes an ever cheaper commodity the more goods he creates. The *devaluation* of the human world increases in direct relation with the *increase in value* of the world of things. Labour does not only create goods; it also produces itself and the worker as a *commodity*, and indeed in the same proportion as it produces goods.

This fact simply implies that the object produced by labour, its product, now stands opposed to it as an *alien being*, as a *power independent* of the producer. The product of labour is labour which has been embodied in an object and turned into a physical thing; this product is an *objectification* of labour. The performance of work is at the same time its objectification. The performance of work appears in the sphere of political economy as a *vitiation* of the worker, objectification as a *loss* and as *servitude to the object*, and appropriation as *alienation*.

So much does the performance of work appear as vitiation that the worker is vitiated to the point of starvation. So much does objectification appear as loss of the object that the worker is deprived of the most essential things not only of life but also of work. Labour itself becomes an object which he can acquire only by the greatest effort and with unpredictable interruptions. So much does the appropriation of the object appear as alienation that the more objects the worker produces the fewer he can possess and the more he falls under the domination of his product, of capital.

All these consequences follow from the fact that the worker is related to the *product of his labour* as to an *alien* object. For it is clear on this presupposition that the more the worker expends himself in work the more powerful becomes the world of objects which he creates in face of himself, the poorer he becomes in his inner life, and the less he belongs to himself. It is just the same as in religion. The more of himself man attributes to God the less he has left in himself. The worker puts his life into the object, and his life then belongs no longer to himself but to the object. The greater his activity, therefore, the less he possesses. What is embodied in the product of his labour is no longer his own. The greater this product is, therefore, the more he is diminished. The *alienation* of the

worker in his product means not only that his labour becomes an object, assumes an *external* existence, but that it exists independently, *outside himself*, and alien to him, and that it stands opposed to him as an autonomous power. The life which he has given to the object sets itself against him as an alien and hostile force.

Let us now examine more closely the phenomenon of *objectification*; the worker's production and the *alienation* and *loss* of the object it produces, which is involved in it. The worker can create nothing without *nature*, without the *sensuous external world*. The latter is the material in which his labour is realized, in which it is active, out of which and through which it produces things.

But just as nature affords the *means of existence* of labour, in the sense that labour cannot *live* without objects upon which it can be exercised, so also it provides the *means of existence* in a narrower sense; namely the means of physical existence for the *worker* himself. Thus, the more the worker *appropriates* the external world of sensuous nature by his labour the more he deprives himself of *means of existence*, in two respects: first, that the sensuous external world becomes progressively less an object belonging to his labour or a means of existence of his labour, and secondly, that it becomes progressively less a means of existence in the direct sense, a means for the physical subsistence of the worker.

In both respects, therefore, the worker becomes a slave of the object; first, in that he receives an *object of work*, i.e. receives *work*, and secondly, in that he receives *means of subsistence*. Thus the object enables him to exist, first as a *worker* and secondly, as a *physical subject*. The culmination of this enslavement is that he can only maintain himself as a *physical subject* so far as he is a *worker*, and that it is only as a *physical subject* that he is a worker.

(The alienation of the worker in his object is expressed as follows in the laws of political economy: the more the worker produces the less he has to consume; the more value he creates the more worthless he becomes; the more refined his product the more crude and misshapen the worker; the more civilized the product the more barbarous the worker; the more powerful the work the more feeble the worker; the more the work manifests intelligence the more the worker declines in intelligence and becomes a slave of nature.)

Political economy conceals the alienation in the nature of labour in so far as it does not examine the direct relationship between the worker (work) and production. Labour certainly produces marvels for the rich but it produces privation for the worker. It produces palaces, but hovels for the worker. It produces beauty, but deformity for the worker. It replaces labour by machinery, but it casts some of the workers back into a barbarous kind of work and turns the others into machines. It produces intelligence, but also stupidity and cretinism for the workers.

The direct relationship of labour to its products is the relationship of the worker to the objects of his production. The relationship of property owners to the objects of production and to production itself is merely a *consequence* of this first relationship and confirms it. We shall consider this second aspect later.

Thus, when we ask what is the important relationship of labour, we are concerned with the relationship of the *worker* to production.

So far we have considered the alienation of the worker only from one aspect; namely, *his relationship with the products of his labour.* However, alienation appears not merely in the result but also in the *process* of production, within

productive activity itself. How could the worker stand in an alien relationship to the product of his activity if he did not alienate himself in the act of production itself? The product is indeed only the *résumé* of activity, of production. Consequently, if the product of labour is alienation, production itself must be active alienation—the alienation of activity and the activity of alienation. The alienation of the object of labour merely summarizes the alienation in the work activity itself.

What constitutes the alienation of labour? First, that the work is *external* to the worker, that it is not part of his nature; and that, consequently, he does not fulfill himself in his work but denies himself, has a feeling of misery rather than well-being, does not develop freely his mental and physical energies but is physically exhausted and mentally debased. The worker, therefore, feels himself at home only during his leisure time, whereas at work he feels homeless. His work is not voluntary but imposed, *forced labour.* It is not the satisfaction of a need, but only a *means* for satisfying other needs. Its alien character is clearly shown by the fact that as soon as there is no physical or other compulsion it is avoided like the plague. External labour, labour in which man alienates himself, is a labour of self-sacrifice, of mortification. Finally, the external character of work for the worker is shown by the fact that it is not his own work but work for someone else, that in work he does not belong to himself but to another person.

Just as in religion the spontaneous activity of human fantasy, of the human brain and heart, reacts independently as an alien activity of gods or devils upon the individual, so the activity of the worker is not his own spontaneous activity. It is another's activity and a loss of his own spontaneity.

We arrive at the result that man (the worker) feels himself to be freely active only in his animal functions—eating, drinking and procreating, or at most also in his dwelling and in personal adornment—while in his human functions he is reduced to an animal. The animal becomes human and the human becomes animal.

Eating, drinking and procreating are of course also genuine human functions. But abstractly considered, apart from the environment of human activities, and turned into final and sole ends, they are animal functions.

We have now considered the act of alienation of practical human activity, labour, from two aspects: (1) the relationship of the worker to the *product of labour* as an alien object which dominates him. This relationship is at the same time the relationship to the sensuous external world, to natural objects, as an alien and hostile world; (2) the relationship of labour to the *act of production* within *labour*. This is the relationship of the worker to his own activity as something alien and not belonging to him, activity as suffering (passivity), strength as powerlessness, creation as emasculation, the *personal* physical and mental energy of the worker, his personal life (for what is life but activity?), as an activity which is directed against himself, independent of him and not belonging to him. This is *self-alienation* as against the above-mentioned alienation of the *thing*.

We have now to infer a third characteristic of *alienated labour* from the two we have considered.

Man is a species-being not only in the sense that he makes the community (his own as well as those of other things) his object both practically and theoretically, but also (and this is simply another expression for the same thing) in the sense that he treats himself as the present, living species, as a *universal* and consequently free being.

Species-life, for man as for animals, has its physical basis in the fact that

man (like animals) lives from inorganic nature, and since man is more universal than an animal so the range of inorganic nature from which he lives is more universal. Plants, animals, minerals, air, light, etc. constitute, from the theoretical aspect, a part of human consciousness as objects of natural science and art; they are man's spiritual inorganic nature, his intellectual means of life, which he must first prepare for enjoyment and perpetuation. So also, from the practical aspect, they form a part of human life and activity. In practice man lives only from these natural products, whether in the form of food, heating, clothing, housing, etc. The universality of man appears in practice in the universality which makes the whole of nature into his inorganic body: (1) as a direct means of life; and equally (2) as the material object and instrument of his life activity. Nature is the inorganic body of man; that is to say nature, excluding the human body itself. To say that man *lives* from nature means that nature is his *body* with which he must remain in a continuous interchange in order not to die. The statement that the physical and mental life of man, and nature, are interdependent means simply that nature is interdependent with itself, for man is a part of nature.

Since alienated labour: (1) alienates nature from man; and (2) alienates man from himself, from his own active function, his life activity; so it alienates him from the species. It makes *species-life* into a means of individual life. In the first place it alienates species-life and individual life, and secondly, it turns the latter, as an abstraction, into the purpose of the former, also in its abstract and alienated form.

For labour, *life activity, productive life*, now appear to man only as *means* for the satisfaction of a need, the need to maintain his physical existence. Productive life is, however, species-life.

It is life creating life. In the type of life activity resides the whole character of a species, its species-character; and free, conscious activity is the species-character of human beings. Life itself appears only as a *means of life*.

The animal is one with its life activity. It does not distinguish the activity from itself. It is *its activity*. But man makes his life activity itself an object of his will and consciousness. He has a conscious life activity. It is not a determination with which he is completely identified. Conscious life activity distinguishes man from the life activity of animals. Only for this reason is he a species-being. Or rather, he is only a self-conscious being, i.e. his own life is an object for him, because he is a species-being. Only for this reason is his activity free activity. Alienated labour reverses the relationship, in that man because he is a self-conscious being makes his life activity, his *being*, only a means for his *existence*.

The practical construction of an *objective world*, the *manipulation* of inorganic nature, is the confirmation of man as a conscious species-being, i.e. a being who treats the species as his own being or himself as a species-being. Of course, animals also produce. They construct nests, dwellings, as in the case of bees, beavers, ants, etc. But they only produce what is strictly necessary for themselves or their young. They produce only in a single direction, while man produces universally. They produce only under the compulsion of direct physical needs, while man produces when he is free from physical need and only truly produces in freedom from such need. Animals produce only themselves, while man reproduces the whole of nature. The products of animal production belong directly to their physical bodies, while man is free in face of his product. Animals construct only in accordance with the standards and needs of the species to which they belong, while man knows how to produce in accordance with the standards of every species and knows how to apply the appropriate standard to the object. Thus man constructs also in accordance with the laws of beauty.

It is just in his work upon the objective world that man really proves himself as a *species-being*. This production is his active species-life. By means of it nature appears as *his* work and his reality. The object of labour is, therefore, the *objectification of man's species-life*; for he no longer reproduces himself merely intellectually, as in consciousness, but actively and in a real sense, and he sees his own reflection in a world which he has constructed. While, therefore, alienated labour takes away the object of production from man, it also takes away his *species-life*, his real objectivity as a species-being, and changes his advantage over animals into a disadvantage in so far as his inorganic body, nature, is taken from him.

Just as alienated labour transforms free and self-directed activity into a means, so it transforms the species-life of man into a means of physical existence.

Consciousness, which man has from his species, is transformed through alienation so that species-life becomes only a means for him. (3) Thus alienated labour turns the *species-life of man*, and also nature as his mental species-property, into an *alien* being and into a *means* for his *individual existence*. It alienates from man his own body, external nature, his mental life and his *human life*. (4) A direct consequence of the alienation of man from the product of his labour, from his life activity and from his species-life, is that *man is alienated from other men*. When man confronts himself he also confronts *other* men. What is true of man's relationship to his work, to the product of his work and to himself, is also true of his relationship to other men, to their labour and to the objects of their labour.

In general, the statement that man is alienated from his species-life means that each man is alienated from others, and that each of the others is likewise alienated from human life.

Human alienation, and above all the relation of man to himself, is first realized and expressed in the relationship between each man and other men. Thus in the relationship of alienated labour every man regards other men according to the standards and relationships in which he finds himself placed as a worker.

We began with an economic fact, the alienation of the worker and his production. We have expressed this fact in conceptual terms as *alienated labour*, and in analysing the concept we have merely analysed an economic fact.

Let us now examine further how this concept of alienated labour must express and reveal itself in reality. If the product of labour is alien to me and confronts me as an alien power, to whom does it belong? If my own activity does not belong to me but is an alien, forced activity, to whom does it belong? To a being *other* than myself. And who is this being? The *gods?* It is apparent in the earliest stages of advanced production, e.g. temple building, etc. in Egypt, India, Mexico, and in the service rendered to gods, that the product belonged to the gods. But the gods alone were never the lords of labour. And no more was *nature*. What a contradiction it would be if the more man subjugates nature by his labour, and the more the marvels of the gods are rendered superfluous by the marvels of industry, the more he should abstain from his joy in producing and his enjoyment of the product for love of these powers.

The *alien* being to whom labour and the product of labour belong, to whose service labour is devoted, and to whose enjoyment the product of labour goes, can only be *man* himself. If the product of labour does not belong to the worker, but confronts him as an alien power, this can only be because it belongs to *a man other than the worker*. If his activity is a torment to him it must be a source of *enjoyment* and pleasure to another. Not the gods, nor nature, but only man himself can be this alien power over men.

Consider the earlier statement that the relation of man to himself is first *realized, objectified*, through his relation to other men. If he is related to the product of his labour, his objectified labour, as to an *alien*, hostile, powerful and independent object, he is related in such a way that another alien, hostile, powerful and independent man is the lord of this object. If he is related to his own activity as to unfree activity, then he is related to it as activity in the service, and under the domination, coercion and yoke, of another man.

Every self-alienation of man, from himself and from nature, appears in the relation which he postulates between other men and himself and nature. Thus religious self-alienation is necessarily exemplified in the relation between laity and priest, or, since it is here a question of the spiritual world, between the laity and a mediator. In the real world of practice this self-alienation can only be expressed in the real, practical relation of man to his fellow men. The medium through which alienation occurs is itself a *practical* one. Through alienated labour, therefore, man not only produces his relation to the object and to the process of production as to alien and hostile men; he also produces the relation of other men to his production and his product, and the relation between himself and other men. Just as he creates his own production as a vitiation, a punishment, and his own product as a loss, as a product which does not belong to him, so he creates the domination of the non-producer over production and its product. As he alienates his own activity, so he bestows upon the stranger an activity which is not his own.

We have so far considered this relation only from the side of the worker, and later on we shall consider it also from the side of the non-worker.

Thus, through alienated labour the worker creates the relation of another man, who does not work and is outside the work process, to this labour. The relation of the worker to work also produces the relation of the capitalist (or whatever one likes to call the lord of labour) to work. *Private property* is, therefore, the product, the necessary result, of *alienated labour*, of the external relation of the worker to nature and to himself.

Private property is thus derived from the analysis of the concept of *alienated labour*; that is, alienated man, alienated labour, alienated life, and estranged man.

We have, of course, derived the concept of *alienated labour* (*alienated life*) from political economy, from an analysis of the *movement of private property*. But the analysis of this concept shows that although private property appears to be the basis and cause of alienated labour, it is rather a consequence of the latter, just as the gods are *fundamentally* not the cause but the product of confusions of human reason. At a later stage, however, there is a reciprocal influence.

Only in the final stage of the development of private property is its secret revealed, namely, that it is on one hand the *product* of alienated labour, and on the other hand the *means* by which

labour is alienated, *the realization of this alienation.*

This elucidation throws light upon several unresolved controversies—

1. Political economy begins with labour as the real soul of production and then goes on to attribute nothing to labour and everything to private property. Proudhon, faced by this contradiction, has decided in favour of labour against private property. We perceive, however, that this apparent contradiction is the contradiction of *alienated labour* with itself and that political economy has merely formulated the laws of alienated labour.

We also observe, therefore, that *wages* and *private property* are identical, for wages, like the product or object of labour, labour itself remunerated, are only a necessary consequence of the alienation of labour. In the wage system labour appears not as an end in itself but as the servant of wages. We shall develop this point later on and here only bring out some of the consequences.

An enforced *increase in wages* (disregarding the other difficulties, and especially that such an anomaly could only be maintained by force) would be nothing more than a *better remuneration of slaves*, and would not restore, either to the worker or to the work, their human significance and worth.

Even the *equality of incomes* which Proudhon demands would only change the relation of the present-day worker to his work into a relation of all men to work. Society would then be conceived as an abstract capitalist.

2. From the relation of alienated labour to private property it also follows that the emancipation of society from private property, from servitude, takes the political form of the *emancipation of the workers*; not in the sense that only the latter's emancipation is

involved, but because this emancipation includes the emancipation of humanity as a whole. For all human servitude is involved in the relation of the worker to production, and all the types of servitude are only modifications or consequences of this relation.

17

The Metropolis and Mental Life

GEORG SIMMEL

The deepest problems of modern life derive from the claim of the individual to preserve the autonomy and individuality of his existence in the face of overwhelming social forces, of historical heritage, of external culture, and of the technique of life. The fight with nature which primitive man has to wage for his *bodily* existence attains in this modern form its latest transformation. The eighteenth century called upon man to free himself of all the historical bonds in the state and in religion, in morals and in economics. Man's nature, originally good and common to all, should develop unhampered. In addition to more liberty, the nineteenth century demanded the functional specialization of man and his work; this specialization makes one individual incomparable to another, and each of them indispensable to the highest possible extent. However, this specialization makes each man the more directly dependent upon the supplementary activities of all others. Nietzsche sees the full development of the individual conditioned by the most ruthless struggle of individuals; socialism believes in the suppression of all

competition for the same reason. Be that as it may, in all these positions the same basic motive is at work: the person resists to being leveled down and worn out by a social-technological mechanism. An inquiry into the inner meaning of specifically modern life and its products, into the soul of the cultural body, so to speak, must seek to solve the equation which structures like the metropolis set up between the individual and the super-individual contents of life. Such an inquiry must answer the question of how the personality accommodates itself in the adjustments to external forces. This will be my task today.

The psychological basis of the metropolitan type of individuality consists in the *intensification of nervous stimulation* which results from the swift and uninterrupted change of outer and inner stimuli. Man is a differentiating creature. His mind is stimulated by the difference between a momentary impression and the one which preceded it. Lasting impressions, impressions which differ only slightly from one another, impressions which take a regular and habitual course and show regular and habitual contrasts—all these use up, so to speak, less consciousness than does the rapid crowding of changing images, the sharp discontinuity in the grasp of a single glance, and the unexpectedness of onrushing impressions. These are the psychological conditions which the metropolis creates. With each crossing of the street, with the tempo and multiplicity of economic, occupational and social life, the city sets up a deep contrast with small town and rural life with reference to the sensory foundations of psychic life. The metropolis exacts from man as a discriminating creature a different amount of consciousness than does rural life. Here the rhythm of life and sensory mental imagery flows more slowly, more habitually, and more evenly. Precisely in this connection the sophisticated character of metropolitan psychic life becomes understandable—as over against small town life which rests more upon deeply felt and emotional relationships. These latter are rooted in the more unconscious layers of the psyche and grow most readily in the steady rhythm of uninterrupted habituations. The intellect, however, has its locus in the transparent, conscious, higher layers of the psyche; it is the most adaptable of our inner forces. In order to accommodate to change and to the contrast of phenomena, the intellect does not require any shocks and inner upheavals; it is only through such upheavals that the more conservative mind could accommodate to the metropolitan rhythm of events. Thus the metropolitan type of man—which, of course, exists in a thousand individual variants—develops an organ protecting him against the threatening currents and discrepancies of his external environment which would uproot him. He reacts with his head instead of his heart. In this an increased awareness assumes the psychic prerogative. Metropolitan life, thus, underlies a heightened awareness and a predominance of intelligence in metropolitan man. The reaction to metropolitan phenomena is shifted to that organ which is least sensitive and quite remote from the depth of the personality. Intellectuality is thus seen to preserve subjective life against the overwhelming power of metropolitan life, and intellectuality branches out in many directions and is integrated with numerous discrete phenomena.

The metropolis has always been the seat of the money economy. Here the multiplicity and concentration of economic exchange gives an importance to the means of exchange which the scantiness of rural commerce would not have allowed. Money economy and the dominance of the intellect are intrinsically connected. They share a matter-of-fact attitude in dealing with men and with things; and, in this attitude, a formal justice is often coupled with an inconsiderate hardness. The intellectually sophisticated person is indifferent to all genuine individuality, because relationships and reactions result from it which cannot be exhausted with logical operations. In the same manner, the individuality of phenomena is not commensurate with the pecuniary principle. Money is concerned only with what is common to all: it asks for the exchange value, it reduces all quality and individuality to the question: How much? All intimate emotional relations between persons are founded in their individuality, whereas in rational relations man is reckoned with like a number, like an element which is in itself indifferent. Only the objective measurable achievement is of interest. Thus metropolitan man reckons with his merchants and customers, his domestic servants and often even with persons with whom he is obliged to have social intercourse. These features of intellectuality contrast with the nature of the small circle in which the inevitable knowledge of individuality as inevitably produces a warmer tone of behavior, a behavior which is beyond a mere objective balancing of service and return. In the sphere of the economic psychology of the small group it is of importance that under primitive conditions production serves the customer who orders the good, so that the producer and the consumer are acquainted. The modern metropolis, however, is supplied almost entirely by production for the market, that is, for entirely unknown purchasers who never personally enter the producer's actual field of vision. Through this anonymity the interests of each party acquire an unmerciful matter-of-factness; and the intellectually calculating economic egoisms of both parties need not fear any deflection because of the imponderables of personal relationships. The money economy dominates the metropolis; it has displaced the last survivals of domestic production and the direct barter of goods; it minimizes, from day to day, the amount of work ordered by customers. The matter-of-fact attitude is obviously so intimately interrelated with the money economy, which is dominant in the metropolis, that nobody can say whether the intellectualistic mentality first promoted the money economy or whether the latter determined the former. The metropolitan way of life is certainly the most fertile soil for this reciprocity, a point which I shall document merely by citing the dictum of the most eminent English constitutional historian: throughout the whole course of English history, London has never acted as England's heart but often as England's intellect and always as her money-bag!

In certain seemingly insignificant traits, which lie upon the surface of life, the same psychic currents characteristically unite. Modern mind has become more and more calculating. The calculative exactness of practical life which the money economy has brought about corresponds to the ideal of natural science: to transform the world into an arithmetic problem, to fix every part of the world by mathe-matical formulas. Only money economy has filled the days of so many people with weighing, calculating, with numerical determinations, with a reduction of qualitative values to quantitative ones. Through the calculative nature of money a new precision, a certainty in the definition of identities and differences, an unambiguousness in agreements and arrangements has been brought about in the relations of life-elements—just as externally this precision has been effected by the universal diffusion of pocket watches. However, the conditions of metropolitan life are at once cause and effect of this trait. The relationships and affairs of the typical metropolitan usually are so varied and complex that without the strictest punctuality in promises and services the whole structure would break down into an inextricable chaos. Above all, this necessity is brought about by the aggregation of so many people with such differentiated interests, who must integrate their relations and activities into a highly complex organism. If all clocks and watches in Berlin would suddenly go wrong in different ways, even if only by one hour, all economic life and communication of the city would be disrupted for a long time. In addition an apparently mere external factor: long distances, would make all waiting and broken appointments result in an ill-afforded waste of time. Thus, the technique of metropolitan life is unimaginable without the most punctual integration of all activities and mutual relations into a stable and impersonal time schedule. Here again the general conclusions of this entire task of reflection become obvious, namely, that from each point on the surface of existence—however closely attached to the surface alone—one may drop a sounding into the depth of the psyche so that all the most banal externalities of life finally are connected with the ultimate decisions concerning the meaning and style of life. Punctuality, calculability, exactness are forced upon life by the complexity and extension of metropolitan existence and are not only the most intimately connected with its money economy and intellectualistic character. These traits must also color the contents of life and favor the exclusion of those irrational, instinctive, sovereign traits and impulses which aim at determining the mode of life from within, instead of receiving the general and precisely schematized form of life from without. Even though sovereign types of personality, characterized by irrational impulses, are by no means impossible in the city, they are, nevertheless, opposed to typical city life. The passionate hatred of men like Ruskin and Nietzsche for the metropolis is understandable in these terms. Their natures discovered the value of life alone in the unschematized existence which cannot be defined with precision for all alike. From the same source of this hatred of the metropolis surged their hatred of money economy and of the intellectualism of modern existence.

The same factors which have thus coalesced into the exactness and minute precision of the form of life have coalesced into a structure of the highest impersonality; on the other hand, they have promoted a highly personal subjectivity. There is perhaps no psychic phenomenon which has been so unconditionally reserved to the metropolis as has the blasé attitude. The blasé attitude results first from the rapidly changing and closely compressed contrasting stimulations of the nerves. From this, the enhancement of metropolitan intellectuality, also, seems originally to stem. Therefore, stupid people who are not intellectually alive in the first place usually are not exactly blasé.

A life in boundless pursuit of pleasure makes one blasé because it agitates the nerves to their strongest reactivity for such a long time that they finally cease to react at all. In the same way, through the rapidity and contradictoriness of their changes, more harmless impressions force such violent responses, tearing the nerves so brutally hither and thither that their last reserves of strength are spent; and if one remains in the same milieu they have no time to gather new strength. An incapacity thus emerges to react to new sensations with the appropriate energy. This constitutes that blasé attitude which, in fact, every metropolitan child shows when compared with children of quieter and less changeable milieus.

This physiological source of the metropolitan blasé attitude is joined by another source which flows from the money economy. The essence of the blasé attitude consists in the blunting of discrimination. This does not mean that the objects are not perceived, as is the case with the half-wit, but rather that the meaning and differing values of things, and thereby the things themselves, are experienced as insubstantial. They appear to the blasé person in an evenly flat and gray tone; no one object deserves preference over any other. This mood is the faithful subjective reflection of the completely internalized money economy. By being the equivalent to all the manifold things in one and the same way, money becomes the most frightful leveler. For money expresses all qualitative differences of things in terms of "how much?" Money, with all its colorlessness and indifference, becomes the common denominator of all values; irreparably it hollows out the core of things, their individuality, their specific value, and their incomparability. All things float with equal specific gravity in the constantly moving stream of money. All things lie on the same level and differ from one another only in the size of the area which they cover. In the individual case this coloration, or rather discoloration, of things through their money equivalence may be unnoticeably minute. However, through the relations of the rich to the objects to be had for money, perhaps even through the total character which the mentality of the contemporary public everywhere imparts of these objects, the exclusively pecuniary evaluation of objects has become quite considerable. The large cities, the main seats of the money exchange, bring the purchasability of things to the fore much more impressively than do smaller localities. That is why cities are also the genuine locale of the blasé attitude. In the blasé attitude the concentration of men and things stimulates the nervous system of the individual to its highest achievement so that it attains its peak. Through the mere quantitative intensification of the same conditioning factors this achievement is transformed into its opposite and appears in the peculiar adjustment of the blasé attitude. In this phenomenon the nerves find in the refusal to react to their stimulation the last possibility of accommodating to the contents and forms of metropolitan life. The self-preservation of certain personalities is bought at the price of devaluating the whole objective world, a devaluation which in the end unavoidably drags one's own personality down into a feeling of the same worthlessness.

Whereas the subject of this form of existence has to come to terms with it entirely for himself, his self-preservation in the face of the large city demands from him a no less negative behavior of a social nature. This mental attitude of metropolitans toward one another we may designate, from a formal point of view, as reserve. If so many inner reactions were responses to the continuous external contacts with innumerable people as are those in the small town, where one knows almost everybody one meets and where one has a positive relation to almost everyone, one would be completely atomized internally and come to an unimaginable psychic state. Partly this psychological fact, partly the right to distrust which men have in the face of the touch-and-go elements of metropolitan life, necessitates our reserve. As a result of this reserve we frequently do not even know by sight those who have been our neighbors for years. And it is this reserve which in the eyes of the small-town people makes us appear to be cold and heartless. Indeed, if I do not deceive myself, the inner aspect of this outer reserve is not only indifference but, more often than we are aware, it is a slight aversion, a mutual strangeness and repulsion, which will break into hatred and fight at the moment of a closer contact, however caused. The whole inner organization of such an extensive communicative life rests upon an extremely varied hierarchy of sympathies, indifferences, and aversions of the briefest as well as of the most permanent nature. The sphere of indifference in this hierarchy is not as large as might appear on the surface. Our psychic activity still responds to almost every impression of somebody else with a somewhat distinct feeling. The unconscious, fluid and changing character of this impression seems to result in a state of indifference. Actually this indifference would be just as unnatural as the diffusion of indiscriminate mutual suggestion would be unbearable. From both these typical dangers of the metropolis, indifference and indiscriminate suggestibility, antipathy protects us. A latent antipathy and the preparatory stage of practical antagonism effect the distances and aversions without which this mode of life could not at all be led. The extent and the mixture of this style of life, the rhythm of its emergence and disappearance, the forms in which it is satisfied—all these, with the unifying motives in the narrower sense, form the inseparable whole of the metropolitan style of life. What appears in the metropolitan style of life directly as dissociation is in reality only one of its elemental forms of socialization.

This reserve with its overtone of hidden aversion appears in turn as the form or the cloak of a more general mental phenomenon of the metropolis: it grants to the individual a kind and an amount of personal freedom which has no analogy whatsoever under other conditions. The metropolis goes back to one of the large developmental tendencies of social life as such, to one of the few tendencies for which an approximately universal formula can be discovered. The earliest phase of social formations found in historical as well as in contemporary social structures is this: a relatively small circle firmly closed against neighboring, strange, or in some way antagonistic circles. However, this circle is closely coherent and allows its individual members only a narrow field for the development of unique qualities and free, self-responsible movements. Political and kinship groups, parties and religious associations begin in this way. The self-preservation of very young associations requires the establishment of strict boundaries and a centripetal unity. Therefore they cannot allow the individual freedom and unique inner and outer development. From this stage social development proceeds at once in two different, yet corresponding, directions. To the extent to which the group grows—numerically, spatially, in significance and in content of life—to the same degree the group's direct, inner unity loosens, and the rigidity of the original demarcation against others is softened through mutual relations and connections. At the same time, the individual gains freedom of movement, far beyond the first jealous delimitation. The individual also gains a specific

individuality to which the division of labor in the enlarged group gives both occasion and necessity. The state and Christianity, guilds and political parties, and innumerable other groups have developed according to this formula, however much, of course, the special conditions and forces of the respective groups have modified the general scheme. This scheme seems to me distinctly recognizable also in the evolution of individuality within urban life. The small-town life in Antiquity and in the Middle Ages set barriers against movement and relations of the individual toward the outside, and it set up barriers against individual independence and differentiation within the individual self. These barriers were such that under them modern man could not have breathed. Even today a metropolitan man who is placed in a small town feels a restriction similar, at least, in kind. The smaller the circle which forms our milieu is, and the more restricted those relations to others are which dissolve the boundaries of the individual, the more anxiously the circle guards the achievements, the conduct of life, and the outlook of the individual, and the more readily a quantitative specialization would break up the framework of the whole little circle.

The ancient *polis* in this respect seems to have had the very character of a small town. The constant threat to its existence at the hands of enemies from near and afar effected strict coherence in political and military respects, a supervision of the citizen by the citizen, a jealousy of the whole against the individual whose particular life was suppressed to such a degree that he could compensate only by acting as a despot in his own household. The tremendous agitation and excitement, the unique colorfulness of Athenian life, can perhaps be understood in terms of the fact that a people of incomparably individualized personalities struggled against the constant inner and outer pressure of a de-individualizing small town. This produced a tense atmosphere in which the weaker individuals were suppressed and those of stronger natures were incited to prove themselves in the most passionate manner. This is precisely why it was that there blossomed in Athens what must be called, without defining it exactly, "the general human character" in the intellectual development of our species. For we maintain factual as well as historical validity for the following connection: the most extensive and the most general contents and forms of life are most intimately connected with the most individual ones. They have a preparatory stage in common, that is, they find their enemy in narrow formations and groupings the maintenance of which places both of them into a state of defense against expanse and generality lying without and the freely moving individuality within. Just as in the feudal age, the "free" man was the one who stood under the law of the land, that is, under the law of the largest social orbit, and the unfree man was the one who derived his right merely from the narrow circle of a feudal association and was excluded from the larger social orbit—so today metropolitan man is "free" in a spiritualized and refined sense, in contrast to the pettiness and prejudices which hem in the small-town man. For the reciprocal reserve and indifference and the intellectual life conditions of large circles are never felt more strongly by the individual in their impact upon independence than in the thickest crowd of the big city. This is because the bodily proximity and narrowness of space makes the mental distance only the more visible. It is obviously only the obverse of this freedom if, under certain circumstances, one nowhere feels as lonely and lost as in the metropolitan crowd. For here as elsewhere it is by no means necessary that the freedom of man be reflected in his emotional life as comfort.

It is not only the immediate size of the area and the number of persons which, because of the universal historical correlation between the enlargement of the circle and the personal inner and outer freedom, has made the metropolis the locale of freedom. It is rather in transcending this visible expanse that any given city becomes the seat of cosmopolitanism. The horizon of the city expands in a manner comparable to the way in which wealth develops; a certain amount of property increases in a quasi-automatical way in ever more rapid progression. As soon as a certain limit has been passed, the economic, personal, and intellectual relations of the citizenry, the sphere of intellectual predominance of the city over its hinterland, grow as in geometrical progression. Every gain in dynamic extension becomes a step, not for an equal, but for a new and larger extension. From every thread spinning out of the city, ever new threads grow as if by themselves, just as within the city the unearned increment of ground rent, through the mere increase in communication, brings the owner automatically increasing profits. At this point, the quantitative aspect of life is transformed directly into qualitative traits of character. The sphere of life of the small town is, in the main, self-contained and autarchic. For it is the decisive nature of the metropolis that its inner life overflows by waves into a far-flung national or international area. Weimar is not an example to the contrary, since its significance was hinged upon individual personalities and died with them; whereas the metropolis is indeed characterized by its essential independence even from the most eminent individual personalities. This is the counterpart to the independence, and it is the price the individual pays for the independence, which he enjoys in the metropolis. The most significant characteristic of the metropolis is this functional extension beyond its physical boundaries. And this efficacy reacts in turn and gives weight, importance, and responsibility to metropolitan life. Man does not end with the limits of his body or the area comprising his immediate activity. Rather is the range of the person constituted by the sum of effects emanating from him temporally and spatially. In the same way, a city consists of its total effects which extend beyond its immediate confines. Only this range is the city's actual extent in which its existence is expressed. This fact makes it obvious that individual freedom, the logical and historical complement of such extension, is not to be understood only in the negative sense of mere freedom of mobility and elimination of prejudices and petty philistinism. The essential point is that the particularity and incomparability, which ultimately every human being possesses, be somehow expressed in the working-out of a way of life. That we follow the laws of our own nature—and this after all is freedom—becomes obvious and convincing to ourselves and to others only if the expressions of this nature differ from the expressions of others. Only our unmistakability proves that our way of life has not been superimposed by others.

Cities are, first of all, seats of the highest economic division of labor. They produce thereby such extreme phenomena as in Paris the remunerative occupation of the *quatorzième*. They are persons who identify themselves by signs on their residences and who are ready at the dinner hour in correct attire, so that they can be quickly called upon if a dinner party should consist of thirteen persons. In the measure of its expansion, the city offers more and more the decisive conditions of the division of labor. It offers a circle which through its size can absorb a highly diverse variety of services. At the same time, the concentration of individuals and their struggle for customers compel the individual to specialize in a function from which he cannot be readily displaced by another. It is decisive that city life has transformed the struggle with nature for livelihood into an inter-human struggle for gain, which here is not granted by nature but by other men. For specialization does not flow only from the competition for gain but also from the underlying fact that the seller must always seek to call forth new and differentiated needs of the lured customer. In order to find a source of income which is not yet exhausted, and to find a function which cannot readily be displaced, it is necessary to specialize in one's services. This process promotes differentiation, refinement, and the enrichment of the public's needs, which obviously must lead to growing personal differences within this public.

All this forms the transition to the individualization of mental and psychic traits which the city occasions in proportion to its size. There is a whole series of obvious causes underlying this process. First, one must meet the difficulty of asserting his own personality within the dimensions of metropolitan life. Where the quantitative increase in importance and the expense of energy reach their limits, one seizes upon qualitative differentiation in order somehow to attract the attention of the social circle by playing upon its sensitivity for differences. Finally, man is tempted to adopt the most tendentious peculiarities, that is, the specifically metropolitan extravagances of mannerism, caprice, and preciousness. Now, the meaning of these extravagances does not at all lie in the contents of such behavior, but rather in its form of "being different," of standing out in a striking manner and thereby attracting attention. For many character types, ultimately the only means of saving for themselves some modicum of self-esteem and the sense of filling a position is indirect, through the awareness of others. In the same sense a seemingly insignificant factor is operating, the cumulative effects of which are, however, still noticeable. I refer to the brevity and scarcity of the inter-human contacts granted to the metropolitan man, as compared with social intercourse in the small town. The temptation to appear "to the point," to appear concentrated and strikingly characteristic, lies much closer to the individual in brief metropolitan contacts than in an atmosphere in which frequent and prolonged association assures the personality of an unambiguous image of himself in the eyes of the other.

The most profound reason, however, why the metropolis conduces to the urge for the most individual personal existence—no matter whether justified and successful—appears to me to be the following: the development of modern culture is characterized by the preponderance of what one may call the "objective spirit" over the "subjective spirit." This is to say, in language as well as in law, in the technique of production as well as in art, in science as well as in the objects of domestic environment, there is embodied a sum of spirit. The individual in his intellectual development follows the growth of this spirit very imperfectly and at an ever increasing distance. If, for instance, we view the immense culture which for the last hundred years has been embodied in things and in knowledge, in institutions and in comforts, and if we compare all this with the cultural progress of the individual during the same period—at least in high status groups—a frightful disproportion in growth between the two becomes evident. Indeed, at some points we notice a retrogression in the culture of the individual with reference to spirituality, delicacy, and idealism. This discrepancy results essentially from the growing division of labor. For the division of labor demands from the individual an ever more one-sided accomplishment, and the greatest advance in a one-sided pursuit only too frequently means dearth to the personality of the individual. In any case, he can cope less and less with the overgrowth of objective culture. The individual is reduced to a negligible quantity, perhaps less in his consciousness than in his practice and in the totality of his obscure emotional states that are derived from this practice. The individual has become a mere cog in an enormous organization of things and powers which tear from his hands all progress, spirituality, and value in order to transform them from their subjective form into the form of a purely objective life. It needs merely to be pointed out that the metropolis is the genuine arena of this culture which outgrows all personal life. Here in buildings and educational institutions, in the wonders and comforts of space-conquering technology, in the formations of community life, and in the visible institutions of the state, is offered such an overwhelming fullness of crystallized and impersonalized spirit that the personality, so to speak, cannot maintain itself under its impact. On the one hand, life is made infinitely easy for the personality in that stimulations, interests, uses of time and consciousness are offered to it from all sides. They carry the person as if in a stream, and one needs hardly to swim for oneself. On the other hand, however, life is composed more and more of these impersonal contents and offerings which tend to displace the genuine personal colorations and incomparabilities. This results in the individual's summoning the utmost in uniqueness and particularization, in order to preserve his most personal core. He has to exaggerate this personal element in order to remain audible even to himself. The atrophy of individual culture through the hypertrophy of objective culture is one reason for the bitter hatred which the preachers of the most extreme individualism, above all Nietzsche, harbor against the metropolis. But it is, indeed, also a reason why these preachers are so passionately loved in the metropolis and why they appear to the metropolitan man as the prophets and saviors of his most unsatisfied yearnings.

If one asks for the historical position of these two forms of individualism which are nourished by the quantitative relation of the metropolis, namely, individual independence and the elaboration of individuality itself, then the metropolis assumes an entirely new rank order in the world history of the spirit. The eighteenth century found the individual in oppressive bonds which had become meaningless—bonds of a political, agrarian, guild, and religious character. They were restraints which, so to speak, forced upon man an unnatural form and outmoded, unjust inequalities. In this situation the cry for liberty and equality arose, the belief in the individual's full freedom of movement in all social and intellectual relationships. Freedom would at once permit the noble substance common to all to come to the fore, a substance which nature had deposited in every man and which society and history had only deformed. Besides this eighteenth-century ideal of liberalism, in the nineteenth century, through Goethe and Romanticism, on the one hand, and through the economic division of labor, on the other hand, another ideal arose: individuals liberated from historical bonds now wished to distinguish themselves from one another. The carrier of man's values is no longer the "general human being" in every individual, but rather man's qualitative uniqueness and irreplaceability. The external and internal history of our time takes its course within the struggle and in the changing entanglements of these two ways of defining the individual's role in the whole of society. It is the function of the metropolis to provide the arena for this struggle and its reconciliation. For the metropolis presents the peculiar conditions which are revealed to us as the opportunities and the stimuli for the development of both these ways of allocating roles to men. Therewith these conditions gain a unique place, pregnant with inestimable meanings for the development of psychic existence. The metropolis reveals itself as one of those great historical formations in which opposing streams which enclose life unfold, as well as join one another with equal right. However, in this process the currents of life, whether their individual phenomena touch us sympathetically or antipathetically, entirely transcend the sphere for which the judge's attitude is appropriate. Since such forces of life have grown into the roots and into the crown of the whole of the historical life in which we, in our fleeting existence, as a cell, belong only as a part, it is not our task either to accuse or to pardon, but only to understand.

18

The Anomie of Modern Life

EMILE DURKHEIM

No living being can be happy or even exist unless his needs are sufficiently proportioned to his means. In other words, if his needs require more than can be granted, or even merely something of a different sort, they will be under continual friction and can only function painfully. Movements incapable of production without pain tend not to be reproduced. Unsatisfied tendencies atrophy, and as the impulse to live is merely the result of all the rest, it is bound to weaken as the other relax.

In the animal, at least in a normal condition, this equilibrium is established with automatic spontaneity because the animal depends on purely material conditions. All the organism needs is that the supplies of substance and energy constantly employed in the vital process should be periodically renewed by equivalent quantities; that replacement be equivalent to use. When the void created by existence in its own resources is filled, the animal, satisfied, asks nothing further. Its power of reflection is not sufficiently developed to imagine other ends than those implicit in its physical nature. On the other hand, as the work demanded of each organ itself depends on the general state of vital energy and the needs of organic equilibrium, use is regulated in turn by replacement and the balance is automatic. The limits of one are those of the other; both are fundamental to the constitution of the existence in question, which cannot exceed them.

This is not the case with man, because most of his needs are not dependent on his body or not to the same degree. Strictly speaking, we may consider that the quantity of material supplies necessary to the physical maintenance of a human life is subject to computation, though this be less exact than in the preceding case and a wider margin left for the free combinations of the will; for beyond the indispensable minimum which satisfies nature when instinctive, a more awakened reflection suggests better conditions, seemingly desirable ends craving fulfillment. Such appetites, however, admittedly sooner or later reach a limit which they cannot pass. But how determine the quantity of well-being, comfort or luxury legitimately to be craved by a human being? Nothing appears in man's organic nor in his psychological constitution which sets a limit to such tendencies. The functioning of individual life does not require them to cease at one point rather than at another; the proof being that they have constantly increased since the beginnings of history, receiving more complete satisfaction, yet with no weakening of average health. Above all, how establish their proper variation with different conditions of life, occupations, relative importance of services, etc.? In no society are they equally satisfied in the different stages of the social hierarchy. Yet human nature is substantially the same among all men, in its essential qualities. It is not human nature which can assign the variable limits necessary to our needs. They are thus unlimited so far as they depend on the individual alone. Irrespective of any external regulatory force, our capacity for feeling is in itself an insatiable and bottomless abyss.

But if nothing external can restrain this capacity, it can only be a source of torment to itself. Unlimited desires are insatiable by definition and insatiability is rightly considered a sign of morbidity. Being unlimited, they constantly and infinitely surpass the means at their command; they cannot be quenched. Inextinguishable thirst is constantly renewed torture. It has been claimed, indeed, that human activity naturally aspires beyond assignable limits and sets itself unattainable goals. But how can such an undetermined state be any more reconciled with the conditions of mental life than with the demands of physical life? All man's pleasure in acting, moving and exerting himself implies the sense that his efforts are not in vain and that by walking he has advanced. However, one does not advance when one walks toward no goal, or—which is the same thing—when his goal is infinity. Since the distance between us and it is always the same, whatever road we take, we might as well have made the motions without progress from the spot. Even our glances behind and our feeling of pride at the distance covered can cause only deceptive satisfaction, since the remaining distance is not proportionately reduced. To pursue a goal which is by definition unattainable is to condemn oneself to a state of perpetual unhappiness. Of course, man may hope contrary to all reason, and hope has its pleasures even when unreasonable. It may sustain him for a time; but it cannot survive the repeated disappointments of experience indefinitely. What more can the future offer him than the past, since he can never reach a tenable condition nor even approach the glimpsed ideal? Thus, the more one has, the more one wants, since satisfactions received only stimulate instead of filling needs. Shall action as such be considered agreeable? First, only on condition of blindness to its uselessness. Secondly, for this pleasure to be felt and to temper and half veil the accompanying painful unrest, such unending motion must at least always be easy and unhampered. If it is interfered with only restlessness is left, with the lack of ease which it, itself, entails. But it would be a miracle if no insurmountable obstacle were ever encountered. Our thread of life on these conditions is pretty thin, breakable at any instant.

To achieve any other result, the passions first must be limited. Only then can they be harmonized with the faculties and satisfied. But since the individual has no way of limiting them, this must be done by some force exterior to him. A regulative force must play the same role for moral needs which the organism plays for physical needs. This means that the force can only be moral. The awakening of conscience interrupted the state of equilibrium of the animal's dormant existence; only conscience, therefore, can furnish the means to re-establish it. Physical restraint would be ineffective; hearts cannot be touched by physio-chemical forces. So far as the appetites are not automatically restrained by physiological mechanisms, they can be halted only by a limit that they recognize as just. Men would never consent to restrict their desires if they felt justified in passing the assigned limit. But, for reasons given above, they cannot assign themselves this law of justice. So they must receive it from an authority which they respect, to which they yield spontaneously. Either directly and as a whole, or through the agency of one of its organs, society alone can play this moderating role; for it is the only moral power superior to the individual, the authority of which he accepts. It alone has the power necessary to stipulate law and to set the point beyond which the passions must not go. Finally, it alone can estimate the reward to be prospectively offered to every class of human functionary, in the name of the common interest.

As a matter of fact, at every moment of history there is a dim perception, in the moral consciousness of societies, of the respective value of different social services, the relative reward due to each, and the consequent degree of comfort appropriate on the average to workers in each occupation. The different functions are graded in public opinion and a certain coefficient of well-being assigned to each, according to its place in the hierarchy. According to accepted ideas, for example, a certain way of living is considered the upper limit to which a workman may aspire in his efforts to improve his existence, and there is another limit below which he is not willingly permitted to fall unless he has seriously demeaned himself. Both differ for city and country workers, for the domestic servant and the day-laborer, for the business clerk and the official, etc. Likewise the man of wealth is reproved if he lives the life of a poor man, but also if he seeks the refinements of luxury overmuch. Economists may protest in vain; public feeling will always be scandalized if an individual spends too much wealth for wholly superfluous use, and it even seems that this severity relaxes only in times of moral disturbance.[1] A genuine regimen exists, therefore, although not always legally formulated, which fixes with relative precision the maximum degree of ease of living to which each social class may legitimately aspire. However, there is nothing immutable about such a scale. It changes with the increase or decrease of collective revenue and the changes occurring in the

moral ideas of society. Thus what appears luxury to one period no longer does so to another; and the well-being which for long periods was granted to a class only by exception and supererogation, finally appears strictly necessary and equitable.

Under this pressure, each in his sphere vaguely realizes the extreme limit set to his ambitions and aspires to nothing beyond. At least if he respects regulations and is docile to collective authority, that is, has a wholesome moral constitution, he feels that it is not well to ask more. Thus, an end and goal are set to the passions. Truly, there is nothing rigid nor absolute about such determination. The economic ideal assigned each class of citizens is itself confined to certain limits, within which the desires have free range. But it is not infinite. This relative limitation and the moderation it involves, make men contented with their lot while stimulating them moderately to improve it; and this average contentment causes the feeling of calm, active happiness, the pleasure in existing and living which characterizes health for societies as well as for individuals. Each person is then at least, generally speaking, in harmony with his condition, and desires only what he may legitimately hope for as the normal reward of his activity. Besides, this does not condemn man to a sort of immobility. He may seek to give beauty to his life; but his attempts in this direction may fail without causing him to despair. For, loving what he has and not fixing his desire solely on what he lacks, his wishes and hopes may fail of what he has happened to aspire to, without his being wholly destitute. He has the essentials. The equilibrium of his happiness is secure because it is defined, and a few mishaps cannot disconcert him.

But it would be of little use for everyone to recognize the justice of the

---

[1] Actually, this is a purely moral reprobation and can hardly be judicially implemented. We do not consider any reestablishment of sumptuary laws desirable or even possible.

hierarchy of functions established by public opinion, if he did not also consider the distribution of these functions just. The workman is not in harmony with his social position if he is not convinced that he has his desserts. If he feels justified in occupying another, what he has would not satisfy him. So it is not enough for the average level of needs for each social condition to be regulated by public opinion, but another, more precise rule, must fix the way in which these conditions are open to individuals. There is no society in which such regulation does not exist. It varies with times and places. Once it regarded birth as the almost exclusive principle of social classification; today it recognizes no other inherent inequality than hereditary fortune and merit. But in all these various forms its object is unchanged. It is also only possible, everywhere, as a restriction upon individuals imposed by superior authority, that is, by collective authority. For it can be established only by requiring of one or another group of men, usually of all, sacrifices and concessions in the name of the public interest.

Some, to be sure, have thought that this moral pressure would become unnecessary if men's economic circumstances were only no longer determined by heredity. If inheritance were abolished, the argument runs, if everyone began life with equal resources and if the competitive struggle were fought out on a basis of perfect equality, no one could think its results unjust. Each would instinctively feel that things are as they should be.

Truly, the nearer this ideal equality were approached, the less social restraint will be necessary. But it is only a matter of degree. One sort of heredity will always exist, that of natural talent. Intelligence, taste, scientific, artistic, literary or industrial ability, courage and manual dexterity are gifts received by each of us at birth, as the

heir to wealth receives his capital or as the nobleman formerly received his title and function. A moral discipline will therefore still be required to make those less favored by nature accept the lesser advantages which they owe to the chance of birth. Shall it be demanded that all have an equal share and that no advantage be given those more useful and deserving? But then there would have to be a discipline far stronger to make these accept a treatment merely equal to that of the mediocre and incapable.

But like the one first mentioned, this discipline can be useful only if considered just by the peoples subject to it. When it is maintained only by custom and force, peace and harmony are illusory; the spirit of unrest and discontent are latent; appetites superficially restrained are ready to revolt. This happened in Rome and Greece when the faiths underlying the old organization of the patricians and plebeians were shaken, and in our modern societies when aristocratic prejudices began to lose their old ascendancy. But this state of upheaval is exceptional; it occurs only when society is passing through some abnormal crisis. In normal conditions the collective order is regarded as just by the great majority of persons. Therefore, when we say that an authority is necessary to impose this order on individuals, we certainly do not mean that violence is the only means of establishing it. Since this regulation is meant to restrain individual passions, it must come from a power which dominates individuals; but this power must also be obeyed through respect, not fear.

It is not true, then, that human activity can be released from all restraint. Nothing in the world can enjoy such a privilege. All existence being a part of the universe is relative to the remainder; its nature and method of manifestation accordingly depend not only on itself but on other beings, who consequently restrain and regulate it. Here there are only differences of degree and form between the mineral realm and the thinking person. Man's characteristic privilege is that the bond he accepts is not physical but moral; that is, social. He is governed not by a material environment brutally imposed on him, but by a conscience superior to his own, the superiority of which he feels. Because the greater, better part of his existence transcends the body, he escapes the body's yoke, but is subject to that of society.

But when society is disturbed by some painful crisis or by beneficent but abrupt transitions, it is momentarily incapable of exercising this influence; thence come the sudden rises in the curve of suicides which we have pointed out above.

In the case of economic disasters, indeed, something like a declassification occurs which suddenly casts certain individuals into a lower state than their previous one. Then they must reduce their requirements, restrain their needs, learn greater self-control. All the advantages of social influence are lost so far as they are concerned; their moral education has to be recommenced. But society cannot adjust them instantaneously to this new life and teach them to practice the increased self-repression to which they are unaccustomed. So they are not adjusted to the condition forced on them, and its very prospect is intolerable; hence the suffering which detaches them from a reduced existence even before they have made trial of it.

It is the same if the source of the crisis is an abrupt growth of power and wealth. Then, truly, as the conditions of life are changed, the standard according to which needs were regulated can no longer remain the same; for it varies with social resources, since it largely determines the share of each class of producers. The scale is upset; but a new scale cannot be immediately improvised. Time is required for the public conscience to reclassify men and things. So long as the social forces thus freed have not regained equilibrium, their respective values are unknown and so all regulation is lacking for a time. The limits are unknown between the possible and the impossible, what is just and what is unjust, legitimate claims and hopes and those which are immoderate. Consequently, there is no restraint upon aspirations. If the disturbance is profound, it affects even the principles controlling the distribution of men among various occupations. Since the relations between various parts of society are necessarily modified, the ideas expressing these relations must change. Some particular class especially favored by the crisis is no longer resigned to its former lot, and, on the other hand, the example of its greater good fortune arouses all sorts of jealousy below and about it. Appetites, not being controlled by a public opinion become disoriented, no longer recognize the limits proper to them. Besides, they are at the same time seized by a sort of natural erethism simply by the greater intensity of public life. With increased prosperity desires increase. At the very moment when traditional rules have lost their authority, the richer prize offered these appetites stimulates them and makes them more exigent and impatient of control. The state of de-regulation or anomy is thus further heightened by passions being less disciplined, precisely when they need more disciplining.

But then their very demands make fulfillment impossible. Overweening ambition always exceeds the results obtained, great as they may be, since there is no warning to pause here. Nothing gives satisfaction and all this agitation is uninterruptedly maintained without appeasement. Above all, since this race for an unattainable goal can give no other pleasure but that of the race itself, if it is one, once it is interrupted the participants are left empty-handed. At the same time the struggle grows more violent and painful, both from being less controlled and because competition is greater. All classes contend among themselves because no established classification any longer exists. Effort grows, just when it becomes less productive. How could the desire to live not be weakened under such conditions?

This explanation is confirmed by the remarkable immunity of poor countries. Poverty protects against suicide because it is a restraint in itself. No matter how one acts, desires have to depend upon resources to some extent; actual possessions are partly the criterion of those aspired to. So the less one has the less he is tempted to extend the range of his needs indefinitely. Lack of power, compelling moderation, accustoms men to it, while nothing excites envy if no one has superfluity. Wealth, on the other hand, by the power it bestows, deceives us into believing that we depend on ourselves only. Reducing the resistance we encounter from objects, it suggests the possibility of unlimited success against them. The less limited one feels, the more intolerable all limitation appears. Not without reason, therefore, have so many religions dwelt on the advantages and moral value of poverty. It is actually the best school for teaching self-restraint. Forcing us to constant self-discipline, it prepares us to accept collective discipline with equanimity, while wealth, exalting the individual, may always arouse the spirit of rebellion which is the very source of immorality. This, of course, is no reason why humanity should not improve its material condition. But though the moral danger involved in every growth of prosperity is not irremediable, it should not be forgotten.

If anomy [normlessness: lack of rules governing behavior] never appeared except, as in the above instances, in intermittent spurts and acute crisis, it might cause the social suicide-rate to vary from time to time, but it would not be a regular, constant factor. In one sphere of social life, however—the sphere of trade and industry—it is actually in a chronic state.

For a whole century, economic progress has mainly consisted in freeing industrial relations from all regulation. Until very recently, it was the function of a whole system of moral forces to exert this discipline. First, the influence of religion was felt alike by workers and masters, the poor and the rich. It consoled the former and taught them contentment with their lot by informing them of the providential nature of the social order, that the share of each class was assigned by God himself, and by holding out the hope for just compensation in a world to come in return for the inequalities of this world. It governed the latter, recalling that worldly interests are not man's entire lot, that they must be subordinate to other and higher interests, and that they should therefore not be pursued without rule or measure. Temporal power, in turn, restrained the scope of economic functions by its supremacy over them and by the relatively subordinate role it assigned them. Finally, within the business world proper, the occupational groups by regulating salaries, the price of products and production itself, indirectly fixed the average level of income on which needs are partially based by the very force of circumstances. However, we do not mean to propose this organization as a model. Clearly it would be inadequate to existing societies without great changes. What we stress is its existence, the fact of its useful influence, and that nothing today has come to take its place.

Actually, religion has lost most of its power. And government, instead of regulating economic life, has become its tool and servant. The most opposite schools, orthodox economists and extreme socialists, unite to reduce government to the role of a more or less passive intermediary among the various social functions. The former wish to make it simply the guardian of individual contracts; the latter leave it the task of doing the collective bookkeeping, that is, of recording the demands of consumers, transmitting them to producers, inventorying the total revenue and distributing it according to a fixed formula. But both refuse it any power to subordinate other social organs to itself and to make them converge toward one dominant aim. On both sides nations are declared to have the single or chief purpose of achieving industrial prosperity; such is the implication of the dogma of economic materialism, the basis of both apparently opposed systems. And as these theories merely express the state of opinion, industry, instead of being still regarded as a means to an end transcending itself, has become the supreme end of individuals and societies alike. Thereupon the appetites thus excited have become freed of any limiting authority. By sanctifying them, so to speak, this apotheosis of well-being has placed them above all human law. Their restraint seems like a sort of sacrilege. For this reason, even the purely utilitarian regulation of them exercised by the industrial world itself through the medium of occupational groups has been unable to persist. Ultimately, this liberation of desires has been made worse by the very development of industry and the almost infinite extension of the market. So long as the producer could gain his profits only in his immediate neighborhood, the restricted amount of possible gain could not much overexcite ambition. Now that he may assume to have almost the entire world as his customer, how could passions accept their former

confinement in the face of such limitless prospects?

Such is the source of the excitment predominating in this part of society, and which has thence extended to the other parts. There, the state of crisis and anomy is constant and, so to speak, normal. From top to bottom of the ladder, greed is aroused without knowing where to find ultimate foothold. Nothing can calm it, since its goal is far beyond all it can attain. Reality seems valueless by comparison with the dreams of fevered imaginations; reality is therefore abandoned, but so too is possibility abandoned when it in turn becomes reality. A thirst arises for novelties, unfamiliar pleasures, nameless sensations, all of which lose their savor once known. Henceforth one has no strength to endure the least reverse. The whole fever subsides and the sterility of all the tumult is apparent, and it is seen that all these new sensations in their infinite quantity cannot form a solid foundation of happiness to support one during days of trial. The wise man, knowing how to enjoy achieved results without having constantly to replace them with others, finds in them an attachment to life in the hour of difficulty. But the man who has always pinned all his hopes on the future and lived with his eyes fixed upon it, has nothing in the past as a comfort against the present's afflictions, for the past was nothing to him but a series of hastily experienced stages. What blinded him to himself was his expectation always to find further on the happiness he had so far missed. Now he is stopped in his tracks; from now on nothing remains behind or ahead of him to fix his gaze upon. Weariness alone, moreover, is enough to bring disillusionment, for he cannot in the end escape the futility of an endless pursuit.

We may even wonder if this moral state is not principally what makes economic catastrophes of our day so fertile in suicides. In societies where a man is subjected to a healthy discipline, he submits more readily to the blows of chance. The necessary effort for sustaining a little more discomfort costs him relatively little, since he is used to discomfort and constraint. But when every constraint is hateful in itself, how can closer constraint not seem intolerable? There is no tendency to resignation in the feverish impatience of men's lives. When there is no other aim but to outstrip constantly the point arrived at, how painful to be thrown back! Now this very lack of organization characterizing our economic condition throws the door wide to every sort of adventure. Since imagination is hungry for novelty, and ungoverned, it gropes at random. Setbacks necessarily increase with risks and thus crises multiply, just when they are becoming more destructive.

Yet these dispositions are so inbred that society has grown to accept them and is accustomed to think them normal. It is everlastingly repeated that it is man's nature to be eternally dissatisfied, constantly to advance, without relief or rest, toward an indefinite goal. The longing for infinity is daily represented as a mark of moral distinction, whereas it can only appear within unregulated consciences which elevate to a rule the lack of rule from which they suffer. The doctrine of the most ruthless and swift progress has become an article of faith. But other theories appear parallel with those praising the advantages of instability, which, generalizing the situation that gives them birth, declare life evil, claim that it is richer in grief than in pleasure and that it attracts men only by false claims. Since this disorder is greatest in the economic world, it has most victims there.

Industrial and commercial functions are really among the occupations which furnish the greatest number of suicides. . . . Almost on a level with the liberal professions, they sometimes surpass them; they are especially more afflicted than agriculture, where the old regulative forces still make their appearance felt most and where the fever of business has least penetrated. Here is best recalled what was once the general constitution of the economic order. And the divergence would be yet greater if, among the suicides of industry, employees were distinguished from workmen, for the former are probably most stricken by the state of anomy. The enormous rate of those with independent means (720 per million) sufficiently shows that the possessors of most comfort suffer most. Everything that enforces subordination attenuates the effects of this state. At least the horizon of the lower classes is limited by those above them, and for this same reason their desires are more modest. Those who have only empty space above them are almost inevitably lost in it, if no force restrains them.

19

Science and the Disenchantment of the World

MAX WEBER

Scientific progress is a fraction, the most important fraction, of the process of intellectualization which we have been undergoing for thousands of years and which nowadays is usually judged in such an extremely negative way. Let us first clarify what this intellectualist rationalization, created by science and by scientifically oriented technology, means practically.

Does it mean that we, today, for instance, everyone sitting in this hall, have a greater knowledge of the conditions of life under which we exist than has an American Indian or a Hottentot? Hardly. Unless he is a physicist, one who rides on the streetcar has no idea how the car happened to get into motion. And he does not need to know. He is satisfied that he may "count" on the behavior of the streetcar, and he orients his conduct according to this expectation; but he knows nothing about what it takes to produce such a car so that it can move. The savage knows incomparably more about his tools. When we spend money today I bet that even if there are colleagues of political economy here in the hall, almost every one of them will hold a different answer in readiness to the question: How does it happen that one can buy something for money—sometimes more and sometimes less? The savage knows what he does in order to get his daily food and which institutions serve him in this pursuit. The increasing intellectualization and rationalization do *not*, therefore, indicate an increased and general

From *From Max Weber, Essays in Sociology*, edited and translated by H. H. Gerth and C. Wright Mills. Copyright © 1946 by Oxford University Press, Inc. Excerpted by permission.

knowledge of the conditions under which one lives.

It means something else, namely, the knowledge or belief that if one but wished one *could* learn it at any time. Hence, it means that principally there are no mysterious incalculable forces that come into play, but rather that one can, in principle, master all things by calculation. This means that the world is disenchanted. One need no longer have recourse to magical means in order to master or implore the spirits, as did the savage, for whom such mysterious powers existed. Technical means and calculations perform the service. This above all is what intellectualization means.

Now, this process of disenchantment, which has continued to exist in Occidental culture for millennia, and, in general, this "progress," to which science belongs as a link and motive force, do they have any meanings that go beyond the purely practical and technical? . . . What is the value of science?

Here the contrast between the past and the present is tremendous. You will recall the wonderful image at the beginning of the seventh book of Plato's *Republic:* those enchained cavemen whose faces are turned toward the stone wall before them. Behind them lies the source of the light which they cannot see. They are concerned only with the shadowy images that this light throws upon the wall, and they seek to fathom their interrelations. Finally one of them succeeds in shattering his fetters, turns around, and sees the sun. Blinded, he gropes about and stammers of what he saw. The others say he is raving. But gradually he learns to behold the light, and then his task is to descend to the cavemen and to lead them to the light. He is the philosopher; the sun, however, is the truth of science, which alone seizes not upon illusions and shadows but upon the true being.

Well, who today views science in such a manner? Today youth feels rather the reverse: the intellectual constructions of science constitute an unreal realm of artificial abstractions, which with their bony hands seek to grasp the blood-and-the-sap of true life without ever catching up with it. But here in life, in what for Plato was the play of shadows on the walls of the cave, genuine reality is pulsating; and the rest are derivatives of life, lifeless ghosts, and nothing else. How did this change come about?

Plato's passionate enthusiasm in *The Republic* must, in the last analysis, be explained by the fact that for the first time the *concept,* one of the great tools of all scientific knowledge, had been consciously discovered. Socrates had discovered it in its bearing. He was not the only man in the world to discover it. In India one finds the beginnings of a logic that is quite similar to that of Aristotle's. But nowhere else do we find this realization of the significance of the concept. In Greece, for the first time, appeared a handy means by which one could put the logical screws upon somebody so that he could not come out without admitting either that he knew nothing or that this and nothing else was truth, the *eternal* truth that never would vanish as the doings of the blind men vanish. That was the tremendous experience which dawned upon the disciples of Socrates. And from this it seemed to follow that if one only found the right concept of the beautiful, the good, or, for instance, of bravery, of the soul—or whatever—that then one could also grasp its true being. And this, in turn, seemed to open the way for knowing and for teaching how to act rightly in life and, above all, how to act as a citizen of the state; for this question was everything to the Hellenic man, whose thinking was political throughout. And for these reasons one engaged in science.

The second great tool of scientific work, the rational experiment, made its appearance at the side of this discovery of the Hellenic spirit during the Renaissance period. The experiment is a means of reliably controlling experience. Without it, present-day empirical science would be impossible. There were experiments earlier; for instance, in India physiological experiments were made in the service of ascetic yoga technique; in Hellenic antiquity, mathematical experiments were made for purposes of war technology; and in the Middle Ages, for purposes of mining. But to raise the experiment to a principle of research was the achievement of the Renaissance. They were the great innovators in *art,* who were the pioneers of experiment. Leonardo and his like and, above all, the sixteenth-century experimenters in music with their experimental pianos were characteristic. From these circles the experiment entered science, especially through Galileo, and it entered theory through Bacon; and then it was taken over by the various exact disciplines of the continental universities, first of all those of Italy and then those of the Netherlands.

What did science mean to these men who stood at the threshold of modern times? To artistic experimenters of the type of Leonardo and the musical innovators, science meant the path to *true* art, and that meant for them the path to true *nature.* Art was to be raised to the rank of a science, and this meant at the same time and above all to raise the artist to the rank of the doctor, socially and with reference to the meaning of his life. This is the ambition on which, for instance, Leonardo's sketch book was based. And today? "Science as the way to nature" would sound like blasphemy to youth. Today, youth proclaims the opposite: redemption from the intellectualism of science in order to return to one's own nature and therewith to nature in general. Science as a way to art? Here no criticism is even needed.

But during the period of the rise of the exact sciences one expected a great deal more. If you recall Swammerdam's statement, "Here I bring you the proof of God's providence in the anatomy of a louse," you will see what the scientific worker, influenced (indirectly) by Protestantism and Puritanism, conceived to be his task: to show the path to God. People no longer found this path among the philosophers, with their concepts and deductions. All pietist theology of the time, above all Spener, knew that God was not to be found along the road by which the Middle Ages had sought him. God is hidden, His ways are not our ways, His thoughts are not our thoughts. In the exact sciences, however, where one could physically grasp His works, one hoped to come upon the traces of what He planned for the world. And today? Who—aside from certain big children who are indeed found in the natural sciences—still believes that the findings of astronomy, biology, physics, or chemistry could teach us anything about the *meaning* of the world? If there is any such "meaning," along what road could one come upon its tracks? If these natural sciences lead to anything in this way, they are apt to make the belief that there is such a thing as the "meaning" of the universe die out at its very roots.

And finally, science as a way "to God"? Science, this specifically irreligious power? That science today is irreligious no one will doubt in his innermost being, even if he will not admit it to himself. Redemption from

the rationalism and intellectualism of science is [considered] the fundamental presupposition of living in union with the divine. . . . The only thing that is strange is the method that is now followed: the spheres of the irrational, the only spheres that intellectualism has not yet touched, are now raised into consciousness and put under its lens. For in practice this is where the modern intellectualist form of romantic irrationalism leads. This method of emancipation from intellectualism may well bring about the very opposite of what those who take to it conceive as its goal.

After Nietzsche's devastating criticism of those "last men" who "invented happiness," I may leave aside altogether the naive optimism in which science—that is, the technique of mastering life which rests upon science— has been celebrated as the way to happiness. Who believes in this?—aside from a few big children in university chairs or editorial offices. Let us resume our argument.

Under these internal presuppositions, what is the meaning of science as a vocation, now after all these former illusions, the "way to true being," the "way to true art," the "way to true nature," the "way to true God," the "way to true happiness," have been dispelled? Tolstoi has given the simplest answer, with the words: "Science is meaningless because it gives no answer to our question, the only question important for us: 'What shall we do and how shall we live?' " That science does not give an answer to this is indisputable. The only question that remains is the sense in which science gives "no" answer, and whether or not science might yet be of some use to the one who puts the question correctly.

Today one usually speaks of science as "free from presuppositions." Is there such a thing? It depends upon what one understands thereby. All scientific work presupposes that the rules of logic and method are valid; these are the general foundations of our orientation in the world; and, at least for our special question, these presuppositions are the least problematic aspect of science. Science further presupposes that what is yielded by scientific work is important in the sense that it is "worth being known." In this, obviously, are contained all our problems. For this presupposition cannot be proved by scientific means. It can only be *interpreted* with reference to its ultimate meaning, which we must reject or accept according to our ultimate position towards life.

Furthermore, the nature of the relationship of scientific work and its presuppositions varies widely according to their structure. The natural sciences, for instance, physics, chemistry, and astronomy, presuppose as self-evident that it is worth while to know the ultimate laws of cosmic events as far as science can construe them. This is the case not only because with such knowledge one can attain technical results but for its own sake, if the quest for such knowledge is to be a "vocation." Yet this presupposition can by no means be proved. And still less can it be proved that the existence of the world which these sciences describe is worth while, that it has any "meaning," or that it makes sense to live in such a world. Science does not ask for the answers to such questions. . . . Natural science gives us an answer to the question of what we must do if we wish to master life technically. It leaves quite aside, or assumes for its purposes, whether we should and do wish to master life technically and whether it ultimately makes sense to do so. . . .

First, of course, science contributes to the technology of controlling life by calculating external objects as well as man's activities. . . .

Second, science can contribute . . .

methods of thinking, the tools and the training for thought. . . .

Fortunately, however, the contribution of science does not reach its limit with this. We are in a position to help you to a third objective: to gain *clarity*. Of course, it is presupposed that we ourselves possess clarity. As far as this is the case, we can make clear to you the following:

In practice, you can take this or that position when concerned with a problem of value—for simplicity's sake, please think of social phenomena as examples. *If* you take such and such a stand, then, according to scientific experience, you have to use such and such a *means* in order to carry out your conviction practically. Now, these means are perhaps such that you believe you must reject them. Then you simply must choose between the end and the inevitable means. Does the end "justify" the means? Or does it not? The teacher can confront you with the necessity of this choice. He cannot do more, so long as he wishes to remain a teacher and not to become a demagogue. He can, of course, also tell you that if you want such and such an end, then you must take into the bargain the subsidiary consequences which according to all experience will occur. Again we find ourselves in the same situation as before. These are still problems that can also emerge for the technician, who in numerous instances has to make decisions according to the principle of the lesser evil or of the relatively best. Only to him one thing, the main thing, is usually given, namely, the end. But as soon as truly "ultimate" problems are at stake for us this is not the case. With this, at long last, we come to the final service that science as such can render to the aim of clarity, and at the same time we come to the limits of science.

Besides we can and we should state: In terms of its meaning, such and such a practical stand can be derived with inner consistency, and hence integrity, from this or that ultimate *weltanschauliche* position. Perhaps it can only be derived from one such fundamental position, or maybe from several, but it cannot be derived from these or those other positions. Figuratively speaking, you serve this god and you offend the other god when you decide to adhere to this position. And if you remain faithful to yourself, you will necessarily come to certain final conclusions that subjectively make sense. This much, in principle at least, can be accomplished. Philosophy, as a special discipline, and the essentially philosophical discussions of principles in the other sciences attempt to achieve this. Thus, if we are competent in our pursuit (which must be presupposed here) we can force the individual, or at least we can help him, to give himself an *account of the ultimate meaning of his own conduct.* This appears to me as not so trifling a thing to do, even for one's own personal life. Again, I am tempted to say of a teacher who succeeds in this: he stands in the service of "moral" forces: he fulfills the duty of bringing about the self-clarification and a sense of responsibility. And I believe he will be the more able to accomplish this, the more conscientiously he avoids the desire personally to impose upon or suggest to his audience his own stand.

This proposition, which I present here, always takes its point of departure from the one fundamental fact, that so long as life remains immanent and is interpreted in its own terms, it knows only of an unceasing struggle of these gods with one another. Or speaking directly, the ultimately possible attitudes toward life are irreconcilable and hence their struggle can never be brought to a final conclusion. Thus it is necessary to make a decisive choice. Whether, under such conditions, science is a worthwhile "vocation" for somebody, and whether science itself has an objectively valuable "vocation" are again value judgments about which nothing can be said in the lecture-room. To affirm the value of science is a presupposition for teaching there. I personally by my very work answer in the affirmative, and I also do so from precisely the standpoint that hates intellectualism as the worst devil, as youth does today, or usually only fancies it does. In that case the word holds for these youths: "Mind you, the devil is old; grow old to understand him." This does not mean age in the sense of the birth certificate. It means that if one wishes to settle with this devil, one must not take to flight before him as so many like to do nowadays. First of all, one has to see the devil's ways to the end in order to realize his power and his limitations.

Science today is a vocation organized in special disciplines in the service of self-clarification and knowledge of interrelated facts. It is not the gift of grace of seers and prophets dispensing sacred values and revelations, nor does it partake of the contemplation of sages and philosophers about the meaning of the universe. This, to be sure, is the inescapable condition of our historical situation. We cannot evade it so long as we remain true to ourselves. And if Tolstoi's question recurs to you: as science does not, who is to answer the question: "What shall we do, and, how shall we arrange our lives?" or, in the words used here tonight: "Which of the warring gods should we serve? Or should we serve perhaps an entirely different god, and who is he?" then one can say that only a prophet or a savior can give the answers. If there is no such man, or if his message is no longer believed in, then you will certainly not compel him to appear on this earth by having thousands of professors, as privileged hirelings of the state, attempt as petty prophets in their lecture-rooms to take over his role. All they will accomplish is to show that they are unaware of the decisive state of affairs: the prophet for whom so many of our younger generation yearn simply does not exist. But this knowledge in its forceful significance has never become vital for them. The inward interest of a truly religiously "musical" man can never be served by veiling to him and to others the fundamental fact that he is destined to live in a godless and prophetless time by giving him the *ersatz* of armchair prophecy. The integrity of his religious organ, it seems to me, must rebel against this. . . .

The fate of our times is characterized by rationalization and intellectualization and, above all, by the "disenchantment of the world." Precisely the ultimate and most sublime values have retreated from public life either into the transcendental realm of mystic life or into the brotherliness of direct and personal human relations. It is not accidental that our greatest art is intimate and not monumental, nor is it accidental that today only within the smallest and intimate circles, in personal human situations, in *pianissimo*, that something is pulsating that corresponds to the prophetic *pneuma*, which in former times swept through the great communities like a firebrand, welding them together. If we attempt to force and to "invent" a monumental style in art, such miserable monstrosities are produced as the many monuments of the last twenty years. If one tries intellectually to construe new religions without a new and genuine prophecy, then, in an inner sense, something similar will result, but with still worse effects. And academic prophecy, finally, will create only fanatical sects but never a genuine community.

To the person who cannot bear the fate of the times like a man, one must say: may he rather return silently, without the usual publicity build-up of renegades, but simply and plainly. The arms of the old churches are opened widely and compassionately for him. After all, they do not make it hard for him. One way or another he has to bring his "intellectual sacrifice"—that is inevitable. If he can really do it, we shall not rebuke him. For such an intellectual sacrifice in favor of an unconditional religious devotion is ethically quite a different matter than the evasion of the plain duty of intellectual integrity, which sets in if one lacks the courage to clarify one's own ultimate standpoint and rather facilitates this duty by feeble relative judgments. In my eyes, such religious return stands higher than the academic prophecy, which does not clearly realize that in the lecture-rooms of the university no other virtue holds but plain intellectual integrity. Integrity, however, compels us to state that for the many who today tarry for new prophets and saviors, the situation is the same as resounds in the beautiful Edomite watchman's song of the period of exile that has been included among Isaiah's oracles: "He calleth to me out of Seir, Watchman, what of the night? The watchman said, The morning cometh, and also the night: if ye will enquire, enquire ye: return, come."

The people to whom this was said has enquired and tarried for more than two millennia, and we are shaken when we realize its fate. From this we want to draw the lesson that nothing is gained by yearning and tarrying alone, and we shall act differently. We shall set to work and meet the "demands of the day," in human relations as well as in our vocation. This, however, is plain and simple, if each finds and obeys the demon who holds the fibers of his very life.

Part Three

Sociology of

Contemporary Society

INTRODUCTION

Life in contemporary society is, of course, the subject of most sociological analysis. Sociologists describe and explain the structure and change of contemporary social life, including the kinds of groups, social processes, and institutions that are predominant in today's world. Sociologists in North America and Western Europe generally concentrate on the study of their own urban-industrial societies, describing and explaining these as they move toward the metropolitan, bureaucratic, automated world that some have called the postmodern society.[1] The groups of essays in this, the largest section of the book, describe and explain some important aspects of life in this society.

Scientific analysis of any kind is a cooperative, progressive endeavor in which descriptions are made more accurate and explanations more complete as scientists check and expand one another's observations. The social sciences, however, have the special problem that their subject matter is in the process of transformation as they observe it. The social scientist is very much in the position described by the ancient Greek philosopher Heraclitus, who likened life to a river and pointed out that a man, here an observer of life, could never step into the "same" river twice, for each time he walked into it, it actually would be a different river, the part that he originally had observed already having moved on toward the sea. The sociologist studying social classes or suburban communities in America, for example, should know that what he is looking at has probably changed since the last group of sociologists studied it and will be still different if he comes back to restudy it in a few years.[2]

Sociologists and other social scientists must have the courage to face this rapid obsolescence of their data. At the same time, they need to concentrate on the discovery of basic processes at work in contemporary social life so they can identify the over-all trends of change in the postmodern society. In this way, their studies will become less time-bound and more relevant to the de-

[1] See, for example, David Cooperman and E. V. Walter, *Power and Civilization*, Part II, "The Postmodern World" (New York: Thomas Y. Crowell Company, 1962).
[2] Perhaps even more intriguing is the possibility that social life may be changed as a result of being observed and reported on by sociologists. For a good discussion of this question, see John R. Seeley, "Social Science? Some Probative Problems" in *Sociology on Trial*, eds. Maurice R. Stein and Arthur J. Vidich (Englewood Cliffs, N.J.: Prentice-Hall, Inc., 1963).

veloping future, as it can be discerned in the living present. For Part Three, the largest portion of the book, we have sought analyses that not only describe aspects of society today, but that also attempt to project its future trends. In other words the selections here are both fundamental—in that they deal with basic processes, groups, and institutions of modern society—and future-oriented —in that they attempt to describe what our social life is becoming.

This part of the book concentrates on those groups, processes, and institutions that are most important to the postmodern societies coming into existence in North America and Western Europe. The dominant forms of social organization in this kind of society include the metropolis, bureaucracy, social classes, and ethnic groups; basic institutions of contemporary social life include the family, education, the economy, the state, and the military; and fundamental social processes include socialization, stratification, conflict, and change. Although important sociological studies exist of industrial socialist societies and nonindustrial societies of the underdeveloped third world, they are not represented here owing to lack of space. We believe, however, that postmodern societies of the West show some important trends that will develop in advanced societies generally. These include metropolitanization, bureaucratization, and totalization, all of which are described in the readings we have selected. Let us now briefly review the topics that are discussed in the readings of this section.

Families and schools are groups within which the young are *socialized*—that is, prepared for adult life in society as it is presently organized. The kinship and educational systems of our societies are, therefore, secondary institutions that prepare people for life in society but do not significantly shape the over-all structure of society or determine the direction of its change. Religion is also regarded, at least in the United States, as an important socializing institution: Americans report they go to church because it is good for the children to have some religious training. The groups forming these institutions—churches, schools, particular families—prepare individuals to take roles and enact them successfully in a society whose basic structure and direction of change are determined mainly by people's activities in the primary institutions: the economy, government, and the military. Youth is the period of life in which people are making the transition from these socialization institutions to participation in the major institutions of society and the creation of their own families. Sex roles, as defined both in the family and in the society at large, are changing today in response to the structural shifts in social institutions, thereby altering the life conditions of the men and women who will play these roles.

The community is the habitat of the members of a society, the physical and social environment in which they carry out the important activities of their lives: earning a living, raising their families, governing themselves, and educating their children. For primitive man the community—that is, the roving band or the settled village—often constituted the largest social unit and so was synonymous with "society" as a whole. In feudal Europe, the communities were the manors of the nobility and clergy or the towns of the tradesmen and merchants. Industrialization created the factory city as the place of residence of most members of early modern society. Postmodern society is in the process of metropolitanization, as most communities are developing into metropolitan areas that fan out around large central cities and come to include satellite cities, suburbs, and even country towns within the web of their social and economic, although not political, organization. Sociological studies of communities, consequently, are recognizing that particular cities, towns, and villages have to be understood in their metropolitan contexts as specialized parts of the social and economic life of the entire metropolitan area into which they are being integrated. The habitat of postmodern man is becoming the highly integrated metropolitan complex, rather than the distinctive and separate individual communities of the past.

Bureaucracy is the typical form of group structure in most institutional areas of advanced industrial societies. The economy, the government, the military, education, and even religion become bureaucratically organized in both socialist and capitalist countries as they develop toward the advanced industrial form of society. In fact, the only institutional area that has not become bureaucratically organized in advanced societies is the kinship system. Families survive as one of the few nonbureaucratic groups in postmodern society. The trend toward bureaucratization has numerous causes, among the most important of which are the increasing size of the population and the increasing complexity of modern technology. Bureaucracy is the only form of social organization that has so far been invented to handle the large-scale administrative tasks that increasing size and complexity create for modern man in most areas of his social life. Bureaucracy's ability to organize the activities of many different people toward the accomplishment of some common end—such as producing and selling automobiles, governing a city, or fighting a war—results from its formal, rational organization, in which the activities of the participants are governed by sets of rigid rules. Interaction among bureaucratic role players is standardized and impersonal, based on strictly limited areas of competence in which the bureaucrat is expected to be an expert. The effectiveness of bureaucracy comes from the specialization of each participant in some small area of activity in which he becomes an expert and the coordination of the efforts of many such experts toward the achievement of a common goal. Bureaucracy is becoming the organizational environment of postmodern man, and understanding its functioning and its effects on people is necessary for any grasp of the structure of contemporary society and the psychology of contemporary man.

Social class, religion, race, and national origin have long provided bases of group organization in the large nations of Western Europe and North America. Relations among the different classes, races, and ethnic groups (those sharing a common national origin, language, and religion) have provided some of the basic dynamics of conflict, accommodation, and change in the lives of these nations. The United States of America and Canada, for example, were first settled by people from many European countries; in America, some people imported African Negroes to work the plantations of the southern states. Orientals later were brought to the United States to provide labor for the economic enterprises of the western states. Negroes and Orientals today constitute segregated groups forced to live apart from the "white," or Caucasian, populations in residential and general social segregation. The Caucasian populations of these countries are themselves divided into different ethnic groups, each with its distinctive subculture: the French-Canadians and the Jews of large cities in the United States and Canada, for example. And people of Italian, Irish, German, Scandinavian, Polish, and Hungarian backgrounds as well have formed social groups in cities and towns of different parts of these countries. To a greater or lesser degree, these ethnic groups have created organizations in which they carry on separate social lives and through which they promote their interests. Blacks, the most numerous racial minority in the United States, are creating and using organizations of their own to promote the interests of the group as a whole. Racial and ethnic groups probably will continue for some time to provide important forms of association for their members and the dynamics of group conflict in the United States and Canada.

Criminal and other forms of deviant behavior, which contravene the prevailing norms of society, are universal social occurrences. All human societies, therefore, have created mechanisms to prevent, punish, and otherwise control the behavior of their members in light of the prevailing normative system. The police, courts, and prisons of advanced societies form part of a social control apparatus that seeks to deal with violations of society's legal norms. Other institutions, such as mental hospitals, drug and alcohol rehabilitation centers, suicide "hot lines," and psychotherapy, have been developed in advanced societies to deal with the types of deviance prevalent in them. Some types of deviant behavior are very much integrated into parts of the social structure of the society. Organized crime, for example, among other things provides illegal, but wanted, goods and services including gambling, prostitution, and loan sharking to the population. Societies seem to generate different rates of more individual types of deviant behavior, such as mental illness, drug addiction, and suicide, which are said to measure to some extent the effects on individuals of the more stressful aspects of life in a particular society. As a result, rates of different types of deviant behavior tend to be differentially distributed by ethnic group, social class, and sex and age in contemporary societies. In sociological study, the emphasis traditionally has been on discovering how the workings of the social system and the culture generate the patterns of deviant behavior found in the society.

Social class divisions have developed along similar lines in the various industrial capitalist nations of the West. These include an upper class of industrialists, financiers, and merchants, the owners of the means of economic production and exchange; a broad middle class of managers, government officials, small merchants, professional people, salesmen, clerks, and other lower white-collar workers; a working class of factory operatives, laborers, and service workers; and a lower class of people employed in marginal and seasonal work or unable to obtain employment at all. Western European nations have small classes of aristocrats, generally landowners whose estates and titles are survivals from preindustrial society. The extent to which the different classes have formed themselves into social groups actively promoting their common economic interests has differed from class to class and from one time to another. The upper classes have generally formed informal, loose associations of overlapping groups whose unity is based on common social backgrounds of the members and their common interests. The working class in these countries has occasionally formed revolutionary groups seeking to take power by force; however, in the recent past, it more commonly has formed political parties to seek power through the electoral processes. In all countries of the West, the working class has formed labor unions through which it seeks to promote the economic and sometimes political interests of its members. Some parts of the middle class, notably such high-status professional people as doctors and lawyers, have formed strong associations to protect and promote the interests of their professions as they see them. Managers, small merchants, government officials, and white-collar workers have not, for the most part, formed groups to promote their common class interests. Today, class-based social groups appear to be diminishing in number and importance even though major economic inequalities continue to exist in most societies of the West.

The political, economic, and military institutions of the industrial capitalist countries are the primary institutional areas of these societies. Men's actions in the groups that make up these institutions generally shape the organization and functioning of the societies as a whole and the personal experience of the people living in them. These societies, in fact, are in a permanent state of change arising from men's activities in these institutional areas. Other institutions, including the family, education, and religion, must change to accommodate themselves to changes in social life caused by the operation of the primary institutions, although their adaptive changes, as in the case of changes in the birth rate, eventually react on the primary institutions. Economic institutions include all the groups engaged in the production and distribution of material goods and related services in the society. Political institutions include all groups involved in the processes of distribution and exercise of legitimate power in the society. Military institutions include the groups that control the most powerful of the legitimate means of violence in the society.

We have included a discussion of the basic institutions under the single heading of "The Political Economy" because they all must be considered in their interrelations in order to understand their organization and operation today. Western European and North American countries are all welfare states today in which the national governments formally have assumed responsibility for assuring by one means or another the economic well-being of the population and the efficient functioning of the national economy as a whole. The military services, since World War II and during the long cold war, have become the largest branch of the federal government in the United States and a major influence in the national economy. They spend more than sixty billion dollars a year, about twenty-five billion of which is used for procurements from private business and industry. The business corporations themselves exercise significant social, as well as economic, influence through their pricing, investment, and production decisions, which are privately made within the corporations but have great public consequences. The economies of the advanced industrial capitalist countries are becoming more and more organized into a small number of very large corporations. The largest 150 corporations in the United States control more than 60 per cent of the productive assets of that country and about 25 per cent of those of the entire noncommunist world.[3] These corporations are becoming truly international organizations with significant economic interests in so many countries that they cannot be said to "belong" to any one country. Sociologists are just beginning to study this new form of social organization in the world.

The character of social life in a particular era is determined by the structure and processes of interaction in the major social groups and institutions of that period. In assessing the nature of social experience for the individual in our society, it is necessary to summarize its basic trends and point out their consequences for the individual participant in social life. Social scientists and social commentators have, in recent years, pointed out trends toward what have been

[3] See, for example, the essays in Andrew Hacker, ed., *The Corporation Take-Over* (New York: Harper and Row, Publishers, 1964).

called the "organized," or "total," society and the "mass" society.[4] By organized society, or total society, they refer to the tendency for social life to become organized into large-scale, impersonal bureaucracies. In bureaucracies, power is vested in the top positions; the people in these positions make the basic decisions for the organization and these are passed down as orders to people in subordinate positions. The activities of most participants in bureaucracies are determined by these orders and the formal rules, which define the rights and duties of their positions. A kind of bureaucratic totalism develops when most people's lives become organized by large bureaucracies and as individuals they are relatively powerless. If, at the same time, other groups in society, such as associations, informal groups, and interest groups are disappearing or else becoming large-scale bureaucracies themselves, some sociologists feel we have the conditions for the development of the mass society. This is a society in which, outside of the formal organization of the bureaucracies and the personal privacy of the home, social life becomes atomized into a mass of unorganized, only casually related individuals. Mass communication, including television, radio, newspapers, and large-circulation magazines, is seen as the means by which a leveling to a common "mass culture" occurs for these highly differentiated, unrelated individuals. A mass-total society, then, is one in which the individuals are relatively powerless, relate to others primarily in limited bureaucratic roles, and are reduced to a common cultural level by the agencies of the mass media.

Sociology is one of man's instruments for understanding his collective life. Its purposes include discovering the basic character and changes in societies and assessing the consequences of these for man's life. With his perspective on the whole of social life, we feel the sociologist has a special responsibility to try to discern the basic direction of social change and to show contemporary man the kind of society he is creating by his current activities. This is certainly one of the important roles of sociology in modern society.

[4] See, for example, C. Wright Mills, *The Power Elite* (New York: Oxford University Press, Inc., 1956); Paul Goodman, "Youth in the Organized Society," *Commentary*, 95–107 (Feb. 1960); and Harold L. Wilensky, "Mass Society and Mass Culture," *American Sociological Review*, 29: 173–196 (April 1964). Many essays on these topics are collected in Phillip Olsen, ed., *America As a Mass Society* (New York: The Free Press, 1963).

A The Family, Socialization, and Sex Roles

INTRODUCTION

Kinship and education are the basic socialization institutions of contemporary society; and youth is the time in life when people are completing this socialization and moving toward adulthood. The family provides new members for society, as well as the very earliest training of new members in the society's culture. It is the one institution that is not becoming bureaucratically organized and, thus, is one of the few sources of intimate, personal, emotionally involving and expressive social interaction in postmodern society. Education, on the other hand, is becoming one of the major "industries" of contemporary Western societies in the sense that, as more people are going to school for longer periods of time, educational organizations are becoming major employers and spenders of private and public money. Youth is a transitional period between childhood and adulthood that, in our society, has developed a number of *subcultures*, or special worlds, within the larger society, such as those of "teenagers," "juvenile delinquents," and "hippies." Some aspects of these subcultures have been adopted in the larger society, thereby making it possible for older people to participate in them.

Dennis Wrong, in his review of Philippe Ariès's history of the family, *Centuries of Childhood*, reminds us that the family as we know it is actually a recent social invention. The premodern "household" of late medieval times was a very loosely defined unit including parents and their children, perhaps some other blood relatives, business associates such as apprentices and journeymen in the household of a master artisan, and servants of the house, among whom social and sexual relations were often what to us would appear unstructured and promiscuous. According to Ariès, childhood in premodern Europe was not perceived as a special period of life; children were actually thought of and treated as "little adults."

Leo Zakuta describes the trend toward social equality between husbands and wives and the decreasing social distance between parents and children in the nuclear family that is becoming typical of urban North America. This family contrasts strikingly with the large households of premodern Europe and with the extended families of primitive peoples that might include as many as sixty people, and corresponds, it is interesting to note, to the biologically based family unit that has been identified as characteristic of higher primates and some other mammals. The free choice of partners in forming this union, the small size of the family unit, and the increasing physical mobility of the family in modern America, Zakuta claims, all contribute to increasing the intimacy and emotional interdependence of family members. This, he believes, has led to the extension of the ideal of romantic love from courtship into the married life of the couple and to closer, less authoritarian relations between parents and their children.

Harry Gracey provides a case study of socialization processes in American elementary schools today. The first thing children are asked to learn in school, he claims, is how to play the *role of student.* With an account of a day in a kindergarten, he shows that this role includes conformity to an adult-imposed routine, unquestioning obedience to authority, participation in rituals that have no intrinsic meaning for the children, and their creation of private, meaningful social interaction in the interstices of a social and physical environment imposed by adults. Gracey contends that these requirements of the student role are commensurate with the requirements of role playing in bureaucracies generally, and that school today involves preparation for a social life that will be spent mostly in large bureaucratic organizations.

Ulf Hannerz lived in the Washington, D.C., black ghetto for two years studying the subculture there and paying particular attention of the socialization of boys in that community. It has been argued, most notably in the American government's Moynihan Reports on the black family, that because a permanent father was so often lacking, boys growing up in the black inner-city neighborhoods were deprived of male models necessary for their socialization. It was contended that such deprivation would put these boys at a distinct disadvantage in making their way in the adult world, especially outside the ghetto. Hannerz, by contrast, found through his participant observation in the ghetto community itself that, although the actual fathers often were absent from homes with children, there were many males in the local community with whom the boys did interact and from whom they apparently learned the norms of masculine behavior in the subculture. Hannerz also observed that the boys' mothers and other female relatives with whom they had close relationships treated them as boys, or men-children, expecting their behavior to be different from the girls. In this way, the women showed the growing boys what was expected from men in the community.

Suzanne Keller identifies what she considers to be the constant and the variable aspects of the woman's role in contemporary American society. Sex roles, or the activities each society reserves for each gender, are highly variable, she points out, and only minimally related to biological differences between men and women. Since the industrial revolution, when economic activities became separated from the home, the woman's role in the West has been chiefly "maternal, wifely, and erotic." In this generation, she points out, educated women from the affluent sectors of postindustrial society are acting in concert to change the definition of their role to include careers and power in the other institutions of society. Keller identifies some of the personal and social consequences of this shift in societal sex-role definitions.

20

A Social History of the Family

DENNIS H. WRONG

The average social scientist is thoroughly ignorant of Western social history. He is likely to know more about the kinship system of the Trobriand Islanders and the sexual mores of the Eskimos than he knows of the attitudes toward children or the kind of school system that existed in western Europe before the 19th century. Philippe Ariès' *Centuries of Childhood*, which intensively explores the last subjects, among others, is bound therefore to come as something of a revelation, casting a new light on the contemporary sociologist's favorite generalizations about recent trends in parent-child relations, the connection between the family and the larger society, and the "socialization" of the young in general.

That marriage and the family are universal institutions and that all societies must make provision for the maintenance and socialization of children (which, indeed, is what primarily accounts for the universality of marriage and the family) are today sociological commonplaces. It is also well known that our contemporary laws governing marriage, divorce and the rights and obligations of parenthood, our kinship nomenclature and the balance we strike between the family group created by

marriage and the extended family of affinal relatives ("in-laws") are deeply rooted in the Western past, stemming from Hebrew, Christian and classical influences. Demographic historians have, however, only recently become fully aware of the distinctiveness of the Western family as an enduring "structural type" when contrasted with the joint family systems of the great Asian civilizations. The Western family, they have concluded, stresses to a unique degree the priority of the marriage relation over ties of unilateral descent and thus grants greater economic and residential independence to the married pair and their offspring than is common in the Orient, where the nuclear group is absorbed into a larger household of paternal kin.

The interest of demographic historians has centered on the different effects of the Western and Asian family systems on the level of the birth rate and attitudes toward procreation, a difference that may have considerable bearing on the future of the underdeveloped countries now experiencing a population explosion that began in the West nearly two centuries ago. The Western family type was, of course, firmly established long before Europe's demographic revolution, and it may well have provided a favorable setting for the eventual mass adoption of birth control that has curtailed rapid Western growth in the present century. In fact, the recent work of several demographic and economic historians contains the germs of a "familistic" theory, not only of the Western population transition but also of the genesis of capitalism and the Industrial Revolution themselves, which have so often been treated as independent causes of demographic change.

Ariès is a demographic historian, the author of an important study of French population since the 18th century. It was "the study of modern demographic phenomena," he tells us, that led him to conclude that "the family occupied a tremendous place in our industrial societies and that it had perhaps never before exercised so much influence over the human condition." Such a conclusion flatly contradicts the widely held view that the family has suffered a decline in industrial society, that—in the language of an influential school of family sociologists—it has been "losing its functions" and becoming in consequence a less significant focus of our lives. Accordingly, although Ariès' point of departure was demographic history, he has gone beyond it in an attempt "to look back into our past to find out whether the idea of the family had not been born comparatively recently. . . ." The result is a book that, although of limited interest to the population specialist, is endlessly fascinating to students of the family, of life in the premodern West in general and of the changing sensibilities of Western man as expressed in his manners, morals, art and religion.

The hard facts of demography and the only slightly less firm data on the formal structure of the family are quickly passed over as the author attempts to trace a moral revolution in the evaluation of childhood, the treatment of children and the significance attached to family life. Personal memoirs and correspondence, family portraits, the echoes of the past buried in colloquial speech, the subjects and genres of classical painting, religious and "profane" iconography, manuals of etiquette, the published sermons of moralists, old school registers, official histories of educational institutions— these are his sources, as they must necessarily be those of social historians studying beliefs and customs that were so taken for granted as the backdrop of daily life they left few enduring records of their existence in an age antedating universal literacy, the ubiquity of the printing press and the omnivorous fact-collecting of modern social science.

How did our European cultural and biological ancestors evaluate childhood as a period of life in the 16th, 17th and 18th centuries, the era that is the seedbed of so much of the "modern" and the graveyard of so much of the "medieval"? When did they first begin to see childhood as an irrecoverably precious age, worthy of celebration and fixation in art, requiring enrichment by parental solicitude and protection from too early exposure to the corruptions and workaday cynicism of adult life? Was the late medieval and early modern world addicted to the extreme age-grading we take so much for granted today? ("How old are you?" is usually the first question we put to a child we have just met.) How did the grouping of children into school classes differentiated by both age level and progressively more "advanced" subjects of study evolve— a feature of modern schooling that has not been questioned even by the most radical educational reformers? Is the notion of the family as the arena of an intense "private life," a fortress protecting the individuality of the person, truly an ancient heritage of Western culture, as is so often assumed by writers bewailing the forces of "mass society" that are today allegedly breaching its walls?

These are the main questions to

which Ariès addresses himself. His answers reveal a fundamental change of outlook, a transformation of sensibility, that took place in the period he covers. This change occurred within the structural type of the Western family institution, which remained constant throughout. Ariès' data therefore suggest that crucial historical shifts in feeling and imagination may escape the notice of contemporary sociologists whose "structural bias" disposes them to stress enduring institutional forms subject at most to gradual modifications of type. "Not that the family did not exist as a reality," he observes of the period preceding the changes he has described, "but it did not exist as a concept."

Nor does Ariès find that the demographic changes of the early modern period account for the revolution in sensibility he records; it would be highly plausible to interpret an increased concern with childhood and a new solicitude for children as results of the decline in infant mortality that made it easier for parents to cherish each child as an irreplaceable individual by reducing the risk of early death and the resulting shock of bereavement. But Ariès finds that the new interest in the child preceded by more than a century the medical and public health discoveries that decisively reduced infant mortality. He suggests, in fact, that the causal link may have run in the other direction, with increased concern for children producing a state of mind favorable to all hygienic precautions and to the rapid spread of such particular innovations as smallpox vaccination.

Centuries of Childhood is divided into three sections. The first deals with "the idea of childhood." Evidence ranging from iconography depicting the "ages of life" to the history of games and children's dress is surveyed to show the evolution from the complete lack of attribution of any special character

to childhood in medieval society to the intense preoccupation with the physical, moral and—more recently—psychological welfare of children that had developed by the 18th century and still obsesses us today. The second section, occupying roughly half the book, is a history of schooling from the Middle Ages to the end of the *ancien régime*, comprehensively tracing the growth of different types of school and their curriculums, the origins of the school class, the progress of discipline and the development of age-grading in education. The book's final section discusses the family, particularly the "concept of the family." We are shown the metamorphosis of the great, sprawling aristocratic and middle-class households of the late Middle Ages, scarcely distinguishing between members of the family, servants and regular visitors, into the sharply defined unit of the married couple and their children, ensconced in the absolute privacy of their "home," that constitutes the modern family.

Ariès draws his material primarily from French sources, particularly in the section on the school, although he makes a sustained effort to cover developments in England as well. Germany, Switzerland, the Low Countries and Italy are referred to occasionally, usually when the evidence is iconographic. The Latin texts of the Church fathers and the later Renaissance humanists were influential, of course, throughout western Europe, so that much of Ariès' account of early postmedieval society refers to general conditions and needs no specific geographic reference.

Artists in the Middle Ages were not even capable of correctly drawing children. They pictured them as little men, fully equipped with the muscular development and bodily proportions of adults. And children were pictured only in religious art; although adult portraiture was popular, no effort was made to preserve the transitory likeness of the child until funeral effigies of dead children became common in the 16th centure. Before this time and for a considerable period afterward in the lower classes and rural areas, the child was regarded at most as a charming little plaything, a domestic pet, and his death was not much more of an occasion for grief and mourning than is that of a pet dog or cat today.

In the Middle Ages children were weaned rather later—at about the age of seven—than is the custom today, but as soon as weaning was completed they were removed from the care of their mothers or nurses and plunged straight into adult life. There were no special games or pastimes considered to be exclusively appropriate for children. Games like blindman's bluff or hide-and-seek, which later were regarded solely as childish diversions, and which are still part of the strangely traditional and autonomous culture of childhood, were originally played by adults too. Conversely, children of five and six played chess, danced complicated ballet steps and learned to perform on the lute and violin.

No effort was made to conceal the facts of sexuality from small children. Their sex organs were fondled and joked about by adults. The lack of privacy in the medieval household, where any room might serve temporarily as a bedroom and where adults and children commonly shared the same bed, made it difficult for adults to conceal their sexual activities from children; indeed, they had little inclination to do so. Freud's once shocking discovery of infantile and childish curiosity about sex was no more than a rediscovery of what medieval parents and nurses matter-of-factly assumed. In this sense the now vanished Victorian belief in childish innocence did not exist in medieval society, although open references to sexuality before children were permitted

because it was thought that children lacked all true sexual motivation before the age of puberty. There was no awareness of the connection between infantile and adult sexuality on which psychoanalysis so strongly insists.

The change from the casual medieval attitude toward childhood to our current tense concern with it passed through several stages. By the 16th century adult expressions of pleasure at the playfulness and prattling of small children, a pleasure that had previously "formed part of the huge domain of unexpressed feelings," amounted virtually to a "cult of the child" in upper-class families. No less a personage than Montaigne protested irritably: "I cannot abide that passion for caressing newborn children, which have neither mental activities nor recognizable bodily shape by which to make themselves lovable, and I have never willingly suffered them to be fed in my presence." Yet, as Ariès points out, Montaigne's very annoyance at the "coddling" of children "was as novel as 'coddling,' and even more foreign . . . to the indifferent attitude of people in the Middle Ages." His wish to segregate children from adults was shared by the 17th-century moralists and pedagogues whose "fondness for children and its special nature no longer found expression in amusement and 'coddling' but in psychological interest and moral solicitude."

These moralists and pedagogues—of whom the Jesuits and the Jansenists of Port Royal were the most important in France—eventually won the day. Their victory resulted in the creation of a system of schooling conceived of as being a careful, methodical preparation of the child for adult life. The contrast with the old free mingling of children and adults in the Middle Ages could scarcely have been greater. Moreover, the goals of education were no longer merely intellectual or vocational but included the shaping of the child's moral character as well. Thus the school became a thoroughly authoritarian institution in which a corps of disciplinarian masters ruled over a "proletariat" of powerless children. The old freebootery of student life in the Middle Ages—next to which the much deplored hedonism and irresponsibility of our contemporary adolescent and college-age youth seem tame —became a thing of the past. The shutting off of the child in a separate, hierarchical world outside the family reached its zenith in the boarding schools of the 19th century, of which the great English public schools are the best-known examples. The reaction to this incarceration of the child in educational prisons came at the end of the 19th century, when "the family was substituted for the school as the predominant moral setting."

Most of the developments I have summarized applied to boys alone. Girls remained comparatively undifferentiated from women for a longer time: in dress; in the more tenacious belief that, except for religious instruction, they needed no special education outside the family, which effectively delayed the extension of schooling to girls until the late 18th and early 19th centuries; and in the survival through the 17th century of an exceedingly early age at marriage for females—13- and 14-year-old brides were by no means uncommon.

The interest in childhood, first manifest in the 16th century, was part of a developing interest in the family—that is, the "nuclear family" of parents and children—that originated in the 15th century, coinciding with a decline in the value attached to the hereditary line. The hereditary line had been glorified in medieval society, although it had never been the basis for the household group and so lacked the "functional" economic and child-rearing significance of the Oriental unilineal descent group. The Church disapproved of the emphasis on the "pagan" blood ties of the hereditary line, but it did not assume full control of marriage, transforming it into a sacrament, until the 13th century. And it was not until the 16th century that the family became a theme of religious iconography. At the same time, the practice of private family prayers and worship became common, indicating the new value attached to a group that had previously "existed in silence," failing to "awaken feelings strong enough to inspire poet or artist."

But before the family could come to be regarded as the virtual extension of the self that it is today, or even the lair from which one sallied forth to engage the outside world of the Victorian period, more mundane changes in the conditions of life had to take place. The houses of the rich until the end of the 17th century "sheltered, apart from the family proper, a whole population of servants, employees, clerics, clerks, shopkeepers, apprentices and so on." No clear distinctions were made between social, professional and private life, which brought together much the same people in any case. All activities were carried on in the family's living quarters, where the same rooms served successively—and often simultaneously —as salons, offices and bedrooms. It was the social (and often enough sexual) promiscuity of life in the big houses that spurred the clerical pedagogues to their task of building a school system that would effectively remove the child from the family during what were regarded as his formative years. In spite of the earlier development of new emotional relation between parents and children, it was not until the 18th century that "the family began to hold society at a distance, to push it back beyond a steadily extending zone of private life." The change was reflected in the new structure of the house: the old all-purpose rooms disappeared to be replaced by specialized bedrooms and dining rooms, and the rooms now opened off a central corridor, so that it was no longer necessary to pass through each room in traversing the house. Privacy and domesticity, those two prized and interlinked modern values, were born together.

It is not feasible to summarize all the information assembled by Ariès that challenges the stereotyped view of the past held even by most scholars and social scientists. One major conclusion suggests itself, although my own ignorance may have given me an exaggerated view of its novelty. We are accustomed to regarding the Middle Ages as an "age of faith" and to seeing our subsequent history as a steady movement away from a spiritually unified medieval Christendom toward the pluralistic, secularized, science-centered world of the present. The Renaissance, the Reformation, the Enlightenment and the Industrial Revolution are seen as successive stages in this movement. But Ariès' data suggest that Christian ideas and sensibility had little vital influence on social relations and daily life until the 16th century. Although the Church was a crucial unifying and centralizing institution in the polycentric world of medieval feudalism, its relation to daily life, to the web of custom, resembled more closely the relation of the Catholic Church today to the syncretic culture of the part-Indian, part-Negro populations of Central America than it resembled the later clerical reshaping of domestic habits achieved by the reformers of the Reformation and the Counter Reformation. Thus our modern sensibility, while it may properly be described as post-Christian, is in no sense postmedieval. In our attitudes toward the family and childhood we stand in vital respects closer to Christian thought and feeling, even in its more

moralistic and puritanical forms that we see ourselves as reacting against, than to the gay, casual, frequently coarse outlook of the Middle Ages, which cannot even be characterized as the reverse of "child-centered" since it lacked any distinct conception of childhood.

Social history of the kind Ariès gives us reveals more fully than other kinds of history the value of what is called historical perspective. It does so because in exploring the world of childhood and the family, a world in which we are all intimately involved, it succeeds in communicating more profoundly a sense of the strangeness of time and change in the life of man and society. Our familiarity with the subject is enhanced because it is the life of our own historical ancestors that is described in *Centuries of Childhood*. Echoes of that life persist today in the form of beliefs, archaisms of speech and minor customs, twisted and distorted in the crucible of historical transformation, surviving in "form" but not in "function," as the anthropologist would put it. Yet the very fact that this is so, that we are tied to the men and women of the Middle Ages by a thread of cultural continuity, enables us to experience more deeply what the anthropologist calls "culture shock" in confronting these lives so different from ours and yet marked with faint but decisive traces of similarity. No reading of anthropological materials on the kinship systems and domestic lives of primitive peoples can have such an impact. Nor, with all his opportunities for field observation, is it as easy for the anthropologist to succeed in discovering in his data "the tremor of life that he can feel in his own existence," to quote Ariès' brilliant summation of the ultimate aim of the social historian.

21

Equality in North American Marriages

LEO ZAKUTA

During the past several generations there have been important changes in North American family relationships. While this essay emphasizes the husband-wife relation, its main perspectives also apply to the relations between parents and children. The "data" presented here come from the casual observations of family life that are made by everyone, rather than from a formal empirical study of the family. Accordingly, I am assuming that these observations of the North American, urban, middle-class family—the only one that I know at first hand—are sufficiently well known that they can be discussed here without that careful documentation of actual behavior that eventually will be necessary.

My central point is that certain changes in the behavior of family members toward each other stem from alterations in their mutual sentiments—or feelings toward one another; these feelings, in turn, are closely linked to shifts in their standards and forms of family organization. For the sake of economy, these standards and forms will be taken as given, as will be the general conditions out of which they arise: namely, the growth of democratic ideology, cities, and industry; the mobility and mixture of people; and the development of an essentially new society. I will not try to explain why the values and forms have changed, but will simply describe the new ones briefly and concentrate on how they have affected family sentiments and thereby behavior.

Reprinted from *Social Research*, 30: 157–170 (Summer 1963), with permission of the author and the publisher.

Ideological Changes and Romantic Marriage

I have been trying in vain to recall from whom I first heard the suggestion that our fiction—popular as well as "serious"—provides an intriguing symptom of how significantly the married relation has changed in our society. The argument, which is perhaps familiar, goes as follows: In the past, love stories were ordinarily about courtship, and they usually concluded with marriage. The emotional relations of the married were of much less consuming interest, presumably on the assumption that they contained little of comparable fascination. In contrast, today's fiction, drama, and movies frequently center on the emotional relation between husband and wife; typically, they are already married when the story begins. The inference obviously is that those intense feelings which we think of as romance now occur much more often within marriage than they once did. If this inference is valid, why does contemporary marriage produce feelings of romantic involvement or such distress at their departure that the couple may dissolve or seriously consider dissolving their marriage? To pursue this question one must find the structural and ideological conditions which seem most closely associated with romance in general first, then those with its growing importance in contemporary marriage.

In general, romance seems to occur where the partners feel that they choose each other freely rather than where others, usually the parents, do the choosing. (Whether the choice is really "free" is not only beyond proof but,

from the perspective of the social scientist, as totally irrelevant as whether
man's will is really "free." It is the
actor's sense or feeling of being free
to choose that matters, just as a man's
view of whether another's will is free
or not governs his feelings and behavior towards him.)

The suggestion that romantic feelings are linked to a sense of free choice
raises a parenthetical quarrel and question. The quarrel is with those exhorta-
tory treatises on marriage and the family, unfortunately so numerous in the
social sciences, that almost invariably
warn the reader about the "romantic
fallacy" and the dangers of "building"
a marriage on so feeble a foundation as
romance instead of on presumably
more solid stuff, such as similar views
about money, in-laws, child-rearing,
and religion. One wonders how many
of these writers have been sufficiently
inspired by their own preaching to put
it into practice.

The quarrel aside, the question is:
If the "romantic fallacy" refers to expectations that are quite unlikely to be
realized, why select these as if they
were somehow unique? Are people not
constantly launching new enterprises,
activities, and organizations with the
highest (one could almost say the
"wildest") of hopes, some of which we
label "utopian"? And don't many of
these bodies, like most marriages, survive despite the subsequent abatement
of their members' initial hopes? But
who in our fraternity is ready to counsel against this general human tendency? Perhaps romance or falling in
love may occur whenever people commit themselves, with a sense of free
choice, to any undertaking about which
they have great expectations. If so, the
numerous parallels which have been
drawn between "conversion" and "falling in love" should not be surprising.

Returning to the main question, how
does the sense of free choice affect ro-

mance in marriage? Many obvious circumstances make divorce or separation
seem much more feasible to a contemporary couple than to their grandparents and thus give them a greater feeling of choice than was once the case.
The argument, however, that ideological and structural changes are responsible for the development of, or concern about, romance in marriage must
rest on some distinctive grounds. These
are more easily seen if we compare
those two familiar models—the "patriarchal" and "contemporary" family
types.

Three structural changes from the
first type to the second seem to be
closely linked to the growing importance of romantic feelings within marriage. They are, in ascending order of
importance: the family's smaller size,
the greater mobility of the family, and
the equality of the married couple.
These features have been termed structural solely as a matter of economy;
properly, they should be called "ideo-
logical-structural," since each one of
the changes in family form has occurred because the people concerned
felt that they should.

The family's contraction results from
fewer children and fewer relatives in
the household. As a result, the child
may become more deeply involved with
the fewer remaining adults so that in
his subsequent marriage he seeks the
intensity of emotional involvement
which he has already experienced.
Framed in this way—the more adults
in the family, the greater the dispersal
of emotional involvement—this argument does not seem very convincing.
The reduction in family size may not
be important in itself. But it has been
accompanied by another, though somewhat unrelated, change, which has
made it important—the growing equality between parents and children which
tends to intensify their mutual involvement by lowering the barriers that au-

thority usually creates. Once the generations can become closer, numbers become important because the typical family contains fewer adults to serve as the focus for the children's involvement.

The family's greater mobility also tends to intensify the mutual involvement of its members by throwing them together more than would a more stable existence. If the unit which moves is usually the nuclear family, then it cuts itself off from its closest relatives as well as from its whole network of friends and acquaintances. Weakened ties with outsiders increase the members' mutual dependence and reduce their avenues of escape from one another. Although many families may not move, the growth of so many large organizations, including government, with their numerous branches probably means that increasing numbers regard relocation as a distinct possibility. If so, it need not be actually moving, but merely the prospect that heightens the married couple's feeling of how much their happiness hinges on the "success" of this one tie which not only endures when all others are severed but which, by the very breaking of other ties, becomes all the more important. Under these circumstances, would they not count somewhat more heavily on the congeniality of this relation?

It is the third condition of equality that merits the most serious consideration. Its general effect is similar to that of the other two—it brings people together more often and more intimately. Status differences everywhere seem to inhibit free and easy association, and the more pronounced they are, the more separate are the parties, except where their association is formally specified. This principle is built into the official military structure in the form of separate messes that limit extracurricular association and therefore presumably personal involvement across hierarchical levels. We see it arise somewhat more spontaneously in the cafeterias of work organizations and in relations between racial and ethnic groups—in the latter cases, it is called segregation.

Consequences of Inequality. In an apparent paradox, the barriers to ease and intimacy are often less where the status differences are very great, so that a man may have a much freer and easier relation with his slave or servant than he does with his employee or even with his children, or, in some family systems, with his mistress than with his wife. These considerations, incidentally, should warn us against dismissing too lightly the statements of those white Southerners who claim that they love their Negroes. Before condemning the unspoken qualification, "in their place," as hypocrisy, we should ask if this is really very different from the parent who loves his children but who would be furious if they began to do certain things conventionally reserved for adults. P. G. Wodehouse has persistently rung one change on this theme in the delicately balanced relations between Jeeves, the manservant who is equal to every occasion, and his master, Bertie Wooster, who is equal to none of them. Jeeves' invariable way of demonstrating his displeasure with his master—of punishing him, as we say in our flat sociological speech—is by a cool but courteous refusal to exceed his station by offering the advice and suggestions that Bertie requires to cope with his current crisis. Thus, as in many accounts of the Negro in the old South and of others in servitude, Jeeves owes not only his intimacy with his master but also his considerable influence over him to the fact that he not only knows his place, but likes it.

What permits ease and intimacy in these various instances is, of course, that status differences are so large and clear that a more relaxed relation brings no suggestion of fundamental equality between the parties. Furthermore, the relaxation of formalities in relations of this type is ostensibly subject to the pleasure of the superior, and the parties do not associate as equals in any of the situations in which friends ordinarily meet. These considerations indicate that the links between friendship, sociability, and equality deserve a comprehensive examination.

The main point, however, is that if separate activities and restrained relations arise out of status differences, then separation and restraint should be much more prominent in the "patriarchal" than in the "contemporary" family. A casual glance at Toronto's large, post-war, Italian immigrant district shows how obviously they are more prominent. True to the traditions of their Italian patriarchal rural society, males congregate sociably in exclusively masculine groups in the streets and restaurants and the women presumably stay home. If the customers in the restaurants are couples, it is fairly certain that they are not first generation Italians. That the present Toronto pattern is not unusual is clear from William F. Whyte's portrait of comparable Italian groups in Boston in the 1930s.[1] His account, by the way, suggests another parallel between the gang and family. In both cases, the lower status members stay close to home, while the others feel free to roam. The Italian segregation of the sexes has innumerable counterparts the world over, including the British working man's pub and the exclusively male clubs of his "betters." (It is tempting to observe how neatly the proverbial closeness between the British wife and her "mum" and the alleged fondness of Englishmen for their dogs both fit into the general pattern. But this may be merely circulating the stereotype.)

[1] *Street Corner Society* (Chicago: University of Chicago, 1943).

If status differences lead to segregation because people usually seek the companionship of their "equals," then the marital relation in the patriarchal family should display the same kind of separation in matters of sex and companionship as it does in most other activities. And, by all accounts, it does. Allowing for whatever exaggeration is introduced to achieve humor or drama, the stories, movies, and literature of continental Europe in the Victorian age or of contemporary rural society in France, Italy, and elsewhere indicate both the prevalence and the relative openness—the two are obviously interdependent—of extra-marital affairs for men. The relatively open acceptance of prostitution and of having a mistress on the grounds that "boys will be boys" or, less indulgently perhaps, "men are like that," coupled with the clear understanding that girls should be "ladylike," suggests once more the link with status differences. Again, it is the higher status category that is permitted freedom; who can roam, perhaps symbolically; and who at least feel that they have a choice that is less readily available to the lower status group.

One test of this general argument would involve looking at family systems with varying degrees of status difference between the spouses in order to examine the accompanying patterns of sexual fidelity. Thus, in the traditional Chinese family, in which the husband's standing was especially lofty, concubinage was apparently much more acceptable than was its counterpart in Europe, and the concubine's position was correspondingly higher. In the Chinese family, though below the level of a wife, the concubine was often brought into the household and, significantly, her children were considered legitimate. Wifely infidelity, as one would expect, was regarded as more outrageous and disastrous than it was in the European family. The elevated status of the Japanese *geisha* is another case in point. (It would be interesting to know how the occupation of the *geisha* has been affected by the reported rapid "Westernization" of the Japanese family.) Whether polygamy is a further point along this same continuum should be relatively easy to determine by determining whether it is always associated with even greater male dominance.

The contemporary "American" pattern, in which husband and wife are much closer in standing, fits neatly into this scheme on the other side of this argument. Whether extra-marital affairs are less frequent in this system is impossible to say because of their more clandestine nature, but the secrecy itself is the best evidence of its greater unacceptability to all concerned. Were it possible to know, one would expect that infidelity is also more evenly distributed between the sexes in this system than in the patriarchal.

I have pursued this theme in order to show both the extent of separation between wives and husbands in the patriarchal system as well as the link between separateness and relative rank. Relations between the sexes, married or unmarried, between the old and young, and between countless other groups all display essentially the same pattern. Our assumptions about what it is natural for people to do together obviously involve assumptions about their relative status. In most parts of the world, as introductory sociology students soon learn, men and women do not ordinarily dance, walk, or spend their leisure time together. Frequently, they do not even eat together—that seemingly universal expression of equality—and, in the more patriarchal homes in the North American society, parents and children eat separately much more regularly. Finally, our conventional assumption that sex relations,

at least in marriage, are highly personal hardly corresponds to that of many males in the more patriarchal societies who make the distinction between duty and pleasure or between work and play that so often differentiates the formal from the informal.

Consequences of Equality. The extended remarks about the consequences of inequality are a background against which we can see more clearly the consequences, in sentiment and behavior, of greater equality. For various reasons, the status of women and wives in Western and Westernized societies has increased considerably while that of men and husbands has dropped somewhat so that a woman's relationship to them in marriage has become much closer to equal. By reducing the distance which inequality imposes, both the range of association and of reciprocal emotional involvement increase. By emotional involvement, I refer not only to feelings of affection but also to their opposite. Both are likely to grow within the same relation. The central argument is that since mutual involvement increases and becomes more complex, feelings of antagonism and hatred are also likely to become intensified. (The reciprocity of involvement requires emphasis to distinguish these instances from those enduring relations characterized by intense involvement on one side and a much more casual attitude on the other. These asymmetrical feelings are common in authority relations, in which the superior ordinarily looms much larger in the mind of his subordinate than vice versa. Employees and boss, child and parent, and wife and husband in the older family system of the Orient are all instances of this type of unequal emotional involvement.)

As their positions become more equal, the prospect of informal or sociable association seems more natural and appealing to husbands and wives.

In effect, they now view their prospective relation in terms of something like friendship, the main requisite of which is, of course, status equality. As a result, wives and husbands tend to leave their sexually compartmentalized worlds and to do many things together which their grandparents did not. Ideologically, this change is expressed in such phrases as "partnership, companionship," and even "togetherness." Their companionship, we have seen, is fostered not only by their greater equality but also by being more cut off from relatives and friends, including the adult kin who have disappeared from the household. The possibilities of friendship—perhaps it had better be called companionship—are further augmented by some blurring of their former distinctive roles and activities. Not only is the wife freer to venture from the home to work for pay, or on behalf of "worthy causes," or simply to play—all, incidentally, formerly reserved for higher status groups, either men or women of the wealthy leisure class—but her husband is also more likely to participate in the formerly exclusively wifely tasks—in the kitchen, nursery, or even in public by sharing the shopping. Thus, like friends and equals, they do numerous similar things, many of them together.

The combination of these conditions —a smaller, more mobile, and more equalitarian family—leads not only to a more informal, intimate, and complex marital relation; it also leads to a new conception of what that relation ought to be, that is, to new standards of what constitutes a successful marriage. Both partners are likely to expect and to want the more intense mutual involvement that the altered structure of the marriage relation facilitates and to judge the success of their marriage in terms of the extent and the character of that involvement.

Under these circumstances, the sense of personal congeniality or, in the more usual phrase, "compatibility," becomes a, or perhaps the, central criterion on which the partners assess the success of their marriage and decide on its future.

Those who regard these developments with dismay or distaste usually conclude that marriage has come to mean less to the contemporary couple since so many do decide to terminate it. The advocates of the new often argue, on the other hand, that these decisions indicate the very opposite; namely, that people now expect more from their marriage and are unwilling to settle for the unhappy relations that previous generations endured. But this argument, like any evaluative one, is insoluble and beside the point. It is not a matter of greater or lesser expectations but of different ones. And the heavy emphasis placed on personal congeniality means that many of the relations that do not measure up to the expectations of at least one of the partners will be terminated.

Furthermore, the new marital structure and expectations create additional hazards to the permanence of the relation. By facilitating very strong involvement, they are likely to lead, at least on occasion, to more intense antagonism and bitter clashes. Feelings of equality contribute to this possibility by removing or threatening to remove ultimate authority from the husband and thereby open the way to struggle for power, since the right to decide is no longer vested in a position but in each individual's conviction of what should be done. Finally, if their relation "goes sour" chronically, both partners are likely to feel the consequences as more devastating than did their grandparents. Unlike the latter, they have fewer avenues of escape from each other, they face the agonies of decision about the formal status of their marriage, and their deeper mutual involvement tends to produce stronger friction and animosity. It is therefore hardly surprising that, under these conditions, so many contemporary couples find their marriages too intolerable to endure. (In addition, if equality tends to reduce or conceal the incidence of husbands' infidelity, it simultaneously increases its seriousness as an offence and thus its threat to the continuation of the marriage.)

Thus instead of regarding a "high" rate of divorce and separation as a somewhat alien virus which has managed to infect the North American marriage system, we may, perhaps more profitably, view it as an inevitable outcome of the distinctive ideology, structure, and sentiments of that system.

I have suggested previously that the sense of free choice seems a necessary condition for romance—whether before or within marriage. Several obvious conditions provide this sense to the contemporary married couple. Among them are, of course, the greater prevalence and acceptability of divorce, one further instance of how an effect is also a cause, as well as the greater earning power of women, that facilitates the step for both partners. If I seem to have underemphasized this last condition, it was mainly out of reluctance to overemphasize it. While it seems extremely important, its exact significance is very difficult to determine since divorce and women's earning power have both risen considerably over the long run. Unless one can somehow separate these variables, precise statements about their relation seem impossible. These considerations naturally lead to speculation about Hollywood, where both divorce and the earning power of women seem to have reached unprecedented heights. Here is the community in which the status and income of women is least dependent on their husbands and where equality between the married partners and the sense of free choice about continuing the marriage are at a peak. It is under these circumstances, I would guess, that the concern about romance in marriage is most intense since the feeling of great freedom makes the continuity of the marriage contingent on little else. And despite all of the tongue-clucking about Hollywood, it seems clear that marriage still rates very highly there. How else can we account for Hollywood's apparently endless optimism about marriage in the face of such seemingly overwhelming odds.

The shifts in the standards and structure within the family, and more generally between the sexes, and between adults and children have several other effects on sentiments and behavior that seem worthy of note. As a result of the diminishing status distance between the sexes, in general, and between the various age levels, males and females seem increasingly at ease with each other and so do the young with their elders, though the reverse is not necessarily as true.

More specifically, greater equality seems to reduce the fear, deference, and perhaps even awe that children once had toward their parents and possibly wives toward their husbands. The contemporary father who lectures his son, "I would never have dared speak to *my* father as you do to me," may be doing something more than repeating a universal and timeless lament of fathers; he may, for a change in this endless litany, be uttering a simple truth. Correspondingly, husbands are more likely to be attentive and sensitive to the wishes, tastes, and viewpoints of their wives and children than they have been in the past, one example of which is the new ideology of sex relations in the twentieth century.[2] Status equality seems to be the central condition for reciprocal sensitivity to the wishes and feelings of others. And this is a point that warrants fuller examination than is possible in this short essay.

How these shifts in structure and sentiment affect the cohesion of the family merits some special consideration. In this matter I take as my whipping boy George Homans, as a perverse repayment for the considerable debt that this paper obviously owes him. In *The Human Group* he refers to the contemporary family as one of "low integration" and to its more patriarchal predecessor as one of "high integration." [3] But is "integration," or whatever we call the binding ties, all of a piece and thus simply a matter of more or less? In the older family type, cohesion or integration depended more heavily on specialized and physically interdependent roles with a fairly clear, if elaborate, chain of command, as well as, of course, considerable emotional involvement and interdependence. In the contemporary family, specialized roles, physical interdependence, and authority are all still of central importance, but the balance has been shifting away from these aspects towards the emotional involvement on which

the cohesion of more informal groups depends. In brief, the family has been moving away from the elaborate, formal, and involuntary structure characteristic of large and stable organizations toward the smaller, more intense, and more volatile association composed of freely consenting equals which is characteristic of more informal groups.

Conclusion

I will conclude with a venture into the more fanciful, where the sociologist can treat more easily than he can test. If changes in the relations between the sexes can affect their conscious sentiments toward each other, then why can they not similarly affect those feelings that are more buried and which are manifested only indirectly in overt behavior? If males have experienced a loss of status relative to females, then one should expect that at least some—like any group which has suffered a loss of status—would exhibit various forms of compensation for the loss and resentment toward the usurpers, and that these forms would be perhaps partly in the realm of fantasy.

Possibly the popularity of magazines of the *Playboy* type represents such a reaction. After all, the central themes of these magazines can be interpreted easily enough in terms of both compensation and resentment. There is self-enhancement through the vicarious association with the habits and objects of the rich and lofty. But the outstanding "plaything" of the "playboy" is women. His sure and easy "way with women" is perhaps his chief qualification for solid standing as a "playboy." The growing discrepancy between the fantasy—the smooth, self-assured, sophisticated, and uninvolved male mastery of uniformly devoted and eager women—and the increasingly free and equal relations between the sexes may

[2] Significantly, that ideology emphasizes "sensitivity" for the male, "freedom" for the woman, and reduction of the traditional or stereotyped differences in their sexual roles and responses. And, as might be expected, the evidence of Alfred Kinsey and his associates strongly suggests that these modes of behavior are much more prevalent in the middle class, especially among the more highly educated.

[3] *The Human Group* (New York: Harcourt, Brace, 1950), p. 280. The essay's general indebtedness to the writings of Ernest Burgess and Talcott Parsons on the family and marriage will be sufficiently obvious to most readers so that specific references have seemed unnecessary.

be the source of the apparent popularity of these periodicals. Another branch of this type of periodical—a "lower" one by popular repute—expresses the male's resentment much more directly,

sexual "sadism" permitting him to participate vicariously in a more vigorous revenge on those who have robbed him of his glorious patrimony.

22

Learning the Student Role: Kindergarten as Academic Boot Camp*

HARRY L. GRACEY

Introduction

Education must be considered one of the major institutions of social life today. Along with the family and organized religion, however, it is a "secondary institution," one in which people are prepared for life in society as it is presently organized. The main dimensions of modern life, that is, the nature of society as a whole, is determined principally by the "primary institutions," which today are the economy, the political system, and the military establishment. Education has been defined by sociologists, classical and contemporary, as an institution which serves society by socializing people into it through a formalized, standardized procedure. At the beginning of this century Emile Durkheim told student teachers at the University of Paris that education "consists of a methodical socialization of the younger generation." He went on to add:

It is the influence exercised by adult generations on those that are not ready for social life. Its object is to arouse and to develop in the child a certain number of physical, intellectual, and moral states that are demanded of him by the political society as a whole and by the special milieu for which he is specifically destined. . . . To the egotistic and asocial being that has just been born, (society) must, as rapidly as possible, add another, capable of leading a moral and social life. Such is the work of education.[1]

The educational process, Durkheim said, "is above all the means by which society perpetually recreates the conditions of its very existence." [2] The contemporary educational sociologist, Wilbur Brookover, offers a similar formulation in his recent textbook definition of education:

Actually, therefore, in the broadest sense education is synonymous with socialization. It includes any social behavior that assists in the induction of the child into membership in the society or any behavior by which

* This article is based on research conducted with the Bank Street College of Education under NIMH Grant No. 9135. The study is more fully reported in Harry L. Gracey, *Curriculum or Craftsmanship: Elementary School Teacher in a Bureaucratic System*. Chicago, University of Chicago Press, 1972.

[1] Emile Durkheim, *Sociology and Education* (New York: The Free Press, 1956), pp. 71–72.
[2] *Ibid.*, p. 123.

the society perpetuates itself through the next generation.[3]

The educational institution is, then, one of the ways in which society is perpetuated through the systematic socialization of the young, while the nature of the society which is being perpetuated —its organization and operation, its values, beliefs and ways of living—are determined by the primary institutions. The educational system, like other secondary institutions, *serves* the society which is *created* by the operation of the economy, the political system, and the military establishment.

Schools, the social organizations of the educational institution, are today for the most part large bureaucracies run by specially trained and certified people. There are few places left in modern societies where formal teaching and learning is carried on in small, isolated groups, like the rural, one-room schoolhouses of the last century. Schools are large, formal organizations which tend to be parts of larger organizations, local community School Districts. These School Districts are bureaucratically organized and their operations are supervised by state and local governments. In this context, as Brookover says:

the term education is used . . . to refer to a system of schools, in which specifically designated persons are expected to teach children and youth certain types of acceptable behavior. The school system becomes a . . . unit in the total social structure and is recognized by the members of the society as a separate social institution. Within this structure a portion of the total socialization process occurs.[4]

Education is the part of the socialization process which takes place in the

[3] Wilbur Brookover, *The Sociology of Education* (New York: American Book Company, 1957), p. 4.
[4] *Ibid.*, p. 6.

schools; and these are, more and more today, bureaucracies within bureaucracies.

Kindergarten is generally conceived by educators as a year of preparation for school. It is thought of as a year in which small children, five or six years old, are prepared socially and emotionally for the academic learning which will take place over the next twelve years. It is expected that a foundation of behavior and attitudes will be laid in kindergarten on which the children can acquire the skills and knowledge they will be taught in the grades. A booklet prepared for parents by the staff of a suburban New York school system says that the kindergarten experience will stimulate the child's desire to learn and cultivate the skills he will need for learning in the rest of his school career. It claims that the child will find opportunities for physical growth, for satisfying his "need for self-expression," acquire some knowledge, and provide opportunities for creative activity. It concludes, "The most important benefit that your five-year-old will receive from kindergarten is the opportunity to live and grow happily and purposefully with others in a small society." The kindergarten teachers in one of the elementary schools in this community, one we shall call the Wilbur Wright School, said their goals were to see that the children "grew" in all ways: physically, of course, emotionally, socially, and academically. They said they wanted children to like school as a result of their kindergarten experiences and that they wanted them to learn to get along with others.

None of these goals, however, is unique to kindergarten; each of them is held to some extent by teachers in the other six grades at the Wright School. And growth would occur, but differently, even if the child did not attend school. The children already know how to get along with others, in their families and their play groups. The unique job of the kindergarten in the educational division of labor seems rather to be teaching children the student role. The student role is the repertoire of behavior and attitudes regarded by educators as appropriate to children in school. Observation in the kindergartens of the Wilbur Wright School revealed a great variety of activities through which children are shown and then drilled in the behavior and attitudes defined as appropriate for school and thereby induced to learn the role of student. Observations of the kindergartens and interviews with the teachers both pointed to the teaching and learning of classroom routines as the main element of the student role. The teachers expended most of their efforts, for the first half of the year at least, in training the children to follow the routines which teachers created. The children were, in a very real sense, *drilled* in tasks and activities created by the teachers for their own purposes and beginning and ending quite arbitrarily (from the child's point of view) at the command of the teacher. One teacher remarked that she hated September, because during the first month "everything has to be done rigidly, and repeatedly, until they know exactly what they're supposed to do." However, "by January," she said, "they know exactly what to do [during the day] and I don't have to be after them all the time." Classroom routines were introduced gradually from the beginning of the year in all the kindergartens, and the children were drilled in them as long as was necessary to achieve regular compliance. By the end of the school year, the successful kindergarten teacher has a well-organized group of children. They follow classroom routines automatically, having learned all the command signals and the expected responses to them. They have, in our terms, learned the student role. The follow-

ing observation shows one such classroom operating at optimum organization on an afternoon late in May. It is the class of an experienced and respected kindergarten teacher.

An Afternoon in Kindergarten

At about 12:20 in the afternoon on a day in the last week of May, Edith Kerr leaves the teachers' room where she has been having lunch and walks to her classroom at the far end of the primary wing of Wright School. A group of five- and six-year-olds peers at her through the glass doors leading from the hall cloakroom to the play area outside. Entering her room, she straightens some material in the "book corner" of the room, arranges music on the piano, takes colored paper from her closet and places it on one of the shelves under the window. Her room is divided into a number of activity areas through the arrangement of furniture and play equipment. Two easels and a paint table near the door create a kind of passageway inside the room. A wedge-shaped area just inside the front door is made into a teacher's area by the placing of "her" things there: her desk, file, and piano. To the left is the book corner, marked off from the rest of the room by a puppet stage and a movable chalkboard. In it are a display rack of picture books, a record player, and a stack of children's records. To the right of the entrance are the sink and clean-up area. Four large round tables with six chairs at each for the children are placed near the walls about halfway down the length of the room, two on each side, leaving a large open area in the center for group games, block building, and toy truck driving. Windows stretch down the length of both walls, starting about three feet from the floor and extending almost to the high ceilings. Under the windows are long shelves on which are kept all the toys, games, blocks, paper, paints and other equipment of the kindergarten. The left rear corner of the room is a play store with shelves, merchandise, and cash register; the right rear corner is a play kitchen with stove, sink, ironing board, and bassinette with baby dolls in it. This area is partly shielded from the rest of the room by a large standing display rack for posters and children's art work. A sandbox is found against the back wall between these two areas. The room is light, brightly colored and filled with things adults feel five- and six-year-olds will find interesting and pleasing.

At 12:25 Edith opens the outside door and admits the waiting children. They hang their sweaters on hooks outside the door and then go to the center of the room and arrange themselves in a semi-circle on the floor, facing the teacher's chair which she has placed in the center of the floor. Edith follows them in and sits in her chair checking attendance while waiting for the bell to ring. When she has finished attendance, which she takes by sight, she asks the children what the date is, what day and month it is, how many children are enrolled in the class, how many are present, and how many are absent.

The bell rings at 12:30 and the teacher puts away her attendance book. She introduces a visitor, who is sitting against the right wall taking notes, as someone who wants to learn about schools and children. She then goes to the back of the room and takes down a large chart labeled "Helping Hands." Bringing it to the center of the room, she tells the children it is time to change jobs. Each child is assigned some task on the chart by placing his name, lettered on a paper "hand," next to a picture signifying the task—e.g., a broom, a blackboard, a milk bottle, a flag, and a Bible. She asks the children who wants each of the jobs and rearranges their "hands" accordingly.

Returning to her chair, Edith announces, "One person should tell us what happened to Mark." A girl raises her hand, and when called on says, "Mark fell and hit his head and had to go to the hospital." The teacher adds that Mark's mother had written saying he was in the hospital.

During this time the children have been interacting among themselves, in their semi-circle. Children have whispered to their neighbors, poked one another, made general comments to the group, waved to friends on the other side of the circle. None of this has been disruptive, and the teacher has ignored it for the most part. The children seem to know just how much of each kind of interaction is permitted—they may greet in a soft voice someone who sits next to them, for example, but may not shout greetings to a friend who sits across the circle, so they confine themselves to waving and remain well within understood limits.

At 12:35 two children arrive. Edith asks them why they are late and then sends them to join the circle on the floor. The other children vie with each other to tell the newcomers what happened to Mark. When this leads to a general disorder Edith asks, "Who has serious time?" The children become quiet and a girl raises her hand. Edith nods and the child gets a Bible and hands it to Edith. She reads the Twenty-third Psalm while the children sit quietly. Edith helps the child in charge begin reciting the Lord's Prayer, the other children follow along for the first unit of sounds, and then trail off as Edith finishes for them. Everyone stands and faces the American flag hung to the right of the door. Edith leads the pledge to the flag, with the children again following the familiar sounds as far as they remember them. Edith then asks the girl in charge what song she wants and the child replies, "My Country." Edith goes to the piano and plays "America," singing as the children follow her words.

Edith returns to her chair in the center of the room and the children sit again in the semi-circle on the floor. It is 12:40 when she tells the children, "Let's have boys' sharing time first." She calls the name of the first boy sitting on the end of the circle, and he comes up to her with a toy helicopter. He turns and holds it up for the other children to see. He says, "It's a helicopter." Edith asks, "What is it used for?" and he replies, "For the army. Carry men. For the war." Other children join in, "For shooting submarines." "To bring back men from space when they are in the ocean." Edith sends the boy back to the circle and asks the next boy if he has something. He replies "No" and she passes on to the next. He says "Yes" and brings a bird's nest to her. He holds it for the class to see, and the teacher asks, "What kind of bird made the nest?" The boy replies, "My friend says a rain bird made it." Edith asks what the nest is made of and different children reply, "mud," "leaves" and "sticks." There is also a bit of moss woven into the nest and Edith tries to describe it to the children. They, however, are more interested in seeing if anything is inside it, and Edith lets the boy carry it around the semi-circle showing the children its insides. Edith tells the children of some baby robins in a nest in her yard, and some of the children tell about baby birds they have seen. Some children are asking about a small object in the nest which they say looks like an egg, but all have seen the nest now and Edith calls on the next boy. A number of children say, "I know what Michael has, but I'm not telling." Michael brings a book to the teacher and then goes back to his place in the circle of children. Edith reads the last page of the book to the class. Some children tell of books which they have

at home. Edith calls the next boy, and three children call out, "I know what David has." "He always has the same thing." "It's a bang-bang." David goes to his table and gets a box which he brings to Edith. He opens it and shows the teacher a scale-model of an old-fashioned dueling pistol. When David does not turn around to the class, Edith tells him, "Show it to the children," and he does. One child says, "Mr. Johnson [the principal] said no guns." Edith replies, "Yes, how many of you know that?" Most of the children in the circle raise their hands. She continues, "That you aren't supposed to bring guns to school?" She calls the next boy on the circle and he brings two large toy soldiers to her which the children enthusiastically identify as being from "Babes in Toyland." The next boy brings an American flag to Edith and shows it to the class. She asks him what the stars and stripes stand for and admonishes him to treat it carefully. "Why should you treat it carefully?" she asks the boy. "Because it's our flag," he replies. She congratulates him, saying, "That's right."

"Show and Tell" lasted twenty minutes and during the last ten one girl in particular announced that she knew what each child called upon had to show. Edith asked her to be quiet each time she spoke out, but she was not content, continuing to offer her comment at each "show." Four children from other classes had come into the room to bring something from another teacher or to ask for something from Edith. Those with requests were asked to return later if the item wasn't readily available.

Edith now asks if any of the children told their mothers about their trip to the local zoo the previous day. Many children raise their hands. As Edith calls on them, they tell what they liked in the zoo. Some children cannot wait to be called on, and they call out things to the teacher, who asks them to be quiet. After a few of the animals are mentioned, one child says, "I liked the spooky house," and the others chime in to agree with him, some pantomiming fear and horror. Edith is puzzled, and asks what this was. When half the children try to tell her at once, she raises her hand for quiet, then calls on individual children. One says, "The house with nobody in it"; another, "The dark little house." Edith asks where it was in the zoo, but the children cannot describe its location in any way which she can understand. Edith makes some jokes but they involve adult abstractions which the children cannot grasp. The children have become quite noisy now, speaking out to make both relevant and irrelevant comments, and three little girls have become particularly assertive.

Edith gets up from her seat at 1:10 and goes to the book corner, where she puts a record on the player. As it begins a story about the trip to the zoo, she returns to the circle and asks the children to go sit at the tables. She divides them among the tables in such a way as to indicate that they don't have regular seats. When the children are all seated at the four tables, five or six to a table, the teacher asks, "Who wants to be the first one?" One of the noisy girls comes to the center of the room. The voice on the record is giving directions for imitating an ostrich and the girl follows them, walking around the center of the room holding her ankles with her hands. Edith replays the record, and all the children, table by table, imitate ostriches down the center of the room and back. Edith removes her shoes and shows that she can be an ostrich too. This is apparently a familiar game, for a number of children are calling out, "Can we have the crab?" Edith asks one of the children to do a crab "so we can all re-

member how," and then plays the part of the record with music for imitating crabs by. The children from the first table line up across the room, hands and feet on the floor and faces pointing toward the ceiling. After they have "walked" down the room and back in this posture they sit at their table and the children of the next table play "crab." The children love this; they run from their tables, dance about on the floor waiting for their turns and are generally exuberant. Children ask for the "inch worm" and the game is played again with the children squirming down the floor. As a conclusion Edith shows them a new animal imitation, the "lame dog." The children all hobble down the floor on three "legs," table by table, to the accompaniment of the record.

At 1:30 Edith has the children line up in the center of the room; she says, "Table one, line up in front of me," and children ask, "What are we going to do?" Then she moves a few steps to the side and says, "Table two over here, line up next to table one," and more children ask, "What for?" She does this for table three and table four and each time the children ask, "Why, what are we going to do?" When the children are lined up in four lines of five each, spaced so that they are not touching one another, Edith puts on a new record and leads the class in calisthenics, to the accompaniment of the record. The children just jump around every which way in their places instead of doing the exercises, and by the time the record is finished, Edith, the only one following it, seems exhausted. She is apparently adopting the President's new "Physical Fitness" program in her classroom.

At 1:35 Edith pulls her chair to the easels and calls the children to sit on the floor in front of her, table by table. When they are all seated she asks, "What are you going to do for work-time today?" Different children raise their hands and tell Edith what they are going to draw. Most are going to make pictures of animals they saw in the zoo. Edith asks if they want to make pictures to send to Mark in the hospital, and the children agree to this. Edith gives drawing paper to the children, calling them to her one by one. After getting a piece of paper, the children go to the crayon box on the right-hand shelves, select a number of colors, and go to the tables, where they begin drawing. Edith is again trying to quiet the perpetually talking girls. She keeps two of them standing by her so they won't disrupt the others. She asks them, "Why do you feel you have to talk all the time," and then scolds them for not listening to her. Then she sends them to their tables to draw.

Most of the children are drawing at their tables, sitting or kneeling in their chairs. They are all working very industriously and, engrossed in their work, very quietly. Three girls have chosen to paint at the easels, and having donned their smocks, they are busily mixing colors and intently applying them to their pictures. If the children at the tables are primitives and neo-realists in their animal depictions, these girls at the easels are the class abstract-expressionists, with their broad-stroked, colorful paintings.

Edith asks of the children generally, "What color should I make the cover of Mark's book?" Brown and green are suggested by some children "because Mark likes them." The other children are puzzled as to just what is going on and ask, "What book?" or "What does she mean?" Edith explains what she thought was clear to them already, that they are all going to put their pictures together in a "book" to be sent to Mark. She goes to a small table in the play-kitchen corner and tells the children to bring her their pictures when they are

finished and she will write their message for Mark on them.

By 1:50 most children have finished their pictures and given them to Edith. She talks with some of them as she ties the bundle of pictures together—answering questions, listening, carrying on conversations. The children are playing in various parts of the room with toys, games and blocks which they have taken off the shelves. They also move from table to table examining each other's pictures, offering compliments and suggestions. Three girls at a table are cutting up colored paper for a collage. Another girl is walking about the room in a pair of high heels with a woman's purse over her arm. Three boys are playing in the center of the room with the large block set, with which they are building walk-ways and walking on them. Edith is very much concerned about their safety and comes over a number of times to fuss over them. Two or three other boys are pushing trucks around the center of the room, and mild altercations occur when they drive through the block constructions. Some boys and girl are playing at the toy store, two girls are serving "tea" in the play kitchen and one is washing a doll baby. Two boys have elected to clean the room, and with large sponges they wash the movable blackboard, the puppet stage, and then begin on the tables. They run into resistance from the children who are working with construction toys on the tables and do not want to dismantle their structures. The class is like a room full of bees, each intent on pursuing some activity, occasionally bumping into one another, but just veering off in another direction without serious altercation. At 2:05 the custodian arrives pushing a cart loaded with half-pint milk containers. He places a tray of cartons on the counter next to the sink, then leaves. His coming and going is unnoticed in the room (as, incidentally, is the presence of the observer, who is completely ignored by the children for the entire afternoon).

At 2:15 Edith walks to the entrance of the room, switches off the lights, and sits at the piano and plays. The children begin spontaneously singing the song, which is "Clean up, clean up. Everybody clean up." Edith walks around the room supervising the clean-up. Some children put their toys, the blocks, puzzles, games, and so on back on their shelves under the windows. The children making a collage keep right on working. A child from another class comes in to borrow the 45-rpm adaptor for the record player. At more urging from Edith the rest of the children shelve their toys and work. The children are sitting around their tables now and Edith asks, "What record would you like to hear while you have your milk?" There is some confusion and no general consensus, so Edith drops the subject and begins to call the children, table by table, to come get their milk. "Table one," she says, and the five children come to the sink, wash their hands and dry them, pick up a carton of milk and a straw, and take it back to their table. Two talking girls wander about the room interfering with the children getting their milk and Edith calls out to them to "settle down." As the children sit many of them call out to Edith the name of the record they want to hear. When all the children are seated at tables with milk, Edith plays one of these records called "Bozo and the Birds" and shows the children pictures in a book which go with the record. The record recites, and the book shows the adventures of a clown, Bozo, as he walks through a woods meeting many different kinds of birds who, of course, display the characteristics of many kinds of people or,

more accurately, different stereotypes. As children finish their milk they take blankets or pads from the shelves under the windows and lie on them in the center of the room, where Edith sits on her chair showing the pictures. By 2:30 half the class is lying on the floor on their blankets, the record is still playing and the teacher is turning the pages of the book. The child who came in previously returns the 45-rpm adaptor, and one of the kindergarteners tells Edith what the boy's name is and where he lives.

The record ends at 2:40. Edith says, "Children, down on your blankets." All the class is lying on blankets now, Edith refuses to answer the various questions individual children put to her because, she tells them, "it's rest time now." Instead she talks very softly about what they will do tomorrow. They are going to work with clay, she says. The children lie quietly and listen. One of the boys raises his hand and when called on tells Edith, "The animals in the zoo looked so hungry yesterday." Edith asks the children what they think about this and a number try to volunteer opinions, but Edith accepts only those offered in a "rest-time tone," that is, softly and quietly. After a brief discussion of animal feeding, Edith calls the names of the two children on milk detail and has them collect empty milk cartons from the tables and return them to the tray. She asks the two children on clean-up detail to clean up the room. Then she gets up from her chair and goes to the door to turn on the lights. At this signal the children all get up from the floor and return their blankets and pads to the shelf. It is raining (the reason for no outside play this afternoon) and cars driven by mothers clog the school drive and line up along the street. One of the talkative little girls comes over to Edith and pointing out the window says,

"Mrs. Kerr, see my mother in the new Cadillac?"

At 2:50 Edith sits at the piano and plays. The children sit on the floor in the center of the room and sing. They have a repertoire of songs about animals, including one in which each child sings a refrain alone. They know these by heart and sing along through the ringing of the 2:55 bell. When the song is finished, Edith gets up and coming to the group says, "Okay, rhyming words to get your coats today." The children raise their hands and as Edith calls on them, they tell her two rhyming words, after which they are allowed to go into the hall to get their coats and sweaters. They return to the room with these and sit at their tables. At 2:59 Edith says, "When you have your coats on, you may line up at the door." Half of the children go to the door and stand in a long line. When the three o'clock bell rings, Edith returns to the piano and plays. The children sing a song called "Goodbye," after which Edith sends them out.

Training for Learning and for Life

The day in kindergarten at Wright School illustrates both the content of the student role as it has been learned by these children and the processes by which the teacher has brought about this learning, or, "taught" them the student role. The children have learned to go through routines and to follow orders with unquestioning obedience, even when these make no sense to them. They have been disciplined to do as they are told by an authoritative person without significant protest. Edith has developed this discipline in the children by creating and enforcing a rigid social structure in the classroom through which she effectively controls the behavior of most of the children for most of the school day. The "living with others in a small society" which the school pamphlet tells parents is the most important thing the children will learn in kindergarten can be seen now in its operational meaning, which is learning to live by the routines imposed by the school. This learning appears to be the principal content of the student role.

Children who submit to school-imposed discipline and come to identify with it, so that being a "good student" comes to be an important part of their developing identities, *become* the good students by the school's definitions. Those who submit to the routines of the school but do not come to identify with them will be adequate students who find the more important part of their identities elsewhere, such as in the play group outside school. Children who refuse to submit to the school routines are rebels, who become known as "bad students" and often "problem children" in the school, for they do not learn the academic curriculum and their behavior is often disruptive in the classroom. Today schools engage clinical psychologists in part to help teachers deal with such children.

In looking at Edith's kindergarten at Wright School, it is interesting to ask how the children learn this role of student—come to accept school-imposed routines—and what, exactly, it involves in terms of behavior and attitudes. The most prominent features of the classroom are its physical and social structures. The room is carefully furnished and arranged in ways adults feel will interest children. The play store and play kitchen in the back of the room, for example, imply that children are interested in mimicking these activities of the adult world. The only space left for the children to create something of their own is the empty center of the room, and the materials at their disposal are the blocks, whose use causes anxiety on the part of the teacher. The room, being carefully organized physically by the adults, leaves little room for the creation of physical organization on the part of the children.

The social structure created by Edith is a far more powerful and subtle force for fitting the children to the student role. This structure is established by the very rigid and tightly controlled set of rituals and routines through which the children are put during the day. There is first the rigid "locating procedure" in which the children are asked to find themselves in terms of the month, date, day of the week, and the number of the class who are present and absent. This puts them solidly in the real world as defined by adults. The day is then divided into six periods whose activities are for the most part determined by the teacher. In Edith's kindergarten the children went through Serious Time, which opens the school day, Sharing Time, Play Time (which in clear weather would be spent outside), Work Time, Clean-up Time, after which they have their milk, and Rest Time, after which they go home. The teacher has programmed activities for each of these Times.

Occasionally the class is allowed limited discretion to choose between proffered activities, such as stories or records, but original ideas for activities are never solicited from them. Opportunity for free individual action is open only once in the day, during the part of Work Time left after the general class assignment has been completed (on the day reported the class assignment was drawing animal pictures for the absent Mark). Spontaneous interests or observations from the children are never developed by the teacher. It seems that her schedule just does not allow room for developing such unplanned events. During Sharing Time, for example, the child who brought a bird's nest told Edith, in reply to her question of what kind of bird made it, "My friend says it's a rain bird." Edith does not think to ask about this bird, probably because the answer is "childish," that is, not given in accepted adult categories of birds. The children then express great interest in an object in the nest, but the teacher ignores this interest, probably because the object is uninteresting to her. The soldiers from "Babes in Toyland" strike a responsive note in the children, but this is not used for a discussion of any kind. The soldiers are treated in the same way as objects which bring little interest from the children. Finally, at the end of Sharing Time the child-world of perception literally erupts in the class with the recollection of "the spooky house" at the zoo. Apparently this made more of an impression on the children than did any of the animals, but Edith is unable to make any sense of it for herself. The tightly imposed order of the class begins to break down as the children discover a universe of discourse of their own and begin talking excitedly with one another. The teacher is effectively excluded from this child's world of perception and for a moment she fails to dominate the classroom situation. She reasserts control, however, by taking the children to the next activity she has planned for the day. It seems never to have occurred to Edith that there might be a meaningful learning experience for the children in re-creating the "spooky house" in the classroom. It seems fair to say that this would have offered an exercise in spontaneous self-expression and an opportunity for real creativity on the part of the children. Instead, they are taken through a canned animal imitation procedure, an activity which they apparently enjoy, but which is also imposed upon them rather than created by them.

While children's perceptions of the world and opportunities for genuine spontaneity and creativity are being systematically eliminated from the kindergarten, unquestioned obedience to authority and rote learning of meaningless material are being encouraged. When the children are called to line up in the center of the room they ask "Why?" and "What for?" as they are in the very process of complying. They have learned to go smoothly through a programmed day, regardless of whether parts of the program make any sense to them or not. Here the student role involves what might be called "doing what you're told and never mind why." Activities which might "make sense" to the children are effectively ruled out and they are forced or induced to participate in activities which may be "senseless," such as the calisthenics.

At the same time the children are being taught by rote meaningless sounds in the ritual oaths and songs, such as the Lord's Prayer, the Pledge to the Flag, and "America." As they go through the grades children learn more and more of the sounds of these ritual oaths, but the fact that they have often learned meaningless sounds rather than meaningful statements is shown when they are asked to write these out in the sixth grade; they write them as groups of sounds rather than as a series of words, according to the sixth grade teachers at Wright School. Probably much learning in the elementary grades is of this character, that is, having no intrinsic meaning to the children, but rather being tasks inexplicably required of them by authoritative adults. Listening to sixth grade children read social studies reports, for example, in which they have copied material from encyclopedias about a particular country, an observer often gets the feeling that he is watching an activity which has no intrinsic meaning for the child. The child who reads, "Switzerland grows wheat and cows and grass and makes a lot of cheese" knows the dictionary meaning of each of these words but

may very well have no conception at all of this "thing" called Switzerland. He is simply carrying out a task assigned by the teacher *because* it is assigned, and this may be its only "meaning" for him.

Another type of learning which takes place in kindergarten is seen in children who take advantage of the "holes" in the adult social structure to create activities of their own, during Work Time or out-of-doors during Play Time. Here the children are learning to carve out a small world of their own within the world created by adults. They very quickly learn that if they keep within permissible limits of noise and action they can play much as they please. Small groups of children formed during the year in Edith's kindergarten who played together at these times, developing semi-independent little groups in which they created their own worlds in the interstices of the adult-imposed physical and social world. These groups remind the sociological observer very much of the so-called "informal groups" which adults develop in factories and offices of large bureaucracies.[5] Here too, within authoritatively imposed social organizations people find "holes" to create little subworlds which support informal, friendly, nonofficial behavior. Forming and participating in such groups seems to be as much part of the student role as it is of the role of bureaucrat.

The kindergarten has been conceived of here as the year in which children are prepared for their schooling by learning the role of student. In the classrooms of the rest of the school grades, the children will be asked to submit to systems and routines imposed by the teachers and the curriculum. The days will be much like those of kindergarten, except that academic subjects will be

[5] See, for example, Peter M. Blau, *Bureaucracy in Modern Society* (New York: Random House, 1956), Chapter 3.

substituted for the activities of the kindergarten. Once out of the school system, young adults will more than likely find themselves working in large-scale bureaucratic organizations, perhaps on the assembly line in the factory, perhaps in the paper routines of the white collar occupations, where they will be required to submit to rigid routines imposed by "the company" which may make little

sense to them. Those who can operate well in this situation will be successful bureaucratic functionaries. Kindergarten, therefore, can be seen as preparing children not only for participation in the bureaucratic organization of large modern school systems, but also for the large-scale occupational bureaucracies of modern society.

23

Roots of Black Manhood

ULF HANNERZ

Some 5.7 million people were simply not counted in the 1960 census, and most of them, it now appears, were Negro men living in northern cities. This statistical oversight, if that is what it was, is not unique to the government's census takers. Ever since the beginnings of the scholarly study of black people in the Americas, there has been an interesting fascination with the differences between the family life of Negroes and that of their white counterparts, the chief difference being seen as the dominant, not to say dominating, role of women in black families.

From E. Franklin Frazier's pioneering 1932 study of The Negro Family in Chicago through Melville Herskovits' The Myth of the Negro Past in 1941 to the so-called Moynihan Report of 1965, social scientists have been repeatedly rediscovering, analyzing and worrying over the crucial role of the mother (or grandmother) in the family structure

of blacks in the New World. Herskovits saw the centrality of the mother as an African vestige, typical of the polygymous marriage in which every woman, with her offspring, formed a separate unit. Frazier is generally regarded as the first to ascribe to the institution of slavery itself the strongest influence in undetermining the stability of marriage, an influence that was later reinforced when blacks encountered what Frazier perceived as the peculiarly urban evils of anonymity, disorganization and the lack of social support and controls. Moynihan, like Frazier, sees the matriarchal family as being practically without strengths, at least in the context of the larger American society, but his Report emphasizes the ways in which employer discrimination and, more recently, welfare policies have contributed to the breaking up (or foreclosure) of the male-dominated family unit among blacks.

In all of these studies, however, the black *man*—as son, lover, husband, father, grandfather—is a distant and shadowy figure "out there somewhere"

. . . if only because his major characteristic as far as the household is
concerned is his marginality or absence.

I do not mean to suggest that the
black man is undiscovered territory.
Obviously he is not. His popular image
was fixed for one (long) era in *Uncle
Tom's Cabin* and prophetically fashioned for our own time in Norman
Mailer's essay "The White Negro."
Here is Mailer's Hipster, modeled on
the Negro: "Sharing a collective disbelief in the words of men who had too
much money and controlled too many
things, they knew almost as powerful a
disbelief in the socially monolithic ideas
of the single mate, the solid family and
the respectable love life." And here is
Mailer's black man:

Knowing in the cells of his existence that
life was war, nothing but war, the Negro
(all exceptions admitted) could rarely afford
the sophisticated inhibitions of civilization,
and so he kept for his survival the art of
the primitive, he lived in the enormous
present, he subsisted for his Saturday night
kicks, relinquishing the pleasures of the mind
for the more obligatory pleasures of the
body, and in his music he gave voice to
the character and quality of his existence,
to his rage and the infinite variations of joy,
lust, languor, growl, cramp, pinch, scream
and despair of his orgasm.

Certainly there is poetic exaggeration
in Mailer's description, and perhaps a
conscious effort to mythicize his subject; and certainly too there is a great
deal of stereotyping in the general public's imagery of the people of the black
ghetto. But hardly anyone acquainted
with life in the ghetto can fail to see
that Mailer's portrait captures much of
the reality as well. Lee Rainwater's
sketch of the "expressive life-style" of
the black male shows a trained social
scientist's analysis that is remarkably
similar to Mailer's. And undoubtedly
there *is* a sizable segment of the black
male population that is strongly con-

cerned with sex, drinking, sharp clothes
and "trouble"; and among these men
one finds many of those who are only
marginally involved with married life.
Of course, ghetto life styles are heterogeneous, and there are many men who
live according to "mainstream" values;
but it is to the ones who do not that
we should turn our attention if we want
to understand what kinds of masculinity
go with the female-dominated family.

This essay is an attempt to outline
the social processes within the ghetto
communities of the northern United
States whereby the identity of streetcorner males is established and maintained. To set the stage and state the
issues involved in this essay, I'd like
to look at the views of two other observers of the ghetto male. One is
Charles Keil, whose *Urban Blues* (1966)
is a study of the bluesman as a "culture
hero." According to Keil, the urban
blues singer, with his emphasis on sexuality, "trouble" and flashy clothes, manifests a cultural model of maleness that
is highly valued by ghetto dwellers and
relatively independent of the mainstream cultural tradition. Keil criticizes
a number of authors who, without
cavilling at this description of the male
role, tend to see it as rooted in the individual's anxiety about his masculinity.
This, Keil finds, is unacceptably ethno-
centric:

Any sound analysis of Negro masculinity
should first deal with the statements and
responses of Negro women, the conscious
motives of the men themselves and the
Negro cultural tradition. Applied in this
setting, psychological theory may then be
able to provide important new insights in
place of basic and unfortunate distortions.

Keil, then, comes out clearly for a
cultural interpretation of the male role
we are interested in here. But Elliot
Liebow in *Tally's Corner* (1967), a
study resulting from the author's participation in a research project that

definitely considered ghetto life more in terms of social problems than as a culture, reaches conclusions which, in some of their most succinct formulations, quite clearly contradict Keil's:

Similarities between the lower-class Negro father and son . . . do not result from "cultural transmission" but from the fact that the son goes out and independently experiences the same failures, in the same areas, and for much the same reasons as his father.

Thus father and son are "independently produced look-alikes." With this goes the view that the emphasis on sexual ability, drinking and so forth is a set of compensatory self-deceptions which can only unsuccessfully veil the streetcorner male's awareness of his failure.

Keil and Liebow, as reviewed here, may be taken as representatives of two significantly different opinions on why black people in the ghettos, and in particular the males, behave differently than other Americans. One emphasizes a cultural determinism internal to the ghetto, the other an economic determinism in the relationship between the ghetto and the wider society. It is easy to see how the two views relate to one's perspective on the determinants of the domestic structure of ghetto dwellers. And it is also easy to see how these perspectives have considerable bearing on public policy, especially if it is believed that the ghetto family structure somehow prevents full participation by its members in the larger American society and economy. If it is held, for example, that broad social and economic factors, and particularly poverty, make ghetto families the way they are—and this seems to be the majority opinion among social scientists concerned with this area—then public policy should concentrate on mitigating or removing those elements that distort the lives of black people. But if the style of life in the ghetto is cul-

turally determined and more or less independent of other "outside" factors, then public policy will have to take a different course, or drop the problem altogether *qua* problem.

Admittedly, the present opportunity structure places serious obstacles in the way of many ghetto dwellers, making a mainstream life-style difficult to accomplish. And if research is to influence public policy, it is particularly important to point to the wider structural influences that *can* be changed in order to give equal opportunity to ghetto dwellers. Yet some of the studies emphasizing such macrostructural determinants have resulted in somewhat crude conceptualizations that are hardly warranted by the facts and which in the light of anthropological theory appear very oversimplified.

First of all, let us dispose of some of the apparent opposition between the two points of view represented by Keil and Liebow. There is not necessarily any direct conflict between ecological-economic and cultural explanations; the tendency to create such a conflict in much of the current literature on poverty involves a false dichotomy. In anthropology, it is a commonplace that culture is usually both inherited and influenced by the community's relationship to its environment. Economic determinism and cultural determinism can go hand in hand in a stable environment. Since the ecological niche of ghetto dwellers has long remained relatively unchanged, there seems to be no reason why their adaptation should not have become in some ways cultural. It is possible, of course, that the first stage in the evolution of the specifically ghetto life-style consisted of a multiplicity of identical but largely independent adaptations from the existing cultural background—mainstream or otherwise—to the given opportunity structure, as Liebow suggests. But the second stage of adaptation—by the following generations—involves a perception of the first-stage adaptation as a normal condition, a state of affairs which from then on can be expected. What was at first independent adaptation becomes transformed into a ghetto heritage of assumptions about the nature of man and society.

Yet Liebow implies that father and son are independently produced as streetcorner men, and that transmission of a ghetto-specific culture has a negligible influence. To those adhering to this belief, strong evidence in its favor is seen in the fact that ghetto dwellers —both men and women—often express conventional sentiments about sex and other matters. Most ghetto dwellers would certainly agree, at times at least, that education is a good thing, that gambling and drinking are bad, if not sinful, and that a man and a woman should be true to each other. Finding such opinions, and heeding Keil's admonition to listen to the statements and responses of the black people themselves, one may be led to doubt that there is much of a specific ghetto culture. But then, after having observed behavior among these same people that often and clearly contradicts their stated values, one has to ask two questions: Is there any reason to believe that ghetto-specific behavior is cultural? And, if it *is* cultural, what is the nature of the coexistence of mainstream culture and ghetto-specific culture in the black ghetto?

To answer the first question, one might look at the kinds of communications that are passed around in the ghetto relating to notions of maleness. One set of relationships in which such communications occur frequently is the family; another is the male peer group.

Deficient Masculinity?

Much has been made of the notion that young boys in the ghetto, growing up in matrifocal households, are somehow deficient in or uncertain about their masculinity, because their fathers are absent or peripheral in household affairs. It is said that they lack the role models necessary for learning male behavior; there is a lack of the kind of information about the nature of masculinity which a father would transmit unintentionally merely by going about his life at home. The boys therefore supposedly experience a great deal of sex-role anxiety as a result of this cultural vacuum. It is possible that such a view contains more than a grain of truth in the case of some quite isolated female-headed households. Generally speaking, however, there may be less to it than meets the eye. First of all, a female-headed household without an adult male in residence but where young children are growing up—and where, therefore, it is likely that the mother is still rather young—is seldom one where adult males are totally absent. More or less steady boyfriends (sometimes including the separated father) go in and out. Even if these men do not assume a central household role, the boys can obviously use them as source material for the identification of male behavior. To be sure, the model is not a conventional middle-class one, but it still shows what males are like.

Furthermore, men are not the only ones who teach boys about masculinity. Although role-modeling is probably essential, other social processes can contribute to identity formation. Mothers, grandmothers, aunts and sisters who have observed men at close range have formed expectations about the typical behavior of men which they express and which influence the boys in the household. The boys will come to share in the women's imagery of men, and often they will find that men who are not regarded as good household partners (that is, "good" in the conventional sense) are still held to be attractive company. Thus the view is easily imparted that the hard men, good talkers, clothes-horses and all, are not altogether unsuccessful as men. The women also act more directly toward the boys in these terms—they have expectations of what men will do, and whether they wish the boys to live up (or down) to the expectations, they instruct them in the model. Boys are advised not to "mess with" girls, but at the same time it is emphasized that messing around is the natural thing they will otherwise go out and do—and when the boys start their early adventures with the other sex, the older women may scold them but at the same time point out, not without satisfaction, that "boys will be boys." This kind of maternal (or at least adult female) instruction of young males is obviously a kind of altercasting, or more exactly, socialization to an alter role—that is, women cast boys in the role complementary to their own according to their experience of man-woman relationships. One single mother of three boys and two girls put it this way:

You know, you just got to act a little bit tougher with boys than with girls, 'cause they just ain't the same. Girls do what you tell them to do and don't get into no trouble, but you just can't be sure about the boys. I mean, you think you're OK and next thing you find out they're playing hookey and drinking wine and maybe stealing things from cars and what not. There's just something bad about boys here, you know. But what can you say when many of them are just like their daddies? That's the man in them coming out. You can't really fight it, you know that's the way it is. They know, too, but you just got to be tougher.

This is in some ways an antagonistic socialization, but it is built upon an expectation that it would be unnatural for men not to turn out to be in some ways bad—that is fighters, drinkers, lady killers and so forth. There is one thing worse than a no-good man—the sissy, who is his opposite. A boy who seems

weak is often reprimanded and ridiculed not only by his peers but also by adults, including his mother and older sisters. The combination of role-modeling by peripheral fathers or temporary boy-friends with altercasting by adult women certainly provides for a measure of male role socialization within the family.

And yet, when I said that the view of the lack of models in the family was too narrow, I was not referring to the observers' lack of insight into many matrifocal ghetto families as much as I was to the emphasis they placed on the family as *the* information storage unit of a community's culture. I believe it is an ethnocentrism on the part of middle-class commentators to take it for granted that if information about sex roles is not transmitted from father to son within the family, it is not transmitted from generation to generation at all. In American sociology, no less than in the popular mind, there is what Ray Bird-whistell has termed a "sentimental model" of family life, according to which the family is an inward-turning isolated unit, meeting most of the needs of its members, and certainly their needs for sociability and affection. The "sentimental model" is hardly ever realistic even as far as middle-class American families are concerned, and it has even less relevance for black ghetto life. Ghetto children live and learn out on the streets just about as much as within the confines of the home. Even if mothers, aunts and sisters do not have streetcorner men as partners, there is an ample supply of them on the front stoop or down at the corner. Many of these men have such a regular attendance record as to become quite familiar to children and are frequently very friendly with them. Again, therefore, there is no lack of adult men to show a young boy what men are like. It seems rather unlikely that one can deny all role-modeling effect of these men on their young neighbors. They may be missing in the United States census records, but they are not missing in the ghetto community.

Much of the information gained about sex roles outside the family comes not from adult to child, however, but from persons in the same age-grade or only slightly higher. The idea of culture being stored in lower age-grades must be taken seriously. Many ghetto children start participating in the peer groups of the neighborhood at an early age, often under the watchful eye of an elder brother or sister. In this way they are initiated into the culture of the peer group by interacting with children —predominantly of the same sex— who are only a little older than they are. And in the peer-group culture of the boys, the male sex role is a fairly constant topic of concern. Some observers have felt that this is another consequence of the alleged sex role anxiety of ghetto boys. This may be true, of course, at least in that it may have had an important part in the development of male peer-group life as a dominant element of ghetto social structure. Today, however, such a simple psychosocial explanation will not do. Most ghetto boys can hardly avoid associating with other boys, and once they are in the group, they are efficiently socialized into a high degree of concern with their sex role. Much of the joking, the verbal contests and the more or less obscene songs among small ghetto boys, serve to alienate them from dependence on mother figures and train them to the exploitative, somewhat antagonistic attitude toward women which is typical of streetcorner men.

"Mother!"

This is not to say that the cultural messages are always very neat and clear-cut. In the case of the kind of insult contest called "playing the dozens,"

"sounding" or (in Washington, D.C.) "joning," a form of ritualized interaction which is particularly common among boys in the early teens, the communication is highly ambiguous. When one boy says something unfavorable about another's mother, the other boy is expected either to answer in kind or to fight in defense of his honor (on which apparently that of his mother reflects). But the lasting impression is that there is something wrong about mothers—they are not as good as they ought to be ("Anybody can get pussy from your mother"), they take over male items of behavior and by implication too much of the male role ("Your mother smokes a pipe"). If standing up for one's family is the manifest expected consequence of "the dozens," then a latent function is a strengthening of the belief that ghetto women are not what they ought to be. The other point of significance is that the criteria of judgment about what a good woman should be like are apparently like those of the larger society. She should not be promiscuous, and she should stick to the mainstream female role and not be too dominant.

The boys, then, are learning and strengthening a cultural ambivalence involving contradictions between ideal and reality in female behavior. I will return to a discussion of such cultural ambivalence later. But the point remains that even this game involves continuous learning and strengthening of a cultural definition of what women are like that is in some ways complementary to the definition of what men are like. And much of the songs, the talk and the action—fighting, sneaking away with girls into a park or an alley or drinking out of half-empty wine bottles stolen from or given away by adult men—are quite clearly preparations for the streetcorner male role. If boys and men show anxiety about their masculinity, one may suspect that this is induced as much by existing cultural standards as by the alleged nonexistence of models.

This socialization within the male peer group is a continuing process; the talk that goes on, continuously or intermittently, at the street corner or on the front steps may deal occasionally with a football game or a human-interest story from the afternoon newspaper, but more often there are tales from personal experience about adventures of drinking (often involving the police), about women won and lost, about feminine fickleness and the masculine guile (which sometimes triumphs over it), about clothing, or there may simply be comments on the women passing down the street. "Hi ugly . . . don't try to swing what you ain't got."

This sociability among the men seems to be a culture-building process. Shared definitions of reality are created out of the selected experiences of the participants. Women are nagging and hypocritical; you can't expect a union with one of them to last forever. Men are dogs; they have to run after many women. There is something about being a man and drinking liquor; booze makes hair grow on your chest. The regularity with which the same topics appear in conversation indicates that they have been established as the expected and appropriate subjects in this situation, to the exclusion of other topics.

• Mack asked me did I screw his daughter, so I asked: "I don't know, what's her name?" And then when I heard that gal was his daughter all right, I says, "Well, Mack, I didn't really have to take it, 'cause it was given to me." I thought Mack sounded like his daughter was some goddam white gal. But Mack says, "Well, I just wanted to hear it from you." Of course, I didn't know that was Mack's gal, 'cause she was married and had a kid, and so she had a different name. But then you know the day after when I was out there a

car drove by, and somebody called my name from it, you know, "hi darling," and that was her right there. So the fellow I was with says, "Watch out, Buddy will shoot your ass off." Buddy, that's her husband. So I says, "Yeah, but he got to find me first!"

• Let me tell you fellows, I've been arrested for drunkenness more than two hundred times over the last few years, and I've used every name in the book. I remember once I told them I was Jasper Gonzales, and then I forgot what I had told them, you know. So I was sitting there waiting, and they came in and called "Jasper Gonzales," and nobody answered. I had forgotten that's what I said, and to tell you the truth, I didn't know how to spell it. So anyway, nobody answered, and there they were calling "Jasper Gonzales. Jasper Gonzales!" So I thought that must be me, so I answered. But they had been calling a lot of times before that. So the judge said, "Mr. Gonzales, are you of Spanish descent?" And I said, "Yes, your honor, I came to this country thirty-four years ago." And of course I was only thirty-five, but you see I had this beard then, and I looked pretty bad, dirty and everything, you know, so I looked like sixty. And so he said, "We don't have a record on you. This is the first time you have been arrested?" So I said, "Yes, your honor, nothing like this happened to me before. But my wife was sick, and then I lost my job you know, and I felt kind of bad. But it's the first time I ever got drunk." So he said, "Well, Mr. Gonzales, I'll let you go, 'cause you are not like the rest of them here. But let this be a warning to you." So I said, "Yes, your honor." And then I went out, and so I said to myself, "I'll have to celebrate this." So I went across the street from the court, and you know there are four liquor stores there, and I got a pint of wine and next thing I was drunk as a pig.

• Were you here that time a couple of weeks ago when these three chicks from North Carolina were up here visiting Miss Gladys? They were really gorgeous, about 30–35. So Charlie says why don't we stop by the house and he and Jimmy and Deekay can go out and buy them a drink. So they say they have to go and see this cousin first, but then they'll be back. But then Brenda (Charlie's wife) comes back before they do, and so these girls walk back and forth in front of the house, and Charlie can't do a thing about it, except hope they won't knock on his door. And then Jimmy and Deekay come and pick them up, and Fats is also there, and the three of them go off with these chicks, and there is Charlie looking through his window, and there is Brenda looking at them too, and asking Charlie does he know who the chicks are.

Groups of one's friends give some stability and social sanction to the meanings that streetcorner men attach to their experiences—meanings that may themselves have been learned in the same or preceding peer groups. They, probably more than families, are information storage units for the ghetto-specific male role. At the same time, they are self-perpetuating because they provide the most satisfactory contexts for legitimizing the realities involved. In other words, they suggest a program for maleness, but they also offer a haven of understanding for those who follow that program and are criticized for it or feel doubts about it. For of course all street-corner males are more or less constantly exposed to the definitions and values of the mainstream cultural apparatus, and so some cultural ambivalence can hardly be avoided. Thus, if a man is a dog for running after women—as he is often said to be among ghetto dwellers—he wants to talk about it with other dogs who appreciate that this is a fact of life. If it is natural for men to drink, let it happen among other people who

understand the nature of masculinity. In this way the group maintains constructions of reality, and life according to this reality maintains the group.

It is hard to avoid the conclusion, then, that there is a cultural element involved in the sex roles of streetcorner males, because expectations about sex are manifestly shared and transmitted rather than individually evolved. (If the latter had been the case, of course, it would have been less accurate to speak of these as roles, since roles are by definition cultural.) This takes us to the second question stated above, about the coexistence of conventional and ghetto-specific cultures. Streetcorner men certainly are aware of the male ideal of mainstream America—providing well for one's family, remaining faithful to one's spouse, staying out of trouble, etc. —and now and then every one of them states it as his own ideal. What we find here, then, may be seen as a bicultural situation. Mainstream culture and ghetto-specific culture provide different models for living, models familiar to everyone in the ghetto. Actual behavior may lean more toward one model or more toward the other, or it may be some kind of mixture, at one point or over time. The ghetto-specific culture, including the streetcorner male role, is adapted to the situation and the experience of the ghetto dweller; it tends to involve relatively little idealization but offers shared expectations concerning self, others and the environment. The mainstream culture, from the ghetto dweller's point of view, often involves idealization, but there is less real expectation that life will actually follow the paths suggested by those ideals. This is not to say that the ghetto-specific culture offers no values of its own at all, or that nothing of mainstream culture ever appears realistic in the ghetto; but in those areas of life where the two cultures exist side by side as alternative guides to action (for naturally, the ghetto-specific culture, as distinct from mainstream culture, is not a "complete" culture covering all areas of life), the ghetto-specific culture is often taken to forecast what one can actually expect from life, while the mainstream norms are held up as perhaps ultimately more valid but less attainable under the given situational constraints. "Sure it would be good to have a good job and a good home and your kids in college and all that, but you got to be yourself and do what you know." Of course, this often makes the ghetto-specific cultural expectations into self-fulfilling prophecies, as ghetto dwellers try to attain what they believe they can attain; but, to be sure, self-fulfilling prophecies and realistic assessments may well coincide.

"Be Yourself"

On the whole, one may say that both mainstream culture and ghetto-specific culture are transmitted within many ghetto families. I have noted how socialization into the ghetto male role within the household is largely an informal process, in which young boys may pick up bits and pieces of information about masculinity from the women in the house as well as from males who may make their entrances and exits. On the other hand, when adult women—usually mothers or grandmothers—really "tell the boys how to behave," they often try to instill in them mainstream, not to say puritanical norms—drinking is bad, sex is dirty and so forth. The male peer groups, as we have seen, are the strongholds of streetcorner maleness, although there are times when men cuss each other out for being "no good." Finally, of course, mainstream culture is transmitted in contacts with the outside world, such as in school or through the mass media. It should be added, though, that the latter may be used selectively to strengthen some ele-

ments of the streetcorner male role; ghetto men are drawn to Westerns, war movies and crime stories both in the movie house and on their TV sets.

Yet, even if the nature of men's allegiance to the two cultures makes it reasonably possible to adhere, after a fashion, to both at the same time, the bicultural situation of streetcorner males involves some ambivalence. The rejection of mainstream culture as a guide to action rather than only a lofty ideal is usually less than complete. Of course, acting according to one or the other of the two cultures to a great extent involves bowing to the demands of the social context, and so a man whose concerns in the peer-group milieu are drinking and philandering will try to be "good" in the company of his mother or his wife and children, even if a complete switch is hard to bring about. There are also peer groups, of course, that are more mainstream-oriented than others, although even the members of these groups are affected by streetcorner definitions of maleness. To some extent, then, the varying allegiance of different peer groups to the two cultures is largely a difference of degree, as the following statement by a young man implies.

Those fellows down at the corner there just keep drinking and drinking. You know, I think it's pretty natural for a man to drink, but they don't try to do nothing about it, they just drink every hour of the day, every day of the week. My crowd, we drink during the weekend, but we can be on our jobs again when Monday comes.

However, although where one is or who one is with does bring some order into this picture of bicultural ambivalence, it is still one of less than perfect stability. The drift between contexts is itself not something to which men are committed by demands somehow inherent in the social structure. Ghetto men may spend more time with the family, or more time with the peer group, and the extent to which they choose one or the other, and make a concomitant cultural selection, still appears to depend much on personal attachment to roles, and to changes in them. The social alignments of a few men may illustrate this. One man, Norman Hawkins, a construction laborer, spends practically all his leisure time at home with his family, only occasionally joining in the streetcorner conversations and behavior of the peer group to which his neighbor, Harry Jones, belongs. Harry Jones, also a construction worker, is also married and has a family but stays on the periphery of household life, although he lives with his wife and children. Some of the other men in the group are unmarried or separated and so seldom play the "family man" role which Harry Jones takes on now and then. Harry's younger brother, Carl, also with a family, used to participate intensively in peer group life until his drinking led to a serious ailment, and after he recuperated from this he started spending much less time with his male friends and more with his family. Bee Jay, a middle-aged bachelor who was raised by his grandmother, had a job at the post office and had little to do with street life until she died. Since then, he has become deeply involved with a tough, hard-drinking group and now suffers from chronic health problems connected with his alcoholism. Thus we can see how the life careers of some ghetto men take them through many and partly unpredictable shifts and drifts between mainstream and ghetto-specific cultures, while others remain quite stable in one allegiance or another.

Two Cultures

The sociocultural situation in the black ghetto is clearly complicated. The community shows a great heterogeneity of life-styles; individuals become committed in some degree to different ways of being by the impersonally-enforced structural arrangements to which they are subjected, but unpredictable contingencies have an influence, and their personal attachments to life-styles also vary. The socioeconomic conditions impose limits on the kinds of life ghetto dwellers may have, but these kinds of life are culturally transmitted and shared as many individuals in the present, and many in the past, live or have lived under the same premises. When the latter is the case, it is hardly possible to invent new adaptations again and again, as men are always observing each other and interacting with each other. The implication of some of Frazier's writings, that ghetto dwellers create their way of life in a cultural limbo—an idea which has had more modern expressions—appears as unacceptable in this case as in any other situation where people live together, and in particular where generations live together. The behavior of the streetcorner male is a natural pattern of masculinity with which ghetto dwellers grow up and which to some extent they grow into. To see it only as a complex of unsuccessful attempts at hiding failures by self-deception seems, for many of the men involved, to be too much psychologizing and too little sociology. But this does not mean that the attachment to the ghetto-specific culture is very strong among its bearers.

The question whether streetcorner males have mainstream culture or a specific ghetto culture, then, is best answered by saying that they have both, in different ways. There can be little doubt that this is the understanding most in line with that contemporary trend in anthropological thought which emphasizes the sharing of cultural imagery, of expectations and definitions of reality, as the medium whereby individuals in a community interact. It is noteworthy that many of the commentators who have been most skeptical of the idea of a ghetto-specific culture, or more generally a "culture of poverty," have been those who have taken a more narrow view of culture as a set of values about which an older generation consciously instructs the younger ones in the community.

Obviously, the answer to whether there is a ghetto-specific culture or not will depend to some extent on what we shall mean by culture. Perhaps this is too important a question to be affected by a mere terminological quibble, and perhaps social policy, in some areas, may well proceed unaffected by the questions raised by a ghetto-specific culture. On the other hand, in an anthropological study of community life, the wider view of cultural sharing and transmission which has been used here will have to play a part in our picture of the ghetto, including that of what ghetto males are like.

24

The Woman's Role: Constants and Change

SUZANNE KELLER

The status of women is under review in many parts of the world today. Discussions about true or spurious femininity, women's duties, women's natural proclivities, their lesser sexuality, their greater sexuality, are topics that apparently command endless interest. The growing preoccupation with this question—not only among women—suggests that the traditional answers no longer ring true to a growing number of contemporary citizens.

In 1970, Benjamin Spock, a widely influential American pediatrician, saw fit to recant some of his earlier pronouncements about women by admitting that they had been less factual and more prejudiced than he had realized.

Reprinted from *Women in Therapy: New Psychotherapies for a Changing Society.* Ed. by Violet Franks and Vasanti Burtle. Copyright © 1974 by Brunner/Mazel, New York. Reprinted with minor deletions by permission of the publisher.

His current change of heart led him to find some "of these opinions . . . embarrassing . . . to acknowledge now." "It is obvious," he confessed in belated candor, "that I, like most men and women up to a couple of years ago, harbored an underlying sexism [prejudice in favor of the dominant sex] in some matters" (Spock, 1971). This included such widespread beliefs as that "women will always play the major role in childcare," or that the mother rather than the father must give up whatever career time is necessary for the care of small children, or that the husband's work must always come first. Still going along with the conventional wisdom, Spock also warned mothers about playing a dominant role in their households. "I was right," he later reflected, "in speaking of the unhealthy effects of domineering mothers and submissive fathers, but I forgot to mention the unhealthiness of the opposite." In his current view, that is, excessive dominance and submissiveness are seen as unhealthy for both sexes.

This suggests that, as traditional assumptions about the female role are being critically reexamined, so are certain traditional beliefs about the biological determinants of sex roles.

As the evidence accumulates, it becomes clear that the biology of gender is a pretext for wide variations in cultural response, and not even that indisputable constant, the female monopoly on pregnancy and childbirth, can escape the imprint of culture and social structure. This reluctantly accepted truth precludes our predicting the personal and social traits of men and women from the sheer fact of their biological differentiation. Even in our own time we note remarkable variations in the traits attributed to women in different societies, as some cultures attribute to them what others firmly deny.

Hence one cannot generalize about women across cultures or subcultures and all such generalizations are highly selective and distort the multifaceted reality. In this discussion of the female role, therefore, I will try to confine myself to industrialized societies, especially to the contemporary United States. I will begin by sketching out the core elements of the female role and then consider the variations and departures from it.

Some Definitions

There is considerable confusion in existing discussions due to the absence of common definitions. At times, different terms refer to the same phenomenon or, conversely, the same terms are used to denote different things. To facilitate matters, I will use the following working definitions in this paper.

Following Robert Stoller, let us use gender and sex role as follows (Stoller, 1968):

Gender refers to the psychological connotations of maleness or femaleness which result in masculinity and femininity.

Gender identity refers to the awareness of belonging to one of the two sexes, an awareness which becomes quite complex in time. From the simple dichotomy at age two of "I am male or female," one proceeds to various qualifications such as "I am strongly or weakly feminine or masculine," or, "I like or dislike being a boy, a girl"; or "I'm not really a boy or girl, I'm only pretending." According to Stoller and others of the Johns Hopkins Group that did pioneering research on transsexualism, a core gender identity (the conviction that I am female and not male and vice versa) is established somewhere around ages two to three.

Gender role refers to the overt behavior one displays to others to indicate one's gender to them. Since others validate one's self-perception, their reactions are an important source of gender validation. If they are not reinforcing, one's gender identity may be confused or shifting.

Finally, there is *sex role*, often erroneously used to denote gender role whereas it serves as a standard for these. Sex roles are the parts society reserves for each gender. These standards will serve as guides to individuals and groups as to what is ideally desirable, not what is actually possible. If we wish to understand why Frenchmen behave differently from American men, though both are biologically male, we need to look at the standards or social expectations governing masculinity in their respective societies. At the same time, however, these general guides are no more than a rough outline of how individual men in each society will behave and react. For these will translate the cultural script to suit particular subcultural and individual circumstances.

Hence the terms masculine and feminine have a number of different connotations:

(a) male and female as sexually different;
(b) male and female as reproductively different;
(c) masculine and feminine as subjective identity;
(d) masculine and feminine as social identity or role.

Core Elements of the Female Role

In discussing contemporary problems experienced by men and women, it is not unusual to refer to sex roles as an explanatory concept for their behavior. So we are told that the differential socialization of boys and girls stems from the different role expectations entertained by parents or that the feminine self-image is shaped by contradictory role demands. However, despite these references, the concept of sex role itself is left rather vague and poorly defined, and the use of the general label obscures ignorance about significant components of gender-related expectations in different groups and settings. Hence we need a more subtle and diversified image of the female role, whose core and variable elements will now be discussed.

The core aspects of the female role in the United States currently—as gleaned from the ideals held out to women in the society at large—include the following:

(1) a concentration on marriage, home, and children as the primary focus of feminine concern.
(2) a reliance on a male provider for sustenance and status. This important component of the wife role is symbolized by the woman taking her husband's name and sharing her husband's income.

(3) an expectation that women will emphasize nurturance and life-preserving activities, both literally as in the creation of life and symbolically, in taking care of, healing, and ministering to the helpless, the unfortunate, the ill. Preeminent qualities of character stressed for women include sympathy, care, love, and compassion, seemingly best realized in the roles of mother, teacher, and nurse.
(4) an injunction that women live through and for others rather than for the self. Ideally, a woman is enjoined to lead a vicarious existence—feeling pride or dismay about her husband's achievements and failures or about her children's competitive standing.
(5) a stress on beauty, personal adornment, and eroticism, which, though a general feature of the female role, is most marked for the glamour girl.
(6) a ban on the expression of direct assertion, aggression, and power strivings except in areas clearly marked woman's domain—as in the defense of hearth and home. There is a similar ban on women taking the direct (but not indirect) sexual initiative.

In the three themes stressed for the female role—maternal, wifely, and erotic—primary emphasis is supposed to be given to the maternal and wifely aspects, though at certain stages of the life cycle, the erotic component may be preeminent. However, this exclusive preoccupation with maternity and wifedom is not as old as we like to pretend. As Viola Klein (1971) has repeatedly reminded us, we are victims of two serious shortcomings in reconstructing history: short memories and poor information. For, historically, women have played a great variety of significant economic and productive roles in addition to their reproductive ones. The chief dividing line seems to be the industrial revolution and the physical separation between home and workplace which gradually led to the familiar current division of work by gender.

The ensuing diminution of women's public roles coincided with an intensification of the private domestic sphere which exaggerated both the physical and the emotional isolation of women. Gradually, moreover, the very process which relieved the household of productive work and otherwise reduced its responsibilities in religion, education, and recreation also deprived of its former social significance. Hardest hit by this deflation of what had previously been an essential, indeed indispensable, contribution to human welfare were women in the middle classes who experienced these shifts and contradictions most keenly. Overeducated for domesticity yet insufficiently educated for rewarding work in the higher occupational ranks, this led to the characteristic "woman problem" among them.

Klein considers this an illustration of a cultural lag as women continue to be tied down to the household and family whereas men are already caught up in non-family institutions. Hence men are likely to feel a tug of war between family and job concerns, or between job-related travel and the domestically-based household, which women do not as yet experience. On the other hand, women are confronted by role conflict engendered by the contraction of previous responsibilities and their isolation from significant portions of public experience and participation. Nonetheless the domestic ideal persists as a cultural ideal, albeit one often bypassed or altered by structured departures from the *female core role*.

Variants of the Female Role

The female core role thus has two basic aspects—an economic-work aspect and an erotic-procreative one. Of the two major departures or variants, one challenges women's economic dependency, the other their sexual dependency on men. The self-supporting divorcée or the aspiring career girl are instances of the first category. The courtesan or prostitute are examples of the second. These modifications lead, in time, to the emergence of various hybrid or social types that combine the overarching feminine ideal with particular personal and social necessities. The working wife, the part-time mother and the successful professional woman are typical examples of how the female role may be alternatively structured.

In the following summary of sociological variants of the female role in American society we see that even in a single society one may talk of woman's role but not thereby be able to generalize to all women. The wife of the affluent executive and the wife of a modestly paid worker, for example, experience the feminine role in very different ways even though they might share certain general objectives regarding home and family life.

Affluent Wives. The first example comprises women married to men in the top economic ranks, specifically, men earning at least $100,000 per year. A study of 400 such women (Wyse, 1970) showed that they can reject the more onerous routines of domesticity in favor of esthetic preoccupations. Home is not primarily perceived a shelter, this security being taken for granted, but a place of retreat, comfort, and a setting for self-expression and display. Indeed it is not always clear to which of several dwellings the term home applies, for three-fifths of the sample had at least two places they called home.

Not surprisingly, all of these women had hired help for the heavier household tasks and their domestic pursuits centered on entertaining and creating an attractive setting for themselves and their children. They are thus far less domestic than the suburban housewife but probably more so than their affluence requires.

Life consists of travel, home entertaining, charity work, and such hobbies as reading, sports, and artistic endeavors. The division of work by sex turns out to be fairly extensive in some respects and slight in others. The most striking sex differentiation concerns remunerative employment outside of the home, with the husbands clearly being worker-providers and the wives, consumer-spenders. In this sense the division of labor parallels that prevalent in the society at large but at a more affluent scale. As for the division of labor within the home, here we find much less sex-typing and the sexes clearly socialize together.

How ready would these women be to earn their own living? Not very, judging from the fact that only ten per cent are engaged in any kind of paid employment now, although four-fifths of them had had training as teachers, nurses, and secretaries, in that order. Only one-sixth, in fact, looked favorably upon the idea of a career for themselves. Part of their reluctance is probably due to the fact that their husbands support them in such grand style. Nearly half pay their bills and debts outright and three-tenths give them an allowance with which to do so on their own. Two-thirds own wealth jointly with their husbands, and one-third have their own stocks, bonds, houses, and boats. All in all these women felt happy with their way of life and expressed no major complaints about the roles assigned them.

Workingmen's Wives. By contrast, consider working class women whose worlds are bounded by family and local neighborhood and increasingly by poorly paid jobs taken out of necessity rather than desire. Whether or not they hold jobs, they must generally do all of the housework including cooking,

washing, cleaning, and mending. Material survival and bringing up their children are their major preoccupations and interests. Giving top priority to the wife-mother role, they judge men by their ability to fulfill their roles as family providers. Unlike middle class wives, however, they are far less wrapped up in their husbands' jobs or their children's inner lives as long as both live up to expectations. Also, in contrast to the more affluent, home is a symbol of security and shelter, and is reserved for entertaining one's own family. There is sharp sex-typing of work and of interests, resulting in considerable role segregation between men and women.

The really interesting question is how much do these two types of women have in common? Is the biology of gender a common bond? Is their formal rank *vis-à-vis* men a common bond? Or does social class constitute a permanent wedge to any potential unity between them, therefore precluding our classifying them under a single category called women?

One shared attribute concerns consumer power. Both types of women are likely to be the spenders of the money earned by their men. Working class women, in particular, have the power of the purse and more so than middle class wives set the general pattern of family life (Komarovsky, 1964, Rainwater, 1959, Shostak, 1969). Still, despite pervasive differences in life-styles and resources by social class, one feels that the middle class ideal, extolling domesticity and maternity, exerts a strong influence on both groups of women.

A contrasting pattern exists in more rigid class systems where one often finds several cultural images, each salient for a particular class, competing for national allegiance. In Greece, for example, according to an analysis of a series of films examined by Safilios-

Rothschild, we find a clear-cut distinction between two prominent feminine prototypes. One is the "good" girl—shy, sexually inexperienced, nurturant, and faithful—who is also poor and without social and family connections. Her antithesis is the emancipated, independent, and self-directing "bad" girl, who does not subscribe to the sexual double standard and who initiates and terminates her love affairs at will, expecting men to adjust to her pattern of life. Rich girls are able to pick and choose, there being "a distinct relationship between the amount of wealth and social status a girl possesses and the degree of social and sexual freedom to which she may be entitled (Safilios-Rothschild, 1968).

The rich-bad girl is very attractive to Greek men despite the fact that they are warned about her ruthlessness and her tendency to "exploit and use them as playthings" (Safilios-Rothschild, 1968). For a poor man without money or connections she is a desirable marital prospect. The poor-good girl, on the other hand, is expected to subordinate herself totally to the man's needs and interests, reassuring him by her selfless and quasi-maternal devotion. Each of these images of femininity monopolizes powerful themes in Greek life—limitless love and acceptance versus fortune and success. In recent movies, notes Safilios-Rothschild, there seems to be a fusion of previously antithetical images as class patterns converge in response to the spread of the modern ethos.

Ethnic subcultures likewise constitute points of departure from the idealized feminine prototype. In America's Black community, for example, women seem to give much greater emphasis to autonomy than is true in other subcommunities. "The strongest conception of womanhood . . . among all preadult females is that of how the woman has to take a strong role in the family" (Ladner, 1971). The symbol of the "resourceful woman" is very influential in their lives, as is the stress on self-support and hard work. Women's key duties include the conventional ones of keeping a home and caring for children, but also, if necessary, that of financially supporting a family.

The procreative powers of women are greatly and positively emphasized in this subculture and the main line of gender demarcation is not work but the female power to bear children. Along with this there is a strong accent on the erotic components of femininity —beauty, self-adornment, and sexual freedom. Thus the Black feminine ideal —to be strong, responsible, autonomous, maternal, and sensual—rewards qualities quite antithetical to the white middle class ideal.

It is evident that the three subcultural variants depart in significant ways from the cultural stereotypes of femininity. A lot seems to hinge on whether or not male providers are willing and able to assume the responsibilities of economic support. If not, women are compelled to leave their domestic havens for paid employment, thereby introducing major role modifications. And here we note an interesting division between occupations considered appropriate or inappropriate for women. Appropriate ones seem to tap some of the same qualities that adhere to the conventional image of femininity, as expressed in teaching, nursing, or the theater. Inappropriate are all the fields tagged "masculine." The distinction between the two is clearly cultural, not motivational. Dancers, singers, and entertainers, for example, are considered feminine despite their often conspicuous success and affluence gained via fierce competitiveness and ambition, whereas business and professional women are stigmatized for venturing into "masculine" territory.

The career-woman seems to be a particularly unappealing model in industrial societies, mainly it would seem because she challenges the cultural formula for the sex-typing of work and rank. Recently, of course, new avenues have opened up in previously closed spheres and the career girl as distinct from the less flattering career woman has emerged as a more acceptable type. Though women are by now engaged in virtually every occupational category, few of them manage to get into the leading ranks. Those that do form yet another social type as members of a somewhat exclusive club of queen-beedom in which they appear to have the best of both worlds. "I masquerade in vain as an old bachelor," wrote the incomparable Colette who was one of that rare hybrid, "it is still a very feminine pleasure that I enjoy in being the only woman at the Goncourt lunches, surrounded by an Areopagus of men. Five, six, eight, nine men— real men—and age has nothing to do with it—the faults and seductiveness of men . . ." (Crossland, 1953). . . .

Power of the Female Role

One point of considerable controversy regarding the female role concerns its potential for the exercise of power. For some the dependency built into the role is proof of a lack of power while for others the capacity to demand support and sustenance proves just the opposite.

Each stand has evidence in its favor. Those who see women as powerless cite their economic dependency on men, their legal subordination, their more limited opportunities for earning and learning, and their formal powerlessness. Those who see them as powerful cite various rights—to vote, to inherit property, to work divorce laws in their favor, and to obtain economic support for themselves and their children. In addition to such formal rights there are also various kinds of deference and pro-

tection, access to wealth and status without self-exertion, emotional power in the family, and erotic power over men. Not to be ignored is the well-known phenomenon of ambitious women acting as powers behind the throne, propelling men to elaborate undertakings and often reducing them to mere figureheads for their own power strivings. These indirect forms of power are often neglected or dismissed as insignificant, a neglect which may seriously distort the assessment of power by gender.

Before taking sides on the issue, it is necessary first to clarify the meaning and forms of power we are willing to acknowledge. Power may be divided into several kinds. There is institutional and personal power, for example, the first referring to the capacity to mobilize and direct social forces towards collective ends, the second devoted to dominating one's personal environment. Institutional power is vested in formal social positions in the economy, the polity, and the military sectors among others, whereas personal power is not attached to formal positions but to personal qualities. The two may interpenetrate but they do so imperfectly and unpredictably. Women who rarely possess formal institutional power in modern societies may nonetheless command a great deal of personal power.

Another distinction to keep in mind concerns the reach and scope of power. Power may be awesome in terms of the resources at its command and yet not be able to touch the inner lives of individuals, whereas it may be virtually invisible and yet work its way into the deepest levels of consciousness. Here, too, the sexes divide in predictable ways in the contemporary world: some men possess enormous institutional power that affects the fate of millions of individuals but lack the power to penetrate to the core of the self, a power that women command by virtue of their emotional centrality in the family and in the sphere of erotic intimacy.

Family Power. Both as wives and mothers, women may derive a sense of power from organizing households, dominating kinship networks, disposing of family budgets, making demands on husbands, and supervising their children's lives. Of course family and wife power depend first of all on being married and having offspring and secondly on the significance of the family in the life of society. As this significance declines, the power that rests upon it does likewise, which may be one source of the current dissatisfaction with the traditional female role. However, it is the role of mother which offers women the most extensive opportunities for the exercise of direct and overt power. In their impact on their children, mothers can and have shaped history. It is interesting that Freud and Jung, two pioneers of psychoanalysis, divide sharply on where they consider the center of family power to reside. For Freud it was clearly the father and for Jung just as clearly the mother. The mother archetype is an image "sung and praised in all tongues." The memory of mother love "is among the most touching and most unforgettable memories of the adult human being: it is the secret root of all birth and of all transformation; it means for us the homecoming, and is the silent primordial source of every beginning and every end. Mother is mother-love; it is my experience and my secret" (Jacobi, 1958).

Many writers take the dependency and formal subordination of women rather too literally. They thereby miss the possibilities for women's exercise of power behind the facade of male supremacy. Thus alongside the meek and submissive wife must be placed the family despot and henpecked husband. In this light, Italy has been described as a "cryptomatriarchy" by one of its most astute observers, where men may be conspicuous but women are predominant (Barzini, 1964). And a study of American popular literature of the nineteenth century showed that the best-selling domestic novels of the day dealt frankly with the doctrine of complete female domestic domination (Peck, 1971). The plots of these novels, as indeed the lives of their authors, centered on the shared myth of the competent and resourceful heroine and the weak, sick, immoral, or missing male. In the ensuing struggle for power, the morally superior female always triumphs. "In all of these books a mature sexual relationship between a man and a woman is never really the goal or the ideal. The surface is sentiment and piety, but the subject is always power" (Peck, 1971).

Erotic Power. Quite a different form of power available to women is erotic power or the power to arouse, withhold, or gratify sexual desire and emotional longings in men. If women are made to depend on men economically and legally in patriarchal and quasi-patriarchal societies, men are made to depend on women erotically.

In most discussions of the woman question, the erotic power of women does not receive the emphasis it deserves. It is either ignored entirely or seen solely from the perspective of men's exploitation of erotic favors. This bias underestimates the equivalent exploitation of men by women. Today as throughout the patriarchal era, Eros is woman, a fact lost neither on the women who make use of it nor on the men in awe of it.

One supreme contemporary example of this kind of personal, magnetic feminine power concerns the impact of Um Khaltoum, the world famous siren of the Middle East, whose name is known to more Arabs than anyone else's. Now in her sixties, she holds her voluntary subjects enthralled by her monthly Thursday evening performance in Cairo, when public life virtually comes to a standstill. It is said that high government officials and politicians seek her advice or at least her blessings for important undertakings. "Miss Khaltoum is more popular than Nasser and Farouk together . . . No Egyptian leader could survive if she made it known that she was against him" (Tanner, 1967).

In sum, the female role does not, as is often claimed, preclude the exercise of power but its form tends to be personal, indirect, and emotionally highly penetrative. If one confines the term power only to its formal and institutional aspects, one will either ignore or underestimate other kinds without, however, diminishing their considerable importance. Which form of power one considers most impressive largely depends on one's convictions and values and perhaps opportunities for exercising one or another form. At this time I do not believe it possible to choose among different forms of power on objective grounds, though men seem to pay more attention to that reserved for their gender. There are limits to every form of power and there are special rewards associated with each. Indeed if one covets a feeling of being powerful in the lives of known individuals, personal power would seem to be both more immediate and more compelling. Hence the female role has its own special possibilities for domination. And while one can agree with John Stuart Mill in his speech to the House of Commons in 1867: "Sir, it is true that women have great power. It is part of my case that they have great power; but they have it under the worst possible conditions, because it is indirect and therefore irresponsible" (Beasley, 1968, p. 158), one should nevertheless give it its just due.

Increasingly, women are growing restive with their traditional roles and thus presumably with the power regarding family, children, and community based upon them. As a consequence of their growing contacts with the wider world of employment and enterprise, their ambitions are kindled for the exercise of institutional forms of power. This is particularly true for women in milieus where men are primed to management and leadership.

Indeed, the traditional female role appears to be less satisfactory and appealing to women who have more rather than less of the good things of life, particularly if they have either special talents or great aspirations for worldly success. Thus it is the educated, talented, middle and upper class women who are most impatient with the limits society imposes on female accomplishments. Bred in milieus where ambition, initiative, and success are most encouraged and admired, they are, by contrast with their brothers and male friends, prohibited from their realization. Thus, while absolutely better off than lower class women, they are, relative to men and to the values internalized as members of their class, worse off. This makes the conventional female role less gratifying and its rejection, in whole or in part, more tempting.

For the lower classes quite the opposite would seem to hold true. Here the men suffer both absolute deprivation in earnings and status and relative deprivation by comparison with more successful men and cultural ideals of successful masculinity. By comparison, women's work, hard though it be, centered on making a home and raising children, may seem more life-affirming and rewarding.

Self-Esteem and the Female Role

No matter what private advantage may be derived from a judicious manipulation of feminine opportunities in a culture overtly androcentric, the prevalent cultural favoritism is bound to undermine self confidence and self-esteem in women. This is not to say that most men will have self-esteem in such a culture but only that their roles provide them with a pretext for it.

In contemporary societies, despite changing priorities, most women cannot avoid realizing that they not only have a different destiny from that of men but in certain important respects a lesser one. This lesson is not always crystal clear but it is probably unavoidable in societies that seek not so much to demean women as to exalt, shore up, and elevate men.

Women come to terms with this message in a number of ways. For a few, this cultural slight is a spur to extraordinary efforts designed to prove their worthiness by conspicuous achievements. But most women, as indeed most men, will prune their ambitions to their opportunities. This leads to the familiar denial of self, of ambitions nipped in the bud, of projects abandoned, or of steps not taken. Initially the inhibition comes from parents, teacher, or other social authority, but later one's inner arbiter takes over and what was once second nature now becomes primary impulse to self-effacement. Few find it possible to suppress ambitions at age three only to reverse this attitude at age twenty.

The conditions for low self-esteem among women are difficult to assess. In order to discover its prevalence, one needs to know how the cultural message is perceived and interpreted by particular women, and the saliency of family, love, or career in their lives.

Keeping in mind the difficulties of assessing role satisfaction and self-esteem, it is not too surprising that existing studies exhibit quite contradictory findings. One oft cited study, by Rosencrantz and his co-workers, showed that both sexes assigned less valued traits to the female than to the male role. However, these were female college students who, in light of the theory of relative deprivation referred to earlier, should react most acutely to the limitations and restrictions placed in their path (Rosencrantz, 1968). Moreover, in this and other studies, it is not always clear whether the respondents are assessing sex roles cognitively or emotionally. Though they may know that the culture assigns a lower or more ambiguous value to the female role, they may still not value it less personally.

A more comprehensive, large-scale study of high school students, for example, found no less self-esteem among girls than among boys (Rosenberg, 1965). Indeed social class turned out to be far more important for self-esteem than sex. Moreover, both boys and girls had almost identical responses as to who had been their parents' favorite child, most naming a younger sibling of the opposite sex as their fathers' and mothers' favorite child.

Social class affected the pattern of self-esteem by sex, with upper class boys having somewhat higher self-esteem than upper class girls, with lower class girls reversing this pattern by exhibiting higher self-esteem than lower class boys.

These and other data, sporadic and incomplete though they be, suggest that women may find fault with various aspects of their roles without, however, rejecting the role itself. Femininity, though hard to define, is generally perceived as something positive and desirable (Hartley, in Seward and Williamson, 1970). It appears to involve early commitment to activities and symbols defined as feminine—beauty, grace, style, love—qualities perceived as intrinsically gratifying.

In fact, it has been shown that women are the key reference group for women and men alike. Using figure drawing tests, McAdoo found that both boys and girls drew women rather than men when asked to draw a figure, and 5th grade boys were twice as likely to draw a person of the opposite sex than were girls (McAdoo, 1971). The difference was that boys drew essentially maternal types of women, whereas girls drew glamour girls. And a study of face-saving behavior showed that, contrary to the investigator's expectations, women turned out to have a particular need to save face before a female rather than before a male audience, expecting the former to be more critical (Brown, 1971). If this is confirmed, it may help account for the so-called preference for male over female bosses, not because women do not admire other women but because they fear they will be more demanding.

Costs and Benefits of the Female Role

At this writing the liabilities of the female role are being highlighted, perhaps to make up for the long period in which its presumed benefits had been overemphasized. Since both costs and benefits are discernible, however, it might be useful to draw up a balance sheet comparing them.

Benefits. As will be evident, the advantages to be listed may be seen as disadvantages when assessed from a different perspective, which only underlines the fact that there are no absolute or objective ways to assess human values apart from the affinities and desires of the assessing person. What such a list can do, however, is to stimulate discussion and public debate. Among the benefits I have selected are:

(1) Economic security—which does not necessarily mean economic well-being but rather the absence of pressures to assume onerous responsibilities and risk difficult economic decisions. Until recently, women who held jobs to help support households that lacked adequate male providers resembled men who "help" with the housework. Their efforts were commendable but not obligatory. I believe that this aspect of the female role and its converse, pressures on men to assume heavy economic obligations for their families, have not received adequate attention.

(2) Emotional security: Women are permitted a wider range of emotional expression than are men and their roles accentuate the giving and receiving of love and affection—towards parents, mates, and children. Hence the sphere of intimacy is more accessible to them and they have more outlets for anxieties and tensions.

(3) The cult of beauty: This, as indeed most everything, can be overdone, of course, but the accent on appearance and style may be a creative experience in a number of ways. Beauty and attractiveness arouse favorable responses in others and are thus intrinsically gratifying. Moreover, the stress on being beautiful and desirable permits, indeed encourages, women to be self-indulgent and thus promotes a socially sanctioned narcissism that feeds the ego.

(4) A number of other qualities stressed for the female role, such as nurturance, warmth, and sympathy, are intrinsically pleasant both to exercise and to acquire.

(5) Finally, the lack of pressure to achieve: not needing to succeed in worldly terms means that women can be more relaxed, less driven, more person-oriented, and in some ways more individualistic than men. Of course this will not be a benefit for women who do seek worldly success.

Costs of the Female Role. The disadvantages of the female role may be summed up as follows:

(1) Lesser autonomy (by comparison with the male role): This means more restrictions and constraints on

self-development which is especially difficult for independent, self-propelled, ambitious women not content with family and erotic power.

(2) Ignorance and lack of training: Women acquire less formal training and know-how to cope with an increasingly technical and complicated world. As the arena of work and of public life becomes more complex relative to the domestic household, women will find themselves increasingly at a disadvantage.

(3) Categorical subordination to men: This is especially the case for the married woman for whom this subordination was in a sense designed. This affects not only the formal, legal aspects of life but one's self-conception and human relationships.

In essence it seems that the female role exchanges autonomy for security. Whether this is a good or a bad bargain depends on what sort of world one inhabits. In an age of famine, danger, and war, it may well be comforting to have someone else assume responsibility for survival. Protection from the struggle for existence in a cruel and difficult world certainly makes life easier.

These very gains, however, become obstacles and inequities for women who seek autonomy and are willing to confront the struggle for existence head-on. And even the women who welcome the protectiveness built into their role may wish to forego it if it comes to signify second class citizenship.

As women move beyond the domestic arena their dissatisfactions are likely to increase for a time because it is then that they are likely to discover the full measure of their inadequacies to cope with the world. The legal and social discrimination against women, only because they are women, may not be fully apparent to women staying close to home amidst like-minded others. Once they expand their contacts, however, they also become aware, often painfully so, of closed worlds and missed opportunities.

Another source of contemporary dissatisfaction with the female role stems from the declining importance, hence prestige, of maternal and housekeeping duties, as a lifetime focus on maternity diminishes. This is bound to erode the sense of worth of women otherwise perfectly content with domesticity and maternity. When children were a supremely valued social resource, women felt proud about their monopoly in providing them. Today, with the advent of zero population growth the whole symbolic complex of childbirth and child-rearing is losing its central hold. Already we find it difficult to respond to Colette's memory of her pregnancy as a "long holiday of privileges and attentions."

Moreover, when motherhood was of supreme social significance, women's categorical subordination to men may well have been compensated for by their "natural" superiority. But now, as lifetime maternity is being phased out of history, women are victims of a cultural lag as well as of social inferiority.

There are, furthermore, serious discontinuities in female socialization between childhood expectations and adult realities (Hartley, 1970, p. 144 ff). One concerns their lack of preparation to earn their own living if need be or to cope with life if Prince Charming does not chance by. Expecting to find a nest with built-in male provider may set up false hopes and virtually guarantee later disappointments. The insistence, by the mass media and schools, among others, that women prefer to be safely tucked away in their suburban castles may strike some powerful sentimental chords but it is totally out of step with a reality in which some two-fifths of

American women are employed full-time outside these castles.

And where women do pursue serious social or professional ambitions, they soon learn that there are quotas and exclusion devices of which they had been unaware. There is also of course the painful discovery of their lack of preparation, emotional and educational, to cope with a world geared to male patterns of achievement. In part this is linked to a discontinuity in the authority figures in women's lives and the need to replace the powerful mother of childhood with powerful males of adult life. We know all too little about how successfully they manage to do this.

There is also the discontinuity, first noticed by Freud, of erotic focus. Unlike men, women must shift their primary emotional attachment from mother to men. Men, who have serious discontinuities of their own, do not confront this particular problem since their primary caretaker and their later love-objects are both female. Some women, according to Freud, never make the transition while others only pretend to, expressing their confusion and reluctance in sexual coldness towards men or in a permanent attachment to the mothers of their childhoods.

These are among the reasons why women may be expected to suffer certain role-determined symptoms and maladjustments. Nonetheless, as was pointed out earlier, the deficiencies of the female role do not, apparently, lead to mass defections from it. Girls seem to develop positive gender identifications which give them a sense of selfhood strong and rewarding enough to withstand their later disappointments and difficulties in a remarkable way (Stoller, 1968). Also, surprisingly, in spite of male privilege, few women wish to be men. Rather they seek certain opportunities and rights as women. One psychoanalyst noted, on the basis of several decades of clinical experience, that he has never encountered a woman who would like her body to become male though he has known some who would like to add certain male features to the bodies they already possess. In other words, women may desire to be both male and female at the same time (Lederer, 1968). The various sex changes, incidentally, are, so far at least, nearly all requested by males who want to become females.

Conclusion

Many basic changes are under way in the areas of family, work, child-rearing, and erotic relations which will create pressures to redesign the female (as well as the male) role so as to be better suited to emerging realities. Already there is growing pressure from educated middle and upper class women for status and equality before the law, while their less educated and less skilled peers strive for more congenial conditions of employment. A labor shortage in some areas will work to the advantage of some women, while the decline of lifetime maternity will make for a large-scale exodus into new fields of interests and commitment for others. Along with occupational and economic changes, there are changes in labor laws, sex discrimination, educational opportunities, and marriage and divorce laws.

The social revolution affecting marriage, maternity, and employment cannot be ignored by those helping professionals of which psychotherapy is a part. It is clearly not realistic to perceive women in the traditional 19th century terms—themselves oversimplified and unreal—as dependent, domesticated and submissive. To still view women in this old-fashioned light attests to the power of habit and ignores the complexities introduced by the transition in which women find themselves. This raises the question of how psychotherapy, still largely guided by such traditional images of women, can help them resolve their problems.

In particular we must ask what typical problems confront women in these changing times and how different women try to cope with them. Here, too, it is important to be sensitized to women's multiple social guises. The fact that there are predictable differences by social class, educational level, age, and life style should not be irrelevant for psychotherapy. Patients from different social terrains may require quite different strategies of treatment.

In this paper I have tried to spell out the constants and variants of the female role so as to permit a more complex, and in that sense truer, grasp of the current realities affecting them. I hope that this effort to delineate a less global model of conceptions of womanhood will help those concerned with theory and practice in the healing arts.

References

ALBERT, ETHEL M. The roles of women: Question of values. In Seymour M. Farber and Roger H. Wilson (eds.), *The Potential of Woman*. Hightstown, N. J.: McGraw-Hill, 1963, pp. 105–115.

BART, PAULINE B. The myth of a value-free psychotherapy. In Wendell Bell and A. Mau (eds.), *The Sociology of the Future*. New York: Russell Sage Foundation, 1972, pp. 113–159.

BARZINI, LUIGI. *The Italians*. New York: Atheneum, 1964.

BIDDLE, BRUCE, J. and THOMAS, EDWIN J. (eds.) *Role Theory: Concepts and Research*. New York: Wiley, 1966.

BROWN, BERT R. Saving face. *Psychology Today*, 55–59, 86, May, 1971.

COLEMAN, JAMES S., *et al.* Leading crowds in ten Midwestern High Schools and emphasis upon personality and attractiveness. In Bernard Farber (ed.), *Kinship and Family Organization*. New York: Wiley, 1966, pp. 378–387.

CROSLAND, MARGARET. *Madame Colette*. London: Peter Owen, 1953, p. 198.

HARTLEY, RUTH. American core culture: Changes and continuities. In G. H. Seward and R. C. Williamson (eds.), *Sex Roles in Changing Society*. New York: Random House, 1970, pp. 126–150.

JACOBI, JOLANDE (ed.). *Psychological Reflections*. New York: Torchbooks, 1958, p. 89.

KLEIN, VIOLA. *The Feminine Character*. Chicago: University of Illinois Press, 1971.

KOMAROVSKY, MIRRA. *Blue-collar Marriage*. New York: Random House, 1964.

LADNER, JOYCE A. *Tomorrow's Tomorrow, The Black Woman*. New York: Doubleday, 1971.

LYND, HELEN MERRELL. *On Shame and the Search for Identity*. New York: Wiley, 1958.

MCADOO, B. *Self Esteem in Children's Human-Figure Drawings*. Senior Thesis, Dept. of Sociology, April, 1971.

MYRDAL, ALVA and KLEIN, VIOLA. *Women's Two Roles*. London: Routledge and Kegan Paul, 1966.

PECK, ELLEN. Review of happy endings by Helen W. Papashvily. *Central New Jersey N.O.W. Newsletter*, April, 1971, p. 12.

RAINWATER, LEE. *Working Class Wife*. Chicago: Oceana Publications, 1959.

ROSENBERG, MORRIS. *Society and the Adolescent Self-Image*. Princeton, N. J.: Princeton University Press, 1965.

ROSENKRANTZ, P. S., BEE, H., VOGEL, S. R., BROVERMAN, I. K., and BROVERMAN, D. M. Sex role stereotypes and self-concepts in college students. *Journal of Consulting and Clinical Psychology*, 32, 287–295, 1968.

SAFILIOS-ROTHSCHILD, CONSTANTINA. Good and bad girls in modern Greek movies. *The Journal of Marriage and the Family*, 1968.

SARBIN, THEODORE R. Role theory. In Gardner Lindzey (ed.), *Handbook of Social Psychology*, Vol. I, Reading, Mass.: Addison-Wesley, 1954, p. 223.

SHEED, WILFRED. The good word: Men's women, women's men. *The New York Times Book Review*, May 2, 1971, p. 2.

SHOSTAK, ARTHUR B. *Blue-Collar Life*. New York: Random House, 1968.

SPOCK, BENJAMIN M. Male chauvinist Spock recants—Well, almost. *The New York Times Magazine*, September 12, 1971, pp. 98 ff.

STOLLER, ROBERT. *Sex and Gender*. New York: Science House, 1968.

TANNER, HENRY. An Arab singer stirs pandemonium in Paris hall. *New York Times*, November 17, 1967, p. 43.

WOLFGANG, LEDERER. *The Fear of Women*. New York: Harcourt Brace Jovanovich, 1968.

WYSE, LOIS. *Mrs. Success*. New York: World Publishing Co., 1970.

B The Community

INTRODUCTION

Communities are populations that occupy a common territory and gain a living from the environment through their cooperative efforts. For primitive man, the community was often simply a temporary settlement of a few families who stopped in one place until they used up the available food supply, hunting birds and animals and gathering whatever fruits, nuts, and roots grew there, and then moved to a new location for a new supply of food. Permanent settlements of large populations became possible with the invention of agriculture. In general, the more fertile and extensive the farmland and the more efficient the means of transportation, the larger the human settlements that became possible. In larger settlements, a more complex division of labor developed and men became more dependent on one another. The large cities of modern society require a high degree of coordination of individual activities in order to achieve the intricate integration of the whole required for their effective functioning.

The community, or the neighborhood if the settlement is very large, is the next social group beyond the family that the individual encounters as he grows up. The sociologist Charles Horton Cooley pointed out the importance of the small community or neighborhood in the formation of individual personality and in socializing children and young people to the culture of the group. The quality of community life, therefore, affects the development of individual personality as well as the group's efficiency in gaining a living from nature.

Sidney Aronson takes a fresh look at the city, the dominant form of community life in today's industrialized societies, reminding us that the city always has been the center of man's civilization, the place where all the arts and artifacts of civilized cultures have been created. He points out that cities serve as the creative centers of societies because of the great variety of stimuli they provide man, the wide range of choices they present to urban dwellers, and the possibility of finding audiences or associates for almost any kind of activity. Variety, stimulation, creativity, and privacy, Aronson reminds us, are positive values of urban life that tend to be ignored by critics of cities today.

While the world is becoming urbanized today, the advanced industrial countries are becoming metropolitanized. William Dobriner shows how the

251

communities of the United States, for example, are becoming organized into metropolitan areas around a small number of major cities. In such metropolitan areas, a division of labor develops between communities. Central cities about which the metropolitan areas are integrated specialize in finance, in wholesale and retail trade, and, to a certain extent, in manufacturing. Smaller cities become specialized manufacturing satellites of the central cities, or sometimes residential suburbs, while new suburbs spring up rapidly in a "residential ring" of the metropolitan area. Communities on the "rur-urban fringe" of the metropolitan area may become residences of executives and professionals who can afford to travel long distances to work in the central cities, homes of people working in the satellite cities, or specialized suppliers of agricultural products or recreational facilities to the populations of the metropolitan areas. Small towns beyond the metropolitan areas, many of which are losing population even as the national population grows, sometimes disappear altogether, as when dams are built across valleys to provide water and electric power for the city and areas of the countryside are reforested to furnish recreation facilities for city people.

As Dobiner anticipates, recent data show that the suburbs are the fastest growing parts of metropolitan areas in North America. Herbert Gans, in his article, shows how selective suburban growth is in terms of race and social class of the people moving to them. Initially white middle- and upper-middle class communities, suburbs now house many white families from the lower middle class and the affluent American working class. Poor people are excluded by economic reasons from suburban residence, and black people have been excluded from most white suburbs on racial grounds, even when they were affluent. Gans critically examines two options open to social policy, especially with regard to the poor and the poor black inner-city dwellers: the proposal for the federal government to subsidize suburban housing for such families, and the idea of massive economic development programs in the central cities to raise the income of the poor and give them more options about where they can live.

Arthur Vidich and Joseph Bensman describe the integration of the small country town into the metropolitan economy. The town they studied specialized in one agricultural product, milk, which was sold on a metropolitan market, whereas most of the products consumed by the community were imported from the metropolitan centers. The country town was also a residence for families of men working in the industries of nearby cities. The small town, Vidich and Bensman point out, even imports its image of itself from the urban centers. Articles, stories in magazines, and programs on radio and television that describe and evaluate small-town life are assembled in the editorial rooms and studios located in the metropolitan centers and transmitted to the countryside.

Lawrence Susskind, in the last selection of this section, enumerates the varied purposes that have been served by the construction of totally planned new communities in modern industrial societies. He points out that the construction of these complete communities provides a golden opportunity for the application of social science knowledge—especially from microsociology and social psychology—to human living environments in order to influence the behavior patterns that emerge in these communities. Susskind discusses some of the surprising problems he sees as standing in the way of this practical use of scientific knowledge.

25

The City: Illusion, Nostalgia, and Reality

SIDNEY H. ARONSON

How different would our view of the city be, had the Jewish scribes who wrote the Book of Genesis been urban dwellers rather than members of a nomadic, desert tribe; had they located paradise amid the marketplace or the theatre of a thriving town rather than in a pastoral Garden of Eden; had they not held up to an impressionable posterity the "cities of the valley"—Sodom and Gemorah—as archetypal images of appalling evil? We can only speculate on the answers to such questions while knowing full well that we are both the spiritual and lineal descendants of people who deeply distrusted the life of cities and who imaged the Golden Age of freedom and happiness as a sylvan oasis. The City of God was a self-evident self-contradiction.

Historical attempts to deal with the city's origins have always been in the nature of guesswork and ingenious speculation based on the most fragmentary of evidence. For the first few thousand years of its existence the archaeological record of city life is a record more of gaps than of facts. Nor has the analysis of the modern city always been on firmer ground informed as so much of it has been, especially in America, by the antiurban bias that pervades so much of our history and our social attitudes, a bias that has effectively obscured the nature of the city and led to an obsession with its worst features to the almost complete neglect of its best. The standard, contemporary sociological view of the city sees it rather as a human theatre of horrors than as the matrix of inexhaustible choices and

From Dissent (1971). Reprinted by permission.

opportunities, the provider of endless stimulation, and the seedbed of all that goes by the name "civilization."

Yet the city's origin and its early history may be worth brief attention if only because such an examination may uncover aspects of the city which have too long been obscured or casually assumed. Then too, an historical perspective should make it easier to avoid that reverse evolutionary thinking which, beginning with Hesiod and the Book of Genesis, has placed man's Golden Age in the past and has gone on to yearn for what Roger Starr has called the "City of the Imagination." This is not to deny the real things that are wrong with the cities of today but to suggest that that is only one facet of the story and not perhaps the most important one.

For most of his time on earth man was a roving hunter and predator, forced to wander and to forage for food because the latter was so limited and the competition for it so fierce that even the most bountifully supplied areas could support no more than a handful of people. The first permanent settlements (not cities, to be sure) probably began as resting places in a nomadic existence and as burial sites. At some point in the development of man's mind, he had attributed to the spirits of the dead such powers over the living that the former had to be ceremonially buried, commemorated, and propitiated. What converted these temporary settlements into permanent ones was that series of events, occurring during the Neolithic Period, which we are justified in calling the "Agricultural Revolution": the domestication of plants and animals and, ultimately, man himself.

The resulting increased food production made possible the support of a larger population than ever before and made it both necessary and possible to excuse some of the adult population from the food-growing process and to divert their energies to the process and storage of food and to the maintenance of the settlement itself. While the greater food supply made such specialization possible, the specialization, in its turn, led to more efficient food production and utilization thus setting in motion those cycles, vicious or beneficial depending on one's point of view, that have remained with us to this day. Lewis Mumford's definition of the city as a container of containers reflects implicitly the greater complexity and differentiation of village life.

The invention of the plow and, perhaps, of the political institution of kingship made it possible for the village to develop into the town, and ultimately the city, by producing, on the one hand, a food surplus large enough to free whole groups from direct involvement with food production and, on the other, by creating an instrumentality that could effectively organize and utilize surplus resources. In consequence the village artisan, once a part-time peasant, became a full-time craftsman producing for a more or less dependable "market." It was not long thereafter that fairs and regular markets supplanted the system of barter between individuals.

Whether between the village and the true city there is an homology or only an analogy remains a matter of dispute among historians and urbanists but we know that in the city the natural features of the landscape to which the villages resorted for protection gave way to well-planned fortresses or citadels, temporary markets, to permanent, regulated ones (the sine qua non of a city for Max Weber), and wooden altars to imposing stone temples. At this point in history political institutions were not differentiated from religious ones—the king was at the same time the chief priest of the cult and was often himself considered divine—and under the threat of religious sanction the people of the city and the surrounding hinterland that depended on it (the suburbs of an earlier era) could be made to build those imposing monuments that ever since have denoted the beginnings of civilization. Civilization is coeval with the city; the etymological connection between the two words is far from gratuitous.

For Emile Durkheim, on the other hand, the key to urbanism was not in monuments or material artifacts but in the social processes that underlay them and, specifically, in the division of labor that made possible such complex living arrangements. For Durkheim the city was, above all, a place where different people did different things and by so doing developed relationships of mutual interdependence. But this is tantamount to saying that the city by its very nature creates diversity. For the division of labor, by producing different kinds of work, created different personalities since every work situation shapes human character congruent with its own demands. Thus, the greater the variety of social processes in a society, the more distinctive and varied are the psychological types that it exhibits. What could truly be said of the peasant, that he "looks into his neighbor's face and sees his own image" was no longer true for the city dweller. The city thus became an inexhaustible spectacle.

Concomitant with this increase in size and diversity that in part defines the city went an equal increase in "impersonality" or "anonymity." Where a large population inhabits a confined area (and most premodern cities were quite small in area primarily because of the needs of defense), it becomes impossible for the individual, in Weber's terms, to have "personal reciprocal acquaintance" of all or any substantial part of his fellow inhabitants. In other words, the individual often finds himself a stranger in his own city, an insight forcefully developed by Weber's contemporary Georg Simmel.

In considering those features of the city that seemed to make urban living so eminently desirable to many of our ancestors, we must be careful to distinguish between the advantages of life in permanent settlements as such from the advantages to be derived from living in true cities. Many of the benefits of settled life were available to the inhabitants of hamlets and villages in almost equal measure to city dwellers. These included a respite from wandering, relative safety, and the comforts of a permanent dwelling. What the city added to these and what the village and hamlet could never supply were diversity, a superabundance of choices, an incomparable range of opportunities: economic, political, artistic, and religious; and a setting in which one could exploit and exchange the fruits of one's creativity, whatever its form. Furthermore, there was the stimulation that inevitably arose from living among diverse types of people, of being at the center of power, commerce, and the arts, of meeting visitors from the other great cities of the world. To live in a city was thus to be present at the creation and the endless recreation of all that the world civilization connotes.

But the advantages of life in permanent settlements were not all on the side of the city nor did the advantages of the city necessarily increase in lineal fashion as the latter grew larger. Village life meant more comfortable and secure living for its inhabitants at the same time that its small size permitted villages the luxury of certain dangerous habits. The sloppy housekeeping customs villagers carried over from their nomadic past were tolerable in the relatively uncrowded conditions of village life. Nor did villages and small towns present the kind of tempting targets to marauders as did wealthy and populous cities. If the city nurtured civilization it also and simultaneously encouraged warfare, often for the same reasons.

Cities were thus beset by hazards within and enemies without. The more people were crowded into urban centers the more hazardous did the traditional habits of housekeeping become. The disposal of refuse was not perceived as a problem by the early urbanite, in fact, in the ancient city, human excreta and other wastes were customarily thrown into the street in front of one's dwelling and were removed only through biological degrading and the medium of rain, or, occasionally, of flooding. The hazards to health posed by this method of waste disposal are obvious and plagues were correspondingly common. The appearance of New York City's streets during the sanitation strike of early 1969 may give one a faint idea of what the streets of ancient metropoli were like year after year, although, in fairness, most of the waste produced in the premodern city was of an organic character and did ultimately decay.

Even the introduction of indoor plumbing—which occurred as early as the Minoan Period (circa 3000 B.C.), did little to improve the problem of waste disposal since it was available only to the rich while the poor continued to use the streets as a convenient refuse dump. This was true even in Athens of Pericles and the Rome of the Empire. Meanwhile, the invention of the high-rise apartment building—the Roman "Insula"—so discouraged what little care had been exercised in the process of garbage disposal that new laws had to be passed, forbidding the emptying of chamber pots from the upper story windows of such buildings onto whatever unfortunates happened to be passing in the streets below. And, as has been a persistent irony of technological innovation, what improved one condition simultaneously worsened another: the water which flushed privies in Roman *Insulae* was later used for washing and cooking drawn as it was from the same conduits and streams. And so the city became the seedbed of disease and pestilence as well as of civilization, able to maintain its population only as a result of high birth rates and of a constant influx of rural inhabitants drawn by the city's myriad attractions and opportunities.

The greatest threat to early cities was, however, other cities. "In reality," wrote Plato, "every city is in a natural state of war with every other." For urbanization and the political development that accompanied it also produced the capacity to organize larger and more effective armies than ever before. In consequence, cities, the storehouses of wealth and political power, became irresistible targets for those who sought one or another or both. The history of civilization is replete with the sacking and plundering of great cities, the slaughter and enslavement of their inhabitants. In premodern time Babylon, Nineveh, Carthage, Rome, Jerusalem, Ch'angan, Baghdad, and Constantinople all suffered such a fate at least once.

One of the more paradoxical aspects of the city's history, considering its seminal role in the rise of civilization, is what a relatively small percentage of the world's total population has actually resided in cities. Most of the people who have ever inhabited this planet have not been urbanites. Until the 19th century all but a relatively few of the world's cities, by the standards of today, were no larger than fair-sized towns. The earliest cities, those that arose some 5,000 to 8,000 years ago in the Mesopotamian culture area, probably did not contain populations much in excess of 5,000. Even in the first millen-

nium B.C., when city life was at least 2,000 years old it was only the exceptional urban center that could boast a population larger than some 30,000, although Periclean Athens at the height of its power and influence may have had a population of as much as 300,000 including slaves and metics. The only two premodern cities that seem at all comparable to those of the industrial age are Rome of the second century A.D. (especially the period of Trajan) and Ch'angan of the first half of the T'ang Dynasty, each of which appears to have had a million or more inhabitants. But even in the heyday of the Roman Empire and the urban development it fostered most cities were modest in size and most Romans did not live in them. With the invasions from the North, the disintegration of the Roman Empire, and the consequent disruption of commerce, urban life in Western Europe entered on a half-millennium period of decline as many city-dwellers returned to the towns and the countryside and took up once again an agricultural life. Many cities, including Rome itself, were reduced to a fraction of the population they had once supported. It was not until the 10th century, with the reopening of the Mediterranean to western traders and the general revival of economic life consequent upon that event, that cities entered upon a renaissance. Most of the later Medieval and Renaissance cities of Europe contained fewer than 50,000 inhabitants. As had always been the case up to that time the vast majority of the world's population lived physically if not politically, economically, and spiritually apart from the cities.

The Industrial Revolution radically and rapidly changed that state of affairs. Just as the expansion of commerce and trade had spurred urbanization in the preindustrial age so did industrialization lead, everywhere in the world, to the rise and growth of the modern city. Beginning in England in the late 18th century the Industrial Revolution spread first to Western Europe and then to America despite Thomas Jefferson's admonition to "let our workshops remain in Europe." It brought in its wake a profound and thoroughgoing restructuring of virtually every human activity and social institution—in agriculture, manufacturing, business organization, transportation, communication, government, religion, and family life. The city-building which the Industrial Revolution set in motion differed from that of the preindustrial age in that industrialization and its accompanying changes made possible the concentration of millions of people within the metropolis itself and of further millions, economically and socially dependent on the city, in adjacent suburbs. We have at last reached the point at which every region of the world has its megalopolis and it has become customary to speak of the "urbanization of the world," to refer to the spread and growth of cities as "irreversible and inexorable" and to predict that eventually three fourths of the world's population will live in cities of more than 500,000 inhabitants.

The industrial metropolis that was often superimposed on an existing preindustrial city overwhelmed existing urban institutions that had, at best, been no more than adequate to their tasks. This would have been true even if the source of the rapidly increasing urban population had been primarily or entirely from the natural increase of the existing urban population (that is, from an accelerating increase of the birth rate over the death rate). But, in fact, most of the tens of millions who flooded into the cities in the aftermath of industrialization were drawn from the ranks of peasants, farmers, and landless agricultural laborers for whom the countryside had no further use or who had no further use for the countryside. Throughout the Western world, and

especially in the United States, the rustic, the yokel, the country bumpkin —scarcely characterized by "urbanity" —became the typical new city dweller. In the American case the inevitable problems posed by the differing values and life styles of urban-born and rural-born groups were aggravated by the fact of the huge foreign immigration that began in earnest after the mid-1840's. Yet, the peasant is always a foreigner in the city and European cities were not appreciably better off simply because of their greater ethnic homogeneity. In every major city the problem of acculturation of rural immigrants has been a real and pressing one. In American society the movement from rural areas to the cities has gone on virtually to the present day although, since the 1920's, the chief source of this migration has shifted from foreign-born peasants to native-born rural blacks.

The great transformation of the city in the drive toward mature industrialization was experienced so acutely by both European and American sociologists that it became a dominant concern— almost an obsession—of modern sociology (an intellectual activity which is itself a product of the conflict of ideologies that ushered in the industrial age). Many sociologists, writing from the essentially Romantic ideological position, deplored the loss of warm, intimate, primary group relations and that sense of belonging to an organic, solidary community which they believed —or affected to believe—to have characterized earlier small town and rural life. In its place they depicted a fragmented and impersonal urban society in which isolated, anonymous individuals had only the most temporary and superficial contact with one another.

Following the first World War, Robert Park and his colleagues at the University of Chicago, strongly influenced by the German tradition of Tonnies and Simmel, tried to provide the empirical evidence that would support the more philosophical and impressionistic analyses of the European sociological Romantics. In the America of Harding and Coolidge—the redoubt of "normalcy"—they found cities (more particularly, Chicago) characterized by slums and racial ghettos, by bohemias and skid rows, by crime and delinquency, by jack-rollers and hoboes, by prostitutes, taxi-dancers, and schizophrenics. Although the members of the Chicago School felt bound by the canons of dispassionate scientific inquiry to maintain a semblance of objectivity in their writings they could scarcely conceal their dismay. Surely this was not what Durkheim meant when he said that the moral order of modern society was based on the division of social labor. Urban dwellers seemed able to sustain only impersonal, fleeting, and exploitative relations with one another. City dwellers, wrote Park, were like so many guests in a hotel "meeting but not knowing one another."

Thus, the Chicago School brought the prestige of science (in an age enamored of science and "scientism") to the support of an anti-urban tradition in America that long antedated the development of sociology and that had numbered among its adherents some of America's most creative and influential thinkers. Surely the city has changed (if not always for the better) since Jefferson in the early 19th century warned of its poverty, depravity, and corruption but that characterization of American urban life has enjoyed remarkable continuity both in our philosophical and literary traditions. This may suggest that the preindustrial city despite several millennia of history had still not become the truly congenial home for man or there may even be biological reasons, as some evolutionary biologists have suggested, why even confirmed and satisfied city dwellers yearn for the quiet and beauty of the countryside even though their only real concession to such a desire may be a tree planted in the back yard of a Manhattan brownstone. The rapid and momentous changes wrought by the Industrial Revolution were, in most instances, forced upon a set of living and working arrangements that had never been able to make its residents feel "urbane."

And so instead of celebrants the American city has had little but critics —often vitriolic ones—from Thomas Jefferson to Frank Lloyd Wright and Lewis Mumford. The case for the city as a kind of a 20th century version of Dante's Inferno is too well known and too depressing to bear detailed review here. Any hardened urbanite would readily recognize the chief counts of the indictment: poverty, ugliness, filth, violence, substandard housing, foul air, nerve shattering noise, political corruption (*the* shame of the cities for Lincoln Steffens and the Muckrakers of the Progressive Era), crime, drug addiction, mutual fear, crowds, loneliness, exasperating traffic jams, inadequate health and welfare services, inadequate transportation facilities, mediocre public schools, a criminal justice system so overburdened and ineffectual that all but a handful of crimes go unpunished, and everywhere a pervasive incivility of man to man. As has always been so, these failings and inadequacies are not evenly distributed among all the residents and residential areas of the city but fall most heavily on the poor and, especially, on the blacks and other ethnic minorities who form an ever increasing proportion of the United States' central city's population.

Even those problems once thought definitely solved threaten to recur. The provision of enclosed sewer systems, first introduced in mid-19th century London (such a system had existed in Kanossos of the Minoans but that was in another country and besides, the civilization was dead), and the later chemical purification of water effectively put an end to the ages-old threat of cholera and typhus epidemics. But now detergent residues flood the sewers and even seep into the drinking water of cities and the ground water of the countryside itself. Natural epidemics may thus be replaced by man-made epidemics. Solid wastes, most of which used to be organic in character, now are composed largely of glass, metal, and plastic containers that will not decay for hundreds of years, if ever, leading to the creation of unsightly and undisposable mountains of refuse. And the excreta deposited every day by scores of thousands of pet dogs on the streets of every major American city serves to give each resident and visitor a faint idea of what the streets of most ancient cities probably were like.

As though this indictment were not devastating enough there are those who believe that the city's greatest offense is the absence of "community" or, in other terms, the presence of widespread "anomie," social disorganization or social and psychological isolation. In the eyes of its authors, the City of the Imagination was always characterized by geographically compact, close-knit groups of kinsmen and neighbors who satisfied the ubiquitous and imperious human need for emotional warmth, friendship, and protection. In such an ideal city all the needs of its inhabitants were satisfied by those who knew and cared for the individual personally without any intervention by formal, impersonal service organizations. Paradoxically unlike most of the other urban maladies, it is the economically better-off residents who are said to suffer most acutely from the decline of the old neighborhood community. Although those who hold this view do not specify by what processes it comes to pass, they appear to believe that poverty, crowding, and the deprivation of human dignity encourage the development of communal sentiments and institutions. Would Katherine Genovese, the most striking symbol of the breakdown of community in the American city, have been saved from death had she resided in a black or Puerto Rican ghetto rather than in a middle-class white neighborhood?

It was the German philosopher-sociologist Georg Simmel who, in his 1918 essay "The Metropolis and Mental Life," provided the first coherent characterization of the city as an arena of impersonality, secondary relationships, and anomie. (In fact Simmel did not use the word "anomie" but his characterization is close enough to the accepted meaning of that word so that we may use the latter as a convenient shorthand.) Twenty years later his student, Louis Wirth, repeated and embellished Simmel's analysis in his well-known article, "Urbanism as a Way of Life." It was through Wirth and his writings that this ideological position (for that is what it is) passed into the main stream of American sociology under the guise of factual descriptions. Precisely because this ideology has been so prominent and persistent both in American sociology and popular social criticism it deserves some close scrutiny.

There is little doubt that the quantitative increase in the population of a city ultimately causes qualitative changes in the life of the city's inhabitants, a point that Marx made in a more general sense in the mid-19th century. At some critical point in the growth of a city (it is not necessary for the argument to be able to identify that point precisely), it becomes impossible for every inhabitant to know everyone else even by reputation. Attention to sheer numbers does not, of course, deny the importance of other sociological variables in understanding the life of a city or the attitudes of its inhabitants. Once passed the critical point cities become composed essentially of strangers, that is, individuals who tend to be suspicious of and even hostile to those they do not know personally. When, in addition, the strangers are of different races, ethnic groups, or social classes competing for scarce and limited resources the possibilities of misunderstanding and conflict increase exponentially.

The effect of increasing numbers on the character of urban life is to increase the probability that certain events or types of events will occur and that certain conditions will prevail while decreasing the probability of certain other kinds of events. For example, increasing the numbers and thus the density of a population of any given area will increase the probability of a high noise level, of large accumulations of refuse, of traffic jams, of overcrowded public transportation facilities at peak travel hours, of crowding in stores on weekends, and of long ticket lines for popular plays, movies, and sporting events. The very same conditions will, on the other hand, decrease the probability that any two randomly selected inhabitants will meet on the street and will similarily decrease the likelihood that one will be intimately acquainted with all of one's coworkers or physically close neighbors. Furthermore, an increase in the number of inhabitants will tend to increase the absolute numerical representation of many types of people whose proportion of the total population may be very small. Thus, every city of substantial size has its set population of psychopaths, drug addicts, hoodlums, lovers, lawyers, prostitutes, homosexuals, hippies, and so on *ad infinitum*. Finally, as with all voluntary migrations, that to the city was selective and thus increased some probabilities while decreasing others. Historically, it has always been the younger, the more energetic, the more ambitious, the more restless (accounting perhaps for the competitive atmosphere associated with cities), and

the more unscrupulous who have been attracted to the city; but also those whose deviance or idiosyncracies could only be tolerated in the atmosphere of privacy (for which anonymity is but a pejorative name) that the numbers, the diversity, and the psychological distance of the city makes possible.

But these very same factors account for the existence of an entirely different city: the city of the museum and the cathedral, of the playhouse and concert hall, of the bookstore and the research laboratory, in summary, that seedbed and storehouse of the products of man's most creative impulses. Cities provide not only the time but the physical and psychological conditions necessary for the creation of art: large numbers of people from whom the gifted can be selected; teachers and critics; physical facilities and money; literacy; the stimulation of exhibits and performances and of people meeting people. While some of the opportunities offered by the city attract the anti-social, others attract another kind of deviant: the talented provincial. And, in fact, the two are often the same. Essential for the creation of art or of any high culture is the availability of audiences—those willing and able to buy or support the work of artists. Much has been made of the fact that relative to the total population of a city the proportion who support the "art trade" is small; that may well be but the absolute number is large, large enough to provide an adequate market for most creative artists. The village, the town, even small cities produce only the dilettante and the amateur, not the artist; orchestras and theatrical performances, but not music or drama. First rate artists may be found in towns and small cities but only after they have been formed in the crucible of the metropolis.

Once the city is viewed as composed of an almost infinite number of publics making almost an infinite number of choices, many of the amenities and delights of urbanity become clear. The diversity of publics is assured by that very migration to the industrial city that has made it into a living ethnographic museum. For example, the glossary in Kate Simon's *New York Places and Pleasures* directs the reader to places that sell attayef, barracuda loafs, bialys, boccie balls, bouillabaisse, brioche, cherimoyas, cholent, chladdegh ring, couscous, decoupage, fhidara, ipon, kimchee, kompe, kouraber, and scores of other things that demonstrate that the city remains what it has always been: the great bazaar of infinite choices. Indeed, the audiences for such urban amenities gradually grow larger not only because the cosmopolitanism of the city exposes people to the exotic but also because the increasing prosperity makes it possible for many who previously could not afford to be part of a particular audience to join in. As Roger Starr has observed, the increase in the number of customers for the products of the city further alienates its critics either because the latter, usually arguing from an aristocratic position, object to the leveling of taste or because they are inconvenienced by the heavy demand. They are totally unaware that the essential diversity of city life depends on the existence of many substantial publics. For example, even with an attendance of 250,000 the New York flower show of 1970 lost money. The greatest threat to urbanity would seem to lie not in the excessive size of publics but in the danger that those publics will not be large and diverse enough to sustain the multiplicity of markets and choices.

This image of the city as a crosscutting system of publics, markets, and choices clearly runs counter to the prevailing dreary view that social *dis*-organization is the defining characteristic of city life, if indeed, disorganization can be a defining characteristic of any

viable institution. Present evidence suggests that the city still *is* viable, though ailing. From this point of view the *organization* of urban life seems a far more prominent characteristic than its *dis*-organization.

Unfortunately, not all urbanites share equally in the remarkable range of choices offered by the city. True, the decades since 1940 have produced a growing middle class which is both able and eager to enjoy the diversity of city life and to make use of the choices it offers. But for the poor, the excluded, and the disadvantaged the city remains a giant tease, offering much enticement but little fulfillment. The future of the city depends heavily on the capacity of its leadership to make those groups into publics able to participate in the city's diversity and able to make meaningful choices from among alternatives which it offers.

At the same time as the city increases the chances the individual will be able to satisfy his tastes and interests whatever they may be, it is also able, for the same reasons, to satisfy the human need for other people. Since its very invention the city has been a gathering place for different kinds of people, and the industrial metropolis especially, as we have seen, attracts and concentrates every conceivable personality type. This means that any individual urbanite, whatever his attitudes and behavior idiosyncrasies, has a reasonable chance to find congenial others to share those attitudes and idiosyncrasies. The other side of that cohesion and face-to-face intimacy so extolled by the champions of the village and the small town was that it forcibly imposed a set of attitudes and values on all its members and inhibited the expression of any views and feelings that were not consonant with the dominant ethos. It is not accidental that the one aspect of the small town that is not idealized by its nostalgic defenders is the difficulty of escaping the watchful eye of the community. Sherwood Anderson's *Winesburg, Ohio* serves as a model of the small town's hostility not only to deviance but to difference.

Despite this, critics of the city continue to "view with alarm" what they call the impersonal, fragmented quality of urban life and compare it unfavorably with the warm, face-to-face relationships they believe to have characterized villages, towns, and even the urban neighborhoods of half a century or more ago. They contend that the extended family, the single most important primary group, has disintegrated and dispersed under the impact of large scale industrialization as its constituent units, responding to opportunities presented by economic development, have scattered across the landscape. Although more recent studies have demonstrated that the American conjugal family is less isolated than once believed and although new types of primary groups have been discovered by sociologists, the latter have tended to see these as "temporary systems," shifting task and friendship groupings, grounded either in work situations or informal activities rather than in perduring groups such as the nuclear family. Sociologists, bemused by the confusion between physical and psychological closeness, have almost completely overlooked how large scale urban life makes it possible for the urbanite to take advantage of the multitude of human choices the city offers him.

The urbanite can become an integral part of a network of satisfying human relationships precisely because there exists in the city publics of every conceivable taste and interest and because forms of transportation and communication—especially the telephone—makes it possible for the individual to extend his range of personal associations far beyond the limits of his physical area of residence ("his neighborhood" in its original meaning). Unlike the town dweller, the urbanite can form primary groups based on personal attraction and shared interests rather than solely on the accident of physical propinquity. The very density of urban population makes it impossible to know all one's physical neighbors even if one wished to do so and makes of every street and virtually every building a physical point at which dozens or even hundreds of social networks intersect.

Some sociologists now speak of "dispersed" social networks to denote that many urbanites form primary groups with others who are scattered throughout the metropolitan area, groups which interact as much over the telephone as in face-to-face gatherings. From the point of view of the individual such groups constitute his "psychological neighborhood" as opposed to his physical neighborhood of residence. Modern transportation, of course, makes it possible for such groups to foregather in person but it seems doubtful that such dispersed groups could long remain cohesive without the communication made possible by the telephone. The city has not lost community, it has rather developed a different kind of community more appropriate to its physical setting.

Sociologists have only recently discovered these "telephone communities" (as Suzanne Keller calls them) and their precise character still remains obscure. I myself have discovered one such "neighborhood" that consists of a group of elderly widows living alone who maintain scheduled daily telephone contact as a means of insuring the safety, health, and emotional security of the group's members. The telephone also plays a key role in maintaining the cohesion of physically dispersed families: private telephone calls seem to be made most frequently among close relatives with mother-daughter calls probably the most frequent of all.

Of course, psychological closeness not dependent on the telephone is also pos-

sible in the modern city and probably exists in a few neighborhoods such
as the Chinatowns of New York and
San Francisco and the Italian North
End of Boston. In addition, the communes that have recently sprung up in
various parts of the country represent
a new form of primary group, one that
differs both from the preindustrial extended family and the conjugal family
of industrial society. What the future
of this new form will be and how successful it will be in meeting psychological as well as the physical needs of its
members remains to be seen.

If we are to believe the ideology which
has come to surround it, rural life provided emotional security at the expense
of privacy and individuality; the modern city, on the other hand, can provide both physical privacy, even amidst
high density living, and intimacy
within one's psychological neighborhood or neighborhoods. Needless to say,
this arrangement does not always work
satisfactorily: there are times, as the
Genovese case showed us, when a neighbor in the old fashioned sense of the
word is sorely needed. But it is just as
easy to blame such incidents on the
lack of adequate police protection, a
protection needed the more as the
meaning of "community" shifts from
physical to psychological and as many
of the activities that used to be the
province of informal neighborhood
groupings are assumed by large-scale,
bureaucratic governmental organizations. Moreover in the modern industrial city it is virtually impossible to
determine who speaks for "the community" since each psychological
neighborhood draws its residents from
diverse parts of the metropolitan area.

Those critics engaged in writing the
city's obituary speak as though the chief
hope of the future lies in alternative
living arrangements. Much has been
made of the recent census findings
(both 1960 and 1970) that show de-

cline in the population of many American central cities and a more than
corresponding rise in the suburban
population. Yet many of those who
flock to the suburbs are the middle and
upper middle class supporters of the
"art trade" and the "great bazaar." To
ask how quickly such people would live
in small towns not situated near a major
metropolis is at the same time to answer
the question. Those who have chosen
suburban life have not created new
institutions but have tended to make
second-hand imitations of existing urban
forms. The suburban shopping center
offers convenience and adequate parking space but at the price of a narrower
range of choices than those offered by
central city department stores and specialty shops. Suburbs are widely believed to offer superior public education
and that belief has itself been a major
motive for the exodus from the central
city. But except for towns such as
Newton, Massachusetts and 'Scarsdale,
New York, there is precious little evidence for the superiority of suburban
over central city schools. We now know
that middle-class suburban schools attract eager, highly motivated, well socialized white students; but the quality
of education in blue collar suburbs is
no better than that of urban schools
which cater to similar populations.

It is, of course, possible that increasing dissatisfaction with the quality of
urban life may produce a new migration out toward the suburbs and exurbs
which, in its magnitude, may be comparable to that which created the industrial city as we know it. Some demographers and sociologists have claimed to
see evidence of such a migration in the
results of the 1970 census, results which
disclosed that America's suburban population (exceeding 71 million) is now
its largest single sector. In comparison,
the central cities now contain some 59
million people while another 71 million
live in the nation's smaller cities, towns,

and genuinely rural areas. Should such a suburban or exurban migration prove, in fact, to be the trend of the future, the ultimate result will be the gradual filling of the relatively sparsely settled countryside, the still further diffusion of standardized housing developments and shopping centers, a still greater dependence on the automobile, and the total uglification of the American landscape. It may be little enough to say in its favor, but at least the concentration of the American population in large metropolitan areas has preserved a real distinction between the urban and the rural. That in itself may be a positive value.

But perhaps the most remarkable tribute to the city is the ability of its inhabitants to endure and to surmount virtually every catastrophe, every abomination, every one of the many affronts to their senses, to adapt to each successive trial, to survive and, by surviving, to triumph. As always, wars remain the greatest threat to the city, yet war has come to be accepted, much as fire used to be, as the "ultimate municipal germicide." The typical New Yorker, that intrepid veteran of municipal crises, has become a master of survival. At the Museum of Modern Art recently, I observed an elderly woman demonstrating to a companion the best way to keep a robber from making off with a handbag. Millions of subway riders know that any day they may be trapped in their trains and forced to exit through the labyrinth of tracks, tunnels, and underground passageways—as many thousands already have. And all city dwellers know that from time to time, as the result of strikes, job actions, and political disputes they will have to make do

for shorter or longer periods without essential services. The dream of permanently leaving New York is but the New Yorker's latest wish-fulfilling fantasy and has replaced the older dream of leaving the employ of another and starting one's own business.

Recently, in the *New York Times*, John Canaday wrote something that may sum up both the glory and the horror of the contemporary American city. He wrote of the increase in his rent, the mugging of his mother-in-law, of subway delays, and of a pickpocket in the elevator, but then he added: "in how many towns outside New York would 15th century prayer books and Japanese screens attract the large audiences they do here?" Where else but in New York or, more generally, in a true city? Such experiences incarnate the uniqueness of the urban experience: the coexistence at the same time in the same place of the wonders and the terrors of human life— the visionary and his audience side by side with the criminal and his victims.

Speculation over the supposed obsolescence of the city and its ultimate decline seems both premature and unfruitful. Around the world a new wave of the great urban migration is gathering force and the clamor for those products of civilization that only the city can provide rises apace. Robert Park, despite his concern over the city's anomie, was one of the first to realize that as a result of living in the city man produced civilization. The end of the city might well signify the end of that civilization. The task of this generation is not to bury or to replace the city but to humanize it, to make of it a decent home for all its residents, to make it urbane as well as urban.

26

The Growth and Structure of Metropolitan Areas

WILLIAM M. DOBRINER

In 1900, metropolitan areas claimed 31 percent of the total population. Today, 2 out of 3 Americans live in urban places, but over 60 percent of the total population lives in metropolitan areas. Census forecasts suggest that by 1975 the population of the United States will exceed 220 million, an increase of roughly 40 million over 1960, 63 percent of whom will live in metropolitan areas.

The growth of metropolitan centers, however, is merely one facet of the urban revolution of the last sixty years. Although metropolitan areas have demonstrated amazing growth, the component parts are by no means growing at the same rate. In 1900, for example, the population of the *central cities* of metropolitan areas constituted 61.9 percent of the total metropolitan unit while the suburban and fringe areas outside of the cities were only 38.1 percent of the total area. By 1960, however, the picture had changed. Central cities claimed barely half of the total population of metropolitan areas.

The 1960 Census for the New York Standard Metropolitan Statistical Area dramatically illustrates the national trend. While New York City lost a total of 109,973 persons between 1950 and 1960, its suburban counties were registering spectacular gains. Nassau County increased 93 percent over the decade. Rockland 53 percent, Suffolk 141 percent, and Westchester 29 percent. In this manner, while New York City lost about one and a half percent of its population during the decade, its suburbs increased by 75 percent.

William M. Dobriner, *Class in Suburbia*, © 1963. By permission of Prentice-Hall, Inc., Englewood Cliffs, N.J.

From 1900 until 1920 central cities were growing faster than their tributary rings. However, in each decade since 1920 the rings have been growing faster than the central cities. Thus, the comparative growth rates between central cities and their rings have now become considerable. In the decade between 1940 and 1950, rings grew almost two and a half times as fast as central cities. The result has been that the suburban population alone is estimated at more than 50 million. The trends in the New York metropolitan area are clearly reflected on the national level. According to the 1960 Census, about 84 percent of the 28 million population increase during the decade 1950–60 occurred in the nation's metropolitan areas. However, the increase in these areas from 89,316,903 in 1950 to 112,885,178 in 1960 (26.4 percent) saw the suburban rings growing at a much faster rate than central cities. The increase of central cities in the decade (5.6 million) to a total of 58 million by 1960 constituted a 10.7 percent increase; in contrast, outlying suburban areas grew from 36.9 million population in 1950 to 54.9 million in 1960 for an increase of 48.6 percent.

The growth rates for central cities are clearly continuing to decline. Indeed, the trend is for the central cities of the largest metropolitan areas to have even slower rates of growth than the central cities of smaller metropolitan areas. We have already noted that New York City lost population during the 1950–1960 decade. In the five metropolitan areas of 3,000,000 or more the growth in central cities was only 1 percent. In contrast, however, the growth of the suburban rings of these great metropolitan centers was 71 percent. As size declines, the growth rate of central cities increased in relation to the suburban areas. In the case of the smaller metropolitan areas of less than 100,000, the growth rate (29 percent) exceeded the suburban rate (11 percent).

It is clear that population is moving toward the suburbs and the claim of central cities is decreasing. For the country as a whole, the outlying rings of metropolitan centers accounted for about two thirds of the total U.S. population increase since 1950 and for more than three-fourths of the total increase within metropolitan areas. Furthermore, the trend of central city loss and suburban gain is expected to continue. By 1975, the Committee for Economic Development estimates the central city population will have dropped to 42 percent of the metropolitan total, while the suburban and fringe areas outside will have grown to 57 percent of the entire metropolitan complex. This almost reverses the central city-suburban population proportions established for metropolitan areas at the turn of the century.

Although cities, as a distinguishable community form, have existed for over five thousand years, the city in its metropolitan guise is scarcely one hundred years old. . . . the metropolitan area may be regarded as a vast spatial structure consisting of functionally interdependent economic, political, and social subsystems. The result may be a super-organized concentration that takes in portions of two or three states in a highly specialized and differentiated functional integration of areas that go well beyond the political limits of the core city.

Indeed, the process of metropolitan growth has proceeded so far that the unit "metropolitan area" in the aforementioned sense may no longer apply to the larger, integrated metropolitan aggregates that are flowing into each other across the nation. The "boundaries" of metropolitan areas are fusing to form super-metropolitan entities that have been called "strip cities" or, as Jean Gottmann has termed the integration of metropolitan areas from southern New Hampshire all the way to the Appalachian foothills in Virginia, "Megalopolis."

According to a study made by U.S. News and World Report (Sept. 18, 1961; see Figure 1) the thirteen major "strip cities" in the United States— Boston to Washington, Albany to Erie, Cleveland to Pittsburgh, Toledo to Cincinnati, Detroit to Muskegon, Chicago–Gary to Milwaukee, St. Louis to Peoria, Seattle to Eugene, San Francisco to San Diego, Kansas City to Sioux Falls, Fort Worth–Dallas–San Antonio–Houston, Miami–Tampa–Jacksonville, and Atlanta to Raleigh—contain half the population of the country (89,395,496) and have increased more than 25 percent from 1950. Of the total 212 metropolitan areas in the nation, 119 fall within 13 giant strip city patterns. Not only did half the population live within these super-metropolitan constellations, but 109 billion dollars in retail trade at 54.7 percent of the total consumer market was expended there. . . .

Although their language varies, ecologists, demographers, economists, sociologists, and political scientists think of the metropolitan area in terms of three differentiated zones. We can, therefore, assume that this view of metropolitan centers is generally useful. Since there is general agreement that the zones are there, but not complete accord on the terms used to describe these areas, we shall identify them as (1) the Central Core, (2) the Suburban Zone, and (3) the Rural-Urban Fringe. Having identified these zones, however, the logical task is to inquire into those factors which have led to the

Figure 1
The thirteen major strip cities in the United States. (*Courtesy of the Department of Commerce, Bureau of the Census.*)

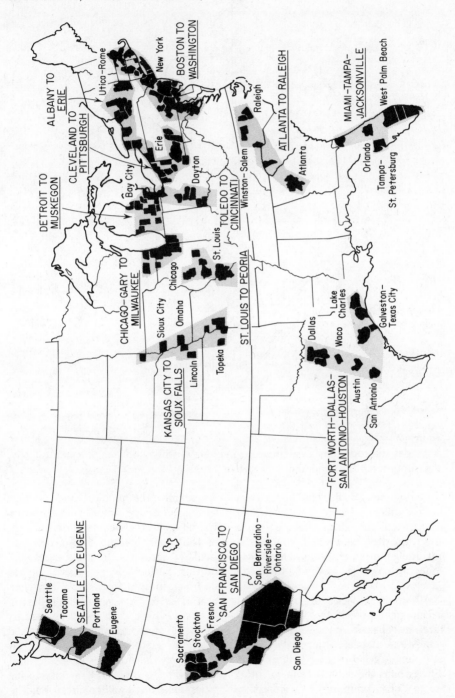

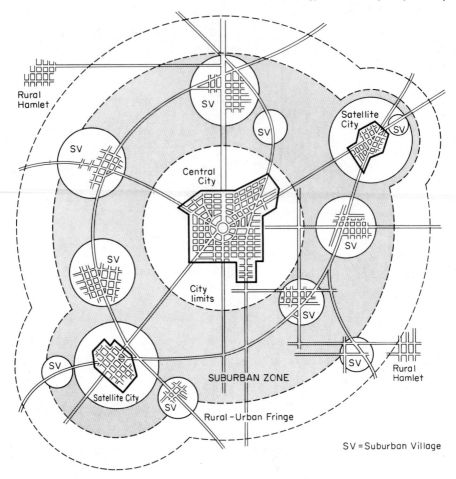

Figure 2
A model metropolitan area showing the relationship between the central city, the suburban zone, and the rural-urban fringe.

three-ring view of metropolitan centers. In the interest of brevity we shall take the central city—the core area—as a given quantity and shall concentrate our discussion on the communities and zones which lie beyond the core city. . . .

All of these views of the suburbs, which are representative of the literature, rest heavily on two basic characteristics—characteristics which critically, or as Martin says "definitively," differentiate the suburb from all other forms of community organization.

These are: the physical and political separation of the suburb from the central city, and the economic dependence of the suburb on the core city as particularly seen in the suburban commuting pattern. Suburbs may indeed be much more than this, but if a community is to be regarded as suburban in its simplest and most elementary form, it must be physically removed from the central city and it must rely heavily on the urban economy. . . .

Satellites [smaller manufacturing cities of a metropolitan area] tend to be older than residential suburbs and are found most often in industrialized sections of the northeast and north-central areas of the nation. In addition, suburbs and satellite cities tend to have contrasting types of populations. In general, satellites contain younger populations than do residential suburbs with a trend toward the lower socioeconomic class and status groups. Along similar lines, the population of satellite cities, contrasted with a model residential suburb, have a lower average education, lower average rent levels, high proportions of foreign-born whites, higher fertility rates, higher percentages of tenant-occupied buildings, and a work force in which two out of three workers are in the blue collar occupations.

In contrasting the comparative growth rates of residential suburbs and the employing satellites, Schnore demonstrated that the suburbs were growing almost twice as fast as the satellites. Furthermore, the suburbs were becoming even more residential in character, while the satellite areas, in addition to the central cities, were becoming more industrialized.

In the zonal view of the patterning of metropolitan areas [see Figure 2] Zone I consists of the densely populated and highly commercialized and industrialized core, while Zone II consists of a belt or rapidly growing suburban communities and industrialized satellite cities. Of the two, suburbs and satellites, the suburbs seem to predominate slightly on the national average.

Beyond the suburban belt lies the third zone of the metropolitan area which goes by a variety of names. Some call it "the rural ring," "urban fringe," "the outer ring," "the rural-urban fringe," and the like. We have called it the "rural-urban fringe" and by that we identify it as the last belt or area in which metropolitan or urban patterns are still evident. Essentially this belt consists of a geographic area in which the prevailing use of land is neither clearly urban nor suburban (residential, industrial, commercial) or rural (agricultural). It is that area where the expanding metropolis is currently waging its imperialistic war. This is the belt where the new suburban colonies and satellite cities will emerge in a few years. Thus, from an ecological view, the rural-urban fringe represents that spatial dimension of the entire area in which new urban functions, largely in the form of suburban residential areas and employing satellites, eat into the rural countryside. As such, it is a heterogeneous area of instability and change. On one side of the illusive and fragmentary boundary of the urban fringe lies the ring of suburban villages and satellite cities and on the other, beyond suburbia and the interurban railways, past the commuter railroad, the expressway and parkway systems, the mass-produced subdivisions, the land opens up and the signs of the city fade. Beyond the rural-urban fringe all volatile and unstable, lie the small villages, the pokey economies and the sleepy roadways of rural America. . . .

27

The Future of the Suburbs

HERBERT J. GANS

In this unpredictable world, nothing can be predicted quite so easily as the continued proliferation of suburbia. Not only have American cities stopped growing for more than a generation, while the metropolitan areas of which they are a part were continuing to expand lustily, but there is incontrovertible evidence that another huge wave of suburban home building can be expected in the coming decade.

Between 1947 and about 1960, the country experienced the greatest baby boom ever, ending the slowdown in marriages and childbirths created first by the Depression and then by World War II. Today, the earliest arrivals of that baby boom are themselves old enough to marry, and many are now setting up housekeeping in urban or suburban apartments. In a few years, however, when their first child is two to three years old, and the second is about to appear, many young parents will decide to buy suburban homes. Only simple addition is necessary to see that by the mid-seventies, they will be fashioning another massive suburban building boom, provided of course that the country is affluent and not engaged in World War III.

The new suburbia may not look much different from the old; there will, however, be an increase in the class and racial polarization that has been developing between the suburbs and the cities for several generations now. The suburbs will be home for an ever larger

proportion of working-class, middle-class and upper-class whites; the cities, for an ever-larger proportion of poor and nonwhite people. The continuation of this trend means that, by the seventies, a great number of cities will be 40 to 50 percent nonwhite in population, with more and larger ghettos and greater municipal poverty on the one hand, and stronger suburban opposition to open housing and related policies to solve the city's problems on the other hand. The urban crisis will worsen, and although there is no shortage of rational solutions, nothing much will be done about the crisis unless white America permits a radical change of public policy and undergoes a miraculous change of attitude toward its cities and their populations.

Another wave of suburban building would develop even if there had been no post-World War II baby boom, for American cities have always grown at the edges, like trees, adding new rings of residential development every generation as the beneficiaries of affluence and young families sought more modern housing and "better" neighborhoods. At first, the new rings were added inside the city limits, but ever since the last half of the nineteenth century, they have more often sprung up in the suburbs. . . .

Moreover, studies of housing preferences indicate that the majority of Americans, including those now living in the city, want a suburban single family house once they have children, and want to remain in that house when their children have grown up. This urge for suburban life is not limited to the middle class or just to America; the poor would leave the city as well if they could afford to go, and so would many Europeans. . . .

Obviously, the popular antisuburban literature, which falsely accuses the suburbs of causing conformity, matriarchy, adultery, divorce, alcoholism, and other standard American pathologies, has not kept anyone from moving to the suburbs, and even the current predictions of land shortages, longer commuting, and urban congestion in the suburbs will not discourage the next generation of home buyers. Most, if not all, metropolitan areas still have plenty of rural land available for suburban housing. Moreover, with industry and offices now moving to the suburbs, new areas previously outside commuting range become ripe for residential development to house their employees. . . .

Of course, all this leads to increasing suburban congestion, but most suburbanites do not mind it. They do not leave the city for a rural existence, as the folklore has it; they want a half acre or more of land and all their favorite urban facilities within a short driving distance from the house. . . .

It goes without saying that almost all the new suburbanites—and the developments built for them—will be white and middle-income for, barring miracles in the housing industry and in Federal subsidies, the subdivisions of the seventies will be too expensive for any family earning less than about [$12,000]. Thus, even if suburbia were to be racially integrated, cost alone would exclude most nonwhites. Today, less than 5 percent of New York State's suburban inhabitants are nonwhite, and many of them live in ghettos and slums in the small towns around which suburbia has developed.

Nevertheless, the minuscule proportion of nonwhite suburbanites will increase somewhat in the future, for, if the current affluence continues, it will benefit a small percentage of Negroes and Puerto Ricans. Some of them will be able to move into integrated suburban communities, but the majority will probably wind up in existing and new middle-class ghettos.

If urban employment is available, or if the ongoing industrialization of the South pushes more people off the land, poverty-stricken Negroes will continue to come to the cities, overcrowding and eventually enlarging the inner-city ghettos. Some of the better-off residents of these areas will move to "outer-city" ghettos, which can now be found in most American cities; for example, in Queens. And older suburbs like Yonkers and Mount Vernon will continue to lose some of the present residents and attract less affluent newcomers, as their housing, schools and other facilities age. As a result of this process, which affects suburbs as inevitably as city neighborhoods, some of their new inhabitants may be almost as poor as inner-city ghetto residents, so that more and more of the older suburbs will face problems of poverty and social pathology now thought to be distinctive to the city.

That further suburban growth is practically inevitable does not mean it is necessarily desirable, however. Many objections have been raised, some to suburbia itself, others to its consequences for the city. For example, ever since the rise of the postwar suburbs, critics have charged that suburban life is culturally and psychologically harmful for its residents, although many sociological studies, including my own, have shown that most suburbanites are happier and emotionally healthier than when they lived in the city. In addition, the critics have charged that suburbia desecrates valuable farm and recreation land, and that it results in "suburban" sprawl.

Suburbia undoubtedly reduced the supply of farm acreage, but America has long suffered from an oversupply of farmland, and I have never understood why allowing people to raise children where other people once raised potatoes or tomatoes desecrates the land. Usually, the criticism is directed to "ugly, mass-produced, look-alike little boxes," adding a class bias to the charges, as if people who can only afford mass-produced housing are not entitled to live where they please, or should stay in the city. . . .

The harmful effects of suburbia on the city are a more important criticism. One charge, made ever since the beginning of suburbanization in the nineteenth century, is that the suburbs rob the city of its tax-paying, civic-minded and culture-loving middle class. Actually, however, middle-class families are often a tax liability for the city; they demand and receive more services, particularly more schools, than their taxes pay for. Nor is there any evidence that they are more civic-minded than their non-middle-class neighbors; they may be more enthusiastic joiners of civic organizations, but these tend to defend middle-class interests and not necessarily the public interest. Moreover, many people who live in the suburbs still exert considerable political influence in the city because of their work or their property holdings and see to it that urban power structures still put middle-class interests first, as slum organizations, whose demands for more antipoverty funds or public housing are regularly turned down by city hall, can testify.

The alleged effect of the suburbs on urban culture is belied by the vast cultural revival in the city which occurred at the same time the suburban exodus was in full swing. Actually, most suburbanites rarely used the city's cultural facilities even when they lived in the city, and the minority which did, continues to do so, commuting in without difficulty. Indeed, I suspect that over half the ticket buyers for plays, art

movies, concerts and museums, particularly outside New York, are—and have long been—suburbanites. Besides, there is no reason why cultural institutions cannot, like banks, build branches in the suburbs, as they are beginning to do now. Culture is no less culture by being outside the city.

A much more valid criticism of suburbanization is its effect on class and racial segregation, for the fact that the suburbs have effectively zoned out the poor and the nonwhites is resulting in an ever-increasing class and racial polarization of city and suburb. In one sense, however, the familiar data about the increasing polarization are slightly misleading. In years past, when urban census statistics showed Negroes and whites living side by side, they were actually quite polarized socially. On New York's Upper West Side, for example, the big apartment buildings are de facto segregated for whites, while the rotting brownstones between them are inhabited by Negroes and Puerto Ricans. These blocks are integrated statistically or geographically, but not socially, particularly if white parents send their children to private schools.

Nor is suburbanization the sole cause of class and racial polarization; it is itself an effect of trends that have gone on inside the city as well, and not only in America. When people become more affluent and can choose where they want to live, they choose to live with people like themselves. What has happened in the last generation or two is that the opportunity of home buyers to live among compatible neighbors, an opportunity previously available only to the rich, has been extended to people in the middle- and lower-middle-income brackets. This fact does not justify either class or racial segregation, but it does suggest that the polarization resulting from affluence would have occurred even without suburbanization.

Class and racial polarization are harmful because they restrict freedom of housing choice to many people, but also because of the financial consequences for the city. For one thing, affluent suburbia exploits the financially bankrupt city; even when payroll taxes are levied, suburbanites do not pay their fair share of the city's cost in providing them with places of work, shopping areas and cultural facilities and with streets and utilities, maintenance, garbage removal and police protection for these facilities.

More important, suburbanites live in vest-pocket principalities where they can, in effect, vote to keep out the poor and the nonwhites and even the not very affluent whites.

As a result, the cities are in a traumatic financial squeeze. Their ever more numerous low-income residents pay fewer taxes but need costly municipal services, yet cities are taking in less in property taxes all the time, particularly as the firms that employ suburbanites and the shops that cater to them also move to the suburbs. Consequently, city costs rise at the same time as city income declines. To compound the injustice state and Federal politicians from suburban areas often vote against antipoverty efforts and other Federal funding activities that would relieve the city's financial troubles, and they also vote to prevent residential integration.

These trends are not likely to change in the years to come. In fact, if the present white affluence continues, the economic gap between the urban have-nots and the suburban haves will only increase, resulting on the one hand in greater suburban opposition to integration and to solving the city's problems, and on the other hand to greater discontent and more ghetto rebellions in the city. This in turn could result in a new white exodus from the city, which, unlike the earlier exodus, will be based almost entirely on racial fear, making suburbanites out of the middle-aged

and older middle-class families who are normally reluctant to change communities at this age and working-class whites who cannot really afford a suburban house. Many of them will, however, stay put and oppose all efforts toward desegregation, as indicated even now by their violent reaction to integration marches in Milwaukee and Chicago, and to scattered-site public housing schemes which would locate projects in middle-income areas in New York and elsewhere.

Ultimately, these trends could create a vicious spiral, with more ghetto protest leading to more white demands, urban and suburban, for repression, resulting in yet more intense ghetto protests, and culminating eventually in a massive exodus of urban whites. If this spiral were allowed to escalate, it might well hasten the coming of the predominantly Negro city.

Today, the predominantly Negro city is still far off in the future, and the all-Negro city is unlikely. Although Washington, D.C.'s population is about . . . [70] percent Negro, and several other cities, including Newark, Gary and Richmond, hover around the 50 percent mark, [in 1970, 13] of the 130 cities with over 100,000 population [were] 40 percent or more Negro. . . . (New York's Negro population was [21] percent in [1970], although in Manhattan, the proportion of Negroes was 27 percent and of Negroes and Puerto Ricans, 39 percent.)

Moreover, these statistics only count the nighttime residential population, but who lives in the city is, economically and politically, a less relevant statistic than who works there, and the daytime working population of most cities is today, and will long remain, heavily and even predominantly white.

Still, to a suburbanite who may someday have to work in a downtown surrounded by a black city, the future may seem threatening. A century ago, native-born WASPs must have felt similarly, when a majority of the urban population consisted of foreign-born Catholics and Jews, to whom they attributed the same pejorative racial characteristics now attributed to Negroes. The city and the WASPs survived, of course, as the immigrants were incorporated into the American economy, and suburban whites would also survive. . . .

Unfortunately, present governmental policies, local, state and Federal, are doing little to reverse the mounting class and racial polarization of city and suburb. Admittedly, the strong economic and cultural forces that send the middle classes into the suburbs and bring poor nonwhite people from the rural areas into the city in ever larger numbers are difficult to reverse even by the wisest government action.

Still, governmental policies have not been especially wise. The major efforts to slow down class and racial polarization have been these: legislation to achieve racial integration; programs to woo the white middle class back to the city; plans to establish unified metropolitan governments, encompassing both urban and suburban governmental units. All three have failed. None of the open housing and other integration laws now on the books have been enforced sufficiently to permit more than a handful of Negroes to live in the suburbs, and the more recent attempt to prevent the coming of the predominantly black city by enticing the white middle class back has not worked either.

The main technique used for this last purpose has been urban renewal, but there is no evidence—and, in fact, there have been no studies—to show that it has brought back a significant number of middle-class people. Most likely, it has only helped confirmed urbanites find better housing in the city. The attractions of suburbia are simply too persuasive for urban renewal

or any other governmental program to succeed in bringing the middle class back to the city. . . .

Metropolitan government is, in theory, a good solution, for it would require the suburbs to contribute to solving the city's problems, but it has long been opposed by the suburbs for just this reason. They have felt that the improvements and economies in public services that could be obtained by organizing them on a metropolitan basis would be offset by what suburbanites saw as major disadvantages, principally the reduction of political autonomy and the loss of power to keep out the poor and the nonwhites.

The cities, which have in the past advocated metropolitan government, may become less enthusiastic as Negroes obtain greater political power. Since the metropolitan area is so predominantly white, urban Negroes would be outvoted every time in any kind of metropolitan government. Some metropolitanization may nevertheless be brought about by Federal planning requirements, for as Frances Piven and Richard Cloward point out in a recent New Republic article, several Federal grant programs, particularly for housing and community facilities, now require a metropolitan plan as a prerequisite for funding. Piven and Cloward suggest that these requirements could disfranchise the urban Negro, and it is of course always possible that a white urban-suburban coalition in favor of metropolitan government could be put together deliberately for precisely this purpose. Under such conditions, however, metropolitan government would only increase racial conflict and polarization.

What then, can be done to eliminate this polarization? One partial solution is to reduce the dependence of both urban and suburban governments on the property tax, which reduces city income as the population becomes poorer, and forces suburbs to exclude low-income residents because their housing does not bring in enough tax money. If urban and suburban governments could obtain more funds from other sources, including perhaps the Federal income tax, parts of the proceeds of which would be returned to them by Washington, urban property owners would bear a smaller burden in supporting the city and might be less opposed to higher spending. Suburbanites would also worry less about their tax rate, and might not feel so impelled to bar less affluent newcomers, or to object to paying their share of the cost of using city services.

Class polarization can be reduced by rent- or price-supplement programs which would enable less affluent urban-ites to pay the price of suburban living and would reduce the building and financing costs of housing. But such measures would not persuade the sub-urbs to let in Negroes; ultimately, the only solution is still across-the-board residential integration.

The outlook for early and enforce-able legislation toward this end, how-ever, is dim. Although election results have shown time and again that North-ern white majorities will not vote for segregation, they will not vote for in-tegration either. I cannot imagine many political bodies, Federal or other-wise, passing or enforcing laws that would result in significant amounts of suburban integration; they would be punished summarily at the next elec-tion.

For example, proposals have often been made that state and Federal gov-ernments should withdraw all subsidies to suburban communities and builders practicing de facto segregation, thus depriving the former of at least half their school operating funds, and the latter of Federal Housing Authority (FHA) insurance on which their build-ing plans depend. However desirable as such legislation is, the chance that it would be passed is almost nil. One can also argue that Washington should of-fer grants-in-aid to suburban govern-ments which admit low-income resi-dents, but these grants would often be turned down. Many suburban munici-palities would rather starve their public services instead, and the voters would support them all the way.

The best hope now is for judicial ac-tion. The New Jersey Supreme Court ruled some years back that builders relying on FHA insurance had to sell to Negroes, and many suburban sub-divisions in that state now have some Negro residents. The United States Supreme Court has just decided that it will rule on whether racial discrimi-nation by large suburban developers is unconstitutional. If the answer turns out to be yes, the long, slow process of implementing the Court's decisions can at least begin.

In the meantime, solutions that need not be tested at the ballot box must be advanced. One possibility is new towns, built for integrated populations with Federal support, or even by the Federal Government alone, on land now va-cant. Although hope springs eternal in American society that the problems of old towns can be avoided by starting from scratch, these problems seep easily across the borders of the new commu-nity. Even if rural governments can be persuaded to accept new towns in their bailiwicks and white residents could be attracted, such towns would be viable only if Federal grants and powers were used to obtain industries—and of a kind that would hire and train poorly skilled workers.

Greater emphasis should be placed on eliminating job discrimination in suburban work places, particularly in industries which are crying for workers, so that unions are less impelled to keep out nonwhite applicants. Mass transit systems should be built to enable city dwellers, black and white, to obtain suburban jobs without necessarily living in the suburbs.

Another and equally important solution is more school integration—for example, through urban-suburban educational parks that will build up integrated student enrollment by providing high-quality schooling to attract suburban whites, and through expansion of the bussing programs that send ghetto children into suburban schools. Although white suburban parents have strenuously opposed bussing their children into the city, several suburban communities have accepted Negro students who are bussed in from the ghetto; for example, in the Boston area and in Westchester County.

And while the Supreme Court is deliberating, it would be worthwhile to persuade frightened suburbanites that, as all the studies so far have indicated, open housing would not mean a massive invasion of slum dwellers, but only the gradual arrival of a relatively small number of Negroes, most of them as middle-class as the whitest suburbanite. A massive suburban invasion by slum dwellers of any color is sheer fantasy. Economic studies have shown the sad fact that only a tiny proportion of ghetto residents can even afford to live in the suburbs. Moreover, as long as Negro workers lack substantial job security, they need to live near the center of the urban transportation system so that they can travel to jobs all over the city.

In addition, there are probably many ghetto residents who do not even want suburban integration now; they want the same freedom of housing choice as whites but they do not want to be "dispersed" to the suburbs involuntarily. Unfortunately, no reliable studies exist to tell us where ghetto residents do want to live, but should they have

freedom of choice, I suspect many would leave the slums for better housing and better neighborhoods outside the present ghetto. Not many would now choose predominantly white areas, however, at least not until living among whites is psychologically and socially less taxing, and until integration means more than just assimilation to white middle-class ways.

Because of the meager success of past integration efforts, many civil rights leaders have given up on integration and are now demanding the rebuilding of the ghetto. They argue persuasively that residential integration has so far and will in the future benefit only a small number of affluent Negroes, and that if the poverty-stricken ghetto residents are to be helped soon, that help must be located in the ghetto. The advocates of integration are strongly opposed. They demand that all future housing must be built outside the ghetto, for anything else would just perpetuate segregation. In recent months, the debate between the two positions has become bitter, each side claiming only its solution has merit.

Actually there is partial truth on both sides. The integrationists are correct about the long-term dangers of rebuilding the ghetto; the ghetto rebuilders (or separatists) are correct about the short-term failure of integration. But if there is little likelihood that the integrationists' demands will be carried out soon, their high idealism in effect sentences ghetto residents to remain in slum poverty.

Moreover, there is no need to choose between integration and rebuilding, for both policies can be carried out simultaneously. The struggle for integration must continue, but if the immediate prospects for success on a large scale are dim, the ghetto must be rebuilt in the meantime.

The primary aim of rebuilding, however, should not be to rehabilitate houses or clear slums, but to raise the standard of living of ghetto residents. The highest priority must be a massive antipoverty program which will, through the creation of jobs, more effective job-training schemes, the negative income tax, children's allowances and other measures, raise ghetto families to the middle-income level, using outside resources from government and private enterprise and inside participation in the planning and decision-making. Also needed are a concerted effort at quality compensatory education for children who cannot attend integrated schools; federally funded efforts to improve the quality of ghetto housing, as well as public services; some municipal decentralization to give ghetto residents the ability to plan their own communities and their own lives, and political power so that the ghetto can exert more influence in behalf of its demands.

If such programs could extend the middle-income standard of living to the ghetto in the years to come, residential integration might well be achieved in subsequent generations. Much of the white opposition to integration is based on stereotypes of Negro behavior—some true, some false—that stem from poverty rather than from color, and many of the fears about Negro neighbors reflect the traditional American belief that poor people will not live up to middle-class standards. Moreover, even lack of enthusiasm for integration among ghetto residents is a result of poverty, they feel, rightly or not, that they must solve their economic problems before they can even think about integration.

If ghetto poverty were eliminated, the white fears—and the Negro ones—would begin to disappear, as did the pejorative stereotypes which earlier Americans held about the "inferior races"—a favorite nineteenth-century term for the European immigrants—until they achieved affluence. Because attitudes based on color differences are harder to overcome than those based on cultural differences, the disappearance of anti-Negro stereotypes will be slower than that of anti-immigrant stereotypes. Still, once color is no longer an index of poverty and lower-class status, it will cease to arouse white fears, so that open-housing laws can be enforced more easily and eventually may even be unnecessary. White suburbanites will not exclude Negroes to protect their status or their property values, and many, although not necessarily all, Negroes will choose to leave the ghetto.

Morally speaking, any solution that does not promise immediate integration is repugnant, but moral dicta will neither persuade suburbanites to admit low-income Negroes into their communities, nor entice urbane suburbanites to live near low-income Negroes in the city. Instead of seeking to increase their middle-income population by importing suburban whites, cities must instead make their poor residents middle-income. The practical solution, then, is to continue to press for residential integration, but also to eliminate ghetto poverty immediately, in order to achieve integration in the future, substituting government antipoverty programs for the private economy which once created the jobs and incomes that helped poorer groups escape the slums in past generations. Such a policy will not only reduce many of the problems of the city, which are ultimately caused by the poverty of its inhabitants, but it will assure the ultimate disappearance of the class and racial polarization of cities and suburbs. . . .

28

The Country Town and the Mass Society

ARTHUR J. VIDICH AND JOSEPH BENSMAN

The Ambivalent Attitude to Mass Society

Springdalers have a decided respect for the great institutions that characterize American society. The efficiency, organizational ability and farflung activities of giant government and business enterprise inspire them with awe. The military might of the nation and the productive capacity of industry lend a Springdaler a sense of pride and security, and the continuous development and successful application of science assure him that he is a participant in the most forward-looking and progressive country in the world. Anyone who would attack the great institutions of America would have no audience in Springdale: "Everybody knows this country wouldn't be what it is if it weren't for free enterprise and the democratic form of government." When the Springdaler is on the defensive he will tell the critic, "If you don't like it here you can go back to where you came from."

The Springdaler also sees that the urban and metropolitan society is technically and culturally superior to his own community. He sees this in his everyday life when he confronts the fact that his community [a small country town of 3000 people] cannot provide him with everything he needs: almost everyone goes to the city for shopping or entertainment; large numbers of peo-

Selections from Arthur J. Vidich and Joseph Bensman, *Small Town in Mass Society: Class, Power and Religion in a Rural Community* (rev. edn. copyright © 1968 by Princeton University Press; Princeton Paperback, 1968), pp. 79–93, 95–102, 104–105. Reprinted by permission of Princeton University Press.

ple are dependent on the radio and television; and everyone realizes that rural life would be drastically altered without cars and refrigerators. Springdalers clearly realize how much of local life is based on the modern techniques, equipment and products which originate in distant places.

The community is constantly dependent on cultural and material imports and welcomes these as a way of "keeping up with the times." However, they believe that the very technical and cultural factors that make for the superiority of the "outside" also account for the problems of living that cities exhibit. The "city masses," while they have easier access to progress, are also the ready-made victims of the negative aspects of progress. In contrast, rural life, because it is geographically distant, can enjoy progress and avoid the worst features of the industrial mass society; Springdalers can believe that they are in a position to choose and utilize only the best of two worlds, that the importations, if properly chosen, need not affect the inner life of the community.

Because it is possible to choose only the best, the Springdaler can believe, that in spite of some disadvantages, his is the better of two worlds. This belief in the autonomy or, at worst, the self-selective dependency of rural life makes it possible for the community member publicly to voice the following conceptions concerning the relationships between his town and mass society:

1. That the basic traditions of American society—"grassroots democracy," free and open expression, individualism—are most firmly located in rural

society. The American heritage is better preserved in the small town because it can resist bad city influences and thereby preserve the best of the past.

2. That the future hope of American society lies in rural life because it has resisted all "isms" and constitutes the only major bulwark against them.

3. That much of the progress of society is the result of rural talent which has migrated to the cities. In this way rural society has a positive influence on urban life; rural migrants account for the virtues of city life. "Everyone knows that most of the outstanding men in the country were raised in small towns" and Springdalers proudly point to several local names that have made good on the outside.

4. That "when you live in a small town you can take or leave the big cities —go there when you want to and always come back without having to live as they do." There is the belief that "if more people lived in small towns, you wouldn't have all those problems."

These summarize the types of beliefs that are frequently stated in public situations. The observer who is willing to go beyond the public statements discovers that Springdale has a great variety of direct and intimate connections with a wide range of institutions of the mass society. Moreover, these institutions affect many phases of the community, have consequences for its internal local functioning and in some ways control the direction of social change within it.

Springdale is connected with the mass society in a variety of different forms. The cumulative effect of these various connections makes possible the continuous transmission of outside policies, programs and trends into the community, even though the effects of the transmis-

sion and the transmitting agents themselves are not always seen. Outside influences can be transmitted directly by a socially visible agent such as the extension specialist who lives in the community for the purpose of acting upon it. Outside interests and influences can also be expressed indirectly through members of the community: policies and programs of relatively invisible outside interests are transmitted by *heads* of local branches of state and national organizations, by *heads* of local businesses dependent on outside resources and by *heads* of churches attached to larger organizations. In some instances the community is affected by the consequences of decisions made by business and government which are made with specific reference to the community, i.e., the decision to build a state road through the community or the decision to close down a factory. Plans and decisions that refer directly to the community are made from a distance by invisible agents and institutions. Perhaps most important are the mass decisions of business and government which are transmitted to the rural scene by the consequences of changes in prices, costs and communications. These affect the town even though they are not explicitly directed at it, and they comprise the invisible social chain reactions of decisions that are made in centers of power in government, business and industry. The invisible social chain reactions emanating from the outside no doubt alter the life of the community more seriously than the action of visible agents such as the extension specialist.

These types of transmission do not represent mutually exclusive channels, but rather exist in complex interrelationship with each other. They merely suggest the major ways in which the community is influenced by dynamics which occur in the institutions of mass society. How these combined dynamics in their various combinations affect the fabric of life in Springdale can be seen by examining the way in which cultural importations and economic and political connections shape the character of community life. In their net effect they influence the psychological dimensions of the community.

Cultural Importations from Mass Society

The external agents of cultural diffusion range from specific observable individuals placed in the local community by outside institutions to the impact of mass media of communications and successive waves of migration. The consequence of these modes of diffusion lies in the effect which they have on local styles of living.

Formal Organizations. The adult extension program of the land grant college is mediated at the local level by the county agent and the home demonstration agent who respectively are concerned with farming methods and production, and patterns of home-making and family life. These agents carry out their program through the Farm and Home Bureau organizations. In Springdale township these agencies have a membership of 300–400 adults. The county agent is primarily concerned with introducing modern methods of farm production and operation and with fostering political consciousness among the farmers. As a type of executive secretary to the local Farm Bureau, whose officers are local farmers, the agent acts as an advisor in planning the organization's program, which includes such items as production and marketing problems, parity price problems and taxation problems.

The organizational structure of the Home Bureau parallels the Farm Bureau. From skills and techniques and personnel available at the extension center, local programs consist, for example, of furniture refinishing or alu-

minum working as well as discussions on such topics as child-rearing, nutrition, penal institutions and interior design. The Home Bureau extension specialist trains a local woman in information and techniques which are reported back to the local club. This program, geared as it is to modern home-making, child-rearing and the feminine role, has the effect of introducing new styles and standards of taste and consumption for the membership.

Other institutional connectors similar to the above in organizational structure account for the introduction of still other social values and social definitions. The 4-H Club, the Future Farmers of America and the Boy and Girl Scouts, as well as the Masons, Odd Fellows, American Legion, Grange and other local branches of national organizations and their auxiliaries, relate the Springdaler to the larger society through the social meanings and styles of activity defined in the programs, procedures and rituals of the national headquarters. State and national conventions, but not office holding, of these as well as church organizations directly link individuals to the outside. In effect these arrangements regularize and institutionalize the communication and organizational nexus between the small town and the point of origin of new ideas and values.

New cultural standards are also imported by agents who are not permanent residents of the town or who have only a transient relationship with it. These include the teachers at the central school, many of whom view their jobs as a temporary interlude in a progression of experience which will lead to a position in a city system. The other agents of contact are a wide variety of salesmen and "experts" who have a regular or irregular contact with business, government and private organizations. From the surrounding urban centers and the regional sales offices of

farm implement and automobile manufacturers and nationally branded products, modern methods of merchandizing
and business practice are introduced.
Experts in civil defense, evangelism,
fire-fighting, gardening, charity drives,
traffic control and youth recreation introduce new techniques and programs
to the local community. This great variety and diversity of semi-permanent and
changing contacts in their cumulative
effect act as a perpetual blood transfu-
sion to local society. The net effect that
these agents have as transmitters of life
styles depends in a measure on their
position and prestige in the community.
The differential effect of these cultural
contacts is treated below.

The Mass Media. Social diffusion
through the symbols and pictorial
images of the mass media of communications has permeated the community, reducing the local paper to reporting of social items and local news
already known by everyone. Few individuals read only the local weekly paper;
the majority subscribe to dailies published in surrounding cities and in the
large metropolitan areas. This press,
itself part of larger newspaper combines,
presents an image of the passing scene
in its news and nationally syndicated
features to which the population of an
entire region is exposed.

The mass culture and mass advertising of television and radio reach Springdale in all their variety. Television,
particularly, is significant in its impact
because for the first time the higher art
forms such as ballet, opera and plays
are visible to a broad rural audience.
National events such as party conventions, inaugurations and investigative
hearings are visible now to an audience
which was previously far removed from
the national centers of action and
drama. Because of the relative geographic isolation of Springdale, television has made available entirely new
areas of entertainment, information and

education. It has created new leisure-
time interests, has introduced new
modes of leisure-time consumption and
has led to the acceptance of standardized entertainment models. Wrestling,
Arthur Godfrey and Howdy-Doody are
common symbols of entertainment.
Equally available and pervasive among
the classes and individuals to whom
they appeal are pocket books, comic
books, and horror and sex stories. Micky
Spillane, Willie Mays, Davy Crockett
and other nationally prominent personages as well as nationally branded
products are as well known and available to the small town as they are to
the big city. The intrusion of the mass
media is so overwhelming that little
scope is left for the expression of local
cultural and artistic forms.

However, the diffusion of the printed
word is not limited to the mass media;
it is present also in the realm of education, both religious and secular. The
state department of education syllabus
defines minimum standards and content for subject matter instruction.
Courses of Sunday School instruction
are available for all age levels, and each
faith secures its material from its own
national religious press. In each of
these major institutional areas the standards and *content* of instruction are
defined in sources available only in
standardized form. . . .

The Immigrant As Cultural Carrier.
Specific individuals are carriers of cultural diffusion, and the volume and extent of migration in and out of the
community suggests the degree and intimacy of its contact with the mass
society. In a community which is regarded as stable and relatively unchanging by its own inhabitants, only
25 percent of its population was born
locally. Another 25 percent has moved
into the community since 1946 and 55
percent are new to the community since
1920. Moreover, of the 45 percent who
have moved to the community since

1932, more than 30 percent have lived for a year or longer in cities with populations in excess of 25,000; 7 percent in cities with populations in excess of one-half million.

Each decade and each generation introduces a new layer of immigrants to the community. The agricultural and business prosperity of the 1940's and early 1950's has brought city dwellers to farms and to businesses on main street, and the housing shortage has led workers to reclaim long-abandoned farm dwellings. The 12 percent of new people who moved into Springdale in the Thirties came in response to the effects of the depression. From 1918 to 1928 the Poles moved onto farms abandoned by descendants of original settlers. Indeed, the ebb and flow of migration extends back to such eras of political and economic upheaval as the depression of the 1890's, the civil war, the depression of the 1830's, and the mass movement of people during the Indian Wars and the opening of the territory in the early 1800's. Each new wave of migrants, bringing with it the fashions and thought styles of other places, influences the cultural development of the community.

The cumulative consequences of these channels of diffusion and the quantity and quality of the "material" diffused denies the existence of a culture indigenous to the small town. In almost all aspects of culture, even to speech forms, and including technology, literature, fashions and fads, as well as patterns of consumption, to mention a few, the small town tends to reflect the contemporary mass society.

Basically, an historically indigenous local culture does not seem to exist. The cultural imports of each decade and generation and the successive waves of migration associated with each combine to produce a local culture consisting of layers or segments of the mass culture of successive historical eras. In the small town the remaining elements of the gay-ninety culture are juxtaposed against the modern central school. The newer cultural importations frequently come in conflict with the older importations of other eras. The conflict between "spurious" and "genuine" culture appears to be a conflict between two different ages of "spurious" culture.

The Economic Nexus: Occupational Gatekeepers to the Mass Society

Simply because individuals pursue given occupations, their interconnections with mass society follow given patterns. They may be direct employees of specific organizations of the mass society; they may be the objects and targets of the programs of mass organizations; they may be trained by and in great institutions or their skills may be utilized only in urban areas. Because of these occupational characteristics they are specially qualified, accessible and available as transmitters of specific organizational and cultural contacts and contents.

Because these individuals in their occupational roles as gatekeepers are treated as specialists by both the community and mass society, occupation even more than life style becomes a crucial dimension of community life. The content, quality and amount of cultural importation accounted for by an individual is a function of the specific occupational nexus which he has to both the community and mass society.

The Professionals. A number of institutional representatives who are residents of the town receive their position in the community by virtue of their connections with outside agencies. Their position in the community is secured in part by the institution to which they are connected and by the evaluation of the role they are imputed to have in the agency which they locally represent.

The group of individuals who possess a borrowed prestige based on their external affiliations fall largely in the professional category. They are individuals who uniformly possess a college education. Among their ranks are included lawyers, ministers, doctors, teachers, engineers, and a variety of field representatives of state and federal agencies who settle in the community for occupational purposes. All of these individuals, except one or two, have migrated to the community as adults. In addition to the prestige which they are accorded by virtue of being "educated," their overwhelming characteristic as a group lies in the influence which they have in mediating between the town and the larger society. They possess the knowledge and techniques necessary for connecting the small town to the intricate organization of the mass bureaucratic society. They possess "contacts" with outside agencies and their role requires an ability to understand "official" documents and forms, and to write appropriate letters to appropriate bureaus. Thus, for example, the lawyer is counsel to political bodies as well as to free associations and other local organizations, in which capacities he gains an extensive and intimate knowledge of affairs of the town and thereby acquires a position of influence. In like manner the technical knowledge of state educational regulations and policies possessed by the high-school principal is indispensable to the locally constituted school board.

In addition to the prestige and influence which segments of this group possess by virtue of their education and institutional role, they are accorded a respect and, in some cases, awe because of the power which they are imputed to have in manipulating the outside world; they can accomplish things for the community which no one else can.

Moreover, this professional group as a whole, including the relatively transient teaching staff, are felt to have access to styles of taste and consumption which are considered different from those available to the rest of the community. As a result these institutional connectors are considered outside the ordinary realm of prestige assignments and social stratification. That is, their social position in the community is not guaranteed by conforming to standards which are indigenous to the community but, rather, by imputed conformance to "alien" or "exotic" standards of urban life.

As a result of this dual position, individuals in this group, especially those who have come from or have resided for some time outside the community, are able to influence styles of consumption and thought in the community. They do this in three main areas of activity: in organizational activities, community projects and social fashions. They have been prime movers in setting up a formal program of youth recreation and in vigorously participating in and supporting local cultural activities such as plays, recitals and educational talks. In the P.T.A. they constitute the block favoring those modern methods and programs which bring the outside world to the small town—talks by foreign university students, race relations discussions and socio-dramas in dating and parent-child relationships. Ideas for the development of a community center and adult education programs emanate from and are supported by them. In terms of dress styles and personal adornment as well as home furnishings and styles of party giving, this group is in the forefront of innovation.

This innovating group of middle-class newcomers is supported by a group of college-educated locals who act as a bridge between the new standards and local society. In supporting these new standards, the local group absorbs some of the resentment which is directed at the innovating group by both the farmers and merchants. . . .

It must be noted that the professionals' psychological orientation to accentuate the "elite" cultural values of mass society is more than merely a product of their residence, education or background in the mass society. The limitations on economic success and the limited professional opportunities in the community means that the drive toward success through work and investment is not fully available to them. The possession of alien cultural standards makes it possible for the professionals to reject the success drive by accepting meaningful standards alternative to those available to the rest of the community; they distinguish themselves in the community by their identification with external values.

Businessmen. For storekeepers, filling station operators, appliance dealers, automobile and farm equipment dealers and feed mill operators, the external world is a source of supply for the goods and commodities which they sell on the local market. Their position in relation to their source of supply and the overall condition of the national economy determines the level of their business activity, ceilings on their potential income, and hence indirectly their style of life. To analyze this group we must consider separately the position of the independent shopkeeper, the businessman who operates on a franchise and the feed mill and farm implement dealer.

The shopkeepers who make up the bulk of the business community have experienced a slow and gradual decline in their class position relative to other groups in the community. This is mainly due to the breakdown of their monopolistic position with respect to the local market, but it is also related to the rise of other groups. The development of the automobile, the appearance of the chain stores in surrounding areas and the expansion of mail order sales have placed them in a competitively disadvantageous position. Moreover, the nationally branded and advertised product, with its fixed profit margin determined by the producer, has tended in a general way to determine his volume/profit ratio in a way increasingly disadvantageous to him. His decrease in profits in relation to volume has driven him to greater competition with other local shopkeepers—a competition which takes place in the form of despecialization, greater reliance on credit trade and keeping his shop open for long hours. The first two of these responses to his dilemma have further depressed his profit/volume ratio: in the one case by reducing his return on his investment and in the other case by increased losses due to bad debts. He keeps his business open in an effort to improve his investment/profit ratio and this he can do only by staying in the store himself. . . .

The position of the businessman who operates on a *franchise* is more obviously linked to the mass society. Usually he not only has a single source of supply, but also his source of supply (a petroleum company, for example) specifies the business practices and standards which must be maintained in order to retain the franchise. If the retail outlet is owned by the supplier (as with some filling stations) rents may be charged on a sliding scale according to volume of business—less volume, less rent—with the consequence that the profit margin of the local operator is not fixed. . . . As individuals they are relatively unimportant to the community since there is a high rate of turnover of franchises.

There are three individuals in the business class who are exceptions. These are the feed mill operators and the farm implement dealers who in Springdale consist of one feed mill operator located on the periphery of the township, one implement dealer located in the village, and one large-scale combined feed mill, housing supply and farm implement partnership. Because they service an agricultural industry which since the early Forties has been prosperous, they are favorably situated in the local economy.

In terms of their customer relationships they are most intimately tied to the farmers, especially to the prosperous farmers, who do most of the buying. Because of their market position their economic fate is intimately related to that of the farmers. In the period of farm ascendancy at the time of the study, they too were prosperous and exhibited all of the same aspects of expansion, investment and opportunity-consciousness already described for the farmer. In addition, however, because they are businessmen and the most successful businessmen, they have achieved the respect, admiration and enmity of the business community as well as of the town at large.

They are the most heavily capitalized group of individuals in the community and play an important credit function in the local agricultural economy. Because of the farmer's economic dependence on them and the interlocking character of their mutual fate, the feed mill and the implement dealers identify themselves with the farmer's interests. In local politics they are in a position to provide the leadership in organizing the farmer's interests and frequently act as spokesman for the farm community. . . .

Industrial Workers. Industrial workers represent a curious gap in the relationship of the rural community to mass society. Individuals who live in Springdale but work outside on products which are geared to a national market are not understandable to other members of the community because the rural community lacks the perceptual apparatus necessary to understand industry and the industrial process. The industrial worker lives in the community, but the occupational basis of his existence is not subject to the social pigeon-holing by others necessary to making judgments and assessments of him.

Industrial workers consist mainly of individuals and their families who have migrated to the community in an effort to escape city life and to seek cheaper housing as well as land for home gardens. Due to the ecological conditions of the rural community (a large number of abandoned farm dwellings and the breakup of large houses into apartments), in-migrating as well as native industrial workers live in a scattered pattern throughout the township. As a consequence of their work routine, which involves, in addition to their work in a factory, one or two hours of commuting plus, in many cases, the operation of an extensive garden, home improvements and the care of livestock or a secondary occupation, this group tends to be relatively socially isolated in its day-to-day contact with the rest of the community. Their work carries them to the city where they can do their shopping and engage in city activities. As individuals some of the industrial workers strive to become involved in community activities and many of them maintain an affiliation with one of the local churches. . . .

Farmers. As noted earlier, there are two classes of farmers, the rational and the traditional. A major difference between them is the way they organize their production in relation to the mass market and government regulations.

Those who gear themselves to the mass market address themselves to favorably pegged prices, subsidies and quotas. As a consequence when prices and regulations are favorable they accept the favorable environment as a condition for their operations. They invest and expand, work hard and are successful. Their success stimulates confidence and buoyancy and produces an expansionist psychology. . . .

To show how the internal status position of the farmer is related to the institutional structure of the larger society, account must be taken of the fluctuations in the agricultural economy over the past thirty years. The agricultural depression beginning after World War I and extending to the beginning of World War II placed the farmer in a depressed (indebted) economic position. The decline of the farmer in Springdale was more extreme than in the nation at large during this period because Springdale is a marginal agricultural area with relatively poor land and a high rate of feed purchases. Farmers were either dispossessed, displaced or they retrenched to a heavily indebted minimum standard of consumption and operation. In this period the farmer verged on being declassed or actually was declassed.

Today the farmer is an important and ascendant segment of the rural middle class. From a position of near bankruptcy in 1933 he had risen (at the time of the field work for this study) to a position of heavy capitalization and social prominence. His rise coincided with the rationalization of marketing procedures (The Federal Milk Price Order in the New York Milk Shed), federal agricultural policies, and the rise in the market value of his products since the early 1940's. Specific agricultural policies which have contributed to his rise include the price support program, farm credit programs, and fertilizer and other land improvement give-aways. A little recognized source of preferential treatment given him by an outside agency lies in the structure of United States income tax laws, which allow for rapid depreciation of plant and equipment, little accountability on cash sales and a broad base of allowable operating expenses.

Although the status of all farmers is equally linked to decisions and policies of these larger institutional structures (the price structure and federal agricultural legislation), all farmers do not equally orient their operations to legislation and regulations oriented to them. At this point the rate of status ascendancy of the individual farmer is probably directly related to the extent to which he accepts the preferential treatment accorded him in these larger policy decisions. Those who have been most swift and efficient in adjusting to the changing conditions of the agricultural economy over the past twenty years constitute the most rapidly ascending segment of farmers.

As a consequence of the character of the institutional connectors which link the farmer to the great society, the status of the farmer relative to other local groups is relatively independent of local community forces. By the same token, his status is directly related to price structures and mass decisions and policies. Alterations in these external forces, such as a tumbling in farm prices, can cause an upheaval in the status of the local community.

The Political Surrender to Mass Society

Local political institutions consist of a village board, a town board and local committees of the Republican and Democratic parties. The jurisdiction of the village board includes powers of control and regulation over a variety of community facilities and services— street lighting, water supply, fire protection, village roads, street signs and parks. To carry out the functions empowered to it, it possesses the power of taxation. The town board is concerned chiefly with fire protection, the construction and maintenance of roads; through its participation on the county board of supervisors, it participates in programs connected with welfare, penal and other county services.

However, at almost every point in this seemingly broad base of political domain the village and town boards adjust their action to either the regulations and laws defined by state and federal agencies which claim parallel functions on a statewide or nationwide basis or to the fact that outside agencies have the power to withhold subsidies to local political institutions.

Local assessment scales and tax rates are oriented to state equalization formulas which partially provide the standardized basis on which subsidies are dispersed by the state. State highway construction and development programs largely present local political agencies with the alternative of either accepting or rejecting proposed road plans and programs formulated by the state highway department.

The village board, more than the town board, is dependent on its own taxable resources (taxes account for almost half its revenues) and best illustrates the major dimensions of local political action. The village board in Springdale accepts few of the powers given to it. Instead, it orients its action to the facilities and subsidies controlled and dispensed by other agencies and, by virtue of this, forfeits its own political power. Solutions to the problem of fire protection are found in agreements with regionally organized fire districts. In matters pertaining to road signs and street signs action typically takes the form of petitioning state agencies to fulfill desired goals "without cost to the taxpayer." On roads built and maintained by the state there is no recourse but to accept the state traffic bureau's standards of safety. A problem such as snow removal is solved by dealing directly with the foreman of the state highway maintenance crew

through personal contacts: "If you treat him right, you can get him to come in and clear the village roads." In other areas of power where there are no parallel state agencies, such as for garbage collections or parks, the village board abdicates its responsibility.

As a consequence of this pattern of dependence, many important decisions are made for Springdale by outside agencies. Decisions which are made locally tend to consist of approving the requirements of administrative or state laws. In short the program and policies of local political bodies are determined largely by acceptance of grants-in-aid offered them—i.e., in order to get the subsidy specific types of decisions must be made—and by facilities and services made available to them by outside sources.

Psychologically this dependence leads to an habituation to outside control to the point where the town and village governments find it hard to act even where they have the power. Legal jurisdictions have been supplanted by psychological jurisdictions to such an extent that local political action is almost exclusively oriented to and predicated on seeking favors, subsidies and special treatment from outside agencies. The narrowing of legal jurisdictions by psychologically imposed limits lead to an inability to cope with local problems if outside resources are not available.

Power in local political affairs, then, tends to be based on accessibility to sources of decision in larger institutions. Frequently this accessibility consists merely of the knowledge of the source, or it may mean a personal contact, or an ability to correspond to get necessary information. Under these circumstances, power in the political arena is delegated to those with contacts in and knowledge of the outer world and to those who are experts in formal communication with impersonal bureaucratic offices. These are, on the individual level, the lawyer and, on an institutional level, the political party. The lawyer gains his paramountcy through technical knowledge and personalized non-party contacts up the political hierarchy with other lawyers. He is the mediator between the local party and the party hierarchy, and transforms his personalized contacts into political indispensability in the local community. His access to outside sources of power determines his power and predominance in the local community.

The Social Psychological Consequences of the Rural Surrender

A central fact of rural life, then, is its dependence on the institutions and dynamics of urban and mass society. The recognition of this dependence and the powerlessness associated with it give to the agents and institutions of the great society a degree of respect and admiration which, however, does not always connote approval. Rather, there is a high degree of ambivalence with respect to these agents and institutions. They have respect because of their power and wealth, and because their norms have the legitimacy of acceptance in wide areas of the society at large. On the other hand, the very dominance of the mass institution causes resentments, since, in the light of this dominance, rural life in its immediacy is devalued. Hence, for example, although the standards of the land grant college are accepted, the institution and its agents may be resented for the role they play in innovation.

The phenomenon of psychological ambivalence to the mass society is particularly reinforced by the fact that slight changes in the policies and dynamics of the mass institutions can

have profound effects on the rural way of life and on its major social and economic classes—i.e., parity policies industrial relocations, new state roads and state subsidization formulas. In response to these conditions, the members of the rural community and their political spokesmen resent their dependency and powerlessness and channnelize it into anti-urban politics and policies. In relation to the outer world, there exist two types of political victory; when rural rather than urban areas get a disproportionately large share of the benefits of the state budget and when the city can be made the object of investigation on grounds of corruption or vice by politicians surrounded by a halo of rural images. At the same time a personal identification with important urban political officials lends an individual prestige in the rural community.

But this continuous transvaluation of the attitudes toward urban life and its representatives are never so simple as the dependence-resentment mechanism would suggest. For such political and psychological currents are supported by intricately articulated images of the mass society and rural self images . . . which for the purposes of this discussion can be termed counterimages.

These images, themselves, are a product of complex institutional developments and reflect the process of urban penetration. For it is uniquely ironical that the self-image of the rural community and its image of urban life are in part the products of the penetration of urban mass media. Through these media the people of Springdale see urban life dominated by crime, dirt, filth, immorality, vice, corruption and anti-Americanism. The urban center is seen as a jungle of man's inhumanity to man; the large political center as a "dog-eat-dog" world of investigations and counterinvestigations with few clearly defined heroes. It sees the urban middle classes confronted by apparently hopeless personal problems and moving from crisis to crisis without end. It is because of the mechanism of resentment that the Springdaler can see wide class differences in urban society and be unaware of class in his own environment.

Contrariwise, the mass media frequently present rural life in idyllic terms. The *Saturday Evening Post* cover brings forth the image of the cracker barrel, the virtues of life close to soil and stream and of healthy, simple, family living. The weekly press carries syndicated columnists who extol the virtues of ruralism. Political as well as feature speakers who come to town invariably reinforce the town's image of itself: "The false life of cities," "If America were made up of small towns like Springdale, this would be a better country." "The goodness of America lies in the small town where life and nature meet to make for genuine living." The urban man of knowledge and the university scientist verbalize their own image of rural life and in doing so shape the self-image of the rural audience. . . .

The farmer [for example] is strong, self-reliant and capable. He is warm, affectionate and devoted but these characteristics are frequently hidden under a crusty, gruff exterior. He is a good businessman and a sharp trader capable in the final analysis of outwitting others, especially the city slicker. Outside of a few old gossips, community life is richly warm and filled with a wide variety of social interchange, gatherings and genuinely spontaneous self-expression. The rural dweller is religious, moral and upright, though capable of "cutting-up" in a way which is both amusing and tolerable. . . .

From the standpoint of the producer of mass media, to complete the picture, the image presented of rural life and life in general reflects not only his estimate of his audience (since not all of the mass media are specifically aimed at the rural market) but also the psychological climate of the urban centers where images of rural life are produced. The romanticization of rural life in press and radio reflects the need of the urban dweller to conceive of rural life as simpler and freer from the complexities, tensions and anxieties which he faces in his own world. Rural life is thus conceived as a counter-image which highlights his own situation. However, when presented to the rural resident, it serves as an image which enables the rural dweller to form symbolic and ideological resistance to urban society. It is thus through the mass media that the negative reactions to mass society of both the rural and urban dweller are linked; and it is as sets of similar responses to the negative aspects of urbanism that both urban and rural dwellers find a common symbolic meeting ground. . . .

Hence, those factors which appear to be decisive in determining the action of the rural community are factors which originate in areas outside the rural community. Thus, even when the rural community attacks the urban mass society, the nature of the attack, its intensity and the situations which bring it forth are, in large part, the products of urban mass society. Rural life, then, can be seen as one area in which the dynamics of modern urban mass society are worked out. . . .

29

Planning for New Towns: The Gap Between Theory and Practice*

LAWRENCE SUSSKIND

New towns have been built for many reasons: to relieve congestion and overcrowding in large urban centers (Britain), to develop frontier regions (the Soviet Union), to exploit concentrated resources (Venezuela), to defend captured territories (Israel), to provide a showcase for technological innovations (United States), to symbolize a new political or economic orientation (Turkey), and to absorb and acculturate migrants (Australia).[1] However, many of the ideas upon which planners have based their designs have not been subjected to rigorous analysis. This is particularly true in so far as the social organization of planned communities is concerned. This paper identifies several concepts of social organization that new town planners have deployed for their purposes—largely unsuccessfully. There are some interesting parallels between the ideas of the new town planners and the work of community sociologists, although there appear to be few if any direct linkages.

Reprinted with permission of Macmillan Publishing Co., Inc. from *The Community, Approaches and Applications* by Marcia Pelly Effrat. Copyright © 1974 by Sociological Inquiry.
* I am indebted to Professor Lloyd Rodwin for his advice and encouragement; although we disagree on some of the points presented in this paper, his thinking on the subject has strongly influenced my own.
1 William Alonso, "What Are New Towns For?" *Urban Studies*, Vol. II, No. 1, January, 1970, pp. 37–55; William Alonso, "Needed and Spontaneous New Towns," in Harvey Perloff and Neil Sandberg (eds.), *New Towns—Why and For Whom* (New York: Praeger), 1973, pp. 237–241. For a brief description of the international new towns movement see Pierre Merlin, *New Towns* (London: Methuen), 1971. For more detailed materials on the British new towns see Lloyd Rodwin, *The British New Towns Policy* (Cambridge: Harvard University Press), 1966 and Frederic J. Osborn and Arnold Whittick, *The New Towns: The Answer to Megalopolis* (London: Leonard Hill, 1963; Harold Orlans, *Stevenage: A Sociological Study of a New Town* (London: Routledge), 1962. Useful case studies of new town development in other countries includes Erika Speigel, *New Towns in Israel* (New York: Praeger), 1967; U.N. Department of Social Affairs, *Planning of Metropolitan Areas and New Towns* (New York: United Nations), 1967; Lloyd Rodwin and Associates, *Planning Urban Growth*

Self-Containment, Social Balance, and the Neighborhood Unit

In their study of Springdale (an upstate New York town) Vidich and Bensman identified a number of institutional mechanisms by which small communities sustain the illusion that the pressures of urbanization, industrialization, and bureaucratization are subordinate to local demands.[2] Although the reverse is more likely to be true, the extent to which local activity patterns can reinforce certain life-styles points to the highly sophisticated process of

and Regional Development (Cambridge: M.I.T. Press), 1969. The American new town experience is described in Edward Eichler and Marshall Kaplan, *The Community Builders* (Berkeley: University of California Press), 1967; Clarence Stein, *Toward New Towns for America*, 2nd edition (Cambridge: M.I.T. Press), 1966; and James Clapp, *New Towns and Urban Policy* (New York: Dunellen), 1971.
2 Arthur J. Vidich and Joseph Bensman, *Small Town in Mass Society* (Garden City: Doubleday), 1960. Originally published by Princeton University Press in 1958.

socialization that takes place at a community level.

Vidich and Bensman did not publish their study of *Small Town in Mass Society* until the late 1950s, but earlier versions of the same idea are not difficult to spot. Their diagnosis is reminiscent, for example, of the ideas advanced by one of the earliest community sociologists—Ferdinand Tönnies. In his major work, *Gemeinshaft und Gesellschaft*, Tönnies argued that "members of a community are relatively immobile in a physical and a social way: individuals neither travel far from their locality of birth nor do they rise up the social hierarchy." [3] Hillary's exhaustive review of the literature suggests that most community studies assume that a person's fate depends more on local patterns of local interaction than on broader societal forces.[4]

What Vidich and Bensman labeled the myth of local autonomy recalls Ebenezer Howard's original proposal for self-contained garden cities. Howard's proposal, aimed originally at decanting London's large and growing population, called for the development of new self-contained communities of approximately 30,000 people. Each community was to be surrounded by a permanent greenbelt and equipped to meet a full range of social, economic, and cultural needs. Unified land ownership and clearly articulated neighborhood units were intended to capture the most desirable aspects of city and country living. Howard assumed that each

new town would be able to meet all the social needs of its residents and to recapture the simpler life of pre-industrial England.[5]

To the extent that planned communities have lured families away from overcrowded metropolitan areas, they have done so by creating and sustaining the illusion that it is possible to escape the pervasive influences of mass society. This has been accomplished by suggesting that everyone can find better housing and higher-paying jobs merely by moving to a new town; assurances have been offered that a planned community can control its destiny through the manipulation of land uses and careful adherence to a master plan. In a very real sense, the success of a new town depends on the developer's ability to market the illusion of local autonomy. From the planners' standpoint, social networks and supporting institutions must be established that will engender a common sense of purpose and a shared image of how the community should look in the distant future.

A second new town planning concept is the notion of social balance. Socially balanced communities are those which provide a mix of places to work and to live as well as a population that is heterogeneous with respect to age, occupation, income, ethnicity, and class. J. S. Buckingham's plan for New Victoria (1849), for example, called for

An entirely new town . . . peopled by an adequate number of inhabitants with such due proportions between the agricultural and manufacturing classes and between possessors of capital, skill, and labour as to provide . . . the highest degree of health, contentment, morality, and enjoyment yet seen in any existing community.[6]

[3] J. C. McKinney and C. P. Loomis, "The Application of Gemeinschaft and Gesellschaft as Related to Other Typologies," in the introduction to the American Edition of Ferdinand Tönnies, *Community and Society* (New York: Harper Torchbook), 1963, pp. 12–29. Originally published by Michigan State University Press, East Lansing, 1957.

[4] George A. Hillery, *Communal Organizations: A Study of Local Societies* (Chicago: University of Chicago Press), 1968.

[5] Ebenezer Howard, *Garden Cities of Tomorrow* (London: Faber), 1945; 3rd edition (Cambridge: MIT Press), 1965.

[6] J. S. Buckingham, "National Evils and Practical Remedies," London, 1849, p. 141, quoted in Harold Orlans, *op. cit.*

Howard's garden city proposal suggested the desirability of including "all true workers of whatever grade."

The Reith Committee, set up in 1945 to plan the development of the British new towns program, suggested that the main problem was "one of class distinctions . . . if the community is to be truly balanced, so long as social classes exist, all must be represented in it. A contribution is needed from every type and class of person, the community will be poorer if all are not there." [7] The Committee seemed to accept the need for social balance without any reservation.

The balanced community explicitly recognizes the existence of class distinctions but attempts to induce social mixing through physical proximity and the sharing of facilities. It has been suggested by many new town planners that there are good reasons for seeking such balance: the upper and middle classes provide models for emulation, models of enterprise, and to a lesser extent, models of behavior. Balance also implies social harmony. Moreover, the economic life of a new town might be seriously jeopardized without a diversity of skill groups in the local population. Still other interpretations have been ventured. Ruth Glass argues that a balanced community provides for social control (under the guise of leadership) that would otherwise be lacking in the working class, which, if brought together without the restraints of the old established community, might constitute a threat to the established order.[8] Similar arguments, implicitly supporting the *embourgeoisement* of the working class, have found their way into planning strategies designed to promote social balance in American new towns.[9]

Implicit theories of community stratification provide a scaffolding upon which the concept of social balance rests. The presumption that various social groups have different childrearing practices and social service needs is basic to the programming of new town facilities. Warner, Hollingshead, Lenski, Landecker, and others have argued that in every community an unambiguous class structure exists based on differentials in social position, family status, and relative influence in local affairs; this sustains the planners' presuppositions.[10] Although stratification studies have come under increasing fire within the sociological profession in recent years, the news has yet to penetrate the planning literature. Indeed, the possibility that planners may be reinforcing some aspects of stratification by freezing class differentials into rigid physical designs is rarely discussed in planning circles.

To planners involved in the creation of new towns, social balance implies reproducing some standard or average demographic profile.

[9] Herbert Gans, "The Balanced Community: Homogeneity or Heterogeneity in Residential Areas," in *People and Plans* (New York: Basic Books), 1968, pp. 166–182.
[10] W. Lloyd Warner and Paul S. Lunt, *The Social Life of a Modern Community* (New Haven: Yale University Press), 1941; W. Lloyd Warner and Paul S. Lunt, *The Status System of a Modern Community* (New Haven: Yale University Press), 1942; A. B. Hollingshead, *Elmtown's Youth* (New York: John Wiley), 1949; Gerhard E. Lenski, "American Social Classes: Statistical Strata or Social Groups," *American Journal of Sociology*, LVIII, Nov. 1, 1952, pp. 139–144; Warner S. Landecker, "Types of Integration and Their Measurement," in Roland Warren (ed.), *Perspectives on the American Community* (Chicago: Rand McNally and Co.), 1966, pp. 227–238.

[7] Committee on the New Towns, Final Report, Comd. 6876, p. 10.
[8] Ruth Glass, "Urban Sociology," *Current Sociology*, Vol. 4, No. 4, 1955, pp. 14–19.

In the development of Crawley New Town the aim was to achieve a similar balance to that of England and Wales in the local (new town) population. In social class terms, a balanced community is thus one which conforms to the class characteristics of England and Wales. . . .[11]

Social balance can refer to the population mix in the town as a whole (what Gans calls macro-integration) or to the mix of social groups within residential or neighborhood clusters (micro-integration).

Micro-integration carries with it the possibility of actual integration; it means that people of different classes and races will be sharing those physical spaces in which potential integration could become actual integration. Micro-integration does not automatically require actual integration, however, for even next door neighbors can avoid social intercourse. Nevertheless, such avoidance is not easy, and more important, it is not pleasant, for most people want to be friendly with their neighbors if at all possible. Macro-integration puts less pressure on people to engage in actual integration, without, however, precluding it. Instead they have the opportunity to engage in social relations with heterogeneous community members on a voluntary basis.[12]

The principles of micro-integration were given their classic formulation by Clarence Perry in what he defined as the neighborhood unit:

a residential area which provides housing for the population for which one elementary school is ordinarily required, its actual area depending on its population density . . . bounded on all sides by arterial streets

sufficiently wide to facilitate its bypassing instead of penetration by through traffic. . . . Sites for the school and other institutions having service spheres coinciding with the limits of the unit should be suitably grouped around a central point.[13]

Most new town plans call for little more than a collection of neighborhood units organized around a central business district. For example, the British new town of Harlow is divided into four neighborhood clusters of 20,000 people each. The clusters are made up of two, three, or four small neighborhoods of 5,000 to 6,000 based on the size of catchment areas for primary education.

In the smaller neighborhoods, which remain the basic planning units, the primary school is brought within safe walking distance for children, and the housewife is never more than one-half kilometer from a small group of shops. At the same time the neighborhood center placed at the principal focus within the cluster can support a very considerable range of community services.[14]

Each neighborhood is intended to facilitate close social interaction among families presumed to share the same set of values and life expectations. There have been serious disagreements on the appropriate size of neighborhoods. Proposals range from 5,000 or even less up to 20,000. Those favoring smaller neighborhoods argue that they are more cohesive and offer more intimate contact. Others argue that 15,000 to 20,000 people are required to support an effective and varied neighborhood center.[15] Population arrangements are en-

[11] B. J. Heraud, "Social Class and the New Towns," in Urban Studies, Vol. 5, No. 1, February 1968, pp. 33–58.

[12] Herbert Gans, "The Possibilities of Class and Racial Integration in American New Towns: A Policy-Oriented Analysis," in Perloff and Sandberg (eds.), op. cit., pp. 137–157.

[13] Richard Dewey, "The Neighborhood, Urban Ecology, and City Planning," in Paul K. Hatt and Albert J. Reiss, Cities and Society (New York: The Free Press), 1951, p. 786.

[14] Lesley E. White, "The Social Factors Involved in the Planning and Development of New Towns," in U.N. Department of Social Affairs, op. cit., pp. 194–200.

[15] Ibid.

forced through the design and pricing of residential units. The key assumption in neighborhood planning is that most people will value convenience, that is, a shorter distance from home to services and amenities, more than they will value extremely low densities.[16]

The neighborhood concept was not invented by sociologists, but various interpretations of the neighborhood principle (ranging from the notion of a service area designed to reduce unnecessary expenditures of time and energy to an effort to recreate a rural way of life with its closely compacted primary groups) find indirect support in classic studies of social stratification.[17] This is true not only in terms of what sociologists have identified as the need for separate settings for different groups in the same community but also in terms of the conflicts that sociologists have warned are likely to arise if incompatible groups are forced to live at close quarters.

The neighborhood unit was discarded in plans for the new town of Corby (England), for Cumbernauld (Scotland), and, more recently, in the new town of Skelmersdale (England). The planning consultants involved pointed out that increasing car ownership has created a more mobile population better able to satisfy its interests over a wider field. This seems to make sense. Nevertheless, the neighborhood unit has reappeared in almost all recent master plans for American new towns.[18] Perhaps its reappearance suggests a hidden agenda. The neighborhood unit may be the only acceptable means of achieving social balance without opening up the floodgates of indiscriminate mixing of social classes.

To understand why and how key concepts have found their way into the planning field, Gans suggests that it is important to ask who the planners are, what means they have at their disposal, and what interest groups they feel they are serving.[19] Most planners bring a middle-class view of city life to their professional careers and are beholden to government agencies and private developers for their jobs. Gans suggests that the neighborhood boundaries typically drawn by professional planners tend to ignore class divisions in the population, except those manifested by differences in housing type.

Favoring low density and small-town living, the planners seek to achieve the cessation of residential mobility and the control and minimization of future growth. The only land uses programmed for future growth [are] those favored by affluent residents, high-status industrial and commercial establishments, and real estate interests catering to these and the tax collector.[20]

His caricature is probably overdrawn, but it does raise some important questions. If the British experience is any indication, new town planners in the United States are likely to have considerable difficulty trying to make their new town plans work. The next section of this paper examines some of the problems involved and possibilities of implementing the concepts mentioned above.

The Gap Between Theory and Practice

As a means of promoting economic development in lagging regions and of

[16] Margaret Willis, "Sociological Aspects of Urban Structure," The Town Planning Review, Vol. 39, No. 4, January 1969, pp. 296–306.
[17] James Dahir, The Neighborhood Unit Plan, Its Spread and Acceptance (New York: Russell Sage Foundation), 1947. Also see Reginald Isaacs' well-known critique of the neighborhood unit in "The Neighborhood Theory," Journal of the American Institute of Planners, XIV, Spring 1948, pp. 15–23.
[18] Willis, op. cit., p. 296.
[19] Herbert Gans, "City Planning in America: A Sociological Analysis," in People and Plans, op. cit., pp. 57–77.
[20] Ibid., p. 62.

organizing additional growth in metropolitan areas, new towns have worked reasonably well.[21] The first generation of British new towns, for example, proved that public development was a decidedly feasible strategy.[22] As examples of physical design, new towns have not been extraordinarily exciting, but there have been instances of highly competent and imaginative architecture.

To get a sense of what new towns have been able to do, it is necessary to look at their overall impact on national growth patterns, or at the very least, their influence on development trends within key metropolitan areas.[23] In Britain the initial function of the new towns effort was to service the overspill population of London and to tidy up the excesses of speculative development. The most significant possibility—that of guiding, perhaps even dominating, critical interregional and intraregional relationships—did not come into play until the initiation of a second generation of new towns in the mid-1960s.[24]

One element of the success of the British new towns program was the government's willingness to provide incentives for industrial relocation. When a system of depreciation allowances (permitting write-offs of new investments against taxes) proved inadequate, the government offered more powerful grants-in-aid and tax incentives to help with the initial costs of capital construction. The British experience supports the planners' assertion that new towns can be used to implement national development policies as long as the public sector plays a leading role. This is not to say that private interests need not be involved. However, if public policy had not informed decisions regarding the number, scale, and location of planned new towns, the relative advantages of this form of development would never have been realized.

The new city of Ciudad Guayana in Venezuela attests to the fact that it may be possible to realize a "social profit" via public land ownership and intelligent tax policy.[25] Late in 1960 the Venezuelan government set up the Corporation Venezolana de Guayana (CVG) to develop the Guayana region, one of the country's greatest natural resource areas. The CVG was given the job of planning and building a major new city. Since the government owned the land, CVG was able to preserve the essence of its plan through public land ownership. The Corporation kept the land it needed for community purposes. Above all, public ownership offered CVG an opportunity to capture a reasonable share of the income and concentration of values it helped to create. Since commercial land and some of the better quality residential and industrial sites were likely to be the most profitable, CVG retained this land and sold the remainder (subject to restrictions on its use).

Although the opportunity to build a new city from the ground up seemed at the outset to be the answer to a planner's dream, there were serious stumbling blocks. The absence of trained technicians and workers, established community relations and loyalties, basic consumer and business services, and adequate community facilities created certain strains. Attracted by the prospect of jobs, poor migrants invaded the area, putting up makeshift shelters and complicating the task of organizing land uses and public services. Because of the great distance to an established city

---

[21] Lloyd Rodwin, *Nations and Cities* (Boston: Houghton-Mifflin), 1970.

[22] Lloyd Rodwin, *The British New Towns Policy, op. cit.*

[23] Arie Shachar, "The Role of New Towns in National and Regional Development: A Comparative Study," in Perloff and Sandberg (eds.), *op. cit.*, pp. 30–47.

[24] Rodwin, *Nations and Cities, op. cit.*

[25] Rodwin, *Planning Urban Growth and Regional Development, op. cit.*, Chapter 1.

center, the initial cost of development was enormously inflated. Nevertheless, by the early 1970s, the city was well on its way to achieving its projected population of 250,000. The natural riches of the area were successfully drawn into the mainstream of the Venezuelan economy.

Offset against these partial successes have been a series of difficult problems. The experience to date confirms the early predictions of the new town critics who claimed that (1) small size and low density would not be essential to the design of desirable living environments; (2) investments in new towns would shortchange inner city redevelopment efforts; (3) serious problems of adjustment would plague new residents during the first stages of development; and (4) difficult social issues would arise which had been overlooked entirely.

Sufficient evidence has now accumulated to support many of these predictions. First, limitations on size and density have indeed created problems. For one thing, the cost of living in new towns has been somewhat higher than in big cities. Although individual neighborhoods were organized around compact service centers, overall densities have been relatively low and have resulted in higher prices not only for housing, but also for many public services spread out over larger areas.[26] Higher costs, in turn, have narrowed the range of residents, lopping off any chance of relocation for the lowest income groups. Lower densities have also minimized the attractiveness of certain industrial sites. Industries looking for densely settled areas to provide outlets for their products, proximity to smaller supporting firms, and highly specialized labor have not been attracted to new towns.

Restrictions on horizontal or slightly

upward mobility from one job to another have handicapped new town residents expecting to live near their place of work. Increased mobility, in fact, has been a key factor in shattering the self-containment concept in Britain. A recent study shows that in the eight original new towns built around London "there are 76 persons who live in a new town and work outside it or commute to a new town for work, for every 100 who both live and work in the same new town." [27] The relatively small size of most new towns has also minimized the chances of providing diversified services and amenities. Specialty shops and cultural activities have been difficult to sustain outside high density urban centers. As it turns out, small size and relatively low density, even in a totally planned environment, only make sense when one assumes that the residents will settle into a job, a house, and a neighborhood for all time to come.

The second prediction that came true was that new towns would undercut efforts to rebuild central cities. Not only have new town planning programs siphoned off money that might have been used to rehabilitate deteriorating core areas, but they also have skimmed off upwardly mobile workers who otherwise might have stayed behind and tried to improve matters. Certain industries intent on expanding were lured to new towns on the outskirts of metropolitan areas and subsidized by the government while the fiscal capacities of central cities continued to erode. In what may have been the most unexpected blow, new towns riveted public attention on the suburbs and promoted the fantasy of garden city living, thus drawing a curtain over the difficulties plaguing big cities.

A number of studies have reported a phenomenon known as the "new town

26 Nathaniel Litchfield, "Economic Opportunity in New Towns" in Perloff and Sandberg (eds.), op. cit., pp. 48–67.

27 Ira M. Robinson, "Small, Independent, Self-contained and Balanced New Towns: Myth or Reality?" in Perloff and Sandberg (eds.), op. cit., pp. 2–27.

blues" or "transitional neurosis." [28]
Early new town residents have had great
difficulty making friends. They feel cut
off from long-standing social ties. Wives
in particular are lonely. Lives in general
are more strained. Shops and public
houses, close at hand in old inner city
neighborhoods, are nonexistent or more
distant in new towns and thus unable
to serve as social centers. [29] To a great
extent these problems are transitory,
but in a larger sense the migration to
new towns has ripped apart the close-
knit fabric of kin and neighbors in
many cities. While some degree of dis-
orientation has always accompanied a
move, families in difficulty in new towns
are not likely to find helping institutions to fall back on.

Other social issues have also arisen
for which the planners were not prepared. In his study of two British new
towns, Willmott identifies a number of
problems, including imbalance in the
population structure and the difficulty
of integrating social groups via the
neighborhood unit. [30] People moving to
new towns have been predominantly
young couples with small children. This
age bias has created an early demand
for extensive social services and facilities
that quickly become outmoded as the
population matures. [31] It has also generated a lack of diversity in social activities. [32]

Few of the assumptions regarding the
importance of the neighborhood unit
as a socializing device have been borne
out. [33] As a way of structuring community life around the provision of schools,
shops, and other services, the concept
has not worked particularly well. Perhaps it has been applied too inflexibly.
In England, the emphasis on the distinctiveness of neighborhood populations did not fit with the patterns of
social interaction that developed. [34] Perhaps, too, the neighborhood unit was
too large a locality (5,000 to 10,000
residents) for most people. The residents did not identify with the neighborhoods laid out by the planners. [35]
Part of the problem stemmed from the
surprising degree of cross-commuting
into and out of many new towns. [36] In
any event, the neighborhood unit is not
the locus of informal social relations it
was supposed to be.

The problems of achieving social balance and of organizing a community
into manageable parts have taken their
toll of new town planning theory. The
search for fresh paradigms of social and
economic organization goes on. In the
meantime, preliminary results of privately financed efforts to build new
towns in the United States suggest two
other difficulties. The first is race relations. The second is the problem of
maintaining the myth of local autonomy in the face of encroaching social
disorganization.

Too little is known about attitudes
toward racial integration and about behavior in integrated situations to permit firm conclusions about whether or
not racial integration is possible in new
towns. [37] However,

[28] Peter Willmott, "Social Research and
New Communities," in the *Journal of the
American Institute of Planners*, Vol. 33,
1967, Nov., pp. 387–398.
[29] Herbert Gans, *The Levittowners* (New
York: Pantheon), 1967.
[30] Peter Willmott, "Housing Density and
Town Design in a New Town," *Town
Planning Review*, Vol. XXXIII, July 1962,
pp. 115–127.
[31] Norman Pritchard, "Planned Social Provision in New Towns," *Town Planning Review*, Vol. XXXVIII, No. 1, April 1967,
pp. 25–34.
[32] Jennifer Moss, "New and Expanded
Towns: A Survey of the Demographic Characteristics of Newcomers," *Town Planning
Review*, Vol. XXXIX, No. 2, July 1968, pp.
117–139.

[33] Willis, *op. cit.*
[34] Heraud, *op. cit.*
[35] Willmott, "Housing Density and Town
Design in a New Town," *op. cit.*
[36] A. A. Ogilvy, "The Self-Contained New
Towns" in *Town Planning Review*, Vol.
XXXIX, No. 1, April 1968, pp. 38–54.
[37] Herbert Gans, "The Possibilities of Class
and Racial Integration," *op. cit.*

Racial micro-integration is rare, except temporarily when communities are in racial transition and until the "tipping point" is reached, and it is rare in most new towns because it has not often been tried, except on a token basis. Still, it exists in new towns such as Columbia, Reston, and the Levitt-built Willingboro, but partly because the blacks who moved into these towns were of high status.[38]

What seems to be emerging is general agreement on at least one point: racial integration among neighborhoods or residential clusters will be most feasible when there are no significant class differences between the races, or when minority racial groups are of higher status than the whites.[39] Gans suggests that racial integration will probably be most feasible in upper-middle-class areas. This is not very promising, however, because the new towns program in the United States is supposed to provide housing for low- and moderate-income groups and particularly for minority groups trapped in the central city. The task of weaving low-income minority families into the social fabric of a new town is beyond anything planners can handle at the present time.

The notion of the new town as a sanctuary from overcrowding and urban blight is already breaking down in the United States. In Columbia, Maryland, one of the few American new towns to reach a preliminary population threshold of 10,000, the problems of crime, vandalism, and racial tension have already surfaced.[40] Future efforts to market planned communities as morally cohesive minisocieties immune to larger social problems will become increasingly difficult. Developers must find new ways of sustaining the myth of local autonomy, otherwise they will lose their drawing power.

One last problem also deserves attention. Private developers in the United States and public development corporations in other countries have all had great difficulty finding ways to involve new town residents in community governance. Unless community residents are involved at least to some extent in development decisions and ongoing management operations they can impede the pace of development.[41] The negative aura of community dissent can also sabotage a new town's marketability, to say nothing of the corrosive effects such confrontation can have on the fragile bonds of trust and friendship that new residents must try to build.

In summary, there appear to be at last three major obstacles to implementing the concepts of social organization implicit in most new town plans. The first is the lack of sufficiently powerful implementation mechanisms. Techniques for attracting and maintaining a heterogeneous population have no more than a hit-or-miss quality about them. There are neither incentives nor controls strong enough (except in a totalitarian regime) to induce balanced migration or social interaction among groups that prefer not to mix. Efforts to organize local patterns of family life around neighborhood service centers have faltered: first, because they have failed to take account of sharp discontinuities in the age structure; and second, because the trade-off between density and convenience has not been

[38] Ibid.

[39] Study prepared by the Metropolitan Applied Research Center for the U.S. Department of Housing and Urban Development cited in Jack Underhill, "The New Community Development Process" in an unpublished volume of essays edited by Gideon Golany, Penn State University.

[40] Jay Rosenthal, "A Tale of One City," New York Times Magazine, December 26, 1971.

[41] David Godschalk, "Participation, Planning, and Exchange in Old and New Communities: A Collaborative Paradigm," unpublished Ph.D. dissertation, Department of City and Regional Planning, University of North Carolina, 1972.

as important as the planners originally suspected. Finally, the problem of maintaining the illusion of economic opportunity and self-sufficiency in the face of preliminary signs of social deterioration has become more difficult than ever. Greater mobility, the increasing impact of mass communications, and the footloose character of a highly urbanized population make it extremely difficult to pretend that new towns can somehow be shielded from social problems typically found in central cities.

A second obstacle is the lack of a grounded theory of social interaction at the neighborhood level. We have yet to discover how to organize supporting institutions to help ease the process of entry. Moreover, there does not seem to be any general agreement about the best way of arranging social services and community facilities. Most new towns are organized around the neighborhood unit (which in turn assumes that elementary education is the key to social organization). In addition, it is impossible to disregard the often violent reactions of suburban dwellers to the inmigration of blacks, the poor, and other minority groups. In the United States, civil rights groups have spearheaded efforts for many years to pierce the exclusivity of the suburbs. Racial equality, fair housing, and integration have been their bywords. Today, however, the passion for ethnic autonomy has confused the issue. With political control of several major cities practically within their grasp, many black leaders are extraordinarily wary of new town proposals which they view as part of a dispersal or integrationist strategy. Anything that threatens to dilute their emerging political majority is subject to careful scrutiny and, more often than not, severe criticism. It is not clear whether one segment or the other of the black community will dominate, or whether an alliance will be forged that can somehow reinforce their separate objectives.

Nor is it clear how other groups will react to this situation. It may be, however, that various minority groups will prefer to build new towns that they can control and in which they can remain relatively separate.[42]

A third obstacle is the problem of responding to resident demands for participation in local affairs. The financial feasibility of a new town as well as its hope for a more efficiently organized land use pattern, hinge on adherence to a master plan. This seems to preclude any significant role for new community residents in the decision making process. Moreover, in light of the fact that the first wave of residents may want to "pull up the drawbridge," this is a particularly knotty problem. These are indeed serious problems, and they threaten the success of the fledgling new towns program in the United States. There may be a number of ways, however, of overcoming these obstacles and of narrowing the gap between theory and practice.

The Transformational Possibilities

The concept of planning has broadened over time, escalating from an early preoccupation with town and county problems, to a regional and even a national concern for the formulation of overall growth strategies. While efforts to build small, self-contained new communities were supported originally as a way of decentralizing big cities, recent generations of planners have argued for larger new towns which they hope will act as magnets pulling growth to lagging regions. The problems of planning for social aspects of community life, however, are still as intractable as ever.

The British new towns program was launched on the assumption that the

---

[42] One suggestion along these lines was made by Ervin Golantay, "Black New Towns," *Progressive Architecture*, August, 1968, pp. 126–131.

long-term problems caused by the industrial revolution could be solved by restoring people to the land and by financing continuing city improvements out of the increment in land values collected via rents (public ownership). Social problems, to the extent that they were considered at all, were correlated with unlimited city size, high neighborhood density, and the great distance between job opportunities and residential areas. While big cities implied unlimited size and high densities, new towns would be programmed to achieve an optimal size and density. The problematic journey to work would be eliminated because people would live where they worked. The neighborhood unit was selected as the basic building block in the planners' design, representing a coherent clustering of social groups with relatively similar needs and expectations. It all seemed to make such good sense, yet the outcome has been surprisingly unsuccessful. In what ways were the new town planners misdirected? Might it be possible to adjust the new towns policy recently adopted in the United States in order to avoid many of the same disappointments?

New town development in the United States began in earnest with the passage of the Urban Growth and New Community Development Act of 1970. This act provides attractive incentives to public and private entrepreneurs and investors interested in the planned development of "socially and economically sound new communities." The U.S. Department of Housing and Urban Development is empowered to provide loans, grants, and interest subsidies for the development of new-towns-in-town (the clearance and redevelopment of "functionally obsolete properties" in the central cities), planned suburban communities, and new towns or growth centers in rural areas. As of June, 1973, the federal government had committed upwards of $250 million to fourteen new towns scattered throughout the United States (Table 1). Unfortunately, no justification for the selection of sites or the approval of plans has been forthcoming.[43]

The new towns program in the United States will be judged in several ways. First, by the extent to which it serves the poor and the disadvantaged. The fourteen new towns approved thus far (with a population of 800,000 projected over the next thirty years) are scheduled to provide roughly 65,000 units of housing for families with low and moderate incomes. Of the 200,000 new jobs likely to be created, it is not clear what proportion will be accessible to those who are currently unemployed or unskilled. Another measure of success will be the extent to which the new towns can link to recuperative efforts in the central city. Few new towns approved to date have been designed to revitalize decaying central city areas. A third, and probably the most important test of the new towns program, will be whether or not the planners are able to discover appropriate techniques for re-creating social networks and stimulating positive social interaction at something approximating a neighborhood level. Will it be possible to develop more sophisticated theories grounded in a better understanding of social dynamics at the community level? Although lip service has been given to the notion of technological innovation, almost no attention has been paid to the problems and prospects of serious social experimentation.

New communities provide special opportunities for social learning.[44] Although discussions have centered around

[43] Lloyd Rodwin and Lawrence Susskind, "The Next Generation of New Towns" in James Bailey (ed.), *New Towns in America* (New York: John Wiley), 1973.

[44] The possibilities of experimentation in new towns were first discussed by this author in Lawrence Susskind and Gary Hack, "New Towns in a National Urban Growth Strategy," *Technology Review*, February, 1972, pp. 30–42.

Table 1
Summary of New Towns Approved and Subsidized by the U.S. Department of Housing and Urban Development

COMMUNITY	PROJECTED POPULATION	PROJECTED JOBS	DWELLING UNITS	PER CENT OF HOUSING FOR LOW AND MODERATE INCOME FAMILIES	LOCATION	DATE AND AMOUNT HUD GUARANTEE COMMITMENT (IN THOUSANDS)
Jonathan, Minn.	49,996	18,152	5,500 in 10 years	25	20 mi. SW of Minneapolis	21,000 2/70
St. Charles Communities, Md.	79,145	14,890	25,000 in 20 years	20	25 mi. SE of Wash., D.C.	24,000 6/70
Park Forest South, Ill.	110,000	N.A.	35,000 in 15 years	16	30 mi. S of Chicago	30,000 6/70
Flower Mound, Tex.	64,141	16,454	18,000 in 20 years	20	20 mi. NW of Dallas	18,000 12/70
Maumelle, Ark.	45,000	N.A.	14,000 in 20 years	23	12 mi. NW of Little Rock	7,500 12/70
Cedar-Riverside, Minn.	31,250	14,609	12,500 in 20 years	44	downtown Minneapolis	24,000 6/71
Riverton, N.Y.	25,632	11,180	8,000 in 16 years	40	10 mi. S of Rochester	12,000 12/71
San Antonio Ranch, Tex.	87,972	17,990	28,000 in 30 years	35	20 mi. NW of San Antonio	18,000 2/72
Woodlands, Tex.	150,000	40,000	49,160 in 20 years	27	30 mi. NW of Houston	50,000 4/72
Gananda, N.Y.	55,808	12,890	17,200 in 20 years	21	12 mi. N of Rochester	22,000 4/72
Soul City, N.C.	44,000	18,000	12,096 in 30 years	37	45 mi. NW of Raleigh-Durham	14,000 6/72
Lysander, N.Y.	18,355	N.A.	5,000 in 20 years	50	12 mi. NW of Syracuse	*
Harbinson, S. C.	21,343	6,100	6,500 in 20 years	35	8 mi. NW of Columbia	13,000 10/72
Welfare Is., N.Y.	17,000	7,500	5,000	55	East River between Manhattan and Queens, N.Y.C.	†

Source: Office of New Communities Development, U.S. Department of Housing and Urban Development, as of January, 1973.
* Funded by the New York State Urban Development Corp., approved by HUD June, 1972.
† Funded by the New York State Urban Development Corp., approved by HUD December, 1972.

the possibility of testing new technological hardware, new waste control systems, industrialized housing and other building systems, and new modes of transportation, the potential for deploying sophisticated technology is not the central issue. Important as such innovations may seem, it is the process of managing social and economic develop- ment that requires special attention. New towns can provide an opportunity to study the process of working back and forth between what is desirable and what is feasible. It is at this nexus that planners and sociologists can collaborate in interesting and important ways.

Two decisions usually made early in

the planning process have an almost irreversible impact upon the ultimate character of a community: the selection of a site and the amount and nature of the financing commitment. Experiments might be aimed at opening up these decisions to the ultimate users who, quite literally, have to live with the consequences. It might be possible, for instance, to identify the potential users of a new town so that they could help design the community before a final decision on site selection was made. The planners of Soul City have considered ways of identifying prospective residents so that they can be involved in the initial planning stages.[45] If this is too difficult, consultants and advisors might be selected whose interests are similar to those likely to live in the new town. (One word of warning here: involvement of surrogate users must go beyond the traditional market survey; they must have a part in generating the range of options as well as evaluating specific alternatives.) Either strategy should yield much needed information on social service preferences and the extent to which different groups will cluster when given the opportunity.

Another useful strategy would be to defer as many decisions as possible which affect the form of development until residents are on the scene. Indeed, the initial development might include temporary quarters for residents (short-term rentals) while they become directly involved in planning activities. Designs might be sought which break down what are presently large capital investments such as sewer and road systems into smaller components which may (or may not) be added incrementally, thereby avoiding long-term commitments to an overall physical form.

[45] David Godschalk, *The Planning Process for New Town Development: Soul City*, Department of City and Regional Planning, University of North Carolina, Chapel Hill, 1969.

Still another possible approach might be to build several smaller neighborhoods simultaneously, so that each could offer very different combinations of site and cash flow characteristics. Neighborhoods which are deliberately planned to grow slowly (temporary users might be allowed to pay for the carrying costs of the land) might be paired with others which are planned to grow as rapidly as possible. Financing commitments might vary accordingly. These suggestions imply great flexibility in holding open site and cash flow arrangements—flexibility which only government backing can help to ensure. In each case it should be possible to adjust physical designs to respond to emerging activity patterns and to learn more about the processes by which neighborhood groups sort themselves out.

The development of more permanent institutions in a new community provides another opportunity for experimentation. Preventive health care on a community scale (as in Columbia, Maryland) and prepaid group practice arrangements might become a major part of a plan for the delivery of health services. Various ownership formats—condominiums, cooperatives, etc.—and other mechanisms for local control could be tested along with institutional innovations such as:

Small quasigovernmental units. Can control over services traditionally provided by city-wide governments be dispersed to small groups of residents or to neighborhood associations? What are the effects of disaggregation?

Special service districts or corporations. Can local development corporations be designed to control the delivery of services? Can debt repayment be transferred from the developer to the community or service districts in small increments?

Crisis management. Can better ways be found of raising issues of community concern, disseminating information, and resolving conflict through neighborhood forums, ombudsmen, or new forms of media, particularly cable television?

From experiments such as these it should be possible to discover which forms of community organization provide adequate support for newcomers and which contribute most to the satisfaction of various resident groups.

Most, if not all of these experiments presume that social researchers will be able and willing to evaluate the process of new town development. New towns are obviously more conducive to this kind of research than established neighborhoods. Reactions to continuous probing are likely to be less severe in a new town than in an established inner city area. Moreover, developers often make it clear from the outset that part of the price of living in a new town will be a continuous bombardment of surveys and questionnaires. Participant observers can move into a new town somewhat less obtrusively. The most important difference, however, is that the evolution of social arrangements in a new town is relatively transparent whereas in older neighborhoods, successive waves of immigration, the interplay of impinging pressures from nearby communities, and the time-bound hierarchy of residency make it difficult to study the *process* of social transformation.

Experiments in new town design are different from experiments in the physical sciences in at least three ways: the large number of variables involved in any situation makes it virtually impossible to undertake classical matched-pair experiments; "scaling up" may change the nature of the problem and invalidate the results of a pilot experiment, and since humans are involved,

successes and failures are always relative and subjective concepts.[46] Nevertheless, experiments in institutional design and the study of their subsequent impact on social organization are an absolutely necessary step in building more sophisticated theories of new town planning.

A rigorous monitoring system is also a prerequisite for learning from new town experiments. Monitoring should indicate the performance of the community at the local level, where feedback will allow for frequent adjustments, and at the national level where alternative new town development strategies can be evaluated. Since communities take years to develop, long-term recording of events, perceptions, and changes will be required. The process of research should begin with each initial participant in the development process recording his or her expectations: designers ought to spell out the various opportunities they envision for each new town, and investors ought to be specific about profit expectations. Monitoring should include the periodic collection of photographic, visual, and verbal records of the community, and an archivist should be designated to collect and hold impressions and records in every new town.

What has been missing is a sense that we know what community life should be like—for one or for all segments of the population. Unfortunately, we do not. To the extent that new towns start out representing different models of social and economic activity, they provide an opportunity to gauge the probable reactions of various population groups. Most attempts to construct social experiments have failed; partly because the risks involved are great and partly because planners and social scientists have been too timid to

[46] Donald Schon, "On Bringing Technology to Social Problems," *Technology Review*, February, 1971, pp. 46–51.

suggest such large-scale ventures. New towns can change all that, first, because no one need be an unwitting captive of a new town experiment and second, because the climate is obviously ripe for such bold adventures. We need to advance our understanding about possible ways of improving the quality of community life. The burden is now on the shoulders of those who have hidden behind the protective covering of descriptive research. Much as they despise the thought, there is no way to avoid the need for policy-oriented or prescriptive experimental research.

New town planners may well be guilty of replacing one illusion with another. A fresh start will not necessarily produce better results, especially if no one is clear about what he is striving for. The only way to reduce the chance of failure is to develop a better process of social learning. In so far as new town development is concerned, experimentation might help to generate a clearer perception of the real value of alternative new town designs. This is an effort, though, that will require an input from planners whose implicit social theories are rarely grounded in systematic research and from community sociologists who have often failed to focus on the process of social change. If the two professions are unable to work in tandem the gap between theory and practice is likely to become even wider.

C Bureaucracy

INTRODUCTION

Bureaucracy is a form of social organization that men have invented for carrying out administrative tasks in large, complex societies. Bureaucracy was used by the ancient Egyptians for organizing the complex economy of the Nile Valley and the empire; the emperors and empresses of ancient China used a bureaucratic form of organization to govern their vast empires; and the Romans used bureaucracy to administer their far-flung territories, as well as to organize the provision of large cities and the command of the Legions. Today, as human societies become large and complex the world over, most of the important areas of social life within them are becoming bureaucratically organized.

The governments of modern cities and nations are composed of large numbers of administrative bureaucracies through which all the varied tasks of government are carried out. Business enterprises in the capitalist nations are becoming organized into large-scale corporate bureaucracies, the largest of which employ more people and have larger budgets than states of the United States and half the nations of the world. In socialist countries, economic activity is organized in the bureaucracies of the national government. Modern military establishments are the epitome of authoritarian bureaucracies, where total control is vested in the top positions and relations between superior and subordinate are almost purely ones of command and obedience. Education systems, even when administered on the local community level as in the United States, develop into bureaucracies simply because the communities are large and the task of educating people for life in our technologically advanced society is very complex, requiring the services of many specialists whose activities must be integrated. The modern university is a vast bureaucratic structure, administering the education of as many as forty thousand students at a time. Religious denominations in modern Western societies find they must organize central bureaucracies to administer standard policies throughout the denomination. The Roman Catholic Church provides one of the oldest models of bureaucratically organized religious groups.

Max Weber was the first sociologist to make a systematic study of bureaucratic organization, both in ancient societies and in the modern West. It is his contention that bureaucracy provides the most efficient means for carrying out large-scale administrative tasks. He attributes the efficiency of bureaucracy to the basic characteristics of its structure. He identifies these characteristics as the distribution of the work in a fixed division of labor among offices; a hierarchical ordering of offices so that the work of each employee is supervised by another; a set of formal, rational rules that governs the work of all employees; objectivity and impersonality in the conduct of the affairs of each office; the filling of positions in the bureaucracy by people possessing the certified technical qualifications to carry out the work; and the definition of bureaucratic office holding as a secure full-time career for the individual in order to motivate him to work efficiently. Weber shows how each of these basic characteristics of bureaucratic organizations contributes to the over-all efficiency and effectiveness of administration.

Seymour Martin Lipset discusses the common predicament of a new group of top officers coming into a bureaucratic organization and finding that career bureaucrats have effective control. The new top officers find they must somehow gain the cooperation of these bureaucrats before they can use the organization to carry out new programs they want to institute. Lipset provides a case study of this process in a Canadian provincial government bureaucracy that had developed under many years of Conservative government rule and suddenly was asked, as the result of a Socialist party election victory, to administer a series of radical government programs. The resistance that the newly elected politicians met from the bureaucrats in this case is not different in kind from that that might be met by a new group of officers taking charge of a business corporation with the goal of changing its ways of operating, or by a new president of a large university wanting to reform its educational program.

Bureaucracy, as has been said, dominates modern society as the form of organization of most of our large-scale enterprises. As business and industry have become large-scale enterprises, with the rise of corporate capitalism in the West, they too have taken on the bureaucratic form of organization. Reinhard Bendix, in the article reprinted here, documents the growing bureaucratization of business and industry in America and discusses some of its consequences for the operation of industrial organizations, including the stratification of their hierarchies of offices and recruitment of people into managerial positions.

Eliot Freidson, on the other hand, identifies what he sees as a trend in "post-industrial" society toward the professionalization of white-collar occupations and discusses some of the possible consequences of this trend for bureaucratic structures. In particular, he sees professional work as incongruent with traditional authority relations in bureaucratic organizations. He thinks that new forms of coordination and control will have to be developed for the organization of professionalized occupations.

Alfred Weber, the younger brother of Max Weber, discusses the implications of bureaucracy for the continuation of freedom in modern societies. The hierarchical organization of bureaucracy, he points out, requires the making of decisions and the exercise of control over the organization by those in top positions, leaving those in lower positions generally powerless. This centralization has the further consequence of discouraging individual initiative in the development of new ideas and practices in the organization. The standardization of bureaucratic procedures and practices has the consequence, Weber claims, of developing uniformity in thought and behavior throughout the society. Weber sees these consequences of bureaucracy in advanced capitalist and socialist countries today and argues that only a structural reorganization of these societies can preserve freedom in the modern world.

30
Formal Characteristics of Bureaucracy

MAX WEBER

Modern officialdom functions in the following specific manner:

I. There is the principle of fixed and official jurisdictional areas, which are generally ordered by rules, that is, by laws or administrative regulations. (1.) The regular activities required for the purposes of the bureaucratically governed structure are distributed in a fixed way as official duties. (2.) The authority to give the commands required for the discharge of these duties is distributed in a stable way and is strictly delimited by rules concerning the coercive means, physical, sacerdotal, or otherwise, which may be placed at the disposal of officials. (3.) Methodical provision is made for the regular and continuous fulfilment of these duties and for the execution of the corresponding rights; only persons who have the generally regulated qualifications to serve are employed.

In public and lawful government these three elements constitute 'bureaucratic authority.' In private economic domination, they constitute bureaucratic 'management.' Bureaucracy, thus understood, is fully developed in political and ecclesiastical communities only in the modern state, and, in the private

From *From Max Weber: Essays in Sociology*, edited and translated by H. H. Gerth and C. Wright Mills. Copyright © 1946 by Oxford University Press, Inc. Reprinted by permission.

economy, only in the most advanced institutions of capitalism. Permanent and public office authority, with fixed jurisdiction, is not the historical rule but rather the exception. This is so even in large political structures such as those of the ancient Orient, the Germanic and Mongolian empires of conquest, or of many feudal structures of state. In all these cases, the ruler executes the most important measures through personal trustees, table-companions, or court-servants. Their commissions and authority are not precisely delimited and are temporarily called into being for each case.

II. The principles of office hierarchy and of levels of graded authority mean a firmly ordered system of super- and subordination in which there is a supervision of the lower offices by the higher ones. Such a system offers the governed the possibility of appealing the decision of a lower office to its higher authority, in a definitely regulated manner. With the full development of the bureaucratic type, the office hierarchy is monocratically organized. The principle of hierarchical office authority is found in all bureaucratic structures: in state and ecclesiastical structures as well as in large party organizations and private enterprises. It does not matter for the character of bureaucracy whether its authority is called 'private' or 'public.'

When the principle of jurisdictional

'competency' is fully carried through, hierarchical subordination—at least in public office—does not mean that the 'higher' authority is simply authorized to take over the business of the 'lower.' Indeed, the opposite is the rule. Once established and having fulfilled its task, an office tends to continue in existence and be held by another incumbent.

III. The management of the modern office is based upon written documents ('the files'), which are preserved in their original or draught form. There is, therefore, a staff of subaltern officials and scribes of all sorts. The body of officials actively engaged in a 'public' office, along with the respective apparatus of material implements and the files, make up a 'bureau.' In private enterprise, 'the bureau' is often called 'the office.'

In principle, the modern organization of the civil service separates the bureau from the private domicile of the official, and, in general, bureaucracy segregates official activity as something distinct from the sphere of private life. Public monjes and equipment are divorced from the private property of the official. This condition is everywhere the product of a long development. Nowadays, it is found in public as well as in private enterprises; in the latter, the principle extends even to the leading entrepreneur. In principle, the executive office is separated from the household, business from private correspondence, and business assets from private fortunes. The more consistently the modern type of business management has been carried through the more are these separations the case. The beginnings of this process are to be found as early as the Middle Ages.

It is the peculiarity of the modern entrepreneur that he conducts himself as the 'first official' of his enterprise, in the very same way in which the ruler of a specifically modern bureau-cratic state spoke of himself as 'the first servant' of the state. The idea that the bureau activities of the state are intrinsically different in character from the management of private economic offices is a continental European notion and, by the way of contrast, is totally foreign to the American way.

IV. Office management, at least all specialized office management—and such management is distinctly modern —usually presupposes a thorough and expert training. This increasingly holds for the modern executive and employee of private enterprises, in the same manner as it holds for the state official.

V. When the office is fully developed, official activity demands the full working capacity of the official, irrespective of the fact that his obligatory time in the bureau may be firmly delimited. In the normal case, this is only the product of a long development, in the public as well as in the private office. Formerly, in all cases, the normal state of affairs was reversed: official business was discharged as a secondary activity.

VI. The management of the office follows general rules, which are more or less stable, more or less exhaustive, and which can be learned. Knowledge of these rules represents a special technical learning which the officials possess. It involves jurisprudence, or administrative or business management.

The reduction of modern office management to rules is deeply embedded in its very nature. The theory of modern public administration, for instance, assumes that the authority to order certain matters by decree—which has been legally granted to public authorities— does not entitle the bureau to regulate the matter by commands given for each case, but only to regulate the matter abstractly. This stands in extreme contrast to the regulation of all relationships through individual privileges and bestowals of favor, which is absolutely dominant in patrimonialism, at least in so far as such relationships are not fixed by sacred tradition.

All this results in the following for the internal and external position of the official.

I. Office holding is a 'vocation.' This is shown, first, in the requirement of a firmly prescribed course of training, which demands the entire capacity for work for a long period of time, and in the generally prescribed and special examinations which are prerequisites of employment. Furthermore, the position of the official is in the nature of a duty. This determines the internal structure of his relations, in the following manner: Legally and actually, office holding is not considered a source to be exploited for rents or emoluments, as was normally the case during the Middle Ages and frequently up to the threshold of recent times. Nor is office holding considered a usual exchange of services for equivalents, as is the case with free labor contracts. Entrances into an office, including one in the private economy, is considered an acceptance of a specific obligation of faithful management in return for a secure existence. It is decisive for the specific nature of modern loyalty to an office that, in the pure type, it does not establish a relationship to a *person*, like the vassal's or disciple's faith in feudal or in patrimonial relations of authority. Modern loyalty is devoted to impersonal and functional purposes. Behind the functional purposes, of course, 'ideas of culture-values' usually stand. These are *ersatz* for the earthly, or supra-mundane personal master: ideas such as 'state,' 'church,' 'community,' 'party,' or 'enterprise' are thought of as being realized in a community; they provide an ideological halo for the master.

The political official—at least in the fully developed modern state—is not considered the personal servant of a ruler. Today, the bishop, the priest, and the preacher are in fact no longer, as in early Christian times, holders of purely personal charisma. The supra-mundane and sacred values which they offer are given to everybody who seems to be worthy of them and who asks for them. In former times, such leaders acted upon the personal command of their master; in principle, they were responsible only to him. Nowadays, in spite of the partial survival of the old theory, such religious leaders are officials in the service of a functional purpose, which in the present-day 'church' has become routinized and, in turn, ideologically hallowed.

II. The personal position of the official is patterned in the following way: (1.) Whether he is in a private office or a public bureau, the modern official always strives and usually enjoys a distinct *social esteem* as compared with the governed. His social position is guaranteed by the prescriptive rules of rank order and, for the political official, by special definitions of the criminal code against 'insults of officials' and 'contempt' of state and church authorities.

The actual social position of the official is normally highest where, as in old civilized countries, the following conditions prevail: a strong demand for administration by trained experts; a strong and stable social differentiation, where the official predominantly derives from socially and economically privileged strata because of the social distribution of power; or where the costliness of the required training and status conventions are binding upon him. The possession of educational certificates—to be discussed elsewhere —are usually linked with qualification for office. Naturally, such certificates or patents enhance the 'status element' in the social position of the official. For the rest this status factor in individual cases is explicitly and impassively acknowledged; for example, in the prescription that the acceptance or rejection of an aspirant to an official career depends upon the consent ('election') of the members of the official body. This is the case in the German army with the officer corps. Similar phenomena, which promote this guild-like closure of officialdom, are typically found in patrimonial and, particularly, in prebendal officialdoms of the past. The desire to resurrect such phenomena in changed forms is by no means infrequent among modern bureaucrats. For instance, they have played a role among the demands of the quite proletarian and expert officials (the *tretyj* element) during the Russian revolution.

Usually the social esteem of the officials as such is especially low where the demand for expert administration and the dominance of status conventions are weak. This is especially the case in the United States; it is often the case in new settlements by virtue of their wide fields for profit-taking and the great instability of their social stratification.

(2.) The pure type of bureaucratic official is *appointed* by a superior authority. An official elected by the governed is not a purely bureaucratic figure. Of course, the formal existence of an election does not by itself mean that no appointment hides behind the election—in the state, especially, appointment by party chiefs. Whether or not this is the case does not depend upon legal statutes but upon the way in which the party mechanism functions. Once firmly organized, the parties can turn a formally free election into the mere acclamation of a candidate designated by the party chief. As a rule, however, a formally free election is turned into a fight, conducted according to definite rules, for votes in favor of one of two designated candidates.

In all circumstances, the designation of officials by means of an election among the governed modifies the strictness of hierarchical subordination. In principle, an official who is so elected has an autonomous position opposite the superordinate official. The elected official does not derive his position 'from above' but 'from below,' or at least not from a superior authority of the official hierarchy but from powerful party men ('bosses'), who also determine his further career. The career of the elected official is not, or at least not primarily, dependent upon his chief in the administration. The official who is not elected but appointed by a chief normally functions more exactly, from a technical point of view, because, all other circumstances being equal, it is more likely that purely functional points of consideration and qualities will determine his selection and career. As laymen, the governed can become acquainted with the extent to which a candidate is expertly qualified for office only in terms of experience, and hence only after his service. Moreover, in every sort of selection of officials by election, parties quite naturally give decisive weight not to expert considerations but to the services a follower renders to the party boss. This holds for all kinds of procurement of officials by elections, for the designation of formally free, elected officials by party bosses when they determine the slate of candidates, or the free appointment by a chief who has himself been elected. The contrast, however, is relative: substantially similar conditions hold where legitimate monarchs and their subordinates appoint officials, except that the influence of the followings are then less controllable.

Where the demand for administration by trained experts is considerable, and the party followings have to recognize an intellectually developed, educated, and freely moving 'public opinion,' the use of unqualified officials falls back upon the party in power at the next election. Naturally, this is more likely to happen when the officials are appointed by the chief. The demand for a trained administration now exists in the United States, but in the large cities, where immigrant votes are 'corraled,' there is, of course, no educated public opinion. Therefore, popular elections of the administrative chief and also of his subordinate officials usually endanger the expert qualification of the official as well as the precise functioning of the bureaucratic mechanism. It also weakens the dependence of the officials upon the hierarchy. This holds at least for the large administrative bodies that are difficult to supervise. The superior qualification and integrity of federal judges, appointed by the President, as over against elected judges in the United States is well known, although both types of officials have been selected primarily in terms of party considerations. The great changes in American metropolitan administrations demanded by reformers have proceeded essentially from elected mayors working with an apparatus of officials who were appointed by them. These reforms have thus come about in a 'Caesarist' fashion. Viewed technically, as an organized form of authority, the efficiency of 'Caesarism,' which often grows out of democracy, rests in general upon the position of the 'Caesar' as a free trustee of the masses (of the army or of the citizenry), who is unfettered by tradition. The 'Caesar' is thus the unrestrained master of a body of highly qualified military officers and officials whom he selects freely and personally without regard to tradition or to any other considerations. This 'rule of the personal genius,' however, stands in contradiction to the formally 'democratic' principle of a universally elected officialdom.

(3.) Normally, the position of the official is held for life, at least in public bureaucracies; and this is increasingly the case for all similar structures. As a factual rule, *tenure for life* is presupposed, even where the giving of notice or periodic reappointment occurs. In contrast to the worker in a private enterprise, the official normally holds tenure. Legal or actual life-tenure, however, is not recognized as the official's right to the possession of office, as was the case with many structures of authority in the past. Where legal guarantees against arbitrary dismissal of transfer are developed, they merely serve to guarantee a strictly objective discharge of specific office duties free from all personal considerations. In Germany, this is the case for all juridical and, increasingly, for all administrative officials.

Within the bureaucracy, therefore, the measure of 'independence,' legally guaranteed by tenure, is not always a source of increased status for the official whose position is thus secured. Indeed, often the reverse holds, especially in old cultures and communities that are highly differentiated. In such communities, the stricter the subordination under the arbitrary rule of the master, the more it guarantees the maintenance of the conventional seigneurial style of living for the official. Because of the very absence of these legal guarantees of tenure, the conventional esteem for the official may rise in the same way as, during the Middle Ages, the esteem of the nobility of office rose at the expense of esteem for the freemen, and as the king's judge surpassed that of the people's judge. In Germany, the military officer or the administrative official can be removed from office at any time, or at least far more readily than the 'independent judge,' who never pays with loss of his office for even the grossest offense against the 'code of honor' or against social conventions of the salon. For this reason, if other things are equal, in the eyes of the master stratum the judge is considered less qualified for social intercourse than are officers and administrative officials, whose greater dependence on the master is a greater guarantee of their conformity with status conventions. Of course, the average official strives for a civil-service law, which would materially secure his old age and provide increased guarantees against his arbitrary removal from office. This striving, however, has its limits. A very strong development of the 'right to the office' naturally makes it more difficult to staff them with regard to technical efficiency, for such a development decreases the career-opportunities of ambitious candidates for office. This makes for the fact that officials, on the whole, do not feel their dependency upon those at the top. This lack of a feeling of dependency, however, rests primarily upon the inclination to depend upon one's equals rather than upon the socially inferior and governed strata. The present conservative movement among the Badenia clergy, occasioned by the anxiety of a presumably threatening separation of church and state, has been expressly determined by the desire not to be turned 'from a master into a servant of the parish.'

(4.) The official receives the regular *pecuniary* compensation of a normally fixed *salary* and the old age security provided by a pension. The salary is not measured like a wage in terms of work done, but according to 'status,' that is, according to the kind of function (the 'rank') and, in addition, possibly, according to the length of service. The relatively great security of the official's income, as well as the rewards of social esteem, make the office a sought-after position, especially in countries which no longer provide opportunities for colonial profits. In such countries, this situation permits relatively low salaries for officials.

(5.) The official is set for a '*career*' within the hierarchical order of the public service. He moves from the lower, less important, and lower paid to the higher positions. The average official naturally desires a mechanical fixing of the conditions of promotion: if not of the offices, at least of the salary levels. He wants these conditions fixed in terms of 'seniority,' or possibly according to grades achieved in a developed system of expert examinations. Here and there, such examinations actually form a character *indelebilis* of the official and have lifelong effects on his career. To this is joined the desire to qualify the right to office and the increasing tendency toward status group closure and economic security. All of this makes for a tendency to consider the offices as 'prebends' of those who are qualified by educational certificates. The necessity of taking general personal and intellectual qualifications into consideration, irrespective of the often subaltern character of the educational certificate, has led to a condition in which the highest political offices, especially the positions of 'ministers,' are principally filled without reference to such certificates.

31

Bureaucracy and Social Reform

SEYMOUR MARTIN LIPSET

Various writers and social scientists have long called attention to the fact that, in large-scale social organizations, administrative functions cannot be separated from policy-making power.[1] It is impossible to understand the operation of a government purely by analyzing the goals of the politicians in power, and the nongovernmental pressures on them. The members of the administrative bureaucracy, the Civil Service, constitute one of the major "Houses" of government, and as such have the power to initiate, amend, and veto actions proposed by other branches. The goals and values of the Civil Service are at least as important a part of the total complex of forces responsible for state policy as those of the ruling political party.

The political problem of the power and influence of a permanent Civil Service is not important as long as the social and economic values of the bureaucracy and the governing politicians do not seriously conflict. The problem becomes crucial, however, when a new political movement takes office and proposes to enact reforms which go beyond the traditional frame of reference of previous government activity. It is especially important today, when the explicit formal goals of many democratic states are changing from the *laissez-faire* policeman regulation of society to those of the social-welfare-planning state.[2]

The tradition and concept of a merit nonpatronage Civil Service developed in many countries as a result of the needs of the dominant business groups which demanded cheap, efficient, and predictable service from the state. Kingsley has shown how in Great Britain, the policy of the impartial Civil Service grew with the increase in political power of the business class.[3] Business men desired an efficient state which would facilitate and protect the development of commerce. Permanent, nonpolitical officials insured continuity of government regulations and practices and made for stable relations with the state, regardless of party fortunes. The policy of the merit Civil Service was not challenged as long as party politics remained contests between groups which accepted the basic orientation and activities of the state and society.[4]

The establishment of reform and socialist governments, which propose radical changes in the functions of the state, necessarily raises the problem of whether the reforms that these governments are pledged to carry out can successfully be initiated and administered by a bureaucratic structure, which is organized to regulate a different set of

Reprinted from *Research Studies*, Washington State University, 17: 11–17 (1949), with permission of the publisher and the author. This paper is a summary of a chapter in *Agrarian Socialism* by Seymour Martin Lipset (Berkeley: University of California Press, 1950) Anchor Book edition 1967.

[1] See Harold Laski, *Democracy in Crisis* (London: George Allen and Unwin, Ltd., 1933), pp. 99–104; Max Weber, *Essays in Sociology* ed. by H. Gerth and C. W. Mills (New York: Oxford University Press, 1946), pp. 232–233; Herman Finer, *The Future of Government* (London: Methuen and Co., 1946), pp. 12–13.

[2] See J. Donald Kingsley, *Representative Bureaucracy* (Yellow Springs: The Antioch Press, 1944), pp. 287–305.
[3] *Ibid.*, pp. 42–72.
[4] See L. D. White and T. V. Smith, *Politics and Public Service* (New York: Harper and Brothers, 1939), pp. 132–33.

norms, and whose members possess different values from those of the "radical" politicians.

Since the days of Karl Marx, some socialists have maintained that a successful socialist state "must destroy the old state apparatus," that is, erect a new administrative organization. In recent times, various individuals who have served in or studied socialist or "social welfare" governments have suggested that one crucial reason for their failure to proceed more vigorously toward the attainment of their goals has been the "bureaucratic conservative" influence of permanent Civil Servants. This point has been made about the Social-Democratic governments in Weimar (Germany), the various Labor governments in Great Britain, Australia, and New Zealand, the Popular Front governments in France, and the New Deal in the United States.[5]

The validity of the hypothesis about the "conservative" role of a permanent Civil Service was tested by the author in the course of a research study of a social-democratic movement which secured power towards the end of the last war.

The Cabinet Ministers in this government anticipated "sabotage" and resistance to their plans by the permanent Civil Service. In a pre-election speech, the head of the government stated his belief that the Civil Service must be sympathetic to the objectives of the government:

[5] See Arnold Brecht, "Bureaucratic Sabotage," *Annals of American Academy of Political and Social Science* (January, 1937), p. 5; Edgar Lansbury, *George Lansbury, My Father* (London: Sampson Low Masston and Co., Ltd., no date), p. 197; Charles Aiken, "The British Bureaucracy and the Origin of Parliamentary Policy, *American Political Science Review*, XXXIII (Feb., 1939), pp. 40–41; V. G. Childe, *How [Australian] Labour Governs* (London: Labour Publishing Co., Ltd., 1923), p. 16; J. Donald Kingsley, *op. cit.*, p. 274; and Leon Blum, *For All Mankind* (London: Victor Gollancz, 1946), p. 59.

It is most necessary for any government that those in charge of various departments shall be competent and capable of absorbing new ideas and techniques. No matter how good legislation is, if those in charge of administering it are unsympathetic or incapable of a new approach, little good will come of it.

The government ministers entered office ready to change key Civil Servants as soon as they showed any signs of opposition to government proposals. The ministers, however, envisaged opposition as deliberate "sabotage" and explicit defiance of government proposals. The key Civil Servants, on the other hand, expected to be discharged or demoted soon after the socialists took office. A number of them, therefore had begun to look for other jobs or planned to retire. In the hope of maintaining their positions, however, many of these Civil Servants began to ingratiate themselves with their ministers.

Almost all of the leading Civil Servants were outwardly obsequious, flattered their ministers, and in general, did everything they could to convince the Cabinet that they were cooperative. In many departments, during the early period of the new government, the best "socialists" were in the top ranks of the government bureaucracy. The administratively insecure Cabinet ministers were overjoyed at the response which they secured from the Civil Servants. They were happy to find people in their departments who were friendly and helpful. To avoid making administrative blunders which would injure them in the eyes of the public and the party, the ministers gradually began to depend on the Civil Servants, who never criticized and knew the internal operations of the department.[6]

[6] "[Specialist] Ministers are likely to arrive in office, not with a complete body of specific plans, but with some general principles which the departments will be asked to test

The failure to change key members of the Civil Service had important consequences for the future work of the government, as it was interpreted by many of the officials as revealing personal weakness on the part of their ministers and a lack of political strength on the part of the movement. The Civil Servants, soon realizing that there was no danger of being discharged, fell back into the bureaucratic pattern of maintaining the traditional practices and the equilibrium of their departments. Some Civil Servants succeeded in convincing their ministers that various proposed changes were administratively infeasible, or that they would incur too much opposition from important groups in the community. Top-ranking Civil Servants exchanged information with each other on their techniques of "controlling" their ministers. It is difficult to demonstrate concretely and it would be revealing confidential information to do so, but it is a fact that in conversations with others, key officials have boasted of "running my department completely," and of "stopping harebrained radical schemes."

The resistance of top-level Civil Servants to proposed new reforms was not necessarily a result of their conscious anti-socialist sympathies. Though there were probably instances in which direct partisan sabotage of the government took place, the most significant "bureaucratic conservative" influence on the government does not appear to be a result of attempts to injure the government. Many of the leading officials appeared to be honestly concerned with doing their jobs. These Civil Servants would probably have attempted to modify schemes of conservative governments which appeared unworkable to them. The bureaucracy, however, had become institutionalized under conservative governments. Its pattern of reacting to problems had been routinized. New methods of administration were often considered difficult or "impossible" to the incumbent bureaucrat, either because they had never been tried before, or because they would require the revamping of the work of a department. By opposing such changes, the Civil Servant was only taking the easy way out of preserving the *status quo* in his own area of working and living. Harold Laski has pointed this out as a characteristic of bureaucracy in general:

In all large scale enterprise men who are desirous of avoiding great responsibility (and the majority of men is so desirous) are necessarily tempted to avoid great experiments. In a political democracy this obviously becomes an official habit where there is a . . . bureaucratic system. . . .

The tendency accordingly has been a certain suspicion of experimentalism, a benevolence toward the 'safe' man. . . . Administrative codes . . . are applied simply from the conservatism of habit.[7]

Civil Service modification of government goals took three major forms: (1) the continuation by government departments of traditional and, from the socialist point of view, "reaction-

against the facts before they are given the share of a concrete measure. The inevitable tendency of the departments will be, for the Minister's own sake, to minimize the break with tradition. . . . They will be passionately and laudably anxious to save him from failure. Unless they share his own outlook— and this is unlikely enough—they will want time where he demands speed, the attack on the narrow front, where his instruction is for comprehensiveness.

". . . . this attitude in the civil service is wholly compatible with the tradition of neutrality. . . . My point is the quite different one that . . . the whole ethos of the service becomes one of criticism which looks towards delay instead of encouragement which looks toward action." Harold Laski, *op. cit.*, pp. 103–04.

[7] Harold Laski, "Bureaucracy," in *Encyclopedia of the Social Sciences*, Volume III, ed. by Edwin R. A. Seligman (New York: The Macmillan Company, 1935), p. 72.

ary" modes of procedures; (2) changes in the intent of new laws and regulations through administrative practices; and (3) direct and indirect methods of influencing Cabinet members to adopt policies advocated by top-level Civil Servants. Each of the above statements will be documented in a larger study of the work of this government.[8]

The sources of Civil Service action cannot be found in an unidimensional analysis. Civil Servants, like all individuals, do not operate in a social vacuum (though one suspects that some advocates of the "impartial" Civil Service believe that they do). Their opinions about relative "right" and "wrong" on a particular issue are determined by various pressures existing in their social milieu. A department official is not only interested in whether a minister's proposals can be effectively put into operation, but must also be concerned with the effect of such policies on the traditional practices of the department, and of the long-term relations of the department with other groups in the government and in the community. A reform which may be socially desirable, but which disrupts the continuity of practices, and inter-personal relations within the department, will often be resisted by a top-ranking Civil Servant. He is obligated to protect those beneath him in the administrative hierarchy from the negative consequences of a change in policy.

Second, and as important in influencing the decisions of government officials, is the fact that their opinion of the feasibility of any proposal is necessarily colored by their social and political outlook and by the climate of opinion in the social group in which they move. Many of the top-ranking Civil Servants are members of the upper class socially in the capital city in which they live. Their social contacts are largely with people who believe that they will be adversely affected by many socialist policies. Civil Servants cannot avoid being influenced by the predicament of their own social group. Those government officials who belong to professional or economic groups, whose power or privileges are threatened by government policies, tend to accept the opinion of their group that reforms which adversely affect the group are wrong and will not work.[9] There are a number of examples of Civil Servants reducing the significance of reforms directed against their own groups.

The failure of this government to change the character of the top-level Civil Service precipitated a major conflict within the party between the Cabinet ministers and the majority of the non-office holding leaders of the movement. The majority of the members of the party's legislative group, the party executive, and annual convention delegates have demanded that the government replace old administrators by more sympathetic personnel. The members of these groups usually cite many examples of actions by the Civil Service which they consider to be "administrative sabotage." The attacks on the Cabinet by the rest of the party has gradually forced the Cabinet to modify its public position on the question, and in the last two years it has accepted the principle of a partially politicized bureaucracy and has appointed a number of sympathetic experts to leading positions in the administrative apparatus.

Many of the new "radical" Civil Servants have suggested new policies or specific means of carrying out overall government policy which would probably never have been proposed if policy formation had been left to the Cabinet and the permanent Civil Service. The ministers did not have the technical knowledge to suggest needed

---

[8] S. M. Lipset, *Agrarian Socialism, op. cit.*

[9] See Max Weber, *op. cit.*, p. 234.

changes in their own field, and the old Civil Servants were not imbued with the social-democratic values of finding means to reduce the wealth and power of private-interest groups and of using the agencies of the government to increase the standards of living of the people. In at least two departments the differences in orientation of the new and old Civil Service resulted in the two groups engaging in a covert struggle to determine department policy. The permanent Civil Servants in these departments repeatedly brought their ministers into contact with representatives of the more conservative groups in their field, whereas the new Civil Servants encouraged supporters of reform to visit the minister and impress him with the widespread public support for changes. Examination of the work of many government departments makes it apparent that there is a direct relationship between the extent and vigor of reform, and the degree to which the key administrative positions in a department are staffed by persons who adhered to the formal goals of the government.

In recent years many individuals have become concerned with the problem of "bureaucratic domination" in large-scale society. The justified concern with the dangers of oligarchic or "bureaucratic" domination of social organization has, however, led many persons to ignore the fact that it does make a difference to society which set of "bureaucrats" controls its destiny. To suggest, as many social scientists have, that trade unions, co-operatives, corporations, political parties, and states are large social organizations which must develop a bureaucratic structure in order to operate efficiently still leaves a large area of indeterminate social action for a bureaucratically organized society. No matter how structured a situation, every individual and group acts somewhat differently within

it, as determined by his past background and present social pressures.

The emphasis on a single theory of bureaucracy has been encouraged by the lack of a sociological approach on the part of political scientists working in the field of governmental bureaucracies. For the most part, they have not raised questions about the social origins and values of government administrators and about the relationship of such factors to government policy.[10] The determinants of the role played by the Civil Servant in affecting government policy are analyzed largely on the bureaucratic level; that is, the actions of the bureaucracy are explained in terms of the self-preservation and efficiency goals of the Civil Service. These interests may be defined in terms of prestige and privilege, preservation of existent patterns of organization or relationships within a department, or maintenance of department traditions and policies. There is as yet little formal recognition that the behavior of a governmental bureaucracy also varies with the nongovernmental social background and interests of those inhabiting the bureaucratic structure. Members of a Civil Service—like members of the judiciary, trade-unions, or business corporations—are also members of other nongovernmental social groups and classes. Social pressures from the multi-group affiliations and loyalties of individuals will determine their behavior. The behavior of an individual or group in a given situation cannot be considered as if the individual or group members had no other life outside of the given situation one is analyzing.

A permanent governmental bureauc-

[10] For two studies by sociologists which deal with this problem, see Reinhard Bendix, *Higher Civil Servants in American Society* (Boulder: University of Colorado Press, 1949), and Philip Selznick, *T.V.A. and the Grass Roots* (Berkeley: University of California Press, 1949).

racy which is part of or loyal to a minority social group can be an effective check against social reforms desired by the majority in a period of changing social values such as the present. There is no simple solution to the dilemma of keeping government administration efficient, as well as responsive to the will of the electorate. The increase in the power, functions, and sheer size of modern government necessitates the search for some means of controlling the bureaucracy. It is utopian to think that the electorate's changing the inexpert politician who formally heads the bureaucracy will by itself

change the course of the activities of the government. As Max Weber stated:

> The question is always who controls the existing bureaucratic machinery. And such control is possible only in a very limited degree to persons who are not technical specialists. Generally speaking, the trained permanent official is more likely to get his way in the long run than his nominal supervisor, the Cabinet Minister, who is not a specialist.[11]

[11] *The Theory of Social and Economic Organization*, translated by Talcott Parsons and A. R. Henderson (New York: Oxford University Press, 1947), p. 128.

32

Bureaucratization in Industry

REINHARD BENDIX

The bureaucratization of modern industry has increased over the last half century. At the same time the changes of industrial organization which have accompanied this development have contributed to industrial peace. The following essay is designed to explore some background factors which tend to support these two propositions. It seeks to establish that industrial entrepreneurs considered as a class have undergone major changes since the beginning of the 19th century. These changes have culminated in the development of an industrial bureaucracy. The consequences of this bureaucratization may be observed in the changing system of supervision as well as in the transfor-

Reprinted from *Industrial Conflict*, by Kornhauser, et al., pp. 164–75. Copyright 1954 by McGraw-Hill, Inc. Used with permission of the McGraw-Hill Book Company.

mation of the prevailing ideology of industrial managers.

Introduction

Webster's Collegiate Dictionary defines "bureaucracy" as routine procedure in administration, as a system of carrying on the business of government by means of bureaus, each controlled by a chief. This definition reflects the fact that it has not been customary to speak of bureaucracy in industry. Traditionally, the term has been applied to the activities of government; it has been broadened to include large-scale organizations generally only in recent years.

The polemic implications of the term bureaucracy obscure its use in a descriptive sense, and yet it is important to use it in that sense. "A system of carrying on the business of industry and government by means of bureaus" is a definition of "administration" as well as of bureaucracy. Yet the two terms are not synonymous. Bureaucracy suggests in addition that the number of bureaus has increased, that their functions have become specialized as well as routinized, and that increasing use is made of technical apparatus in the performance of these specialized functions, which is in turn related to the increasing use of expert, technical knowledge. The use of technical knowledge in the administration of industry implies the employment of specialists, whose work presupposes the completion of a course of professional training. The work of these specialists entails the subdivision and consequent elaboration of the managerial functions of planning, production organization, personnel selection, and supervision.

These developments have many ramifications. They depend, on the one side, on the growth of training facilities in many fields of applied science. They make possible a centralization of authority in industrial management, which can be made effective only by a simultaneous delegation of circumscribed authority to specialized bureaus or departments. This encourages the substitution of deliberately planned methods of procedure for rule-of-thumb "methods," and this in turn promotes the utilization of mechanical devices. But the adoption of rational procedures achieves greater operating efficiency than is possible in less elaborated organizational structures at the constant risk of more bureaucracy, in the negative sense.

These remarks give an idea of the complexity of the process called "bureaucratization." Little is gained, however, by adopting a concise definition of this term. It is rather intended as the common denominator of many related tendencies of administrative procedure which have characterized government and industry in recent decades.

But while the term itself remains vague, its component elements do not.

The following aspects of bureaucratization will be considered in this essay. In the first section it is shown that industrial entrepreneurs as a group have been transformed since the inception of modern industry at the beginning of the 19th century. This has resulted in the elaboration of managerial functions in industry. In the second section an attempt is made to sketch the changes of managerial ideology which have accompanied bureaucratization. The first section characterizes the development of industrial bureaucracy. In the second section certain ideological consequences are analyzed which are especially relevant for an understanding of peace and conflict in industrial relations.

Changes in Managerial Functions

The growing bureaucratization of industry may be analyzed in a variety of ways. The role of the employer has changed fundamentally since the rise of modern industry. The manager or owner of old, who knew and directed every detail of his enterprise, has become the modern industrialist who is above all else a specialist in business administration. Evidence for this transformation of the entrepreneur may be reviewed briefly.

In a report for 1792 Robert Owen states that it took him 6 weeks of careful observation to become thoroughly familiar with every detail of an enterprise employing 500 men. An enterprise employing 500 men could be comprehended and managed at one time by a man of talent and experience. It is improbable that the same could be done today. A manager of a plant with 500 employees cannot be in daily touch with the details of the manufacturing process as Owen was. He will have various subordinates to supervise this process for him; also, this manager has lost most or all of his personal contacts with the workers in the plant. And although labor may be as efficient as it had been before this depersonalization of the employment relationship, this same efficiency is now obtained "at an increased cost in supervisory staff, complicated accounting methods, precise wage systems, liberal welfare provisions, checks and balances, scheduling and routine." The point to emphasize is that bureaucratization of industry is not simply synonymous with the increasing size of the enterprise but with the growing complexity of its operation.

The bureaucratization of industry is, therefore, not simply the outcome of a recent development. In his analysis of the Boulton and Watt factory in 1775–1805 Erich Roll has described an elaborate system of keeping records, which was used as a basis of wage-determination, of cost-calculation, and of planning new methods of production. It is probable that this system was introduced when the firm passed from the original founders, who were in close contact with every operation of their enterprise, into the hands of the younger generation, who were not in touch with every operation and who, therefore, needed such a system of control. At that time few firms were organized as efficiently as Boulton and Watt, but the case illustrates the fact that the bureauc-

ratization of industry is not synonymous with the recent growth in the size of the large enterprises.

Corroborative evidence on this point is also contained in a study of American business leaders in the railroads and in the steel and textile industries, in the decade 1901–1910. The careers of 185 prominent industrialists were classified in terms of whether they had made their way in business by their own efforts exclusively, whether they had made their way in a family-owned enterprise, or whether they had risen through the ranks of an industrial bureaucracy; the results of the classification are shown in Table 1. These data make it apparent that prominent industrialists have had a bureaucratic career pattern at a relatively early time.

Occupational statistics reflect this decline of the independent enterpriser and the increase of the "industrial bureaucrat," especially in the heavy industries. In the period 1910–1940 the number of independent industrial enterprisers declined from about 425,000 in 1910 to 390,000 in 1930 and 257,000 in 1940, in manufacturing, construction, and mining. In the same industries the number of managerial employees increased from 375,976 in 1910 to 769,-749 in 1930 and 802,734 in 1940.

The bureaucratization of industry has also profoundly altered the job environ-

Table 1

American Business Leaders, by Type of Career and Date of Birth *

TYPE OF CAREER	BEFORE 1841 %	1841–1850 %	1851–1860 %	AFTER 1860 %
Independent	26	19	11	8
Family	22	24	42	36
Bureaucratic	52	57	47	56
	—	—	—	—
Total cases (= 100%)	23	59	55	25

* William Miller, "The Business Elite in Business Bureaucracies," in William Miller (ed.), *Men in Business*, Cambridge, Mass., Harvard University Press, 1952, p. 291. Reprinted by permission.

ment of the lowest rung on the managerial ladder. Until about a generation or two ago the foreman occupied a position of real importance in industry, especially with regard to the management of labor. In the majority of cases the foreman would recruit workers, he would train them on the job, he would supervise and discipline them, which included such handling of grievances as was permitted, and he would pay their wages on a time basis.

Today the foreman performs the functions of the immediate supervisor of the workers, who is in effect the executive agent of various supervisory departments. And it is increasingly a matter of discretion for these departments whether or not they decide to consult the foreman. The following summary based on a study of 100 companies which were sampled for the purpose of analyzing the *best* practices in American industry, illustrates this point clearly:

Hiring. In two-thirds of the companies replying, the personnel department interviews and selects new employees, while the foreman has final say; but in one-third the foreman has no voice in hiring.

Discharge. Foremen have some say in discharge, but only in one-tenth of all cases can they discharge without any consultation.

Pay Increases and Promotion. These must almost always be approved by other authorities.

Discipline. In only one-tenth of all cases do foremen have complete charge of discipline.

Grievances. Discussion with the foreman is generally the first step in the grievance procedure, but the extent to which he settles grievances is not clear. A small sample in the automotive-aircraft industries shows that this may range from 45 to 80%.

Policy-making. Only 20% of the companies replying held policy meetings with foremen.

These findings make it apparent that the "average" foreman's responsibilities

have remained, while his authority has been parceled out among the various supervisory departments. It is not surprising that this bureaucratization of supervisory functions has entailed inescapable tensions between the various departments performing these functions as well as tensions between these departments and the foremen. The latter have had to surrender their authority to the supervisory departments, but their responsibility for the execution of decisions has remained.

The changes in managerial functions which have grown out of the increasing division of labor within the plant and which are evident in the changing activities and career patterns of business executives and foremen are reflected also in the rise of "administrative overhead." A recent study of the rise of administrative personnel in American manufacturing industries since 1899 makes it clear that this rise has occurred throughout the economy (Table 2).

A detailed examination reveals that this over-all increase in the ratio of administrative and production personnel is *not* systematically related to any one factor except size. Melman finds, somewhat paradoxically, that administrative cost as a proportion of production cost is lower in large than in small firms, despite the general upward trend in administrative personnel. His explanation is that all firms have shown an absolute increase in administrative overhead but that at any one time large firms as a group have a proportionately lower administrative overhead than small firms. This relative advantage of the larger firms is attributed to skill in organization. In the long run, however, all firms must anticipate an increase in administrative cost.

It should be added that a comparative study of administrative personnel in the manufacturing industries of other countries reveals similar trends, though

Table 2

All Manufacturing Industries: Composition of Work Force in Administration
and Production Categories, 1899–1947 (In Thousands) *

PERSONNEL	1899	1909	1923	1929	1937	1947
Administration	457	886	1,345	1,562	1,567	2,672
Production	4,605	6,392	8,261	8,427	8,602	12,010
Administration personnel, as per cent of production personnel	9.9%	13.9%	16.3%	18.5%	18.2%	22.2%

* Seymour Melman. "The Rise of Administrative Overhead in the Manufacturing Industries
of the United States 1899–1947," *Oxford Economic Papers*, Vol. 3, No. 1 (February, 1951),
p. 66. Reprinted by permission of the Oxford University Press.

it is noteworthy that the ratio of administrative as compared with productive personnel has increased more in the United States than in France, Germany, or England. Melman's summary figures for a nationwide sample of manufacturing industries do not reveal the striking differences between industries and it may therefore be helpful to cite a few sample figures from his data (Table 3). These figures make it apparent that the over-all upward trend of administrative overhead covers a great diversity of particular developments. Although it is true that the average proportion of administration to production personnel has increased, there are significant differences between industries, and important fluctuations of this ratio have also occurred within an industry over time.

It may be useful to enumerate, in addition, some of the factors which are relevant for the interpretation of these statistics. Economically, it makes a great

Table 3

Sampled Manufacturing Industries: Administration and Production
Personnel, 1899–1937 *

INDUSTRY	Administration Personnel As Per Cent of Production Personnel				
	1899	1909	1923	1929	1937
Agricultural implements	22.1	18.6	19.8	18.3	20.6
Boots and shoes	6.2	8.1	10.8	11.0	8.5
Boxes, paper	6.3	9.1	13.6	14.4	16.1
Cash registers and business machines	15.9	23.8	23.2	36.9	37.7
Drugs and medicines	45.7	69.2	51.3	61.5	58.1
Electrical machinery	12.5	20.7	31.4	24.6	26.7
Explosives	17.3	12.3	33.6	38.2	44.4
Glass	4.5	5.3	8.6	9.7	11.5
Lighting equipment	12.8	20.1	22.9	20.6	19.2
Locomotives, not built in railroad shops	3.9	13.6	9.5	20.9	29.8
Meat packing, wholesale	15.3	20.1	24.8	22.8	29.2
Motor vehicles	13.1	13.3	11.5	14.8	16.9
Petroleum refining	10.0	19.3	24.1	35.6	45.3

* Seymour Melman. "The Rise of Administrative Overhead in the Manufacturing Industries
of the United States 1899–1947," *Oxford Economic Papers*, Vol. 3, No. 1 (February, 1951),
p. 66. Reprinted by permission of the Oxford University Press.

difference whether administrative personnel in industry increases together with a rapidly or a slowly expanding work force. That is to say, increasing administrative expenditures can be easily sustained in a rapidly expanding industry. Also, the increases of personnel in administration are accompanied by capital investments. Today, a given number of clerks can do a great deal more work than formerly, with the aid of various computing and multigraphing machines. As a group they also do a greater variety of work, owing to specialization and partial mechanization. However, neither the greater complexity of administrative work nor the various efforts at standardization and routinization can be measured by the number of clerks employed. The increase of administrative personnel is, therefore, only a proximate measure of bureaucratization.

Managerial Ideology and Bureaucracy

The general trend is in the direction of an increase in the complexity of managerial tasks. To assess the problems created by this trend, it is not sufficient, for example, to describe how the functions of hiring and discharge, of administering an equitable wage structure, and of processing grievances and disciplining workers have become the special tasks of separate departments. In order to understand the modern problems of management, we must realize that this separation of functions has created for all ranks of management an ambiguity which is in many respects similar to, though it is not so intense as, that of the foreman. The over-all managerial problem has become more complex because each group of management specialists will tend to view the "interests of the enterprise" in terms which are compatible with the survival and the increase of its special function. That is, each group will have a trained capacity for its own function and a "trained incapacity" to see its relation to the whole.

The problem of industrial management is to subdivide, as well as to coordinate, the tasks of administration and production and then to maximize the efficiency of each operation. In so doing it employs specialists, and each group of specialists must exercise considerable discretion in order to get the work done. That is to say, with each step toward specialization the centrifugal tendencies and, hence, the coordinating tasks of central management increase. Bureaucratization has accompanied the whole development of industry, but it has increased more rapidly since the inception of scientific management in the 1890's. The major development of trade-unions has occurred during the same period. If we consider these parallel changes it becomes apparent that the greater complexity of the managerial task has consisted in the need for intramanagerial coordination at a time when managerial leadership was challenged by the organizing drives of trade-unions as well as by the ideological attacks of the muckrakers. Hence the ideology of business leaders, their justification of the authority they exercise and of the power they hold, has gradually assumed a double function: (1) to demonstrate that the authority and power of the industrial leader is legitimate and (2) to aid the specific job of managerial coordination.

Until recently the ideologies of the industrial leaders did not serve this double function. In the past their leadership was justified by a reiteration of time-tested shibboleths which would make clear what was already self-evident to all but the most die-hard radicals. Success is virtue, poverty is sin, and both result from the effort or indolence of the individual. Together with this belief went the idea that every use made of poverty was beneficial to the social welfare, as long as it resulted in an increase of wealth. These ideas, which justified the authority and power of the industrial leaders, established a goal in life for everyone. The tacit assumption was that in the prevailing economic order the chances of each "to get to the top" were the same. Hence the success of the industrial leader was itself the token of his proved superiority in a struggle between equals. To question this was to bar the way of those who would succeed after him.

These ideas have never really died; there is much contemporary evidence to show that the beliefs of industrial leaders have remained essentially the same. Successful industrialists as a group have always tended to express views which ranged from the belief that their virtue had been proved by their works and that their responsibilities were commensurate with their wealth to the assertion that their eminence was self-evident and that their privileges could not be questioned. They would speak with Andrew Carnegie of the "trusteeship of wealth" and point to their benevolent relations to their employees, their philanthropic activities, and their great contributions to the nation's wealth as evidence of their worth. Others would think of themselves as "Christian men to whom God in his infinite wisdom has given the control of the property interest of the country." Nor can we dismiss the possibility that some of these industrial giants would say the first and think the second.

Fifty years later the same opinions are expressed, albeit in modern dress. Alfred P. Sloan writes:

those charged with great industrial responsibility must become industrial statesmen. . . . Industrial management must expand its horizon of responsibility. It must recognize that it can no longer confine its activities to the mere production of goods and services. It must consider the impact of its operations on the economy as a whole in relation to the social and economic welfare of the entire community.

On the other hand, Tom Girdler has written of his role in the company town which he had helped to develop:

In fact I suppose I was a sort of political boss. Certainly I had considerable power in politics without responsibility to "the people." But who were the people in question? An overwhelming majority of them were the men for whom the company aspired to make Woodlawn the best steel town in the world . . . What did it matter if the taxes were soundly spent? What did it matter if Woodlawn had just about the best school system in Pennsylvania? What did it matter if there were no slums, no graft, no patronage, no gambling houses, no brothels? What did it matter if it was a clean town?

If all these wonderful things were done by the company for the people of Woodlawn, what did it matter that the company and its managers were not responsible to the people? As an Episcopalian vestry man, Girdler could also speak of Christian men who, by the grace of God, controlled the property interests of the community on behalf of the people.

Businessmen express themselves with the intention of demonstrating statesmanship and intransigeance, then as now. Yet even the celebration of the industrial leader has had to accommodate, albeit tardily, the Puritan virtues of hard work, frugality, and unremitting effort to the qualities useful in a bureaucratic career. As the size and bureaucratization of business increased, this ideological accommodation could no longer be accomplished on the model of the Horatio Alger story. Of course, the idea of success as a reward of virtue is as much in evidence today as it was 100 years ago. But the celebration of the industrial leader can no longer suffice; it is accompanied today by a celebration of the organization and of the opportunities it has to offer. When A. P. Sloan writes that "the corporation [is] a pyramid of opportunities from the bottom to the top with thousands of chances for advancement" he refers to the promise of a bureaucratic career not to the earlier image of the individual enterpriser. And when he adds that "only capacity limited any worker's chance to improve his own position," he simply ignores the fact that the methods of promotion themselves are bureaucratized, that they are regarded as a legitimate object of collective-bargaining strategies between union and management, and that under these circumstances minimum rather than maximum capacity is often a sufficient basis for promotion. At any rate, the idea of thousands of chances for promotion is different from the idea of individual success. Outstanding industrial leaders of today will reflect this difference in their attempts to define the image of success in an era of bureaucratization.

It is important to recognize that today managerial ideology performs a second function. While it is still designed to inspire confidence in the leaders of industry, it should also aid modern managers to achieve effective coordination within their enterprises, which is today a far more difficult task than it was formerly. There is a literature of advice to the ambitious young man which has accompanied the development of industry. In this literature the hero cult of the industrial leader has been abandoned gradually, and advice well suited to the industrial bureaucrat has taken its place. Hero cult and advice to the industrial bureaucrat involve partly incompatible themes. The qualities of ruthlessness and competitive drive, while appropriate for the "tycoon," are ill suited for his managerial employees. This does not mean that these qualities are no longer useful but that they no longer provide a workable rationale for the majority of industrial managers.

It may be useful to put formulations of these two themes side by side. The classic text of the individual enterpriser is *Self-help with Illustrations of Character, Conduct and Perseverance*, written by Samuel Smiles in 1859 and copied interminably ever since. Its purpose was,

to re-inculcate these old-fashioned but wholesome lessons . . . that youth must work in order to enjoy—that nothing creditable can be accomplished without application and diligence—that the student must not be daunted by difficulties, but conquer them by patience and perseverance—and that, above all, he must seek elevation of character, without which capacity is worthless and worldly success is naught.

The classic text of the industrial bureaucrat is *Public Speaking and Influencing Men in Business*, written by Dale Carnegie in 1926 and used as the "official text" by such organizations as the New York Telephone Company, the America Institute of Banking, the YMCA schools, the National Institute of Credit, and others. Though there is no single statement of purpose which can be cited, the following summary statement will suffice: "We have only four contacts with people. We are evaluated and classified by four things: by what we do, by how we look, by what we say, and how we say it." In his foreword to this book Lowell Thomas has written a testimonial to Dale Carnegie which gives the gist of this and many similar books with admirable clarity:

Carnegie started at first to conduct merely a course in public speaking: but the students who came were businessmen. Many of them hadn't seen the inside of a class room in thirty years. Most of them were paying their tuition on the installment plan. They wanted results; and they wanted them quick —results that they could use the next day in business interviews and in speaking before groups.

So he was forced to be swift and practical. Consequently, he has developed a
system of training that is unique—a striking combination of Public Speaking, Salesmanship, Human Relationship, Personality
Development and Applied Psychology. . . .
Dale Carnegie . . . has created one of the
most significant movements in adult education.

This new ideology of personality
salesmanship appeared to put within
reach of the average person the means
by which to climb the ladder to success. No doubt this accounts for its
popularity. But it should be added that
its public acceptance implied a prior
disillusion with the more old-fashioned
methods of achieving success. The bureaucratization of modern industry has
obviously increased the number of steps
from the bottom to the top at the same
time that it has made the Puritan virtues largely obsolete. It is probable,
then, that the techniques of personality
salesmanship became popular when the
ideal of individual entrepreneurship
ceased to be synonymous with success,
while the image of a career of promotions from lower to higher positions became of greater significance. From the
standpoint of the individual these techniques became a means of career advancement; from the standpoint of
management they seemed to facilitate
the coordination of a growing and increasingly specialized staff. In the context of American society this new
ideology reflected the increasing importance of the service trades as well as
the growing demand for skill in personnel relations.

These considerations place the hu-
man-relations approach to the problems
of labor management in a historical
perspective. Attention to human relations has arisen out of the managerial
problems incident to the bureaucratization of industry. It has also arisen out
of the discrepancy between a people's
continued desire for success and the

increasing disutility of the Puritan virtues or of the tenets of Darwinian
morality. But whatever their origins,
the "personality cult" as well as the
more sophisticated philosophies of personnel management have helped to
make more ambiguous the position of
the industrial manager. In giving orders
to his subordinates in the past, the manager could claim to derive his authority
from the rights of ownership conferred
on him. For a long time the managerial
employee had represented the "heroic
entrepreneur," and he had justified his
own actions by the right which success
had bestowed upon him. But with the
dispersion of ownership this justification
became increasingly tenuous. Strictly
speaking, the old ideology of success no
longer applied to the managers since
theirs was a bureaucratic, not an entrepreneurial, success. As the human-rela-
tions approach is extended downward
from the office staff to the work force,
managers come to attenuate their tough-
minded conception of authority. But
in so doing they are never single-minded.
Their careers are often inspired by the
older belief in the self-made man,
though this belief is more and more at
variance with their own experience in
industry. In asserting their authority
over subordinates as if they were the
successful entrepreneurs of old, they
come into conflict with the bureaucratic
reality of their own careers. Yet if they
adjust their beliefs to that reality, then
they are faced with the dilemma of
exercising authority while they deny the
traditional claims which had hitherto
justified this authority.

It is at this point that managers are
divided today in their attitudes toward
their employees and toward their own
exercise of authority. Many continue to
believe in the heroic entrepreneur whose
success is justification in itself, and they
consequently resist the "tender-minded"
approach to human relations in industry. They also resist recognition of the

fact that the industrial environment has changed. Others have begun to reformulate the older statements of "business statesmanship" and "business responsibility" in keeping with the realities of industry in an era of bureaucratization. But in their attempts to do so they have had to demonstrate the self-evident truths once more that the economy provides ample opportunities, given drive and talent, and that those who succeed deserve to do so and provide a model to be followed. To develop an ideology along these lines by advertising the techniques of personality salesmanship and by celebrating the career opportunities of an industrial bureaucracy implies an interest in industrial peace, for these techniques and opportunities are beside the point under conditions of conflict. The new ideology is less combative than the old; but it is also insufficient because its appeals are more readily applicable to the salaried employee than to the industrial worker. The idea that all employees are members of "one big happy family" is a case in point, for the efforts to make this idea meaningful to the workers frequently take the form of personalizing an impersonal employment relationship. Perhaps this is appropriate for the managerial and ideological coordination of the salaried employees. It is, moreover, not surprising that the idea of the "family of employers and employees" often becomes the fighting creed of hard-pressed executives who seek to solidify their enterprises against the competing appeals of the trade-unions. But there is an element of cant in this approach which does not make it a promising foundation for a new ideology as long as democratic institutions prevail. Perhaps Horatio Alger is so reluctant to pass into limbo because his image implied an idealistic message. Perhaps it is the absence of such a message which makes the appeal to employees as members of a family so questionable. The ideological rationale of an economic order should have a positive meaning for everyone. The fact is that in this era of bureaucratization the industrialist does not have a fighting creed.

33

Professionalization and the Organization of Middle-Class Labour in Postindustrial Society*

ELIOT FREIDSON

Every generation considers itself to be new and modern. And this is proper,

Reprinted from The Sociological Review Monograph no. 20: "Professionalization and Social Change," University of Keele, 1973.
* I wish to thank Arlene K. Daniels for comments on an earlier version of this paper.

for the contemporary is by definition what is only just being experienced in the knife-edge of the present. The problem for the participant and the analyst alike, however, is to determine whether the present is 'really' new and modern, or whether it is, as the elderly are characteristically inclined to believe, just variation on settled and familiar themes. If it is merely the latter, then there is no serious point to changing our way of looking at the present or of assuming that it is leading us toward some qualitatively different future. But if it is the former, then we must ask what the genuinely new means for the future—whether it is part of a trend which leads to far-reaching shifts of emphasis in basic social institutions, or whether it is an isolated event. And if it appears to be part of a distinct trend, we must, as scholars and scientists, examine the value of our conceptual equipment for analyzing it. Unfortunately, our conceptual equipment at any particular time is far more likely to be useful for ordering the past events it was created to deal with than it is for understanding genuinely new events of the present or the future.

Our own time seems to be one in which something genuinely new is emerging. Many analysts believe that major changes are taking place in the most advanced industrial societies. Those changes are seen to be as basic and far-reaching as those which occurred two hundred years ago and which are now summed up as the Industrial Revolution. Various writers have struggled to find an appropriate name for the emergent society, but it seems to me that until future historians, from their more advantageous, backward-looking perspective, create and agree on their own epithet, Bell's term, 'postindustrial,' is the most useful, avoiding neologism while at the same time connoting departure from the society we know. (Bell, 1967.) I shall use it throughout this paper.

But while many analysts seem agreed that what is new and modern in our time is something with profound consequences for the nature of society, their discussions remain fixed on substance. They are not concerned about the ab-

stract analytical implications of those changes for the basic sociological concepts we have used to analyse the mechanisms ordering industrial society. These analysts discuss technology, including data-processing, automation and communications, they discuss its foundation in 'technique' and special knowledge, and they discuss the economy, but they do not consider the social forms by which all will be organized and dispensed. They pay little attention to social organization, apparently assuming that traditional forms will persist. But if change is to be so radical, should we expect that our present received concepts of social organization are of such universal pertinence that they can be applied without question? Is it not quite plausible that habits of thought, strategies, foci and concepts developed for the analysis of industrial society may *not* be equally useful and well-fitted to the analysis of postindustrial society?

I shall argue in this paper that if what is being said about postindustrial society is true, then very basic sociological concepts for the analysis of the social organization of work must be reconsidered. One of the most basic of such concepts is that of the division of labour and, particularly, the principle of authority which establishes, coordinates and controls specialized labour. Since the Industrial Revolution, administrative authority has been emphasized. However, in this paper I wish to suggest that a key to concepts better fitted to the emergent new society lies in the logic embedded in the concept of professionalization, which stresses a different principle of authority over labour. To show this, I shall briefly review what most writers agree are the important characteristics of the emergent society. Next, I shall point out what this view implies about the usefulness of what is by now our almost instinctive reliance on the concepts of administrative authority forged for the analysis of industrial society. Then I shall discuss how the concept of the authority of institutionalized expertise implicit in the idea of professionalization may prove far more useful and fitting than the traditional concept of rational-legal administrative authority.

The Prototypical Postindustrial Worker

Some of the elements of the postindustrial society are predicated on the assumption that the trends of the past few decades will continue and even accelerate until a basic point of balance is passed. In this situation, formerly minor segments of the work force will become critical. The decline of agricultural labour and the rise of industrial labour created such a change of balance between types of workers in the development of industrial society. In the present-day, prophets note the decline of industrial or manufacturing labour as a trend indicating that future workers will be engaged primarily in clerical, sales and service work. (Fuchs, 1966.) Massive as the manufacturing or industrial base of the society will remain, its labour requirements will both decline and change, as machines tend themselves and other machines, and as the demand for highly trained labour expands while that for unskilled and semiskilled labour contracts. Just as men are still engaged in agricultural work now in advanced industrial society, so will men still be engaged in manufacturing in the future, but the bulk of men will be engaged in other kinds of work, and factory labour will cease to be archetypal in the emerging age.

If this redistribution occurs, who will be the archetypal worker in postindustrial society? Most writers emphasize the significance of workers practising complex skills for which higher education is thought necessary. (Cf. Bell, 1968; Lane, 1966; Etzioni, 1968.) Virtually all see the new society as being 'knowledge-based', but some emphasize one kind of knowledge-based worker while others emphasize another. Those like John Kenneth Galbraith (1968), who are interested in state and corporate manufacturing and commercial enterprise, emphasize the role of the expert who plans and makes decisions, and are prone in that context to use the word 'technocrat'. (Cf. Touraine, 1971.) The workers they refer to are engineers, economists, systems analysts, and specially trained managers. Others, like Bennis (Bennis and Slater, 1969), Bell (1968) and Lane (1966) are somewhat more general, emphasizing a broad class of professional-technical workers, and the educational and scientific estate (Price, 1965) which trains them and creates their knowledge. Still others, and most especially Halmos (1970), emphasize the role of the professional and semiprofessional personal service worker—the teacher, physician, social worker, nurse, counsellor, and the like who are connected with the social, psychological, medical and other 'helping' services of the welfare state.

Each writer on the postindustrial society has a particular issue in mind, and so properly emphasizes one kind of worker over another. While all workers may be alike in possessing higher education, they are educated in quite different subjects and by quite different methods, they perform quite different kinds of work, and have quite different kinds of responsibility. Higher education, as such, no matter what the curriculum and the job prepared for, does not discriminate analytic differences in function as basic as that between manager and worker. That difference is the key to understanding how work gets organized. And it is also the key to discerning how postindustrial society may differ from industrial society in ways not recognized by those who stress the role of knowledge in the abstract without asking how knowledge gets organized as work.

What is the traditional difference between manager and worker? In industrial society, managers, administrators, supervisors, or other officials of the formal productive organization exercise authority over workers. They establish the organization, determine the set of tasks necessary to attain their production goals, employ, train, assign and supervise men to perform those tasks, and coordinate the interrelations of the various tasks so as to gain their ends. The worker, on the other hand, is the one who performs those directly productive tasks which have been organized, supervised and coordinated by the manager. It is this by-now self-evident distinction which becomes problematic in the postindustrial society.

What is of great importance about the forecasts of postindustrial labour is that they imply that large numbers of the prototypical 'knowledge-based' tasks are *productive* rather than managerial. Research scientists, teachers and physicians, for example, characteristically perform a kind of productive labour, even if the labour is not necessarily manual and oriented to the production of services rather than goods. In contrast, other knowledge-based workers perform managerial functions, setting up frameworks of authority and communication to facilitate the performance of labour. Each has a generically different function, the task of one being to organize the labour of the other. What is different in the forecasts of the postindustrial society is that they imply that *the capacity of managers to control the productive workers* is open to serious question in ways that have not really existed in industrial society.

In industrial society, the prototypical productive worker—the lower class factory hand—is ordered and controlled ever more systematically by management. But the prototypical productive worker of the postindustrial society— the middle class knowledge-based worker —may be in a position to resist much managerial authority and control. Even now, the ambiguous position of knowledge-based productive labour in the present conventional industrial scheme of administration is mirrored by its anomalous classification as 'staff' rather than as 'line'. The *jobs* or organizational positions are dependent on management for capital, supportive services and at least some lines of communication, but the *tasks* of these workers are not. Their tasks are not created by or dependent on management, nor are the qualifications to perform them so dependent. Finally, evaluation of the performance of those tasks does not rest solely with management.

In essence, the prototypical worker of industrial society operates clearly and unambiguously under the authority of management, but the prototypical workers of postindustrial society may work in a radically different way which limits seriously the traditional authority of management. Whereas 30 or 40 years ago one could talk of the 'revolution' whereby management took authority from the owner, (Burnham, 1960) writers like Galbraith can now write that the 'technostructure . . . not management, is the guiding intelligence—the brain—of the [business] enterprise'. (Galbraith, 1968, p. 82.) Being the brain is not the same thing as setting goals and being in charge, but it does make the authority of management problematic. In earlier industrial enterprises, management was the brain as well as the authority.

The Limitation of Managerial Rationalization

Apparently, neither the tasks nor the status of these postindustrial workers seem amenable to the kind of rationalization that was applied by management to the factory line worker in industrial society. Indeed, it is precisely crisis in managerial rationalization and control (Cf. Berkley, 1971) which prophets of a new society imply when they point to the emergence of a growing collection of increasingly strategic productive workers whose comparatively abstract skills require long training and are surrounded by a mystique of the esoteric and the complex. Those strategic skills are of such a nature that they resist managerial rationalization as manual and clerical skills have not been able to do. They do so in part because of their intrinsically complex character, but even more because of the occupational organization which grows up around them. Their occupational organization is a function of professional socialization rather than on-the-job training. Some of the motivation to identification with institutionalized skills and to solidarity with colleagues stems from the requirement of a long period of formal education. Long training is a socially, economically and psychologically costly investment which virtually presupposes expectation of a stable life-long career, and fairly extensive bonds and common interests shared with others going through the same process. Higher vocational education does not merely insert 'knowledge' into people's heads, but also builds expectations and commitments not easily overcome by managerial or policy rationalization. Organized specialized occupational identities get constructed. Knowledge gets institutionalized as expertise. The structure of meanings and commitments can override organizational goals or commitments.

The sociological rather than merely technical or economic significance of a long period of training in putatively complex and abstract skills—that is, of 'knowledge-based' skill—lies in its tendency to develop institutionalized commitments on the part of those trained.

Such trained workers are inclined to identify with their skill and with their fellows with the same training and skill. They are prone to develop not merely general *skill-class*, or mass solidarity, as is sometimes the case with industrial workers in trade unions, but *disciplinary* or occupational solidarity. Their skill is not merely abstractly there as a potential, but it is institutionalized as a stable discipline or occupation. Such trained workers do not constitute a class of labour which can be treated as mere hands, to perform whatever tasks management may invent for them and then train them for. Rather, they are a kind of labour with preexistent skills for which management may have a need, but which management must take more or less as given. Their tasks are instituitionalized occupationally, and thus resist simplification, fragmentation, mechanization or some other mode of managerial rationalization of labour.

The Limitation of Managerial Authority

If it is true that a new kind of highly educated labour with specialized skills is becoming more important to the emergent society, and that the skills involved resist managerial rationalization, what are the consequences? Even now we can see some of them. The character of managerial or administrative authority which developed in the Industrial Revolution is at present experiencing such radical changes that the traditional concepts of managerial authority and formal corporate structure are being questioned. Indeed, an increasing number of writers argue that reality has deviated so far from the concepts of monocratic, 'rational-legal' administration, formal organization, hierarchical order and bureaucracy that new concepts are needed which pick out the analytically significant elements of the emergent forms of organization. Such new concepts must, of course, perform the same analytical function as traditional ones, the most important of which is to specify the nature and source of the control and coordination of various kinds of specialized labour so that some productive goal can be reached. If traditional managerial or administrative authority has lost much of its strength, but specialization and division of labour continue unabated, what does organize labour and how is it coordinated? This question has barely been considered by writers on the postindustrial society other than on the very broad and vague level of societal or social policy goals. An answer to the question on a more concrete level is hinted at, however, by passing references to professionalization.

As I have already noted, most writers agree on the strategic importance of workers with skills requiring long formal education, skills rather more esoteric and abstract than the manual and clerical skills organized and even imparted by management in the past. The problem is how, if not by management, such special skills get organized and coordinated. A number of writers have implied the answer. Ellul wrote, 'technique always creates a kind of secret society, a closed fraternity of its practitioners'. (Ellul, 1964, p. 162.) Skill can form the focus, in short, of an occupational group which then claims the authority of its institutionalized expertise over the performance of its work. This tendency is recognized by Galbraith in his observation that men of the technostructure are inclined to identify themselves with their department or function rather than with the corporation as a whole (Galbraith, 1968, pp. 162–168) and by Bennis in his delineation of 'pseudo-species' as 'bands of specialists held together by the illusion of a unique identity and with a tendency to view other pseudo-species with suspicion and mistrust'. (Bennis and Slater, 1968, p. 66.) The

suggestions all point to the development of solidarity among workers practising the same specialized skill, an organized solidarity strong enough to resist the pressure toward integration and rationalization exerted by management. The solidarity is of specialty, as discussed by Durkheim (1964), not of skill-class. Such solidarity suggests that professionalization will be a critical element in the organization of production in postindustrial society.

'Profession', 'professionalization', and 'professional' are all extremely ambiguous words, much of their stubborn imprecision hinging on their confusing and sometimes incompatible multiple connotations. But there is no other word in the English language which can be used to represent an occupation so well organized that its members can realistically envisage a career over most of their working years, a career during which they retain a particular occupational identity and continue to practise the same skills no matter what the institution they work in. A similar form of organization is to be found in the skilled trade or craft, though the craft cannot claim the same kind of knowledge-based skill as can the profession.

Such organized occupations can be contrasted with traditional industrial labour. As opposed to organized occupations with concrete and particular identity, much industrial labour revolves around forms of work which are rather more appropriately called jobs or positions than occupations, since they are merely specially constituted tasks in a division of labour created, coordinated and controlled by management. Those jobs are created, dissolved and reconstituted by management on the basis of changing production goals or needs, changing technology, or further rationalization for the end of greater productivity or lower cost. They have no social or economic foundation for their persistence beyond the plants, agencies or firms in which they exist. The persons performing concrete tasks constituted as jobs may not perform them for long, since the job can get eliminated or reconstituted. The workers are identified primarily by the general substance and level of their skill—e.g., manual or clerical, unskilled or semiskilled or skilled—and if they are organized into such corporate associations as unions, it is more on the basis of industry or skill-class than on the basis of substantive skill and training. Such labour organizations are far more concerned with wages, working conditions, job security and advancement than with control over tasks constituting jobs.

For industrially organized workers the substance of the work and who can do it are established and controlled by the manager or administrator. Tasks are planned around some managerial goal and men hired and trained to perform them. This is the norm for the way the Industrial Revolution has, historically, rationalized labour by first dissolving preindustrial functional differentiation by craft and land, and then reorganizing the labour of massed, undifferentiated workers around managerial authority. But workers organized by professional or craft associations both now and in the past establish and control the substance of their work as well as who can do it. Specialized fragments of the labour market split off and become organized and stabilized around tasks which the workers have institutionalized. (Cf. Kerr, 1954.) Organized occupations like professions and crafts which institutionalize specialization are at once a survival and a revival of preindustrial modes of organizing work. They are alternatives to administrative rationalization.

The key to assessing whether or not the organized occupation will gain even more strength in the future society is the degree to which all work can be rationalized and therefore reconstituted and controlled by management. It seems to be implicit in discussions of the prototypical worker of the postindustrial society that knowledge-based work, the work of middle-class experts, professionals and technicians, is by its very nature *not* amenable to the mechanization and rationalization which industrial production and commerce have undergone over the past century. If it is true that management cannot rationalize such work—whether for technological, economic, political-legal or even ideological or class reasons—then it can only maintain an administrative framework around it. Management remains dependent for attaining its goals on the worker but is unable to really control who performs the work and how it is done. Instead of an industrial bureaucratic structure, with authority organized vertically, management can only organize supportive services vertically, leaving authority over the work to the workers themselves. Management may set goals, but it may not set means or connect means to goals.

Coordination of the Division of Labour

But if management cannot exercise much authority over task, how are varied tasks coordinated? How is the division of labour organized? Traditionally, the division of labour has been seen as a purely functional array of interdependent tasks performed by an aggregate of individuals possessing the necessary skills. For Adam Smith, the division of labour meant individual men competing with each other for employment to perform more or less abstractly conceived specialized and interdependent tasks. Coordination of all tasks was supposed to take place in part by the natural operation of the forces of the free market and in part, albeit implicitly, by entrepreneurs who invent cheaper ways of producing goods. Any explicit social combination of the participants in the division of labour was considered unnatural. But in reality, if only out of economic self-interest, both labour and capital were prone to organize into combinations designed to influence the labour market in ways that aggregates of competing individuals could not. While Smith's *concept* of the division of labour ruled out social organization, in the historical *reality* of the Industrial Revolution the division of labour has been continuously subject to socially organized forces and has never been a merely technical arrangement of specialized, interdependent tasks. Empirically, we must treat the division of labour as a social organization.

Historically, the social organization of the division of labour has been constituted by interaction between two radically different ways of organizing the human labour necessary to perform interdependent tasks, and of defining the tasks themselves. The common terms 'bureaucratization' and 'professionalization' denote, albeit crudely, those two different modes of organization. In the former case, the character of the task, who will perform it, the way it is performed and evaluated, and the way it will be related to others is created by management. The worker is recruited and organized to perform it. The worker and his labour are mere plastic materials for management, materials organized into jobs by managerial conceptions of the tasks necessary for the production of some good or service for the market. This mode of organizing the division of labour is implicit in Smith, and it is the mode characteristic of industrial society. Coordination of the division of labour in an industrial organization can easily be seen as a function of managerial or bureaucratic authority. In the case of professionalization, however, the task, who is to perform it, and the way it is performed and evaluated is controlled by the men who actually perform the productive labour. Labour is organized into specialized occupations which control their own tasks, and the division of labour is constituted as a congeries of such organized occupations. In this case, however, the mechanism by which the work of the various occupations are coordinated appears problematic. How can any regulation exist *between* occupations without the monocratic authority of management?

If, as is characteristically the case for *industrial* labour, the authority for the definition of tasks and their organization into jobs lies in management, then the division of labour can be seen to be constituted by the jobs which management creates, defines and maintains. Managerial authority coordinates the relationships between the productive tasks accomplished by every job. Bureaucratization refers to a monocratic ordering of functions into jobs governed by particular rational-legal rules. If, on the other hand, as may characteristically be the case for *postindustrial* society, the authority for definition and organization of task comes from the prototypical workers themselves, then the division of labour must be seen to be constituted by the occupations into which work is organized and the relationship between occupations defined and ordered by the jurisdictions established among occupations. Those jurisdictions can be established in a variety of ways, the most formal being by exclusive licensing and by contract.

Occupational jurisdictions must be seen as establishing the boundaries of institutionalized tasks and also, what is often overlooked, the occupational authority to coordinate interrelated tasks. They establish, in short, their own species of hierarchical authority in the division of labour, authority predicated on institutionalized expertise rather than on that of bureaucratic office. Such authority gives some occupations the legitimate right to command the work of other occupations. Even now, as a class, the professions provide examples of how a structure of occupations can be ordered and coordinated hierarchically by the authority of institutionalized expertise. Medicine, for example, gives orders to a wide variety of other workers in an interdependent technical enterprise, and does so even when those workers are in the employ of others. In medicine, the division of labour is ordered and coordinated by a dominant profession rather than by management. (Freidson, 1970.) The division of labour thus does not need management for its coordination; an at least logically possible alternative to management exists in the form of the occupational principle of authority over work (Freidson, 1973.) Prophecies of postindustrial society suggest that there is a very real empirical possibility that the new division of labour may in fact require a shift from managerial to occupational authority.

The Social Role of Knowledge

In this paper I have argued that if the 'knowledge-based' worker is to be prototypical in the postindustrial society, then concepts of the mechanisms by which productive labour is organized, controlled and coordinated must be examined closely. I suggested that the prime mechanism of the Industrial Revolution was administrative or bureaucratic authority, the strength of which was predicated on its capacity to rationalize tasks into jobs for which it could itself mobilize and train labour. 'Knowledge-based' labour, however, may be resistant to rationalization both by the very nature of the skill and knowledge it possesses, and by its tendency to organize itself into stable occupations similar to those of present-day professions. Indeed, I suggested that the mechanism for organizing, controlling and even coordinating specialized labour to be found among professions today—the authority of institutionalized expertise—may be far more useful for visualizing the substance of the Postindustrial Revolution than reliance on now-traditional notions of rational-legal authority and bureaucracy.

Underlying the analysis in this paper is the assumption that knowledge is a problematic concept with implications which cannot be seen clearly until translated into human activity—into men who are recruited, trained and then led to engage in the work of producing, communicating or practising knowledge, technique or skill. It is assumed, furthermore, that work is analyzed inadequately if it is seen as an individual activity, that when more than one person does the same work, the possibility exists that the aggregate of workers will form a group. Should this occur, the purely rational, functional, technical quality thought to inhere in the work itself becomes incorporated into and transformed by a social, political and economic enterprise. It loses its abstract purity and maybe even its virtue. Thus, whether or not one sees hope for a future in which 'knowledge' becomes the critical guiding force of postindustrial society depends on how one can visualize the ways in which the use of that knowledge is likely to be organized and controlled.

References

BELL, DANIEL: 'Notes on the Post-Industrial Society', *The Public Interest*, 6 (Winter), pp. 24–45 and 7 (Spring), pp. 102–118, 1967.

BELL, DANIEL: 'The Measurement of Knowledge and Technology', pp. 145–246 in E. B. Sheldon and W. E. Moore, eds., *Indicators of Social Change*. Russell Sage Foundation, New York, 1968.

BENNIS, W. G. and SLATER, P. E., *The Temporary Society*, Harper and Row, New York, 1969.

BERKLEY, G. E.: *The Administrative Revolution*, Prentice-Hall, Englewood Cliffs, 1971.

BURNHAM, JAMES: *The Managerial Revolution*, Indiana University Press, Bloomington, 1960.

DURKHEIM, EMILE: *The Division of Labor in Society*, The Free Press, New York, 1964.

ELLUL, JACQUES: *The Technological Society*, Vintage Books, New York, 1964.

ETZIONI, AMITAI: *The Active Society*, The Free Press, New York, 1968.

FREIDSON, ELIOT: *Professional Dominance*, Aldine-Atherton, Chicago, 1970.

FRIEDSON, ELIOT: 'Professions and the Occupational Principle', in E. Friedson (ed.): *The Professions and Their Prospects*, Sage Publications, Beverly Hills, California, 1973.

FUCHS, V. R.: 'The First Service Economy', *The Public Interest* 2 (Winter), 7–17, 1966.

GALBRAITH, J. K.: *The New Industrial State*, New American Library, New York, 1968.

HALMOS, PAUL: *The Personal Service Society*, Schocken Books, New York, 1970.

KERR, CLARK: 'The Balkanization of Labor Markets', pp. 92–110 in E. W. Bakke (ed.): *Labor Markets and Economic Opportunity*, John Wiley &-Sons, New York, 1954.

LANE, R. E.: 'The Decline of Politics and Ideology in a Knowledgeable Society', *American Sociological Review*, 31, pp. 649–662, 1966.

PRICE, D. K.: *The Scientific Estate*, Harvard University Press, Cambridge, 1965.

TOURAINE, A.: *The Post-Industrial Society*, Random House, New York, 1971.

34

Bureaucracy and Freedom

ALFRED WEBER

It is almost commonplace to observe that we live in an era of increasing bureaucratization of our existence. To discuss bureaucracy and freedom meaningfully is to inquire into the common

Reprinted from the *Modern Review*, 3–4: 176–186 (March–April 1948), by permission of the publisher.

conditions of social life that are conducive to such bureaucratization; to ask what specific forms it assumes and to what extent it is avoidable and escapable; how we can evade the obvious implicit danger of its degenerating into totalitarianism or even terrorism; in brief, how to preserve liberty.

Historically, bureaucracy is not a

novel phenomenon. Indeed, the history of advanced human civilization began with bureaucracies that upheld and gave shape to the entire social life of the time. The hieratically-organized priesthood that created and guarded the magically-sanctified way of life, under pharaohs and emperors in ancient Egypt and Babylon, was probably the most "totalitarian" bureaucracy history has ever known. In its all-pervading forms and formulae, it conditioned not only the outer but also the inner manifestations of life—which in their totality could not be tampered with if its magic forces were to be kept intact. But this apparatus required no special instrument of self-perpetuation—neither a strong police nor a standing army. Only some 1500 years later, about 2000 b.c., were such special institutions established in defense against the nomads pressing in from without. These first great totalitarian bureaucratic structures could afford not to stain themselves with instruments of compulsion; they never experienced freedom as their antagonist.

The primary civilizations of China and India were likewise permeated with a strong bureaucratic web, similarly established on a basis of magic acceptance. In India, it was at an early point replaced by the caste system developed by the carriers of this magic faith—the Brahmins—who utilized the primitive belief in the transmigration of the soul and infused a solid skeleton of hieratic, functional division of labor into the existential matrix. There was no longer any need for a distinct layer of professional officialdom. Little remained of individual freedom of action in either the practical or even the political sphere. But considerable intellectual freedom could thrive, particularly under the influence of the surviving noble caste of the Kshatriya. In China, the mandarins came to form a strata of learned scribes, supported by the magistic hierocracy. An extraordinarily powerful bureaucracy

emerged; its enemy, however, is not to be found in the masses yearning for freedom but always in the imperial seraglio with its eunuchs. Yet considerable leeway remained for freedom in practice. And, just as in India, a culture of great spontaneity, permeating all strata of society, could develop within this still relatively loose bureaucratic framework.

The ancient civilizations of the Middle East—above all, that of Persia—were also almost all built on a foundation of bureaucracy. But in the Persian Empire itself bureaucracy was not hieratically sanctified. Far-reaching tolerance and only loose cohesion among its components remained characteristic of the great empire. The Persian emperor did not become a semi-divinity or vicar of god equipped with a supporting and all-encompassing bureaucracy. The distinct ways of life among the conquered nationalities were left virtually untouched or even revived, as was best exemplified by the liberation of the Jewish aristocracy from Babylonic exile and the re-establishment of Jerusalem.

But neither this Jewish nor any other "unbureaucratized" state or social organism had any conscious notions of personal freedom. Among the Jews in particular, an inner and outer activity was far too ritualized and placed under the control, first of the Levites, later of the learned scribes. Spiritual effort was harnessed not for the achievement of personal freedom but for the collective fulfillment of the religious mission and its ethically-conceived unfolding and deepening. The struggle was not being waged for freedom as such.

The ancient Jewish community was one of the first highly-developed state edifices without a proper bureaucracy. But owing to the peculiar manner in which individualism and collectivism were here intertwined, it stood entirely outside the contest of freedom versus bureaucracy.

The first societies that were aware of this contest and whose consciousness of freedom grew and sharpened upon this awareness, were ancient Greece and Rome. Neither of them needed bureaucracy since both had found a suitable form of social organization in the *polis* and *urbs*, with their honorary offices, and required no rational division of functions or professional specialization in public life. With lesser success in Greece and with greater success in Rome, this social organization met the test. The priestly hierocracy remained almost unseen—mysticism, sacrifices, and oracles notwithstanding—since it found no means for its propagation into the workaday life in the form of a temporal bureaucracy. It remained impotent, deprived of the opportunity to limit the range of free decisions in any manner.

The concept of freedom, taken for granted ever since the days of the earlier horsemen, continued to be recognized in the continual social struggle which accompanied the transformations that both the Roman and the Greek state underwent on the thoroughly rational basis of liberty. It was this notion of freedom that became the articulate intellectual slogan voiced in the great fight against the bureaucratic east, a fight waged not only for the preservation of national independence but quite specifically directed against a world of "unfreedom." Herodotus was aware of this, and this Thucydides put into Pericles' mouth in his funeral oration: ". . . freely we order the commonwealth" and "not fetched by imitation of others, we are rather a model for them."

Leaving aside the worlds of Islam and Russia, which are too complex to be treated briefly, let us look at the Western world. While one does encounter strongly bureaucratic forms of organization in that part of the West which was once occupied by the Roman Em-

pire, the West, both at its inception and for a considerable time thereafter, was as good as devoid of officialdom. For feudalism was the very opposite of bureaucracy, since it represented the non-professional and non-specialized execution of functions. And this is why within and alongside the form of reciprocal feudal relationships—contractual, hence originally based on the premise of freedom—with the revival of classicism, the ancient consciousness of liberty could be revived and renewed. It could produce a symbiosis of the pre-cultural sense of freedom, on the one hand, and a more deeply comprehensible and comprehended freedom produced by Christianity, on the other. In bending the old concept of natural rights to its ends, it could unfold the ideas of liberty and equality of a Locke.

Such was the great contest of bureaucracy and freedom in the past. The rise of the modern state was the occasion, and provided the framework for that strata of professional officialdom that was imported into the West from Byzantium over the Italian universities. This is also whence came its metaphysical sanction.

Less attention is usually paid to the fact that the bureaucratic stratification in the modern state has been produced as much by the emergence of standing armies as by the rise of civil officialdom. It is no accident that the modern standing army, with its rational gradations and schematic unification, has found its most striking expression in the military *casern*—admittedly, a factory with a bureaucratic head.

Since the latter half of the nineteenth century, the bureaucratic stranglehold has rapidly spread, as if endowed with mystic power, from administrative offices and army barracks into almost all fields of human endeavor. It has increasingly penetrated, affected, and transformed relations between man and man. Today industry is in large segments no less bureaucratic than are the public health services, in whose barrack-like hospitals the disease, and not the sick human being, assumes individuality—where, so to speak, the object replaces the subject. The same is true of modern social legislation, of the compulsory insurance schemes with their gigantic machines; of such labor organizations as trade unions, with their bureaucratic heads; of popular political organizations, with their caucuses. Not only the state and other official bureaucracies continue to swell in accordance with the "law of growing state functions" first formulated by Adolf Wegner; next to them we witness a growth —a rank growth—of innumerable private bureaucracies, which everywhere offer the same picture: the emergence of a closed bureaucratic leadership, largely autocratic in practice, and as specialized a division of labor as is rationally necessary or possible. In recent decades, the number of officials and civil servants has been growing far more rapidly than the number of workers. What we witness is a tremendous inflation of the bureaucratic head topping a more slowly growing body. And this, despite all democratic sugar-coating, means: the spread of authoritarian leadership through small cliques and staffs, tending not only rationally to divide the fulfillment of functions horizontally, if you will, but also to permeate it vertically in such a manner as to assure the uppermost bureaucratic nucleus, due to its organizational-technical position, of preponderance against any endeavor to shape and express the will from below. This is the hidden master key to the over-all trends of present-day social organization.

If we ask for the way out, for an antitoxin, we must first take account of the following. Our modern world, interdependent as it has become, organized in large and increasingly inclusive units, necessarily bringing a specialization of functions in society, cannot be controlled except by large-scale formations, inherently gradated and bureaucratic in management. This is certainly true of the general organization of services and supplies. Just like the Egyptians and Babylonians of old, with their canal system which had to be bureaucratically managed, so we "moderns" are caught in the gigantic web of railroads, postal services, electricity, and what not—a web which spans and upholds our very existence, a web within whose framework we live and die, and which by its very nature commands central bureaucratic direction and rational subdivision. On our level of civilization, this framework of social existence has become an artificially rational and bureaucratic stockade from which there is no escape.

Just as inescapably, the great dimensions of our world and the concomitant huge organizations that belong in it result in the transformation of a previously diversified society of individuals into a uniform mass. This is also inherent in the very nature of these vast dimensions, since they bracket and uniformly affect great masses of human beings in a standardized fashion. It is an optical illusion to see this trend toward mass uniformity only in its most obvious and almost accidental manifestation, namely, the uprooted, intermingled and compressed masses of our cities and industrial centers. Less visibly but just as effectively, this schematizing trend affects that part of the population which has remained geographically dispersed but is being supplied—day after day, hour after hour—with the same uniformly-prepared set of experiences and information—and this in such a manner that the victims are being flattened out, as if by a steamroller, without being capable of resisting this process. Today they cannot but react as a mass, which is being swayed daily and hourly in similar rhythm. Not to face this reality is to indulge in romantic self-deception.

But once we recognize how a limited number of central agencies can make and break public opinion and decisively shape the mental habitat of the masses, we understand how natural it is to try and utilize these psychic potentialities through appropriate organs and methods specifically patterned for this purpose. One more step, and an effort is made to recast this outwardly uniform mass into one that is a herd in inherent constitution and behavior—and thus gain complete control over it. The resulting political conception is the specific modern authoritarian party, with its various appendages such as the rational system of "party cells" and control by "block wardens." Intensive propaganda turns into terrorism. This is the base on which the modern terroristic dictatorships have flourished. In a sense, they are the sole alternative and antipode to democracy. Modern bureaucratization of all forms of life not only makes it possible to "lead" the masses but also is susceptible of becoming the tool of a demagogic clique and the authoritarian organization associated with it, for the definitive eviction of freedom.

I would not think of proclaiming this transformation of modern bureaucracy and rationalization into dictatorship as inevitable. After the terrible example which mankind recently experienced with the substitution of terroristic dictatorship for democracy in Germany, I will still maintain that those countries are, above all, most immune to it which have a historically-rooted tradition of liberty or, whenever challenged, have proved capable of soon re-establishing it anew. For countries like Switzerland or the Netherlands, for Sweden and Norway, for England and the United States, political freedom as a decisive counterweight to totalitarianism is virtually innate, as far as we can see

today; their peoples seem to take freedom as much for granted as they do the limbs for the survival of the body. The problem facing *these* countries is limited to the first two aspects outlined above: the challenge of weakening, narrowing, and atrophying private initiative due to an unhealthy growth of bureaucracy and uniformity through modern techniques of standardization. But all three consequences must be understood as elements present in modern society, and must be grasped in their technical aspects as well.

Next to the *casern*, the factory provided the second locus around which the modern trend toward rationalization and mechanization could crystallize. Historically, it is matter of sheer accident that the factory system arose, of all things, under modern capitalism. Generally speaking, the factory is a purely cultural product: a Socialist system employing techniques and rational organization needs it as imperatively as does capitalism. But to the extent to which our large-scale existence demands effective organization in large units—for rational reasons of competition as well as because of the inherent nature of its dimensions—the principles of the factory system and the concomitant bureaucratization of institutions cannot be evaded. Perhaps spontaneous and free motivating forces of unbureaucratic hue could be injected into our social bloodstream. But even these must fit in with the overall skeleton—unless we wish artificially to preserve elements incommensurate with the great dimensions of our days; unless, so to speak, we choose to perpetuate forcibly isolated little hothouses around which the air of the wide spaces is allowed freely to circulate. Today most of the problems we here face can be correctly seen, felt, and dealt with only within this larger radius. Not only in the technical but especially in the mental and political realm there are definite limits beyond which there is no escape from the organization of society into large units, no escape from the bureaucratization connected with it.

Let us draw the consequences.

There exist today very substantial tendencies which, while of sharply anti-fascist and anti-Nazi persuasion, *should* be anti-totalitarian as well, but which in effect represent but a different form of totalitarianism. Or else, in the sincere belief of working for human liberty and emancipation, they paradoxically further a process of all-bureaucratic enslavement, because they ignore the dangers outlined above. One such trend is Communism, in its current edition at least; official contemporary Democratic Socialism is the other.

Both are fanatically centralist and rationalist. Therein they are the genetic heirs of the nineteenth century. Present-day Communism sacrifices the rights of the individual and freedom in favor of the complete liquidation of the upper classes and the elimination of all productive private capital. This transformation, it holds, can be achieved only by totalitarian means, and for its achievement no sacrifice is too great. One cannot argue with such a radical attitude, as it is based on a peculiar scale of values. "Classical" Socialism, on the other hand, today passionately defends the democratic scale of values. But its actions lead it to a double paradox.

Constricted to the old, mid-nineteenth century formulae which stem from Marx' revelation of the nature of capitalism, this classical socialism looks for its panacea to the "*socialization* of the means of production," which is to bring in the wake of the elimination of private capital's power position the emancipation of the proletariat. This slogan, intentionally couched in very general and vague terms by Marx and Engels, is so fascinating in an atmosphere imbued with the tradition of class struggle that when the modern Socialist seeks to mold it into a plank or political program, can think of nothing better than the nationalization—or, coin a term, *etatization*—of the means of production. Enraptured as he is, he fails to perceive the danger of the unheard-of strengthening of concentrated and ubiquitous bureaucracy, which would transform the anticipated emancipation of the masses into its antithesis. The classical Socialist is oblivious of the danger of enslavement by the State and does not notice that he is in effect advocating state socialism—on the model once favored by those to whom civil liberties mattered little and the authoritarian state meant much. He who really should know something about historical dialectics, fails to perceive that he becomes its victim.

The other paradox consists in the sign of equality which the contemporary Social-Democrat, taking the State to be his only universe of discourse, places between public planning and Socialism. Planned economy as such—as imperative as it may be within limits under the present circumstances—has little to do with Socialism, *i.e.* with the emancipation of the masses. Planning in the economic sphere may mitigate crimes and blunt the impact of the resulting phenomenon of mass unemployment. But beyond this, it is merely a technique arising from such deficiency situations as result from war and economic disorder. That is why today planning is so widely accepted. But its impressive propagation, in turn, is apt to lead once again towards omnipotent bureaucracy, killing off in the process the end goal of Socialism—Freedom.

We who see these dangers—what can we do about them? Some will tell us that what we need is to organize society in smaller units, substitute federalism for centralism with its lethal tendencies. The limits within which this recipe can be carried out have already been outlined. They are—to repeat myself—partly material, and just as important, partly psychological and mental. Federalism creates, not less bureaucracy, but more. Under it, the unpenetrable abodes of officialdom multiply, in which decisions of greatest portent are made without the participation of the public. The same is true whenever a great-dimensional whole is split up under the slogan of federalism. The necessary decisions will still have to be made at the center in a bureaucratic manner. What you have then accomplished is the replacement of one bureaucracy by several superimposed bureaucracies—those of the subordinate limbs and that at the center—which co-exist under superfluous and paralyzing complications. The material limits for all forms of federalism are thus clearly indicated.

The over-expansion of the federative idea is just as dangerous in the political and mental sense. It fosters and facilitates rule and abuse by all sorts of small bureaucratic cliques. What we need today in the sphere of mind and politics is not the confinement to small empty rooms but, on the contrary, the approximation of the global and telluric, the espousal of dimensions which encompass all humanity. There, on the higher rung, federalism for the new and greater entities is again indicated. Federalism on such a higher level is probably the only salvation for Europe.

Of course every nation should organize on the richest possible communal and regional basis; and, depending on its traditions, it may follow the pattern of federation and Bundesstaat: of course, local government should remain as untouched as possible and be permitted to mold itself independently to a maximal extent. Of course small, historically warranted states have a right to exist today—especially today—along with the emerging supernational federations; above all, they have a moral function to fulfill. One must not forget,

however, that those questions which are of moral and political importance are being settled not in small but in increasingly large entities and demand solution on such vast dimensions.

The most radical enemy of modern bureaucracy, one who has recognized its menace with considerable clairvoyance, is neo-liberalism. In strange ways this new and growing school of thought is at times wedded to the neo-federalist trend. The reason for this alliance is the tendency to misread the signs of the time—a tendency noticeable in both these movements. In neo-federalism it is the vision of an organically-germinating, easily scannable small unit of social organization that distorts the outlook, as it appears to require little bureaucracy and would seem to engender democratic spontaneity. In neo-liberalism it is romantic oblivion to the fact that since the 19th century we have had monopoly capitalism, which cannot be done away with by evading the word "capitalism" or by prohibiting its symptoms—cartels, syndicates, and trusts—and seeking to re-establish free competition with all its rules of the game. Such business combinations are but the forms in which the accumulative tendencies of capital find expression, which aim at the establishment of overt or covert monopolies and, in one form or another, do indeed, set up monopolies—unless they themselves are extinguished. Pretty verbiage about the restitution of competition and the prohibition of monopolies are of no use. Such legislation merely trims the beard, so to speak, without touching the foundations on which monopolies thrive. All sacrifices before the altar of competition are doomed to be futile whenever the market is dominated by some four or ten big business enterprises whose captains, over a glass of whiskey, can decide upon the conditions under which they will supply the market in what amounts to monopolistic or quasi-monopolistic manner. The efforts of the neo-liberals, well-meant as they are, can therefore be of only limited practical value, for they come as little to grips with the bases of bureaucratization as with the effective diversion of totalitarianism, whose menace they see but fail to trace to the end. Their approach is romantic—and this is an age which, whether it likes it or not, requires economic planning.

I can see but one effective barrier to these dangers: a new form of Socialism, distinct from its classical form. It must be a Socialism which, taking account of the social framework within which bureaucracy exists as a universal and inescapable trend, infuses organized counterforces into this framework in order to salvage liberty and accordingly seeks to exert a systematic influence on state and society. It must *socialize* all those segments of economy which have become monopolistic, bureaucratic, hence ripe for socialization —and thereby shatter the power of capitalist bureaucracy. It must do so not in order to replace private bureaucracy with state bureaucracy—*i.e.* merely change masters—in order to establish a society in which (along with a necessarily nationalized and bureaucratic transportation, communications, and supply system) all other monopolies are broken, dissolved into public, corporate-socialist, autonomous units which as free units on the market can survive in the form of such rationally-necessary technical organisms as public foundations, socially-useful concessions, or public corporations which would be constrained to adopt socialist behavior and organization. *This means above all: production without the capitalist profit motive; election of boards of directors by those concerned; a voice, and concern for the furtherance of the interests of the workers.* Such socialist organs, freely co-existing, would have to be under the control of economic senates, part of the judicial arm, which would be entirely independent of

all influence of political parties. This would be a form of industrial organization which, once the above conditions are fulfilled, could even make possible the reduction of bureaucratic planning along socialist lines, after the elimination of present economic shortages of production. Next to these organs there must be "democratic partnership" of employees in the economic sphere, on the model of most recent English practice in the non-socialized branches of economy; and the establishment of a network of production co-operatives in agriculture so as to reduce even there the bureaucracy of planning. It must be a Socialism whose *political* orientation would aim at undermining bureaucracy's intellectual and moral tendency to domineer. It must aim at reducing bureaucracy to its necessary technical functions.

These are but a few practical features, easy to multiply, of such a new, thoroughly realistic, Socialist orientation, which would aim at the emancipation, not only of the working class, but of the population as a whole. To this end—by transformation or, whenever impossible, by restrictions—it would infuse spontaneous forces in order to counteract the bureaucratization of societal life, to render totalitarianism impossible and, at the same time, to realize freedom for all mankind.

I have been compelled to ask myself bluntly whether human history is to end where it began more than 5,000 years ago; whether mankind is to lose the freedom it gained at such a high price in the course of its existence; whether it is to trade in its liberty for a man-made dungeon just as it once exchanged the barbaric absence of restrictions for a hierocracy that guided and shaped its existence? Such a monstrous and grotesque parody of all meaningful history is not inevitable. What I have sought to do is to stake out the road along which, perhaps, it is possible to escape it.

D Race, Ethnicity, and Religion

INTRODUCTION

Virtually all modern nations include peoples of different racial, ethnic, and religious backgrounds. These differences sometimes are regarded as historical accidents, in contrast to the social class differences created and perpetuated by the major institutional structures of a society. Yet, the populations of all civilized societies, even the very earliest ones, have been ethnically diverse. The earliest civilizations came into being by absorbing and welding together numerous primitive societies, each of which contributed elements of its own distinctive culture. Empires and, at a later date, nation-states expanded by conquering alien peoples. In modern history, mass migrations have added to the ethnic diversity of national populations. It is true that ethnic differences often have become attenuated over time. The development of a loyalty to a national culture that takes precedence over attachments to previously independent local cultures is a major consequence of modern nation building. Yet, new ethnic divisions arise in a nation when it expands its territory or attracts immigrants from outside its borders after older divisions have become little more than historical memories. Thus, ethnic diversity always has been a feature of civilized societies, as ubiquitous as class divisions. The enormous variety of historical processes that create ethnically and, in particular, racially diverse national populations are reviewed by Everett C. Hughes in the first selection reprinted here.

The term *ethnic group* has come to mean any group within a national society possessing elements of a distinctive culture that are the source of solidarity among its members. The combination of a shared language, national origin, and religion is the most common and durable cultural bond fostering ethnic solidarity. Ethnic groups account for different proportions of the populations of various modern nation-states. In some, a single ethnic group may form a majority of the population, as Englishmen do in Great Britain. Other nations, such as the United States, contain many groups, none of which constitutes a majority. Ethnic differences may be associated with, or even grow out of, either racial or religious differences, or both. In one of our readings, Lester Singer argues that the racial discrimination suffered by American Blacks has given them a distinctive minority culture and group consciousness. Religious oppression or segregation often has had similar consequences, as the history of the Jews in both Christian

344

and Moslem societies attests. But both racial and religious differences often exist independently of more inclusive group differences.

In our second selection, Nathan Glazer and Daniel Patrick Moynihan survey ethnic differences in world perspective, much as Hughes reviews racial differences in the first reading. They cite evidence that ethnic identities and conflicts in the contemporary world are becoming more rather than less salient, contradicting traditional liberal and Marxist expectations that ethnicity was destined to disappear in the course of modernization and secularization. Glazer and Moynihan also note that in the United States ethnic attachments have, in recent years, achieved new and unprecedented recognition and legitimacy.

Race is a biological rather than a cultural phenomenon. A race is a population possessing some genes in common that create physical resemblances among its members. The social visibility of racial differences, engraved as they are on the very physiques of human beings, makes it possible for races to perpetuate their sense of difference from one another. When one race is the more powerful and cherishes a belief in its innate superiority, it can create a whole structure of permanent institutions imposing severe disabilities on racial minorities. American Blacks, Orientals, Mexicans, and Indians have experienced such disabilities. Their situation is, thus, not comparable to that of European nationality groups who suffered a rejection by native-born Americans that was bound to diminish in force as second- and third-generation descendants of immigrants became fully Americanized.

All traces of the original African culture of American Negroes were destroyed when they were captured and brought to the New World and forced to endure the long ordeal of slavery. The experience of slavery and of the racial discrimination that survived its abolition have given Negroes a distinctive version of American culture. Gradually, Negroes have developed a strong sense of group solidarity in combatting the deprivations and indignities they have suffered, a process that Lester Singer calls *ethnogenesis*. The rise of an organized black protest movement was the major domestic political event in the United States in the 1960's.

All four of the readings included in this section discuss at least some aspect of the circumstances of the American Negro. Hughes compares the positions of American Blacks and French Canadians within their respective national societies and the protest movements each of these peoples has created to change and improve their position. Professor Hughes has been kind enough to write an additional two paragraphs to his original 1963 paper in which he summarizes his view of more recent developments. Glazer and Moynihan note the effects of black protest in the 1960's on American governmental policy and also comment on the degree to which ethnic movements abroad have imitated the forms of American black protest.

In our last selection, Robert N. Bellah discusses the new religious sects and cults that have appeared in America in the 1970's, some of them representing Christian revivals, others the appeal of a variety of oriental religions. Although only a minority of the population has been engaged, these new movements have had a special appeal to young people. Bellah, indeed, regards them as successor movements to the short-lived student New Left and youth counterculture of the 1960's. However, he also regards them as evidence of the widespread decline of belief in the distinctive American combination of Biblical religion and utilitarian individualism that traditionally has served to legitimate our major institutions. Until the 1960's, the United States, in contrast to many European countries, had been spared the experience of the withdrawal of faith in its established order on the part of large segments of the population. Bellah doubts that a restoration of confidence in what used to be called the American Way of Life is likely and suggests that the new religious consciousness points to several alternative future possibilities.

35

Race Relations in World Perspective

EVERETT C. HUGHES

What is there new to say about race relations? A colleague with great knowledge and deep experience of American race relations—he is a Negro—asked me that. I could have answered that new things are happening in race relations here and all over the world; things from which we can still learn.

A younger colleague who builds models and tries them out in the laboratory wanted to know to what general theoretical problem I would direct this discussion. I could have answered that race relations are so much a feature of most societies, and that they are in such flux that one could find in them a living laboratory for almost any problem of social interaction, social identity and social structure which one could imagine.

While these points are indeed part of my discussion, a deeper question concerning sociology and social life lurks in the background: Why did social scientists—and sociologists in particular—not foresee the explosion of collective action of Negro Americans to-

Reprinted from Everett C. Hughes, "Race Relations and the Sociological Imagination," *American Sociological Review*, 28: 879–887 (Jan. 1964), with permission of the author and the publisher.

ward immediate full integration into American society? It is but a special instance of the more general question concerning sociological foresight of and involvement in drastic and massive social changes and extreme forms of social action.

Robert E. Park defined race relations thus:

. . . the term . . . includes all the relations which exist between members of different ethnic and genetic groups which are capable of provoking race conflict and race consciousness, or of determining the relative status of the racial groups of which a community is composed.[1] . . .

Park's definition makes study of race relations a part of the study of society itself, not a peculiar problem requiring special concepts for its analysis.

In the same paper Park—it was in 1939—spoke of a great movement among "national minorities to control and direct their own destinies;" a

[1] Robert E. Park, "The Nature of Race Relations," pp. 3–45 in E. T. Thompson (ed.), *Race Relations and the Race Problem*. Durham, N.C.: Duke University Press, 1939. Reproduced in Park, *Race and Culture*, Glencoe, Ill.: The Free Press, 1950, pp. 81–116. See p. 82.

movement "which began in Europe in the early part of the last century, and has now spread, as if it were contagious, to every part of the world; every part of the world at any rate, which has felt or still feels itself oppressed in its provincial, autonomous life, or for any other reason, inferior in its international status." [2]

We of this country ushered in that great movement for national independence a little earlier than the beginning of the 19th century. Never ethnically homogeneous, we become less so by swallowing the remnants of Spanish and French empires, by importing black labor from Africa, and by encouraging immigration from Europe and, for a time, from Asia. The movement continued in Central and South America; those new states were also, all of them, racially mixed. The Spanish- or Portuguese-speaking cities were surrounded by latifundia with indigenous, African or mixed labor force, beyond which generally there lay a back country whose inhabitants were not part of any body politic. As in North America, immigration from Europe and even from Asia continued. To our North, Canada gradually took on national status, by a confederation of provinces, the oldest of which was French-speaking Quebec.[3]

In Europe the continental Empires began to break up; Belgium, Greece, Italy, Norway, Finland and the Balkan states became nation-states. At the end of the First World War, the process went on until a belt of independent states was formed between Russia and the west. Established in the name of the self-determination of peoples—of people of common language and culture governing themselves on their historic territory—not one of those nation-states corresponded to the ideal. Every one contained some minority of another people than the one in whose name independence had been claimed. Nor, indeed, was any one of the dominant states from which these peoples had got independence, made into a country of one language and people by this cleansing. Germany tried to reverse the trend under Hitler, but ended up smaller than ever, as two states each racially purer —in our broad sense—than any in Europe. In that sense, Hitler won.

The victors of the First World War were proponents of the self-determination of European peoples, but all had overseas empires to which they did not apply that principle—as Max Weber pointed out in a speech at the time.[4] Their turn came after World War II. Their Asiatic, Oceanic and African possessions then sought and got political independence. None of these former colonies is racially homogeneous. India, Indonesia, the Philippines all contain a variety of languages, historic religions, cultures and tribes. Mass migrations, some voluntary, some forced, have, if anything, made people more aware of those divisions. In the little artificial states of the old French Asiatic colonies, probably few people know what state they do live in. In the Near East and northern Africa, a series of states, supposedly Muslim in religion and Arab in culture, are in fact a mosaic of languages, sects, tribes, races, classes and "communities." Israel, enclaved among them, is itself an ethnic pressure-cooker; linguistic and patriotic conformity are insisted upon.

In the oldest state south of the Sahara, South Africa, the European population is divided into majority and

[2] Loc. cit.
[3] New Zealand, Australia and the Union of South Africa became, like Canda, self-governing states with minorities, either indigenous or European, or both.

[4] Max Weber, "Deutschland unter den europäischen Weltmächten (October, 1916)," pp. 73–93 in Gesammelte Politische Schriften. Munich: Drei Masken Verlag, 1921. See pp. 89–90.

minority, which are numerically but a fraction of the total population of the country. The black Africans, once tribal, are being welded into something like an entity by the effort of the Europeans to keep them from it. Among the Europeans themselves, the former minority of Afrikaners has become the dominant group in politics, although English South Africans still dominate the economy. The other countries and the few remaining colonies in sub-Saharan Africa are all diverse in language, culture, tribal loyalties and degree of integration into modern urban economy and life. So diverse are they that the language of the battle for independence is generally that of the oppressor from whom they seek emancipation; language, that is, in both senses, of letters and words and of political and social philosophy. A bit of African chant and rhythm make the rhetoric seem more indigenous than it is. Portugal has thus far saved her empire by not teaching the language of independence, in either sense, to her African subjects.

All of these African countries are observation posts for those interested in the process of nation-making on which Bagehot wrote a classic essay a century ago. The development of a feeling of national, rather than local or tribal, identity proceeds but painfully in some of them.[5] Lucy Mair thinks its growth depends not upon a state of mind induced by propaganda, but upon social structure. Cities, communications, education and experience of industrial employment will create people who identify themselves with a nation. "The structure of an industrial society," she says, "is such that no section of it can pursue its interests by trying to cut itself off from the rest."[6] Whether or not she is right on that point, certainly the new African states are not yet nations. It may be that the state makes the nation, and not the reverse.

This tremendous burgeoning of so-called nation-states took place in a time of colossal migrations, voluntary or forced, of people seeking land or wanted as labor for industrial agriculture, the extractive or more advanced industries. Migration makes diversified populations. Even Japan, of all nations perhaps the one with the strongest myth of national homogeneity, got a large population of strange people as she became industrial and an empire—Koreans, Okinawans, her traditional Eta and her tribal Ainu have given the Japanese something on which to exercise their racial exclusiveness. As a final twist, some of the centers of erstwhile empires are now getting a reverse migration from their former colonies. West Indian Negroes are entering the British labor force at the bottom, as are Algerians in France and Puerto Ricans in New York.

The very era in which the concept of nation-state has been so powerful has been one of empire-building and empire-breaking; an era in which the idea has spread, as Park said, like a contagion; a queer contagion, since the European countries which spread it did their best to prevent others—those in their own empires, at any rate—from catching it. The nation-state, far from eliminating race relations, intensifies them; its ideology of the correspondence of cultural and racial with political boundaries makes internal problems of what were external or international problems in the days of empire or in the more primitive times of tribal rule. It has made great numbers of human individuals aware of race as a fateful personal characteristic, determining the terms of their struggle for a place. It has made whole groups of people conscious of themselves as having a status, not merely in their own

[5] Walter Bagehot, *Physics and Politics.* Chapters III and IV, "Nation-Making."
[6] Lucy Mair, "Divide and Rule in the New Countries?" *New Societies,* No. 37 (June 13, 1963), p. 18.

region, but in the world. Race, in our broad sense, has been made a part of the political, economic and social processes of much of the world. The United Nations has become an organ of world opinion which makes every domestic racial problem again a diplomatic and international one as well.

The relations among races are now even more disturbed than when Park wrote. They offer a richer and more varied living laboratory than ever for any of us sociologists who would consider going abroad other than to attend conferences. But it is not precisely a laboratory which they offer, for we have but one chance to observe, to understand and to act.

Of course, we need not go abroad. Racial turmoil is here at home. In North America, two elderly nation-states—as those things go—contain two of the oldest established minorities of the world, Negro Americans and French Canadians. When I call them old, I refer to the duration of their position in the nation-states of which they are a part. Negro Americans, aided by some others, are engaged in their most massive, determined, urgent and detailed struggle for equality. French Canadians are vigorously demanding an overhaul of the century-old bargain sealed by the Confederation of the provinces into a single dominion.

Although there have always been agitators in both minorities, there have been long periods of quiet in which there was an entente between the leading classes of each minority and the dominant groups and implicit acceptance of it by the masses of the people. During these periods the dominant group apparently thought that an equilibrium had been established for an indefinite period, with changes going on so slowly as not to upset it. One might have said of both American and Canadian society what Park says of all:

Every society represents an organization of elements more or less antagonistic to each other but united for the moment, at least, by an arrangement which defines the reciprocal relations and respective sphere of action of each. This accommodation, this *modus vivendi*, may be relatively permanent as in a society constituted by castes, or quite transistory as in societies made up of open classes. In either case, the accommodation, while it is maintained, secures for the individual or for the group of recognized status.

In the accommodation, then, antagonism of the hostile elements is, for the time being, regulated, and conflict disappears as overt action, although it remains latent as a potential force. With a change in the situation, the adjustments that had hitherto held in control the antagonistic forces fail. There is confusion and unrest which may result in open conflict. Conflict . . . invariably issues in a new accommodation or social order, which in general involves a changed status in the relations among the participants.[7]

Park's view of society is that status arrangements are always tentative and likely to be questioned. In our two minorities, many of the younger people are questioning the bargain—the status arrangement—made by their forebears and consented to by their elders (for failure to act is considered consent). But what is the time perspective of parties to a bargain? The group with the greatest interest in the status quo may be expected to think of the arrangement as permanent, and to justify it by various devices—such as the doctrine of racial superiority and inferiority. The group disadvantaged in status may use some principle of permanency, which has been violated by the status-bargain forced upon them. Thus a national minority, such as the French Canadian, will prove that it was there first; that it is an older nation than the oppressor. The function of folklore is to establish antiquity and the rights

[7] R. E. Park and E. W. Burgess, *Introduction to the Science of Sociology*, Chicago: University of Chicago Press, 1921, p. 665.

based upon it. Colonial tribal minorities can achieve a sort of apocalyptic eternity, as Nadine Gordimer says so well of Africans:

You can assure yourself of glory in the future, in a heaven, but if that seems too nebulous for you—and the Africans are sick of waiting for things—you can assure yourself of glory in the past. It will have exactly the same sort of effect on you, in the present. You'll feel yourself, in spite of everything, worthy of either your future or your past.[8]

In both our minorities, the Negro-American and the French-Canadian, the time perspectives of past bargains are being called into question; in both cases, the dominant group asks either that the bargain be permanent or that it be changed but slowly.

Why the great outbreak of unrest and demand for change in those two minorities at just this moment? Certainly there have been great changes in the situation of both. At the last census, French Canadians had become more urban than other Canadians; Negroes, more urban than other Americans. With the precipitous drop in the agricultural labor force of both countries, these minorities have undergone changes of occupational structure probably greater than those of the rest of the population. Both minorities, in the industrial and urban order in which their fate now lies, are concentrated at lower points of the socio-economic scale than are the dominant groups.

These similarities may appear strained. They cover great differences. French Canadians do not, and never have, suffered civil or personal disabilities; they have not had to give deference to others. No social rank inheres in being French Canadian; the only aristocracy Canada ever had was French.

8 Nadine Gordimer, *Occasion for Loving*, New York: Viking, 1960, pp. 9–10.

French institutions in Canada are more venerable than English. French Canadians have headed the national government and always control the governments of their province and of most cities within it.

The two minorities are alike in that they have gone from a rural condition to an urban and see themselves as thereby put into a position of increased disadvantage; and at precisely that time in history when such disadvantage is no longer a purely domestic matter. But they seek opposite remedies. The Negro Americans want to disappear as a defined group; they want to become invisible as a group, while each of them becomes fully visible as a human being. Only so will they, in the myriad relations of American life, be judged by the characteristics pertinent to each. They want to be seen, neither as Negroes nor as if they were not; but as if it did not matter. The French Canadians, on the other hand, struggle not for survival as individuals—in which their problems are those of other Canadians —but for survival as a group with full social, economic and political standing.

These two apparently opposite goals represent one of the dialectics of human beings and the groups with which they identify themselves and are identified. How like others, how different from them shall I, shall we, can I, can we, be? And in what respects? Jews in the western world are generally thought to find these questions difficult, and the solutions unstable. Such a group as Negro Americans is at one pole—where all is to be gained from reduction of the social perception of differences. Their end will have been gained when Negroid characteristics and African descent matter no more and no less than other physical traits and quirks of ancestry. At that point, there would be no racial bargain. Whether all persons known as Negroes—and their descendants of that future day—would be content to wipe out their collective past and all features of Negro-American culture is another matter.

Some Negro Americans have given up hope that white Americans will ever live up to the bargain of the American ideology of equal rights for all. They reject everything American—the country, the Christian religion, their Anglo-Saxon names; as so-called Black Muslims they claim complete and eternal difference from white Americans and seek to develop such solidarity among Negroes as will enable them to fight and bargain for a separate realm. To support their claim, they have imagined themselves a glorious past as the Muslims who were the scourge of Europe and Christianity throughout the centuries. They project themselves into an apocalyptic future when, in cargo-cult fashion, their ship will come in and the evil white race will be destroyed.[9] This, mind you, is not in the South Seas, in Black Africa or among dispossessed American Indians, but among urban Americans. The question one must ask is this: at what point do people so far lose confidence in the "others" with whom they are destined to live as to reject all the collective symbols of their common society, and to erase from their talk all phrases which imply common humanity. Such symbolic Apartheid has not been the prevailing mind of Negro Americans, but it lurks ready to be called into the open with every alienating rebuff. The balance is still with the movement for complete integration.

Indeed it is so much so that some

[9] M. Eliade, " 'Cargo-Cults' and Cosmic Regeneration," pp. 139–143 in S. L. Thrupp (ed.), *Millennial Dreams in Action. Comparative Studies in Society and History,* Supplement II, The Hague, 1962. See other articles in this volume. The members of such cults are enjoined to prepare for the great day, not by political action, but by strict abstinence from all contact with the enemy and his works.

Negroes are claiming special treatment in order to make the integration more rapid, on the ground that past discrimination has loaded them with a competitive disadvantage which it will take a long time to overcome. Thus, for the moment, they appear to be asking that their Negro-ness be not forgotten, in order that, in the long run, it may be. It is the vigor and urgency of the Negro demand that is new, not its direction or the supporting ideas. It was that vigor and urgency that sociologists, and other people, did not foresee, even though they knew that Negroes would not be content forever with their situation, and should have sensed that the contradiction between "speed" and "deliberate" would become the object of both wit and anger.

In Canada, the tension between French and English has always existed, and has always turned upon the question of the survival and status of the French as a linguistic, cultural and political entity. French Canadians believe that a large proportion of English Canadians assume that French Canada will and ought to cease to exist, just as English Canadians believe that many Americans assume that Canada itself will and ought to cease to exist. From time to time, the tension becomes great and various French nationalist movements arise. In time of war, English Canadians accuse French Canadians of less than full devotion to the cause, while French Canadians resent the attempt of the others to tell them their duty. In the great depression there was tension over jobs and the burden of unemployment centering about the fact that management and ownership of industry were English, while labor was French.

The present movement is the first major one in time of peace and prosperity, when critics can say, and do, "They never had it so good. What do they want anyway?" To be sure it is a *drôle de paix* in which some other Canadians wish the French might join more heartily in the campaign against Castro—as they ought, it is said, being Catholics and therefore presumably leaders in the battle against Communism. Not only are the circumstances different from the times of earlier national upsurgings, but the very rhetoric is contrary, and some of the most ardent of earlier leaders are dubbed compromisers, or even traitors.

Most earlier French nationalist leaders called upon their fellow Canadians to respect the bargain of Confederation everywhere in Canada; bilingualism and public support of Catholic schools should prevail, or at least be tolerated, everywhere, not only in Quebec. The French were to have parity, their just proportion of all positions in government, and eventually in business and industry. But to merit their survival French Canadians should retain their rural virtues, including a high birth rate which would win for them, in due time, a victory of the cradle. To retain those virtues, their unemployed and the extra sons of farmers should go north to clear and settle new lands. Only so would they save themselves from the vices of the city, which were alleged to be English, American—and Jewish. To document their charter-membership of Canada, they cultivated folklore and song; their novelists wrote of the clearing of the land, of the drive of logs down the rivers after the spring thaw, of the land passing from father to son. They emphasized their place as the true Canadians—*Canadiens* without qualifying adjective—while English Canadians were *Anglais*, or perhaps *Canadiens anglais*.

Thus equal rights with English in a common country was the theme of most of the earlier leaders, and was the sentiment of most French Canadians, whether active in any movement or not. But the new movement talks of separation of the State, not Province, of Quebec from Canada; if not separation, then a new constitution giving Quebec a special status. It calls the French people of Quebec by the name *Québecois*. English Canadians are called Canadians, with English spelling, and the French word Canadien, is avoided. The government in Ottawa is spoken of as an alien power maintaining unjust colonial rule; the *Québecois* are chid for allowing themselves to remain the only white colonized people in the world and, indeed, one of the few colonized peoples, white or colored. Instead of seeking bilingualism everywhere in Canada, the more extreme wing—and even some quite conservative groups—ask for a Quebec with one language, French, and complete fiscal independence from Canada. The movement takes the doctrine of the nation-state in its extreme form as defining the goal to be attained.

Instead of praising rural life, they speak of an urban and industrial Quebec, which will solve its problem by becoming master in its own house. They dismiss return to the land and the victory of the cradle as dreams that divert French Canadians from attaining realistic goals. Those goals of well-being for an urban and industrial people are to be gained by socialistic means, and by breaking the power of Yankee capitalism.

Some talk of Freud, Marx and alienation. In literary criticism, they talk of emancipation from obsession with the past, the frontiers, the land and France; not of denying the past and French identity, but of taking them for granted while they deal with their problems as North American city dwellers, as a people who need no justification except that they exist and have the same problems to write about as do others.

The new rhetoric may not be used in extreme form by many, but it has permeated a great deal of French-

Canadian writing and political talk. It has spread much more rapidly than any one expected. There are indeed some extreme groups who have turned to the bombing of symbols of British hegemony—a statue of Queen Victoria, an army recruiting station, and mailboxes in what is considered a well-to-do English quarter. The members of this small terrorist sect are not the leaders of the separatist movement, but their existence and temper indicate the intensity of the general feeling of malaise. Those arrested and accused of the bombings are alienated young men of the city, not intellectuals, but part of the white-collar Lumpenproletariat, semi-employed. It has been said that the whole separatist movement is one of the little bureaucrats of business and government. In its more moderate form, the movement has certainly been joined by many people of various classes, whose rhetoric also turns in the direction of a special status for the State of Quebec, of a renegotiation of the terms of Confederation.

To return to this country, the new things about the Negro movement are not its ultimate goals and its rhetoric, but its immediate goals, its mass and its structure. It got under way and took on mass as a struggle for the equal right to consume goods and services—food, transportation, education, housing and entertainment. This is a goal of people with at least some money to spend and with the aspiration to spend as others do. The Negro Americans who led those first sit-ins were indeed so American that they seem more humiliated by not being able to spend the dollar than they would be at not having a dollar to spend. "My money is as good as the other fellow's," is probably the ultimate expression of American democracy. Here we meet the great paradox in American social structure. While our race line is, next to South Africa's, the world's tightest, we have the times-over largest Negro middle

class in the world, and the largest group of Negroes approaching middle-class western tastes and with the money to satisfy them in some measure. This may be due to the fact that we are that country in which industry first depended upon its own workers to be its best customers, and in which movement has gone farthest in that direction.[10] Handicapped though Negro Americans are in employment and income, they are well-enough off to resent the barriers which prevent them from keeping up with the white Joneses. This reflects a great change in the Negro social structure itself; goal and social structure are doubtless functions of each other. In the struggle for consumption it appears generally to have been true that the Negro participants were of higher social class than the whites who have set upon them, or perhaps it is that racial struggles bring out the low-class side of white people.

Now that the movement for equality of the right to consume has moved into high gear—and especially in the South —the movement for equality in employment has taken on new momentum in the North. When, during the war, a number of us worked to get Negroes employed in industry in Chicago, our first objective was to get them moved into semi-skilled production jobs, and out of maintenance and unskilled work. The effort now is aimed higher—at the kinds of work controlled by craft unions, and especially those in construction. For in the precariously seasonal construction trades apprentice-

[10] F. P. Spooner shows that in South Africa the high standard of living of Whites rests upon the poverty of the Blacks; seven-eighths of the labor in mining, the industry that brings money to the country, is Black. The consumption industries import raw materials with the foreign exchange earned by mining, and produce at prices which only Whites can afford. *South African Predicament. The Economics of Apartheid*, New York: Praeger, 1960, pp. 181 *et seq.*

ships and jobs are notoriously held tightly in ethnic and family cliques. The battle for equality of right to consume may be essentially won long before access to all kinds of training and jobs is open. There are many inaccessible crevices in the American labor market. I have seen no good account of who the people are who are demonstrating at construction sites, but apparently many have been drawn in who never took part in demonstrations before. We may expect, I believe, that each new immediate objective, whether for the right to consume or to work, will draw in new kinds of participants.

One of the most striking cases of this is the apparent mobilization of the National [Negro] Medical Association. It was reported in the press that members of the National Medical Association were to picket the convention of the American Medical Association in Atlantic City and their headquarters in Chicago. The permanent executive secretary of the Negro association declared himself against the picketing as it would embarrass his good friends in the American Medical Association; but the young president was reported to have said he would himself lead the picketing. Negro physicians have been notoriously conservative in their attack on racial discrimination—even against themselves. Safely ensconced in general practice with patients whom white physicians did not want, they enjoyed a certain security provided they were content to practice in their own offices or in segregated hospitals, letting such Negro patients as could get into other hospitals go to white physicians. But that security is in danger. Negro physicians no longer have a near monopoly on Negro patients, for the patients may be part of insurance schemes which give them access to clinics or hospitals and which will pay their bills. The few segregated Negro hospitals are in generally sad and declining condition.

Young Negro physicians do not want to tie their professional fate to them. Back of all this, however, lies a general change in the structure of medical organization. The capital goods of medicine are concentrated more and more in hospitals and clinics; patient and physician meet where the tools and machines and auxiliary personnel are found. If the Negro patient has more access to them than the Negro physician, the latter is in a poor position. Thus a general change in the social structure of medical institutions strikes hard at the position of one of the Negro-American elites. If the younger Negro physicians are to survive, they must get into the main institutions of modern medicine; that means specialization, access to clinics, hospitals and laboratories, membership of various colleague groups and ability to move freely. The American Medical Association is the bastion of the older organization of medicine, for the power to accept members lies completely in the hands of county medical associations, dominated by local physicians out of sympathy with the modern trends in medicine as well as likely to be opposed to recognizing Negroes as full colleagues.

Perhaps it took this combination of changes in the structure of medical institutions, plus the momentum of a great social movement to stir the relatively well-off and well-entrenched to such undignified action as picketing. The change in medical institutions gives the younger Negro physician a motive for rejecting the bargains of the older ones; the new movement gives them the will and the courage.

The older Negro middle class—in the clergy, teaching, law, medicine, insurance and undertaking—had its being in segregated institutions. They got support from white people and organizations with an implicit bargain that there was to be no Negro middle class except what could be supported by giving services to Negro clients and customers; as Park said, the accommodation gave certain Negroes a defined place and field of activity. Now that these institutions are undergoing changes much like those in medicine, the very basis of the older Negro elite would be shaky even without changes in the race line itself.[11]

But that line is changing. With every increase of access of Negroes to consumption and service institutions; the security of the older Negro middle class, which depended upon segregated delivery of services takes another blow; and another front is opened in the battle for equality in the production and distribution of goods and services. Like so many battles in time of great change, it is in part a battle of the generations. In the larger, more itinerant and cosmopolitan system of distributing professional services in which younger men must make their careers, sponsorship of specialized colleagues and the good opinion of their peers about the country counts more than favor with a local clientele or local white leader. While the standards of judgment among professional peers are in some respects objective and universal, yet the specialized colleagueships of the academic, scientific and professional world are small and relations are quite personal. People are loath to hire a stranger. This is the front on which Negro scholars and professional men have to move forward.[12]

[11] E. Franklin Frazier, *The Black Bourgeoisie*, New York: The Free Press, 1957. That was the middle class of which Frazier wrote so mordantly.

[12] I have not commented on the role in this movement of the older organizations established to improve the condition of Negroes, to win their rights, or to consolidate their position. The Urban Leagues originally had the form of social agencies, with boards of leading citizens and support by community chests as well as by gifts. The National As-

Another new feature of the present movement is that some white people have joined not merely in financial support but in direct action itself. A few white Protestant, Catholic and Jewish religious dignitaries have lent not merely their voices, but also their bodies to the demonstrations. Larger numbers of young white persons, mainly students, have joined, perhaps at somewhat greater risk, in marches, demonstrations and sit-ins in both South and North. This is another matter on which Park commented, in 1923, just 40 years ago:

What has happened to other peoples in this modern world, has happened, is happening, to the Negro. Freedom has not given him the opportunity for participation in the common life of America and of the world that he hoped for. Negroes are restless and seeking. We are all restless, as a matter of fact.

In some respects, however, it seems to me the Negro, like all the other disinherited peoples, is more fortunate than the dominant races. He is restless, but he knows what he wants. The issues in his case, at least, are clearly defined. More than that, in this racial struggle, he is daily gaining not merely new faith in himself, but new faith in the world. Since he wants nothing except what he is willing to give to every other man on the same terms, he feels that the great forces that shape the destinies of peoples are on his side. It is always a source of great power to any people when they feel that their interests, so far from being antagonistic, are actually identified with the interests of the

sociation for the Advancement of Colored People was originally both a fighting and an elite organization without the features of a philanthropic agency; it became the organ of legal action. The new direct action has been led by new people. A division of labor seems to be emerging among them, with the whole enlivened by the popular direct action. This is a common enough feature of social movements; as some organizations settle down to one style of negotiation or action, new styles of action spring up around new, unofficial, charismatic leaders.

antagonists. We of the dominant, comfortable classes, on the other hand, are steadily driven to something like an obstinate and irrational resistance to the Negro's claims, or we are put in the position of sympathetic spectators, sharing vicariously in his struggles but never really able to make his cause whole-heartedly our own.[13]

The obstinate and irrational resistance of which Park spoke is certainly in evidence, and apparently more on the consumption front than on the job front. Perhaps the American ego is more centered on symbolic consumption of housing among the right neighbors than on having the right job and colleagues. But what about those white people who join in the lively action on behalf of Negro equality? Are they really nothing more than sympathetic spectators? This raises questions concerning the part of people without status disadvantage in the struggles of those who have a disadvantage. The clergy and many white people are, for the first time, going into overt action on behalf of an eternal principle which they presumably believed and preached all the time. In this case, conscience seems to have been aroused only after the movement, initiated and led by the injured party, got momentum and showed some signs of success. This somewhat cynical suggestion is no answer to this problem: What circumstances so re-define a social situation that some espoused eternal moral principle is considered not merely to apply to it, but to require immediate drastic

[13] Robert E. Park, "Negro Race Consciousness as Reflected in Race Literature," *American Review*, I (Sept.–Oct. 1923), 505–516, reproduced in R. E. Park, *Race and Culture*, New York: The Free Press, 1950, pp. 284–300.

action of kinds the keepers of the principle ordinarily would not consider proper? . . .

*   *   *

In 1963, when this paper was written, the balance of Negro American sentiment appeared to fall in the direction of integration; but it was on the verge of turning toward symbolic and organizational separation. The turn came quickly, sometimes with violence.

The organizational separation sought was not return of the old segregated schools, churches, and hospitals. It was rather a separation within existing institutions. The symbol of the new attitude is the name *Black*, which, more than the moderate word "Colored" and the exotic Portuguese word "Negro," makes the difference between the races polar—as distant as black from white. The immediate popular organizational goal is reorganization of many existing institutions so as to allow Blacks control of their own segment, with Black teaching Black about Blacks in the schools and universities, Blacks delivering professional services to Blacks, Blacks selling to Blacks. But one should be careful about predicting that this mood will continue or that all Blacks share it now or will share it in the future.

Some do, and more may, desire to play the game of equality and identity on the larger stage of all humanity. The aim of such a paper as mine was not to make predictions of events, but rather to develop sensitivity to the turns things may take, and to emphasize, as did Park, that "status arrangements are always tentative and likely to be questioned."

36

Why Ethnicity Today?

NATHAN GLAZER AND
DANIEL P. MOYNIHAN

Ethnicity seems to be a new term. In the sense in which we use it—the character of quality of an ethnic group—it does not appear in the 1933 edition of the *Oxford English Dictionary*, and only makes its appearance in the 1972 *Supplement*, where the first usage recorded is that of David Riesman in 1953. It is included in *Webster's Third New International*, 1961, but did not find its way into the *Random House Dictionary of the English Language* of 1966, nor the *American Heritage Dictionary of the English Language*, 1969. It did, however, make the 1973 edition of the *American Heritage Dictionary*, where it is defined as: "1. The condition of belonging to a particular ethnic group; 2. Ethnic pride." One senses a term still on the move. The first of these two definitions fits well with our own: an objective condition. The second, however, is decidedly *subjective*: "pride." How very different from an old meaning, "obs. rare" as the *OED* has it, "heathendom: heathen superstition." At the very least, a change of relative status is going on here, and a shift in the general understanding of ethnic groups. Where they were formerly seen as survivals from an earlier age, to be treated variously with toleration, annoyance, or mild celebration, there is now a growing sense that they may be forms of social life that are

Reprinted by permission of the publishers from *Ethnicity: Theory and Experience*, Edited by Nathan Glazer and Daniel P. Moynihan, Cambridge, Massachusetts: Harvard University Press, 1975, as adapted in *Commentary*, October, 1974. Copyright © 1974 by the President and Fellows of Harvard College.

capable of renewing and transforming themselves.

Still, one may wonder how useful this new term really is. Does it describe a new reality, or is it simply a new way of describing something old? Is it not a matter of age-old human characteristics and sentiments, finding expression, perhaps, in new settings, but in themselves nothing new? We think not. In our judgment, something new *has* appeared. A reader of the early 19th century, encountering the assertion that industrialization was shaping distinctive social classes, could well have shrugged it off with the thought that there had always been social ranks, always different ways of earning a living. Yet to have done so would have been to miss a big event of that age. Similarly, we feel that to see only what is familiar in the ethnicity of our time is to miss the emergence of a new social category as significant for the understanding of the present-day world as that of social class itself.

Perhaps the best way of getting at what is new here is by reference to the prevailing ideas of most contemporary social scientists regarding the course of modern social development. One such idea has been called by Milton Gordon the "liberal expectancy"—the expectation that the kinds of features which distinguish one group from another would inevitably lose their weight and sharpness in modern and modernizing societies, that there would be increasing emphasis on achievement rather than ascription, that common systems of education and communication would wipe out group differences, that nationally uniform economic and political systems would have the same effect. Under these circumstances the "primordial" (or in any case antecedent) differences between groups would become less and less significant. This "liberal expectancy" flowed into the "radical expectancy"—that class would become the main line of division between people, erasing the earlier lines of tribe, language, religion, national origin, and that these class divisions would themselves, after the Revolution, disappear. Thus Karl Marx and his followers reacted with impatience to the heritage of the past, as they saw it, in the form of ethnic attachments. *Interest* should guide rational men in social action; and interest was determined by economic position.

Yet one of the striking characteristics of the present situation is the extent to which the ethnic group itself is now behaving as an interest group. Interest is pursued effectively by ethnic groups today as well as by interest-defined groups: indeed, perhaps it can be pursued even more effectively. As against class-based forms of social identification and conflict—which of course continue to exist—we have been surprised by the persistence and salience of ethnic-based forms of social identification and conflict.

Thus, whereas in the past religious conflicts were based on such issues as the free and public practice of a religion, today they are based—like the one which is tearing Northern Ireland apart—on the issue of which group shall gain benefits or hold power. Language conflicts—as in India—today have little to do with the right to the public use of the language, as they did in the 19th century when, for example, there were efforts to Russify the Russian Empire and Magyarize the Hungarian Kingdom. They have more to do with which linguistic group shall have the best opportunity to get which job. It would be wrong to insist on too sharp a distinction: certainly the prestige of one's religion and language is involved in both kinds of conflict. Nevertheless the weight has shifted from an emphasis on culture, language, religion, *as such*, to an emphasis on the economic and social interests of the members of the linguistic or religious group.

There are two related explanations which may account for this development. The first is the evolution of the welfare state in the more advanced economies of the world and the advent of the socialist state in the underdeveloped economies. In either circumstance, the *state* becomes a crucial and direct influence on economic well-being, as well as on political status and everything flowing from that. In such a situation it is usually not enough, or not enough for long enough, to assert claims on behalf of large but loosely aggregated groups such as "workers," "peasants," "white-collar employees." Claims of this order are too broad to elicit a very satisfactory response, and even when they do, the benefits are necessarily diffuse and often evanescent, having the quality of an across-the-board wage increase which produces an inflation that leaves everyone about as he was. As a matter of strategic efficacy, it becomes necessary to disaggregate, to assert claims for a group small enough to make significant concessions possible and, equally, small enough to produce some gain from the concessions made. A British Prime Minister who does "something for the workers" probably doesn't do much and almost certainly does even less for his party. Doing something for the Scots, however, becomes an increasingly attractive and real option for Westminster. *That* much in the way of resources can be found, and the Scots are likely both to know about it and to consider it a positive gain, at least past the point of the next general election.

The welfare state and the socialist state appear to be especially responsive to ethnic claims. This is everywhere to be encountered: an Indian minister assuring his parliament that "Muslims, Christians, and other minorities" will receive their "due and proper share" of railroad jobs; a Czech government choosing a Slovak leader; a Chinese prime minister in Singapore choosing an Indian foreign minister; and so on. Leaders of groups are aware that political skills in pressing such claims vary, and occasionally voice their concern, as reported in a recent Associated Press dispatch from Los Angeles:

The Asian-American community leaders have accused the U.S. Department of Labor of exploiting their inexperience in "the political game" to exclude them when allocating federal funds.
"We Asians have always been a quiet minority. We've always been taken for granted, and we always get the crumbs," Miss ———, a leader of the Chinese Community Council, told newsmen.
Miss ——— was referring to the distribution of $314,000 in federal funds for career counseling projects. The council leaders accused the U.S. manpower area planning council of doing "a tremendous wrong" in giving the funds away entirely to Black and Chicano groups, whose project proposals were more professionally drafted.

The strategic efficacy of ethnicity as a basis for asserting claims against government has its counterpart in the seeming ease whereby government employs ethnic categories as a basis for distributing its rewards. Nothing was more dramatic than the rise of this practice on the part of the American government in the 1960's, *at the very moment it was being declared abhorrent and illegal*. The Civil Rights Act of 1964 was the very embodiment of "the liberal expectancy." "Race, color, religion, sex, national origin": all such ascriptive categories were abolished. No one was to be classified by such primi-

tive terms. In particular, government was to become color blind. Within hours of the enactment of the statute, in order to enforce it, the federal government, for the first time, began to require ever more detailed accountings of subgroups of every description, job trainees, kindergarten children, kindergarten teachers, university faculties, front-office secretaries in terms of—race, color, sex. (We have not yet proceeded to religion and national origin.) The expectancy that such characteristics would be ignored—in the immediate postwar years governments were busy eliminating all references to race and religion from official forms, even forbidding universities to request photographs of applicants for admission—was instantly replaced by the requirement that they not only be known but the facts as to distribution justified. Random distributions would not do: quotas appeared in American society, the instrument of national social policy designed ostensibly to prevent discrimination by going—inevitably, perhaps—beyond that to positive efforts on behalf of those presumptively discriminated against, a list which in short order commenced to lengthen.

Statutes began to reflect this new strategy. A small example: the Drug Abuse Education Act of 1970 provides "for the use of adequate personnel from similar social, cultural, age, ethnic, and racial backgrounds as those of the individuals served under any such program." In other words, the federal government was not only to know the peculiar ethnic patterns of various kinds of drug abuse, but was to match the therapists with the patients: Azerbaijani junkie, Azerbaijani counselor. In a variation of folk medicine, it was judged that wherever a malady was found, there too would a remedy reside. Which may or may not be nonsense: what is not to be denied is that the statute appropriated many millions of dollars for social services which were going to end up in the pockets of those who would dispense them, and these could be concentrated in specific ethnic groups. If government was doing a group a favor by providing special therapeutic services, it could compound the favor by concentrating the patronage involved within the very same group.

In addition to the strategic efficacy of ethnicity in making claims on the resources of the modern state, another reason for the shift to ethnicity as the organizing principle of interest conflicts concerns the issue of equality. Men are not equal; neither are ethnic groups. Whether they should be, or shouldn't be, is, of course, a wholly different question. If one is to describe the way the world is, one describes people everywhere ranked in systems of social stratification in which one person is better or worse off than another. This is the empirical fact. As with individuals, so with groups of individuals, with social groups defined by ethnic identity. We follow Ralf Dahrendorf in holding that inequalities among groups arise in the same way as he says they do among individuals: from differential success in achieving norms. Dahrendorf's thesis is that every society establishes norms selected from a universe of possible values. There seems no end to human ingenuity in thinking of characteristics that can be described as desirable or undesirable. It can be thought a good thing to be wealthy, or to be poor; to be dark or to be light; to be skinny or fat; generous or mean; religious or atheistic; fun-loving or dour; promiscuous or chaste. However, once a selection is made as to what is good and what is bad, individuals—and, we add, ethnic groups—have different levels of success in attaining the desired condition. Woe to blacks in Rhodesia; pity the white in Uganda. Pity the Nepalese in Bhutan who labors on

construction gangs before the eyes of a landowning peasantry which despises such servility; woe to the Malay facing the onslaught of Chinese industriousness.

In Dahrendorf's account the individual encounters the norms of his society *and* the "sanctions designed to enforce these principles." Some do better than others and reap the rewards; some suffer the punishments. But as between different ethnic groups, which have made quite different selections from the universe of possibilities, the norms of one are likely to be quite different from those of another, such that individuals who are successful by the standards of their own groups will be failures by those of the others. In a situation where one group is dominant—which is to say that its norms are seen as normal not just for them, but for everyone—there follows an almost automatic consignment of other groups to inferior status. This is not an entirely automatic consequence, since some groups will discover that they are good at achieving the norms of the dominant group, and may even be better than the group that laid down those "laws." In Kenya the Indians were evidently better at trading than the Africans, and so the Indians are being expelled. Jews have known the experience, Japanese, Chinese: who has not? (There are, of course, situations in which no one group is dominant, and where differing norms compete with one another, but this makes if anything for less social peace, as no one is ever quite certain what constitutes success or failure.)

Herein lies the dynamic element in the system. Dahrendorf writes that "Inequality always implies the gain of one group at the expense of others; thus every system of social stratification generates protest against its principles and bears the seeds of its own suppression." It is not perhaps necessary to assert that *every* system of social stratification generates protest against its principles. Some may not. But most that we run into in the 20th century seem to do so. This is to say that a *different* set of norms is set forth as desirable. Struggle ensues. Changes occur, not infrequently changes that favor those previously unsuccessful. Things *they* are good at come to be labeled good.

At this point we come back to the strategic efficacy of ethnicity as an organizing principle. In the most natural way the unsuccessful group has the best chance of changing the system if it behaves *as a group*. It is as a group that its struggle becomes not merely negative, but positive also, not merely against the norms of some other group, but in favor of the already existing norms of its own. One of the difficulties of social class as an organizing principle surely is that there just isn't that much conflict of norm between most social classes. In the West intellectuals and others at the top of the social stratification will fantasize about the differences between the values of those at the bottom and those in the middle—always to the advantage of the former—but it usually turns out that those at the bottom pretty much share notions of desirable and undesirable with those in the middle. Ethnic groups, however, often do differ as to what is desirable and what is undesirable.

Marxists thought ethnic groups would disappear. Why on earth would one wish to be a Pole when one could be a Worker? One reason, we are suggesting, is that being a Pole—or a Sikh, or a Mestizo—frequently involves a distinctive advantage or disadvantage, and that remaining a Pole, or a Sikh, or a Mestizo is just as frequently a highly effective way either to defend the advantage or to overcome the disadvantage.

Some individuals opt otherwise. They "pass" out of their own ethnic group into another, typically one that offers greater advantages. This process of absorption is extremely powerful: in the United States, at least, it is probably still quite the most important social process. Americans become more "American" and less ethnic all the time. But they may also—and simultaneously—become more ethnic. This was most dramatically the experience of Negro Americans during the 1960's—they even changed their name to "blacks" to establish that new assertion of distinctiveness—and other groups followed suit, or accompanied them on parallel tracks. As with student activism, this was a phenomenon whole parts of the world were experiencing, and any explanation that depends solely on local elements is not likely to remain satisfactory for long. Something larger was going on: something so large that Ralf Dahrendorf has recently referred to the "refeudalization" of society, the return of ascribed rather than achieved characteristics as determinants of social stratification. It may be that ethnicity is merely part of this larger development.

In a most tentative way one further suggestion may be advanced concerning the new saliency of ethnicity. Dahrendorf notes that for almost two centuries —"from Locke to Lenin"—"property dominated social and political thought: as a source of everything good or evil, as a principle to be retained or abolished." Yet, he continues, in societies such as those of the Soviet Union, Yugoslavia, and Israel, where private property has been reduced to "virtual insignificance," social stratification— class—persists, even flourishes. Further, we would add, the new stratification is to a considerable extent correlated with ethnicity. It probably always was, but the preoccupation with property relations obscured ethnic ones, which, typically, were seen either as derivative of the former, or survivals from a pre-contractual age. Now—as Yugoslav Communists struggle hopelessly (or so it would seem) to achieve some equity of development and living standard as between Bosnia-Herzegovina, Croatia, Macedonia, Montenegro, Serbia, and Slovenia; as Israeli socialists look with alarm at the persisting differences in the "social class status" of "European" Jews as against "Oriental" Jews in their homeland; as Great Russians prattle on about the equality of ethnic groups in the Soviet Union, while Ukrainians in Washington rally in protest at the *Russian* Embassy, and Jews in Moscow demand to be allowed to emigrate to Israel—it is property that begins to seem derivative, and ethnicity a more fundamental source of stratification.

This phenomenon is likely to be as much in evidence in an advanced capitalistic society where property relations are attenuated, as in a Communist or socialist society where they are abolished. But it is the Communist nations which have shown the more pronounced concern with ethnic matters, possibly because ethnic reality is so at odds with Marxist-Leninist theory. (Otto Bauer, one of the few Communist theorists to attempt to incorporate "nationalities" into Communist theory was, perhaps significantly, a product of the Austro-Hungarian world at a time when Croatia was governed from Vienna.) There are scores of official nationalities in the Soviet Union, and every citizen, at age sixteen, must opt for one such identity, which he retains for life. Similarly, the Chinese, with their great, central Han culture, find themselves paying considerable heed to "minority nationalities." According to a recent news dispatch from Peking:

More than 143,000 people of minority nationalities in the autonomous regions of Sinkiang, Tibet, Inner Mongolia, Kwangsi and Ningsia, and the Province of Yunnan have been admitted into the Communist

Party of China since the Ninth Party Congress in 1969. They include Tibetans, Mongolians, Uighurs, Chuangs, Huis, Koreans, Kazakhs, Yaos, and Miaos.

Most of the new party members are workers and former poor and lower-middle peasants or herdsmen. There is a certain number of revolutionary intellectuals. The new members are both men and women and range in age from young to old.

Many of the new party members from national minorities are emancipated slaves or serfs, or children of former slaves or serfs. They warmly love Chairman Mao, the Party, and the New Society, and hate the old society.[1]

---

[1] Compare the following item taken from a recent issue of *GOP Nationalities News*, a publication of the Republican National Committee:

"*Martin E. Seneca, Jr.*, a Seneca Indian, has been appointed to the important position of Director of Trust Responsibilities, Bureau of Indian Affairs, by BIA Commissioner Morris Thompson. Seneca, with a doctorate of law degree from Harvard, is an Associate Professor of Law at the University of Utah. . . .

"At the April 21 meeting in New York of the newly-formed *Albanian-American Republican Club*, the following slate of officers was elected: *Hamdi H. Oruci*, Chairman; Mrs. *Nejmie Zaimi* and Dr. *Ligoz Buzi*, Vice Chairmen; *Lumo M. Tsungu*, Secretary; and *Mick Kajtazi*, Treasurer.

"Present at the 11th Annual Hungarian Ball of the *Hungarian Freedom Fighters Federation of the U.S.* held in Washington, D.C., on April 20, were Republican Congressman *Larry Hogan* of Maryland; the Director of the RNC Heritage Division and Mrs. *Julian Niemczyk*; and Mr. and Mrs. *Laszlo Pasztor* and Dr. and Mrs. *John B. Genys*, Chairman and Treasurer respectively of the NRHG(N) Council.

"Mrs. *Angela Miller*, of *Colombian* origin, who is vice president of the *Latin American Nationalities Council*, 3rd vice chairman of the Republican Business Women of New York, and president of All Nations Women's Club, Inc., was elected co-chairman of Activities and Planning Committee of the NRHG(N) Council.

"Mrs. *Inese Stokes*, of *Latvian* heritage, recording secretary of the Illinois Republican State Nationalities Council, was elected co-

In short, while religion, language, and concrete cultural differences did decline, at least in the West, as specific foci of attachment and concern (to the extent the "liberal expectancy" was fulfilled), the groups defined by these cultural characteristics were differentially distributed through the social structure. Hence, even as their cultural characteristics were modified by modern social trends and became increasingly "symbolic," they were nevertheless able to serve as a basis for mobilization. Class was once expected to become the focus in the modern world for mobilizing group interests—it related directly to the rational character of society, and the way society generated different interests. Nation was the other great pole around which group interests could be mobilized. We do not in any way suggest that these are not the central categories for understanding modern societies; what we do propose is that ethnicity must now be added as a new major focus for the mobilization of interests, troublesome both to those who wish to emphasize the primacy of class, and those who wish to emphasize the primacy of nation.

But in order to understand why ethnicity has become stronger as a basis of group mobilization, it is necessary to modify the bald assertion that ethnicity serves as a means of advancing group interests—which it does—by insisting that it is not *only* a means of advancing interests. Indeed, one reason that ethnicity has become so effective a means of advancing interests is that it involves more than interests. As Daniel Bell puts it: "Ethnicity has become more salient [than class] because it can combine an interest with an affective tie," while, on the other hand, in the case of class, "what had once been an *ideol-*

ogy has now become almost exclusively an *interest*."

Illuminating as they are, however, such observations do not answer the questions: Why ethnicity? and Why now? Harold Isaacs, describing the making of a basic group identity, begins his analysis with something so immediate as body image. Clearly that, as well as language and intimately transmitted culture, all play a role in the affective component of ethnicity. But in a world of rapid change and shifting identity, any fixed notion of the "primordial" as the basis of group formation is bound to run into trouble. One problem with the primordial is that nowadays we know how recently many "primordial" groups were created. It is also clear that circumstances have much to do with degrees of ethnic attachment, mobilization, and conflict. In some circumstances, there is much; in others, very little.

These are two poles of analysis—the "primordialist" and the "circumstantialist"—between which explanations for the persistence or revival or creation of ethnic identities tend to waver—ours included. We do not celebrate ethnicity as a basic attribute of men which, when suppressed, will always rise again; nor do we dismiss it as an aberration on the road to a rational society in which all such heritages of the past will become irrelevant to social and political action. For as a political idea, as a mobilizing principle, ethnicity in our time has manifested itself under widely disparate conditions with luxuriantly varied results.

Thus, in the United States the rising demands among blacks first for civil rights, then for equality of opportunity, finally for some equality of participation in the social, economic, and political institutions of the country, can be understood in terms of the distinctive history of blacks in the United States. But it is striking that the black movement found an echo among other ethnic groups in the United States—Latin American, American Indian, Oriental, and eventually whites of various kinds. The circumstances of each of these groups were different. Some had been conquered, some had emigrated from colonies, some from free countries, some had met substantial prejudice and discrimination, others nothing much more than the inconvenience of a new country. Yet the form of the mobilized ethnic group seemed, in some degree, to satisfy individuals in each. (Indeed, many had been involved in vigorous ethnic politics for half a century or more. What changed was that such activity was legitimated: previously it had been disapproved and to some degree disavowed.) We do not assert that some common need, some common distress, existed in everybody ready to be evoked. We do not say that ethnicity is something like the identity of parents in Victorian novels which must be discovered lest some nameless distress follow. But on the other hand we do not believe that the new intensity of ethnic identification among a number of groups was merely a matter of imitation, or even of protective mimicry. Some combination of need and imitation seems to have been at work.

The black revolution had as surprising a resonance abroad as at home. A "black power" movement developed in the West Indies, a "civil rights" movement in Northern Ireland, and "Black Panthers" formed in Israel. Once again, as we consider the relative weight of primordial and circumstantial factors, we find a complex interplay. The Catholics of Northern Ireland did not need the black example to teach them that they were aggrieved—their miseries go back farther in history than those of American blacks—nor did the Oriental Jews of Israel need the American blacks

to remind them that something was amiss with their position. Nevertheless through the ever more universally pervasive mass media, the black example exerted its influence to some indeterminate extent, just as on their side American blacks were influenced by certain developments abroad.

The American civil-rights movement, for example, avowedly and explicitly adopted techniques developed in 20th-century India during the struggle against British rule. The more recent (and, it is hoped, marginal) incidents of urban terrorism followed, albeit without any evident awareness of the fact, a model of resistance developed by the Irish in the 19th century, and still dominant there. Underground "commandants" in San Francisco issuing "execution" orders against deviant revolutionaries were acting out the drama of Dublin in 1920. North Africans picked up the technique, or else invented it on their own; and an Italian made a movie, *The Battle of Algiers*, which American revolutionaries were soon trying to imitate. And so exchanges proceeded, with, in our time, ever mounting violence. Hijacking was invented, we believe, by the Palestinians—but Croatian workers resident in Sweden and Moslem dissidents in Ethiopia (to refer only to some of those who have acted out of some ethnic interest) have both made use of it.

What of the future? In the 18th and 19th centuries, international economic developments led to great migrations of labor, which in turn led to the creation of a good number of multi-ethnic states. This process is still going on. Never in history did Western Europe import as much labor as in the years after the Second World War. A new colored population of West Indians, Indians, and Pakistanis was added to England. One-third of the labor force of Switzerland, one-eighth of the labor force of

Germany, and substantial parts of the labor forces of France, Belgium, the Netherlands, and Sweden came to be made up of foreign workers. The legal circumstances of each of these waves of new immigrants varied. Some, like the new colored groups of England, were permanent, and had all the rights of citizenship. Some were from neighboring members of the European Commonwealth, and had claims to full social benefits in any other state of the Commonwealth. Some—like the Algerians in France—came from former colonies and had special rights. Others —Turks and Yugoslavs in Germany— came under permits and, theoretically at least, had no right to any permanent settlement. In other cases, such as Sweden, an egalitarian philosophy of government treated all newcomers, whether Italian or Finnish, generously, both as to social benefits and political rights.

Varied though the patterns are, however, we see everywhere two different approaches in conflict. On the one hand, the common philosophy of egalitarianism asserts that *all* should be treated alike: not only natives and older citizens of a nation, but those who come to work and settle there. On the other hand, Western Europeans have learned that new and permanent settlements of other ethnic groups mean ethnic conflict, and they intend to avoid it if they can. For Great Britain it is too late: although only 2 per cent of the population, the new colored groups already form an issue in British politics that far outweighs their minuscule numbers, and further immigration has virtually been halted. The North Africans, Spanish, and Portuguese in France, and the Italians, Yugoslavs, and Turks in Germany have lesser rights than the West Indians, Pakistanis, and Indians in England, but one wonders whether they will actually be any less permanent a part of those countries. Will the problems arising from the new

heterogeneity of France and Germany— the familiar conflicts over housing, schooling, jobs—really be settled by simple mass expulsions, legal as that may be?

Alone of the major nations in the world, the United States continues to accept large numbers of permanent immigrants. Moreover, these immigrants are of quite different "stock" from those of the past. Most notably, they are Asian, and most notable of all, they are to an unprecedented degree professional, upper-middle-class persons. What this means is that the process of gaining political influence—a process which took even the most successful of earlier groups two generations at least —is likely to be rapid for these most recent newcomers. Thus, however much Western Europeans and others may succeed in protecting themselves from the ethnic storms of the 20th century, we may be sure they will continue to buffet the Great Republic.

Nor, of course, can the remaining nation-states easily succeed in avoiding their share of such difficulties. Since the Second World War almost every new nation—and they far outnumber the older nations—has come into existence with a number of serious ethnic conflicts waiting, as it were, their turn to be the focus of post-independence political life. The old European states, while becoming somewhat more diverse with the addition of new groups, are still in the process of finding out just how diverse they had already become. Add to this the fact—still given surprisingly little attention—that in a world in which each society becomes ethnically more diverse, we have had, since the Second World War, a strong prejudice against the formation of new states organized along ethnic lines. As Samuel Huntington has written, "The 20th-century bias against political divorce, that is, secession, is just about as strong as the 19th-century bias against marital divorce." Bangladesh is an exception, but the general rule remains in force. Certainly these political realities alone seem to provide a good number of the ingredients for a greater degree of ethnic conflict than was experienced, for example, in the world of the Great Depression.

Indeed, there is already evident an increase both in the number and intensity of ethnic conflicts. Walker Conner has undertaken the invaluable task of recording the rise and extent since the French Revolution of what he calls "ethnonationalism." He reports that nearly half of the independent countries of the world have been troubled in recent years by some degree of "ethnically inspired dissonance." We do not have benchmarks for earlier periods, but it seems clear that ethnic conflicts have shown a rise, too, in intensity in the last decade or so. As some examples, consider the Anglophone-Francophone conflict in Canada, Catholic and Protestant in Northern Ireland, Walloon and Fleming in Belgium, Jews and other minority groups versus great Russians in the Soviet Union, Ibo versus Hausa and Yoruba in Nigeria, Bengali versus non-Bengali in Pakistan, Chinese versus Malay in Malaysia, Greek versus Turk in Cyprus. If we had measurements of intensity we would not necessarily find that every one of these conflicts has become uniformly more intense. Some of them seem happily to have peaked (sometimes in war and violent conflict), and measures of harmonization and accommodation seem to have had some effect since these peaks were reached (Nigeria, the United States). In at least one other case—Pakistan—conflict has reached the point of separation, and has subsequently declined in intensity, to be succeeded perhaps by a rise in ethnic discord within each one of the two successor states.

There are those who say that ethnic conflict is simply the form that class conflict has been taking on certain occasions in recent decades, and that without the motor of class exploitation nothing else would follow. Others say that ethnic conflicts must be decomposed into a variety of elements: colonial conflicts; the uprising of the "internally" colonized; the ambition of self-appointed leaders; fashions and fads. To us, however, it seems clear that ethnic identity *has* become more salient, ethnic self-assertion stronger, ethnic conflict more marked everywhere in the last twenty years, and that the reasons include the rise of the welfare state, the clash between egalitarianism and the differential achievement of norms, the growing heterogeneity of states, and the international system of communication. This set of reasons scarcely amounts to a theory, but it does, we believe, suggest that there is a phenomenon here that is, in ways not yet explicated, no mere survival but intimately and organically bound up with major trends of modern societies.

37

Ethnogenesis and Negro-Americans Today

LESTER SINGER

The view of Negro-white relations in American society generally accepted by sociologists is that they are caste relations.[1] A competing view—which has not achieved wide acceptance, although the terminology persists—is that the phenomena are best understood as race relations.[2] The two approaches, regardless of the differences between them, deal primarily with the structure of Negro-white relations and with the factors serving to maintain that relational structure.[3]

My thesis is that these structural models fail to illuminate the character of the entities that occupy the various places in the relational structure. I had asked the question: In sociological terms, *what* are the Negroes in American society? And, at first, the answer appeared to be: They are a caste, or a race—and the whites must be one or the other also. Upon further consideration, however, it became clear that caste —as defined by Warner, Davis and

Myrdal—and race—as defined by Cox —are not answers to the substantive question. The writers answer the question: *Where?* That is to say, they tell us the position of the Negroes in the structure of Negro-white relations. They do not indicate *what* the Negroes are, *what* they constitute as a social entity.

Social Category, Social Entity, and Negro-Americans

Let me make clear the notions that underlie the use of the term "social entity" as contrasted with the term "social category." "Social category" has been defined by Bennett and Tumin as referring to "numbers of people who constitute an aggregate because they have a common characteristic(s) *about which* [italics mine] society expresses some views and which therefore influences their life chances."[4] The "members" of a social category are not necessarily involved in any relationship among themselves. Thus the terms "men," "women," "immigrants," and "divorcees" stand for social categories.[5]

Reprinted from *Social Research*, 29: 422–432 (Winter 1962), with permission of the author and the publisher.

[1] For definitions see as examples W. L. Warner, "Formal Education and the Social Structure," *Journal of Educational Sociology*, vol. 19 (May 1936) pp. 524–31. W. L. Warner and A. Davis, "A Comparative Study of American Caste," in *Race Relations and the Race Problem*, ed. Thompson (Durham, N.C.: Duke University Press, 1939). A. Davis, B. B. and M. R. Gardner, *Deep South* (Chicago, Ill.: University of Chicago Press, 1941). G. Myrdal, *An American Dilemma* (New York: Harper & Bros., 1944).

[2] See as an example O. C. Cox, *Caste, Class, and Race* (New York: Doubleday & Co., Inc., 1948).

[3] This structural emphasis and static quality is especially the case with the caste approach.

[4] J. W. Bennett and M. M. Tumin, *Social Life* (New York: Alfred A. Knopf, Inc., 1949), p. 140. Note that the authors go on to say, "For instance, in our society all people with dark skin may be considered as belonging to a social category."

[5] It may be added that social categories cannot interact in any sociological sense. For example, when we speak of the interaction of men and women, it may sound as if we are referring to the interaction of categories. But actually we are referring to the cumulative interaction of individuals or, more likely, to typical aspects of interaction situations that involve individuals. Certainly such interaction situations are influenced by the beliefs and values attached to the several category definitions but, just as certainly, it

The term "social entity," on the other hand, refers to a number of people manifesting such qualities as patterned relationships, shared values, and self-recognition. Thus a team, a gang, a community, an ethnic group, and a society all constitute recognizable social entities.

For this writer, the nub of the contrast between the two terms is the presence or absence of internal structure and the accompanying cultural, or ideological, elements. This is somewhat like the difference between a bin full of spare parts and an engine which has been assembled from such spare parts. As with the bin full of spare parts, the social category contains elements that have no necessary relations to one another. The social entity, however, like the engine, can only be understood through an understanding of the elements in patterned relations.

In the work of both Myrdal and Cox are to be found the empirical generalizations that express the distinctive social attributes of Negro-Americans. These attributes, when viewed as elements in a pattern rather than separately, make up a picture of Negroes as a social entity on the order of an ethnic group.[6] Among these qualities are, briefly, the following. (1) The existence of a separate Negro prestige continuum, that is "a social-class sys-

tem." (2) The existence of a distinctive Negro culture pattern. [While it is true that the pattern is derived from that of the larger society—Myrdal calls it a "pathological" form and Cox a "truncated" form of the larger American culture pattern—such references to origin indicate, if we disregard their evaluative content, the distinctiveness of this pattern. This is not to say that it is completely different from the larger pattern but, rather, that it is not quite the same.] (3) The existence of various aspects of Negro solidarity vis-à-vis the "whites": its, heretofore, primarily defensive character; its tentativeness; the predominantly compromising nature of Negro leadership; the development of a self-image; the Negroes' conviction of their rights in the larger society; and the direction of collective Negro aspiration toward the realization of these rights within the larger society. (4) The existence of the unaccountable relational networks and organizations (that is the internal structure) which, by virtue of discrimination and the defensive response of Negroes, are manned largely by Negroes.

If this pattern of qualities is significant it means, as I indicated at the outset, that Negroes and, therefore, Negro-white relations, cannot be fully understood if only category concepts are used. The employment of such concepts results in interpretations that are not as inclusive as the data allow. Another important limiting effect of the use of these concepts is an emphasis on the static. Consequently, while a model based on category concepts may prepare the ground, it certainly does not facilitate an examination of process, development, and change.[7] And yet it is in precisely this latter direction that

---

is incorrect to say that the social categories are interacting.

[6] For a definition of ethnic group see note 11. Interestingly enough, both Myrdal and Cox approached the issue of Negroes as an entity, but neither one developed the implications of his own suggestive comments. See Myrdal's references to "a separate community" and "a nation within a nation" (note 1, above), pp. 680, 785, 1003–04 and Cox's reference to a "quasi-society" (note 2, above), p. 503. See also L. Singer, "A Comparative Analysis of Selected Approaches to Negro-White Relations in the United States" (Doctor's dissertation, Columbia University, 1958), pp. 140, 231–32, 270–72.

[7] This is a serious consideration when the investigator's concern is diachronic and developmental. But this is not to say that category concepts are useless, for they are precisely applicable to synchronic analysis.

we must search if social entities, which come into existence and which disappear, are to be adequately understood. Thus, if Negroes in the United States are to be understood as an entity, that is as an ethnic group, it is necessary to attempt to answer such questions as: How did this entity commence to form? What are the factors tending to maintain or change the formative process? What are the circumstances under which such an entity will cease to exist? The remainder of this essay attempts to answer these questions.

Ethnogenesis

During the seventeenth and eighteenth centuries the Africans who were brought to North America, as well as to other parts of the New World, were representatives of a variety of societies, cultural backgrounds, language groups, and so forth. Consequently, *as a totality* they can only be viewed as a social category; that is as "Africans" or "slaves." Removed from their various social contexts and thrown together as enslaved strangers they had, particularly in North America, no internal organization. In fact, the evidence indicates that virtually all traces of African social organization disappeared under the impact of American slavery.[8] One method of accomplishing this was the intentional separation of members of the same society. This was done, among other reasons, to diminish the possibility of revolt. As R. E. Park says, "It was found easier to deal with the slaves, if they were separated from their kinsmen." [9]

[8] See E. F. Frazier, *The Negro in the United States* (New York: The Macmillan Co., 1949), pp. 6–21. This may be contrasted, for example, with Brazilian slavery. See D. Pierson, *Negroes in Brazil* (Chicago: University of Chicago Press, 1942), especially pp. 38–45, IX, and X.

[9] *Race and Culture* (New York: Free Press of Glencoe, Inc., 1950), p. 268.

It should be realized that during the period of slavery the newly arrived Africans came into contact with whites and acculturated slaves. In this way, cut off from their own background, they came to take on the culture of American society in whatever form it was available to them. With Emancipation the former Africans and their descendants became, as the federal government put it, "freedmen." This legal term, however, stands only for a social category; the freedman lacked determinate social group characteristics. But indications of what was to come had been evidenced earlier by the numerous slave revolts,[10] and the participation of runaway slaves and free Negroes in the Abolitionist movement and the Underground Railroad.

Following Emancipation, the group-forming process moved with much greater speed and intensity than before. I propose that this formative process be referred to as "ethnogenesis," meaning by this term the process whereby a people, that is an ethnic group, comes into existence.[11] The process [12] appears to

[10] See H. Aptheker, *American Negro Slave Revolts* (New York: Columbia University Press, 1943).

[11] The term ethnic group is derived from the Greek word *ethnos* meaning "a people." Ethnic group is used here to mean a set of persons that may be distinguished from other such sets by virtue of: (1) a shared pattern of values, beliefs, norms, tastes, and so forth (2) an awareness of their own distinctiveness, partially reflected in a "we-feeling"; (These two distinctions taken together make up their *ethos.*) (3) some structure of relationships among them; and (4) the tendency to maintain generational continuity by marriage within the group. This is very close to E. K. Francis' definition with its emphasis on the *Gemeinschaft* quality of an ethnic group. See, for example, his "The Nature of an Ethnic Group," *American Journal of Sociology*, vol. 52 (March 1947) pp. 393–400 and "The Russian Mennonites: from Religious to Ethnic Group," *American Journal of Sociology*, vol. 54 (September 1948) pp. 101–07. See also the definition given by R. M. MacIver and C. H. Page

have the following form. (1) A portion of a population becomes distinguished, on some basis or bases, in the context of a power relationship. [The particulars are not important for the general outline of the process. The bases may be ideological differences, imputed intrinsic differences, particular functions in the division of labor, and so forth.] (2) The members of this distinguished population segment are "assigned" to a particular social role and fate; [13] that is, the division of labor becomes reorganized.[14] (3) As these people react to the situation in which they find themselves, they become involved with one another, if the situation permits. In other words, social structures develop among them; it is at this point that entity characteristics first become apparent. (4) Then these people become aware of their commonality of fate. The growth of such corporate self-awareness reinforces the structuring tendencies.[15] (5) The further development of the emerging ethnic group will then depend, in part, on the nature of the structures that develop, the content of the group's "self-image," and the shared conception of its destiny. This, of course, emphasizes internal development, which is our present concern. The other big area of causal factors—with which we are not here concerned except to indicate a context of power relations—is the specific character of the relationship with the other segment(s) of the population. Necessarily, internal group development and external (inter-group) relationships influence one another.

It has already been pointed out that the enslaved Africans were not a social group, although from the first they were a distinguishable portion, that is category, of the population. They were not merely physically distinguishable, as has been stressed in the literature, but also socially distinguishable by virtue of their depressed economic situation, with all of the occupational, educational, and associational consequences. With the passage of time it was the latter point that became the most important. Slavery, however, muted the overt, collective responses of the enslaved to the situation. Emancipation altered this picture.

Let us now briefly scan the phases of the processes of ethnogenesis as it has operated in the case of the Negroes.

Reconstruction. During the Reconstruction period the freedmen achieved physical mobility and, consequently, wide-ranging contacts with one another. Also, as a consequence of political participation and the struggle for land, some Negro political leaders emerged. A significant factor that influenced all of the subsequent developments was the failure of the freedman to obtain land and their consequent involvement in cotton farming on, for the most part, the lowest levels of tenancy of the plantation system. It is also significant that

which specifies both primary and secondary relationships in *Society* (New York: Rinehart & Co., Inc.), p. 387. Compare with R. M. Williams, Jr., *The Reduction of Intergroup Tensions* (New York: Social Science Research Council, 1947), p. 42.

[12] This process seems to me to be one of several kinds of "group-forming" processes. Roscoe C. Hinkle, in a private communication, has suggested "socio-genesis" as the generic term.

[13] The distinguished population segment may become dominant, although this is not usually the case. See, for example, MacIver and Page, note 11, p. 388.

[14] In the case of the Africans in the English colonies this would mean, not slavery per se, but the qualities which slavery in America achieved by the end of the seventeenth century. It was only then that the European-Christian "slaves" and the African-heathen "slaves" became differentiated into servants —who would serve for a limited time—and chattel slaves—who would serve for the duration of their lives. See O. Handlin, *Race and Nationality in American Life* (New York: Doubleday Anchor Books, 1957), especially I.

[15] See, for example, A. Rose, *The Negro's Morale* (Minneapolis: University of Minnesota Press, 1949), especially II.

during the Reconstruction period the Negroes had to fight in a variety of ways, including organized militia, against the physical onslaughts of Southern whites.[16]

The National Compromise and After. The Reconstruction governments were overthrown by the end of the third quarter of the nineteenth century, and the last quarter of that century witnessed both the actual restoration and the political assertion of "white supremacy." During this period discriminatory practices increased and there developed a tendency to treat all Negroes alike regardless of social attributes. This marked a change from the previous period (Myrdal, note 1, pp. 578–82). *Pari passu,* behind the growing barriers there were developing distinctive structural and ideological attributes among the Negroes; for example, a "lower class" Negro family pattern, Negro businesses catering to Negroes, the expansion of the Negro Church (with Negro ministers representing the status quo as supernaturally sanctioned), and the emergence of Booker T. Washington as a national Negro leader.

Early Twentieth Century. The peak, or depth, of discriminatory tendencies was reached in the early twentieth century. By this time the Reconstruction state constitutions had been changed, legislation requiring "separate but equal" facilities had been declared constitutional, and in the preceding three decades approximately 2,500 Negroes had been lynched in the South. This last is an index of the community-wide methods of violence and intimidation used by the whites to maintain the situation.

In the first decade of this century, however, there appeared other entity, or ethnic group, characteristics among

the Negroes; for example, organized protest in the form of the Niagara Movement and the National Association for the Advancement of Colored People and the attempts to create economic opportunities for Negroes in the form of the National Urban League. These, in turn, give evidence of the Negroes' conception of their destiny— full and unhampered participation in the larger society. This was first expressed organizationally in the statement of the Niagara Movement in 1905.

World War I and After. At the time of World War I there commenced the "Great Migration" to the Northern cities.[17] The advent of the Negroes was accompanied by a number of severe "race riots." (A "race riot" is a situation in which Negroes fight back against extra-legal mob violence.) As a result of the disappointments and frustrations which followed the move North to "freedom" and the "war to save democracy," the 1920s saw the rise of the Garvey [Back-to-Africa] Movement. Although unsuccessful, it is significant because a fundamental part of the ideology of the movement was anti-white and separatist in orientation. (It is also significant that a movement with this orientation failed.) Further, no whites were involved in the leadership of the movement, as was not the case with the previously mentioned Negro lay organizations nor the Negro Church. This fact demonstrated, for the first time, that Negroes could organize Negroes as such. By this time, as Frazier points out (note 8, p. 531):

---

[16] From one point of view Reconstruction was "a prolonged race riot." G. B. Johnson, cited in Myrdal, note 1, p. 449.

[17] See Myrdal, note 1, pp. 191–96. The bulk of the Negroes are still in the South, although the northward movement continues as well as the movement of Southern Negroes to Southern cities. It might be pointed out that Cox hypothesizes (note 2, p. xxxii) that, "In the future Negroes will probably become more highly urbanized than any other native-born population group in the country."

The impact of urban living . . . [and] . . . conflicts in the North tended not only to intensify the consciousness of being a Negro, but . . . also gave new meaning to being a Negro . . . [it] meant being a member of a group with a cause, if not a history. As in the case of the nationalistic struggles in Europe, the emergence of a . . . literature helped in the development of a consciousness. As we have seen, there appeared a Negro Renaissance following World War I. Much of the literature and art of the Negro Renaissance was not only militant but tended to give the Negro a conception of the mission and destiny of the Negro. The Negro newspapers, which began to influence the masses, tended to create a new . . . consciousness . . . [which] did not have separation from American life.[18]

The recent past and the present continue to yield evidence of both Negro ethnicity and the persistence of ethnogenesis. Such evidence is found in the assaults on the "white primary," segregated education at all levels, the increased efforts of Negroes to get Negroes out to vote, the increasing attempts of Southern Negroes to vote, the "sit-ins" in the South, and the "Freedom Riders." [19]

Summary and Conclusion

To sum up, then, Negro-Americans are an instance of a people: (1) whose ancestors, as recently as four generations ago, showed little in the way of ethnic group characteristics and who in this *ante bellum* period could only be

conceptualized as a social category; (2) who now form a distinct social and subcultural entity within the American society and are in the process of becoming a full-fledged ethnic group; (3) whose character as an emergent ethnic group is the consequence of factors outside themselves as well as their response to these factors.

The earlier ways of conceptualizing Negroes in Negro-white relations in the United States were called into question because they are based on static category concepts and, as such, appear not to do justice to the phenomenon. The available data seem to require an entity concept that will allow the developmental factors to be taken into account. If the ethnogenesis concept, which has been offered to replace these other conceptual tools, is to be properly evaluated, two questions must be answered: Does this new approach encompass the data and relate them adequately to one another? The answer to this is, ultimately, the task of future investigators. How fruitful is this new approach as a source of hypotheses?

This paper will close with some suggestions in answer to the second question.

1. In the light of the above, it may be suggested that the people whom we call the Negroes in this society are not comparable to the so-called Negroes of Brazil, Haiti, or the British West Indies. Negro-Americans are different from Brazilians, Cubans, Haitians, or Jamaicans who may happen to possess some negroid physical traits. In these latter instances, the use of the term Negro lays stress on biological similarities and blurs the sociological, cultural, and psychological differences.

2. Although there have been and are many instances of ethnogenesis,[20] this

---

[18] For a similar view of the social-psychological consequences of the Negro press see Myrdal, note 1, pp. 908–24 and A. Rose, note 15, pp. 102–08.

[19] The "Freedom Riders" have a special significance in that whites are actively participating in the attempt to end discrimination in transportation. Both Myrdal and Cox hypothesize that Negro-Americans cannot achieve their aspirations without overt support from whites. The "sit-ins" are also especially significant because of the youth of the demonstrators.

[20] C. M. Arensberg in a private communication suggests such instances as "Italian-Americans in the U.S.A.; . . . Africans and

particular instance involving the Negroes has a contemporary uniqueness beyond the particularity which inheres in any single case. As stated above, the special aspect in this case resides in the forcible acculturation of the individual African progenitors in a completely strange setting and the loss of their African cultures in the process. An important consequence of this is that when ethnogenesis moved into high gear less than a century ago the freedmen were social persons; that is, they were socialized individuals since they had been members of plantation households. Taken as a whole, however, they comprised a collection of unrelated individuals. Further, this collection of unrelated individuals was without the community of tradition, sentiment, and so forth, that has marked other populations and given rise to ethnic groups such as the Italian immigrants.[21] Thus we have here a case of ethnogenesis starting *ab initio*, unlike all other current instances of ethnogenesis in which members of some ethnic groups become transformed into another ethnic group.[22]

3. To say that Negroes are involved in the process of ethnogenesis is not the same as saying that they are a full-fledged ethnic group. They are not. Full-fledged ethnicity would appear to be characterized by at least two qualities: long tradition and a marked, if not a general, tendency toward self-perpetuation. Concerning tradition, Negro-Americans have neither a legendary nor a long historic past. E. K. Francis writes of what would here be called a full-fledged ethnic group, "Since an ethnic group is based on an elementary feeling of solidarity, we must suppose that mutual adjustment has been achieved over a considerable length of time and that the memory of having possibly belonged to another system of social relationships must have been obliterated. Certainly, this is not the case with Negroes" (note 11, p. 396). As for self-perpetuation, this is usually achieved by endogamy. Now, despite the use of this term with reference to Negro-white relations in the United States, it is quite clear that pressures outside the Negro group are primarily effective in preventing marriages between Negroes and the members of other ethnic groups rather than self-imposed restrictions.[23] The current tendency among Negroes to frown on intermarriage is a defensive *reaction*. It is suggested by various writers that this attitude is neither deep nor abiding (Myrdal, note 1, pp. 56-7 and 62-4 and Cox, note 2, pp. 447-50).

On the basis of the two points of

East Indians in the Caribbean (cf. Trinidad); Hispanos (Puerto Ricans, and so forth) in New York (just started); Pennsylvania Dutch (1600–1800); 'white southerners' paralleling Negroes in the U.S.A.; . . . In Israel, today, the Oriental Jews . . . are being welded into a self-conscious minority vis-à-vis the 'Askenazim' or 'Europeans' by all accounts. . . ."
[21] Beyond the differences in prestige-ranking of field hands and house servants, the only common cultural element was the slave family. On the relative weakness of this structure see Frazier, note 8, II, especially 40–41.
[22] This is the sort of process which E. K. Francis refers to: "Yet even on the ground of our limited knowledge it becomes clear that, generally speaking, the stages of development traversed by ethnic groups are: expansion—fission—new combination." (note 11, p. 398). What we have here called ethnogenesis is related to Francis' sequence at two points. It is, on the one hand, temporally prior in that ethnic groups must

have formed before they could expand. On the other hand, the last stage of the sequence is ethnogenesis. Consequently, the expanded sequence should be: ethnogenesis—expansion—fission—new combination (that is, ethnogenesis).
[23] See, for example, A. Davis and M. and B. Gardner, especially the section, "Endogamy-Keystone of Caste," pp. 24–44. Note also the various state laws, and not only in the deep South, prohibiting intermarriage.

tradition and self-perpetuation, while it is proper to regard the Negroes as an ethnic group, it is also proper to say that they are still in the *process of becoming* an ethnic group, that is, their ethnicity is still *developing*. Paradoxical as the formulation may appear, it is no stranger than applying the term "tree" to a young tree, to a mature tree, and to an old tree. Let us now turn to some predictive notions based on the view of the Negroes as a developing ethnic group.

4. As the Negroes become more of an ethnic group—more focused ,and organized—it may be expected that rather than *re*acting to the actions of white, they will increasingly *act* along paths of action chosen to achieve their goal of full, individual participation in the larger society. It can be added that any successes can be expected to pave the way for increased activity. It may be further hypothesized that, as the barriers to full participation yield and slowly crumble, frustration and impatience over the differences between actuality and aspirations may prompt segments of the Negro group to manifest radical and separatist (anti-white) sentiments, such as the "black Muslim" movement. It is doubtful that any of these organizations will be large. Size, however, should not be confused with importance. By defining one end of the spectrum of Negro responses, such groups will affect the thinking of all Negroes. Further, because of the impact upon the whites, they may contribute to the general struggle for Negro aspirations despite their separatist orientations.

5. A related hypothesis concerns the character of Negro leadership. Negro leaders in the latter part of the nineteenth century typically played the role of justifying the condition of Negroes. Many Negro ministers fell into this category. It is important to add that such leaders were, either directly or as a result of the "veto power," chosen by dominant whites. (This type of leadership is called "accommodating leadership" by Myrdal while Cox refers to it as "the spirit of Uncle Tom.") By the turn of the century, a new kind of leadership had emerged typified by Booker T. Washington. (This type of leaderships is called "conciliatory leadership" by Frazier and "compromising leadership" by Myrdal.) It is Myrdal's thesis, as well as Cox's, that whites were, and are, also influential in the selection of this type of leader. If my thesis is correct, then we may expect that in the coming period the character of Negro leadership will have more of the qualities exemplified earlier by W. E. B. DuBois and today by Martin Luther King, Thurgood Marshall, and James Farmer. We may also expect that the "Uncle Toms" and the conciliators will become fewer and fewer.

6. As a final point, it may be suggested that there are implications for psychological research in the social entity approach to the American Negro. The effects of identifying oneself with an emergent group that is no longer on the defensive but is coming more and more to act for itself as well as with a group that has strong leaders and hero figures should make a significant difference in the personalities of Negro-Americans. Indeed, I believe that as the self-image of the Negroes is internalized by individual Negroes, a redirection and transformation of Negro resentment and hostility and a redefinition of individual Negro selves will surely take place.

38

New Religious Consciousness

ROBERT N. BELLAH

The disturbances and outbursts in America in the 1960s were hardly unique in modern history. Indeed in a century where irrationalities and horrors of all sorts—mass executions, mass imprisonments, wars of annihilation, revolutions, rebellions and depressions—have been common, the events of that decade in America might even be overlooked. But it is precisely the significance of that decade that the irrationalities and horrors of modern history were borne in upon Americans so seriously that for the first time mass disaffection from the common understandings of American culture and society began to occur. Far more serious than any of the startling events of the decade was the massive erosion of the legitimacy of American institutions—business, government, education, the churches, the family—that set in, particularly among young people, and that continues, if public opinion polls are to be believed, in the 1970s even when overt protest has become less frequent.

The erosion of the legitimacy of established institutions among certain sectors of the populations of many European countries—particularly the working class and the intellectuals—began at least 100 years ago. In many of the newer third-world countries, the nation, state and modern institutions have not yet gained enough legitimacy to begin the process of erosion. But in America, in spite of a civil war, major social and religious movements, and minor disturbances of occasionally violent intensity, the fundamental legitimacy of the established order had never

Reprinted by permission of The New Republic, © 1974, The New Republic, Inc.

before been questioned on such a scale. This is in part because that order was itself a revolutionary order, the result of one of the modern world's few successful revolutions. The messianic hope generated by the successful revolution and nurtured by the defeat of slavery in the Civil War, for long made it possible to overlook or minimize the extent to which the society failed to achieve its own ideals. The promise of early fulfillment, which seemed so tangible in America, operated to mute our native critics and prevent mass disaffection, at least for a long time. But in the decade of the '60s for many, not only of the deprived but of the most privileged, that promise had begun to run out.

The interpretations of reality in America that had been most successful in providing meaning and generating loyalty up until the '60s were biblical religion and utilitarian individualism. The self-understanding of the original colonists was that they were "God's new Israel," a nation under God. (From this point of view the addition of the phrase "under God" to the pledge of allegiance in the 1950s was an indication of the erosion of the tradition not because it was an innovation but because it arose from the need to make explicit what had for generations been taken for granted.) In New England this understanding was expressed in the biblical symbol of a covenant signifying a special relationship between God and the people. American society was to be one of exemplary obedience to God's laws and subject to the grace and judgment of the Lord. The notion of Americans as an elect people with exemplary significance for the world was not abandoned but enhanced during the revolution and the period of constructing the new nation. It was dramatically reaffirmed by Lincoln in the Civil War and continued to be expressed in the 20th century in the thought of men like William Jennings Bryan and Woodrow Wilson. This biblical aspect of the national self-understanding was strongly social and collective even though it contained an element of voluntarism from its Protestant roots. Its highest conception of reality was an objective absolute God as revealed in scriptures and its conception of morality was also based on objective revelation.

A second underlying interpretation of reality that has been enormously influential in American history, utilitarian individualism, was never wholly compatible with the biblical tradition, complex as the relations of attraction and repulsion between the two were. This tradition was rooted ultimately in the sophistic, skeptical and hedonistic strands of ancient Greek philosophy but took its modern form initially in the theoretical writings of Thomas Hobbes. It became popular in America mainly through the somewhat softer and less consistent version of John Locke and his followers, a version deliberately designed to obscure the contrast with biblical religion. In its consistent original Hobbesian form, utilitarianism grew out of an effort to apply the methods of science to the understanding of man and was both atheistic and determinist. While the common-sense Lockian version that has been the most pervasive current of American thought has not been fully conscious of these implications, the relation between utilitarianism and Anglo-American social science has been close and continuous from Hobbes and Locke to the classical economists of the 18th and early 19th centures to the social Darwinists of the late 19th century and finally to such influen-

tial present-day sociologists as George Homans.

Whereas the central term for understanding individual motivation in the biblical tradition was "conscience," the central term in the utilitarian tradition was "interest." The biblical understanding of national life was based on the notion of community with charity for all the members, a community supported by public and private virtue. The utilitarian tradition believed in a neutral state in which individuals would be allowed to pursue the maximization of their self-interest and the product would be public and private prosperity. The harshness of these contrasts was obscured, though never obliterated, by several considerations. The biblical tradition promised earthly rewards, as well as heavenly, for virtuous actions. The utilitarian tradition required self-restraint and "morality" if not as ends then as means. But the most pervasive mechanism for the harmonization of the two traditions was the corruption of the biblical tradition by utilitarian individualism so that religion itself finally became for many a means for the maximization of self-interest with no effective link to virtue, charity or community. A purely private pietism emphasizing only individual rewards that grew up in the 19th century and took many forms in the 20th, from Norman Vincent Peale to Rev. Ike, was the expression of that corruption.

The increasing dominance of utilitarian individualism was expressed not only in the corruption of religion but also in the rising prestige of science, technology and bureaucratic organization. The scientific instrumentalism that was already prominent in Hobbes became the central tenet of the most typical late American philosophy, pragmatism. The tradition of utilitarian individualism expressed no interest in shared values or ends since it considered the only significant end to be maximizing individual interest, and individual ends are essentially random. Utilitarianism tended therefore to concentrate solely on the rationalization of means, on technical reason. As a result the rationalization of means became an end in itself. This is illustrated in the story about an American farmer who was asked why he worked so hard. To raise more corn, was his reply. But why do you want to do that? To make more money. What for? To buy more land. Why? To raise more corn. And so on *ad infinitum*. While utilitarian individualism had no interest in society as an end in itself, it was certainly not unaware of the importance of society. Society like everything else was to be used instrumentally. The key term was organization, the instrumental use of social relationships. "Effective organization" was as much a hallmark of the American ethos as technological inventiveness.

The central value for utilitarian individualism was freedom, a term that could also be used to obscure the gap between the utilitarian and the biblical traditions, since it is a central biblical term as well. But for biblical religion, freedom meant above all freedom from sin, freedom to do the right, and was almost equivalent to virtue. For utilitarianism it meant the freedom to pursue one's own ends. Everything was to be subordinate to that: nature, social relations, even personal feelings. The exclusive concentration on means rendered that final end of freedom so devoid of content that it became illusory and the rationalization of means a kind of treadmill that was in fact the opposite of freedom.

That part of the biblical tradition that remained uncorrupted or only minimally corrupted found itself deeply uneasy with the dominant utilitarian ethos. Fundamentalism in America is not simply an expression of backward yokels. Even Bryan's opposition to evo-

lution was in part an opposition to the social Darwinism that he saw as undermining all humane values in America. But that opposition remained largely inchoate, in part because it could not penetrate the facade of biblical symbols that the society never abandoned even when it betrayed them.

It was this dual set of fundamental understandings that the eruption of the 1960s fundamentally challenged. It is important to remember that the events of the '60s were preceded and prepared for by a new articulation of Christian symbolism in the later '50s in the life and work of Martin Luther King. King stood not only for the actualization of that central and ambiguous value of freedom for those who had never fully experienced even its most formal benefits. Even more significantly he stood for the actualization of the Christian imperative of love. For him society was not to be used manipulatively for individual ends. Even in a bitter struggle one's actions were to express that fundamental love, that oneness of all men in the sight of God, that is deeper than any self interest. It was that conception, so close to America's expressed biblical values and so far from its utilitarian practice that, together with militant activism, was so profoundly unsettling.

We are accustomed to thinking of the "costs" of modernization in the developing nations: the disrupted traditions, the break-up of families and villages, the impact of vast economic and social forces that can neither be understood nor adapted to in terms of inherited wisdom and ways of living. Because it is our tradition that invented modernization we have thought that we were somehow immune to the costs or that because the process was, with us, so so slow and so gradual, we had successfully absorbed the strains of modernization. What the '60s showed us was that in America, too, the costs have been high and the strains by no means wholly absorbed. In that decade, at least among a significant proportion of the educated young of a whole generation, occurred the repudiation of the tradition of utilitarian individualism (even though it often persisted unconsciously even among those doing the repudiating) and the biblical tradition too, especially as it was seen, in part realistically, as linked to utilitarianism. Let us examine the critique.

The criticisms of American society that developed in the '60s were diverse and not always coherent, one with another. In many different forms there was a new consciousness of the question of ends. The continuous expansion of wealth and power, which is what the rationalization of means meant in practice, did not seem so self-evidently good. There were of course some sharp questions about the unequal distribution of wealth and power, but beyond that was the question whether the quality of life was a simple function of wealth and power, or whether the endless accumulation of wealth and power was not destroying the quality and meaning of life, ecologically and sociologically. If the rationalization of means, the concern for pure instrumentalism, was no longer self-evidently meaningful then those things that had been subordinated, dominated and exploited for the sake of rationalizing means took on a new significance. Nature, social relations and personal feelings could now be treated as ends rather than means, could be liberated from the repressive control of technical reason.

Among those who shared this general analysis there was a division between those who placed emphasis on overthrowing the present system as a necessary precondition for the realization of a more human society and those who emphasized the present embodiment of a new style of life "in the pores," so to speak, of the old society.

The contrast was not absolute as the effort to create politically "liberated zones" in certain communities such as Berkeley and Ann Arbor indicates. And for a time in the late '60s opposition to the Vietnam war, seen as an example of technical reason gone mad, took precedence over everything else. Yet there was a contrast between those mainly oriented to political action (still, in a way, oriented to means rather than ends, though it was the means to overthrow the existing system) and those mainly concerned with the actual creation of alternative patterns of living. The difference between demonstrations and sit-ins on the one hand, and love-ins, be-ins and rock festivals on the other, illustrates the contrast. Political activists shared some of the personal characteristics of those they fought— they were "uptight," repressed, dominated by time and work. The cultural experimenters, represented most vividly, perhaps, by the "love, peace, groovy" flower children of the middle '60s believed in harmony with man and nature and the enjoyment of the present moment through drugs, music or meditation. In either case there was a sharp opposition to the dominant American ethos of utilitarian instrumentalism oriented to personal success. There was also a deep ambivalence to the biblical tradition to which I will return.

The question of why the old order began to lose its legitimacy just when it did is not one we have felt equipped to answer. Clearly in the '60s there was a conjuncture of dissatisfactions that did not all have the same meaning. The protests of racial minorities, middle-class youth and women had different causes and different goals. In spite of all the unsolved problems the crisis was brought on by the success of the society as much as by its failures. That education and affluence did not bring happiness or fulfillment was perhaps as important as the fact that the society did not seem to be able to solve the problem of racism and poverty. The outbreak of a particularly vicious and meaningless little war in Asia that stymied America's leadership both militarily and politically for years on end, acted as a catalyst but did not cause the crisis. The deepest cause, no matter what particular factors contributed to the actual timing, was, in my opinion, the inability of utilitarian individualism to provide a meaningful pattern of personal and social existence, especially when its alliance with biblical religion began to sag because biblical religion itself had been gutted in the process. I would thus interpret the crisis of the '60s above all as a crisis of meaning, a religious crisis, with major political, social and cultural consequences to be sure.

Religious upheaval is not new in American history. Time and time again, after a period of spiritual dryness, there has been an outbreak of the spirit. But the religious crisis was in more ways a contrast to the great awakenings of the 18th and 19th centuries than a continuation of them. By all the measures of conventional religiosity the early '50s had been a period of religious revival, but the revival of the '50s proved to be as artificial as the Cold War atmosphere that may have fostered it. The '60s saw a continuous drop in church attendance and a declining belief in the importance of religion, as measured by national polls. It is true that conservative and fundamentalist churches continued to grow and that the major losses were in the mainline Protestant denominations and in the Catholic Church after the full consequences of Vatican II began to sink in. But in terms of American culture the latter were far more important than the conservative fringe. Although clergy and laity of many denominations played an important part in the events of the '60s, the churches as such were not the locale of the major changes, even the religious ones.

Indeed it was easier for many in the biblical tradition to relate to the political than to the religious aspect of the developing counterculture. The demand for social justice had a close fit with the prophetic teachings of Judaism and Christianity. The struggle for racial equality and later the struggle against the Vietnam war drew many leaders from the churches and synagogues, even though the membership as a whole remained passive. But in spite of the leadership of Martin Luther King and the martyrdom of divinity students in the civil rights movement, and in spite of the leadership of the Berrigans and William Sloane Coffin in the peace movement, those movements as a whole remained indifferent if not hostile to religion. By the end of the '60s those churchmen who had given everything to the political struggle found themselves without influence and without a following. For most of the political activists the churches remained too closely identified with the established powers to gain much sympathy or interest. As dogmatic Marxism gained greater influence among the activists during the decade, ideological anti-religion increased as well.

But the churches were if anything even less well prepared to cope with the new spirituality of the '60s. The demand for immediate, powerful and deep religious experience, which was part of the turn away from future-oriented instrumentalism toward present meaning and fulfillment, could on the whole not be met by the religious bodies. The major Protestant churches in the course of generations of defensive struggle against secular rationalism had taken on some of the color of the enemy. Moralism and verbalism and the almost complete absence of ecstatic experience characterized the middle-class Protestant churches. The more intense religiosity of black and lower-class churches remained largely unavailable to the white middle-class members of the counterculture. The Catholic Church with its great sacramental tradition might be imagined to have been a more hospitable home for the new movement, but such was not the case. Older Catholicism had its own defensiveness that took the form of scholastic intellectualism and legalistic moralism. Nor did Vatican II really improve things. The Catholic Church finally decided to recognize the value of the modern world just when American young people were beginning to find it valueless. As if all this were not enough, the biblical arrogance toward nature and the Christian hostility toward the impulse life were both alien to the new spiritual mood. Thus the religion of the counterculture was by and large not biblical. It drew from many sources including the American Indian. But its deepest influences came from Asia.

In many ways Asian spirituality provided a more thorough contrast to the rejected utilitarian individualism than did biblical religion. To external achievement is posed inner experience; to the exploitation of nature, harmony with nature; to impersonal organization, an intense relation to a guru. Mahayana Buddhism, particularly in the form of Zen, provided the most pervasive religious influence on the counterculture but elements from Taoism, Hinduism and Sufism were also influential. What drug experiences, interpreted in oriental religious terms, as Leary and Alpert did quite early, and meditation experiences, often taken up when drug use was found to have too many negative consequences, showed was the illusoriness of worldly striving. Careerism and status seeking, the sacrifice of present fulfillment for some ever-receding future goal, no longer seemed worthwhile. There was a turn away not only from utilitarian individualism but from the whole

apparatus of industrial society. The new ethos preferred handicrafts and farming to business and industry and small face-to-face communities to impersonal bureaucracy and the isolated nuclear family. Simplicity and naturalness in food and clothing were the ideal even though conspicuous consumption and oneups-manship (oh, you don't use natural salt, I see) made their inevitable appearance.

Thus the limits were pushed far beyond what any previous great awakening had seen: toward socialism in one direction, toward mysticism in the other. But perhaps the major meaning of the '60s was not anything positive at all. Neither the political movement nor the counterculture survived the decade. Important successor movements did survive, but the major meaning of the '60s was purely negative: the erosion of the legitimacy of the American way of life. On the surface what seems to have been most drastically undermined was utilitarian individualism, for the erosion of the biblical tradition seemed only to continue what had been a long-term trend. The actual situation was more complicated. Utilitarian individualism had perhaps never before been so divested of its ideological and religious facade, never before recognized in all its naked destructiveness. And yet that very exposure could become an ironic victory. If all moral restraints are illegitimate, then why should I believe in religion and morality? If those who win in American society are the big crooks and those who lose do so only because they are little crooks, why should I not try to be a big crook rather than a little one? In this way the unmasking of utilitarian individualism led to the very condition from which Hobbes sought to save us—the war of all against all. Always before, the biblical side of the American tradition has been able to bring antinomian and anarchic tendencies under some kind of control, and perhaps that is still possible today. Certainly the fragile structures of the counterculture were not able to do so. But out of the shattered hopes of the '60s there has emerged a cynical privatism, a narrowing of sympathy and concern to the smallest possible circle, that is truly frightening. What has happened to Richard Nixon should not obscure for us the meaning of his overwhelming victory in 1972. It was the victory of cynical privatism.

In this rather gloomy period of American history, and the mood of the youth culture has been predominantly gloomy—not the hope for massive change that characterized the '60s but the anxious concern for survival, physical and moral—the successor movements of the early '70s take on a special interest. We may ask whether any of them have been able to take up and preserve the positive seeds of the '60s so that under more favorable circumstances they may grow and bear fruit once again. Some of the successor movements clearly do not have that potential. The Weathermen and the SLA on the one hand, the Krishna Consciousness Society and the Divine Light Mission on the other, are parodies of the broader political and religious movements that they represent, too narrow and in some cases too self-destructive to contribute to the future solution of our problems. About others there may be more hope.

To some extent the successor movements, especially the explicitly religious ones, have been survival units in a quite literal sense. They have provided a stable social setting and a coherent set of symbols for young people disoriented by the drug culture or disillusioned with radical politics. What Synanon claims to have done for drug users, religious groups—from Zen Buddhists to Jesus people—have done for ex-hippies.

The Krishna Consciousness Society grew up for example, amidst the disintegration of Haight-Ashbury as a hippie utopia. The rescue mission aspect of the successor movements has had quite tangible results. In many instances reconciliation with parents has been facilitated by the more stable life-style and the religious ideology of acceptance rather than confrontation. A new, more positive orientation toward occupational roles has often developed. In some cases, such as followers of Meher Baba, this has meant a return to school and the resumption of a normal middle-class career pattern. For others, for example, resident devotees of the San Francisco Zen Center or ashram residents of the 3HO movement, jobs are seen only as means to subsistence, having no value in themselves. While the attitude toward work in terms of punctuality, thoroughness and politeness is, from the employer's point of view, positive, the religious devotee has no inner commitment to the job nor does he look forward to any advancement. In terms of intelligence and education the jobholder is frequently "overqualified" for the position he holds but this causes no personal distress because of the meaning the job has for him. For many of these groups the ideal solution would be economic self-sufficiency, so that members would not have to leave the community at all, but few are able to attain this. As in monastic orders some full-time devotees can be supported frugally by the gifts of sympathizers but they are exceptions. Many of the groups also insist on a stable sexual life, in some instances celibate but more usually monogamous, with sexual relations being confined to marriage. Such norms are found not only among Jesus people but in the oriental groups as well.

These features of stability should not be interpreted as simple adaptation to the established society though in some cases that may occur. The human potential movement may serve such an adaptive function, and perhaps Synanon also does to a certain extent. But for the more explicitly religious groups, stable patterns of personal living and occupation do not mean acceptance of the established order. Sympathizers of the oriental religions tend to be as critical of American society as political radicals, far more critical than the norm. While people sympathetic to the Jesus movement are less critical of American society, the Christian World Liberation Front, a Berkeley group, is atypical in being quite critical. All of these movements share a very negative image of established society as sunk in materialism and heading for disaster. Many of them have intense millennial expectations, viewing the present society as in the last stage of degradation before the dawning of a new area. 3HO people speak of the Aquarian age which is about to replace the dying Piscean age. Krishna Consciousness people speak of the present as the last stage of the materialistic Kali-Yuga and on the verge of a new age of peace and happiness. More traditionally biblical expectations of the millennium are common among Jesus people. All of these groups, well behaved as they are, have withdrawn fundamentally from contemporary American society, see it as corrupt and illegitimate, and place their hope in a radically different vision. We should remember that early Christians too were well behaved—Paul advised them to remain in their jobs and their marriages—yet by withholding any deep commitment to the Roman Empire they helped to bring it down and to form a society of very different type.

An important dimension of variation among the groups we have studied is the degree of openness or closure toward the outside world. However some groups with tightly controlled boundaries, that is, specific and demanding requirements for membership, are also highly conversionist, as in the case of Krishna Consciousness and Jesus movements. Nonetheless open boundaries are undoubtedly more conducive to rapid expansion. Transcendental Meditation, which claims not to be a religion and has few if any doctrinal or behavioral requirements, has attracted hundreds of thousands, even though many quickly abandon the practice. The Krishna Consciousness movement on the other hand has remained quite small, perhaps no more than 3000 or 4000 members. Recently this movement has shown distinct introversionist tendencies in sending hundreds of its followers permanently to India.

Some of the more interesting movements show a range of possibilities or a change over time on the dimension of openness and closure. Zen Buddhism is one of the most pervasive influences on the entire range of countercultural developments. Philip Kapleau's *Three Pillars of Zen* was for a time a kind of bible of the counterculture, influencing thousands who had only the most casual acquaintance with Zen meditation. Alan Watts, one of the most influential countercultural gurus, preached essentially a modified Zen. The influence of Zen on everything from psychotherapy to esthetics has been major in the last 10 years. Yet full time membership in a Zen monastery or center is an extremely demanding enterprise, leading in some cases to vows of chastity and poverty. The history of the San Francisco Zen Center from the late '50s to the present shows a continuous movement from general intellectual and cultural interest in Zen to high and demanding standards of practice. Of course Zen, perhaps more than any other movement of oriental origin, exercises an influence out of all proportion to the number of its full time devotees. Just for that reason it represents clearly the tension between general cultural influence and a tightly organized in-group that is to be found in many other movements. 3HO has undergone a shift comparable to the Zen Center in moving away from general yoga practice to the specific beliefs and rituals of Sikhism. A slight tendency in the opposite direction is to be found in the Christian World Liberation Front which has sacrificed some of its "forever family" community for more active ministries especially in the cultural field with its publications and courses. Political groups probably show something of the same spectrum of openness and closedness.

On the whole the human potential groups are open compared to the religious groups, having few requirements for participation though abstention from drugs and alcohol and avoidance of aggressive behavior may be required of participants during the actual period of training. Acceptance of certain frames of reference (I am perfect just as I am) may be a prerequisite if the training is to make sense but these views are not seen as doctrinal requirements. In general the human potential groups, and groups like Transcendental Meditation that are very similar to them, may be seen as cults rather than as sects, in the traditional sociological sense of those terms. The human potential groups are not usually membership groups, except temporarily. Their leaders may be seen as charismatic but more as healers and teachers than as organizational leaders.

Sympathizers of the human potential movement seem to be less alienated from American society than followers of oriental religions or political radicals. They are, nonetheless, more critical than the norm and many of their beliefs contrast sharply with established American ideology. A tension exists within the movement over the issue of latent utilitarianism. If the techniques of the human potential movement are to be used for personal and business success (the training group movement out of which the human potential movement in part derives had tendencies in that direction) then it is no different from the mind cures and positive thinking of the most debased kinds of utilitarian religion in America. But for some in the movement the whole idea of success is viewed negatively and the training is seen in part as a way of gaining liberation from that goal. The high evaluation of bodily awareness and intrapsychic experience as well as non-manipulative interpersonal relations place much of the movement in tension with the more usual orientations of American utilitarian individualism. Here utilitarian individualism is a hydra-headed monster that tends to survive just where it is most attacked.

Immediate experience rather than doctrinal belief continues to be central among all the religious movements, including the Jesus movements, and in the human potential movement as well. Knowledge in the sense of direct first-hand encounter has so much higher standing than abstract argument based on logic that one could almost speak of anti-intellectualism in many groups. Yet it would be a mistake to interpret this tendency as rampant irrationalism. Even though science is viewed ambivalently and the dangers of scientific progress are consciously feared by many in our groups, science as such is not rejected. There is a belief that much of what is experienced could be scientifically validated. Indeed the human potential groups (and Transcendental Meditation) believe that their teachings are in accord with science broadly understood. The study of the physiology of the brain during meditation is seen not as a threat but as a support for religious practice. Since reality inheres in the actual experience, explanatory schemes, theological or scientific, are secondary, though scientific explanations tend to be preferred to theological ones because of the general prestige of science. At a deeper level the lack of interest in critical reflective reason may be a form of anti-intellectualism but the conscious irrationalism of groups such as the romantic German youth movement is quite missing. Similarly there is a complete absence of primordial loyalties and hatreds based on race, ethnic group or even religion.

In spite of the primacy of experience, belief is not entirely missing. In some groups, as we have already seen in the case of 3HO, the stress on doctrine may be increasing. The early phase of the new left was heavily experiential. Unless you had placed your body on the line you could not understand the reality of American society. Consciousness-raising in racial and women's groups continues to emphasize the experiential aspect of oppression and the struggle against it. But new left groups became increasingly doctrinal toward the end of the '60s and remain today more oriented to doctrine than experience in comparison with religious and human potential groups.

A central belief shared by the oriental religions and diffused widely outside them is important because of how sharply it contrasts with established American views. This is the belief in the unity of all being. Our separate selves, according to Buddhism, Hinduism and their offshoots, are not ultimately real. Philosophical Hinduism and Mahayana Buddhism reject dualism. For them ultimately there is no difference between myself and yourself and this river and that mountain. We are all one and the conflict between us is therefore illusory.

While such beliefs are diametrically opposed to utilitarian individualism, for whom the individual is the ultimate ontological reality, there are elements in the Christian tradition to which they are not entirely opposed. Christian theology also felt the unity of Being and the necessity to love beings. The New Testament spoke of the church as one body of which we are all members. But Christianity has tended to maintain the ultimate dualism of creator and creation which the oriental religions would obliterate. Christian mystics have at times made statements (viewed as heretical) expressing the ultimate unity of God and man and, in mediated form, the unity of God and man through Christ is an orthodox belief. Still American Christianity has seldom emphasized the aspect of the Christian tradition that stressed the unity rather than the distinction of divinity and man so that the oriental teachings stand out as sharply divergent.

Much of the countercultural criticism of American society is related to the belief in non-dualism. If man and nature, men and women, white and black, rich and poor are really one then there is no basis for the exploitation of the latter by the former. The ordination of women by Zen Buddhists and 3HO, even though not warranted in the earlier traditions, shows how their American followers interpret the fundamental beliefs. It is significant that from the basis of nondualism conclusions similar to those of Marxism can be reached. But because the theoretical basis is fundamental unity rather than fundamental opposition, the criticism of existing society is non-hostile, non-confrontational and often non-political. Nonetheless the effort to construct a witness community based on unity and identity rather than opposition and oppression can itself have critical consequences in a society based on opposite principles.

Another feature of oriental religions that has been widely influential is their view of dogma and symbol. Believing, as many of them do, that the fundamental truth, the truth of non-dualism, is one, they also accept many beliefs and symbols as appropriate for different groups or different levels of spiritual insight. Dogmatism has by no means been missing in the oriental religions and has been traditionally more important than many of their American followers probably realize. But relative to Christianity and biblical religions generally the contrast holds. Belief in certain doctrinal or historical statements (Jesus is the Son of God, Christ rose from the tomb on the third day) has been so central in Western religion that it has been hard for Westerners to imagine religions for whom literal belief in such statements is unimportant. But the impact of oriental religion coincides with a long history of the criticism of religion in the West in which particular beliefs have been rendered questionable but the significance of religion and myth in human action has been reaffirmed. Post-critical Western religion was therefore ready for a positive response to Asian religions in a way different from any earlier period. Paul Tillich's response to Zen Buddhism late in his life is an example of this. Thomas Merton's final immersion in Buddhism is an even better one. Such tendencies, however, are not to be found in the Christian World Liberation Front or other Jesus movements.

But in many of the oriental groups and certainly in the human potential movement there has been a willingness to find meaning in a wide variety of symbols and practices without regarding them literally or exclusively. The danger here as elsewhere is that post-critical religion can become purely utilitarian. This can happen if one fails to see that any religious symbol or practice, however relative and partial, is an effort to express or attain the truth about ultimate reality. If such symbols and practices become mere techniques for "self-realization" then once again we see utilitarian individualism reborn from its own ashes.

Studies in which I've been engaged began with the thought that the new religious consciousness that seemed to be developing among young people in the San Francisco Bay area might be some harbinger, some straw in the wind, that would tell us of changes to come in American culture and society. We were aware that studies of American religion based on national samples could tell us mainly about what was widely believed in the present and perhaps also in the past, since religious views change relatively slowly. Such samples, however, could not easily pick up what was incipient, especially what was radically new and as yet confined to only small groups. Even our bay area sample, weighted as it was to youth, picked up only a tiny handful of those deeply committed to new forms of religion, although it did lead us to believe that the new groups had gotten a hearing and some sympathy from a significant minority. Our studies of particular groups, based on participant-observation field studies, have told us a great deal about particular groups.

But to assess what we have discovered with respect to possible future trends remains hazardous. We must await other developments in the society as a whole. In trying to assess the possible meaning and role of our groups in the future I would like to outline three possible scenarios for American society: liberal, traditional authoritarian and revolutionary.

The future that most people seem to expect and that the futurologists describe with their projections is very much like the present society only more so. This is what I call the liberal scenario. American society would continue as in the past to devote itself to the accumulation of wealth and power. The mindless rationalization of means and the lack of concern with ends would only increase as biblical religion and morality continue to erode. Utilitarian individualism, with less biblical restraint or facade than ever before, would continue as the dominant ideology. Its economic form, capitalism, its political form, bureaucracy, and its ideological form, scientism, would each increasingly dominate its respective sphere. Among the elite, scientism, the idolization of technical reason alone, would provide some coherent meaning after traditional religion and morality had gone. But technical reason would hardly be a sufficient surrogate religion for the masses. No longer accepting the society as legitimate in any ideal terms, the masses would have to be brought to acquiesce grudgingly by a combination of coercion and material reward. In such a society one could see a certain role for oriental religious groups and the human potential movement—perhaps even for a small radical political fringe. All of these could be allowed within limits to operate and provide the possibility of expressing the frustration and rage that the system generates but in a way such that the individuals concerned were cooled out and the system itself is not threatened. The utilitarian individualism that is latent in all the countercultural successor movements, political and religious, makes this a real possibility. This scenario depicts the society as heading, mildly and gradually, into something like Aldous Huxley's *Brave New World*.

Lately, however, questions have been raised as to the viability of this direction of development. Perhaps there are inner contradictions that will lead to a drastic breakdown in the foreseeable future. Robert Heilbroner has recently predicted such a collapse, largely as a result of ecological catastrope. But Heilbroner also envisages the possibility that tensions between the rich and the poor nations could bring disaster even sooner

than ecological attrition. Even since Heilbroner wrote, the proliferation of atomic weapon capacity in India and the Middle East has strengthened this possibility. Another distinct possibility is worldwide economic collapse bringing social convulsions in train. No matter how the breakdown of the "modernization" syndrome might occur, Heilbroner envisages a relapse into traditional authoritarianism as the most likely result, providing, that is, that the worst outcome, total destruction of life on the planet, is avoided. Simpler, poorer and less free societies might be all that humans would be capable of in the wake of a global catastrophe. The social and personal coherence that the modernizing societies never attained might be supplied by the rigid myths and rituals of a new hierarchical authoritarian society. To put it in terms of the present discussion, the collapse of subjective reason, which is what technical reason ultimately is, would bring in its wake a revival of objective reason in a particularly closed and reified form. Technical reason, because it is concerned not with truth or reality but only with results, not with what is but only with what works, is ultimately completely subjective. That its domineering manipulative attitude to reality in the service of the subjects leads ultimately to the destruction of any true subjectivity is only one of its many ironies. But a new traditional authoritarianism would set up some single orthodox version of what truth and reality are and enforce agreement. Some historically relative creed, belief and ritual would be asserted as identical with objective reality itself. In this way social and personal coherence would be achieved, but ultimately at the expense of any real objectivity.

If a relapse into traditional authoritarianism is a distinct possibility in America, and I believe it is, we might ask what are the likely candidates for the job of supplying the new orthodoxy. Perhaps the most likely system would be right-wing Protestant fundamentalism. We already have a good example of such a regime in Afrikaner dominated South Africa. Conservative Protestant fundamentalism has a large and, by some measures, growing following in America. It has the religious and moral absolutism that a traditional authoritarianism would require, and it is hard to see any close rival on the American scene today. The Catholic Church, which might at an earlier period have been a candidate for such a role, is certainly not, in its post Vatican II disarray. Some of the more authoritarian of our Asian religions might provide a sufficiently doctrinaire model but their small following in comparison with Protestant fundamentalism virtually rules them out. The future for most of the groups we have studied, all but the Jesus movements, would be bleak indeed under such a neo-traditional authoritarianism. It is doubtful if even a group as open as the Christian World Liberation Front could survive. Neo-authoritarian regimes are hard on nonconformity in every sphere. The new Chilean government, for example, not only sets standards of dress and hair style but also persecutes oriental religions.

There remains a third alternative, however improbable. It is this that I am calling revolutionary, not in the sense that it would be inaugurated by a bloody uprising, which I do not think likely, but because it would bring fundamental structural change, socially and culturally. It is to this rather unlikely outcome that most of the groups we have studied, at least the most flexible and open of them, would have most to contribute. Such a new order would involve, as in the case of traditional authoritarianism, an abrupt shift away from the exclusive dominance of technical reason, but it would not involve the adoption of a reified objective reason either. In accord with its concern for ends rather than means alone such a revolutionary culture would have a firm commitment to the quest for ultimate reality. But it would not imagine that any one set of religious or philosophical symbols or beliefs can adequately express that reality. Priorities would shift away from endless accumulation of wealth and power to a greater concern for harmony with nature and between human beings. Perhaps a much simpler, material life, simpler, that is, compared to present middle-class American standards, would result, but it would not be accompanied by an abandonment of free inquiry or free speech. Science, which would ultimately have to be shackled in a traditional authoritarian regime, would continue to be pursued in the revolutionary culture but it would not be idolized as in the liberal model. In all these respects the values, attitudes and beliefs of the oriental religious groups, the human potential movement and even a group like the Christian World Liberation Front, as well as the more flexible of the radical political groups, would be consonant with the new regime and its needs. Indeed many of the present activities of such groups could be seen as experiments leading to the possibility of such a new alternative. Neither safety valve nor persecuted minority, the new groups would be, under such an option, the vanguard of a new age.

Such an outcome would accord most closely with the millennial expectations which we have seen are rife among the new groups. Even if an enormous amount of thought and planning were devoted to such an alternative, thought and planning that the small struggling groups we have been studying are quite incapable at the moment of supplying, the revolutionary alternative seems quite utopian. Perhaps only a major shift in the established biblical religions, a shift away from their uneasy alliance with utilitarian individualism and toward a profound reappropriation of their own religious roots and an openness to the needs of the contemporary world, would provide the mass base for a successful effort to establish the revolutionary alternative. But that shift, too, at present seems quite utopian. It may be, however, that only the implementation of a utopian vision, a holistic reason that unites subjectivity and objectivity, will make human life in the 21st century worth living.

E Crime and Deviance

INTRODUCTION

In all societies, conformity to social norms is a matter of degree rather than an all-or-none question. At one extreme, a few individuals may be seen as exemplifying common ideals to such an exceptional extent that they are eulogized as heroes and saints and held up as models for others to emulate. At the other extreme, those who openly violate the dominant norms are execrated and even regarded as beyond the pale of ordinary humanity. Yet the fate of Aristides the Just and, at a more commonplace level, the discomfort and distaste with which "overachievers" and "goody-goods" are viewed, suggest that exceptional conformity as well as outright nonconformity also meet with social disapproval, although usually of a more latent kind in the case of the former. Deviation from social norms is, in any case, inseparable from the very existence of norms, given the human variety that flourishes in even the smallest societies. The conditions leading to deviation on the part of individuals and groups are inextricably bound up with the very norms, roles, and institutions that constitute the established social order. Deviance is not a mere excrescence, a random occurrence resulting from the unforeseeable peculiarities of a minority of individuals who have failed to be properly "socialized." Daniel Bell, in the first reading, stresses the intimate relationship between organized crime in America and our capitalist economy and cultural ideals of individual opportunity.

Crime is but one form of deviance: namely, conduct that violates the statutes of the criminal law. If deviance in general is, as we have contended, a matter of degree, this does not apply to criminal conduct, for the law and the courts impose an absolute distinction between the illegal and the legal. Particular actions must be adjudicated as criminal or not: one cannot be a little bit in violation of the law. The law *defines* crime as precisely as possible and can even be said to *create* it by so doing. Many laws impose legal sanctions on behavior that is already widely and strongly proscribed by prevailing social norms, essentially those norms that William Graham Sumner called mores. But many laws are created, literally *made*, by legislators and, less directly, judges. Such laws are especially common in advanced industrial societies that undergo fairly rapid social change and consist of diverse subcultural groups that share only a few social norms in common. The law, therefore, not only becomes a major form of social control through the agencies of the police and the courts, but it imposes new norms in situations where no preexisting consensus exists.

Daniel Bell's discussion of organized crime and its connection with "respectable" businessmen and government officials is a classic one of its kind. Bell draws heavily for his data on the U.S. Senate crime hearings conducted by the late Senator Kefauver in the 1950's. There are few more recent discussions of comparable scope and readability, and the main outlines of the picture Bell presents have been reconfirmed since then and do not appear to have changed greatly in the last fifteen years.

Our second reading, by Gresham M. Sykes, describes conditions in a maximum security state penitentiary. Sykes applies to the social structure of the prison some general sociological points about the limitations of force in large organizations and the economic exchanges and tolerated deviance from official rules that are required to supplement force in such coercive systems of total power as prisons.

Many forms of deviance are not criminal. Those that have been studied most extensively by sociologists include mental illness, alcoholism and some forms of drug addiction, sexual aberrancy, suicide, and political and religious radicalism. In recent years, sociologists have devoted enormous attention to the process whereby certain acts and the individuals who perform them become "labeled" as deviant and to the ensuing effects on the person of the label then attached to him or her. Erving Goffman's work has been one of the major influences on so-called labeling theory. In the long discussion of mental illness that we have included as our third reading, Goffman both summarizes the labeling approach and goes beyond its concentration on the labelers and the labeling process, as opposed to the acts and persons labeled. He shows that when a member of a household suddenly begins to act in strange, unconventional, "manic" ways that disrupt household routines, an essentially *political* process of bargaining, collusion, and coalition-forming involving family members, doctors, and other specialists is set in motion, often with the end result that the disrupter is labeled mentally ill. Goffman does not, in contrast to some of the proponents of labeling theory, minimize the pain and disturbance resulting from the disruptive behavior in question in locating it in a larger context that includes the reactions and strategies of others as well.

39

Crime as an American Way of Life

DANIEL BELL

In the 1890's the Reverend Dr. Charles Parkhurst, shocked at the open police protection afforded New York's bordellos, demanded a state inquiry. In the Lexow investigation that followed, the young and dashing William Travers Jerome staged a set of public hearings that created sensation after sensation. He badgered "Clubber" Williams, First Inspector of the Police Department, to account for wealth and property far greater than could have been saved on his salary; it was earned, the Clubber explained laconically, through land speculation "in Japan." Heavy-set Captain Schmittberger, the "collector" for the "Tenderloin precincts"—Broadway's fabulous concentration of hotels, theaters, restaurants, gaming houses, and saloons—related in detail how protection money was distributed among the police force. Crooks, policemen, public officials, businessmen, all paraded across the stage, each adding his chapter to a sordid story of corruption and crime. The upshot of these revelations was reform—the election of William L. Strong, a stalwart businessman, as mayor, and the naming of Theodore Roosevelt as police commissioner.

It did not last, of course, just as previous reform victories had not lasted. Yet the ritual drama was re-enacted. Thirty years ago the Seabury investigation in New York uncovered the tin-box brigade and the thirty-three little McQuades. Jimmy Walker was ousted as Mayor and in came Fiorello LaGuardia. Tom Dewey became dis-

trict attorney, broke the industrial rackets, sent Lucky Luciano to jail, and went to the governor's chair in Albany. Then reform was again swallowed up in the insatiable maw of corruption until in 1950 Kefauver and his committee counsel Rudolph Halley threw a new beam of light into the seemingly bottomless pit.

How explain this repetitious cycle? Obviously the simple moralistic distinction between "good guys" and "bad guys," so deep at the root of the reform impulse, bears little relation to the role of organized crime in American society. What, then, does?

The Queer Ladder

Americans have had an extraordinary talent for compromise in politics and extremism in morality. The most shameless political deals (and "steals") have been rationalized as expedient and realistically necessary. Yet in no other country have there been such spectacular attempts to curb human appetites and brand them as illicit, and nowhere else such glaring failures. From the start America was at one and the same time a frontier community where "everything goes," and the fair country of the Blue Laws. At the turn of the century the cleavage developed between the Big City and the small-town conscience. Crime as a growing business was fed by the revenues from prostitution, liquor, and gambling that a wide-open urban society encouraged and that a middle-class Protestant ethos tried to suppress with a ferocity unmatched in any other civilized country. Catholic cultures have rarely imposed such restrictions and have rarely suffered such

Reprinted with permission of Macmillan Publishing Co., Inc. from *The End of Ideology* by Daniel Bell. Copyright © 1960 by The Free Press, a Corporation.

excesses. Even in prim and proper Anglican England, prostitution is a commonplace of Piccadilly night life, and gambling is one of the largest and most popular industries. In America the enforcement of public morals has been a continuing feature of our history.

Some truth may lie in Max Scheler's generalization that moral indignation is a peculiar fact of middle-class psychology and represents a disguised form of repressed envy. The larger truth lies perhaps in the brawling nature of American development and in the social character of crime. Crime, in many ways, is a Coney Island mirror, caricaturing the morals and manners of a society. The jungle quality of the American business community, particularly at the turn of the century, was reflected in the mode of "business" practiced by the coarse gangster elements, most of them from new immigrant families, who were "getting ahead," just as Horatio Alger had urged. In the older, Protestant tradition the intensive acquisitiveness, such as that of Daniel Drew, was rationalized by a compulsive moral fervor. But the formal obeisance of the ruthless businessman in the workaday world to the church-going pieties of the Sabbath was one that the gangster could not make. Moreover, for the young criminal, hunting in the asphalt jungle of the crowded city, it was not the businessman with his wily manipulation of numbers but the "man with the gun" who was the American hero. "No amount of commercial prosperity," once wrote Teddy Roosevelt, "can supply the lack of the heroic virtues." The American was "the hunter, cowboy, frontiersman, the soldier, the naval hero"—and in the crowded slums, the gangster. He was a man with a gun, acquiring by personal merit what was denied him by complex orderings of stratified society. And the duel with the law was the morality play par excellence: the gangster, with whom ride our own illicit desires, and the prosecutor, representing final judgment and the force of the law.

Yet all this was acted out in a wider context. The desires satisfied in extralegal fashion were more than a hunger for the "forbidden fruits" of conventional morality. They also involved, in the complex and ever shifting structure of group, class, and ethnic stratification, which is the warp and woof of America's "open" society, such "normal" goals as independence through a business of one's own, and such "moral" aspirations as the desire for social advancement and social prestige. For crime, in the language of the sociologists, has a "functional" role in the society, and the urban rackets—the illicit activity organized for continuing profit, rather than individual illegal acts —is one of the queer ladders of social mobility in American life. Indeed, it is not too much to say that the whole question of organized crime in America cannot be understood unless one appreciates (1) the distinctive role of organized gambling as a function of a mass-consumption economy; (2) the specific role of various immigrant groups as they, one after another, became involved in marginal business and crime; and (3) the relation of crime to the changing character of the urban political machines.

Gatsby's Model

As a society changes, so does, in lagging fashion, its type of crime. As American society became more "organized," as the American businessman became more "civilized" and less "buccaneering," so did the American racketeer. And just as there were important changes in the structure of business enterprise, so the "institutionalized" criminal enterprise was transformed too.

In the America of the last fifty years the main drift of society has been toward the rationalization of industry, the domestication of the crude self-made captain of industry into the respectable man of manners, and the emergence of a mass-consumption economy. The most significant transformation in the field of "institutionalized" crime in the 1940's was the increasing importance of gambling as against other kinds of illegal activity. And, as a multi-billion-dollar business, gambling underwent a transition parallel to the changes in American enterprise as a whole. This parallel was exemplified in many ways: in gambling's industrial organization (e.g., the growth of a complex technology such as the national racing-wire service and the minimization of risks by such techniques as lay-off betting); in its respectability, as was evidenced in the opening of smart and popular gambling casinos in resort towns and in "satellite" adjuncts to metropolitan areas; in its functional role in a mass-consumption economy (for sheer volume of money changing hands, nothing has ever surpassed this feverish activity of fifty million American adults); in the social acceptance of the gamblers in the important status world of sport and entertainment, i.e., "café society."

In seeking to "legitimize" itself, gambling had quite often actually become a force against older and more vicious forms of illegal activity. In 1946, for example, when a Chicago mobster, Pat Manno, went down to Dallas, Texas, to take over gambling in the area for the Accardo-Guzik combine, he reassured the sheriff as follows: "Something I'm against, that's dope peddlers, pickpockets, hired killers. That's one thing I can't stomach, and that's one thing the fellows up there— the group won't stand for, things like that. They discourage it, they even go to headquarters and ask them why they don't do something about it."

Jimmy Cannon once reported that when the gambling raids started in Chicago the "combine" protested that, in upsetting existing stable relations, the police were only opening the way for ambitious young punks and hoodlums to start trouble. Nor is there today, as there was twenty or even forty years ago, prostitution of major organized scope in the United States. Aside from the fact that manners and morals have changed, prostitution *as an industry* doesn't pay as well as gambling. Besides, its existence threatened the tacit moral acceptance and quasi-respectability that gamblers and gambling have secured in the American way of life. It was, as any operator in the field might tell you, "bad for business."

The criminal world of the 1940's, its tone set by the captains of the gambling industry, is in startling contrast to the state of affairs in the decade before. If a Kefauver report had been written then, the main "names" would have been Lepke and Gurrah, Dutch Schultz, Jack "Legs" Diamond, Lucky Luciano, and, reaching back a little further, Arnold Rothstein, the czar of the underworld. These men (with the exception of Luciano, who was involved in narcotics and prostitution) were in the main "industrial racketeers." Rothstein, the model for Wolfsheim the gambler in F. Scott Fitzgerald's *The Great Gatsby*, had a larger function: he was, as Frank Costello became later, the financier of the underworld, the pioneer big businessman of crime who, understanding the logic of co-ordination, sought to *organize* crime as a source of regular income. His main interest in this direction was in industrial racketeering, and his entry was through labor disputes. At one time, employers in the garment trades hired Legs Diamond and his sluggers to break strikes, and the Communists, then in control of the cloakmakers union, hired one Little Orgie to protect the pickets and beat up the scabs; only later did both sides learn that Legs Diamond and Little

Orgie were working for the same man, Rothstein.

Rothstein's chief successors, Lepke Buchalter and Gurrah Shapiro, were able, in the early thirties, to dominate sections of the men's and women's clothing industries, of painting, fur dressing, flour trucking, and other fields. In a highly chaotic and cutthroat industry such as clothing, the racketeer, paradoxically, played a stabilizing role by regulating competition and fixing prices. When the NRA came in and assumed this function, the businessman found that what had once been a quasi-economic service was now pure extortion, and he began to demand police action. In other types of racketeering, such as the trucking of perishable foods and waterfront loading, where the racketeers entrenched themselves as middlemen—taking up, by default, a service that neither shippers nor truckers wanted to assume—a pattern of accommodation was roughly worked out, and the rackets assumed a quasi-legal veneer. On the waterfront, old-time racketeers perform the necessary function of loading—but at an exorbitant price—and this monopoly was recognized by both the union and the shippers, and tacitly by the government.

But in the last decade and a half, industrial racketeering has not offered much in the way of opportunity. *Like American capitalism itself, crime shifted its emphasis from production to consumption.* The focus of crime became the direct exploitation of the citizen as consumer, largely through gambling. And while the protection of these huge revenues was inextricably linked to politics, the relation between gambling and "the mobs" became more complicated.

Big-Business Bookies

Although it never showed up in the gross national product, gambling in the last decade was one of the largest industries in the United States. The Kefauver Committee estimated it as a $20 billion business. This figure has been picked up and widely quoted, but in truth no one knows what the gambling "turnover" and "take" actually is nor how much is bet legally (pari-mutuel, etc.) and how much illegally. In fact, the figure cited by the committee was arbitrary and was arrived at quite sloppily. As one staff member said: "We had no real idea of the money spent. . . . The California crime commission said twelve billion. Virgil Peterson of Chicago estimated thirty billion. We picked twenty billion as a balance between the two."

If comprehensive data is not available, we do know, from specific instances, the magnitude of many of the operations. Some indication can be seen from these items culled at random:

James Carroll and the M & G syndicate did a $20 million annual business in St. Louis. This was one of the two large books in the city.

The S & G syndicate in Miami did a $26 million volume yearly; the total for all books in the Florida resort reached $40 million.

Slot machines were present in 69,786 establishments in 1951 (each paid $100 for a license to the Bureau of Internal Revenue); the usual average is three machines to a license, which would add up to 210,000 slot machines in operation in the United States. In legalized areas, where the betting is higher and more regular, the average gross "take" per machine is $50 a week.

The largest policy wheel (i.e., "numbers") in Chicago's "Black Belt" reported taxable net profits for the four-year period from 1946 through 1949, after sizable deductions for "overhead," of $3,656,968. One of the large "white" wheels reported in 1947 a gross income of $2,317,000 and a net profit of $205,-000. One CIO official estimated that perhaps 15 per cent of his union's lower-echelon officials are involved in the numbers racket (a steward, free to roam a plant, is in a perfect situation for organizing bets).

If one considers the amount of dollars bet on sports alone—an estimated six billion on baseball, a billion on football pools, another billion on basketball, six billion on horse racing—then Elmo Roper's judgment that "only the food, steel, auto, chemical, and machine-tool industries have a greater volume of business" does not seem too farfetched.

While gambling has long flourished in the United States, the influx of the big mobsters into the industry—and its expansion—started in the thirties, when repeal of Prohibition forced them to look about for new avenues of enterprise. (The change, one might say crudely, was in the "democratization" of gambling. In New York of the 1860's, 1870's, and 1880's, one found elegant establishments where the wealthy men of the city, bankers, and sportsmen gambled. The saloon was the home of the worker. The middle class of the time did not gamble. In the changing mores of America, the rise of gambling in the 1930's and 1940's meant the introduction of the middle class to gambling and casinos as a way of life.) Gambling, which had begun to flower under the nourishment of rising incomes, was the most lucrative field in sight. To a large extent the shift from bootlegging to gambling was a mere transfer of business operations. In the East, Frank Costello went into slot machines and the operation of a number of ritzy gambling casinos. He also became the "banker" for the Erickson "book," which "laid off" bets for other bookies. Joe Adonis, similarly, opened up a number of casinos, principally in New Jersey. Across the country, many other mobsters went into bookmaking. As other rackets diminished and gambling, particularly horse-race betting, flourished in the forties, a struggle erupted over the control of racing information.

Horse-race betting requires a peculiar industrial organization. The essential component is time. A bookie can operate only if he can get information on odds up to the very last minute before the race, so that he can "hedge" or "lay off" bets. With racing going on simultaneously on many tracks throughout the country, this information has to be obtained speedily and accurately. Thus, the racing wire is the nerve ganglion of race betting.

The racing-wire news service got started in the twenties through the genius of the late Moe Annenberg, who had made a fearful reputation for himself as Hearst's circulation manager in the rough-and-tough Chicago newspaper wars. Annenberg conceived the idea of a telegraphic news service which would gather information from tracks and shoot it immediately to scratch sheets, horse parlors, and bookie joints. In some instances, track owners gave Annenberg the rights to send news from tracks; more often, the news was simply "stolen" by crews operating inside or near the tracks. So efficient did this news distribution system become, that in 1942, when a plane knocked out a vital telegraph circuit which served an Air Force field as well as the gamblers, the Continental Press managed to get its racing wire service for gamblers resumed in fifteen minutes, while it took the Fourth Army, which was responsible for the defense of the entire West Coast, something like three hours.

Annenberg built up a nationwide racing information chain that not only distributed wire news but controlled sub-outlets as well. In 1939, harassed by the Internal Revenue Bureau on income tax and chivvied by the Justice Department for "monopolistic" control of the wire service, the tired and aging Annenberg simply walked out of the business.

He did not sell his interest or even seek to salvage some profit; he simply gave up. Yet, like any established and thriving institution, the enterprise continued, though on a decentralized basis. James Ragen, Annenberg's operations manager and likewise a veteran of the old Chicago circulation wars, took over the national wire service through a dummy friend and renamed it the Continental Press Service.

The salient fact is that in the operation of the Annenberg and Ragen wire service, formally illegal as many of its subsidiary operations may have been (i.e., in "stealing" news, supplying information to bookies, etc.), gangsters played no part. It was a business, illicit, true, but primarily a business. The distinction between gamblers and gangsters, as we shall see, is a relevant one.

In 1946, the Chicago mob, whose main interest was in bookmaking rather than in gambling casinos, began to move in on the wire monopoly. Following repeal, the Capone lieutenants had turned, like Lepke, to labor racketeering. Murray ("The Camel") Humphries muscled in on the teamsters, the operating engineers, and the cleaning-and-dyeing, laundry, and linen-supply industries. Through a small-time punk, Willie Bioff, and union official George Browne, Capone's chief successors, Frank ("The Enforcer") Nitti and Paul Ricca, came into control of the motion-picture union and proceeded to shake down the movie industry for fabulous sums in order to "avert strikes." In 1943, when the government moved in and smashed the industrial rackets, the remaining big shots, Charley Fischetti, Jake Guzik, and Tony Accardo, decided to concentrate on gambling, and in particular began a drive to take over the racing wire.

In Chicago, the Guzik-Accardo gang, controlling a sub-distributor of the racing-news service, began tapping Continental's wires. In Los Angeles, the head of the local distribution agency for Continental was beaten up by hoodlums working for Mickey Cohen and Joe Sica. Out of the blue appeared a new and competitive nationwide racing information and distribution service, known as Trans-American Publishing, the money for which was advanced by the Chicago mobs and Bugsy Siegel, who, at the time, held a monopoly of the bookmaking and wire-news service in Las Vegas. Many books pulled out of Continental and bought information from the new outfit; many hedged by buying from both. At the end of a year, however, the Capone mob's wire had lost about $200,000. Ragen felt that violence would erupt and went to the Cook County district attorney and told him that his life had been threatened by his rivals. Ragen knew his competitors. In June, 1946, he was killed by a blast from a shotgun.

Thereafter, the Capone mob abandoned Trans-American and got a "piece" of Continental. Through their new control of the national racing-wire monopoly, the Capone mob began to muscle in on the lucrative Miami gambling business run by the so-called S & G syndicate. For a long time S & G's monopoly over bookmaking had been so complete that when New York gambler Frank Erickson bought a three months' bookmaking concession at the expensive Roney Plaza Hotel, for $45,000, the local police, in a highly publicized raid, swooped down on the hotel; the next year the Roney Plaza was again using local talent. The Capone group, however, was tougher. They demanded an interest in Miami bookmaking and, when refused, began organizing a syndicate of their own, persuading some bookies at the big hotels to join them. Florida Governor Warren's crime investigator appeared—a friend, it seemed, of old Chicago dogtrack operator William Johnston, who had contributed $100,000 to the Governor's campaign fund—and began raiding bookie joints, but only those that were affiliated with S & G. Then S & G, which had been buying its racing news from the local distributor of Continental Press, found its service abruptly shut off. For a few days the syndicate sought to bootleg information from New Orleans, but found itself limping along. After ten days' war of attrition, the five S & G partners found themselves with a sixth partner, who, for a token "investment" of $20,000, entered a Miami business that grossed $26,000,000 in one year.

Gamblers and Guys

While Americans made gambling illegal, they did not in their hearts think of it as wicked—even the churches benefited from the bingo and lottery crazes. So they gambled—and gamblers flourished. Against this open canvas, the indignant tones of Senator Wiley and the shocked righteousness of Senator Tobey during the Kefauver investigation rang oddly. Yet it was probably this very tone of surprise that gave the activity of the Kefauver Committee its piquant quality. Here were some senators who seemingly did not know the facts of life, as most Americans did. Here, in the person of Senator Tobey, was the old New England Puritan conscience poking around in industrial America, in a world it had made but never seen. Here was old-fashioned moral indignation, at a time when cynicism was rampant in public life.

Commendable as such moralistic fervor was, it did not make for intelligent discrimination of fact. Throughout the Kefauver hearings, for example, there ran the presumption that all gamblers were invariably gangsters. This was true of Chicago's Accardo-Guzik combine, which in the past had its fingers in many kinds of rackets. It was not nearly so true of many of large gamblers in America, most of whom had

the feeling that they were satisfying a basic American urge for sport and looked upon their calling with no greater sense of guilt than did many bootleggers. After all, Sherman Billingsley did start out as a speakeasy proprietor, as did the Kreindlers of the "21" Club; and today the Stork Club and the former Jack and Charlie's are the most fashionable night and dining spots in America (one prominent patron of the Stork Club: J. Edgar Hoover).

The S & G syndicate in Miami, for example (led by Harold Salvey, Jules Levitt, Charles Friedman, Sam Cohen, and Edward [Eddie Luckey] Rosenbaum), was simply a master pool of some two hundred bookies that arranged for telephone service, handled "protection," acted as bankers for those who needed ready cash on hard-hit books, and, in short, functioned somewhat analogously to the large factoring corporations in the textile field or the credit companies in the auto industry. Yet to Kefauver, the S & G men were "slippery and arrogant characters. . . . Salvey, for instance, was an old-time bookie who told us he had done nothing except engage in bookmaking or finance other bookmakers for twenty years." When, as a result of committee publicity and the newly found purity of the Miami police, the S & G syndicate went out of business, it was, as the combine's lawyer told Kefauver, because the "boys" were weary of being painted "the worst monsters in the world." "It is true," Cohen acknowledged, "that they had been law violators." But they had never done anything worse than gambling, and "to fight the world isn't worth it."

Most intriguing of all were the opinions of James J. Carroll, the St. Louis "betting commissioner," who for years had been widely quoted on the sports pages of the country as setting odds on the Kentucky Derby winter book and the baseball pennant races. Senator

Wiley, speaking like the prosecutor in Camus's novel, *The Stranger*, became the voice of official morality:

SENATOR WILEY: Have you any children?

MR. CARROLL: Yes, I have a boy.

SENATOR WILEY: How old is he?

MR. CARROLL: Thirty-three.

SENATOR WILEY: Does he gamble?

MR. CARROLL: No.

SENATOR WILEY: Would you like to see him grow up and become a gambler, either professional or amateur?

MR. CARROLL: No. . . .

SENATOR WILEY: All right. Is your son interested in your business?

MR. CARROLL: No, he is a manufacturer.

SENATOR WILEY: Why do you not get him into the business?

MR. CARROLL: Well, psychologically a great many people are unsuited for gambling.

Retreating from this gambit, the Senator sought to pin Carroll down on his contributions to political campaigns:

SENATOR WILEY: Now this morning I asked you whether you contributed any money for political candidates or parties, and you said not more than $200 at one time. I presume that does not indicate the total of your contributions in any one campaign, does it?

MR. CARROLL: Well, it might, might not, Senator. I have been an "againster" in many instances. I am a reader of *The Nation* for fifty years and they have advertisements calling for contributions for different candidates, different causes. . . . They carried an advertisement for George Norris; I contributed, I think, to that, and to the elder LaFollette.

Carroll, who admitted to having been in the betting business since 1899, was the sophisticated—but not immoral!—counterpoint to moralist Wiley. Here was a man without the stigmata of the underworld or underground; he was worldly, cynical of official rhetoric, jaundiced about people's motives; he was an "againster" who believed that "all gambling legislation originates or stems from some group or some individual seeking special interests for himself or his cause."

Asked why people gamble, Carroll distilled his experiences of fifty years with a remark that deserves a place in American social history: "I really don't know how to answer the question," he said. "I think gambling is a biological necessity for certain types. I think it is the quality that gives substance to their daydreams."

In a sense, the entire Kefauver materials, unintentionally, seem to document that remark. For what the committee revealed time and time again was a picture of gambling as a basic institution in American life, flourishing openly and accepted widely. In many of the small towns, the gambling joint is as open as a liquor establishment. The town of Havana, in Mason County, Illinois, felt miffed when Governor Adlai Stevenson intervened against local gambling. In 1950, the town had raised $15,000 of its $50,000 budget by making friendly raids on the gambling houses every month and having the owners pay fines. "With the gambling fines cut off," grumbled Mayor Clarence Chester, "the next year is going to be tough."

Apart from the gamblers, there were the mobsters. But what Senator Kefauver and company failed to understand was that the mobsters, like the gamblers, and like the entire gangdom generally, were seeking to become quasi-respectable and establish a place for themselves in American life. For the mobsters, by and large, had immigrant roots, and crime, as the pattern showed, was a route of social ascent and place in American life.

The Myth of the Mafia

The mobsters were able, where they wished, to "muscle in" on the gambling business because the established gamblers were wholly vulnerable, not being able to call on the law for protection. The senators, however, refusing to make any distinction between a gambler and a gangster, found it convenient to talk loosely of a nationwide conspiracy of "illegal" elements. Senator Kefauver asserted that a "nationwide crime syndicate does exist in the United States, despite the protestations of a strangely assorted company of criminals, self-serving politicians, plain blind fools, and others who may be honestly misguided, that there is no such combine." The Senate committee report states the matter more dogmatically: "There is a nationwide crime syndicate known as the Mafia. . . . Its leaders are usually found in control of the most lucrative rackets in their cities. There are indications of a centralized direction and control of these rackets. . . . The Mafia is the cement that helps to bind the Costello-Adonis-Lansky syndicate of New York and the Accardo-Guzik-Fischetti syndicate of Chicago. . . . These groups have kept in touch with Luciano since his deportation from the country."

Unfortunately for a good story—and the existence of the Mafia would be a whale of a story—neither the Senate Crime Committee in its testimony, nor Kefauver in his book, presented any real evidence that the Mafia exists as a functioning organization. One finds police officials asserting before the Kefauver committee their *belief* in the Mafia; the Narcotics Bureau *thinks* that a world-wide dope ring allegedly run by Luciano is part of the Mafia; but the only other "evidence" presented— aside from the incredulous responses both of Senator Kefauver and Rudolph Halley when nearly all the Italian gangsters asserted that they didn't know about the Mafia—is that certain crimes bear "the earmarks of the Mafia."

The legend of the Mafia has been fostered in recent years largely by the peephole writing team of Jack Lait and Lee Mortimer. In their *Chicago Confidential,* they rattled off a series of names and titles that made the organization sound like a rival to an Amos and Andy Kingfish society. Few serious reporters, however, give it much credence. Burton Turkus, the Brooklyn prosecutor who broke up the "Murder, Inc." ring, denies the existence of the Mafia. Nor could Senator Kefauver even make out much of a case for his picture of a national crime syndicate. He is forced to admit that "as it exists today [it] is an elusive and furtive but nonetheless tangible thing," and that "its organization and machinations are not always easy to pinpoint." [1] His "evi-

[1] The accidental police discovery of a conference of Italian figures, most of them with underworld and police records, in Apalachin, New York, in November 1957, revived the talk of a Mafia. *Time* magazine assigned a reporter, Serrell Hillman, to check the story, and this what he reported: "I spent some two weeks in New York, Washington and Chicago running down every clue to the so-called Mafia that I could find. I talked to a large number of Federal, state and local law enforcement authorities; to police, reporters, attorneys, detectives, non-profit civic groups such as the Chicago Crime Commission. Nobody from the F.B.I. and Justice Department officials on down, with the exception of a couple of Hearst crime reporters—always happy for the sake of a street sale to associate the 'Mafia' with the most routine barroom shooting—and the Narcotics Bureau believed that a Mafia exists as such. The Narcotics Bureau, which has to contend with a big problem in dope-trafficking, contends that a working alliance oper-

dence" that many gangsters congregate at certain times of the year in such places at Hot Springs, Arkansas, in itself does not prove much; people "in the trade" usually do, and as the loquacious late Willie Moretti of New Jersey said, in explaining how he had met the late Al Capone at a race track, "Listen, well-charactered people you don't need introductions to; you just meet automatically."

Why did the Senate Crime Committee plump so hard for its theory of a Mafia and a national crime syndicate? In part, they may have been misled by their own hearsay. The Senate committee was not in the position to do original research, and its staff, both legal and investigative, was incredibly small. Senator Kefauver had begun the investigation with the attitude that with so much smoke there must be a raging fire. But smoke can also mean a smoke screen. Mob activities is a field in

---

ates between an organized Mafia in Italy and Sicily and a U.S. Mafia. But the Bureau has never been able to submit proof of this, and the F.B.I. is skeptical. The generally held belief is that there is no tightly knit syndicate, but instead a loose "trade association" of criminals in various cities and areas, who run their own shows in their own fields but have matters of mutual interest to take up (as at the Appalachian conference). At any rate, nobody has ever been able to produce specific evidence that a Mafia is functioning."

In early 1959, Fredric Sondern, Jr., an editor of the *Reader's Digest*, published a best-selling book on the Mafia, *Brotherhood of Evil*, but a close reading of Mr. Sondern's text indicates that his sources are largely the files of the Narcotics Bureau, and his findings little more than a rehash of previously publicized material. (For a devastating review of the book, see the *Times Literary Supplement*, London, June 12, 1959, p. 351.) Interestingly enough, in May, 1959, Alvin Goldstein, a former assistant district attorney in New York, who had prosecuted racketeer Johnny Dio, conducted a crime survey of California for Governor Pat Brown and reported that he found no evidence of the existence of a Mafia in California.

which busy gossip and exaggeration flourish even more readily than in a radical political sect.

There is, as well, in the American temper, a feeling that "somewhere," "somebody" is pulling all the complicated strings to which this jumbled world dances. In politics the labor image is "Wall Street" or "Big Business"; while the business stereotype was the "New Dealers." In the field of crime, the side-of-the-mouth low-down was "Costello."

The salient reason, perhaps, why the Kefauver Committee was taken in by its own myth of an omnipotent Mafia and a despotic Costello was its failure to assimilate and understand three of the more relevant sociological facts about institutionalized crime in its relation to the political life of large urban communities in America, namely: (1) the rise of the American Italian community, as part of the inevitable process of ethnic succession, to positions of importance in politics, a process that has been occurring independently but also simultaneously in most cities with large Italian constituencies—New York, Chicago, Kansas City, Los Angeles; (2) the fact that there are individual Italians who play prominent, often leading roles today in gambling and in the mobs; and (3) the fact that Italian gamblers and mobsters often possessed "status" within the Italian community itself and a "pull" in city politics. These three items are indeed related—but not so as to form a "plot."

The Jews . . . the Irish . . . the Italians

The Italian community has achieved wealth and political influence much later and in a harder way than previous immigrant groups. Early Jewish wealth, that of the German Jews of the late nineteenth century, was made largely in banking and merchandising. To that extent, the dominant group in the Jewish community was outside of, and independent of, the urban political machines. Later Jewish wealth, among the East European immigrants, was built in the garment trades, though with some involvement with the Jewish gangster, who was typically an industrial racketeer (Arnold Rothstein, Lepke and Gurrah, etc.). Among Jewish lawyers, a small minority, such as the "Tammany lawyer" (like the protagonist of Sam Orintz's *Haunch, Paunch and Jowl*), rose through politics and occasionally touched the fringes of crime. Most of the Jewish lawyers, by and large the communal leaders, climbed rapidly, however, in the opportunities that established and legitimate Jewish wealth provided. Irish immigrant wealth in the northern urban centers, concentrated largely in construction, trucking, and the waterfront, has, to a substantial extent, been wealth accumulated in and through political alliance, e.g., favoritism in city contracts.

Control of the politics of the city thus has been crucial for the continuance of Irish political wealth. This alliance of Irish immigrant wealth and politics has been reciprocal; many noted Irish political figures lent their names as important window-dressing for business corporations (Al Smith, for example, who helped form the U.S. Trucking Corporation, whose executive head for many years was William J. McCormack, the alleged "Mr. Big" of the New York waterfront), while Irish businessmen have lent their wealth to further the careers of Irish politicians. Irish mobsters have rarely achieved status in the Irish community, but have served as integral arms of the politicians, as strong-arm men on election day.

The Italians found the more obvious big-city paths from rags to riches preempted. In part this was due to the character of the early Italian immigrant.

Most of them were unskilled and from rural stock. Jacob Riis could remark in the nineties, "the Italian comes in at the bottom and stays there." These dispossessed agricultural laborers found jobs as ditch-diggers, on the railroads as section hands, along the docks, in the service occupations, as shoemakers, barbers, garment workers, and stayed there. Many were fleeced by the "padrone" system; a few achieved wealth from truck farming, wine growing, and marketing produce; but this "marginal wealth" was not the source of coherent and stable political power.

Significantly, although the number of Italians in the United States is about a third as high as the number of Irish, and of the thirty million Catholic communicants in the United States, about half are of Irish descent and a sixth of Italian, there is not one Italian bishop among the hundred Catholic bishops in this country or one Italian archbishop among the 21 archbishops. The Irish have a virtual monopoly. This is a factor related to the politics of the American church; but the condition also is possible because there is not significant or sufficient wealth among Italian Americans to force some parity.

The children of the immigrants, the second and third generation, became wise in the ways of the urban slums. Excluded from the political ladder—in the early thirties there were almost no Italians on the city payroll in top jobs, nor in books of the period can one find discussion of Italian political leaders—and finding few open routes to wealth, some turned to illicit ways. In the children's court statistics of the 1930's, the largest group of delinquents were the Italian; nor were there any Italian communal or social agencies to cope with these problems. Yet it was, oddly enough, the quondam racketeer, seeking to become respectable, who provided one of the major supports for the drive to win a political voice for

Italians in the power structure of the urban political machines.

This rise of the Italian political bloc was connected, at least in the major northern urban centers, with another important development which tended to make the traditional relation between the politician and the protected or tolerated illicit operator more close than it had been in the past. This is the fact that the urban political machines had to evolve new forms of fund-raising, since the big business contributions, which once went heavily into municipal politics, now—with the shift in the locus of power—go largely into national affairs. (The ensuing corruption in national politics, as recent Congressional investigations show, is no petty matter; the scruples of businessmen do not seem much superior to those of the gamblers.) One way that urban political machines raised their money resembled that of the large corporations which are no longer dependent on Wall Street: by self-financing—that is, by "taxing" the large number of municipal employees who bargain collectively with City Hall for their wage increases. So the firemen's union contributed money to O'Dwyer's campaign.

A second method was taxing the gamblers. The classic example, as *Life* reported, was Jersey City, where a top lieutenant of the Hague machine spent his full time screening applicants for unofficial bookmaking licenses. If found acceptable, the applicant was given a "location," usually the house or store of a loyal precinct worker, who kicked into the machine treasury a high proportion of the large rent exacted. The one thousand bookies and their one thousand landlords in Jersey City formed the hard core of the political machine that sweated and bled to get out the votes for Hague.

A third source for the financing of these machines was the new, and often illegally earned, Italian wealth. This is

well illustrated by the career of Costello and his emergence as a political power in New York. Here the ruling motive has been the search for an entree—for oneself and one's ethnic group—into the ruling circles of the big city.

Frank Costello made his money originally in bootlegging. After repeal, his big break came when Huey Long, desperate for ready cash to fight the old-line political machines, invited Costello to install slot machines in Louisiana. Costello did, and he flourished. Together with Dandy Phil Kastel, he also opened the Beverly Club, an elegant gambling establishment just outside New Orleans, at which have appeared some of the top entertainers in America. Subsequently, Costello invested his money in New York real estate (including 79 Wall Street, which he later sold), the Copacabana night club, and a leading brand of Scotch whiskey.

Costello's political opportunity came when a money-hungry Tammany, starved by lack of patronage from Roosevelt and LaGuardia, turned to him for financial support. The Italian community in New York has for years nursed a grievance against the Irish and, to a lesser extent, the Jewish political groups for monopolizing political power. They complained about the lack of judicial jobs, the small number—usually one—of Italian congressmen, the lack of representation on the state tickets. But the Italians lacked the means to make their ambition a reality. Although they formed a large voting bloc, there was rarely sufficient wealth to finance political clubs. Italian immigrants, largely poor peasants from southern Italy and Sicily, lacked the mercantile experience of the Jews and the political experience gained in the seventy-five-year history of Irish immigration.

During the Prohibition years, the Italian racketeers had made certain political contacts in order to gain protection. Costello, always the compromiser and fixer rather than the muscle-man, was the first to establish relations with Jimmy Hines, the powerful leader of the West Side in Tammany Hall. But his rival, Lucky Luciano, suspicious of the Irish and seeking more direct power, backed and elected Al Marinelli for district leader on the Lower West Side. Marinelli in 1932 was the only Italian leader inside Tammany Hall. Later, he was joined by Dr. Paul Sarubbi, a partner of gangster Johnny Torrio in a large, legitimate liquor concern. Certainly, Costello and Luciano represented no "unified" move by the Italians as a whole for power; within the Italian community there are as many divisions as in any other group. What is significant is that different Italians, for different reasons and in various fashions, were achieving influence for the first time. Marinelli became county clerk of New York and a leading power in Tammany. In 1937, after being blasted by Tom Dewey, then running for district attorney, as a "political ally of thieves . . . and big-shot racketeers," Marinelli was removed from office by Governor Lehman. The subsequent conviction by Dewey of Luciano and Hines, and the election of LaGuardia, left most of the Tammany clubs financially weak and foundering. This was the moment Costello made his move. In a few years, by judicious financing, he controlled a bloc of "Italian" leaders in the Hall —as well as some Irish on the upper West Side and some Jewish leaders on the East Side—and was able to influence the selection of a number of Italian judges. The most notable incident, revealed by a wire tap on Costello's phone, was the "Thank you, Francisco" call in 1943 by Supreme Court judge nominee Thomas Aurelio, who gave Costello full credit for his nomination.

It was not only Tammany that was eager to accept campaign contributions from newly rich Italians, even though some of these *nouveaux riches* had "arrived" through bootlegging and gambling. Fiorello LaGuardia, the wiliest mind that melting-pot politics has ever produced, understood in the early thirties where much of his covert support came from. (So, too, did Vito Marcantonio, an apt pupil of the master: Marcantonio has consistently made deals with the Italian leaders of Tammany Hall—in 1943 he supported Aurelio and refused to repudiate him even when the Democratic party formally did.) Joe Adonis, who had built a political following during the late twenties, when he ran a popular speakeasy, aided LaGuardia financially to a considerable extent in 1933. "The Democrats haven't recognized the Italians," Adonis told a friend. "There is no reason for the Italians to support anybody but LaGuardia; the Jews have played ball with the Democrats and haven't gotten much out of it. They know it now. They will vote for LaGuardia. So will the Italians."

Adonis played his cards shrewdly. He supported LaGuardia, but also a number of Democrats for local and judicial posts, and became a power in the Brooklyn area. His restaurant was frequented by Kenny Sutherland, the Coney Island Democratic leader; Irwin Steingut, the Democratic minority leader in Albany; Anthony DiGiovanni, later a councilman; William O'Dwyer, and Jim Moran. But, in 1937, Adonis made the mistake of supporting Royal Copeland against LaGuardia, and the irate Fiorello finally drove Adonis out of New York.

LaGuardia later turned his ire against Costello, too. Yet Costello survived and reached the peak of his influence in 1942, when he was instrumental in electing Michael Kennedy leader of Tammany Hall. Despite the Aurelio fiasco, which first brought Costello into notoriety, he still had sufficient power in the Hall to swing votes for Hugo Rogers as Tammany leader in 1948. In those years many a Tammany leader came hat-in-hand to Costello's apartment or sought him out on the golf links to obtain the nomination for a judicial post.

During this period, other Italian political leaders were also coming to the fore. Generoso Pope, whose Colonial Sand and Stone Company began to prosper through political contacts, became an important political figure, especially when his purchase of the two largest Italian-language dailies (later merged into one), and of a radio station, gave him almost a monopoly of channels to Italian-speaking opinion of the city. Through Generoso Pope, and through Costello, the Italians became a major political force in New York.

That the urban machines, largely Democratic, have financed their heavy campaign costs in this fashion rather than having to turn to the "moneyed interests" explains in some part why these machines were able, in part, to support the New and Fair Deals without suffering the pressures they might have been subjected to had their source of money supply been the business groups.[2] Although he has never publicly revealed his political convictions, it is likely that Frank Costello was a fervent admirer of Franklin D. Roosevelt and his efforts to aid the common man. The basic measures of the New Deal, which most Americans today agree were necessary for the public good, would not have been possible

[2] This is an old story in American politics. Theodore Allen, a gambler and saloon keeper, whose American Mabille was an elegant music hall and bordello (he once told a Congressional investigating committee that he was the wickedest man in New York), gave Republican Boss Thurlow Weed a campaign contribution of $25,000 for the re-election of Abraham Lincoln in 1864.

without the support of the "corrupt" big-city machines.

The "New" Money—and the Old

There is little question that men of Italian origin appeared in most of the leading roles in the high drama of gambling and mobs, just as twenty years ago the children of East European Jews were the most prominent figures in organized crime, and before that individuals of Irish descent were similarly prominent. To some extent statistical accident and the tendency of newspapers to emphasize the few sensational figures gives a greater illusion about the domination of illicit activities by a single ethnic group than all the facts warrant. In many cities, particularly in the South and on the West Coast, the mob and gambling fraternity consisted of many other groups, and often, predominantly, of native white Protestants. Yet it is clear that in the major northern urban centers there was a distinct ethnic sequence in the modes of obtaining illicit wealth and that, uniquely in the case of the recent Italian elements, the former bootleggers and gamblers provided considerable leverage for the growth of political influence as well. A substantial number of Italian judges sitting on the bench in New York today are indebted in one fashion or another to Costello; so too are many Italian district leaders—as well as some Jewish and Irish politicians. And the motive in establishing Italian political prestige in New York was generous rather than scheming for personal advantage. For Costello it was largely a case of ethnic pride. As in earlier American eras, organized illegality became a stepladder of social ascent.

To the world at large, the news and pictures of Frank Sinatra, for example, mingling with former Italian mobsters could come somewhat as a shock. Yet to Sinatra, and to many Italians, these were men who had grown up in their neighborhoods and who were, in some instances, by-words in the community for their helpfulness and their charities. The early Italian gangsters were hoodlums—rough, unlettered, and young (Al Capone was only twenty-nine at the height of his power). Those who survived learned to adapt. By now they are men of middle age or older. They learned to dress conservatively. Their homes are in respectable suburbs. They sent their children to good schools and sought to avoid publicity.[3] Costello even went to a psychiatrist in his efforts to overcome a painful feeling of inferiority in the world of manners.

As happens with all "new" money in American society, the rough and ready contractors, the construction people, trucking entrepreneurs, as well as racketeers, polished up their manners and sought recognition and respectability in their own ethnic as well as in

[3] Except at times by being overly neighborly, like Tony Accardo, who, at Yuletide 1949, in his elegant River Forest home, decorated a 40-foot tree on his lawn and beneath it set a wooden Santa and reindeer, while around the yard, on tracks, electrically operated skating figures zipped merrily around while a loudspeaker poured out Christmas carols. The next Christmas, the Accardo lawn was darkened; Tony was on the lam from Kefauver.

the general community. The "shanty" Irish became the "lace curtain" Irish, and then moved out for wider recognition. Sometimes acceptance came first in established "American" society, and this was a certificate for later recognition by the ethnic community, a process well illustrated by the belated acceptance in established Negro society of such figures as Sugar Ray Robinson and Joe Louis, as well as leading popular entertainers.

Yet, after all, the foundation of many a distinguished older American fortune was laid by sharp practices and morally reprehensible methods. The pioneers of American capitalism were not graduated from Harvard's School of Business Administration. The early settlers and founding fathers, as well as those who "won the West" and built up cattle, mining, and other fortunes, often did so by shady speculations and a not inconsiderable amount of violence. They ignored, circumvented, or stretched the law when it stood in the way of America's destiny and their own—or were themselves the law when it served their purposes. This has not prevented them and their descendants from feeling proper moral outrage when, under the changed circumstances of the crowded urban environments, latecomers pursued equally ruthless tactics. . . .

40
Prison and the Defects of Total Power

GRESHAM M. SYKES

"For the needs of mass administration today," said Max Weber, "bureaucratic administration is completely indispensable. The choice is between bureaucracy and dilettantism in the field of administration."[1] To the officials of the New Jersey State Prison the choice is clear, as it is clear to the custodians of all maximum security prisons in the United States today. They are organized into a bureaucratic administrative staff —characterized by limited and specific rules, well-defined areas of competence and responsibility, impersonal standards of performance and promotion, and so on—which is similar in many respects to that of any modern, large-scale enterprise; and it is this staff which must see to the effective execution of the prison's routine procedures.

Of the approximately 300 employees of the New Jersey State Prison, more than two-thirds are directly concerned with the supervision and control of the inmate population. These form the so-called custodian force which is broken into three eight-hour shifts, each shift being arranged in a typical pyramid of authority. The day shift, however—on duty from 6:20 A.M. to 2:20 P.M.—is by far the largest. As in many organizations, the rhythm of life in the prison quickens with daybreak and trails off

"The Defects of Total Power," in Gresham M. Sykes, *The Society of Captives: A Study of Maximum Security Division* (copyrights © 1958 by Princeton University Press; Princeton Paperback, 1971), pp. 40–62. Reprinted by permission of Princeton University Press.
[1] Max Weber, *The Theory of Social and Economic Organization*, edited by Talcott Parsons, New York: Oxford University Press, 1947, p. 337.

in the afternoon, and the period of greatest activity requires the largest number of administrative personnel.

In the bottom ranks are the Wing guards, the Tower guards, the guards assigned to the shops, and those with a miscellany of duties such as the guardianship of the receiving gate or the garage. Immediately above these men are a number of sergeants and lieutenants and these in turn are responsible to the Warden and his assistants.

The most striking fact about this bureaucracy of custodians is its unparalleled position of power—in formal terms, at least—vis-à-vis the body of men which it rules and from which it is supposed to extract compliance. The officials, after all, possess a monopoly on the legitimate means of coercion (or, as one prisoner has phrased it succinctly, "They have the guns and we don't"); and the officials can call on the armed might of the police and the National Guard in case of an overwhelming emergency. The 24-hour surveillance of the custodians represents the ultimate watchfulness and, presumably, noncompliance on the part of the inmates need not go long unchecked. The rulers of this society of captives nominally hold in their hands the sole right of granting rewards and inflicting punishments and it would seem that no prisoner could afford to ignore their demands for conformity. Centers of opposition in the inmate population—in the form of men recognized as leaders by fellow prisoners— can be neutralized through the use of solitary confinement or exile to other

State institutions.[2] The custodians have the right not only to issue and administer the orders and regulations which are to guide the life of the prisoner, but also the right to detain, try, and punish any individual accused of disobedience—a merging of legislative, executive, and judicial functions which has long been regarded as the earmark of complete domination. The officials of the prison, in short, appear to be the possessors of almost infinite power within their realm; and, at least on the surface, the bureaucratic staff should experience no great difficulty in converting their rules and regulations —their blueprint for behavior—into a reality.

It is true, of course, that the power position of the custodial bureaucracy is not truly infinite. The objectives which the officials pursue are not completely of their own choosing and the means which they can use to achieve their objectives are far from limitless. The custodians are not total despots, able to exercise power at whim, and thus they lack the essential mark of infinite power, the unchallenged right of being capricious in their rule. It is this last which distinguishes terror from government, infinite power from almost infinite power, and the distinction is an important one. Neither by right nor by intention are the officials of the New Jersey State Prison free from a system of norms and laws which curb their actions. But within these limitations the bureaucracy of the prison is

organized around a grant of power which is without an equal in American society; and if the rulers of any social system could secure compliance with their rules and regulations—however sullen or unwilling—it might be expected that the officials of the maximum security prison would be able to do so.

When we examine the New Jersey State Prison, however, we find that this expectation is not borne out in actuality. Indeed, the glaring conclusion is that despite the guns and the surveillance, the searches and the precautions of the custodians, the actual behavior of the inmate population differs markedly from that which is called for by official commands and decrees. Violence, fraud, theft, aberrant sexual behavior—all are common-place occurrences in the daily round of institutional existence in spite of the fact that the maximum security prison is conceived of by society as the ultimate weapon for the control of the criminal and his deviant actions. Far from being omnipotent rulers who have crushed all signs of rebellion against their regime, the custodians are engaged in a continuous struggle to maintain order—and it is a struggle in which the custodians frequently fail. Offenses committed by one inmate against another occur often, as do offenses committed by inmates against the officials and their rules. And the number of undetected offenses is, by universal agreement of both officials and inmates, far larger than the number of offenses which are discovered.

Some hint of the custodial bureaucracy's skirmishes with the population of prisoners is provided by the records of the disciplinary court which has the task of adjudicating charges brought by guards against their captives for offenses taking place within the walls. The following is a typical listing for a one-week period:

[2] Just as the Deep South served as a dumping-ground for particularly troublesome slaves before the Civil War, so too can the county jail or mental hospital serve as a dumping-ground for the maximum security prison. Other institutions, however, are apt to regard the Trenton Prison in somewhat the same way, as the report of the Governor's committee to investigate the prison has indicated.

CHARGE	DISPOSITION
(1) Insolence and swearing while being interrogated	(1) Continue in segregation
(2) Threatening an inmate	(2) Drop from job
(3) Attempting to smuggle roll of tape into institution	(3) 1 day in segregation with restricted diet
(4) Possession of contraband	(4) 30 days loss of privileges
(5) Possession of pair of dice	(5) 2 days in segregation with restricted diet
(6) Insolence	(6) Reprimand
(7) Out of place	(7) Drop from job. Refer to classification committee for reclassification
(8) Possession of home-made knife, metal, and emery paper	(8) 5 days in segregation with restricted diet
(9) Suspicion of gambling or receiving bets	(9) Drop from job and change Wing assignment
(10) Out of place	(10) 15 days loss of privileges
(11) Possession of contraband	(11) Reprimand
(12) Creating disturbance in Wing	(12) Continue in segregation
(13) Swearing at an officer	(13) Reprimand
(14) Out of place	(14) 15 days loss of privileges
(15) Out of place	(15) 15 days loss of privileges

Even more revealing, however, than this brief and somewhat enigmatic record are the so-called charge slips in which the guard is supposed to write out the derelictions of the prisoner in some detail. In the New Jersey State Prison, Charge Slips form an administrative residue of past conflicts between captors and captives and the following accounts are a fair sample:

This inmate threatened an officer's life. When I informed this inmate he was to stay in to see the Chief Deputy on his charge he told me if he did not go to the yard I would get a shiv in my back.
      Signed: Officer A_____
Inmate X cursing an officer. In mess hall inmate refused to put excess bread back on tray. Then he threw the tray on the floor. In the Center, inmate cursed both Officer Y and myself.
      Signed: Officer B_____
This inmate has been condemning everyone about him for going to work. The Center gave orders for him to go to work this

A.M. which he refused to do. While searching his cell I found drawings of picks and locks.
      Signed: Officer C_____
Fighting. As this inmate came to 1 Wing entrance to go to yard this A.M. he struck inmate G in the face.
      Signed: Officer D_____
Having fermented beverage in his cell. Found while inmate was in yard.
      Signed: Officer E_____
Attempting to instigate wing disturbance. When I asked him why he discarded [sic] my order to quiet down he said he was going to talk any time he wanted to and _____me and do whatever I wanted in regards to it.
      Signed: Officer F_____
Possession of home-made shiv sharpened to razor edge on his person and possession of 2 more shivs in cell. When inmate was sent to 4 Wing officer H found 3″ steel blade in pocket. I ordered Officer M to search his cell and he found 2 more shivs in process of being sharpened.
      Signed: Officer G_____
Insolence. Inmate objected to my looking at

papers he was carrying in pockets while going to the yard. He snatched them violently from my hand and gave me some very abusive talk. This man told me to_____ myself, and raised his hands as if to strike me. I grabbed him by the shirt and took him to the Center.

Signed: Officer H_____

Assault with knife on inmate K. During Idle Men's mess at approximately 11:10 A.M. this man assaulted Inmate K with a homemade knife. Inmate K was receiving his rations at the counter when Inmate B rushed up to him and plunged a knife in his chest, arm, and back. I grappled with him and with the assistance of Officers S and V, we disarmed the inmate and took him to the Center. Inmate K was immediately taken to the hospital.

Signed: Officer I_____

Sodomy. Found inmate W in cell with no clothing on and inmate Z on top of him with no clothing. Inmate W told me he was going to lie like a_____ _____ _____ _____ to get out of it.

Signed: Officer J_____

Attempted escape on night of 4/15/53. This inmate along with inmates L and T succeeded in getting on roof of 6 Wing and having home-made bombs in their possession.

Signed: Officer K_____

Fighting and possession of home-made shiv. Struck first blow to Inmate P. He struck blow with a roll of black rubber rolled up in his fist. He then produced a knife made out of wire tied to a tooth brush.

Signed: Officer L_____

Refusing medication prescribed by Doctor W. Said "What do you think I am, a damn fool, taking that_____for a headache, give it to the doctor."

Signed: Officer M_____

Inmate loitering on tier. There is a clique of several men who lock on top tier, who ignore rule of returning directly to their cells and attempt to hang out on the tier in a group.

Signed: Officer N_____

It is hardly surprising that when the guards at the New Jersey State Prison were asked what topics should be of first importance in a proposed in-service training program, 98 percent picked "what to do in event of trouble." The critical issue for the moment, however, is that the dominant position of the custodial staff is more fiction than reality, if we think of domination as something more than the outward forms and symbols of power. If power is viewed as the probability that orders and regulations will be observed by a given group of individuals, as Max Weber has suggested,[3] the New Jersey State Prison is perhaps more notable for the doubtfulness of obedience than its certainty. The weekly records of the disciplinary court and Charge Slips provide an admittedly poor index of offenses or acts of noncompliance committed within the walls, for these form only a small, visible segment of an iceberg whose greatest bulk lies beneath the surface of official recognition. The public is periodically made aware of the officials' battle to enforce their regime within the prison, commonly in the form of allegations in the newspapers concerning homosexuality, illegal use of drugs, assaults, and so on. But the ebb and flow of public attention given to these matters does not match the constancy of these problems for the prison officials who are all too well aware that "Incidents"—the very thing they try to minimize—are not isolated or rare events but are instead a commonplace. The number of "incidents" in the New Jersey State Prison is probably no greater than that to be found in most maximum security institutions in the United States and may, indeed, be smaller, although it is difficult to make comparisons. In any event, it seems clear that the custodians are bound to their captives in a relationship of conflict rather than compelled acquiescence, despite the custo-

3 *Ibid.*, p. 324.

dians' theoretical supremacy, and we now need to see why this should be so.

II

In our examination of the forces which undermine the power position of the New Jersey State Prison's custodial bureaucracy, the most important fact is, perhaps, that the power of the custodians is not based on authority.

Now power based on authority is actually a complex social relationship in which an individual or a group of individuals is recognized as possessing a right to issue commands or regulations and those who receive these commands or regulations feel compelled to obey by a sense of duty. In its pure form, then, or as an ideal type, power based on authority has two essential elements: a rightful or legitimate effort to exercise control on the one hand and an inner, moral compulsion to obey, by those who are to be controlled, on the other. In reality, of course, the recognition of the legitimacy of efforts to exercise control may be qualified or partial and the sense of duty, as a motive for compliance, may be mixed with motives of fear or self-interest. But it is possible for theoretical purposes to think of power based on authority in its pure form and to use this as a baseline in describing the empirical case.[4]

It is the second element of authority —the sense of duty as a motive for compliance—which supplies the secret strength of most social organizations. Orders and rules can be issued with the expectation that they will be obeyed without the necessity of demonstrating in each case that compliance will advance the subordinate's interests. Obedience or conformity springs from an internalized morality which transcends the personal feelings of the individual; the fact that an order or a rule is an order or a rule becomes the basis for modifying one's behavior, rather than a rational calculation of the advantages which might be gained.

In the prison, however, it is precisely this sense of duty which is lacking in the general inmate population. The regime of the custodians is expressed as a mass of commands and regulations passing down a hierarchy of power. In general, these efforts at control are regarded as legitimate by individuals in the hierarchy, and individuals tend to respond because they feel they "should," down to the level of the guard in the cellblock, the industrial shop, or the recreation yard.[5] But now these commands and regulations must jump a gap which separates the captors from the captives. And it is at this point that a sense of duty tends to disappear and with it goes that easily-won obedience which many organizations take for granted in the naïveté of their unrecognized strength. In the prison power must be based on something other than internalized morality and the custodians find themselves confronting men who must be forced, bribed, or cajoled into compliance. This is not to say that inmates feel that the efforts of prison officials to exercise control are wrongful or illegitimate; in general, prisoners do not feel that the prison officials have usurped positions of power which are not rightfully theirs, nor do prisoners feel that the orders and regulations which descend upon them from above represent an illegal extension of their rulers' grant of government. Rather, the noteworthy fact about the social system of the New Jersey State Prison is that the bond between recognition of the legitimacy of control and the sense of duty has been torn apart. In these terms the social system of the prison is

---

[4] *Ibid.*, Introduction.

[5] Failures in this process within the custodial staff itself will be discussed in the latter portion of this chapter.

very similar to a *Gebietsverband*, a territorial group living under a regime imposed by a ruling few.[6] Like a province which has been conquered by force of arms, the community of prisoners has come to accept the validity of the regime constructed by their rulers but the subjugation is not complete. Whether he sees himself as caught by his own stupidity, the workings of chance, his inability to "fix" the case, or the superior skill of the police, the criminal in prison seldom denies the legitimacy of confinement.[7] At the same time, the recognition of the legitimacy of society's surrogates and their body of rules is not accompanied by an internalized obligation to obey and the prisoner thus accepts the fact of his captivity at one level and rejects it at another. If for no other reason, then, the custodial institution is valuable for a theory of human behavior because it makes us realize that men need not be motivated to conform to a regime which they define as rightful. It is in this apparent contradiction that we can see the first flaw in the custodial bureaucracy's assumed supremacy.

III

Since the Officials of prison possess a monopoly on the means of coercion, as we have pointed out earlier, it might be thought that the inmate population could simply be forced into conformity

6 *Ibid.*, p. 149.
7 This statement requires two qualifications. First, a number of inmates steadfastly maintain that they are innocent of the crime with which they are charged. It is the illegitimacy of their particular case, however, rather than the illegitimacy of confinement in general, which moves them to protest. Second, some of the more sophisticated prisoners argue that the conditions of imprisonment are wrong, although perhaps not illegitimate or illegal, on the grounds that reformation should be the major aim of imprisonment and the officials are not working hard enough in this direction.

and that the lack of an inner moral compulsion to obey on the part of the inmates could be ignored. Yet the combination of a bureaucratic staff— that most modern, rational form of mobilizing effort to exercise control— and the use of physical violence—that most ancient device to channel man's conduct—must strike us as an anomaly and with good reason. The use of force is actually grossly inefficient as a means for securing obedience, particularly when those who are to be controlled are called on to perform a task of any complexity. A blow with a club may check an immediate revolt, it is true, but it cannot assure effective performance on a punch-press. A "come-along," a straitjacket or a pair of handcuffs may serve to curb one rebellious prisoner in a crisis, but they will be of little aid in moving more than 1200 inmates through the messhall in a routine and orderly fashion. Furthermore, the custodians are well aware that violence once unleashed is not easily brought to heel and it is this awareness that lies behind the standing order that no guard should ever strike an inmate with his hand—he should always use a night stick. This rule is not an open invitation to brutality but an attempt to set a high threshold on the use of force in order to eliminate the casual cuffing which might explode into extensive and violent retaliation. Similarly, guards are under orders to throw their night sticks over the wall if they are on duty in the recreation yard when a riot develops. A guard without weapons, it is argued, is safer than a guard who tries to hold on to his symbol of office, for a mass of rebellious inmates may find a single night stick a goad rather than a restraint and the guard may find himself beaten to death with his own means of compelling order.

In short, the ability of the officials to physically coerce their captives into the paths of compliance is something of an illusion as far as the day-to-day activities of the prison are concerned and may be of doubtful value in moments of crisis. Intrinsically inefficient as a method of making men carry out a complex task, diminished in effectiveness by the realities of the guard-inmate ratio,[8] and always accompanied by the danger of touching off further violence, the use of physical force by the custodians has many limitations as a basis on which to found the routine operation of the prison. Coercive tactics may have some utility in checking blatant disobedience—if only a few men disobey. But if the great mass of criminals in prison are to be brought into the habit of conformity, it must be on other grounds. Unable to count on a sense of duty to motivate their captives to obey and unable to depend on the direct and immediate use of violence to insure a step-by-step submission to the rules, the custodians must fall back on a system of rewards and punishments.

Now if men are to be controlled by the use of rewards and punishments—by promises and threats—at least one point is patent: The rewards and punishments dangled in front of the individual must indeed be rewards and punishments from the point of view of the individual who is to be controlled. It is precisely on this point, however, that the custodians' system of rewards and punishments founders. In our discussion of the problems encountered in securing conscientious performance at work, we suggested that both the penalties and the incentives available to the officials were inadequate. This is also largely true, at a more general level,

with regard to rewards and punishments for securing compliance with the wishes of the custodians in all areas of prison life.

In the first place, the punishments which the officials can inflict—for theft, assaults, escape attempts, gambling, insolence, homosexuality, and all the other deviations from the pattern of behavior called for by the regime of the custodians—do not represent a profound difference from the prisoner's usual status. It may be that when men are chronically deprived of liberty, material goods and services, recreational opportunities and so on, the few pleasures that are granted take on a new importance and the threat of their withdrawal is a more powerful motive for conformity than those of us in the free community can realize. To be locked up in the solitary confinement wing, that prison within a prison; to move from the monotonous, often badly prepared meals in the messhall to a diet of bread and water;[9] to be dropped from a dull, unsatisfying job and forced to remain in idleness—all, perhaps, may mean the difference between an existence which can be borne, painful though it may be, and one which cannot. But the officials of the New Jersey State Prison are dangerously close to the point where the stock of legitimate punishments has been exhausted and it would appear that for many prisoners the few punishments which are left have lost their potency. To this we must couple the important fact that such punishments as the custodians can inflict may lead to an

---

[8] Since each shift is reduced in size by vacations, regular days off, sickness, etc., even the day shift—the largest of the three—can usually muster no more than 90 guards to confront the population of more than 1200 prisoners. The fact that they are so heavily out-numbered is not lost on the officials.

[9] The usual inmate fare is both balanced and sufficient in quantity, but it has been pointed out that the meals are not apt to be particularly appetizing since prisoners must eat them with nothing but a spoon. Cf. Report of the Governor's Committee to Examine the Prison and Parole System of New Jersey, November 21, 1952, pp. 74-79.

increased prestige for the punished in-mate in the eyes of his fellow prisoners. He may become a hero, a martyr, a man who has confronted his captors and dared them to do their worst. In the dialectics of the inmate population, punishments and rewards have, then, been reversed and the control measures of the officials may support disobedi-ence rather than decrease it.

In the second place, the system of rewards and punishments in the prison is defective because the reward side of the picture has been largely stripped away. Mail and visiting privileges, recreational privileges, the supply of personal possessions—all are given to the inmate at the time of his arrival in one fixed sum. Even the so-called Good Time—the portion of the pris-oner's sentence deducted for good be-havior—is automatically subtracted from the prisoner's sentence when he begins his period of imprisonment. Thus the officials have placed them-selves in the peculiar position of grant-ing the prisoner all available benefits or rewards at the time of his entrance into the system. The prisoner, then, finds himself unable to win any signifi-cant gains by means of compliance, for there are no gains left to be won.

From the viewpoint of the officials, of course, the privileges of the prison social system are regarded as rewards, as something to be achieved. That is to say, the custodians hold that recrea-tion, access to the inmate store, Good Time, or visits from individuals in the free community are conditional upon conformity or good behavior. But the evidence suggests that from the view-point of the inmates the variety of benefits granted by the custodians is not defined as something to be earned but as an inalienable right—as the just due of the inmate which should not turn on the question of obedience or disobedience within the walls. After all, the inmate population claims, these benefits have belonged to the prisoner from the time when he first came to the institution.

In short, the New Jersey State Prison makes an initial grant of all its rewards and then threatens to withdraw them if the prisoner does not conform. It does not start the prisoner from scratch and promise to grant its available re-wards one by one as the prisoner proves himself through continued submission to the institutional regulations. As a result a subtle alchemy is set in motion whereby the inmates cease to see the rewards of the system as rewards, that is, as benefits contingent upon per-formance; instead, rewards are apt to be defined as obligations. Whatever justification might be offered for such a policy, it would appear to have a number of drawbacks as a method of motivating prisoners to fall into the posture of obedience. In effect, rewards and punishments of the officials have been collapsed into one and the prisoner moves in a world where there is no hope of progress but only the possibility of further punishments. Since the prisoner is already suffering from most of the punishments permitted by society, the threat of imposing those few remaining is all too likely to be a gesture of futility.

IV

Unable to depend on that inner moral compulsion or sense of duty which eases the problem of control in most social organizations, acutely aware that brute force is inadequate, and lack-ing an effective system of legitimate rewards and punishments which might induce prisoners to conform to institu-tional regulations on the grounds of self interest, the custodians of the New Jersey State Prison are considerably weakened in their attempts to impose their regime on their captive popula-tion. The result, in fact, is, as we have already indicated, a good deal of deviant behavior or noncompliance in a social system where the rulers at first glance seem to possess almost infinite power.

Yet systems of power may be defective for reasons other than the fact that those who are ruled do not feel the need to obey the orders and regulations descending on them from above. Systems of power may also fail because those who are supposed to rule are unwilling to do so. The unissued order, the deliberately ignored disobedience, the duty left unperformed—these are cracks in the monolith just as surely as are acts of defiance in the subject population. The "corruption" of the rulers may be far less dramatic than the insurrection of the ruled, for power unexercised is seldom as visible as power which is challenged, but the system of power still falters.[10]

Now the official in the lowest ranks of the custodial bureaucracy—the guard in the cellblock, the industrial shop, or the recreation yard—is the pivotal figure on which the custodial bureaucracy turns. It is he who must supervise and control the inmate population in concrete and detailed terms. It is he who must see to the translation of the custodial regime from blueprint to reality and engage in the specific battles for conformity. Counting prisoners, periodically reporting to the center of communications, signing passes, checking groups of inmates as they come and go, searching for contraband or signs of attempts to escape—these make up the minutiae of his eight-hour shift. In addition, he is supposed to be alert for violations of the prison rules which fall outside his routine sphere of surveillance. Not only must he detect and report deviant behavior after it occurs;

he must curb deviant behavior before it arises as well as when he is called on to prevent a minor quarrel among prisoners from flaring into a more dangerous situation. And he must make sure that the inmates in his charge perform their assigned tasks with a reasonable degree of efficiency.

The expected role of the guard, then, is a complicated compound of policeman and foreman, of cadi, counsellor, and boss all rolled into one. But as the guard goes about his duties, piling one day on top of another (and the guard too, in a certain sense, is serving time in confinement), we find that the system of power in the prison is defective not only because the means of motivating the inmates to conform are largely lacking but also because the guard is frequently reluctant to enforce the full range of the institution's regulations. The guard frequently fails to report infractions of the rules which have occurred before his eyes. The guard often transmits forbidden information to inmates, such as plans for searching particular cells in a surprise raid for contraband. The guard often neglects elementary security requirements and on numerous occasions he will be found joining his prisoners in outspoken criticisms of the Warden and his assistants. In short, the guard frequently shows evidence of having been "corrupted" by the captive criminals over whom he stands in theoretical dominance. This failure within the ranks of the rulers is seldom to be attributed to outright bribery—bribery, indeed, is usually unnecessary, for far more effective influences are at work to bridge the gap supposedly separating captors and captives.

In the first place, the guard is in close and intimate association with his prisoners throughout the course of the working day. He can remain aloof only with great difficulty, for he possesses few of those devices which normally

[10] Portions of the following discussion concerning the corruption of the guards' authority are to be found in Gresham M. Sykes, *Crime and Society*, New York: Random House, 1956.

serve to maintain social distance between the rulers and the ruled. He
cannot withdraw physically in symbolic
affirmation of his superior position; he
has no intermediaries to bear the brunt
of resentment springing from orders
which are disliked; and he cannot fall
back on a dignity adhering to his office
—he is a *hack* or a *screw* in the eyes
of those he controls and an unwelcome
display of officiousness evokes that great
destroyer of unquestioned power, the
ribald humor of the dispossessed.

There are many pressures in American culture to "be nice," to be a "good
Joe," and the guard in the maximum
security prison is not immune. The
guard is constantly exposed to a sort
of moral blackmail in which the first
signs of condemnation, estrangement,
or rigid adherence to the rules is coun-
tered by the inmates with the threat of
ridicule or hostility. And in this complex interplay, the guard does not always start from a position of determined opposition to "being friendly."
He holds an intermediate post in a
bureaucratic structure between top
prison officials—his captains, lieutenants, and sergeants—and the prisoners
in his charge. Like many such figures,
the guard is caught in a conflict of
loyalties. He often has reason to resent
the actions of his superior officers—
the reprimands, the lack of ready appreciation, the incomprehensible order
—and in the inmates he finds willing
sympathizers: They too claim to suffer
from the unreasonable irritants of
power. Furthermore, the guard in many
cases is marked by a basic ambivalence
toward the criminals under his supervision and control. It is true that the
inmates of the prison have been condemned by society through the agency
of the courts, but some of these prisoners must be viewed as a success in
terms of a worldly system of the values
which accords high prestige to wealth
and influence even though they may

have been won by devious means; and
the poorly paid guard may be gratified
to associate with a famous racketeer.
Moreover, this ambivalence in the
guard's attitudes toward the criminals
nominally under his thumb may be
based on something more than a *sub
rosa* respect for the notorious. There
may also be a discrepancy between the
judgments of society and the guard's
own opinions as far as the "criminality"
of the prisoner is concerned. It is difficult to define the man convicted of
deserting his wife, gambling, or embezzlement as a desperate criminal to
be suppressed at all costs and the crimes
of even the most serious offenders lose
their significance with the passage of
time. In the eyes of the custodian, the
inmate tends to become a man in
prison rather than a criminal in prison
and the relationship between captor and
captive is subtly transformed in the
process.

In the second place, the guard's position as a strict enforcer of the rules is
undermined by the fact that he finds it
almost impossible to avoid the claims
of reciprocity. To a large extent the
guard is dependent on inmates for the
satisfactory performance of his duties;
and like many individuals in positions
of power, the guard is evaluated in
terms of the conduct of the men he
controls. A troublesome, noisy, dirty
cellblock reflects on the guard's ability
to "handle" prisoners and this ability
forms an important component of the
merit rating which is used as the basis
for pay raises and promotions. As we
have pointed out above, a guard cannot
rely on the direct application of force
to achieve compliance nor can he easily
depend on threats of punishment. And
if the guard does insist on constantly
using the last few negative sanctions
available to the institution—if the
guard turns in Charge Slip after Charge
Slip for every violation of the rules
which he encounters—he becomes

burdensome to the top officials of the prison bureaucratic staff who realize only too well that their apparent dominance rests on some degree of cooperation. A system of power which can enforce its rules only by bringing its formal machinery of accusation, trial, and punishment into play at every turn will soon be lost in a haze of pettifogging detail.

The guard, then, is under pressure to achieve a smoothly running tour of duty not with the stick but with the carrot, but here again his legitimate stock is limited. Facing demands from above that he achieve compliance and stalemated from below, he finds that one of the most meaningful rewards he can offer is to ignore certain offenses or make sure that he never places himself in a position where he will discover them. Thus the guard—backed by all the power of the State, close to armed men who will run to his aid, and aware that any prisoner who disobeys him can be punished if he presses charges against him—often discovers that his best path of action is to make "deals" or "trades" with the captives in his power. In effect, the guard buys compliance or obedience in certain areas at the cost of tolerating disobedience elsewhere.

Aside from winning compliance "where it counts" in the course of the normal day, the guard has another favor to be secured from the inmates which makes him willing to forego strict enforcement of all prison regulations. Many custodial institutions have experienced a riot in which the tables are turned momentarily and the captives hold sway over their quondam captors; and the rebellions of 1952 loom large in the memories of the officials of the New Jersey State Prison. The guard knows that he may some day be a hostage and that his life may turn on a settling of old accounts. A fund of good will becomes a valuable form of insurance and this fund is al-

most sure to be lacking if he has continually played the part of a martinet. In the folklore of the prison there are enough tales about strict guards who have had the misfortune of being captured and savagely beaten during a riot to raise doubts about the wisdom of demanding complete conformity.

In the third place, the theoretical dominance of the guard is undermined in actuality by the innocuous encroachment of the prisoner on the guard's duties. Making out reports, checking cells at the periodic count, locking and unlocking doors—in short, all the minor chores which the guard is called on to perform—may gradually be transferred into the hands of inmates whom the guard has come to trust. The cellblock runner, formally assigned the tasks of delivering mail, housekeeping duties, and so on, is of particular importance in this respect. Inmates in this position function in a manner analogous to that of the company clerk in the Armed Forces and like such figures they may wield power and influence far beyond the nominal definition of their role. For reasons of indifference, laziness, or naïveté, the guard may find that much of the power which he is supposed to exercise has slipped from his grasp.

Now power, like a woman's virtue, once lost is hard to regain. The measures to rectify an established pattern of abdication need to be much more severe than those required to stop the first steps in the transfer of control from the guard to his prisoner. A guard assigned to a cellblock in which a large portion of power has been shifted in the past from the officials to the inmates is faced with the weight of precedent; it requires a good deal of moral courage on his part to withstand the aggressive tactics of prisoners who fiercely defend the patterns of corruption established by custom. And if the guard himself has allowed his control to be subverted, he may find that any attempts to undo his error are checked by a threat from the inmate to send a *snitch-kite*—an anonymous note—to the guard's superior officers explaining his past derelictions in detail. This simple form of blackmail may be quite sufficient to maintain the relationships established by friendship, reciprocity, or encroachment.

It is apparent, then, that the power of the custodians is defective, not simply in the sense that the ruled are rebellious, but also in the sense that the rulers are reluctant. We must attach a new meaning to Lord Acton's aphorism that power tends to corrupt and absolute power corrupts absolutely. The custodians of the New Jersey State Prison, far from being converted into brutal tyrants, are under strong pressure to compromise with their captives, for it is a paradox that they can insure their dominance only by allowing it to be corrupted. Only by tolerating violations of "minor" rules and regulations can the guard secure compliance in the "major" areas of the custodial regime. Ill-equipped to maintain the social distance which in theory separates the world of the officials and the world of the inmates, their suspicions eroded by long familiarity, the custodians are led into a modus vivendi with their captives which bears little resemblance to the stereotypical picture of guards and their prisoners.

V

The fact that the officials of the prison experienced serious difficulties in imposing their regime on the society of prisoners is sometimes attributed to inadequacies of the custodial staff's personnel. These inadequacies, it is claimed, are in turn due to the fact that more than 50 percent of the guards are temporary employees who have not passed a Civil Service examination. In 1952, for example, a month and a half before the disturbances which dramatically underlined some of the problems of the officials, the Deputy Commissioner of the Department of Institutions and Agencies made the following points in a report concerning the temporary officer of the New Jersey State Prison's custodial force:

1. Because they are not interested in the prison service as a career, the temporary officers tend to have a high turnover as they are quick to resign to accept more remunerative employment.

2. Because they are inexperienced, they are not able to foresee or forestall disciplinary infractions, the on-coming symptoms of which the more experienced officer would detect and take appropriate preventive measures.

3. Because they are not trained as are the regular officers, they do not have the self-confidence that comes with the physical training and defensive measures which are part of the regular officers' pre-service and in-service training and, therefore, it is not uncommon for them to be somewhat timid and inclined to permit the prisoner to take advantage of them.

4. Because many of them are beyond the age limit or cannot meet the physical requirements for regular appointment as established by Civil Service, they cannot look forward to a permanent career and are therefore less interested in the welfare of the institution than their brother officers.

5. Finally, because of the short period of employment, they do not recognize the individual prisoners who are most likely to incite trouble or commit serious infractions, and they are at a disadvantage in dealing with the large groups which congregate in the cellblocks, the messhall, the auditorium, and the yard.[11]

Now the guard at the New Jersey State Prison receives a salary of $3,240 per year when he is hired and he can

[11] See New Jersey Committee to Examine and Investigate the Prison and Parole Systems of New Jersey, *Report*, November 21, 1952.

reach a maximum of $3,840 per year; and there is little doubt that the low salary scale accounts for much of the prison's high turnover rate. The fact that the job of the guard is often depressing, dangerous, and possesses relatively low prestige adds further difficulties. There is also little doubt that the high turnover rate carries numerous evils in its train, as the comments of the Deputy Commissioner have indicated. Yet even if higher salaries could counterbalance the many dissatisfying features of the guard's job—to a point where the custodial force consisted of men with long service rather than a group of transients—there remains a question of whether or not the problems of administration in the New Jersey State Prison would be eased to a significant extent. This, of course, is heresy from the viewpoint of those who trace the failure of social organizations to the personal failings of the individuals who man the organizational structure. Perhaps, indeed, there is some comfort in the idea that if the budget of the prison were larger, if higher salaries could be paid to entice "better" personnel within the walls, if guards could be persuaded to remain for longer periods, then the many difficulties of the prison bureaucracy would disappear. From this point of view, the problems of the custodial institution are rooted in the niggardliness of the free community and the consequent inadequacies of the institution's personnel rather than flaws in the social system of the prison itself. But to suppose that higher salaries are an answer to the plight of the custodians is to suppose, first, that there are men who by reason of their particular skills and personal characteristics are better qualified to serve as guards if they could be recruited; and second, that experience and training within the institution itself will better prepare the guard for his role, if greater financial rewards could convince him

to make a career of his prison employment. Both of these suppositions, however, are open to some doubt. There are few jobs in the free community which are comparable to that of the guard in the maximum security prison and which, presumably, could equip the guard-to-be with the needed skills. If the job requirements of the guard's position are not technical skills but turn on matters of character such as courage, honesty, and so on, there is no assurance that men with these traits will flock to the prison if the salary of the guard is increased. And while higher salaries may decrease the turnover rate—thus making an in-service training program feasible and providing a custodial force with greater experience —it is not certain if such a change can lead to marked improvement. A brief period of schooling can familiarize the new guard with the routines of the institution, but to prepare the guard for the realities of his assigned role with lectures and discussions is quite another matter. And it seems entirely possible that prolonged experience in the prison may enmesh the guard deeper and deeper in patterns of compromise and misplaced trust rather than sharpening his drive toward a rigorous enforcement of institutional regulations.

We are not arguing, of course, that the quality of the personnel in the prison is irrelevant to the successful performance of the bureaucracy's tasks nor are we arguing that it would be impossible to improve the quality of the personnel by increasing salaries. We are arguing, however, that the problems of the custodians far transcend the size of the guard's pay check or the length of his employment and that better personnel is at best a palliative rather than a final cure. It is true, of course, that it is difficult to unravel the characteristics of a social organization from the characteristics of the individuals who are its members; but there seems to be little reason to believe that a different crop of guards in the New Jersey State Prison would exhibit an outstanding increase in efficiency in trying to impose the regime of the custodians on the population of prisoners. *The lack of a sense of duty among those who are held captive, the obvious fallacies of coercion, the pathetic collection of rewards and punishments to induce compliance, the strong pressures toward the corruption of the guard in the form of friendship, reciprocity, and the transfer of duties into the hands of trusted inmates—all are structural defects in the prison's system of power rather than individual inadequacies.*[12]

[12] Those who are familiar with prison systems such as those of the Federal government or the State of California might argue that I have underestimated the possibilities of improvement which can be won with well-trained, well-paid, well-led guards. They might be right, but I think it is important to stress the serious, "built-in" weaknesses of the prison as a social system.

The question of whether these defects are inevitable in the custodial institution—or in any system of total power—must be deferred to a later chapter. For the moment it is enough to point out that in the New Jersey State Prison the custodians are unable or unwilling to prevent their captives from committing numerous violations of the rules which make up the theoretical blueprint for behavior and this failure is not a temporary, personal aberration but a built-in feature of the prison social system. It is only by understanding this fact that we can understand the world of the prisoners, since so many significant aspects of inmate behavior—such as coercion of fellow prisoners, fraud, gambling, homosexuality, sharing stolen supplies, and so on—are in clear contravention to institutional regulations. It is the nature of this world which must now claim our attention.

41

Mental Illness and the Insanity of Place*

ERVING GOFFMAN

For more than 200 years now the doctrine has been increasingly held that there is such a thing as mental illness, that it is a sickness like any other, and

From *Relations in Public: Microstudies of the Public Order*, by Erving Goffman, © 1971 by Erving Goffman, Basic Books, Inc., Publishers, New York.
* I am much indebted to Edwin Lemert and Sheldon Messinger and to Helen and Stewart Perry for help in writing this paper. It is reprinted with a few editorial changes from *Psychiatry: Journal for the Study of*

that those who suffer from it should be dealt with medically: they should be treated by doctors, if necessary in a hospital, and not blamed for what has befallen them. This belief has social uses. Were there no such notion, we would probably have to invent it.

However, in the last twenty years we

Interpersonal Processes, vol. XXXII, no. 4 (November 1969). Copyright 1969 by the William Alanson White Psychiatric Foundation, Inc.

have learned that the management of mental illness under medical auspices has been an uncertain blessing. The best treatment that money has been able to buy, prolonged individual psychotherapy, has not proven very efficacious. The treatment most patients have received—hospitalization—has proven to be questionable indeed. Patients recover more often than not, at least temporarily, but this seems in spite of the mental hospital, not because of it. Upon examination, many of these establishments have proven to be hopeless storage dumps trimmed in psychiatric paper. They have served to remove the patient from the scene of his symptomatic behavior, which in itself can be constructive, but this function has been performed by fences, not doctors. And the price that the patient has had to pay for this service has been considerable: dislocation from civil life, alienation from loved ones who arranged the commitment, mortification due to hospital regimentation and surveillance, permanent posthospital stigmatization. This has been not merely a bad deal; it has been a grotesque one.

Consequently, in the last decade some important changes have been entertained regarding treatment of the mentally ill. There has been marked improvement in living conditions in mental hospitals, albeit no more so than in other backwashes of American society recently penetrated by secular conceptions of man's inalienable right to recreational facilities. More to the point, there has been some pressure to keep the potential patient in the community as long as possible and to return the hospitalized patient to the community as quickly as possible. The legal rights of persons accused of mental illness have been sharpened—in some states, such as California, to the point where involuntary commitment is quite difficult to arrange. And the notion is abroad that the goal is not to cure the patient but to *contain* him in a niche in free society where he can be tolerated. Where a niche is not available one is sometimes built, as in the institutions of family care and halfway house. And if this new approach places a burden on the patient's home, neighborhood, or work place, there is a current understanding of mental disorder to help justify this: since the patient has been put upon, since he is merely the symptom carrier for a sick set-up, it is only fair that the whole be made to share the burden; it is only fair that the patient and those with whom he is most involved be encouraged, preferably with psychiatric counsel, to work together to work things out.

Given the life still enforced in most mental hospitals and the stigma still placed on mental illness, the philosophy of community containment seems the only desirable one. Nonetheless, it is worth looking at some implications of this approach for the patient's various "others," that is, persons he identifies as playing a significant role in his life. To do this we must examine the meaning of the patient's symptoms for his others. If we do this we will learn not only what containment implies, we will learn about mental disorder.

Before proceeding, I want to introduce one issue and its concepts—an issue regarding the medical world and the doctor-patient relationship.

The ideal behind medical service is much like the ideal behind other legitimate services and, as in their case, is often realized. The patient comes to the doctor on his own, places himself in the doctor's hands, follows the doctor's orders, and obtains results which amply justify the trust and the fee.

Of course there are points of tension. The patient may not know of his need for service; knowing of his need, he may apply to charlatan servers; desiring medical service, he may not be able to afford it; affording it, he may shop around too much before settling on a particular physician; settling on one, he may not follow the advice he gets from him; following the advice, he may find his situation somewhat eased but not basically altered.

More at issue, the two-party dealings and two-party relationship between the doctor and his patient can become complicated in certain ways by other parties. For example: medical group-plans of various kinds can obscure the patient's view of the agency from which he obtains treatment; communicable diseases and suspect wounds oblige the physician to act for the community as well as for the patient. I will focus on one class of these third parties, the patient's daily circles: his service community, his work place, his friendships, and particularly his family.

Traditionally in medical service the patient's family has been given certain functions. For example, very commonly the family is expected to cooperate, to help out, to mobilize the domestic resources necessary to accommodate the special temporary needs of the patient. When the illness is major, the least the family will do is to use its car to bring the patient to the hospital and fetch him therefrom; at most, the household can become a hospital away from the hospital. Whatever the extent of the family help, the physician will usually have to communicate instructions to the helpers, directly or through the patient.

Another function of the family is guardianship. Adult members of the family can be openly called on to act for the patient, typically because he is below the age of discretion or beyond it, ratifying a medical decision ordinarily requiring the free consent of the person directly affected.

Furthermore, should the patient be a full-fledged adult and his situation desperate, the family may be brought into a secret relation with the doctor, who tells them facts about the patient's condition that they need to know for their own good or his, but that the physician feels he cannot on humanitarian or medical grounds tell the patient now. A kind of emergency guardianship is involved requiring collusion between the sick person's kin and the physician. . . .

Signs and symptoms of a *medical* disorder presumably refer to underlying pathologies in the individual organism, and these constitute deviations from biological norms maintained by the homeostatic functioning of the human machine. The system of reference here is plainly the individual organism, and the term "norm," ideally at least, has no moral or social connotation. (Of course, beyond the internal pathology there is likely to be a cause in the external environment, even a social cause, as in the case of infectious or injurious situations of work; but typically the same disorder can be produced in connection with a wide variety of socially different environments.) But what about *mental* symptoms?

No doubt some psychoses are mainly organic in their relevant cause, others mainly psychogenic, still others situational. In many cases etiology will involve all of these causal elements. Further, there seems no doubt that the prepatient—that is, the individual who acts in a way that is eventually perceived as ill—may have any of the possible relations to intentionality: he may be incapable of knowing what he is doing; or he may know the effects of his acts but feel unable to stop himself, or indifferent about stopping himself; or, knowing the effects of certain acts, he may engage in them with malice aforethought, only because of their effects. All of that is not at issue here. For when an act that will later be perceived as a mental symptom is first performed by the individual who will later be seen as a mental patient, the act is not taken as a symptom of illness but rather as a deviation from social norms, that is, an infraction of social rules and social expectations. The perceptual reconstituting of an offense or infraction into a medical, value-free symptom may come quite late, will be unstable when it appears, and will be entertained differently, depending on whether it is the patient, the offended parties, or professional psychiatric personnel doing the perceiving.[1]

This argument, that mentally ill behavior is on its face a form of social deviancy, is more or less accepted in psychiatric circles. But what is not seen —and what will be argued in this paper —is that biological norms and social norms are quite different things, and that ways of analyzing deviations from one cannot be easily employed in examining deviations from the other. . . .

As the law suggests, our response to an individual who physically performs an offensive act is radically qualified by a battery of interpretive considerations: Did he know about the rule he was breaking, and if so, was he aware of breaking it? If he did not appreciate the offensive consequences of his act, ought he to have? And if he did anticipate these offensive results, were they the main purpose of his act or incidental to it? Was it within his physical competence to desist from the offense, and if so, were there extenuating social reasons for not doing so?

The answers to these questions tell us about the actor's *attitude* toward the rule that appears to have been violated, and this attitude must be determined before we can even say what it is that

has happened. The issue is not merely (and often not mainly) whether he conformed or not, but rather in what relationship he stands to the rule that ought to have governed him. Indeed, a significant feature of *any* act is what it can be taken to demonstrate about the actor's relation to such norms as legitimately govern it.

However, the actor's attitude toward a rule is a subjective thing; he alone, if anyone, is fully privy to it. Inevitably, then, an important role will be played by the readings others make of his conduct, and by the clarifying expressions that he contributes, whether to ensure that a proper purpose is not misinterpreted or an improper one is not disclosed. It follows, for example, that if a deviator is suitably tactful and circumspect in his violations, employing secrecy and cover, many of the disruptive consequences of the violation in fact will be avoided. A particular application of the rules is thwarted, but the sanctity of the rule itself is not openly questioned.

A reorientation is therefore to be suggested. An actual or suspected offender is not so much faced with an automatic corrective cycle as with the need to engage in remedial ritual work. Three chief forms of this work are available to him: accounts, apologies, and requests. With accounts he shows that he himself did not commit the offense, or did it mindlessly, or was not himself at the time, or was under special pressure, or did what any reasonable man would have done under the circumstances; [2] with apologies he shows that if indeed he had intended the offense, he now disavows the person that he was, bewails his action, repents, and wants to be given a chance to be what he now knows he should be; with requests

---

[1] Of course, some personal conditions, such as loss of memory or intense anxiety or grandiose persecutory beliefs, are very quickly shifted from offense to symptoms, but even here it is often the case that social rules regarding how a person is properly to orient himself or feel about his situation may be what are initially disturbed.

[2] A discussion of accounts is available in Marvin Scott and Stanford Lyman, "Accounts," *American Sociological Review* XXXIII (1968): 46–62.

he seeks the kind of offer or permission which will transform the act from his offense into the other's boon. With this ritual work, with explanations, propitiations, and pleas, the offender tries to show that the offense is not a valid expression of his attitude to the norms. The impiety is only apparent; he really supports the rules.

Once we see that ritual work bears on the very nature of social acts and considerably loosens what is to be meant by social equilibrium, we can readdress ourselves to the crucial difference between medical symptoms and mental symptoms.

The interesting thing about medical symptoms is how utterly nice, how utterly plucky the patient can be in managing them. There may be physical acts of an ordinary kind he cannot perform; there may be various parts of the body he must keep bandaged and hidden from view; he may have to stay home from work for a spell or even spend time in a hospital bed. But for each of these deviations from normal social appearance and functioning, the patient will be able to furnish a compensating mode of address. He gives accounts, belittles his discomfort, and presents an apologetic air, as if to say that in spite of appearance he is, deep in his social soul, someone to be counted on to know his place, someone who appreciates what he ought to be as a normal person and who is this person in spirit, regardless of what has happened to his flesh. He is someone who does not *will* to be demanding and useless. Tuberculosis patients, formerly isolated in sanitaria, sent home progress notes that were fumigated but cheerful. Brave little troops of colostomites and ileostomites make their brief appearances disguised as nice clean people, while stoically concealing the hours of hellish toilet work required for each appearance in public as a normal person. We even have our Beckett player

buried up to his head in an iron lung, unable to blow his own nose, who yet somehow expresses by means of his eyebrows that a full-fledged person is present who knows how to behave and would certainly behave that way were he physically able.

And more than an air is involved. Howsoever demanding the sick person's illness is, almost always there will be some consideration his keepers will *not* have to give. There will be some physical cooperation that can be counted on; there will be some task he can do to help out, often one that would not fall to his lot were he well. And this helpfulness can be *absolutely* counted on, just as though he were no less a responsible participant than anyone else. In the context, these little bits of substantive helpfulness take on a large symbolic function.

Now obviously, physically sick persons do not always keep a stiff upper lip (not even to mention appreciable ethnic differences in the management of the sick role); hypochondriasis is common, and control of others through illness is not uncommon. But even in these cases I think close examination would find that the culprit tends to acknowledge proper sick-role etiquette. This may only be a front, a gloss, a way of styling behavior. But it says: "Whatever my medical condition demands, the enduring me is to be dissociated from these needs, for I am someone who would make only modest reasonable claims and take a modest and standard role in the affairs of the group were I able."

The family's treatment of the patient nicely supports this definition of the situation, as does the employer's. In effect they say that special license can temporarily be accorded the sick person because, were he able to do anything about it, he would not make such demands. Since the patient's spirit and will and intentions are those of a loyal and seemly member, his old place should be kept waiting for him, for he will fill it well, as if nothing untoward has happened, as soon as his outer behavior can again be dictated by, and be an expression of, the inner man. His increased demands are saved from expressing what they might because it is plain that he has "good" reasons for making them, that is, reasons that nullify what these claims would otherwise be taken to mean. I do not say that the members of the family will be happy about their destiny. In the case of incurable disorders that are messy or severely incapacitating, the compensative work required by the well members may cost them the life chances their peers enjoy, blunt their personal careers, paint their lives with tragedy, and turn all their feelings to bitterness. But the fact that all of this hardship can be contained shows how clearly the way has been marked for the unfortunate family, a way that obliges them to close ranks and somehow make do as long as the illness lasts.

Of course, the foregoing argument must be qualified. In extreme situations, such as the military, when it can be all too plain that the ill person has everything to gain by being counted sick, the issue of malingering may be seriously raised and the whole medical frame of reference questioned.[3] Further, there is the special problem caused by illness directly affecting the face and the voice, the specialized organs of expression. An organic defect in this equipment may be a minor thing according to a medical or biological frame of reference, but it is likely to be of tremendous significance socially. There is no disfigurement of the body that cannot be decorously covered by a sheet and apologized for by a face; but many

disfigurements of the face cannot be covered without cutting off communication, and cannot be left uncovered without disastrously interfering with communication. A person with carcinoma of the bladder can, if he wants, die with more social grace and propriety, more apparent inner social normalcy, than a man with a harelip can order a piece of apple pie.

With certain exceptions, then, persons have the capacity to expressively dissociate their medical illness from their responsible conduct (and hence their selves), and typically the will to do so. They continue to express support of the social group to which they belong and acceptance of their place therein. Their personality or character will be seen to remain constant in spite of changes in their role. This means that the illness may tax the substantive resources of the group, make tragic figures of well members, but still not directly undermine the integrity of the family. In brief, ritual work and minor assistance can compensate for current infractions because an important part of an infraction is what it can be taken to symbolize about the offender's long-range attitude toward maintaining his social place; if he can find alternate ways of conveying that he is keeping himself in line, then current infractions need not be very threatening. Note that the efficacy here of excusing expressions (with the exceptions cited) is due to the fact that medical symptoms involve behavior which is either not an infraction of social norms at all—as in the case of internal tumors of various kinds—or only incidentally so. It is the incidental side effects of the physical deviation that disqualify the person for compliance. When an amputee fails to rise to greet a lady, it is perfectly evident that this failure is only an incidental and unintentional consequence of his condition; no one would claim that he cut off his legs to spite his

[3] Here see the useful paper by Vilhelm Aubert and Shelden Messinger, "The Criminal and the Sick," *Inquiry* I (1958): 137–160.

courtesies. Almost as surely, his disqualification for jobs that require rapid movement can be seen as a side effect of his deviance and not its initial expression. He is a deviator, not a deviant. Here is incapacity, not alienation.

Now turn to symptoms of mental disorder as a form of social deviation. The most obvious point to note is that since there are many kinds of social deviation that have little to do with mental disorder, nothing much is gained by calling symptoms social deviations.

The position can be taken that mental illness, pragmatically speaking, is first of all a social frame of reference, a conceptual framework, a perspective that can be applied to social offenses as a means of understanding them. The offense, in itself, is not enough; it must be perceived and defined in terms of the imagery of mental illness. By definition one must expect that there always will be some liberty and some dissensus in regard to the way this framework is applied. Many important contingencies are known to be involved, some causing the imagery to be applied to psychologically normal behavior with the consequence of reconstituting it into a mental symptom. But given this necessary caveat, we can ask: In our society, what is the nature of the social offense to which the frame of reference "mental illness" is likely to be applied?

The offense is often one to which formal means of social control do not apply. The offender appears to make little effort to conceal his offense or ritually neutralize it. The infractions often occur under conditions where, for various reasons, neither the offended nor the offender can resolve the issue by physically withdrawing from the organization and relationship in which the offense occurs, and the organization cannot be reconstituted to legitimate the new self-assumptions of the offender —or, at least, the participants strongly

feel that these adaptations are not possible. The norms in question are ones which frequently apply and which are constantly coming up for affirmation, since they often pertain to expressive behavior—the behavior which broadcasts to all within range, transmitting warnings, cues, and hints about the actor's general assumptions about himself. Finally, with the exception of paranoia of primary groups (*folie à deux, trois,* etc.), the offense is not committed by a set of persons acting as a team, but rather—or so it is perceived— by an individual acting on his own. In sum, mental symptoms are willful situational improprieties, and these, in turn, constitute evidence that the individual is not prepared to keep his place.[4]

One implication of the offense features I have mentioned should be stressed. Mental symptoms are not, by and large, *incidentally* a social infraction. By and large they are specifically and pointedly offensive. As far as the

---

[4] Although much of mental symptomatology shares these offense features—thereby allowing us to answer to the argument that mental symptoms are not merely any kind of social deviation—it is the case that many social deviations of the situational kind do not qualify as signs of mental illness. We have been slow to learn this, perhaps because mental wards once provided the most accessible source of flagrant situational improprieties, and in such a context it was all too easy to read the behavior as unmotivated, individually generated aberrancy instead of seeing it as a form of social protest against ward life—the protest having to employ the limited expressive means at hand. In the last few years the non-psychiatric character of considerable symptomlike behavior has become much easier to appreciate because situational improprieties of the most flagrant kind have become widely used as a tactic by hippies, the New Left, and black militants, and although these persons have been accused of immaturity, they seem too numerous, too able to sustain collective rapport, and too facile at switching into conventional behavior to be accused of insanity.

patient's others are concerned, the troublesome acts do not merely happen to coincide partly with what is socially offensive, as is true of medical symptoms; rather these troublesome acts are perceived, at least initially, to be intrinsically a matter of willful social deviation.

It is important now to emphasize that a social deviation can hardly be reckoned apart from the relationships and organizational memberships of the offender and offended, since there is hardly a social act that in itself is not appropriate or at least excusable in some social context. The delusions of a private can be the rights of a general; the obscene invitations of a man to a strange girl can be the spicy endearments of a husband to his wife; the wariness of a paranoid is the warranted practice of thousands of undercover agents.

Mental symptoms, then, are neither something in themselves nor whatever is so labeled; mental symptoms are acts by an individual which openly proclaim to others that he must have assumptions about himself which the relevant bit of social organization can neither allow him nor do much about.

It follows that if the patient persists in his symptomatic behavior, then he must create organizational havoc and havoc in the minds of members. Although the imputation of mental illness is surely a last-ditch attempt to cope with a disrupter who must be, but cannot be, contained, this imputation in itself is not likely to resolve the situation. Havoc will occur even when all the members are convinced that the troublemaker is quite mad, for this definition does not in itself free them from living in a social system in which he plays a disruptive part.

This havoc indicates that medical symptoms and mental symptoms are radically different in their social consequences and in their character. It is this havoc that the philosophy of containment must deal with. It is this havoc that psychiatrists have dismally failed to examine and that sociologists ignore when they treat mental illness merely as a labeling process. It is this havoc that we must explore.

The most glaring failure to organize conduct in accordance with assumptions about himself that others accept is to be found in those dramatic cases where the individual, perceived to be in a state of disorganization as an actor, accords himself a personal biographical identity not his own or temporarily reconstitutes himself in accordance with age, sex, and occupational categories for which he does not qualify. Often this is associated with the individual's imputing quite grandiose personal properties to himself. He then makes some effort to treat others accordingly and tries to get them to affirm this identification through their treatment of him.

Note that mental hospitals can manage such diffusions and distortions of identity without too much difficulty. In these establishments much of the person's usual involvement in the undertakings of others and much of his ordinary capacity to make contact with the world are cut off. There is little he can set in motion. A patient who thinks he is a potentate does not worry attendants about their being his minions. That he is in dominion over them is never given any credence. They merely watch him and laugh, as if watching impromptu theater. Similarly, when a mental hospital patient treats his wife as if she were a suspect stranger, she can deal with this impossible situation merely by adjusting downward the frequency and length of her visits.[5] So,

[5] A mental hospital in fact can be defined functionally as a place where persons who are still rightfully part of our daily lives can be held at bay and forced to wait for our occasional visits; and we, instead of sharing

too, the office therapist can withstand the splotches of love and hate that the patient brings to a session, being supported in this disinvolvement by the wonderfully convenient doctrine that direct intercession for the patient, or talk that lasts more than fifty minutes, can only undermine the therapeutic relationship. In all of these cases, distance allows a coming to terms; the patient may express impossible assumptions about himself, but the hospital, the family, or the therapist need not become involved in them.

Matters are quite different, however, when the patient is outside the walls of the hospital or office—outside, where his others commit their persons into his keeping, where his actions make authorized claims and are not symptoms or skits or something disheartening that can be walked away from. Outside the barricades, dramatically wrong self-identification is not necessary in order to produce trouble. Every form of social organization in which the patient participates has its special set of offenses perceivable as mental illness that can create organizational havoc.

One very important organizational locus for mental symptoms consists of public and semipublic places—streets, shops, neighborhoods, public transportation, and the like. In these places a fine mesh of obligations obtains which ensures the orderly traffic and co-mingling of participants. Modes of personal territoriality are delineated, and respect for their boundaries is employed as a key means of ordering mutual presence.

Many classic symptoms of psychosis are precise and pointed violation of these territorial arrangements. There are encroachments, as when a mental patient visiting a supermarket gratuitously riffles through a shopper's cart, or walks behind the counter to examine what is contained there, or openly advances her place in the checkout line, or leans into an ongoing conversation not her own, or addresses a midpassage statement to someone who has not been brought into a state of talk. There are self-contaminations involving exposure or befoulment, as when a patient is denudative, or too easily invites conversational contact from others, or speaks aloud shameful admissions, or smears himself with half-eaten food, or openly toys with his mucus, or takes dirty objects into his mouth. There are "hyperpreclusions," as when a patient declines to acknowledge any conversational overture, or shies away from passing glances, or fights off a medical examination, or will not let go of small personal possessions. . . .

Approach the family—say in the American middle-class version—through conventional sociological terms. When we examine its internal functioning, its internal social economy, we find a legitimated distribution of authority, material resources, work, and free time. There is the obligation of each member to care for and protect the others, insofar as they are in need of this help and a member is able to provide it. There is a normatively established allocation of respect, affection, and moral support. Some common values and special ways of doing things will be maintained. Knowledge of the family biography will be shared, along with memory of joint experiences. A crisscross of personal relationships will be sustained. A common care will be exerted (by all but the very young) so that the damage that could easily occur

_____

existence, can ration it. Of course, patients often can manage to hold their kinsmen at bay, too, simply by declining to meet them off the ward or by becoming upset when they visit. However, the cost of this rejection can be very high—for example, loss of an opportunity to get off the ward for a time and to obtain minor supplies. Further, what the patient can hold off is not life with his loved ones, but visits.

to the household through fire, water, soiling, and breaking will not occur. And each member will be trusted by the others not to exploit any of the lethal instrumentalities readily available in the house for harming himself or the others. Finally, as the special feature of the family as a social organization, each member commits his own feelings and involvements to what he takes to be the personal interests and personal plight of each of the others.

If the behavior of any one member, especially that occurring in the presence of other members, is examined closely, it reveals an expressive style that affirms this allotting of obligations. The maintenance of this style by each member gives the other members constant assurance that their expectations will be lived up to and that things are as they should be. In brief, the activity of each member tends to express that he knows what his social place is in the family and that he is sticking to it. Of course, if an individual member has medical difficulties, he is likely to make extra demands, but part of the safety here is due to the ritual work he engages in which neutralizes these demands as threats to the family's normative order, ensuring constancy to the members' sense of what the ill individual is like as a personality. Nonmedical crises, such as the lengthy absence of a member for military service, can similarly be handled, provided only that appropriate ritual work is done.

Turning to the external economy of the family, we find something similar. Resources which have value in the external environment are budgeted among the members in a conserving and perceivedly equitable manner. The fund of private information about the family possessed by the members is preserved, and a united, somewhat false front is maintained before the world—as if there were a family information rule. Finally, the relationships and work/

school obligations that link individual members to outside persons and organizations comply with established jurisdictional rulings whereby the family retains some rights. In any case, the family member is pulled out of the family space only by real organizations and real persons who have made a real place for him. In brief, nonfamily claims on family members are limited and regularized.

The maintenance of the internal and external functioning of the family is so central that when family members think of the essential character, the perduring personality of any one of their numbers, it is usually his habitual pattern of support for family-organized activity and family relationships, his style of acceptance of his place in the family, that they have in mind. Any marked change in his pattern of support will tend to be perceived as a marked change in his character. The deepest nature of an individual is only skin-deep, the deepness of his others' skin.

In the case of withdrawals—depressions and regressions—it is chiefly the internal functioning of the family that suffers. The burden of enthusiasm and domestic work must now be carried by fewer numbers. Note that by artfully curtailing its social life, the family can conceal these disorders from the public at large and sustain conventional external functioning. Quiet alcoholism can similarly be contained, provided that economic resources are not jeopardized.

It is the manic disorders and the active phases of a paranoid kind that produce the real trouble. It is these patterns that constitute the insanity of place.

The beginnings are unclear and varied. In some cases something causes the prepatient—whether husband, wife, or child—to feel that the life his others have been allowing him is not sufficient, not right, and no longer tenable. He makes conventional demands for relief and change which are not granted, perhaps not even attended. Then, instead of falling back to the *status quo ante*, he begins his manic activity. As suggested, there are no doubt other etiologies and other precipitating sequences. But all end at the same point—the manic activity the family comes to be concerned with. We shall begin with this, although it is a late point from some perspectives.

The manic begins by promoting himself in the family hierarchy. He finds he no longer has the time to do his accustomed share of family chores. He increasingly orders other members around, displays anger and impatience, makes promises he feels he can break, encroaches on the equipment and space allocated to other members, only fitfully displays affection and respect, and finds he cannot bother adhering to the family schedule for meals, for going to bed and rising. He also becomes hypercritical and derogatory of family members. He moves backward to grandiose statements of the high rank and quality of his forebears, and forward to an exalted view of what he proposes soon to accomplish. He begins to sprinkle his speech with unassimilated technical vocabularies. He talks loudly and constantly, arrogating to himself the place at the center of things this role assumes. The great events and personages of the day uncharacteristically evoke from him a considered and definitive opinion. He seizes on magazine articles, movies, and TV shows as containing important wisdom that everyone ought to hear about in detail right now.

In addition to these disturbances of rank, there are those related to the minor obligations which symbolize membership and relatedness. He alone ceases to exercise the easy care that keeps household equipment safe and keeps members safe from it. He alone becomes capricious in performing the little courtesy-favors that all grown members offer one another if only because of the minute cost of these services to the giver compared to their appreciable value to the recipient. And he voices groundless beliefs, sometimes in response to hallucinations, which imply to his kin that he has ceased to regulate his thought by the standards that form the common ground of all those to whom they are closely related.

I repeat that the claims and actions of the ill person are not necessarily bizarre in themselves, merely bizarre when coming from the particular patient addressing himself to his particular family. And bizarreness itself is not the issue. Even when the patient hallucinates or develops exotic beliefs, the concern of the family is not simply that a member has crazy notions, but that he is not keeping his place in relationships. Someone to whom we are closely related is someone who ought not to have beliefs which estrange him from us. The various forms of grandiosity can have the same significance.

The constant effort of the family to argue the patient out of his foolish notions, to disprove his allegations, to make him take a reasonable view—an argumentation so despaired of by some therapists—can similarly be understood as the family's needs and the family's effort to bring the patient back into appropriate relationship to them. They cannot let him have his wrong beliefs because they cannot let him go. Further, if he reverses his behavior and becomes more collected, they must try to get him to admit that he has been ill, else his present saneness will raise doubts about the family's warrant for the way they have been treating him, doubts about their motivation and *their* relationship to him. For these reasons, admission of insanity has to be sought. And what is sought is an extraordinary thing indeed. If ritual work is a means of retaining a constancy of image in the face of deviations in behavior, then a self-admission that one is mentally ill is the biggest piece of ritual work of all, for this stance to one's conduct discounts the greatest deviations. A week of mayhem in a family can be set aside and readied to be forgotten the moment the offender admits he has been ill. Small wonder, then, that the patient will be put under great pressure to agree to the diagnosis, and that he may give in, even though this can mean that he must permanently lower the conception he has of his own character and must never again be adamant in presenting his views.

The issue here is not that the family finds that home life is made unpleasant by the sick person. Perhaps most home life is unpleasant. The issue is that meaningful existence is threatened. The definitions that the sick person tacitly accords the family members are less desirable than the ones they had before and imply that the family members are less connected to him than they had thought. If they accept this revision, then meaningful organization can be re-achieved, as happens, for example, when family cult-formation occurs or folie à ménage. But if they do not, there is trouble.

Let me repeat: the self is the code that makes sense out of almost all the individual's activities and provides a basis for organizing them. This self is what can be read about the individual by interpreting the place he takes in an organization of social activity, as confirmed by his expressive behavior. The individual's failure to encode through deeds and expressive cues, a workable definition of himself, one which closely enmeshed others can accord him through the regard they show his person, is to block and trip up and threaten them in almost every movement that they make. The selves that had been the reciprocals of his are undermined. And that which should

not have been able to change—the character of a loved one lived with—appears to be changing fundamentally and for the worse before their eyes. In ceasing to know the sick person, they cease to be sure of themselves. In ceasing to be sure of him and themselves, they can even cease to be sure of their way of knowing. A deep bewilderment results. Confirmations that everything is predictable and as it should be cease to flow from his presentations. The question as to what it is that is going on is not reduntantly answered at every turn but must be constantly ferreted out anew. And life is said to become like a bad dream—for there is no place in possible realities for what is occurring.

It is here that mental symptoms deviate from other deviations. A person who suddenly becomes selfish, heartless, disloyal, unfaithful, or addicted can be dealt with. If he properly shows cause or contrition he can be forgiven; if he is unrepentant but removable he can be redefined. In either case, his others can come to terms with him, in the sense that the expressions he gives off concerning his definition of himself and them are indications that confirm the relationship they feel they now have to him. The grammaticality of activity is sustained. A patient's mental symptoms, however, are something his others cannot come to terms with. Neither he nor they withdraw from the organization or relationship sufficiently to allow his expression to confirm what his status implies. Thus his behavior strikes at the syntax of conduct, deranging the usual agreement between posture and place, between expression and position.

The domestic disorganization created by the ill person points up an important fact about social control in a unit like the family. Any grown member of the family can leave the household against the will and advice of the family, and, except for exacting financial claims against him, there is nothing that the family can do about it. The power of the leavetaker is especially strong if he departs properly, through channels as it were, with an appropriately staged announcement of intentions. On the other side, there are circumstances (varying in America from state to state) in which a family can have a member removed bodily to a place of detention. However, when, for whatever reason, neither of these forms of socially recognized departure occurs, the family and its household prove to be vulnerable in the extreme. For then the standard notion of social control effected through a corrective cycle becomes quite untenable. The simple fact is that when an offender is disapproved of and punished, and warned what will happen if he persists, it is tacitly assumed that he will be sufficiently committed to the life of the group, and to sustaining those who presume authority in it, to *voluntarily* take the sanction to heart and, whether in good grace or bad, desist from the particular offense. If the family offender elects not to heed the warning, there is then really nothing effective that can be done to him. Sheer manhandling that is not responded to by tacit cooperation requires the full effort of at least two strong adults and even then can only be managed in brief spurts—long enough to remove someone from a house, but not much longer. Even merely to stand watch and guard over a person requires more than a household can usually manage for very long. And the household itself can hardly be run if everything that might be damageable or dangerous must be kept out of an adult's reach.

Households, then, can hardly be operated at all if the good will of the residents cannot be relied on.[6] Inter-

estingly, it is right at the moment of punishment and threat, right when the offender presumably has additional reasons for antagonism, that the family is most clearly dependent on his self-submission to family authority. Punitive action forces the offender either to capitulate and lose face, or to disabuse his opponents of their belief that they have power over him. Just when he is most angry at them he must see that he alone can save their illusions concerning their control over him. Negative sanctions within the context of a household, then, constitute a kind of doomsday machine, forcing the last available opportunity to avoid a breakdown of order upon the stronger of the two parties, who must act as if he is the weaker. Obviously, on occasion he will not be considerate. This vulnerability of family organization is reinforced by the fact that the offender may well give less consideration to his own bodily welfare and his own interests than those who must control him.

I have considered some of the disorganizational consequences of the patient's failure to support the internal order of the family. It is, however, when the family's external functioning is considered that the full derangement is seen.

The social place of a family in the

---

[6] A useful recent description of the structural contingencies of disciplining an unwilling family member is provided in Louise Wilson, *This Stranger, My Son* (New York: G. P. Putnam's Sons, 1968). Mrs. Wilson describes in some detail what a child diagnosed as paranoid schizophrenic can accomplish with the domestic equipment at hand. A full picture is also available in the Bettelheim accounts of the Sonia Shankman Orthogenic School, but in this case, of course, the care that requires the staff's full-time effort *is* their official full-time job. The consequences of attempting discipline of a family member old enough to go to the university but not quite old enough to be defined as independent is beautifully available in the ugly Russier case. See *The Affair of Gabrielle Russier* (New York: Alfred P. Knopf, 1971), and the fine introduction to it written by Mavis Gallant.

community at large is a matter of some delicacy, based as it is on personal and informal control that exposes the family to a thousand possible markets for its various resources—markets which the family itself must deal with prudently if it is to maximize its own long-range interests as these are conventionally defined. It is this circumspection, ordinarily self-imposed, that the active patient transcends.

Misplaced enterprise occurs. Family monies are squandered on little examples of venture capitalism. Grand services and equipment are bought or contracted for, nicely illustrating the democratic, accepting attitude of those who sell things and the personal control that all of us ordinarily maintain. Bargains advertised in the newspaper are ordered in excessive quantity by phone. The occupational and age-grade structure is dipped into far enough down to find commandeers and hirelings for expansive private projects. An unnecessary office or industrial layout is grafted onto the household. The patient finds that his ordinary job is cramping and gives it up or is fired.[7]

[7] A manic patient who can become too large for his home can similarly become too large for his job. Starting with a commendable increase in enthusiasm for his work, he begins to offer fellow workers wanted help and advice, extends this to what is seen as interference in the spheres of others, and finally takes to giving unauthorized directives and acting as a spokesman for his work-organization when he is away from it. During this process of becoming a self-appointed boss, he begins to arrogate to himself more and more equipment, space, and subordinate help. And since his private business and convivial enterprise have greatly expanded and are coming to be very ill-received at home, he shifts more and more of these activities to the work-place, spends more and more time during and after work thus engaged, and soon violates the very delicate norm governing the penetration of private interests into work. He promotes get-togethers of work personnel, and embarrasses status divisions by trying to bring together for conviviality everyone at work who is remotely within his social reach.

A flurry of projects is initiated. A press of occupation occurs.

Contracting is accelerated. The telephone is increasingly used. Each call becomes longer and more calls are made. Favorite recipients are called more and more frequently. When the hour renders local calls a gross violation of informal rules, long-distance calls are made into acceptable time zones; when the hour prevents even these, night telegrams are dispatched. A flood of letter-writing may occur.

Participation is broadened. Assistance is volunteered to persons and organizations undesirous of receiving it from this quarter—the patient appreciating that an offering is a warrantable means of making contact with the recipient. Public life is entered through its least guarded portals: participation in volunteer work; letters to politicians, editors, and big corporations; celebrity hunting; litigation. Critical national events, such as elections, war policy statements, and assassinations, are taken quite personally. Personal appearances on radio and television may be sought; press conferences and press releases may be engineered. Perceived slights in public places lead to scenes and to the patient's making official complaints to officials.

Associating is intensified. Neighbors are dropped in on at unsuitable hours. Parties are arrived at first and left last. There may be a surge of home entertainment that is unstabilizing: properly related friends attend until other commitments cause them to defect; newly formed friends are substituted, but each set wears out more quickly than the last, requiring recruitment from less and less suitable sources; ultimately the gatherings become socially bizarre. Semi-official, public-spirited purposes for home gatherings are increasingly employed, this providing some warrant for the patient's inviting persons he has merely heard about, and for aggregations of persons of widely different social rank. Invitation lists are extended right up to the last minute, as if there were a need to be in touch with all acquaintances and to pack the environment with people. Evenings of commercial recreation and weekend outings are organized repeatedly, involving much recontacting and also the mustering of unacquainted persons into one venture.

Finally, relating is expanded. Courtesy introductions and off-hand referrals by others are followed up and made something of, acquaintanceship is presumed upon, and presuming requests are made across affinal lines to spouses of friends. "Middlemanning" occurs, the ill person attempting to bring into contact persons perceived as having use for each other. The functional specificity of service relations is breached. Advice is proffered to and asked of service personnel on many matters; the use of reciprocal first-naming is suggested; social invitations are extended. Corresponding to this diffusion, personal friends are loaded with service requests and enrolled in schemes and projects. Occasional workers, hired by the patient to help in projects, will be transformed into friends to fill the gap that has developed, but these will now be friends who can be ordered to come and go, there resulting a kind of minionization of the patient's social circle. Minor shortcomings in services received from long-utilized professionals, tradesmen, and repairmen lead to run-ins and the immediate establishment of new service connections. Family secrets are confidentially divulged at informal gatherings to persons who are merely acquaintances. Newly formed friends are enthusiastically praised to the family, giving the impression that the patient's capacity for deep involvement is being exercised capriciously. If the patient is single, unsuitable mating may threaten to occur across age, race, or class lines; if married, then unsuitable re-mating. And some sexual promiscuity may occur of the kind that can be realized at will because it trades on marked status differences. In all of this, the patient either takes advantage of others or places others in a position to take advantage of him, in either case to the deep embarrassment of his family.

A general point can be detected here about the patient's rage for connectedness and position. Since his movement from his allotted place is to be accomplished entirely by the power of self-inclination, two spheres will be in easiest reach for him. One consists of local persons who are appreciably beneath him socially and who are willing to be approached at will because the association can mean some kind of economic gain or social enhancement. The other sphere consists of powerful and well-known personages. Of course, only the most vicarious and attenuated contact can be made with these notables, the channels here being fan letters, telegrams, attendance at personal appearances, unaccepted party invitations, and the like. Nonetheless, when actual social connections become disturbed and insufficient, these figures are there; they acquire a startling immediacy and come to serve as points of reference for self-organization.

The patient, then, is free to move in two directions: downward by means of social trade-offs; upward by means of vicarious or abortive contact. Interestingly, the more trouble at home, the greater the need to move into the lives of friends; the more this is done, the more the second circle will close itself off by virtue of being overtaxed; the more this occurs, the more fully does the patient take flight into unsuitable alliances and vicarious ones. Further, what remains of an inner circle tends to be alienated by what the patient attempts in the next concentric ring; what is there developed is undermined by his antics in a still wider circle. Tentative expansions outward thus reduces what is already possessed, and sharply increases the need to consolidate the new circle. With all of these forces working together, an explosion of dealings results. There is a flight into the community.

Without taking the time to examine in detail any of these over-reachings, or to consider the clinical hypothesis that the patient may be seeking every possible external support for an internal state that is collapsing, let it only be said that so far as family organization is concerned, what happens is that the boundary between it and the community is threatened. In the extreme, the family as a unit that holds itself off from the environing world is forcibly washed away, the members literally displaced from the domestic establishment by a flood of nonmembers and by the sick person's organizational activity.

Note that the community context of family life is such that this sort of diffusion is always possible. The patient does not construct his own avenues of access; he merely uses excessively devices available to anyone in his position. To appreciate this fact, we must look at the community as a system of fences and gates, a system for regulating the formation and growth of social relationships.

A relationship cannot form unless two persons can come into personal contact of some kind (whether face-to-face or mediated), and a relationship cannot develop unless its members can interact over a period of time.

Contact itself is organizationally facilitated in certain basic ways. Contemporary social organization provides that places of residence and work can be reached by phone, telegraph, letters, and personal visits. The necessarily common use of public and semipublic facilities, especially the streets, brings a wide variety of persons within face-to-face reach of one another. The institution of acquaintanceship (estab-lished often through introduction) confers preemptive contact rights. Because of such devices, a very wide potential exists for contact, and through contact the development of relationships.

This potential, in turn, is sharply curtailed by various factors. We do not know the appearance or address of many of those we might want to be in touch with. We are bound by rules which proscribe our initiating talk with unacquainted others except on various good grounds. We are likely to be ignorant of where and when those social occasions will occur where those whose acquaintance we seek will be present, and presence itself allows for the initiation of talk. Knowing where and when, we may not be qualified by money, membership, or invitation to go. Beyond this, there are all the devices used for blocking contacts: disguise of personal appearance, avoidance of public places, nonlisting of telephone numbers, the stationing of gatekeepers to intervene at places of residence and work, segregation by cost and ecology, and so forth. But note, these various blocks to association cannot be allowed to be complete. Any door that completely keeps out undesirables also keeps out some desirables; any means of completely shutting oneself off also shuts out contacts that would be profitable. After all, relationships that come to be close can be traced back to an overture or introduction; service dealings which prove satisfactory can be traced back to an unknown client's or customer's appearing on the telephone; successful projects, to nothing more substantial than announced intentions; valuable publicity for a celebrity, to one among the many phone calls he receives; a warning that one has dropped one's wallet, to a stranger who accosts one on the street. Who knows from whom the next phone call or letter will be and what it will be about? The most careful screening in the world must still expose someone on the staff to *anyone* who bothers to try to make contact. Presentments have to be given a moment's benefit of the doubt, lest that which will come to be desirably realized will not have been able to begin. We must always pause at least for a moment in our oncoming rejection of another in order to check the importuner out. There is no choice: social life must ever expose itself to unwarranted initiatings. A screening device would have no functional value if the only persons who got through it were the persons who got to it.

Mechanisms for facilitating and restricting relationship formation are reinforced by formal legal control, in the sense that persons who decline to be drawn into certain negotiations can be forced to do so by the law, as can those who decline to desist from certain importunings. Much more important, the mechanisms are reinforced by personal control and informal control, resulting in a tacit social contract: a person is obliged to make himself available for contacting and relationship formation, in return for which others are obliged to refrain from taking advantage of his availability. He incidentally can retain the illusion that he does not cut people off; they, that they would not be rejected.

This contract of association is made viable by the allowance of prognosticative expression. An open and friendly address conveys that overtures will be welcomed; a wary and stiff mien, that importunement will result in open rejection. Anyone wending his way through his daily round is guided not only by self-interest but also by these expressions. He avoids accepting subtle invitations that might lead to unsuitable associations and avoids transgressing where subtle warnings have been issued.

He keeps to the straight and narrow. He handles himself ungenerously because on all sides there is something to lose.

It is understandable, then, why the patient finds himself in a disruptable world. Merely by jeopardizing a little more than persons like himself are usually willing to do—through exposing himself either to unsuitable relationships or to insulting rejection—he is in a position to penetrate all social boundaries a little. Whosoever the other, there will always be good reasons to warrant relating to him, and therefore a cover, however quickly discreditable, for the beginning of interaction with him.

A final comment. The manic activity I have described is obviously located in the life of the privileged, the middle and higher classes.[8] I think this ap-

[8] Some empirical evidence for this argument is provided in August Hollingshead and Fredrick Redlich, *Social Class and Mental Illness* (New York: John Wiley & Sons, 1958), p. 288.

For an analytical illustration, consider an extreme comparison: a black wino and a blond model, he in rough clothes and she in the style of the upper middle-class. Compared their public situation—the passage of each across, alongside, or toward the paths of unacquainted others. Consider the eye practices each must face from these walkers-by.

The wino: A walker-by will take care to look at him fleetingly if at all, wary lest the wino find an angle from which to establish eye-to-eye contact and then disturb the passage with prolonged salutations, besmearing felicitations, and other importunements and threats. Should the wino persist in not keeping his place, the discourtesy of outright head-aversion may be necessary.

The model: A walker-by will fix her with an open gaze for as many moments as the passage will allow without his having to turn his head sharply. During this structured moment of staring he may well be alert in fantasy for any sign she makes interpretable as encouraging his attentions. Note that this helter-skelter gallantry remains very well in

parent bias in selecting illustrations is warranted. Social resources must be possessed before they can be handled in the manner that has been considered. Therefore mania would seem to be a disease of persons with social advantages —money, lineage, office, profession, education, sexual attractiveness, and a network of social and familial relationships. Perhaps impoverished expansionists, having few goods to exchange for being taken seriously, are soon forced to make ludicrous presentations, and transform everyone around them into skeptical ward attendants. Thus it could be argued that the well-stationed are prone or at least overrepresented; the insanity of place is a function of position.

I have already touched on some fea-

tures of the family's response to life with the patient. Members feel they are no longer in an easefully predictable environment. They feel bewildered by the change of character and personality that has occurred. Moreover, since the dramatic change has come to a person they feel they should best be able to characterize, cognition itself becomes an issue; the very principles of judgment by which one comes to feel that one knows character and is competent to judge it can become threatened. Consider now some further aspects of the family's response.

One issue concerns the structure of attention. Put simply, the patient becomes someone who has to be watched. Each time he holds a sharp or heavy object, each time he answers the phone, each time he nears the window, each time he holds a cup of coffee above a rug, each time he is present when someone comes to the door or drops in, each time he handles the car keys, each time he begins to fill a sink or tub, each time he lights a match—on each of these occasions the family will have to be ready to jump. And when it is not known where he is or it is known that he is behind a locked door, an alert will have to be maintained for any hint of something untoward. The possibility that the patient will be malicious or careless, that he will intentionally or unintentionally damage himself, the household, or the others, demonstrates that standard household arrangements can be full of danger; obviously, it is the presumption of conventional use that makes us think that these conventional arrangements are safe.[9]

---

check, no danger to the free flow of human traffic, for long ago the model will have learned her part in this ceremony, which is to conduct her eyes downward and unseeing, in silent sufferance of exposure.

Again this structural view of the public situation of the beast and the beauty (illustrating the boundaries of civil inattention), consider the consequence to each of being apparently possessed by an unsuppressed urge to enter into dealings.

Of himself the wino can make a mild nuisance, but nothing much more disarraying than that is likely to be allowed him. The more he rattles the bars of his cage, the more hurrying-by will be done by visitors to the zoo. Social arrangements are such that his screaming right into the face of an unacquainted other may only complete his treatment as someone who does not exist. The friendly model, in contrast, will find that suddenly there are a hundred takers, that strangers of both colors, three sexes, and several age groups are ready to interrupt their course for an adventure in sociability. Where'er she smiles, relationships begin to develop. A wino leaves a narrow trail of persons more fully busying themselves with their initial plans. A manic beauty may not get far enough to leave a trail. She opens up a world that then closes in on her. She clots and entangles the courses of action around her. The more delicate and ladylike, the more she is the peril the Victorian manuals should have warned the city about.

[9] Professionals who manage the actively suicidal are acutely alive to the unconventional lethal possibilities of domestic equipment; indeed, in published case records detail is provided. Less clearly appreciated, perhaps, is that a person with *any* type of actively expressed mental disorder can unhinge the

Three points are to be made concerning the family's watchfulness. First, households tend to be informally organized, in the sense that each member is allowed considerable leeway in scheduling his own tasks and diverting himself in his own directions. He will have his own matters, then, to which he feels a need to attend. The necessity, instead, of his having to stand watch over the patient blocks rightful and pleasurable calls upon time and generates a surprising amount of fatigue, impatience, and hostility. Second, the watching will have to be dissimulated and disguised lest the patient suspect he is under constant surveillance, and this covering requires extra involvement and attention. Third, in order to increase their efficiency and maintain their morale, the watchers are likely to engage in collaboration, which perforce must be collusive.

The family must respond not only to what the patient is doing to its internal life, but also to the spectacle he seems to be making of himself in the community. At first the family will be greatly concerned that one of its emissaries is letting down the side. The family therefore tries to cover up and intercede so as to keep up his front and theirs. This strengthens the collusive alignment in the family against the patient.

As the dispute within the family continues and grows concerning the selves in whose terms activity ought to be organized, the family begins to turn outward, first to the patient's kinsmen, then to friends, to professionals, to employers. The family's purpose is not merely to obtain help in the secretive

management of the patient, but also to get much needed affirmation of its view of events. There is a reversal of the family information rule. Acquaintances or other potential sources of aid who had once been personally distant from the family will now be drawn into the center of things as part of a new solidarity of those who are helping to manage the patient, just as some of those who were once close may now be dropped because apparently they do not confirm the family's definition of the situation.

Finally, the family finds that in order to prevent others from giving weight to the initiatory activity of the patient, relatively distant persons must be let in on the family secret. There may even be necessity for recourse to the courts to block extravagances by conservator proceedings, to undo unsuitable marriages by annulments, and the like. The family will frankly allow indications that it can no longer handle its own problems, for the family cat must be belled. By that time the family members will have learned to live exposed. There will be less pride and less self-respect. They will be engaged in establishing that one of their members is mentally ill, and in whatever degree they succeed in this, they will be exposing themselves to the current conception that they constitute the kind of family which produces mental illness.

While the family is breaking the informational boundary between itself and society—and an appeal to a therapist is only one nicely contained instance of this—it may begin to add some finer mesh as well as some spread to its collusive net. Some of the patient's telephone calls are tapped and some of his letters opened and read. Statements which the patient makes to different persons are secretly polled, with consequent exposure of incongruities. Experiences with the patient are shared in a widening circle in order to

---

meaning of his domestic acts for the other members of the family. What would ordinarily be an uneventful household routine can come to be seen as a deed through which the patient may intentionally or unintentionally damage the equipment at hand, the persons nearby, or himself.

extract and confirm patterns of impropriety. Discreetly planned actions are presented to the patient as unplanned spontaneous ones, or disguised to appear as if originating from a source still deemed innocent by him. This conspiracy, note, is an understandable result of the family's needing very much to know the patient's next move in order to undo it.

A review of the family's response to the patient easily suggests that members will find much cause to feel angry at him. Overlaid, however, there will be other feelings, often stronger. The damage the patient appears to be doing, especially in consequence of his overreachings outside the family, is seen to hurt his own interests even more than those of the rest of the family. Yet for the family this need not produce grim satisfaction or help to balance things out; rather, matters may be made worse. As suggested, it is the distinctive character of the family that its members not only feel responsible for any member in need, but also feel personal identification with his situation. Whenever the patient is out alone in the community, exposed and exposing himself to what can be perceived as a contamination of his self and a diminution of his character, whenever the patient must be left alone at home, exposing himself as well as the household to intended and unintended dangers, the family will know anxiety and fear.

It has been suggested that a family with mania to contend with is likely to form a collusive net, the patient being excolluded.[10] Now turn and take the point of view of the patient.

[10] If the patient is an adult, the consequences for children are especially painful. In order to protect the young from the imperious demands of the patient and from the conception of the patient that would result were his acts taken as serious ones, the young may have to be recruited into the net.

The family's conspiracy is benign, but this conspiracy breeds what others do. The patient finds himself in a world that has only the appearance of innocence, in which small signs can be found—and therefore sought out and wrongly imputed—showing that things are anything but what they seem. At home, when his glance suddenly shifts in a conversation, he may find naked evidence of collusive teamwork against him—teamwork unlike the kind which evaporates when a butt is let in on a good-natured joke that is being played at his expense.[11] He rightly comes to feel that statements made to him are spoken so as to be monitored by the others present, ensuring that they will keep up with the managing of him,

This will also facilitate the collusion by reducing the number of others from whom its operation must be concealed. The children may accept this invitation, decline it, or, if careful enough, give each side the impression that its view is being supported. Whatever the response of the young, adult solidarity is clearly broken and idealization of adults undermined. Children's insubordinate treatment of the ill person can result, the other adults being unable to reinforce demands of the patient. Further, the more the ill person becomes a source of unwarranted demands upon the young, the less the other adults feel they can exert parental discipline where discipline is due.

[11] For this the patient requires no special perceptiveness, sometimes attributed to the insane. It is an empirical fact that in our society the furtive signs through which a collusive alignment is maintained against someone who is present are often crude and easily available to the excolluded. Ordinarily the colluders do not discover that they have been discovered because the excolluded wants to support the surface appearance that he is not so unworthy as to warrant this kind of betrayal. Paradoxically, it is exactly such a surface definition of the situation that the colluders require in order to have something to undercut. I want to add that colluders very often decline to stage their collusion as discreetly as they could. As in many other occasions of false behavior, the manipulators half want their dupe to be aware of what is really thought of him.

and that statements made to others in his presence are designed and delivered for his overhearing. He will find this communication arrangement very unsettling and come to feel that he is purposely being kept out of touch with what is happening.

In addition, the patient is likely to detect that he is being watched, especially when he approaches some domestic device which could be used to harm himself or others, or which is itself valuable and vulnerable to harm. He will sense that he is being treated as a child who can't be trusted to be frankly shown that he is not trusted. If he lights a match or takes up a knife, he may find as he turns from these tasks that others present seem to have been watching him and now are trying to cover up their watchfulness.

In response to the response he is creating, the patient, too, will come to feel that life in the family has become deranged. He is likely to try to muster up some support for his own view of what his close ones are up to. And he is likely to have some success.

The result is two collusive factions, each enveloping the other in uncertainties, each drawing on a new and changing set of secret members. The household ceases to be a place where there is the easy fulfillment of a thousand mutually anticipated proper acts. It ceases to be a solid front organized by a stable set of persons against the world, entrenched and buffered by a stable set of friends and servers. The household becomes a no-man's land where changing factions are obliged to negotiate daily, their weapons being collusive communication and their armor selective inattention to the machinations of the other side—an inattention difficult to achieve, since each faction must devote itself to reading the other's furtive signs. The home, where wounds were meant to be licked, becomes precisely where they are in-flicted. Boundaries are broken. The family is turned inside out.

We see, then, that the domestic manic breeds, and is bred in, organizational havoc, and that this havoc is all too evident. Yet here clinical reports have been very weak. I venture a Durkheimian account.

It is frequently the case that hospitalized patients who have behaved at home in the most exotic and difficult fashion are taken back into the family upon release from the hospital, and that however tentatively they are received, they are given some sort of trial acceptance. Also, it is quite generally the case that before hospitalization, the feeling of the family that the troublesome one is mentally ill will come and go: with each outburst the family will have to face anew the idea that mental illness is apparently involved, but with each moment of the patient's wonted and tranquil behavior, sharp new hope will be experienced by the family— hope that everything is coming back to normal. This readiness to oscillate, this resilience of hope on the family's part, should not be taken particularly as evidence of good will or resistance to bad-naming. In other circumstances, I'm sure, most families would be quite ready to form a rigid and stereotyped view of an offender. But the fact is that there is no stable way for the family to conceive of a life in which a member conducts himself insanely. The heated scramble occurring around the ill person is something that the family will be instantly ready to forget; the viable way things once were is something that the family will always be ready to re-anticipate. For if an intellectual place could be made for the ill behavior, it would not be ill behavior. It is as if perception can only form and follow where there is social organization; it is as if the experience of disorganization can be felt but not retained. When the havoc is at its height, participants are unlikely to find anyone who has the faintest appreciation of what living in it is like. When the trouble is finally settled, the participants will themselves be unable to appreciate why they had become so upset. Little wonder, then, that during the disorganization phase, the family will live the current reality as in a dream, and the domestic routine which can now only be dreamt of will be seen as what is real.

Return now to the earlier discussion of collusive elements in the medical role. Return to the doctor's dilemma.

The traditional picture of mental hospitalization and other psychiatric services involves a responsible person, typically a next of kin, persuading, dragging, conning, or trapping the patient-to-be into visiting a psychiatrist. A diagnostic inspection occurs. It is then that the psychiatrist is likely to begin his collusion with the next of kin, on the grounds that the patient cannot be trusted to act in his own best interests, and that it will not do the patient any good to learn the name and extent of his sickness.[12] The patient, of course, is likely to feel betrayed and conspired against; and he may continue to until he is well enough to see that the collusive action was taken in his own best interests.

The great critics of the collusive management of the mental patient have been the psychoanalysts. They act on the assumption that if a real relationship is to be developed with the client, one allowing the therapist and client to work together profitably, then this relation must not be undercut by the therapist's engaging in collusive communication with the client's responsible

others. If contact is necessary between therapist and patient's kin, then the kin should be warned that the patient must know what has taken place, and what in substance the therapist said to the kin. Therapists realistically appreciate that information about the patient put into the hands of his loved ones might well be used against him. This communications policy cuts the therapist off from many sources of information about the patient, but there is an answer in the doctrine that the patient's trouble is in his style of projecting and relating, and that this can be well enough sampled by means of what is disclosed during private sessions. A parallel can be noted here to what is called hotel anthropology.

I am suggesting that therapists, especially of the psychoanalytical persuasion, appreciate the collusive implication of their contacts with the third party and go far in protecting the patient from this collusion. However, by this very maneuver they help consolidate another collusive relationship, that between themselves and the patient in regard to the responsible others. The practice of trying to get at the patient's point of view, the effort to refrain considerably from passing obvious moral judgments, and the strict obligation on the patient's part to betray all confidences if these seem relevant—all these factors in conjunction with the privacy of the therapeutic setting ensure collusive coalition formation to a degree unappreciated even by the next of kin. (Whereas ordinary relationships give rise to collusive coalitions, the therapeutic situation is a collusion that gives rise to a relationship.) This resembles a domestic handicapping system, whereby the weakest team in the family tournament is given an extra man. Let me add that collusion for hire seems a rum sort of business to be in, but perhaps more good is done than harm.

What has been considered can be

---

12 Surely this practice is not entirely a bad thing, since this information can deeply affect the patient's view of himself, and yet diagnoses seem to vary quite remarkably, depending on the prevailing diagnostic fashion and the tastes of the practitioner.

reduced to a formula. Traditionally the psychotic has been treated through a collusive relation between his therapists and his family and ends up excolluded into the mental hospital, while the neurotic (who is so inclined and can afford it) has been treated to a collusive relation with his therapist against his family or boss and remains in the community.[13]

There is a collusion, then, for psychotics who end up in a mental hospital and for neurotics who stay in the community—the psychiatrist being constrained to engage in one or the other form, depending on his patient and, beyond that, his type of practice. What is to be considered here, however, is the collusion arising when psychotics of the manic kind are managed in the community.

First note that the therapeutic or patient-analyst collusion will have shortcomings. Private talks with the patient will not tell the therapist what is happening to the family or what its urgent needs are. This is indicated by the fact already suggested that psychotherapists have provided hardly any information about the organizational meaning of illness for the units of social organization in which the illness occurs. In any case, since the patient is likely to continue his troublesome activity unabated after beginning therapy, the family will feel that the therapist has become a member of the patient's faction. This is no small matter. The patient's domestic opponents find themselves pressed to the wall of sanity, having to betray a loved one lest his unchar-

[13] Admittedly in recent times some therapists have attempted to treat the same patient in and out of the hospital, in which case the usual alignments are not possible; some have engaged in "family therapy"; and some have attempted a flexible open relationship of access allowing for private and family sessions with the same patient. But even these arrangements, I think, do not prevent collusion problems.

acteristic assumptions about himself make their life unreal. Their social place is being undermined, and the standards they have always used in judging character and identity are in question. The failure of any other person to confirm their view of the patient, even when this failure merely means declining to take sides, adds weight to the hallucinatory possibility that they might be wrong and, being wrong, are destroying the patient. And persons distant from the family will certainly fail to confirm the family's position. A fact about the wider community must here be appreciated. Unless the patient is very ill, those who know him little—even more, those who know him not at all—may not sense that anything is wrong, and with good reason; at least for a time, all they may notice is that an individual is more friendly and outgoing, more approachable than he might be. Those in the community who *do* develop doubts about the patient are likely to be tactful enough to refrain from directly expressing them. After all, easing themselves out of contact with the troublesome one is all that is necessary. The worst that can happen to them is that they will briefly have to face how conditional their concern for another is—conditional on his being willing to withdraw in response to suggestions and hints.

The other type of psychiatric collusion may not be much better. If the family has psychiatric assurance that it is the patient who is crazy and not the family members, this mitigates somewhat their need for confirmation of their position from friends and associates, and in turn mitigates their flight into the community. But in order to contain and discipline the patient, and through this to preserve the possibility of reestablishing the old relationships later, they will feel compelled to tell him he is not himself and that so says the psychiatrist. This won't help very much. The family will almost certainly have to use this club. It won't, however, be the right one. The patient will feel that the family members are concerned not about his illness, but about their pinched status. And the patient by and large will be right. The patient then must either embrace the notion of mental illness, which is to embrace what is likely to be a de-structive conception of his own character, or find further evidence that his close ones have suddenly turned against him.

In summary, the physician finds that he must join the family's faction or the patient's, and that neither recourse is particularly tenable. That is the doctor's dilemma.

F Social Class and Inequality

INTRODUCTION

Although some primitive societies lack class differences, the populations of all known civilized societies have been divided into more or less distinct classes. Yet, sociologists have not always agreed on the meaning of the term *class*, nor on the methods to be used in assigning individuals to particular classes. They have, however, agreed that classes (whatever their other characteristics may be) always consist of groups or categories of people that are *ranked* in relation to one another. Individuals differ in many respects—in age, sex, race, and ethnicity—but such differences do not in themselves constitute class differences. It is only when people are grouped into separate categories on the basis of selected differences and the categories are then ranked as "higher" or "lower," "superior" or "inferior," in relation to each other that we can speak of a class structure. The term *social stratification* is used by sociologists to describe this grouping of individuals into strata regarded as lying above or below one another like geological layers, or, to use a more homely analogy, like the layers of icing in a layer cake. Class systems are hierarchies of such layers that embrace nearly the entire population of a society. The important problem for the sociologist is to determine *which* of the many differences between individuals and groups are the most relevant criteria for classifying them into ranked, societywide strata.

The problem is more easily solved in preindustrial societies than in contemporary industrial societies. In most of the great agrarian civilizations of the past, membership in a class constituted a recognized social role assigning definite rights, privileges, and duties to its incumbents. Class membership was usually assigned to individuals at birth on the basis of the class to which their parents belonged. Stratification systems in which *social mobility*, or the chance to change one's original class in the course of a lifetime, was virtually impossible have been called *caste* systems. The best historical example of such rigid systems is the traditional Indian caste system. Class structures in which an individual can have a higher class position bestowed on him by a ritual ceremony or legal proceeding have been called *estate* systems. Premodern Europe is perhaps the best-known historical example of the estate system. The granting of a title of nobility to an individual and the manumission of a slave are examples of the types of social mobility possible under such a system.

Castes and estates, the basic units in such systems of stratification, were self-conscious, more or less cohesive social groups. Frequently, they created councils and other representative bodies to serve as spokesmen for their collective interests in dealings with other classes and with the political authorities. Yet, caste or estate members were not necessarily equal apart from their common social rank. Penurious noblemen and wealthy commoners existed in feudal Europe, although the former possessed a higher rank than the latter.

In postmodern industrial societies, clearly defined rank orders of groups like the Indian caste or European estate system no longer exist, except as historical survivals in some of the older European countries that, unlike the United States, have a feudal past. Since the French Revolution, nation-states have, in principle, if not always in fact, been committed to the formal legal and political equality of all their citizens. And since the industrial revolution, continuing economic expansion has greatly increased opportunities for individuals to acquire through wealth and occupational success many of the possessions, manners, and attitudes associated with the traditional styles of life of the upper classes. Legal and political equality, the ideology of egalitarianism, a competitive market economy, merit and seniority systems of selecting people for bureaucratic roles, and the influence of mass production and mass communications have blurred older class distinctions.

On the other hand, the relative disappearance of clearly demarcated, cohesive ranked groups has in no sense meant that all men have become equal in wealth, social rank, and power. Nor has it meant, in spite of higher rates of social mobility, that opportunities for achievement are not still for the vast majority primarily determined by parental position—that is, by the stratification level on which people are born. Sociologists have defined three overlapping, yet partially distinct, pyramids of inequality in contemporary industrial societies: one of *wealth;* one of *prestige,* or status; and one of *power.* The wealthy, the highly regarded and socially valued, and the powerful are often not the same persons, which justifies identifying these three separable dimensions of inequality in modern societies.

Our first three selections describe three major groupings in American society that correspond roughly, although in different degrees, to social classes. E. Digby Baltzell describes the American upper class, particularly its Philadelphia branch, a group that in its cohesiveness, wealth, style of life, and stress on family origins resembles older European aristocracies. C. Wright Mills describes the new middle class of managers, salaried employees, and sales and office workers that has grown so rapidly in this century with the increase in the size and number of the bureaucratic organizations requiring their services. In contrast to Baltzell's Proper Philadelphians, Mills finds that this white-collar stratum is internally very heterogeneous in occupation, income, and prestige. Michael Harrington describes the evolution of the "new working class" in America and identifies some of the possible consequences this postindustrial labor force will have for the direction of development in the society.

Of the three groups described, only Baltzell's "business aristocracy" resembles a social class in traditional terms. Thus, we have included as a final reading an analysis by Dennis H. Wrong of the different ways in which the concept of class has been applied to American life and the difficulties of separating the influence of class, as distinct from ethnicity, religion, residence, and generation, on American attitudes and behavior. Wrong concludes that classes in America are regarded most usefully as large aggregates of people who share broadly similar outlooks and life styles as a result of possessing similar life chances that result from their common position in the national market economy.

42

The American Metropolitan Upper Class

E. DIGBY BALTZELL

The wealthier, or, as they would prefer to style themselves the "upper" classes, tend distinctly towards the bourgeois type, and an individual in the bourgeois stage of development, while honest, industrious, and virtuous, is also not unapt to be a miracle of timid and short-sighted selfishness. The commercial classes are only too likely to regard everything merely from the standpoint of "Does it pay?" and many a merchant does not take any part in politics because he is short-sighted enough to think that it will pay him better to attend purely to making money, and too selfish to be willing to undergo any trouble for the sake of abstract duty; while the younger men of this type are too much engrossed in their various social pleasures to be willing to give up their time to anything else.

THEODORE ROOSEVELT

Conceived in a new world which was free of the traditional authority of an established church and a feudal nobility, and born in a revolt from the tyranny of a centralizing government symbolized in the British monarchy and mercantilism, American institutions have, virtually from the beginning, been shaped in a laissez-faire capitalist climate. The merchant, mining, manufacturing, railroad, and finance capitalists, each in their day, were the most powerful members of the elite in nineteenth- and early twentieth-century America. As "old family" is usually found to be synonymous with "old money," the leading capitalists in the pre-Civil War period were the "old-

family" founders in America. In the 1870's, the families of these men and their descendants formed local business aristocracies in the older cities such as Boston, New York, and Philadelphia. Living near one another, on the gentle slope of Murray Hill in New York, on Beacon Street in Boston, or around Rittenhouse Square in Philadelphia, the members of these families knew "who" belonged within this formal and well-structured world of polite society.

In the last two decades of the nineteenth century, these provincial aristocracies of birth and breeding (old money) merged with a new and more conspicuously colorful world known as "Society." It was in the 1880's that New York Society with a capital "S," then moving uptown to the newly fashionable Fifth Avenue district, came under the tutelage of Mrs. Astor and her right-hand man, Ward McAlister. It was Mr. McAlister who coined the snobbish term "Four Hundred" and finally gave his official list to the New York *Times* on the occasion of Mrs. Astor's famous ball on February 1, 1892. During this same period, as millionaires multiplied and had to be accepted, as one lost track of "who" people were and had to recognize "what" they were worth, the *Social Register* became an index of a new upper class in America.

But this new upper class was soon to be organized on a national rather than a local scale. In an age which marked the centralization of economic power under the control of the finance capitalists, the gentlemen bankers and lawyers on Wall Street, Walnut Street, State Street, and La Salle Street began to send their sons to Groton, St. Mark's, or St. Paul's and afterwards to Harvard, Yale, or Princeton where they joined such exclusive clubs as Porcellian, Fence, or Ivy. These polished young men from many cities were educated together, and introduced to one another's sisters at debutante parties and fashionable weddings in Old Westbury, Mount Kisco, or Far Hills, on the Main Line or in Chestnut Hill, in Dedham, Brookline, or Milton, or in Lake Forest. After marriage at some fashionable Episcopal church, almost invariably within this select, endogamous circle, they lived in these same socially circumspect suburbs and commuted to the city where they lunched with their fathers and grandfathers at the Union, Philadelphia, Somerset, or Chicago clubs. Several generations repeat this cycle, and a centralized business aristocracy thus becomes a reality in America. The *Social Register*, first published in 1888, lists the families of this business aristocracy and their relatives and friends, in New York, Chicago, Boston, Philadelphia, Baltimore, San Fran-

cisco, St. Louis, Buffalo, Pittsburgh, Cleveland, Cincinnati-Dayton, and Washington, D.C. In 1940, approximately one-fourth of the residents of these twelve metropolitan areas who were listed in *Who's Who* in that year were also listed in the *Social Register*. Thus the members of this contemporary American upper class, descendants of leaders in American life from colonial times to the present, had considerable influence on the elite in 1940.

In 1940 the Proper Philadelphian tended "distinctly towards the bourgeois type" as Theodore Roosevelt would have put it. While 29 percent of the Philadelphians listed in *Who's Who* were also listed in the *Social Register*, the upper class contributed considerably more than its share of leaders within the business community: 75 percent of the bankers, 51 percent of the lawyers, 45 percent of the engineers, and 42 percent of the businessmen listed in *Who's Who* were also members of the upper class. In addition, of the 532 directorships in industrial and financial institutions reported by *all* the members of the elite, 60 percent were reported by members of the upper class. Finally, the leading bankers and lawyers in the city were members of the upper class. The presidents, and over 80 percent of the directors in the six largest banks were Proper Philadelphians, as were the senior partners in the largest law firms. And Dr. Thomas S. Gates, lawyer, former senior Morgan partner, and President of the University of Pennsylvania in 1940, was not only the most influential and respected member of the upper class but also the most powerful man in the city.

Within the upper class as a whole, moreover, business power tended to be correlated with the various attributes of high social class position. Thus, the members of the business elite, both those in the upper class and the rest, were more likely to live in the more fashionable neighborhoods, to attend the Episcopal churches, to have graduated from the right educational institutions, and to have grown up in the city (see Table 1).

In 1940 the ideal-typical Proper Philadelphian at the apex of the pyramid of social prestige and economic power in the city, may be said to have had the following attributes:

1. Of English or Welsh descent, his great-great-great-grandfather would have been a prominent Philadelphian in the great age of the new republic. Somewhere along the line an ancestor would have made money, or married wisely. And along with money and social position, some good Quaker ancestor would have preferred the Episcopal Church, or have been banished from the Society of Friends for marrying "out of meeting."
2. His family would have been listed

in the Social Register at the turn of the nineteenth century.
3. He would have been born on Walnut Street, facing Rittenhouse Square.
4. After an early education at the Episcopal Academy or some other private school in the city, he would have gone away to one of the fashionable Episcopalian boarding schools in New England.
5. Unless his parents felt an unusual loyalty and pride in local institutions, he would have gone to either Harvard, Yale, or Princeton where he would have belonged to one of the more exclusive clubs.
6. After attending the law school at the University of Pennsylvania, this young Proper Philadelphian would enter one of the fashionable and powerful law firms in the city and eventually become a partner; or enter the field of banking or finance. He would be on the board of directors of several cultural and eco-

Table 1

Philadelphians in *Who's Who* in 1940—Attributes of High Social Class Position As Related to Functional Elites

	SOCIAL CLASS			
	Social Register		*Nonsocial Register*	
ATTRIBUTES OF HIGH SOCIAL CLASS POSITION	BUSINESS ELITE MEMBERS	ALL OTHER ELITE MEMBERS	BUSINESS ELITE MEMBERS	ALL OTHER ELITE MEMBERS
Neighborhood:				
Main Line and Chestnut Hill	80%	44%	32%	14%
Religion:				
Episcopalian	48	37	21	12
Education:				
Private School	44	37	25	12
Harvard-Yale-Princeton	28	18	4	5*
Birthplace:				
Philadelphia	55	49	37	27
(Number of cases)	(107)	(119)	(111)	(433)

* Upper-class graduates of Harvard, Yale, or Princeton go into business, while the other graduates are more likely to go into church or education. This may explain this deviant case.

nomic institutions (Pennsylvania Railroad, a bank such as the Girard Trust Company, and perhaps the Fairmount Park Art Association).

7. Finally, the Proper Philadelphian would live either in Chestnut Hill or the Main Line in 1940, attend the Episcopal Church, be married with three or four children, and walk either up or down Walnut Street to lunch with his peers at the Rittenhouse, or preferably the Philadelphia Club.

As proper Philadelphia has been democratically assimilating new men of power and wealth into its ranks, most of the upper-class members of the elite in 1940, of course, do not measure up to this exalted ideal-typical status. By way of a quantitative summary of the various attributes of social class position discussed throughout this book, the Philadelphia elite as a whole in 1940 has been broken down (in Table 2) into various levels which more or less approach this ideal-typical status. Columns 1 and 3 are made up of upper-class directors in certain prestige institutions discussed in the previous chapter; the men in column 1 were born in Philadelphia and were listed in the 1900 *Social Register*, while those in column 3 were not. Column 1, then, includes old-family men of power while column 3 includes men of newer power and position. The rest of the columns in Table 2 are self-explanatory. As we have said, the Philadelphia Club is both more socially circumspect and more influential than the younger Rittenhouse. In fact, the younger club is best understood as the first rung in the ladder of ascent into the upper class (except for columns 5 and 6, of course, the various subgroups in Table 2 have overlapping and not mutually exclusive memberships).

In a very real sense, Table 2 summarizes this book. Thus Proper Phila-

delphia was a business aristocracy in 1940 wherein social class position and commercial and financial power in the community were positively correlated variables in the total class situation. Throughout its history, and especially since the Civil War, the Philadelphia upper class closely approximated R. H. Tawney's description of the British aristocracy which most American patricians, of course, both emulate and respect: "It is a subtle combination of both—a blend of a crude plutocratic reality with the sentimental aroma of an aristocratic legend—which gives the English class system its peculiar toughness and cohesion. It is at once as businesslike as Manchester and as gentlemanly as Eton. . . ." [1]

After this brief summary of the characteristics of the Philadelphia upper class in 1940, several things pertaining to the American metropolitan upper class as a whole should be emphasized. . . .

It is important to stress once again the fact that, while there are many middle and lower classes in America, and in Philadelphia, there exists one metropolitan upper class with a common cultural tradition, consciousness of kind, and "we" feeling of solidarity which tends to be national in scope. The origin and development of this inter-city moneyed aristocracy in America quite naturally paralleled the rise of rapid communications and the national corporate enterprise. Moreover, just as economic control of the various local firms in the "Yankee Cities" and "Middletowns" of America have gradually gravitated to such metropolitan centers as Boston, New York, or Chicago, so upper-class prestige has, over the years, become increasingly centralized in the fashionable metropolitan suburbs.

[1] R. H. Tawney, *Equality*, New York: Harcourt, Brace & Co., 1931, p. 61.

Table 2
Philadelphians in *Who's Who* in 1940—Attributes of High Social Class
Position As Related to Specified Levels of Prestige and Power

	1	2	3	4	5	6
ATTRIBUTES OF HIGH SOCIAL CLASS POSITION	"OLD FAMILY" PRESTIGE DIRECTORS	PHILA- DELPHIA CLUB MEMBERS	PRESTIGE DIRECTORS, NOT "OLD FAMILY"	RITTEN- HOUSE CLUB MEMBERS	SOCIAL REGISTER	NON- SOCIAL REGISTER
Neighborhood: Main Line and Chestnut Hill	88%	77%	77%	67%	61%	18%
Religion: Episcopalian	70%	58%	50%	41%	42%	14%
Education: Private School	70%	52%	28%	35%	41%	15%
Harvard-Yale-Princeton	33%	37%	33%	21%	22%	5%
Birthplace: Philadelphia	100%	75%	28%	52%	52%	29%
Occupation: Banker	42%	25%	22%	18%	11%	1%
Lawyer	21%	12%	17%	17%	9%	4%
(Number of cases)	(24)	(57)	(18)	(66)	(226)	(544)
Family Size: Mean number of children per Male Parent	3.50	3.30	3.20	2.89	2.80	2.61

The growth and structure of this national upper class has, in turn, been supported by various institutions. First and most important, of course, are the New England boarding schools and the fashionable Eastern universities. Whereas the older generation of Proper Philadelphians were educated at home or in local schools and colleges, at the turn of the century, and especially after the First World War, these national upper-class family-surrogates began to educate the children of the rich and well-born from all cities in ever-increasing numbers. At the same time, the Episcopal Church also developed into a national upper-class institution. By the end of the nineteenth century, the process of upper-class conversion, which had actually begun in the previous century, was virtually complete. In the twentieth century, the fashionable descendants of staunch New England Calvinists or pious Philadelphia Quakers almost invariably worshipped in the Episcopal churches in the metropolitan suburbs of America. And the Episcopal Church is also an important part of the summer social life at such fashionable resorts as Mount Desert [Island, Maine] which do so much to foster inter-city family alliances.

Several things follow from the development of this national upper class and its supporting institutions. On the whole, of course, the family is weakened and increasingly replaced by an associational aristocracy. The family firm gives way to the large and anonymously owned corporation with the attending consequences of declining family pride and responsibility. The entrepreneur who founded the family firm and fortune is replaced by the hired executive, and the corporation soon becomes an impersonal source of dividends which conveniently supports a suitable style of life. At the same time, the fashionable school, college, and club replace the family as the chief status-ascribing institutions: often isolated geographically as well as socially from the rest of the community, these fashionable associations tend to make for less social contact between classes than was the case in an earlier day when the members of polite society, although undoubtedly protected by a formal social distance recognized by all classes, may well have interacted more frequently in the local community with the members of the middle and lower classes. George Wharton Pepper, for instance, met and befriended a Negro boy while he was growing up in the neighborhood of stiff and fashionable Rittenhouse Square; his grandsons, reared in the social homogeneity of the Main Line and a New England boarding school, were more geographically isolated even though born in a more egalitarian age. Finally, the Episcopalianization of the whole American upper class also tends to foster uniformity and class isolation. This is, of course, part of a general trend throughout Protestantism. The Catholic Church has traditionally been an altar before which men of all walks of life bow down together, but the various Protestant denominations have, almost from the beginning, been organized along class lines. Certainly most Protestant churches today are social centers where families of similar backgrounds assemble together for worship. One often wonders if fashionable Episcopalians, in their aversion to the middle-class drabness of the "Protestant ethic," have not thereby substi-

tuted a convenient conventionality for their ancestors' more rigid convictions. At any rate, these developments in upper-class institutions tend to make for an increasing conformity and uniformity, a decline in local color and originality, and perhaps, at the same time, a new snobbishness which inevitably follows the increasing importance now attached to proper associational affiliation.

Arnold Toynbee has written that whereas Western civilization has been preoccupied for several generations with the building of roads, the challenge before us today is one of regulating the traffic thereon. American civilization, led by businessmen of daring enterprise and ingenuity ("know how"), has produced the highest standard of living the world has ever known. And these business leaders and producers of wealth have been the backbone of its upper class. "New occasions teach new duties," however, and today, in the atomic age of abundant consumption, the continuing, or perhaps, new greatness of America will presumably depend on the nation's ability to shoulder the burden of world leadership in creating and defending, to use Toynbee's analogy, some sort of world traffic rules. At the same time, domestic government, at the local, state, and national level, is playing a larger and larger role in the lives of American citizens, both as the defender of law and order and the redistributor of wealth in a host of welfare activities. In short, while entrepreneurial and financial genius may have built up America, statesmen and political leaders are rapidly becoming the most powerful and important members of the contemporary elite.

On the whole, the American upper class, with such outstanding exceptions as the Roosevelts, Adamses, Lodges, and Tafts, has produced few great statesmen in modern times. As we have seen, this has been especially true of

Proper Philadelphia. As young Theodore Roosevelt once wrote: "There are not a few men of means who have always made the till their fatherland, and are always ready to balance a temporary interruption of money-making, or a temporary financial and commercial disaster, against the self-sacrifice necessary in upholding the honor of the nation and the glory of the flag." [2] The vigor and continuity of an upper class depends, not on its social prestige and style of life, but rather on its continuing contribution of men who are both willing and able to assume positions of power and leadership in the world of affairs. As the seat of power moves from State Street to the State House, from Wall Street to Washington, one wonders if the American business aristocracy discussed in this volume will be capable of supplying its share of leaders in local, national, and international governmental affairs. There are several reasons for believing that it will.

First, Philadelphia has been going through a cultural, civic, and political renaissance since the close of the Second World War. The political renaissance has been led by two members of the upper class, Richardson Dilworth, a transplanted member of an old Pittsburgh family, and Joseph Sill Clark, descendant of Enoch W. Clark, founder of one of the city's leading banking families. Both men had distinguished war records; Dilworth with the Marine Corps at Guadalcanal and Clark with the United States Air Force in the Far East. Both were distinguished lawyers and former Republicans who became Democrats rather than attempt to reform the corrupt Republican party from within. Their fight for reform began when Dilworth ran for mayor in 1947 and was defeated by the entrenched

Republican machine. Four years later, however, Clark and Dilworth waged a vigorous campaign and won; Clark became the city's first Democratic mayor in the twentieth century, and Dilworth was elected district attorney. Two years later the local Democratic revival was tested again when in Philadelphia Adlai Stevenson ran 162,000 votes ahead of Dwight D. Eisenhower in a conspicuous reversal of the national Republican landslide. Finally, in 1955, Dilworth was elected to succeed Clark as mayor.[3]

Ever since the reluctant gentlemen-revolutionists founded the Republic in the late eighteenth century, Philadelphians have preferred to have their radical reform movements guided by people of substance and position. While Clark and Dilworth were rejuvenating the Democratic party, other reform groups were forming in the city. Walter Phillips, a Proper Philadelphian and birthright Republican who as a student at Harvard during the Depression came all the way down from Cambridge (much against his father's will) in order to cast his vote for Franklin D. Roosevelt, organized and led the "Republicans for Clark and Dilworth." [4] At the same time, John Frederick Lewis, Jr. and his wife were instrumental in organizing the local

---

[2] Quoted in John P. Mallan, "Roosevelt, Brooks Adams, and Lea: The Warrior Critique of the Business Civilization," *American Quarterly*, 8 (Fall 1956), p. 219.

[3] In this mayoralty contest it is interesting and perhaps a sign of the times, that Richardson Dilworth, one-time end on the Yale football team, and W. Thacher Longstretch, of Princeton gridiron fame, led their respective political parties.

[4] Phillips was also responsible for the founding of Philadelphia's first City Planning Commission (one of the nation's finest today). Appropriately enough, its first Chairman was Edward Hopkinson, Jr. He remained at the helm throughout Mayor Clark's Democratic administration but was replaced by Albert M. Greenfield after Richardson Dilworth became Mayor. Jared Ingersoll announced his resignation from the Commission after Greenfield's appointment as Chairman; such are the ways of social change.

chapter of the Americans for Democratic Action, a so-called radical group with a very responsible and politically concerned membership in Philadelphia.

John Frederick Lewis, Jr. was a wealthy Proper Philadelphia lawyer and philanthropist whose intellectual and nonconformist propensities . . . were more in the tradition of Proper Boston's greatest days when "everybody talked of reform." His grandfather, S. Weir Lewis, founded the family fortune in the China trade before the Civil War . . . and lived a few doors south of Holy Trinity Church on Rittenhouse Square. His father, John Frederick Lewis, Senior, a Philadelphia lawyer, augmented the family fortune by shrewd investments in urban real estate.

The Lewises have been leaders in the cultural life of Philadelphia for two generations. John Frederick Lewis, Senior, was president of the Academy of the Fine Arts, Academy of Music, Mercantile Library, and the Historical Society of Pennsylvania. His son followed in his footsteps as president of the Academy of the Fine Arts and the Academy of Music. In accordance with his civic and cultural interests, John Frederick Lewis, Jr. limited his club memberships to the Franklin Inn and Art Alliance, in both of which he has held the office of president in recent years. The Philadelphia chapter of the Americans for Democratic Action was founded at an informal meeting in the Lewis mansion at 1916 Spruce Street, where the family has lived continuously since 1856.

On the national scene, men of means and background are following the example set by Franklin D. Roosevelt in the 1930's. In fact the Democratic party, in the tradition of Jefferson and that colorful frontier aristocrat, Andrew Jackson (who, of course, appealed to such patrician Philadelphians as Richard Rush and Charles Jared

Ingersoll), has probably taken on more of an aristocratic pattern of leadership than at any other time in its long history. Such men as Adlai Stevenson of Choate School and Princeton, G. Mennen Williams of Salisbury School and Princeton, John F. Kennedy of Choate and Harvard, and both Dean Acheson and Averell Harriman of Groton and Yale are all representative of the trends.[5] Descendants of "robber barons" would hardly be satisfied with the confining life of the corporation executive or a partnership in a large metropolitan law firm.

Even Proper Philadelphians are participating in this trend on the national scene. Apparently the voters of Pennsylvania, who re-elected President Eisenhower by an overwhelming majority, also had enough confidence in Proper Philadelphia's millionaire socialite, Joseph Sill Clark, to send him to Washington as their junior Senator. And he was the descendant of a long line of investment bankers who never had the "itch for public office" in over one hundred years. Finally, of course, America's most important ambassadorial post was held recently by a Proper Philadelphian. The former American Ambassador to Moscow, ex-Philadelphian Charles E. Bohlen, a product of St. Paul's and Harvard (Porcellian), and his brother-in-law, Charles Wheeler Thayer, one of the few Proper Philadelphia graduates of West Point in modern times, are both

[5] A comparison of the biographies of Adlai Stevenson, Averell Harriman, and Dean Acheson as reported in Who's Who (British) and Who's Who in America reveals some interesting cultural contrasts. Hobbies are, of course, reported in the British version only. More interesting, however, is the fact that while all three report their boarding school in their British biographies, none does so in the American volume. One often observes this sort of reverse snobbism in this country where egalitarianism often is preferred to the truth.

thorough students of the Russian language and culture, having long since anticipated the present contest between this country and the Soviet Union. Perhaps gentlemen of means and secure leisure have often been leaders in new movements and ideas. After all, Thomas Jefferson, Oliver Cromwell, Franklin Roosevelt, and George Washington were country squires. Isaiah Berlin may well have a point when he writes:

There is something singularly attractive about men who retained, throughout life, the manners, the texture of being, the habits and style of a civilized and refined *milieu*. Such men exercise a peculiar kind of personal freedom which combines spontaneity with distinction. Their minds see large and generous horizons, and above all, reveal a unique intellectual gaiety of a kind that aristocratic education tends to produce. At the same time, they are intellectually on the side of everything that is new, progressive, rebellious, young, untried, of that which is about to come into being, of the open sea whether or not there is land that lies beyond. To this type belong those intermediate figures, like Mirabeau, Charles James Fox, Franklin Roosevelt, who live near the frontier that divides old from new, between the *douceur de la vie* which is about to pass and the tantalising future, the dangerous new age that they themselves do much to bring into being.[6]

Perhaps America as a whole will benefit from the patrician's modern emancipation from the counting house.

One more question remains to be raised even if it cannot be answered: What is the future function of a predominantly Anglo-Saxon and Protestant upper class in an ethnically and religiously heterogeneous democracy? In many ways, this is the most important question of all. As Joseph Patrick Kennedy, Boston millionaire and American Ambassador to the Court of St.

James under Roosevelt, once put it: "How long does our family have to be here before we are called Americans rather than Irish-Americans?" As has been shown throughout this volume, the American upper class has been from the beginning open to new men of talent and power and their families. By the middle of the twentieth century, however, upper-class status appears to be limited primarily to families of colonial and northern European stock and Protestant affiliations. Glancing back to the turn of the century, when a floodtide of immigrants came to these shores from southern and eastern Europe, to say nothing of the Irish Catholics who came earlier, one wonders if this American democracy has not produced somewhat of a caste situation at the upper-class level. Or are the talented and powerful descendants of these newer immigrants going to be assimilated into some future upper-class way of life and social organization?

It has been shown how parallel upper classes existed in Philadelphia in 1940. On a national scale, "café society" as well as the business executive society of rank, although perhaps not as permanent or community-rooted as the upper class, have been firmly institutionalized in recent decades as parallel social organizations. Whether this contemporary situation is a sign of a healthy social structure of leadership is a problem which needs a great deal of careful research. At any rate, the description of the wealthy and talented expense-account elite in A. C. Spectorsky's *The Exurbanites* or William H. Whyte, Jr.'s *The Organization Man* appears to suggest that large numbers of this new American elite are living in a nightmare of insecurity and conformity.[7] Nor does C. Wright Mills

---

[6] Isaiah Berlin, "A Marvelous Decade (IV)," *Encounter*, 6 (May 1956) p. 21.

[7] A. C. Spectorsky, *The Exurbanites*, Philadelphia: J. B. Lippincott, 1955. William H. Whyte, *The Organization Man*, New York: Simon and Schuster, 1956.

offer much hope; his *The Power Elite* adds up to a "higher immorality." [8]

In closing it should be said that, although a "classless society" is manifestly a contradiction in terms, this democracy surely cannot survive so long as upper-class status is still de-

[8] C. Wright Mills, *The Power Elite*, New York: Oxford University Press, 1956.

nied to those families with minority ethnic and religious affiliations. In this young nation, an ancient mansion of democracy, the stairway of social prestige has been "forever echoing with the wooden shoe going up, and the polished boot descending." When the echoes die, however, the ancient mansion will have been deserted.

43

The New Middle Class

C. WRIGHT MILLS

In the early nineteenth century, although there are no exact figures, probably four-fifths of the occupied population were self-employed enterprisers; by 1870, only about one-third, and in 1940, only about one-fifth, were still in this old middle class. Many of the remaining four-fifths of the people who now earn a living do so by working for the 2 or 3 percent of the population who now own 40 or 50 percent of the private property in the United States. Among these workers are the members of the new middle class, white-collar people on salary. For them, as for wage-workers, America has become a nation of employees for whom independent property is out of range. Labor markets, not control of property, determine their chances to receive income, exercise power, enjoy prestige, learn and use skills.

From *White Collar: The American Middle Classes* by C. Wright Mills. Copyright 1951 by Oxford University Press, Inc. Reprinted by permission.

Occupational Change

Of the three broad strata composing modern society, only the new middle class has steadily grown in proportion to the whole. Eighty years ago, there were three-quarters of a million middle-class employees; by 1940, there were over twelve and a half million. In that period the old middle class in-

The Labor Force

	1870	1940
Old Middle Class	33%	20%
New Middle Class	6	25
Wage-Workers	61	55
Total	100%	100%

New Middle Class

	1870	1940
Managers	14%	10%
Salaried Professionals	30	25
Salespeople	44	25
Office Workers	12	40
Total	100%	100%

creased 135 percent; wage-workers, 255 percent; new middle class, 1600 percent.

The employees composing the new middle class do not make up one single compact stratum. They have not emerged on a single horizontal level, but have been shuffled out simultaneously on the several levels of modern society; they now form, as it were, a new pyramid within the old pyramid of society at large, rather than a horizontal layer. The great bulk of the new middle class are of the lower middle-income brackets, but regardless of how social stature is measured, types of white-collar men and women range from almost the top to almost the bottom of modern society.

The managerial stratum, subject to minor variations during these decades, has dropped slightly, from 14 to 10 percent; the salaried professionals, displaying the same minor ups and downs, have dropped from 30 to 25 percent of the new middle class. The major shifts in over-all composition have been in the relative decline of the sales group, occurring most sharply around 1900, from 44 to 25 percent of the total new middle class; and the steady rise of the office workers, from 12 to 40 percent. Today the three largest occupational groups in the white-collar stratum are schoolteachers, salespeople in and out of stores, and assorted office workers. These three form the white-collar mass.

White-collar occupations now engage well over half the members of the American middle class as a whole. Between 1870 and 1940, white-collar workers rose from 15 to 56 percent of the middle brackets, while the old middle class declined from 85 to 44 percent.

Negatively, the transformation of the middle class is a shift from property to no-property; positively, it is a shift from property to a new axis of stratification, occupation. The nature and well-being of the old middle class can best be sought in the condition of entrepreneurial property; of the new middle class, in the economics and sociology of occupations. The numerical decline of the older, independent sectors of the middle class is an incident in the centralization of property; the numerical rise of the newer salaried employees is due to the industrial mechanics by which the occupations composing the new middle class have arisen.

Industrial Mechanics

In modern society, occupations are specific functions within a social division of labor, as well as skills sold for income on a labor market. Contemporary divisions of labor involve a hitherto unknown specialization of skill: from arranging abstract symbols, at $1000 an hour, to working a shovel, for $1000 a year. The major shifts in occupations since the Civil War have assumed this industrial trend: as a proportion of the labor force, fewer individuals manipulate *things*, more handle *people* and *symbols*.

This shift in needed skills is another way of describing the rise of the white-collar workers, for their characteristic skills involve the handling of paper and money and people. They are expert at dealing with people transiently

The Middle Classes

	1870	1940
Old Middle Class	85%	44%
Farmers	62	23
Businessmen	21	19
Free Professionals	2	2
New Middle Class	15%	56%
Managers	2	6
Salaried Professionals	4	14
Salespeople	7	14
Office Workers	2	22
Total Middle Class	100%	100%

and impersonally; they are masters of the commercial, professional, and technical relationship. The one thing they do not do is live by making things; rather, they live off the social machineries that organize and co-ordinate the people who do make things. White-collar people help turn what someone else has made into profit for still another; some of them are closer to the means of production, supervising the work of actual manufacture and recording what is done. They are the people who keep track; they man the paper routines involved in distributing what is produced. They provide technical and personal services, and they teach others the skills which they themselves practice, as well as all other skills transmitted by teaching.

As the proportion of workers needed for the extraction and production of things declines, the proportion needed for servicing, distributing, and co-ordinating rises. In 1870, over three-fourths, and in 1940, slightly less than one-half of the total employed were engaged in producing things.

	1870	1940
Producing	77%	46%
Servicing	13	20
Distributing	7	23
Co-ordinating	3	11
Total employed	100%	100%

By 1940, the proportion of white-collar workers of those employed in industries primarily involved in the production of things was 11 percent; in service industries, 32 percent; in distribution, 44 percent; and in co-ordination, 60 percent. The white-collar industries themselves have grown, and within each industry the white-collar occupations have grown. Three trends lie back of the fact that the white-collar ranks have thus been the

most rapidly growing of modern occupations: the increasing productivity of machinery used in manufacturing; the magnification of distribution; and the increasing scale of co-ordination.

The immense productivity of mass-production technique and the increased application of technologic rationality are the first open secrets of modern occupational change: fewer men turn out more things in less time. In the middle of the nineteenth century, as J. F. Dewhurst and his associates have calculated, some 17.6 billion horse-power hours were expended in American industry, only 6 percent by mechanical energy; by the middle of the twentieth century, 410.4 billion horse-power hours will be expended, 94 percent by mechanical energy. This industrial revolution seems to be permanent, seems to go on through war and boom and slump; thus 'a decline in production results in a more than proportional decline in employment; and an increase in production results in a less than proportional increase in employment.'

Technology has thus narrowed the stratum of workers needed for given volumes of output; it has also altered the types and proportions of skill needed in the production process. Know-how, once an attribute of the mass of workers, is now in the machine and the engineering elite who design it. Machines displace unskilled workmen, make craft skills unnecessary, push up front the automatic motions of the machine-operative. Workers composing the new lower class are predominantly semi-skilled: their proportion in the urban wage-worker stratum has risen from 31 percent in 1910 to 41 percent in 1940.

The manpower economies brought about by machinery and the large-scale rationalization of labor forces, so apparent in production and extraction, have not, as yet, been applied so extensively in distribution—transportation, communication, finance, and trade. Yet without an elaboration of these means of distribution, the wide-flung operations of multi-plant producers could not be integrated nor their products distributed. Therefore, the proportion of people engaged in distribution has enormously increased so that today about one-fourth of the labor force is so engaged. Distribution has expanded more than production because of the lag in technological application in this field, and because of the persistence of individual and small-scale entrepreneurial units at the same time that the market has been enlarged and the need to market has been deepened.

Behind this expansion of the distributive occupations lies the central problem of modern capitalism: to whom can the available goods be sold? As volume swells, the intensified search for markets draws more workers into the distributive occupations of trade, promotion, advertising. As far-flung and intricate markets come into being, and as the need to find and create even more markets becomes urgent, 'middle men' who move, store, finance, promote, and sell goods are knit into a vast network of enterprises and occupations.

The physical aspect of distribution involves wide and fast transportation networks; the co-ordination of marketing involves communication; the search for markets and the selling of goods involves trade, including wholesale and retail outlets as well as financial agencies for commodity and capital markets. Each of these activities engage more people, but the manual jobs among them do not increase so fast as the white-collar tasks.

Transportation, growing rapidly after the Civil War, began to decline in point of the numbers of people involved before 1930; but this decline took place among wage-workers; the proportion of white-collar workers employed in transportation continued to rise. By 1940, some 23 percent of the people in transportation were white-collar employees. As a new industrial segment of the U.S. economy, the communication industry has never been run by large numbers of free enterprisers; at the outset it needed large numbers of technical and other white-collar workers. By 1940, some 77 percent of its people were in new middle-class occupations.

Trade is now the third largest segment of the occupational structure, exceeded only by farming and manufacturing. A few years after the Civil War less than 5 out of every 100 workers were engaged in trade; by 1940 almost 12 out of every 100 workers were so employed. But, while 70 percent of those in wholesaling and retailing were free enterprisers in 1870, and less than 3 percent were white collar, by 1940, of the people engaged in retail trade 27 percent were free enterprisers; 41 percent white-collar employees.

Newer methods of merchandising such as credit financing, have resulted in an even greater percentage increase in the 'financial' than in the 'commercial' agents of distribution. Branch banking has lowered the status of many banking employees to the clerical level, and reduced the number of executive positions. By 1940, of all employees in finance and real estate 70 percent were white-collar workers of the new middle class.

The organizational reason for the expansion of the white-collar occupations is the rise of big business and big government, and the consequent trend of modern social structure, the steady growth of bureaucracy. In every branch of the economy, as firms merge and corporations become dominant, free entrepreneurs become employees, and the calculations of accountant, statistician, bookkeeper, and clerk in these corporations replace the free 'movement of prices' as the co-ordinating agent of the economic system. The rise of thousands of big and little bureaucracies and the elaborate specialization of the system as a whole create the need for many men and women to plan, co-ordinate, and administer new routines for others. In moving from smaller to larger and more elaborate units of economic activity, increased proportions of employees are drawn into co-ordinating and managing. Managerial and professional employees and office workers of varied sorts—floor-walkers, foremen, office managers—are needed; people to whom subordinates report, and who in turn report to superiors, are links in chains of power and obedience, co-ordinating and supervising other occupational experiences, functions, and skills. And all over the economy, the proportion of clerks of all sorts has increased: from 1 to 2 percent in 1870 to 10 or 11 percent of all gainful workers in 1940.

As the worlds of business undergo these changes, the increased tasks of government on all fronts draw still more people into occupations that regulate and service property and men. In response to the largeness and predatory complications of business, the crises of slump, the nationalization of the rural economy and small-town markets, the flood of immigrants, the urgencies of war and the march of technology disrupting social life, government increases its co-ordinating and regulating tasks. Public regulations, social services, and business taxes require more people to make mass records and to integrate people, firms, and goods, both within government and in the various segments of business and private life. All branches of government have grown, although the most startling increases are found in the executive branch of the Federal Government, where the needs for co-ordinating the economy have been most prevalent.

As marketable activities, occupations change (1) with shifts in the skills required, as technology and rationalization are unevenly applied across the economy; (2) with the enlargement and intensification of marketing operations in both the commodity and capital markets; and (3) with shifts in the organization of the division of work, as expanded organizations require co-ordination, management, and recording. The mechanics involved within and between these three trends have led to the numerical expansion of white-collar employees.

There are other less obvious ways in which the occupational structure is shaped: high agricultural tariffs, for example, delay the decline of farming as an occupation; were Argentine beef allowed to enter duty-free, the number of meat producers here might diminish. City ordinances and zoning laws abolish peddlers and affect the types of construction workers that prevail. Most states have bureaus of standards which limit entrance into professions and semi-professions; at the same time members of these occupations form associations in the attempt to control entrance into 'their' market. More successful than most trade unions, such professional associations as the American Medical Association have managed for several decades to level off the proportion of physicians and surgeons. Every phase of the slump-war-boom cycle influences the numerical importance of various occupations; for instance, the movement back and forth between 'construction worker' and small 'contractor' is geared to slumps and booms in building.

The pressures from these loosely organized parts of the occupational world draw conscious managerial agencies into the picture. The effects of attempts to manage occupational change, directly and indirectly, are not yet great, except of course during wars, when government freezes men in their jobs or offers incen-

ot just market forces.

tives and compulsions to remain in old occupations or shift to new ones. Yet increasingly the class levels and occupational composition of the nation are managed; the occupational structure of the United States is being slowly reshaped as a gigantic corporate group. It is subject not only to the pulling of autonomous markets and the pushing of technology but to an 'allocation of personnel' from central points of control. Occupational change thus becomes more conscious, at least to those who are coming to be in charge of it.

White-Collar Pyramids

Occupations, in terms of which we circumscribe the new middle class, involve several ways of ranking people. As specific activities, they entail various types and levels of *skill*, and their exercise fulfils certain *functions* within an industrial division of labor. These are the skills and functions we have been examining statistically. As sources of income, occupations are connected with *class* position; and since they normally carry an expected quota of prestige, on and off the job, they are relevant to *status* position. They also involve certain degrees of *power* over other people, directly in terms of the job, and indirectly in other social areas. Occupations are thus tied to class, status, and power as well as to skill and function; to understand the occupations composing the new middle class, we must consider them in terms of each of these dimensions.

'Class situation' in its simplest objective sense has to do with the amount and source of income. Today, occupation rather than property is the source of income for most of those who receive any direct income: the possibilities of selling their services in the labor market, rather than of profitably buying and selling their property and its yields, now determine the life-chances of most

of the middle class. All things money can buy and many that men dream about are theirs by virtue of occupational income. In new middle-class occupations men work for someone else on someone else's property. This is the clue to many differences between the old and new middle classes, as well as to the contrast between the older world of the small propertied entrepreneur and the occupational structure of the new society. If the old middle class once fought big property structures in the name of small, free properties, the new middle class, like the wage-workers in latter-day capitalism, has been, from the beginning, dependent upon large properties for job security.

Wage-workers in the factory and on the farm are on the propertyless bottom of the occupational structure, depending upon the equipment owned by others, earning wages for the time they spend at work. In terms of property, the white-collar people are *not* 'in between Capital and Labor'; they are in exactly the same property-class position as the wage-workers. They have no direct financial tie to the means of production, no prime claim upon the proceeds from property. Like factory workers—and day laborers, for that matter—they work for those who do own such means of livelihood.

Yet if bookkeepers and coal miners, insurance agents and farm laborers, doctors in a clinic and crane operators in an open pit have this condition in common, certainly their class situations are not the same. To understand their class positions, we must go beyond the common fact of source of income and consider as well the amount of income.

In 1890, the average income of white-collar occupational groups was about double that of wage-workers. Before World War I, salaries were not so adversely affected by slumps as wages were but, on the contrary, they rather steadily advanced. Since World War I,

Weber's 3-fold approach to stat?

however, salaries have been reacting to turns in the economic cycles more and more like wages, although still to a lesser extent. If wars help wages more because of the greater flexibility of wages, slumps help salaries because of their greater inflexibility. Yet after each war era, salaries have never regained their previous advantage over wages. Each phase of the cycle, as well as the progressive rise of all income groups, has resulted in a narrowing of the income gap between wage-workers and white-collar employees.

In the middle 'thirties the three urban strata, entrepreneurs, white-collar, and wage-workers, formed a distinct scale with respect to median family income: the white-collar employees had a median income of $1,896; the entrepreneurs, $1,464; the urban wage-workers, $1,175. Although the median income of white-collar workers was higher than that of the entrepreneurs, large proportions of the entrepreneurs received both high-level and low-level incomes. The distribution of their income was spread more than that of the white collar.

The wartime boom in incomes, in fact, spread the incomes of all occupational groups, but not evenly. The spread occurred mainly among urban entrepreneurs. As an income level, the old middle class in the city is becoming less an evenly graded income group, and more a collection of different strata, with a large proportion of lumpenbourgeoisie who receive very low incomes, and a small, prosperous bourgeoisie with very high incomes.

In the late 'forties (1948, median family income) the income of all white-collar workers was $4000, that of all urban wage-workers, $3300. These averages, however, should not obscure the overlap of specific groups within each stratum: the lower white-collar people—sales-employees and office workers—earned almost the same as

skilled workers and foremen,[1] but more than semi-skilled urban wage-workers.

In terms of property, white-collar people are in the same position as wage-workers; in terms of occupational income, they are 'somewhere in the middle.' Once they were considerably above the wage-workers; they have become less so; in the middle of the century they still have an edge but the over-all rise in incomes is making the new middle class a more homogeneous income group.

As with income, so with prestige: white-collar groups are differentiated socially, perhaps more decisively than wage-workers and entrepreneurs. Wage earners certainly do form an income pyramid and a prestige gradation, as do entrepreneurs and rentiers; but the new middle class, in terms of income and prestige, is a superimposed pyramid, reaching from almost the bottom of the first to almost the top of the second.

People in white-collar occupations claim higher prestige than wage-workers, and, as a general rule, can cash in their claims with wage-workers as well as with the anonymous public. This fact has been seized upon, with much justification, as the defining characteristic of the white-collar strata, and although there are definite indications in the United States of a decline in their prestige, still, on a nation-wide basis, the majority of even the lower white-collar employees—office workers and salespeople—enjoy a middling prestige.

The historic bases of the white-collar employees' prestige, apart from superior income, have included the similarity of their place and type of work to those of the old middle-classes' which has permitted them to borrow prestige. As

[1] It is impossible to isolate the salaried foremen from the skilled urban wage-workers in these figures. If we could do so, the income of lower white-collar workers would be closer to that of semi-skilled workers.

their relations with entrepreneur and with esteemed customer have become more impersonal, they have borrowed prestige from the firm itself. The stylization of their appearance, in particular the fact that most white-collar jobs have permitted the wearing of street clothes on the job, has also figured in their prestige claims, as have the skills required in most white-collar jobs, and in many of them the variety of operations performed and the degree of autonomy exercised in deciding work procedures. Furthermore, the time taken to learn these skills and the way in which they have been acquired by formal education and by close contact with the higher-ups in charge has been important. White-collar employees have monopolized high school education—even in 1940 they had completed 12 grades to the 8 grades for wage-workers and entrepreneurs. They have also enjoyed status by descent: in terms of race, Negro white-collar employees exist only in isolated instances —and, more importantly, in terms of nativity, in 1930 only about 9 percent of white-collar workers, but 16 percent of free enterprisers and 21 percent of wage-workers, were foreign born. Finally, as an underlying fact, the limited size of the white-collar group, compared to wage-workers, has led to successful claims to greater prestige.

The power position of groups and of individuals typically depends upon factors of class, status, and occupation, often in intricate interrelation. Given occupations involve specific powers over other people in the actual course of work; but also outside the job area, by virtue of their relations to institutions of property as well as the typical income they afford, occupations lend power. Some white-collar occupations require the direct exercise of supervision over other white-collar and wage-workers, and many more are closely attached to this managerial cadre. White-collar

employees are the assistants of authority; the power they exercise is a derived power, but they do exercise it.

Moreover, within the white-collar pyramids there is a characteristic pattern of authority involving age and sex. The white-collar ranks contain a good many women: some 41 percent of all white-collar employees, as compared with 10 percent of free enterprisers and 21 percent of wage-workers, are women.[2] As with sex, so with age: free enterprisers average (median) about 45 years of age, white-collar and wage-workers, about 34; but among free enterprisers and wage-workers, men are about 2 or 3 years older than women; among white-collar workers, there is a 6- or 7-year difference. In the white-collar pyramids, authority is roughly graded by age and sex: younger women tend to be subordinated to older men.

The occupational groups forming the white-collar pyramids, different as they may be from one another, have certain common characteristics, which are central to the character of the new middle class as a general pyramid overlapping the entrepreneurs and wage-workers. White-collar people cannot be adequately defined along any one possible dimension of stratification—skill, function, class, status, or power. They are generally in the middle ranges on each of these dimensions and on every descriptive attribute. Their position is more definable in terms of their relative differences from other strata than in any absolute terms.

On all points of definition, it must be remembered that white-collar people are not one compact horizontal stratum.

[2] According to our calculations, the proportions of women, 1940, in these groups are: farmers, 2.9%; businessmen, 20%; free professionals, 5.9%; managers, 7.1%; salaried professionals, 51.7%; salespeople, 27.5%; office workers, 51%; skilled workers, 3.2%; semi-skilled and unskilled, 29.8%; rural workers, 9.1%.

They do not fulfil one central, positive *function* that can define them, although in general their functions are similar to those of the old middle class. They deal with symbols and with other people, co-ordinating, recording, and distributing; but they fulfil these functions as dependent employees, and the skills they thus employ are sometimes similar in form and required mentality to those of many wage-workers.

In terms of property, they are equal to wage-workers and different from the old middle class. Originating as propertyless dependents, they have no serious expectations of propertied independence. In terms of income, their class position is, on the average, somewhat higher than that of wage-workers. The overlap is large and the trend has been definitely toward less difference, but even today the differences are significant.

Perhaps of more psychological importance is the fact that white-collar groups have successfully claimed more prestige than wage-workers and still generally continue to do so. The bases of their prestige may not be solid today, and certainly they show no signs of being permanent; but, however vague and fragile, they continue to mark off white-collar people from wage-workers.

Members of white-collar occupations exercise a derived authority in the course of their work; moreover, compared to older hierarchies, the white-collar pyramids are youthful and feminine bureaucracies, within which youth, education, and American birth are emphasized at the wide base, where millions of office workers most clearly typify these differences between the new middle class and other occupational groups. White-collar masses, in turn, are managed by people who are more like the old middle class, having many of the social characteristics, if not the independence, of free enterprisers.

44

Old Working Class, New Working Class

MICHAEL HARRINGTON

I.

In recent years the American working class has been called conservative, militant, reactionary, progressive, authoritarian, social democratic, and, the unkindest cut of all, nonexistent. Except for the last, all the labels fit. The labor movement—I sharpen the focus

Reprinted from *Dissent* (Winter 1972), by permission of the publisher, *Dissent Magazine*, New York, N. Y.

on the organized section of the working class—contains more blacks than any other institution in American society, as well as more young whites attracted by the populist racism of George Wallace. Notwithstanding its tendencies toward ethnocentrism and anti-intellectualism, the labor movement has provided a decisive political impetus for whatever democratic planning there is in America. The organized workers are, in short, no one thing; they are a varied, dynamic, contradictory mass whose position in society can drive its members toward a practical social idealism, an anti-social corporatism, or any one of the complicated variants between those extremes.

I believe that the American workers have been a crucial force behind every social gain of the past two generations, and in domestic politics their unions constitute an American kind of de facto social democracy. Perhaps the exigencies of the future will deepen the best impulses within the labor movement, and I am on the side of those within it who are fighting for such a development. But my partisanship does not make me an apologist. Precisely because I am concerned and involved, I cannot afford to gloss over tendencies that run counter to my hopes. I must try to understand the past and present of the working class with as much candor as possible if I am to help those struggling to create its future. In these pages I will try to do that by way of a broad overview of the organized and organizable working class. Insofar as I deal with history, it will be in order to understand the current position of the unions and the various futures it could make possible. But before that can be attempted, I must define a vexing term: the working class. There are serious scholars who argue that it no longer exists in America. My conclusion, however, will be that there is not simply one working class in America but two —an old working class still quite vital and a new working class being created by political and economic evolution.

It is an extraordinary thing that those who argue there is no working class in the United States can be found at the most disparate points of the political spectrum. Herbert Marcuse, who had a notable influence on the New Left youth of the 1960s, writes that " 'the people,' previously the ferment of social

change, have 'moved up' to become the ferment of social cohesion." [1] Paul Sweezy and the late Paul Baran, sympathizers first with Russian, then with Chinese, communism, argued that the organized workers in the United States have been "integrated into the system as consumers and ideologically conditioned members of the society." Arthur Schlesinger, Jr., an activist liberal, says that

the lines of division in our politics have fundamentally altered. The issues are no longer social or economic so much as they are cultural and moral. It is no longer the common men against the boss as much as it is the rational against the indignant, the planner against the spoiler, the humanist against the uneducated, the young against the old.

Perhaps the most emphatic statement of the theme comes from Clark Kerr, a brilliant, pragmatic technocrat. He holds that "the working class not only tends to disappear as a class-conscious and recognizable element in society; it needs to disappear if modern industrial society is to operate with full effectiveness." High technology, he continues, requires consensus and cooperation and therefore cannot tolerate class conflict over basic principles. So even though there are obvious differences between industrialists and file clerks, there are not "any clear class lines to divide them —only infinite gradations."

I disagree with those, from the authoritarian Left to the democratic Center, who think that the American working class does not exist (the Right, which I will not consider here, tends to have a vulgar Marxist, or paranoid, version of the power of organized labor). To use Marx's famous distinction, the

1 Sources for all references within each section are grouped in a bibliographical note at the end of this essay.

working class in this country is not simply a class "in itself"—a mass sharing "a common situation and common interests"—but it is a class "for itself" and the "interests which it defends . . . [are] class interests."

II.

First of all, consider the "old" working class: the primarily blue-collar workers who do physical labor in the industrial economy. It has renewed itself in the last quarter of a century and become a greater force in American politics than at any time in the nation's history.

The total nonagricultural labor force in 1969 numbered 77.902 million men and women. Of these, 48.993 million were "production and nonsupervisory workers on private payrolls," with the 14.647 million in manufacturing the largest single component. Another 12.591 million were employed by federal, state, and local government, and many of them held down such blue-collar and organizable jobs as sanitation man or postman. There were 20.210 million union members, mainly concentrated in machinery, transportation equipment, contract construction, and transportation services.

Among the unorganized one would find the working poor, who numbered close to four million in 1969 according to the government's optimistic definition of poverty. An almost equal number of the "near poor" (who include more whites and tend more to live in families headed by a male than do the poor themselves) were largely outside the unions. Those neither poor nor union members are most numerous in wholesale and retail trade, in finance, insurance, real estate, and the service industries. A good number of these are, of course, white-collar workers, and not a few of them receive wage increases from anti-union employers whenever

organized labor in the industry, or the area, makes a gain.

This working class, both organized and unorganized, has a "common situation and common interests," experienced first and foremost in the reality that it does not have enough money. In 1969 the Bureau of Labor Statistics computed a "modest" budget for an urban family of four at $9,076, an amount in excess of the income of well over half the families in the United States. The trade unionists, most of whom are among the better-off members of the "old" working class, do not achieve this standard: they are neither poor nor affluent but in-between and distinctly deprived. In September 1969 the "average production worker" took home $102.44 for a full week's work, and manufacturing workers, most of whom were organized, received only $106.75. Moreover, since these figures were computed, the cost of living has gone up by almost 20 percent and the real wage of the workers has slightly decreased.

Even if one upgrades all of these numbers because of the enormous increase in the number of working wives —eighteen million of them in 1969, double the figure for 1950—who add an average of 25 percent to their family income, the total still falls short of the government's modest budget. The "modest" standard, it must be emphasized, lives up to its name: it allows for a two-year-old used car and a new suit every four years. In addition to this deficiency in income, most of the union members are employed in manufacturing, construction, and transportation, i.e., in jobs with little intrinsic interest and, in the case of an assembly line in an auto plant, a dehumanizing routine. They are paid not as individuals but as members of a class: after the age of twenty-five, the worker's income does not normally vary with increasing experience, as does that of professional and managerial employees, but usually rises as part of a negotiated group settlement. Indeed, the very fact of being paid a wage by the hour emphasizes another determinant of working-class existence, the vulnerability of the job to the vagaries of the business cycle, the ever-present possibility of being laid off.

Every governmental projection indicates a substantial increase during the next decade in the number of Americans who live under such conditions. The only category of industrial workers that will be in both absolute and relative decline over that period is that of the nonfarm laborers, which is supposed to fall from 3.6 million to 3.5 million. But the number of operatives and craftsmen will increase, and the unions that were created because of the common interest of this great mass are certain to grow in the foreseeable future into the largest membership organizations in the society. In 1980, then, the "old" working class will be larger than ever before in American history.

How is it that such a massive social phenomenon and such obvious trends have been ignored, or declared nonexistent, by many observers? In part, as Penn Kemble has argued, the vantage point of intellectual perception has changed radically during the past thirty years. The social critics of the 1960s and early '70s are relatively affluent compared to the marginality and even joblessness they had experienced during the depression. This change in their own class position may have made them less sensitive to the daily struggles of less-favored people. At the crudest this indifference could be rationalized by confusing the relative decline in manufacturing jobs—they accounted for 39.3 percent of nonagricultural employment in 1919 and for only 28.8 percent in 1969—with an absolute decrease in the number of workers and a consequent

loss of political and social power. This error was sometimes abetted by a failure to explore the fine print in the governmental definitions in which, to take one pertinent example, laundry workers, garage repairmen, and dishwashers in the service industries are not classified as blue collar.

Somewhat more subtly, there were those who acknowledged the existence of the traditional working class but argued that it had become co-opted by the society and therefore lost its distinctive character. But that, as we have just seen, is a misleading simplification. It may be that the workers, as Sweezy and Baran argue, want to be "integrated into the society as consumers," but it is surely of greater moment that the structure of injustice will not allow them, as a rule, even a "modest" income.

Still, the most sophisticated revision of the idea of the working class is based upon a very real, and momentous, shift in class structure (a shift that is also, as will be seen, the key to the emergence of a "new" working class). It is argued that economic classes defined by property relationships—entrepreneurs owning factories, shopkeepers their little businesses, farmers and peasants their plots of land, and workers possessing only their labor power to sell—have become obsolete. The joint stock company, Ralf Dahrendorf holds, separated ownership and control and thereby obviated a theory of class determined by property or the lack of it. He concludes that in the advanced economics authority, not ownership, is central to the formation of social class. And Alain Touraine writes, "It is anachronistic to depict social armies confronting each other. As we pass from societies of accumulation to programmed societies, relationships of power become increasingly more important than opposition between social groups."

These theories are usually developed

with the comment that Marx, fixated as he was upon a primitive model of capitalism, was unaware of such changes. . . . For even granting that there have been profound transformations in the structure of the advanced economies, some of them unforeseen by even so perspicacious a thinker as Marx, what is it that makes the workers I have just described more likely to join unions than any group in society? What predisposes them toward a certain political point of view? The answer, I believe, is embarrassingly old-fashioned. These workers derive their livelihoods almost exclusively from the sale of their labor power in an anonymous, and uncertain, labor market, and it is quite easy to distinguish them from their "fellow employees" who are corporation presidents or managers. There is a social chasm between these groups, not the infinite gradations postulated by Clark Kerr.

To begin with, in the upper reaches of the society property is not quite so passé as the notion of a clear-cut "separation" of ownership and control suggests. A 1967 Fortune survey revealed that 30 percent of the five hundred largest industrial concerns "are clearly controlled by identifiable individuals or by family groups." And, as that survey pointed out, absolute numbers can be more revealing than percentages when one deals with the holdings of the executive officer of a multi-billion-dollar corporation. The board chairman of General Motors at that time "only" owned 0.017 percent of the enterprise over which he presided—but that little fraction was worth $3.917 million. The chairman of Chrysler, with a mere 0.117 percent of his company's stock, had a $2.380 million interest in the business.

More generally, the nonowning managers at the top of the society accumulate wealth. They often enjoy special stock deals and other arrangements: in 1971 the Wall Street Journal reported

that the biggest part of executive pay in the auto industry was a bonus based on the size of profits. So it is that these managers must be counted among the golden elite, the 6.5 percent of the American consumer units which, in December 1962 (there has been no downward redistribution since), had incomes of $50,000 a year or more and owned 57 percent of the wealth of the society. At stake here is not simply the annual pay but, in Herman Miller's definition of wealth, "the sum total of equity in a home or business, liquid assets, investment assets, the value of automobiles owned and miscellaneous assets held in trust, loans to individuals, oil royalties, etc." By that standard, the "nonowning" managers own quite a bit.

The middle levels of management, particularly in the modern corporations, are not so easy to define and will be discussed at greater length in the section on the "new" working class. Now it is enough to note that this labor market is not anonymous, its salaries are not determined on a class basis, as in the case of workers, and it is less subject to the ups and downs of the business cycle. Some of the halcyon notions of the security of these strata were rudely dispelled by the recent Nixon recession, yet no one should have any trouble in distinguishing it from the lot of the wage workers.

So there is a distinct and identifiable universe of the working class even after one has taken into account the tremendous changes in class structure since Marx. The pay is better now, the boom-and-bust rhythm has been attenuated, the famous built-in stabilizers, such as unemployment insurance, are at work. Yet there are crucial elements of working class life—relative deprivation, the impersonality of the work process, greater susceptibility to layoffs than that experienced by other groups in the society, group wages—which remain and are the objective determinants of the class itself. Perhaps one of the best statements of this reality was made in the study of the English affluent worker carried out under the direction of John H. Goldthorpe and David Lockwood.

This project subjected the thesis of the *embourgeoisement* of the working class in that country to a careful empirical examination. It concluded that in England this co-optation simply had not taken place:

A factory worker can double his living standards and still remain a man who sells his labour to an employer in return for wages; he can work at a control panel rather than on an assembly line without changing his subordinate position in the organization of production; he can live in his own house in a "middle class" estate or suburb and still remain little involved in white collar social worlds.

English data cannot, of course, merely be imported to America and applied to the quite different variant of capitalism that exists here. Yet the objective indices show that in the United States as in England the worker is not an integrated participant in affluence but a member of a quite distinct stratum. And this stratum, for the most part, is neither poor nor modestly well off, indeed is better off than ever before—yet still quite deprived. But these statistics are of little political and intellectual significance if they simply describe unrelated facts about an inert mass. One has to come to the second part of Marx's famous distinction: Is the "old" working class a class "for itself," does it act collectively from a consciousness of its position in society?

III.

A preliminary warning: If one looks for a "European"-type class-consciousness in the United States—something like the attitude of that Frenchman, who, when T. S. Eliot accidentally jostled him, responded, "Me, I am a proletarian exploited by the capitalist class"—it cannot be found. It is not even necessary for my purposes that a majority of the workers used the term "working class" to describe their position in society. (When asked to locate themselves on a three-class scale of upper, middle, and lower, the overwhelming majority of Americans, including the members of the AFL-CIO, will say that they are middle-class; but on a five-class scale, on which the working class is in between the poor and the middle class, many more will identify themselves as working class.) I am not in search of a rhetoric but want to describe how workers behave politically in order to maximize goals which go beyond their immediate self-interest, or even the narrow advantage of their craft and skill, and which will have to do with the needs of the entire class and through it of the nation itself.

There are two major lines of argument, sometimes convergent, which hold that, even though there may be objective determinants of class in America, there has either never been or cannot now be any significant mass consciousness of that fact, moving workers to political or social action. On the one hand, it is said that the exceptional historical character of the national experience prevented the development of such a consciousness. On the other hand, it is claimed that the recent evolution of the American economy has produced a consensus in which interest groups compete over the details of the distribution of wealth but classes no longer contest more basic questions of the very mode of allocation itself.

The theory that America has always been immune from the class struggle is the generalization of a profound half-truth.[2] A country without a feudal past, possessing a vast continent to be settled once genocide had been committed

[2] What follows is a summary of a much more detailed, and documented, analysis to be found in my *Socialism* (New York, 1972).

against the Indians, and populated by successive waves of immigrants from the most varied European backgrounds, must differ in a number of crucial ways from the nation-states of the Old World where capitalism first emerged. Lenin wrote of America (and Britain) that there were "exceptionally favorable conditions, in comparison with other countries, for the deep-going and widespread development of capitalism."

Morris Hilquit, theorist of American socialism in the first third of the century, also talked of the "exceptional position" of America with its vast land mass, its prosperous agriculture, its tendency to make wage labor seem only a "temporary condition." But once we grant the apparent uniqueness of American capitalism, is it indeed true that class-consciousness failed to play an important, much less a decisive, role in the nation's history? I think not. The conditions we describe as "American exceptionalism" slowed the emergence of that consciousness and even made its anti-capitalism seem formally pro-capitalist. It did not, however, stop social class from becoming the most important single determinant in our political life.

Moreover, the chief factor inhibiting and distorting working-class self-consciousness was not, as is widely thought, the wealth of the society. Werner Sombart's famous remark that socialism in America ran aground "on shoals of roast beef and apple pie" was made in 1906 and has survived as a myth until this day. But, in a history of American labor (edited by that patriarch of the nonclass interpretation, J. R. Commons), Don Lescohier described as follows the two decades prior to World War I:

Undergoing the vicissitudes of repeated periods of unemployment, experiencing in many occupations a less rapid rise of wages than living costs, [the wage earners] could see that while some groups, like the building mechanics, had made distinct progress, other groups, like the iron and steel workers, employees in meat packing plants, cotton mills, saw mills, tobacco and clothing factories had not held their own against the rapidly rising cost of living.

Indeed, if one compares Germany and the United States between 1890 and 1914, the workers experienced steadily a relative rise in their living standards in the country that produced a mass social democratic movement rather than in the one that did not. But if it was not prosperity that prevented the development of a socialist class-consciousness in America, what was it? Selig Perlman provided part of the answer in his seminal Theory of the Labor Movement:

American labor remains the most heterogeneous laboring class in existence—ethnically, religiously and culturally. With a working class of such composition, to make socialism or communism the official "ism" of the movement would mean, even if other conditions permitted it, deliberately driving the Catholics, who are perhaps a majority in the American Federation of Labor, out of the labor movement, since with them an irreconcilable opposition to socialism is a matter of religious principle. Consequently, the only acceptable "consciousness" for American labor as a whole is "job consciousness" with a limited objective of "wage and job control" . . . .

Perlman was right: heterogeneity made it impossible to organize the great mass of the newly arriving European workers until the '30s and acted, in a thousand different ways, to impede consciousness of membership in a single and united class. Yet Perlman was wrong: even in the '20s when he wrote, and much more so later on, the workers were constantly forced by the exigencies of their class situation to go beyond "wage and job control" and raise class issues about the organization of the entire society. Strangely enough, many scholars failed to take note of this significant phenomenon. For they had adopted, even when they were anti-socialist, the criteria of the left wing of the Socialist party: that class-consciousness must necessarily and exclusively take the form of allegiance to a socialist or worker's party. That party alliance did not come about; class-consciousness did.

So by the early 1920s the majority of the AFL rebelled against Gompers' hostility to social legislation, adopted an approach very much like the one embodied in the socialist proposals that had been rejected during the 1890s, and embarked upon a course that led to an alliance with the Socialist party in the Conference for Progressive Political Action and support for the La Follette campaign in 1924. In 1920 the AFL was in favor of public ownership of the utilities, organization of cooperatives, and workmen's compensation. The railroad men were for the nationalization of their industry, and the Chicago Federation of Labor was in favor of a labor party. The AFL, as Phillip Taft has written of the period, "found itself, against its wishes, propelled into more active political participation." These developments did not, for the reasons Perlman described among others, take place in the guise of a socialist class-consciousness. But they were a clear indication that workers were being driven to consider not simply their jobs but the society as a whole.

The class-conscious movement of the '20s did not succeed and in the latter half of the decade there was a reversion to Gompers' "voluntarist" philosophy. But the reason for this reversal involved a trend that was to prepare the way for the great explosion of working-class militancy in the '30s. With immigration severely restricted after World War I, the expanding economy of the mid-1920s recruited its new workers from the farm and thus tipped the national demographic balance from rural to urban. The initial impact of this progressive turn of events was conservative. Ordinarily, one would have expected the unions to have grown and bettered their wages and working conditions during prosperity, but the influx of farmers, who could be satisfied by cheap wages and were suspicious of group action, depressed the labor market. The war and postwar militancy had driven the average weekly wage in manufacture up to $26.30 in 1920, but in 1921 wages dropped to $22.18 and in 1929 they had only reached $25.03, more than a dollar below the level of 1920.

Still, two momentous events had taken place in the '20s. The American working class was no longer a port of entry for millions of the foreign-born and was becoming, for the first time in its history, homogeneous; and labor was now part of a new urban majority. Once the discrepancy between low wages and high productivity in the '20s helped bring about the Great Depression, these developments were of enormous importance. They helped promote the organization of industrial workers in the CIO and were a major reason why a vast political movement based on class became a crucial feature of politics in the '30s. Richard Hofstadter, one of the few scholars to recognize the importance of this fact, wrote, "The demands of a large and powerful labor movement, combined with the interests of the unemployed, gave the New Deal a social democratic tinge that had never before been present in American reform movements."

IV.

For all the dramatic struggles of the 1930s, it is clear in retrospect that the working class was not in a revolutionary mood. This point must be stressed because many scholarly critics of the notion of a class struggle in the U.S. have unwittingly adopted not simply a Marxian definition of the concept but a "romantic" Marxian definition. For Raymond Aron, a seminal theorist of the notion of "industrial society" (i.e., of consensus capitalism), the class struggle exists only where there is a "fight to the death" between workers and capitalists which eventuates in violence.

Such an idea can indeed be found in *The Communist Manifesto*, for it is a corollary of Marx's youthful error of supposing that society was fast polarizing into only two classes. But the mature Marx did not hold this view and defined the class struggle in a far more subtle and complex fashion which can also serve as an excellent guide to the reality of the American 1930s—and '70s. In his famous Inaugural Address to the International Workingmen's Association, Marx spoke of a campaign to restrict the working day to ten hours in England as "a struggle between the blind rule of supply and demand, which is the political economy of the middle class, and the social control of production through intelligence and foresight, which is the political economy of the working class."

The kind of class struggle envisioned in *The Manifesto* did not emerge in the America of the 1930s or since; the kind analyzed in the Inaugural Address has. Given the obvious exigencies of the situation, the workers were committed as a class—and, with the elections of 1936, organized as a class—to win full-employment policies requiring that the government manage the economy. But if the American workers thus committed themselves to "the social control of production through intelligence and foresight, which is the political economy of the working class," they did not call this policy "socialist." It was not simply that the historic factors identified by Perlman were at work. Beyond that, as Leon Samson has ar-

gued in a fascinating book, Americanism had become a kind of "substitutive socialism." In this country, as distinct from Europe, bourgeois ideology itself stressed equality, classlessness, and the opportunity to share in wealth.

So in the '30s there emerged a mass political movement based upon class institutions (the unions) which demanded not simply narrow legislation related to the needs of this or that trade or craft, but a mode of planned social organization that would give priority to the value of full employment. Since it involves significant modifications of capitalist society as it had existed until then in the United States, this idea met with violent resistance, both physical and ideological, from most employers. They recognized that, even though the worker insisted upon his loyalty to the American ideal, he was reading it in terms of his own class needs.

Thus I would argue that, for all of its truly exceptional characteristics, American capitalism eventually forced its working class to become conscious of itself and to act as a major factor in political life. The theorists of industrial, or post-industrial, society might even grant this historical case. And they would add that in the period after World War II, changes in capitalist society led to the virtual disappearance of that class struggle.

V.

Raymond Aron was an early advocate of this view. Economic conflicts over wages and hours, he said, are quite real.

It is pure hypocrisy to think that they are always resolved in an equitable fashion, pure hypocrisy to deny a struggle over the division of the national income. But it does not thereby happen that, on the strictly economic plane, the group of workers and the group of capitalists oppose one another in a fight to the death, each one having an *essential* interest opposed to the other. The common interest of both, within the framework of the system [*cadre du régime*] is the prosperity of the enterprise and of the economy; it is growth whose necessary conditions correspond simultaneously to the interests of the managers and the employees.

Daniel Bell transposed Aron's thesis for America. There was, he said in the 1950s, an end of ideology. At certain points in his writing that phrase referred to the disappearance of grandiose simplifications about society, a happy event from any point of view. But at other points it announced a controversial trend: the disappearance from Western political life of debate and conflict over fundamental questions, a fading away of the very notion that there should or could be alternative forms of social organization. There was, Bell said,

a rough consensus among intellectuals on political issues: the acceptance of the Welfare State; the desirability of decentralized power; a system of mixed economy and of political pluralism. . . . [And] the workers, whose grievances were once the driving energy for social change, are more satisfied with the society than the intellectuals. The workers have not achieved utopia but their expectations were less than those of the intellectuals and their gains correspondingly larger.

In a much more recent statement of this theme, Bell wrote that the secret of Western society was "productivity." "Economic life could be a non zero-sum game; everyone could end up a winner, though with differential gains." But hardly had the end of ideology been proclaimed than the most tumultuous ideological decade in recent history began—the 1960s. There was a veritable explosion of ideology in the institutions of mass higher education in the advanced economies. And the workers, most dramatically in France and Italy, but in America, too, kept challeng-

ing the differential distribution of gains in strike after strike.

Was this merely a case of groups struggling bitterly over the terms of a consensus? Or, to take Aron's criterion of the most crucial precondition for the existence of a social class, was there a consciousness on the part of those American workers that "their class has a unique destiny and that it cannot fulfill its vocation except by transforming the totality [ensemble] of the social organization"? If the question is posed in this way, so reminiscent of both the early Marx and the early Lukacs, then there was no class struggle in America. Yet it can be demonstrated that American labor was by now more than a mere interest group. Its class-consciousness lies somewhere between the polar extremes of revolutionary transformation and interest politics.

There is, for instance, no question that the intrapersonal culture of the working class has been largely subverted by such changes in class structure as the movement of workers to the suburbs or the achievement of limited access to the consumption-oriented (and rigged) society. As Bennett Berger has documented, it is only in the old working-class neighborhoods, usually ethnic in character, that one finds a face-to-face and daily sense of a common class plight. The old coal-mining towns of Appalachia would be the most obvious example of the vanishing conditions under which social class pervades all aspects of life. But even in looking back, it is wrong to romanticize such working-class neighborhoods or to attribute to them, in Serge Mallet's phrase, a "pseudo-globalness." For instance, the Italian workers who were jammed together in New York before and after World War I were more loyal to their village in the old country, and to the *padroni* who exploited them here, than to their class.

Still, it seems obvious today, in contrast to a generation or two ago, that the worker does not enter a class community when he leaves the factory but rather participates more and more in the nonclass world of consumption. That has its positive side, as Herbert Gans discovered in his study of Levittown. The suburbanized worker, he learned, was not homogenized by the experience as much as critics of the '50s had thought. He became less localistic and suspicious, more inclined to participate in civic and political life. But, I would add, in becoming more of a "citizen" he became less of a worker.

Yet even as there were trends making the impact of classlessness pervasive in the daily life of the individual worker, the labor movement was moving into politics in a much more profound way than in the 1930s. By the end of the '60s, the AFL–CIO, the Auto Workers, and the Teamsters all supported an ongoing political apparatus which, in terms of money, lobbying, campaign workers, and the like, was a major factor in the United States. As David Greenstone documents in his book *Labor in American Politics*, "The emergence of organized labor as a major, nationwide electoral organization of the national Democratic Party was the most important change in the *structure* of the American party system during the last quarter of a century."

This signified the organization of a class, not merely an interest group. An interest group, as Greenstone points out, has very specific demands and avoids committing itself to a single party or a broad social program out of fear that it will compromise its narrow goals. Big corporations, which tend to be Republican, usually maintain a "Democratic" Vice-President to insure access to the White House no matter what. But the unions increasingly have become an organized component of the Democratic party. As Greenstone points out, they could have made a classic

interest-group deal in the '60s. If the AFL–CIO had agreed to let Everett Dirksen's congressional override of the Supreme Court's one man/one vote rule go through, Dirksen would have permitted the repeal of the federal enabling clause for state "right to work" laws. Such action on the latter issue would have meant the successful culmination of a trade-union campaign of more than two decades' duration. Yet labor maximized its long-range political program by standing fast on one man/one vote rather than giving priority to its short-range organizational goals.

The unions thus became a class political force, even if in a fairly undramatic way. There was little rhetoric of class war. Yet the very appearance of national health insurance as a political issue is primarily the result of a campaign waged for years by George Meany and Walter Reuther. Even in the area of race, where so many observers tend to pit blacks against the unions, labor is the most integrated single institution in U.S. society and has done more to raise the living standards of black Americans than any force except the federal government. Part of the confusion over this momentous trend stems from a reliance on polling data in most academic accounts of the labor movement. It is precisely the characteristic of an opinion poll that it reaches a man or woman as he or she is isolated and poses questions in a kind of political and social vacuum. It is therefore admirably suited to reflect the privatized area of a worker's mind but what it omits—as elections do not—is the effect of his participation in a workaday world, his membership in a class.

It is a failure to confront this complex reality that makes Derek Bok and John T. Dunlop miss the significance of trade-union political action in their study of *Labor and the American Community*. They point out that, as re-

His managed society

corded in the opinion polls, the workers have been giving decreasing support to union political action, and that their unions have become more and more political. The polls, I would suggest, do capture some private elements of workers' responses which in recent years have become more marked. But the elections reveal the much more significant fact that by and large those same workers vote massively in national elections for the Democratic candidates endorsed by their union. What Bok and Dunlop miss, then, is the class political attitude of the workers which is not at all the same as, and sometimes even contradicts, the sum totals of their private views. In 1968, for instance, the polls indicated significant support for George Wallace among young white workers in the North during the early fall. Yet when election day came, most of those same workers voted for Hubert Humphrey. Most of them had not changed their personal prejudices in the process, but they had understood that the exigencies of their class situation demanded they vote for a full-employment economy rather than against blacks—i.e., for Humphrey, not Wallace.

This kind of collectivism is far from the romantic Marxian consciousness as defined by Aron, but it is distinctive and clearly goes beyond narrow organizational interests. Moreover, there are a good many indications that the unions will be forced to be even more political in the coming period.

It is now apparent, even to its sophisticated devotees, that the free market is utterly incapable of allocating the resources of a technological society in a rational fashion. In 1971 Daniel Bell, who only a decade earlier had talked of the end of ideology, wrote,

It seems clear to me that, today, we in America are moving away from a society based on a private enterprise market system toward one in which the most important economic decisions will be made at the political level, in terms of consciously defined "goals" and "priorities." In the past there was an unspoken consensus and the public philosophy did not need to be articulated. And this was a strength, for articulation often invites trials for force when implicit differences are made manifest. Today, however, there is a visible change from market to non-market political decision making.

This marks, Bell concludes, "a movement away from governance by political economy to governance by political philosophy."

It is on the basis of this analysis that Bell has been writing about a "post-industrial" society in which the decisive "new men" are the

The 'new class'

scientists, the mathematicians, the economists and the engineers of the new computer technology. . . . The leadership of the new society will rest, not with business or corporations as we have known them (for a good deal of production will be routinized), but with the research corporation, the industrial laboratories, the experimental stations and the universities.

But which values will determine the priorities of these new men? Bell and John Kenneth Galbraith, whose "educational-scientific estate" is another name for the "new men," assume that these educated and generally liberal administrators of power will be able to pursue their own goals. That hope has been around for years and was brilliantly formulated by Thorstein Veblen in his essay collection *The Engineers and the Price System*, which dates back to 1919. The problem is that, from Veblen's day to this, the corporations have been profit-maximizers—more and more sophisticated in their definition of profit, to be sure—and have placed their own interests above those of the society or of the engineers who work for them. The automobile companies, to take a dramatic recent example, have been fighting auto safety and pollution controls for years.

It is at this point that the politics of the American working class become crucial. For if it is indeed true that economic decisions will be increasingly made by a political rather than a market process; if the question is how to manage the economy rather than whether to do so, then what mass force is there in society to fight for social values? Some "new men" might join a progressive political coalition in their off-duty hours but, under present conditions, their working lives will be dominated by corporate values that oppose, or at least would severely limit, any restrictions on the company's freedom of action. Moreover, the corporations tend to favor reactionary Keynesianism, in which the economy is stimulated by incentives to capital rather than through the meeting of human needs, which is social Keynesianism. The largest and most effective force in the society with a commitment to that kind of progressive Keynesianism is the trade-union movement.

In August 1971, when Richard Nixon tacitly admitted the bankruptcy of *laissez-faire* ideas which had created an ingenious recession-inflation, labor reacted in characteristic fashion. Nixon had proposed a federal job cut and a retreat from welfare reform, strict wage controls, vague price controls, and no limit on profits, dividends, and other forms of upper-class compensation. He further proposed an investment tax credit on machinery produced by American companies, a measure that might give business a $5 billion benefit (which would have to be added to the better than $3 billion a year earlier offered by the President in the form of accelerated depreciation for the corporations). The AFL–CIO Executive Council responded:

Instead of extending the helping hand of the federal government to the poor, the unemployed, the financially strapped states and cities, and to the inflation-plagued consumer, the President decided to further enrich big corporations and banks. . . . Mr. Nixon's program is based on the infamous "trickle down" theory. It would give huge sums of money belonging to the people of the United States to big corporations. He would do this at the expense of the poor, the state and local governments and their employees and wage and salary earners.

The AFL–CIO was here articulating what Marx called "the political economy of the working class" as it applies in a post-Keynesian society. This response is rooted in the class position of the members of the labor movement. They stand to gain from redistributionist federal policies favoring those either subaffluent or poor; they are opposed to a management of the economy that maximizes the interests of corporations. The difference between these two versions of Keynesianism is, I would suggest, both profound and systematic. Which one of them prevails will determine much about the shape of the future.

When Irving Louis Horowitz asks skeptically why the "interest-determined demands of the working class are somehow instinctively and intuitively more progressive than those of other sectors," he overlooks the union's stand on such an issue. It is the result, not of instinct or intuition, but of class position. For there is a working class "for itself" with a political consciousness that goes far beyond "job consciousness" and expresses itself in social reformism toward the society as a whole. This class consciousness is not revolutionary but, in practical and programmatic terms, it is remarkably similar to that found among the social democrats of Europe—even when it is sometimes couched in an antisocialist rhetoric. It is not based on that "world apart" of intrapersonal class values which existed at an earlier stage of capitalism. It might be more accurately described, to use a term employed by the British students of the affluent worker, as an "instrumental collectivism."

VI.

This working class, very different from the one studied by Marx, is at the moment going through a new mutation —one that has given rise to theories about a "new" working class.

There is no question that a momentous transformation of the American class structure is taking place. In 1980, according to the projections of the Department of Labor, there will be 15.5 million professional and technical workers and 15.4 million operatives (assemblers, truck drivers, bus drivers). That obviously describes a profound shift away from the industrial proletariat of semiskilled workers. In the decade of the '70s government statisticians expect the labor force to grow by about 25 percent. The categories exceeding that rate are professional and technical workers (50 percent), service workers (45 percent), clerical workers (35 percent), and sales workers (30 percent). Those which will lag behind the national average are managers, officials, and proprietors (22 percent); craftsmen and foremen (22 percent); private household workers (15 percent); operatives (10 percent); nonfarm laborers (−2 percent) and farm workers (−33 percent).

In part, the new patterns of education in the United States are a reflection of these changes in class. In 1940, only 37.8 percent of Americans between twenty-five and twenty-nine years of age had completed four years of high school or more; in 1970 that percentage had jumped to 75.4 percent. In 1940,

5.8 percent of the twenty-five to twenty-nine age group had four years of college or more, in 1970, 16.4 percent (the latter figure underestimates the recent increase in college degrees since it omits those between twenty-one and twenty-five in 1970, i.e., the age group with the highest percentage of graduates). These figures mean, among other things, that many children of the working class are now going to college. In 1969, only 23.7 percent of the family heads of students in college had themselves received a degree, which means they lacked a crucial precondition for middle-class status. The rich were, to be sure, disproportionately represented in higher education: 66 percent of the families with incomes of over $15,000 a year had a child in college in 1969, but only 16.4 percent of those with incomes under $3,000.

Yet when one turns to families with incomes in the general AFL–CIO range, the magnitude of the present social change becomes even more evident. Almost a third of the units in the $5,000–$7,499 group had a child in college, 41.8 percent of those in the $7,499–$9,999 group, and 49.0 percent of those with a $10,000–$15,000 annual income. And since, as Brendan and Patricia Sexton have pointed out, the average trade unionist of today is getting younger, these percentages can be expected to go up as the children of those now youthful workers reach college age.

These trends are likely to continue, and deepen, in the future. Yet there were some specific circumstances in the '60s that might have made these trends seem even more vigorous than they actually are. The tremendous growth in professional and technical employment was, in part at least, caused by federal outlays in space, defense, and education, all of which were cut back in the late '60s. It is sobering to realize that Bell's "new men" and Galbraith's "educational and scientific estate" may have loomed somewhat larger than life because of the impact of such federal policies. Certainly when Washington's cutbacks coincided, not accidentally, with the Nixon recession of the early '70s, there were extremely high rates of unemployment among the educated, including Ph.D.s with scientific and engineering degrees.

The liberal arts component of this surge was unplanned and, in some ways, irrational. As a significant number of such students, or graduates, realize that their education had no functional relationship to the society they were supposed to enter, they dropped out or sought alternative life-styles. One suspects that their plight was a consequence of America's refusal to face up to the revolutionary character of its technology, and disguising what would have been middle-class unemployment as middle-class education. In any case, college spending per student will not continue to increase faster than the Gross National Product, as it did in 1950–1970.

But even with these qualifications, it is clear that the new technology is calling into life a new class structure. The analytic problem arises when one tries to make statements about the political and social behavior of the new strata. In *Toward a Democratic Left* I spoke of these people as a "new class" rather than a "new working class" because I wanted to stress the discontinuities signaled by their appearance. In the present context my focus will be upon those factors which drive such professionals, technicians, and others in a trade-union direction—toward collective bargaining on the job and political pressure for full-employment policies outside the job. So I speak of a new working class. The choice of terms is not crucial; the careful delineation of a new social reality is.

The new strata are not the old middle class, nor the "new middle class" as it was recognized around the turn of the century. The old middle class was composed of men and women of property and income on a small scale. The "new middle class" was an educated salariat, and it was noted by Karl Kautsky as early as the 1890s. When William English Walling popularized Kautsky's views in 1912, he spoke of the possibility of winning the professional classes, the salaried corporation employees, and a large part of the office workers to socialism. But that stratum does not concern us here. The new stratum on which we focus is not based upon property or employment in the private corporation. Its members work, for the most part, in public, or semipublic sectors—education, health, social services, defense and defense-related industries, aerospace—and they are therefore dependent on federal political decisions for their economic well-being. They also tend to be employed by large organizations and often, for all their educational attainments, they are subordinate participants in a hierarchical system.

Let me be more specific.

First, there are those directly engaged in the development of technology, most of them classed as professional and technical workers. One of the most important subcategories of this group includes engineers and scientific technicians. In 1980, according to federal projections, there will be 1.4 million of them, an increase of 50 percent over the 1966 total, and a percentage that will be rising twice as fast as the national labor-force average. Of these, about 40 percent are technicians who will not have been to college but will have received post-high school training or have acquired sophisticated skills on the job. As the aerospace layoffs in 1970 and 1971 demonstrated, many of these workers are exceptionally vulnerable to policy shifts in Washington. Therefore—and in this they are typical of most of the people in the new strata —they offer a political base for a narrow, corporatist kind of lobbying, designed to protect particular jobs without reference to social cost or utility; or they could respond to a movement for democratic and social planning.

Second, there are the educated workers in the service industry, a category that will expand at much better than the average rate (45 percent as against 25 percent) for the decade. There are already two million of them, including schoolteachers in the National Education Association, nurses who belong to associations carrying out "job actions," people who belong to what Bok and Dunlop call "near unions." These groups engage in collective bargaining and political action but refuse, often for reasons of status, to affiliate with the AFL–CIO. But the service category also includes the members of the American Federation of Teachers (which, with more than 200,000 dues payers, is becoming an important union within the AFL–CIO) and the staff members of the Museum of Modern Art who, in September 1971, won a strike as members of a union local.

The trade unionists and the "near unionists" in the service sector tend to be employed, or financed, by the public in education, health care, and the like. There is every reason to expect that they will continue their present tendencies toward job organization and political involvement. Related to them, but not a part of the new strata, are the blue-collar workers in the public sector: policemen, firemen, hospital attendants, sanitation men. Their family backgrounds, education, and income make them a part of the traditional working class. But, like the professional and educated personnel in this area, they also are highly motivated to become active in politics. And by 1980 they will number in the millions.

Third, there are a number of more nebulous categories. In recent years most of the liberal arts students have looked toward teaching as a career. In *Fortune* magazine's 1968 survey of the college campus, 40 percent of the "forerunners"—the two-fifths of the student body who had rejected the vocational-school notion of the college—said that they were interested in teaching. But of the rest only 8 percent were thinking about going into business. Among the 50 percent not accounted for by those two choices will be found dropouts, lifestyle pioneers, artists, workers in communications, etc. They are not as easy to identify as the other groupings, yet they often have served as a cultural vanguard, and their presence should be noted.

Finally, there are deep-going changes taking place in traditional professions. In both the law and medical schools of the late '60s and early '70s there was a demand for more relevant education, and resistance to such established professional organizations as the American Bar Association and the American Medical Association. These trends are much too recent to survey in any but the most superficial of fashions, yet it is likely that the possibilities for legal and medical practice among the poor and the minorities, so important to these students and the young graduates, will depend upon federal decisions with regard to the fight against poverty and for national health care.

We are dealing then with social categories in change, particularly when one talks of the liberal arts students and the radicals in the traditional professions. And it is obvious that in many aspects of their life, above all in their education and income, most of these people more clearly resemble the salaried middle class than the working class. Yet there are important parallels between the new strata and the traditional working class; indeed, they permit one to speak of a "new working class" so long as it is understood that the phrase cannot be taken as a precise definition. Most of the new strata members occupy subordinate positions in large production units, and this is the basis for the unionism and "near unionism" which has already developed among them. Second, almost all of them are in jobs directly dependent upon the political process, and this means that their notion of collective bargaining includes political action from the very outset (indeed, the NEA lobbied long before it began to bargain). At the top of the income scale, particularly among the scientists and the engineers, the new strata shade off into the upper reaches of management; at the bottom, among the scientific technicians without college degrees, they merge with the more skilled members of the traditional working class. But in between those limits there is a large new grouping, numbered in the millions, which, for all its middle-class education and income, is impelled by virtue of its position in society toward collective bargaining and politics.

All of this should not be taken as implying extreme optimism about a future in which a still dynamic old working class will join with the organized new working class to make the good society. There are, as we have seen, status factors that can, and have, kept these groups far apart. There is a tendency toward corporatism in the new strata and in the old working class as well, with an emphasis on a very narrow and self-interested job protection. But there also is at least the possibility that the progressive tendencies in these two working classes, old and new, could provide the basis for a new political coalition in America dedicated to social and democratic—eventually perhaps social democratic—planning.

Bibliographical Note

I. HERBERT MARCUSE, *One-Dimensional Man* (Boston, 1964), p. 256. PAUL SWEEZY and PAUL BARAN, *Monopoly Capital* (New York, 1966), p. 363. ARTHUR SCHLESINGER, JR., "The New Liberal Coalition," the *Progressive*, April 1967, p. 16. CLARK KERR, *Marshall, Marx and Modern Times: The Multi-Dimensional Society* (Cambridge, England, 1969), pp. 36, 83. For Marx on class "in itself" and "for itself," see PROUDHON and MARX, *Misère de la Philosophie, Philosophie de la Misère* (Paris, 1964), p. 490.

II. U.S. BUREAU OF LABOR STATISTICS, *Labor Force Statistics: Handbook of Labor Statistics, 1970* (Washington, D.C.: Government Printing Office, 1970), Table 1, p. 25; Table 38, p. 80; Table 40, p. 83. See also, "24 Million Americans, Poverty in the United States, 1969," in *Working Poor: U.S. Bureau of the Census, Current Population Report*, series P-60, no. 76 (Washington, D.C.: U.S. Government Printing Office, 1970), Table 11, pp. 54–55. For workers' income, see BRENDAN SEXTON, "Middle-Class Workers and the New Politics," *Dissent*, May–June 1969; DEREK C. BOK and JOHN T. DUNLOP, *Labor and the American Community* (New York, 1970), p. 43; RUDOLPH OSWALD, "The City Workers Budget," *Federationist*, February 1968. See also *Wall Street Journal*, March 17, 1969; U.S. DEPARTMENT OF LABOR, *Manpower Projections: U.S. Manpower in the Seventies* (Washington, D.C.: Government Printing Office, 1970). For class income, see S. M. MILLER, "Can Workers Transform Society?" in Sar Levitan, ed., *Blue-Collar Workers* (New York, 1971). On the future of occupational categories, see *Manpower Projections: U.S. Manpower in the Seventies.* See also PENN KEMBLE, "Rediscovering American Labor," *Commentary,* April 1971. On manufacturing jobs, see BUREAU OF LABOR STATISTICS, *Employment and Earnings, U.S., 1909–1970,* Bulletin 1312-7 (Washington, D.C.: Government Printing Office, 1971), Chart I. See RALF DAHRENDORF, *Class and Class-Consciousness in Industrial Society,* rev. ed. (Stanford, 1966), pp. 31, 92–93. ALAIN TOURAINE, *The Post-Industrial Society* (New York, 1971), p. 172. The 1967 *Fortune* study is quoted in RALPH MILIBAND, *The State and Capitalist Society* (London, 1969), pp. 30, 36, no. 1. On executive bonus, see *Wall Street Journal,* September 1, 1971. On wealth, see HERMAN P. MILLER, *Rich Man, Poor Man,* rev. ed. (New York, 1970), p. 157, Table IX-3. See also JOHN H. GOLDTHORPE, DAVID LOCKWOOD, FRANK BECHHOFER, and JENNIFER PLATT, *The Affluent Worker in the Class Structure* (Cambridge, England, 1969), pp. 162–163.

III. V. I. LENIN, *Lenin on the United States* (New York, 1970), p. 24. MORRIS HILQUIT, *History of Socialism in the United States,* rev. ed. (New York, 1965; orig. 1909), pp. 137–139. SOMBART, *Warum gibt es in den Vereinigten Staaten keinen Sozialismus?* (Tübingen, 1906), p. 126. DON LESCOHIER, *History of Labor in the United States, 1886–1932* (New York, 1935), III, p. 60. SELIG PERLMAN, *The Theory of the Labor Movement* (New York, 1949; orig. 1928), pp. 168–169. PHILIP TAFT, *The AF of L in the Time of Gompers* (New York, 1957), p. 476. For IRVING BERNSTEIN on the 1920s, see *The Lean Years* (Boston, 1960), p. 55. On wage statistics in the '20s: U.S. BUREAU OF LABOR STATISTICS, *Historical Statistics of the United States, Colonial Times to 1957* (Washington, D.C.: U.S. Bureau of Labor Statistics, 1960), D626–34, RICHARD HOFSTADTER, *The Age of Reform* (New York, 1955), p. 308.

IV. RAYMOND ARON, *La Lutte des Classes* (Paris, 1964), pp. 106–107, 119–120. For Marx's Inaugural to IWMA, see MEW (Marx and Engels, *Works*), XV, p. 11. For the Employment Act of 1946, see STEPHEN KEMP BAILEY, *Congress Makes a Law* (New York, 1950); LOUIS BLANC, *Organization du Travail,* 5th ed. (Paris, 1848), *passim.* See LEON SAMSON, *Toward a United Front for American Workers* (New York, 1933), pp. 3ff, 21.

V. See RAYMOND ARON, *op. cit.,* pp. 106–107. See DANIEL BELL, *The End of Ideology* (New York, rev. ed., 1961), pp. 397–399; DANIEL BELL, "The Corporation and the Society in the 1970's," *Public Interest,* Summer 1971, p. 9. For Aron's definition of class, see *op. cit.,* p. 120. See BENNETT BERGER, *Working-Class Suburb* (Berkeley, 1960). MALLET, *La Nouvelle Classe Ouvrière* (Paris, 1969), p. 49. See HERBERT GANS, *The Levittowners* (New York, 1967), p. 195. J. DAVID GREENSTONE, *Labor in American Politics* (New York, 1969), *passim* and pp. xii–xiv. See DEREK C. BOK and JOHN T. DUNLOP, *Labor and the American Community* (New York, 1970), chap. 1. BELL, "The Corporation and the Society in the 1970's," *op. cit.,* pp. 31–32. For Bell on new men, see "Notes on the Post-Industrial Society," *Public Interest,* Winter 1967. See JOHN KENNETH GALBRAITH, *The New Industrial State* (Boston, 1967), p. 282ff. See THORSTEIN VEBLEN, *The Engineers and the Price System* (New York, 1933). For instrumental collectivism, see GOLDTHORPE, LOCKWOOD, *et al., op. cit.,* p. 190.

VI. See *Manpower Projections: U.S. Manpower in the Seventies, op. cit.* For educational statistics, see U.S. DEPARTMENT OF COMMERCE, *Characteristics of American Youth*, series P-23, no. 34 (Washington, D.C.: Government Printing Office, 1971).

45

How Important Is Social Class?

DENNIS H. WRONG

The old question of why there has been no socialism in the United States has often been answered by referring to the racial, ethnic, and religious divisions within the ranks of labor, which are the result of successive waves of overseas immigration and the partial incorporation into the labor force of the rural blacks. Accordingly, the American Left has been impatient with the ethnic loyalties and animosities of American workers, seeing them as fossilized survivals that retard the growth of class consciousness. Radicals have charged the ruling classes with deliberately fomenting racial and religious prejudice as part of a divide-and-rule strategy. Yet liberal pluralists have argued that multiple loyalties to class and interest organizations, nationality groups, and churches have enabled the United States to maintain a stable yet flexible social order, and to avoid bitter conflicts in which class, ethnic, and religious divisions are superimposed upon one another. Both radicals and liberals have joined in deploring the race consciousness of American workers, who have so often excluded Negroes, Orientals, and Mexican Americans from their organi-

Reprinted from *Dissent* (Winter 1972), by permission of the publisher, *Dissent Magazine*, New York, N. Y.

zations, thus subjecting these groups to relatively unrestrained exploitation.

These attitudes now have been modified by what Andrew Greeley has called "the legitimation of ethnic self-consciousness." New Left radicals and those liberals influenced by them have supported the growing ethnic solidarity of blacks, Chicanos, and American Indians. But they have looked with disfavor upon the revival of ethnic sentiments among whites—seeing them, not inaccurately, as a response to the new black militancy. Having written off the working class and its unions as a force for major change, the New Left is prone to dismiss the stirrings of ethnic awareness among blue-collar workers as no more than tokens of the incurable racism of the American society. Older socialists, though they have abandoned the millennial expectations of classical Marxism, have retained their attachment to the proletariat, accepting it as it is, "warts and all," as a force for peaceful democratic change. And many of them have, as a result, adopted a newly sympathetic attitude toward the American workers' ethnicities. Both ideological orientations—the emphasis of the New Left on racial pride and Third World nationalism, and older leftists' acceptance of the American working class in its full concreteness—have aroused new interest in the tangled web of class and ethnic identifications in American society.

Less politically committed social analysts also have long tended to minimize the role of ethnic groups in American society, seeing them as destined to disappear within a few generations. In the 1950s, religious identifications were thought to be acquiring new significance in an emerging "mass society" in which even objective class inequalities were supposed to be diminishing. A religious revival was widely proclaimed, and some survey researchers claimed that "religious affiliation" was becoming the crucial "variable," supplanting class, ethnicity, and rural-urban residence in accounting for surviving differences in behavior within an increasingly homogenized society. Religious organizations were seen as replacing the old ethnic associations founded by immigrants in providing individuals with secure group membership and social and emotional support as a protection against the impersonality of the larger society. Will Herberg's *Protestant-Catholic-Jew* and Gerhard Lenski's *The Religious Factor* were the two most impressive books representing these tendencies. Lenski, however, has recently conceded that ". . . *The Religious Factor* is, at best, a picture of an era that has ended." [1]

Sociologists and a host of popular social critics who exaggerated and oversimplified their conclusions called attention in the 1950s to new forms of community life in the expanding suburbs. Although it was recognized that economic and ethnic segregation was maintained and even increased in the suburbs, surburbia was seen primarily as a new and relatively classless way of

life, supplanting the old ethnic urban neighborhoods. It was thought to represent the future to which surviving working-class, lower-class, and ethnic subcultures would eventually succumb under the impact of continuing prosperity. Most of the commentary on suburbia was derisive in tone, and by the early '60s many sociologists were refuting negative stereotypes that had often originated in popularizations of earlier studies by their colleagues.[2]

Some stressed the persistence of class differences, even in suburbia itself, as against the view of a standardized suburban life-style embracing almost everyone. A smaller number argued that ethnic differences had far from disappeared. But even Nathan Glazer, who had insisted for years on the neglected and often subterranean influence of ethnic ties in American life, recently conceded in his introduction to a new edition of *Beyond the Melting Pot* that he and Daniel Patrick Moynihan had underestimated the durability of ethnicity in 1963, when they had concluded the first edition with the sentence "religion and race define the next stage in the evolution of the American peoples." [3]

In the early '60s, attention shifted from religion and suburbia back to the inner city and, to a lesser extent, to the rural and small-town South and the border-state region. The reason, of course, was the black revolution and the rediscovery of poverty. Racial discrimination and economic deprivation, victimizing a sizable minority of the

[1] Gerhard Lenski, "The Religious Factor in Detroit: Revisited," *American Sociological Review*, February 1971, p. 50.

[2] For a summary of this debate, see Dennis H. Wrong, "Suburbs and Myths of Suburbia," in Wrong and Harry L. Gracey, eds., *Readings in Introductory Sociology*, (New York: Macmillan, 1967), pp. 358–64.

[3] Nathan Glazer and Daniel Patrick Moynihan, "Introduction to the Second Edition: New York City in 1970," *Beyond the Melting Pot* (Cambridge, Mass.: MIT Press, 1970), pp. vii–viii.

total population, seemed more significant than the largely symbolic religious and intra-middle class differences stressed in the previous decade. The gradualist view of poverty as confined to "pockets," destined to be wiped out in the course of continued economic growth, no longer seemed plausible. Nor did the comfortable liberal notion that the elimination of racial discrimination constituted the "unfinished business of American democracy," bound to be achieved painlessly within a few decades. By the end of the '60s the student and youth revolts and the emergence of a new feminist movement had added age, generation, and sex to the list of major group identifications seen as shaping values in America.

Clearly, the shifts in the attention of social analysts from class to religious and residential, race, sex, and generational divisions reflect real discontinuities in the recent development of American society. But the mass media, with their voracious appetite for novelty, pick up and publicize each new group that comes into focus, enhancing the impression of discontinuity and casting into outer darkness the "Other Americans" or "forgotten men" or "silent majorities," who then have to be "rediscovered" when the currently fashionable group has been overexposed.

Yet the most scrupulous, perceptive sociological studies of different segments of American society give rise to disagreements as to exactly *which* group memberships or cultural identities account for the attitudes and lifestyles that even their critics concede they accurately describe. I shall give several illustrations of such controversies that arise out of the interpretation of the findings of some of the more influential recent sociological studies, stressing those bearing on class and ethnicity. Sociological research, to be sure, reveals the multiple affiliations and identities of its subjects; but sociologists, sometimes out of a polemical desire to refute prevailing scholarly or popular stereotypes, often stress the primacy of one set of social or cultural determinants over others. Even where this is avoided, the precise way in which age, generation, class, religion, ethnicity, race, and residence interact to produce a subcultural profile poses a difficult problem of analysis.

The sociologist Herbert Gans has insisted on the primacy of class, viewed as the resultant of income and educational and occupational opportunities, in shaping group values and behavior. Gans's first book was *The Urban Villagers*,[4] a study of an Italian community in the West End of Boston, which was influential in mobilizing liberal intellectuals against urban renewal projects that destroyed cohesive neighborhoods. Gans insisted that his subjects' way of life reflected a generic working class rather than a specifically Italian American subculture, pointing to patterns of family structure, sex role and courtship practices, and other values that West Enders shared with a wide variety of ethnically different working-class communities, including the culturally homogeneous British working class. In a review of the book Peter Rossi, one of the few leading American sociologists of Italian American origin, demurred. He invoked "memories of my childhood and adolescence in New York City during the twenties and thirties" to argue that "there is much more characteristically Italian (or perhaps more generally Latin) in the social organization of the West End than Gans would have the reader believe."[5]

In a later study of a planned suburban community in the Philadelphia

[4] New York, Macmillan Free Press, 1962.
[5] From Peter Rossi's review of *The Urban Villagers*, in the *American Journal of Sociology*, November 1964, pp. 381–82.

area, *The Levittowners*,[6] Herbert Gans attacked the "myth of suburbia," arguing that the move to the suburbs had not fundamentally changed class-determined life-styles and that the major conflicts in the multi-class community he studied arose out of clashes between upper-middle-class, on the one hand, and lower-middle and working-class values and interests, on the other. Gans has also been a major critic of the notion that there is an at least semi-autonomous "culture of poverty," insisting that the behavior of the poor is essentially a response to economic deprivation and lack of opportunity.

Bennett Berger's *Working-Class Suburb* was an earlier study attacking the suburban myth. It described, unlike *The Levittowners*, a purely working-class planned development in San Jose, California. Like Gans in *The Urban Villagers*, Berger argued that his subjects embodied an "incipient native white working-class culture" destined to replace older ethnic cultures, although in contrast to Gans the main thrust of his argument was directed against the claims of suburban residence rather than of ethnicity as a shaper of life-styles. "We have no clear images of *American* 'working-class style,'" Berger wrote,

precisely because the lowest positions on our socioeconomic ladder were traditionally occupied by the most recent groups of European immigrants, each of which, as they arrived, pushed earlier groups of immigrants up. Our images of working-class life, consequently, are dominated by ethnic motifs. But the end of mass immigration from Europe may promote the development of an indigenous white working-class culture in the United States in the near future . . . the blue-collar work force is likely to remain at between 20 and 25 million for some time to come, and it is extremely doubtful that Mexicans, Puerto Ricans, and Negroes

will constitute the major part of this industrial labor force. Moreover, the facts of color, marginal occupations (largely not unionized), and ghetto residence are likely to sustain the ethnicity of these groups for the foreseeable future and isolate them from the native, white working-class culture apparently incipient in the San Jose suburb.[7]

Berger's interpretation of his own evidence did not pass unchallenged. In a review Harold Wilensky argued that since Berger's community was only two years old at the time of the study, he had not given its residents sufficient time to develop such suburban middle-class patterns as the *Kaffee Klatsch* among wives, joining voluntary associations, becoming active in the church and PTA, reading consumer-oriented magazines, and raising their aspirations for their children.[8] Wilensky also claimed that Berger's own evidence suggested that some of these patterns were beginning to appear, although they had not been present in the grimy industrial slum Berger's respondents had inhabited before moving to the suburb. Wilensky concluded of Berger's community that "it looks like a suburban variant of lower-middle class culture."

In a later publication, Wilensky forcefully generalized his viewpoint, maintaining that

. . . in the United States and in other rich countries, class consciousness among manual workers is a transitional phenomenon characterizing workers not yet accustomed to the modern metropolis and the modern work place; that a clearly defined working class no longer exists, if it ever did; that much behavior and many attitudes said to be rooted in class are instead a matter of

---

[6] New York: Pantheon Books, 1967.

[7] Bennett Berger, *Working-Class Suburb* (Berkeley and Los Angeles: University of California Press, 1960), p. 95.

[8] From Harold Wilensky's review of *Working-Class Suburb*, in the *American Sociological Review*, April 1961, pp. 310–12.

race, religion, ethnic origin, education, age, and stage in the family life cycle.

Insofar as class categories remain at all useful, the line that divides stably employed, well-educated, well-paid workers from the lower class is becoming more important than the split between upper working class and lower middle class.[9]

The Gans-Rossi difference was over the relative importance of class as against ethnicity, but Berger and Wilensky disagreed over whether there are distinct lower-middle and working-class subcultures, although Wilensky was evidently inclined to attach more importance than either Gans or Berger to suburban residence as producing at least a "variant" of lower-middle-class culture. Wilensky's later statement, however, downgrades the significance of class as such. But he fails to distinguish between politically militant class consciousness in the Marxist sense and the more common emphasis in American sociology on class as the shaper of lifestyles and the source of a diffuse "consciousness of kind" that is hardly the same thing as Marxist class consciousness.

The concept of class has been used with reference to American life in three distinct ways. First, there is the Marxist model of classes as rival groups organized and mobilized for conflict arising out of clashing economic interests. Wilensky correctly questions the importance of this kind of "class consciousness" in the United States today and even in the past. Except perhaps for a few brief moments in the 1930s and in particular regions or industries, the American working class has not conformed to the Marxist model. There has never developed here a network of working-class interest associations and trade-union or party-created institutions sufficiently far-flung and powerful to constitute a distinctive subculture resembling the "nation within a nation" formed around the SPD in Imperial Germany.[10] The distinctive working-class way of life and "we-them" consciousness described by such English writers as Richard Hoggart, Raymond Williams, and E. P. Thompson has scarcely even been present in America.

Most American sociologists have favored a noneconomic conception of "social class," defining classes as aggregates of persons or families differing in values and behavior and forming a rank order of status levels. Most research on class in American communities has employed, at least implicitly, this view of classes as ranked subcultures. The studies of W. L. Warner and his associates in the 1930s and 1940s were pioneering examples. The much-criticized idea of a "culture of poverty" doubtless initially caught on so quickly because it was consistent with this approach.

However, when such sociologists as Herbert Gans and Bennett Berger insist on the importance of class in American life, they suggest a third conception. Essentially, they stress the role of economic inequalities in shaping people's aspirations and outlooks. Classes in this view are neither solidary groups mobilized for social conflict nor more diffuse groups sharing a common life-style and status pride. Rather, classes are groups whose members' aspirations and opportunities, beliefs and life-styles—far from reflecting a coherent self-sustaining culture or subculture—are basically shaped by their market position in the national economy, and, to use a formulation of Max Weber's, by their differential "life-

[9] Harold Wilensky, "Class, Class Consciousness and American Workers," in William Haber, ed., Labor in a Changing America (New York: Basic Books, 1966), pp. 12–28.

[10] Guenther Roth, The Social Democrats in Imperial Germany (Totowa, N.J.: Bedminster Press, 1963).

chances" in the commodity, credit, and labor markets.

Neither the alternative subcultural nor the unequal life-chance views conceive of classes as sharply defined groups inspiring intense loyalties and becoming the focus of self-consciously affirmed identities. True, such analysts as Veblen, the Lynds, Mills, and, more recently, G. William Domhoff have imputed at least a modified form of Marxist class consciousness to American upper or "ruling" classes.[11] And some versions of the subcultural model have pictured classes as membership groups creating strong identifications, at least at the local community level. But these partial exceptions either exclude the vast majority of Americans or confine, in Stanislaw Ossowski's phrase, "class structure in the social consciousness" to the local community.[12]

This is significant because it means that class fails to lend itself to the interpretation most favored by American sociologists to account for both changing and constant group loyalties and the process of identity-formation in America: what might be called the "protection-against-anomie" theory. Sociologists have contended that strong social bonds and identities based on religion, ethnicity, locality, and occupation have persisted or developed in America because they provide emotional security and a sense of community in face of the impersonality and rapid social change of the larger society. The fierce peer-group loyalties—often affirmed as "generational" solidarity—of the young, the appeal of communes, and the new popularity of encounter and sensitivity-training groups, all are recent phenomena readily explained in these terms. The "quest for community" as a reaction to the forces promoting anomie—whether these forces are primarily identified with capitalist market relations, industrialization, urbanization, bureaucratization, or all of these together—has long been a major theme of sociological• thought going back to 19th-century thinkers, in particular to Durkheim and Tönnies.

But the influence of class on conduct in America cannot be understood in terms of this theory, for neither classes nor associations based explicitly on class bonds and interests have been recognized objects of loyalty or membership groups with which people could proudly identify. Frank Tannenbaum's A Philosophy of Labor [13] is one of the very few efforts by an American to present trade unions as Gemeinschaften, protecting their members against the impersonal forces of industrial society rather than as limited economic-interest organizations. But even Tannenbaum was suggesting a potential role rather than describing an actual one. Milton Gordon in his Assimilation in American Life [14] argues that the combination of ethnic origin and class position has produced a group or collectivity he calls an "ethclass," and that this is the largest "reference group" with which Americans feel a positive sense of identification. People define themselves, Gordon maintains, primarily as upper-middle-class Jews, working-class Poles, or lower-class blacks rather than by class or ethnic origin alone.

De Tocqueville was the first to suggest that the leveling of class distinctions in the United States created the risk of an atomized, anonymous society, threatened by the "tyranny of the majority," and he saw the American

11 However, hard-headed corporate elites may have been in protecting and advancing their own interests, even in the 1930s the claim by upper-class conservatives that FDR was "a traitor to his class" had a forced, anachronistic ring.

12 Stanislaw Ossowski, Class Structure in the Social Consciousness (New York: Macmillan Free Press, 1963).

13 New York: Knopf, 1951.

14 New York: Oxford University Press, 1964.

predilection for forming voluntary associations as a response to this situation. Nearly a century later, such European theorists of "mass society" as Emil Lederer and Hannah Arendt held that the decline and breakup of social classes under the impact of war, inflation, and depression had produced a spiritual homelessness conducive to the rise of totalitarian movements that adopted slogans promising the restoration of brotherhood and community. But in America groups other than classes have played an intermediate role between the family and the total society, protecting the individual from anomie.

Sociologists have used the protection-against-anomie theory to account for everything from rises in the birth rate to the appeal of fanatical ideological movements; so it hardly suffices to explain why particular groups become major carriers of identity. "Why," Andrew Greeley asks,

was not social class the membership around which American city dwellers could rally, as it was in England? Why have the trade unions rarely, if ever, played quite the fraternal role in American society that they have in many continental societies? Granted that urban man needed something to provide him with some sort of identification between his family and the impersonal metropolis, why did he stick with the ethnic group when there were other groupings to which he could make a strong emotional commitment? [15]

Why, moreover, do different groups —churches, suburban communities, ethnic groups—appear to succeed one another as centers of "belongingness"? To a degree this is, as I have already noted, a matter of appearance encouraged by fashions in sociological theorizing and the nervous faddishness of the media. As Greeley observes,

The relevant issue for social research is not whether one [means of self-definition] replaces the other or even whether these factors are being replaced by yet another means of self-definition. The important question is, rather, under what sets of circumstances, which kinds of people find what sources of self-definition pertinent. When, for example, do I choose, explicitly or implicitly, to define myself as Irish, when as Catholic, when as Irish Catholic, when as an academic, when a Chicagoan, when as an American? [16]

But what, then, of the current "resurgence of ethnicity," noted by such sociologists as Greeley himself, Glazer and Moynihan, and increasingly publicized by the media? Obviously, the new assertiveness of blacks and the adoption of separatist slogans by some black militants have provided the occasion for a newly self-conscious and unapologetic ethnicity among whites. Yet this cannot be dismissed, as it so often is, as a mere cover for racism. Glazer and Moynihan suggest that

ethnic identities have taken over some of the task in self-definition and in definition by others that occupational identities, particularly working-class identities, have generally played. The status of the worker has been downgraded; as a result, apparently, the status of being an ethnic, a member of an ethnic group, has been upgraded. . . . Today, it may be better to be an Italian than a worker. Twenty years ago, it was the other way around. [17]

Such an emphasis on ethnicity rather than class or occupation reflects a general shift away from work identities and the workplace, which now has been noted in a variety of contexts for two decades. Even New Left radicals have argued that "the community" (the inner-city community, or ghetto) rather than the factory is now the major locus of social conflict. "Member of the com-

15 Andrew M. Greeley, *Why Can't They Be Like Us?* (New York: E. P. Dutton, 1971), p. 40.

16 *Ibid.*, p. 86.
17 Glazer and Moynihan, *op. cit.*, pp. xxxiv-xxxv.

munity" and "community control" have acquired in much radical rhetoric the aura that once attached to "worker" and "workers' control." Christopher Lasch, a spokesman for this outlook, has advocated "building socialism" in the ghetto, although in his critique of black nationalism he asks, "Would self-determination for the ghetto threaten General Motors?" And he answers in the negative—which should be sufficient to dispose of "socialism in one community" as a primary objective in itself.[18]

Recently, the assertion of a "generation gap," in which age and generation are regarded as crucial bases of identity and group allegiance, has been subjected to criticism that in many ways resembles the earlier debunking of the suburban myth.[19] Both critiques emphasized the persistence of class differences within, respectively, the younger generation and suburbia. College youth may have been attracted to the New Left and the counter culture; but, it is pointed out, George Wallace also drew disproportionate support in 1968 from working-class and lower-middle-class youth. These polar outlooks attract, nevertheless, minorities: most young people continue to divide on political and social issues along the same economic and educational lines as their parents.

The restless hunger of many young people for new ideals and new forms of group life has obviously been influential out of proportion to the numbers involved. As if in response, the erosion of familiar moral landmarks has evoked self-conscious reaffirmations of traditional ethnic, religious, and territorial

ties; this has, of course, happened often in the troubled course of modern history. Yet much as it has contributed to our understanding of the stresses of contemporary life, the emphasis of the sociological perspective on anomie and "alienation," "the quest for community," "identity crisis," and "the need for participation" tends to lead to a relative neglect of the importance of the *economic*, of inequality in income and opportunity, as major determinants of the fate of individuals and groups. It has been the special merit of such sociologists as Herbert Gans and S. M. Miller to remind us of the continuing, pervasive influence of economic forces at the national level. . . .

One negative counterpart of close-knit group ties, and the support they provide for the individual, has been the stifling of impulses to freedom, self-determination, and striking out on new paths. If ethnic groups have often, as Greeley acknowledges, been a "mobility trap" for their members, may not heightened ethnic solidarity lead to an even greater sense of imprisonment for working-class boys and, especially, girls, who have become aware in recent years of new options in life-styles and career patterns and a more permissive hedonist ethos? The life-styles of ghetto blacks living on welfare in matrifocal families have often enough been held up by white liberals as models for emulation; and critics of the violence, family instability, lack of achievement orientation, and the many physical and mental pathologies prevalent in the black underclass have been accused of being "hung up on middle-class values." Such anthropological romanticism is unlikely to promote the kind of social change needed to eliminate ghettos, poverty, and racial discrimination. Are we to extend it to white ethnic groups, celebrate the cultural diversity of American society—and ignore its persisting economic injustices and the continuing

18 Christopher Lasch, *The Agony of the American Left* (New York: Knopf, 1969), p. 133.
19 For a brief summary of the evidence, see Seymour Martin Lipset and Earl Raab, "The Non-Generation Gap," *Commentary*, August 1970, pp. 35–39.

arbitrary authority to which workers, both black and white, are subject on the job?

Despite the familiar claim that the ethnic diversity of the American labor force was a barrier to the birth of a powerful socialist movement, it is worth recalling that immigrant groups constituted the bulk of the membership of the newly created Communist party —or parties—after World War I.[20] Even 53 percent of the membership of the indigenous Socialist party was foreign-born by 1920.[21] The core of the New Deal coalition is usually described as consisting of labor and the urban minorities, although, to a considerable degree, these two groups contained the same people. If the Church of England, as the old saw has it, is the Tory party at prayer, it has been almost as true that America's white

ethnic groups have been the Democratic party and the union movement at home. Today "white ethnics" and "blue-collar workers"—when not the invidious "hard hats"—are terms often used interchangeably, each serving as a euphemism for the other in different contexts.

The revival of ethnic sentiments, therefore, need not be an obstacle to a coalition politics working through the Democratic party for reforms. One does not have to choose between extolling the new ethnicity, on the one hand, and ignoring or even deploring it, on the other. But recognition of the reality and the value of ethnic groups is no substitute for improving the school systems, reforming the tax structure, providing better housing, cleaning up the cities, and, in general, redistributing the good things of life in a way that will both increase the opportunities for individuals to escape from their ethnic communities, if they so wish, and improve the levels and quality of living in the ethnic communities themselves.

[20] Nathan Glazer, The Social Basis of American Communism (New York: Harcourt, Brace & World, 1961), chap. 2.
[21] James Weinstein, The Decline of Socialism in America, 1912–1925 (New York: Random House, 1967), p. 328.

G The Political Economy

INTRODUCTION

The social changes of the twentieth century have so increased the interdependence of politics and economics in advanced industrial societies that the old term *political economy* has acquired a new relevance. No longer is it useful to think of the state and the economy as separate, autonomous institutional orders. Indeed, the habit of so conceiving them always led to some distortion of reality and helped provide ideological support for nineteenth-century *laissez-faire* capitalism. It did, however, encourage the growth of economics and political science as specialized disciplines. Yet, today, no economist trying to understand the relations between the supply of goods, consumer demand, savings, and investment in a national economy can ignore the influence of political decisions on these quantities. And no political scientist can fail to see that conflict over the distribution of the national economic product has become the main domestic issue in the politics of democracies—the "democratic class struggle," as it has been aptly called.

The idea of capitalism held by both its defenders and its socialist critics in the nineteenth century has become so obsolete that some writers have claimed that the modern economic order in Western Europe and North America can no longer meaningfully be characterized as "capitalist"—a view at least implied by John Kenneth Galbraith in his discussion of the great American corporations and their industrial planning. The principal changes include the intervention of governments striving to control and even direct the capitalist market economy, the organization of much of the economy into large, powerful corporations—the "corporatization" of the economy—the partial militarization of both government and economy in World War II and the cold war, and the enormously increased complexity of modern technology.

Political democracy has resulted in the organization of parties to advance the interests of those groups suffering most severely from the unregulated workings of the market. Even in countries where these working-class and socialist parties have rarely been elected to office, the necessity of appealing for votes from their adherents has led conservative parties to adopt and enact parts of their program. Thus, government protection of the rights of trade unions, minimum wage laws, social services financed out of taxation, the redistribution of income through taxation, the use of fiscal controls to avert depressions and prevent unemployment, and the nationalization of some public utilities and basic industries have become permanent features of modern government. Collectively, they are often labeled the welfare state.

Welfare-state measures have been more fully accepted in Europe than in the United States, although the latter was the first nation to enact some of them as part of Roosevelt's New Deal in the 1930's. All major European political parties favor preserving and even strengthening the welfare state, whereas significant segments of American conservative opinion remain in opposition even to existing measures. European socialists and even some nonsocialists, as in the French Fifth Republic, are committed to increasing the public sector of the economy and instituting far-reaching national economic planning, measures that would further reduce the autonomy of private capitalists. Powerful support for such a program is lacking in the United States. Although the working class and ethnic minority groups have long supported the Democratic party and the Republican party has always had the support of the business community, socialist ideas and programs have never won a large following in America.

Yet, as Galbraith argues, the huge size of business organizations dictated by the cost and intricacy of the new technology enables them, in effect, to plan their production and sales schedules in virtual independence of autonomous market forces. America's lack of a precapitalist and feudal past accounts for the greater prestige of businessmen in this country. The dominant form of business enterprise, the giant corporation, has been fostered by the size and continental expanse of the American market and the labor shortages that stimulated the invention of mass-production technology. So great is the control of large corporations over the American economy that they possess autonomous decision-making powers in many other areas of social life. Although in no way accountable to political authority, they function as political institutions, deciding issues unrelated to the search for profits as such. Andrew Hacker discusses their role in American society, stressing that they concentrate power in bureaucratic organizations rather than in individuals or families.

In our third reading, Robert Boguslaw considers the unanticipated effects on work and bureaucratic organization of the introduction of high-speed computers. He assesses these effects in the light of rival emphases in sociological theory on *consensus* and *coercion* as alternative bases for holding society together, noting that designers of computer systems often assume that their authority will be accepted by those subject to it rather than experienced as coercive. Yet, neither skilled workers whose skills are made obsolete by computers nor middle-level administrators whose decision-making powers are transferred to computer programmers are likely to greet the new technology with unalloyed approval. Technology, Boguslaw argues, thus becomes a screen for introducing far-reaching changes in the stratification and power relations of large organizations. Boguslaw's analysis is congruent with fears expressed by many social critics today that the increasing implementation of decisions justified on strictly "technical" grounds represents a new way to by-pass democratic debate over, and participation in, social decision making.

The legislator is the prototype of the professional politician in American society. That he does not always feel his lot to be a happy one is suggested by Edward Shils's perceptive analysis of his role. American political parties are such loose coalitions of groups, lacking clear-cut national programs, that the legislator feels himself continuously exposed to the demands of his constituents, who are far from Washington and insensitive to the pressures of all the powerful centralized institutions in American life that are brought to bear on him in Congress. A symbol of democracy and yet often a man from the provinces lacking secure tenure in his job, he feels at an enormous disadvantage in confronting the more urbane and secure representatives of the executive bureaucracy, the Pentagon, and the corporate elite. Small wonder, Shils argues, that he often develops a fear and hatred of those forces identified with the trend toward bigness and centralized power in American life.

Political democracy based on universal suffrage is still less than a century old in most of the Western "bourgeois" democracies. In one selection, Dennis H. Wrong advances a theory as to how it has worked both to encourage and at the same time to limit social change—that is, purposive social change resulting from the political mobilization of the many groups constituting the social order who acquire at least potential power under democratic regimes. Wrong concentrates on the democratic class struggle between dominant and subordinate classes aligned, respectively, with Right and Left ideologies and programs. He draws most of his detailed examples from American political history but does not neglect the other Western democracies and the greater strains to which some of them have been subject in the past.

In the last selection, Christopher Lasch discusses those sudden, violent, politically instituted changes we call revolutions, those attempted total transformations of a society's political economy. Lasch reviews the pattern of the "classical" European revolutions of the eighteenth and nineteenth centuries and contemporary agrarian revolutions and argues the increasing obsolescence of these models for existing advanced industrial societies, especially the United States. He also summarizes and criticizes the conceptions of revolutionary possibility in America that have been prevalent on the political Left in recent years.

46
The New Industrial State

JOHN KENNETH GALBRAITH

1

A curiosity of modern economic life is the role of change. It is imagined to be very great; to list its forms or emphasize its extent is to show a reassuring grasp of the commonplace.

Yet not much is supposed to change. The economic system of the United States is praised on all occasions of public ceremony as a largely perfect structure. This is so elsewhere also. It is not easy to perfect what has been perfected. There is massive change but, except as the output of goods increases, all remains as before.

As to the change there is no doubt. The innovations and alterations in economic life in the last seventy years, and more especially since the beginning of World War II, have, by any calculation, been great. The most visible has been the application of increasingly intricate and sophisticated technology to the production of things. Machines have replaced crude manpower. And increasingly, as they are used to instruct other machines, they replace the cruder forms of human intelligence.

Seventy years ago the corporation was still confined to those industries—railroading, steamboating, steel-making, petroleum recovery and refining, some mining—where, it seemed, production had to be on a large scale. Now it also sells groceries, mills grain, publishes newspapers and provides public entertainment, all activities that were once the province of the individual proprietor or the insignificant firm. The largest firms deploy billions of dollars' worth of equipment and hundreds of thousands of men in scores of locations to produce hundreds of products. The five hundred largest corporations produce close to half of all the goods and services that are available annually in the United States.

Seventy years ago the corporation was the instrument of its owners and a projection of their personalities. The names of these principals—Carnegie, Rockefeller, Harriman, Mellon, Guggenheim, Ford—were known across the land. They are still known, but for the art galleries and philanthropic foundations they established and their descendants who are in politics. The men who now head the great corporations are unknown. Not for a generation have people outside Detroit and the automobile industry known the name of the current head of General Motors. In the manner of all men, he must produce identification when paying by check. So with Ford, Standard Oil and General Dynamics. The men

who now run the large corporations own no appreciable share of the enterprise. They are selected not by the stockholders but, in the common case, by a Board of Directors which narcissistically they selected themselves.

Equally it is a commonplace that the relation of the state to the economy has changed. The services of Federal, state and local governments now account for between a fifth and a quarter of all economic activity. In 1929 it was about eight per cent. This far exceeds the government share in such an avowedly socialist state as India, considerably exceeds that in the anciently social democratic kingdoms of Sweden and Norway, and is not wholly incommensurate with the share in Poland, a Communist country which, however, is heavily agricultural and which has left its agriculture in private ownership. A very large part (between one-third and one-half) of public activity is concerned with national defense and the exploration of space. This is not regarded even by conservatives as socialism. Elsewhere the nomenclature is less certain.

Additionally, in the wake of what is now called the Keynesian Revolution, the state undertakes to regulate the total income available for the purchase of goods and services in the economy. It seeks to insure sufficient purchasing power to buy whatever the current labor force can produce. And, more tentatively and with considerably less sanction in public attitudes, it seeks, given the resulting high employment, to keep wages from shoving up prices and prices from forcing up wages in a persistent upward spiral. Perhaps as a result of these arrangements, and perhaps only to test man's capacity for feckless optimism, the production of goods in modern times has been notably high and remarkably reliable.

Previously, from the earliest appearance of capitalism until the beginning of Hitler's war, expansion and recession had followed each other, at irregular intervals, but in steady procession. The business cycle had become a separate subject of economic study; the forecasting of its course and the explanation of its irregularities had become a modest profession in which reason, divination, incantation and elements of witchcraft had been combined in a manner not elsewhere seen save in the primitive religions. In the two decades following World War II, there was no serious depression; from 1947 until this writing (1966) there has been only one year in which real income in the United States has failed to rise.

Three further changes are less intimately a part of the established litany of accomplishment. First, there has been a further massive growth in the apparatus of persuasion and exhortation that is associated with the sale of goods. Measurement of the exposure, and susceptibility, of human beings to this persuasion is itself a flourishing science.

Second, there has been the beginning of the decline of the trade union. Union membership in the United States reached a peak in 1956. Since then employment has continued to grow; union membership in the main has gone down. Friends of the labor movement, and those who depend on it for a livelihood, picture this downturn as temporary or cyclical. Quite a few others have not noticed it. There is a strong presumption that it is deeply rooted in related and deeper change.

Finally, there has been a large expansion in enrollment for higher education together with a somewhat more modest increase in the means for providing it. This has been attributed to a new and penetrating concern for popular enlightenment. As with the fall in union membership, it has deeper roots. Had the economic system need only for millions of unlettered prole-

tarians, these, very plausibly, are what would be provided.

2

These changes or most of them have been much discussed. But to view them in isolation from each other, the usual practice, is greatly to minimize their effect. They are related to each other as cause to consequence. All are part of a yet larger matrix of change. In its effect on economic society this matrix has been more than the sum of its parts.

Thus mention has been made of machines and sophisticated technology. These require, in turn, heavy investment of capital. They are designed and guided by technically sophisticated men. They involve, also, a greatly increased elapse of time between any decision to produce and the emergence of a salable product.

From these changes come the need and the opportunity for the large business organization. It alone can deploy the requisite capital; it alone can mobilize the requisite skills. It can also do more. The large commitment of capital and organization well in advance of result requires that there be foresight and also that all feasible steps be taken to insure that what is foreseen will transpire. It can hardly be doubted that General Motors will be better able to influence the world around it—the prices and wages at which it buys and the prices at which it sells—than a man in suits and cloaks.

Nor is this all. The high production and income which are the fruits of advanced technology and expansive organization remove a very large part of the population from the compulsions and pressures of physical want. In consequence their economic behavior becomes in some measure malleable. No hungry man who is also sober can be persuaded to use his last dollar for anything but food. But a well-fed, well-clad, well-sheltered and otherwise well-tended person can be persuaded as between an electric razor and an electric toothbrush. Along with prices and costs, consumer demand becomes subject to management. This adds an important further element of control over environment.

When investment in technological development is very high, a wrong technical judgment or a failure in persuading consumers to buy the product can be extremely expensive. The cost and associated risk can be greatly reduced if the state pays for more exalted technical development or guarantees a market for the technically advanced product. Suitable justification—national defense, the needs of national prestige, support to indispensable industries such as supersonic travel—can readily be found. Modern technology thus defines a growing function of the modern state.

And technology and associated requirements in capital and time lead even more directly to the regulation of demand by the state. A corporation, contemplating an automobile of revised aspect, must be able to persuade people to buy it. It is equally important that people be able to do so. This is vital where heavy advance commitments of time and money must be made and where the product could as easily come to market in a time of depression as of prosperity. So there must be stabilization of overall demand.

Affluence adds to the need for such stabilization of aggregate demand. A man who lives close to the margin of subsistence must spend to exist and what he spends is spent. A man with ample income can save, and there is no assurance that what he saves will be offset by the spending or investment of others. Moreover, a rich society owes its productivity and income, at least in part, to large-scale organization—to the corporation. Corporations also have the option of retaining or saving from earnings—and can exercise it with the unique sense of righteousness of men who are imposing thrift on others. There is no guarantee that this corporate saving will be offset by spending. In consequence, in a community of high well-being, spending and hence demand are less reliable than in a poor one. They lose their reliability precisely when high costs and the long period of gestation imposed by modern technology require greater certainty of markets. The Keynesian Revolution occurred at the moment in history when other change had made it indispensable. Like the other changes with which this chapter began, it is intimately a cause and consequence of yet other change.

3

In economics, unlike fiction and the theater, there is no harm in a premature disclosure of the plot: it is to see the changes just mentioned and others as an interlocked whole. I venture to think that modern economic life is seen much more clearly when, as here, there is effort to see it whole.

I am also concerned to show how, in this larger context of change, the forces inducing human effort have changed. This assaults the most majestic of all economic assumptions, namely that man in his economic activities is subject to the authority of the market. Instead, we have an economic system which, whatever its formal ideological billing, is in substantial part a planned economy. The initiative in deciding what is to be produced comes not from the sovereign consumer who, through the market, issues the instructions that bend the productive mechanism to his ultimate will. Rather it comes from the great producing organization which reaches forward to control the markets that it is presumed to serve and, beyond, to bend the customer to its needs. And, in so doing, it deeply influences his values and beliefs—including not a few that will be mobilized in resistance to the present argument. One of the conclusions that follows from this analysis is that there is a broad convergence between industrial systems. The imperatives of technology and organization, not the images of ideology, are what determine the shape of economic society. This, on the whole, is fortunate although it will not necessarily be welcomed by those whose intellectual capital and moral fervor are invested in the present images of the market economy as the antithesis of social planning. Nor will it be welcomed by their disciples who, with lesser intellectual investment, carry the banners of free markets and free enterprise and therewith, by definition, of the free nations into political, military or diplomatic battle. Nor will it be welcomed by those who identify planning exclusively with socialism. These are not, alas, the ideas of the consensus.

Nor is the good fortune unqualified. The subordination of belief to industrial necessity and convenience is not in accordance with the greatest vision of man. Nor is it entirely safe. On the nature of this subjugation, and its consequences, I also dwell at some length.

.   .   .   .

4

Until the end of World War II, or shortly thereafter, planning was a moderately evocative word in the United States. It implied a sensible concern for what might happen in the future and a disposition, by forehanded action, to forestall avoidable misfortune. As persons won credit for competent planning of their lives, so communities won credit for effective planning of their environment. It was thought good to live in a well-planned city. The United States government had a National Resources Planning Board. During the war, postwar planning acquired the status of a modest industry in both the United States and the United Kingdom; it was felt that it would reassure those who were fighting as to the eventual utility as civilians.

With the cold war, however, the word planning acquired ideological overtones. The Communist countries not only socialized property, which seemed not a strong likelihood in the United States, but they planned, which somehow seemed more of a danger. Since liberty was there circumscribed, it followed that planning was something that the libertarian society should avoid. Modern liberalism carefully emphasizes tact rather than clarity of speech. Accordingly it avoided the term and conservatives made it one of opprobrium. For a public official to be called an economic planner was less serious than to be charged with Communism or imaginative perversion, but it reflected adversely nonetheless. One accepted and cherished whatever eventuated from the untrammeled operation of the market. Not only concern for liberty but a reputation for economic hardihood counseled such a course.

For understanding the economy and polity of the United States and other advanced industrial countries, this reaction against the word planning could hardly have been worse timed. It occurred when the increased use of technology and the accompanying commitment of time and capital were forcing extensive planning on all industrial communities. This has now been sensed. And, in many quarters, the word planning is again acquiring a measure of respectability.

Still what is not supposed to exist is often imagined not to exist. In consequence, the role of planning in the modern industrial society remains only slightly appreciated. Additionally, it is the sound instinct of conservatives that economic planning involves, inevitably, the control of individual behavior. The denial that we do any planning has helped to conceal the fact of such control even from those who are controlled.

5

In the market economy the price that is offered is counted upon to produce the result that is sought. Nothing more need be done. The consumer, by his offer to pay, obtains the necessary responding action by the firm that supplies his needs. By offering to pay yet more he gets more. And the firm, in its turn, by similar offers gets the labor, materials and equipment that it requires for production.

Planning exists because this process has ceased to be reliable. Technology, with its companion commitment of time and capital, means that the needs of the consumer must be anticipated—by months or years. When the distant day arrives the consumer's willingness to buy may well be lacking. By the same token, while common labor and carbon steel will be forthcoming in response to a promise to pay, the specialized skills and arcane materials required by advanced technology cannot similarly be counted upon. The needed action in both instances is evident: in addition to deciding what the consumer will want and will pay, the firm must take every feasible step to see that what it decides to produce is wanted by the consumer at a remunerative price. And it must see that the labor, materials and equipment that it needs will be available at a cost consistent with the price it will receive. It must exercise control over what is sold. It must exercise control over what is supplied. It must replace the market with planning.

That, as more time elapses and more capital is committed, it will be increasingly risky to rely on the untutored responses of the consumer needs no elaboration. And this will be increasingly so the more technically sophis-ticated the product. There is a certain likelihood that even two or three years hence there will be a fairly reliable consumer demand for strawberries, milk and fresh eggs. There is no similar assurance that people will want, so spontaneously, an automobile of particular color or contour, or a transistor of particular size or design.

The effect of technology, and related change, in reducing the reliability of the market for labor or equipment and in making imperative the planning of their procurement, is equally clear and can be seen in the simplest case.[1] If men use picks and shovels to build a road, they can be called out on the same morning that the decision is taken to do the job. The picks and shovels serve a variety of purposes; accordingly, the market stocks them in readily available quantities. It will help in getting manpower if, as Marx thought necessary, there is an industrial reserve army of the unemployed. But an equally prompt beginning is possible by raiding the work force of another employer of unskilled labor with the simple market promise of more pay.

When specifications are raised to modern superhighway standards and heavy machinery is introduced, the market no longer works as well. Engineers, draftsmen, drainage experts and those who arrange the elimination of trees, grass, parkland, streams and the other environmental amenities may not be readily available even in response to a substantial advance in pay. Bulldozers and heavy earth-moving equipment cannot be bought with the same facility as picks and shovels. In all of

[1] In technical terms the supply price of highly specialized materials, components and labor is inelastic. So is the demand for highly technical products. In the first instance large (and punishing) increases in prices will bring no added supply. In the second case large (and equally punishing) decreases will bring no added customers.

these cases anticipatory steps must be taken to insure that the necessary supply is available at an appropriate wage or price. Market behavior must be modified by some measure of planning.[2]

For inertial systems engineers, digital circuit design specialists, superconductivity research specialists, aeroelasticity investigators and radio test and evaluation engineers as also for titanium alloys in comparison with steel, and space vehicles as compared with motorcycles, the market is greatly less dependable. Need must be elaborately anticipated and arranged. The language of both industry and government reflects the modern fact. Civil War quartermasters went into the market for their needs. So, in turn, did the contractors who filled these orders. The equivalent procurement would now be programmed.

As viewed by the industrial firm, planning consists in foreseeing the actions required between the initiation of production and its completion and preparing for the accomplishment of these actions. And it consists also of foreseeing, and having a design for meeting, any unscheduled developments, favorable or otherwise, that may occur along the way.[3] As planning is viewed by the economist, political scientist or pundit, it consists of replacing prices and the market as the mechanism for determining what will be produced, with an authoritative determination of what will be produced and consumed and at what price. It will be thought that the word planning is being used in two different senses.

In practice, however, the two kinds of planning, if such they may be called, are inextricably associated. A firm cannot usefully foresee and schedule future action or prepare for contingencies if it does not know what its prices will be, what its sales will be, what its costs including labor and capital costs will be and what will be available at these costs. If the market is unreliable, it will not know these things. Hence it cannot plan. If, with advancing technology and associated specialization, the market becomes increasingly unreliable, industrial planning will become increasingly impossible unless the market also gives way to planning. Much of what the firm regards as planning consists in minimizing or getting rid of market influences.

6

A variety of strategies are available for dealing with the increasing unreliability of markets. Not all, in fact, require their replacement. If the item is unimportant, market uncertainty can be ignored. For General Electric it is a matter of considerable interest to know the price at which it will be able to buy high alloy steel or sell large generators, and the quantities that will be forthcoming or which can be sold. No similar urgency attaches to knowledge of the price at which flatware will be available for the plant cafeterias. And size is a solvent for uncertainty that cannot otherwise be eliminated. In the late nineteen-fifties and early nineteen-sixties, the Convair Division of General Dynamics Corporation lost $425 million on the manufacture of jet transports. Part of this was the result of uncertainties associated with research and de-

---

[2] That planning is necessary does not mean that it is well done. At any given time on any particular construction site, as everyone has observed, nothing much is happening. Planning, to anticipate and arrange material, machinery, manpower and subcontractor requirements, is necessary. But, in context, it is done with great imprecision or incompetence. Accordingly, something is normally being awaited.

[3] "In practice [business management] . . . aims to minimise uncertainty, minimise the consequences of uncertainty, or both." Robin Marris, *The Economic Theory of "Managerial" Capitalism* (New York: The Free Press of Glencoe, 1964), p. 232.

velopment; its 880 and 990 passenger jet cost more to bring into being than expected. But a major factor was the failure of the market—or more precisely default on or failure to obtain the contracts that were meant to reduce market uncertainty. The company did not fail (although it was a near thing) because it had annual revenues of around $2 billion from—in addition to aircraft—such diverse artifacts as missiles, building materials, submarines and telephones.[4] None of these was affected by the misfortunes of Convair. For a smaller company, with one product, a $425 million loss would have been uncomfortable. We have here an important explanation of one of the more notable corporate developments of recent times, the growth of the so-called polyglot corporation. It combines great size with highly diverse lines of manufacture. Thus it can absorb the adverse consequences of uncertainty that cannot otherwise be eliminated. Uncontrolled aversion of customers to one product, such as aircraft, is unlikely to affect telephones or building materials. The effects of market uncertainty are thus contained in what will often be a relatively small part of the total planning unit.

But the more common strategies require that the market be replaced by an authoritative determination of price and the amounts to be sold or bought at these prices. There are three ways of doing this:

(1) The market can be superseded.
(2) It can be controlled by sellers or buyers.
(3) It can be suspended for definite or indefinite periods by contract be-

tween the parties to sale and purchase.

All of these strategies are familiar features of the industrial system.

7

The market is superseded by what is commonly called vertical integration. The planning unit takes over the source of supply or the outlet; a transaction that is subject to bargaining over prices and amounts is thus replaced with a transfer within the planning unit. Where a firm is especially dependent on an important material or product— as an oil company on crude petroleum, a steel firm on ore,[5] an aluminum company on bauxite or Sears, Roebuck on appliances—there is always danger that the requisite supplies will be available only at inconvenient prices. To have control of supply—to rely not on the market but on its own sources of supply—is an elementary safeguard. This does not eliminate market uncertainty; rather, the large and unmanageable uncertainty as to the price of ore or crude is replaced by the smaller, more diffuse and more manageable uncertainties as to the costs of labor, drilling, ore transport and yet more remote raw materials. But this is a highly beneficial exchange. For Socony-Vacuum or Sohio, a change in the cost of crude is a serious matter, a change in the cost of drilling equipment a detail.

As viewed by the firm, elimination

---

[4] Richard Austin Smith, *Corporations in Crisis* (New York: Doubleday, 1963), pp. 91 *et seq.* The company's misfortunes in the sale of aircraft were intimately bound up with the contemporary difficulties of Howard Hughes at TWA.

[5] This problem has been of importance in the difficulties experienced in recent years by Wheeling Steel, a non-integrated producer. "Thus under its contracts Wheeling in the late 1950's and early 1960's, found itself powerless to trim ore supplies as sales fluctuated. . . . Moreover by the early 1960's the operating efficiencies of using beneficiated ores . . . were fully apparent, but Wheeling, tied to outmoded sources of supply, lagged behind many in the industry in using such ores." *Fortune*, June, 1965.

of a market converts an external negotiation and hence a partially or wholly uncontrollable decision to a matter for purely internal decision. Nothing, we shall see, better explains modern industrial policy in regard to capital and labor than the desire to make these highly strategic cost factors subject to purely internal decision.

Markets can also be controlled. This consists in reducing or eliminating the independence of action of those to whom the planning unit sells or from whom it buys. Their behavior being subject to control, uncertainty as to that behavior is reduced. At the same time the outward form of the market, including the process of buying and selling, remains formally intact.

This control of markets is the counterpart of large size and large size in relation to the particular market. A Wisconsin dairy farm cannot influence the price that it pays for fertilizer or machinery. Being small, its decision to purchase or not to purchase is of no appreciable significance to the supplier. The same is true of its sales. Having no control over its suppliers or its customers it pays and receives the going prices.

Not so with General Motors. Its decision to buy or not to buy will usually be very important to its suppliers; it may be a matter of survival. This induces a highly cooperative posture. So with any large firm.[6] Should it be neces-

sary to press matters, General Motors, unlike the dairyman, has always the possibility of supplying a material or component to itself. The option of eliminating a market is an important source of power for controlling it.[7]

Similarly, size allows General Motors as a seller to set prices for automobiles, diesels, trucks, refrigerators and the rest of its offering and be secure in the knowledge that no individual buyer, by withdrawing its custom, can force a change. The fact that GM is one of a few sellers adds to its control. Each seller shares the common interest in secure and certain prices; it is to the advantage of none to disrupt this mutual security system. Competitors of General Motors are especially unlikely to initiate

---

[6] Economists, in the past, have been at pains to disassociate large absolute size from large size in relation to the particular market. "Concentration [i.e. small numbers and hence large size in relation to the market] has nothing to do with size of firms, no matter by what resounding name it is called— big business, colossal corporation, financial giantism, etc. . . . most of my fellow economists would agree that 'absolute size is absolutely irrelevant.'" M. A. Adelman, Hearings before the Subcommittee on Antitrust and Monopoly of the Committee on the Judiciary, United States Senate, Eighty-

Eighth Congress, Second Session, Pursuant to S. Res. 262, Part I. *Economic Concentration. Overall and Conglomerate Aspects* (1964), p. 228. This contention, although wrong, is deeply grounded in contemporary economic attitudes.

Market power is associated by economists not with planning but with monopoly. Market concentration or monopoly in the conventional view is inimical to efficient employment of resources by the market and has strong overtones of illegality. If big business and monopoly power tend to be identical, then all big business is inefficient and presumptively illegal. This, however, given the evident role of large firms in the modern economy is absurd. So disassociation of absolute from relative size is important if traditional antipathy to monopoly is to seem sensible and big business is to be legitimate. In fact, large absolute size and large size relative to the market do go together. Great firms—General Motors, Standard Oil, Ford, United States Steel—are invariably large in relation to their principal markets. On this see the sensible remarks of Carl Kaysen, "The Corporation: How Much Power? What Scope?" in *The Corporation in Modern Society*, Edward S. Mason, ed. (Cambridge: Harvard University Press, 1959), p. 89.

[7] There are similar, although more complex, possibilities for control of the labor market to which I will return.

price reductions that might provoke further and retributive price-cutting. No formal communication is necessary to prevent such actions; this is considered naïve and arouses the professional wrath of company counsel. Everyone knows that the survivor of such a contest would not be the aggressor but General Motors. Thus do size and small numbers of competitors lead to market regulation.

Control of prices is only a part of market control; if uncertainty is to be eliminated there must also be control of the amount sold. But size also makes this possible. It allows advertising, a well-nutured sales organization and careful management of product design which can help to insure the needed customer response. And since General Motors produces some half of all the automobiles, its designs do not reflect the current mode, but are the current mode. The proper shape of an automobile, for most people, will be what the automobile majors decree the current shape to be. The control of demand, as we shall see later, is not perfect. But what is imperfect is not unimportant for reducing market uncertainty.

Finally, in an economy where units are large, firms can eliminate market uncertainty for each other. This they do by entering into contracts specifying prices and amounts to be provided or bought for substantial periods of time. A long-term contract by a Wisconsin dairy farmer to buy fertilizer or sell milk accords no great certainty to the fertilizer dealer or the dairy receiving the milk. It is subject to the capacity of the farmer to fulfill it; death, accident, drought, high feed costs and contagious abortion can all supervene. But a contract with the United States Steel Corporation to supply sheet steel or to take electric power is extremely reliable. In a world of large firms, it follows, there can be a matrix of contracts by which each firm eliminates market uncertainty

for other firms and, in turn, gives to them some of its own.

Outside of the industrial system, most notably in agriculture, the government also intervenes extensively to set prices and insure demand and thus to suspend the operation of the market and eliminate market uncertainty. This it does because the participating units—the individual farms—are not large enough to control prices. Technology and the associated commitment of capital and time require nonetheless that there be stable prices and assured demand. But within the industrial system, similar action is also required where exacting technology, with extensive research and development, mean a very long production period and a very large commitment of capital. Such is the case in the development and supply of modern weapons, in the exploration of space and in the development of a growing range of modern civilian products or services including transport planes, high-speed ground transport and various applied uses of nuclear energy. Here the state guarantees a price sufficient with suitable margin, to cover costs. And it undertakes to buy what is produced or to compensate fully in the case of contract cancellation. Thus, effectively, it suspends the market with all associated uncertainty. One consequence, as we shall see, is that in areas of most exacting and advanced technology the market is most completely replaced and planning is therefore most secure. As a further consequence this has become for the participants a very attractive part of the industrial system. The fully planned economy, so far from being unpopular, is warmly regarded by those who know it best.

8

Two things of some interest are evident from this analysis. It is clear, first of all, that industrial planning is in unabashed alliance with size. The large organization can tolerate market uncertainty as a smaller firm cannot. It can contract out of it as the smaller firm cannot. Vertical integration, the control of prices and consumer demand and reciprocal absorption of market uncertainty by contracts between firms all favor the large enterprise. And while smaller firms can appeal to the state to fix prices and insure demand, this security is also provided by the state to the big industrial firm when it is most needed. Those circumstances—the exacting technology, large commitments of time and capital—make it fairly certain that most of this government work will be done by large organizations.[8]

By all but the pathologically romantic, it is now recognized that this is not the age of the small man. But there is still a lingering presumption among economists that his retreat is not before the efficiency of the great corporation,

or even its technological proficiency, but before its monopoly power. It has superior capacity to extract profits. Therein lies its advantage. "Big business will undertake only such innovations as promise to enhance its profits and power, or protect its market position . . . free competitive men have always been the true innovators. Under the stern discipline of competition they must innovate to prosper and to survive."[9]

This, by the uncouth, would be called drivel. Size is the general servant of technology, not the special servant of profits. The small firm cannot be restored by breaking the power of the larger ones. It would require, rather, the rejection of the technology which since earliest consciousness we are taught to applaud. It would require that we have simple products made with simple equipment from readily available materials by unspecialized labor. Then the period of production would be short; the market would reliably provide the labor, equipment and materials required for production; there would be neither possibility nor need for managing the market for the finished product. If the market thus reigned there would be, and could be, no planning. No elaborate organization would be required. The small firm would then, at last, do very well. All that is necessary is to undo nearly everything that, at whatever violence to meaning, has been called progress in the last half century. There must be no thought of supersonic travel, or exploring the moon, and there will not be many automobiles.

We come thus to the second conclusion which is that the enemy of the

---

[8] In 1960, 384 firms with 5,000 employees or more accounted for an estimated 85 per cent of all industrial research-and-development expenditure. Firms employing fewer than 1,000 people, though numbering 260,000, accounted for only 7 per cent of such expenditure. An estimated 65 per cent of these funds were supplied by the Federal Government. (M. A. Adelman, Hearings before the Subcommittee on Antitrust and Monopoly of the Committee on the Judiciary, United States Senate, Eighty-Ninth Congress, First Session, Pursuant to S. Res. 70, Part III. *Economic Concentration. Concentration, Invention and Innovation* [1965], pp. 1137, 1140.) In recent years the high degree of market security in the use of Federal funds—a secure coverage of all costs and a secure market for the product—has allowed a considerable number of small firms to enter the manufacture of highly technical products. These firms line highways adjacent to major educational centers, most notably in Massachusetts and California, and have encouraged the belief that the small firm has a major foothold in the manufacture of highly technical products and components particularly for defense and space exploration. Their share of the total is, in fact, negligible.

[9] Horace M. Gray, Hearings before the Subcommittee on Antitrust and Monopoly of the Committee on the Judiciary, United States Senate, Eighty-Ninth Congress, First Session, Pursuant to S. Res. 70, Part III. *Economic Concentration. Concentration, Invention and Innovation* (1965), p. 1164.

market is not ideology but the engineer. In the Soviet Union and the Soviet-type economies, prices are extensively managed by the state. Production is not in response to market demand but given by the overall plan. In the western economies, markets are dominated by great firms. These establish prices and seek to insure a demand for what they have to sell. The enemies of the market are thus to be seen, although rarely in social matters has there been such a case of mistaken identity. It is not socialists. It is advanced technology and the specialization of men and process that this requires and the resulting commitment

of time and capital. These make the market work badly when the need is for greatly enhanced reliability—when planning is essential. The modern large corporation and the modern apparatus of socialist planning are variant accommodations to the same need. It is open to every freeborn man to dislike this accommodation. But he must direct his attack to the cause. He must not ask that jet aircraft, nuclear power plants or even the modern automobile in its modern volume be produced by firms that are subject to unfixed prices and unmanaged demand. He must ask instead that they not be produced.

47

The Social and Economic Power of Corporations

ANDREW HACKER

Problems like poverty, civil rights and juvenile delinquency may have been "discovered" only in the past few years, but such can hardly be said about the issue of bigness in American business. On and off, for the last three-quarters of a century, the question has been raised whether the nation's large corporations have reached the point where they can cut a swath through society without having to account for the consequences of their actions.

Allusions to "the trusts," "robber barons" and even "Wall Street" may have an archaic ring. Nevertheless, the frequency and magnitude of recent cor-

Reprinted from "A Country Called Corporate America" by Andrew Hacker in *The New York Times Magazine*, July 3, 1966. Copyright © 1966 by the New York Times Company. Reprinted by permission of the author and the publisher.

porate mergers, the high level of profits despite the persistence of poverty and the latest furor over safety in the country's leading industry are bringing renewed life to a debate that has as much importance for 1966 as did for 1896, 1912 and 1932.

Our large corporations are very large indeed. General Motors, for example, employs more than 600,000 people, a figure exceeding the combined payrolls of the state Governments of New York, California, Illinois, Pennsylvania, Texas and Ohio. The annual sales of Standard Oil of New Jersey are over $10 billion, more than the total tax collections of Wisconsin, Connecticut and Massachusetts, in addition to the six states just mentioned. In fact, our 50 largest companies have almost three times as many people working for them as our 50 states, and their combined sales are over five times greater than the taxes the states collect.

Yet here, as elsewhere, statistics can be made to tell several stories. For example, is big business getting bigger? Between 1957 and 1965, non-agricultural employment in the United States rose by about 10 percent. But during that same period the number of persons employed by the nation's largest industrial companies went up by 15 percent. Measured in this way, the big corporations seem to be taking three steps for every two taken by the economy as a whole.

At the same time it must be acknowledged that corporate America is by no means the fastest-growing sector in the country. Government employment, especially at the local level, is increasing at a higher rate; from 1957 to 1965 the public payroll, excluding the military, rose by 25 percent. Even higher was the percentage increase in service industries. Enterprises like boatyards, car washes and carry-out restaurants—many of them small and locally based—have come to constitute the most vital area of economic growth.

Moreover, the advent of automated processes in large-scale production has actually cut down corporate employment in several dominant industries. At the outset of 1965, for instance, such companies as General Electric and Gulf Oil and United States Steel actually had *fewer* people working for them than they had eight years earlier. While these firms are not yet typical, they may be harbingers of things to come—the apparent ability of corporations to increase their sales, production and profits with a decreasing work force.

If corporate size has a variety of yardsticks, corporate power is beyond precise measurement. It is not an overstatement to say that we know too much about the economics of big business and not nearly enough about the social impact of these institutions. Profes-

sional economists tend to focus on the freedom of large firms to set or manage prices, with the result that attention is deflected from the broader but less tangible role played by corporations in the society as a whole.

By the same token it is all too easy to expose egregious defects in consumer products or advertising or packaging. Congressional hearings make good forums for periodic charges of "irresponsibility," whether the target of the year happens to be automobiles or pharmaceuticals or cigarettes. It is true that the buyer is often stung—and sometimes laid to rest—by the products of even the most prestigeful of corporations. But the quality of merchandise, like the ability to fix prices, is only a secondary aspect of corporate power.

What calls for a good deal more thought and discussion is the general and pervasive influence of the large corporate entity in and on the society. For the decisions made in the names of these huge companies guide and govern, directly and indirectly, all of our lives.

The large corporations shape the material contours of the nation's life. While original ideas for new products may come from a variety of sources, it is the big companies that have the resources to bring these goods to the public. The argument that the consumer has "free will," deciding what he will and will not buy, can be taken just so far. (Too much can be made of the poor old Edsel.) For in actual fact we *do* buy much or even most of what the large corporations put on the shelves or in the showrooms for us.

To be sure, companies are not unsophisticated and have a fair idea of what the consumer will be willing to purchase. But the general rule, with fewer exceptions than we would like to think, is that if they make it we will buy it. Thus we air-condition our bedrooms, watch color television in our living rooms, brush our teeth electrically in the bathroom and cook at eye-level in the kitchen. It is time for frankness on this score: the American consumer is not notable for his imagination and does not know what he "wants." Thus he waits for corporate America to develop new products and, on hearing of them, discovers a long-felt "need" he never knew he had.

And more than any other single force in society, the large corporations govern the character and quality of the nation's labor market. The most visible example of this process has been the decision of companies to introduce computers into the world of work, bringing in train an unmistakable message to those who must earn a living. Millions of Americans are told, in so many words, what skills they will have to possess if they are to fill the jobs that will be available. A company has the freedom to decide *how* it will produce its goods and services, whether its product happens to be power mowers or life insurance or air transportation. And having made this decision, it establishes its recruiting patterns accordingly. Individuals, in short, must tailor themselves to the job if they want to work at all. Most of us and all of our children, will find ourselves adjusting to new styles of work whether we want to or not.

The impact of corporate organization and technology on the American educational system deserves far closer attention than it has been given. Whether we are talking of a vocational high school in Los Angeles or an engineering college in Milwaukee or a law school in New Haven, the shape of the curriculum is most largely determined by the job needs of our corporate enterprises. The message goes out that certain kinds of people having certain kinds of knowledge are needed. All American education, in a significant sense, is vocational. Liberal-arts students may enjoy a period of insulation but they are well aware that they will eventually have to find niches for themselves in offices or laboratories.

While many college graduates go into non-corporate or non-business employment, the fact remains that much of their educational tune is still being determined by corporate overtures. Even the liberal-arts college in which I teach has recently voted to establish within its precincts a department of "computer science." It is abundantly clear that while I.B.M. and Sperry Rand did not command Cornell to set up such a department, the university cannot afford to be insensitive to the changing character of the job market.

Our large firms both have and exercise the power to decide where they will build their new factories and offices. And these decisions, in their turn, determine which regions of the country will prosper and which will stagnate. The new fact of the South is, in largest measure, the result of corporate choices to open new facilities in what was hitherto a blighted area. Not only has this brought new money to the region, but new kinds of jobs and new styles of work have served to transform the Southern mentality. The transition to the 20th century has been most rapid in the communities where national corporations have settled. You cannot remain an unrepentant Confederate and expect to get on in Du Pont.

By the same token the regions which have not prospered in postwar years have been those where corporations have opted not to situate. Too much can be made of the New England "ghost towns." Actually corporations have "pulled out" of very few places; more critical has been their failure to establish or expand facilities in selected parts of the country. Thus patterns of migration—from the countryside to the city and from the city to the suburb—are reflections of corporation decisions on plant and office location. If men adjust to machines, they also move their bodies to where the jobs are.

Related to this have been the corporate decisions to rear their headquarters in the center of our largest cities, especially the East Side of New York. Leaving aside the architectural transformation and the esthetic investment with which we will have to live for many years, the very existence of these prestige-palaces has had the effect of drawing hundreds of thousands of people into metropolitan areas not equipped to handle them. Thus not only the traffic snarls and the commuter crush, but also the burgeoning of suburbs for the young-marrieds of management and the thin-walled apartments for others in their twenties, fifties and sixties.

Much—perhaps too much—has been made of ours being an age of "organization men." Yet there is more than a germ of truth in this depiction of the new white-collar class which is rapidly becoming the largest segment of the American population. The great corporations created this type of individual, and the habits and style of life of corporate employment continue to play a key role in setting values and aspirations for the population as a whole. Working for a large organization has a subtle but no less inevitable effect on a person's character. It calls for the virtues of adaptability, sociability, and that certain caution necessary when one knows one is forever being judged.

The types of success represented by the man who has become a senior engineer at Western Electric or a branch manager for Metropolitan Life are now models for millions. Not only does the prestige of the corporation rub off on the employe, but he seems to be affixed to an escalator that can only move in an upward direction. Too much has been made of the alleged "repudiation"

of business and the corporate life by the current generation of college students. This may be the case at Swarthmore, Oberlin and in certain Ivied circles. But in actual fact, the great majority of undergraduates, who are after all at places like Penn State and Purdue, would like nothing better than a good berth in Ford or Texaco. Indeed, they are even now priming themselves to become the sort of person that those companies will want them to be.

The pervasive influence of the large corporations, in these and other areas, derives less from how many people they employ and far more from their possession of great wealth. Our largest firms are very well-off indeed, and they have a good deal of spare cash to spend as and where they like. These companies make profits almost automatically every year, and they find it necessary to give only a fraction of those earnings back to their stockholders in the form of dividends.

(If the largest companies are "competitive" it is only really in the sense that we all are: all of us have to keep working at our jobs if we are to survive as viable members of the society. Quite clearly the biggest corporations stand no risk of going out of business. Of the firms ranking among the top 40 a dozen years ago all but two are still in preeminent positions. And the pair that slipped—Douglas Aircraft and Wilson meat-packing—continue to remain in the top 100.)

Thus the big firms have had the money to create millions of new white-collar jobs. Department heads in the large companies ask for and are assigned additional assistants, coordinators, planners and programmers who fill up new acres of office space every year. What is ironic, considering that this is the business world, is that attempts are hardly ever made to discover whether these desk-occupiers actually enhance the profitability or the productivity of the company. But everyone keeps busy enough: attending meetings and conferences, flying around the country, and writing and reading and amending memoranda.

White-collar featherbedding is endemic in the large corporation, and the spacious amenities accompanying such employment make work an altogether pleasant experience. The travel and the transfers and the credit-card way of life turn work into half-play and bring with them membership in a cosmopolitan world. That a large proportion of these employes are not necessary was illustrated about 10 years ago when the Chrysler Corporation had its back to the wall and was forced to take the unprecedented step of firing one-third of its white-collar force. Yet the wholesale departure of these clerks and executives, as it turned out, had no effect on the company's production and sales. Nevertheless, Chrysler was not one to show that an empire could function half-clothed, and it hired back the office workers it did not need just as soon as the cash was again available.

If all this sounds a bit Alice-in-Wonderland, it would be well to ponder on what the consequences would be were all of our major corporations to cut their white-collar staffs to only those who were actually needed. Could the nation bear the resulting unemployment, especially involving so many people who have been conditioned to believe that they possess special talents and qualities of character?

Corporate wealth, then, is spent as a corporation wishes. If General Motors wants to tear down the Savoy-Plaza and erect a corporate headquarters for itself at Fifth Avenue and 59th Street, it will go ahead and do so. Quite obviously an office building could, at a quarter of the cost, have been located on Eleventh Avenue and 17th Street. But why should cost be the prime consideration? After all, the stockholders have been paid their dividends, new production facilities have been put into operation, and there is still plenty of money left over. Nor is such a superfluity of spare cash limited to the very largest concerns. Ford, which is generally thought of as General Motors' poor sister, was sufficiently well-heeled to drop a quarter of a billion dollars on its Edsel and still not miss a dividend.

If our large corporations are using their power to reshape American society, indeed to reconstruct the American personality, the general public's thinking about such concentrated influence still remains ambiguous.

There persists, for example, the ideology of anti-trust and the fond place in American hearts still occupied by small business. Thus politicians can count on striking a resonant chord when they call for more vigorous prosecutions under the Sherman Law and for greater appropriations for the Small Business Administration. Most Americans, from time to time, do agree that our largest companies are too big and should somehow or other be broken up into smaller units. But just how strong or enduring this sentiment is is hard to say. No one really expects that Mobil Oil or Bethlehem Steel can or will be "busted" into 10 or a dozen entirely new and independent companies. Thus, if the ideology that bigness equals badness lingers on, there is no serious impetus to translate that outlook into action.

Part of the problem is that if Americans are suspicious of bigness, they are not really clear about just what it is about large corporations that troubles them. Despite the periodic exposures of defective brake cylinders or profiteering on polio vaccine, the big story is not really one of callous exploitation or crass irresponsibility. Given the American system of values, it is difficult to mount a thoroughgoing critique of capitalism or to be "anti-business" in an unequivocal way. The result is that our commentaries in this area are piecemeal and sporadic in character. We have the vocabularies for criticizing both "big government" and "big labor" but the image of the large corporation is a hazy one, and despite its everyday presence in our midst our reaction to its very existence is uncertain.

Take the question of who owns our big enterprises. In terms of legal title the owners are the stockholders, and management is accountable to that amorphous group. But it is well known that in most cases a company's shares are so widely dispersed that the managers of a corporation can run the firm pretty well as they please. Yet even assuming that the executives are acting with the tacit consent of their company's theoretical owners, it is worth inquiring just who these stockholders are.

Interestingly, a rising proportion of the stockholders are not people at all but rather investing institutions. Among these non-people are pension funds, insurance companies, brokerage houses, foundations and universities. Thus some of the most significant "voters" at the annual meetings of the big companies are the Rockefeller Foundation, Prudential Life and Princeton University. And these institutions, out of habit and prudence, automatically ratify management decisions.

It is instructive that the corporations' own public-relations departments have just about given up trying to persuade us that these stockholder gatherings are just another version of the local town meeting. The last report I saw that did this was filled with photographs showing average-citizen stockholders rising to question the board of directors on all manner of company policies. "A sizable number of share-holders participated in the lively discussion periods," the

reader is told. "Many more spoke individually with directors and other executives about the affairs of the company." However, in small type in the back of the report is an accounting of the five votes that were actually taken at the meeting. In no case did the management receive less than 96 percent of the ballots (i.e., shares) that were cast.

From these observations at least one answer is possible: yes, there is a "power élite" presiding over corporate America. Yet the problem with this term is that the "élite" in question consists not so much of identifiable personalities—how many of the presidents of our 20 largest corporations can any of us name?—but rather of the chairs in the top offices.

The typical corporation head stays at his desk for only about seven years. The power he exercises is less discretionary than we would like to believe, and the range of decisions that can be called uniquely his own is severely limited. (It is only in the small companies on the way up, such as the Romney days at American Motors, that the top men impress their personalities on the enterprise.) John Kenneth Galbraith once noted that when a corporation president retires and his successor is named, the price of the company's stock, presumably a barometer of informed opinion, does not experience a perceptible change.

Unfortunately it is far easier to think in terms of actual individuals than of impersonal institutions. Therefore it must be underlined that the so-called "élite" consists not of Frederic Donner and Frederick Kappel and Fred Borch but rather of *whatever* person happens to be sitting in the top seat at General Motors and A.T.&T. and General Electric. We are reaching the point where corporate power is a force in its own right, for all intents and purposes independent of the men who in its name make the decisions.

The modern corporation is not and cannot be expected to be a "responsible" institution in our society. For all the self-congratulatory handouts depicting the large firm as a "good citizen," the fact remains that a business enterprise exists purely and simply to make more profits—a large proportion of which it proceeds to pour back into itself. (True, the big companies do not seek to "maximize" their profits: their toleration of make-work and high living is enough evidence for this.)

But corporations, like all businesses whether large or small, are in the primary business of making money; indeed, they do not even exist to produce certain goods or services that may prove useful or necessary to society. If Eli Lilly or Searle and the other drug companies discovered that they could chalk up larger profits by getting out of vaccines and manufacturing frozen orange juice instead, they would have no qualms or hesitation about taking such a step.

A corporation, then, cannot be expected to shoulder the aristocratic mantle. No one should be surprised that in the areas of civil rights and civil liberties our large companies have failed to take any significant initiative. The men who preside over them are not philosopher-kings, and no expectation should be held out that they may become so. At best they can be counted on to give some well-publicized dollars to local community chests and university scholarships. But after those checks are written (and the handing-over of them has been photographed) it is time to get back to business.

And this is as it should be. Corporate power is great—in fact, far more impressive than corporation executives are willing to admit—and were large corporations to become "socialminded," their impact would be a very mixed blessing. For then the rest of us would have to let corporate management define just what constitutes "good citizenship," and we would have to accept such benefactions without an excuse for comment or criticism.

Therefore, when corporations, in the course of doing their business, create social dislocations there is no point in chiding or exhorting them to more enlightened ways. It would be wrong, of course, to lay the blame for all of our social ills at the doorsteps of the large firms. If the drug companies manufacture cheap and effective birth control pills it is a trifle presumptuous to take them to task for whatever promiscuity occurs as a consequence.

Nevertheless, the American corporation, in the course of creating and marketing new merchandise, presents us with temptations—ranging from fast cars to color television—to which we sooner or later succumb. There is nothing intrinsically wrong with color television. It is, rather, that the money we spend for a new set is money that can no longer be put aside for the college education of our children. (Thus, no one should be surprised when, 15 years from now, there is a demand for full Federal scholarships for college students. Not the least reason for such a demand will be that we were buying color TV back in 1966.)

Specific questions can be framed easily enough. It is the answers that are far from clear. We have unemployment: how far is it because corporations have not been willing or able to create enough jobs for the sorts of people who need them? We have a civil rights problem: how far is it because corporations have been reluctant to hire and train Negroes as they have whites? We have a shortage of nurses: how far is it because corporations outbid and undercut the hospitals by offering girls secretarial jobs at higher pay for less work? We have whole waves of unwanted and unneeded immigrants pouring into our large cities: how far is it because corporations have decided to locate in Ventura County in California rather than Woodruff County in Arkansas?

Questions like these may suggest differing answers but they do add up to the fact that a good measure of laissez-faire continues to exist in our corporate economy. For all their ritual protestations over Government intervention and regulation, our large companies are still remarkably free: free to make and sell what they want, free to hire the people they want for the jobs they have created, free to locate where they choose, free to dispose of their earnings as they like—and free to compel the society to provide the raw materials, human and otherwise, necessary for their ongoing needs.

The task of picking up the pieces left by the wayside belongs to Government. This is the ancient and implicit contract of a society committed to freedom of enterprise. But whether the agencies of Government have the resources or the public support to smooth out the dislocations that have been caused to our economy and society is not at all clear. Negro unemployment, the pollution of the Great Lakes, the architectural massacre of Park Avenue and the wasteland of television seem to be beyond the power and imagination of a Government that has traditionally understood its secondary and complementary role.

Corporate America, with its double-edged benefactions and its unplanned disruptions, is in fact creating new problems at a rate faster than our Governmental bureaus can possibly cope with them. Given that the articulate segments of the American public seem at times to show more confidence in United States Steel than in the United States Senate, the prognosis must be that the effective majority today prefers a mild but apparently bearable chaos to the prospect of serious Government allocation and planning.

The American commitment to private property means, at least for the foreseeable future, that we will be living with the large corporation. On the whole, Americans seem vaguely contented with this development, unanticipated as it may have been. In light of this stolidity the order of the day—to reverse Karl Marx's dictum—is to understand our world rather than change it; to identify, with as much clarity and precision as is possible, the extent to which a hundred or so giant firms are shaping the contours of our contemporary and future society. Only if we engage in such an enterprise will we be able to make any kind of considered judgment concerning the kind of nation in which we wish to live and the sort of people we want to be.

48

The Power of Systems and Systems of Power

ROBERT BOGUSLAW

One of the more popular pastimes developed in the wake of a rapidly burgeoning high-speed computer technology has been the game of "let's play you think computers are bad and I think they are good." In one reported encounter, the protagonists were Norbert Wiener (the father of cybernetics) and Arthur L. Samuel (one of IBM's bright sons). Wiener stated as his thesis that "machines can and do transcend some of the limitations of their designers, and that in doing so they may be both effective and dangerous." [1] Samuel, invoking the familiar argument that "most, if not all, of man's inventions are instrumentalities which may be employed by both saints and sinners," [2] concluded that "the modern digital computer is a modality whose value is overwhelmingly on the side of the good." [3]

History does not record a score for this particular contest, but one is tempted to question whether the game was played in the right ballpark. The Wiener thesis seems to proceed from a perspective that sees the computer as something like a bow-and-arrow contraption possessing more or less indeterminate, boomeranglike performance

characteristics. Samuel seems to see his product essentially as a better mousetrap (and who wants to be on the side of the rats)?

There is, of course, at least one additional perspective from which we may contemplate the computer. This is the perspective that helps us to see it as an integral part of a larger, more encompassing social structure. Computers are not found in nature. They have to be built. And they must take their places within a framework of existing social systems. A decision to place them within a framework redefines existing system arrangements in significant ways. Indeed, as computer complexes assume functions previously performed by bureaucratic hierarchies or disparate units or unorganized work groups, they almost invariably lead to the redesign of existing systems. Specifically, this means changes in information organization (with the aid of computers or other physical equipment), formalized work procedures (that is, customs, computer programs, organizational directives, and so forth), and people.

The process of engaging in this redesign inevitably raises issues about how various system "functions" are to be accomplished. Without becoming embroiled in the intricacies of several hoary controversies among anthropologists and sociologists about the precise meaning of function and the usefulness of "functional analysis" we may note a formulation that defines function as the contribution an activity within a system makes to the whole.[4] This defi-

Robert Boguslaw, The New Utopians: A Study of System Design and Social Change, © 1965, pp. 181–190, 199–200. Reprinted by permission of Prentice-Hall, Inc., Englewood Cliffs, New Jersey.
[1] Norbert Wiener, "Some Moral and Technical Consequences of Automation," in Morris Philipson (ed.), Automation Implications for the Future (New York: Random House, 1962), p. 163.
[2] Arthur L. Samuel, "Some Moral and Technical Consequences of Automation—A Refutation," ibid., p. 179.
[3] Ibid.

[4] Harold Fallding, "Functional Analysis in Sociology," American Sociological Review, 28:1 (February 1963).

nition points up the importance of "specifying precisely both the part and the whole to which a functional statement refers. A practice which is functional within one social region need not be functional in one which is more (or less) inclusive." [5]

The credo of an engineer designing systems composed exclusively of physical or "hardware" components includes the assumption that all functions performed by the components will be *manifest* (that is, "intended and recognized" by the designer).[6] *Latent* functions (those that are neither intended nor recognized) are hopefully omitted. The same credo is held by designers of classical utopias.

The difficulties that arise when computerized systems are designed *without* deviating from this credo have become legend among sophisticates. Suppose, for example, you wish to "automate" the communication functions carried on within a large system. A preliminary step must consist of a detailed specification of the various classes of information currently being communicated. To obtain such a specification, one might examine messages transmitted in the past, and perhaps codify the information normally transmitted over telephone or telegraph lines, and so on. In the process of conducting such an examination, it is all too easy for the neophyte to overlook classes of information characteristically transmitted, let us say, during coffee breaks. Ignoring the latent communicative function of the coffee break can result in a highly complex computerized system that has no way of dealing with some of its most crucial categories of system information.

As Robert K. Merton expressed it

many years ago, "any attempt to eliminate an existing social structure without providing adequate alternative structures for fulfilling the functions previously fulfilled by the abolished organization is doomed to failure." [7]

Now one of the most pervasive characteristics of all social structures is the fact of social differentiation. This, in itself, does not seem very startling. We are accustomed to the notion that some people are old and some young, some female, some male, and so forth. Social differentiation becomes a matter for controversy only after it is used as a basis for social stratification: the distribution of unequal rewards among the various participants in a social system.

Many years ago, two sociologists (Kingsley Davis and Wilbert E. Moore) tried to explain these differences essentially on the basis that

if the more important, highly skilled, and physically and psychologically demanding positions in a complex division of labor are to be adequately filled both from the standpoint of numbers and of minimally efficient performance, *then* there must be *some* unequal rewards favoring these positions over others.[8]

It seems clear that the particular scale of unequal rewards existing in a society tends to be self-perpetuating. People become accustomed to the allocation of certain differences in reward and tend to resist drastic changes.[9] A president of an industrial firm makes more money than a charwoman—this is considered appropriate and fair; and anyone who suggested a reversal in the reward system for our society would encounter serious resistance, not only from presidents, but from most "rea-

---

[5] *Ibid.*, p. 6.
[6] Robert K. Merton, "Manifest and Latent Functions," in *Social Theory and Social Structure*, rev. ed. (New York: Free Press of Glencoe, 1957), p. 51.

[7] *Ibid.*, p. 81.
[8] Cf. Dennis H. Wrong, "The Functional Theory of Stratification: Some Neglected Considerations," *American Sociological Review*, 24:6 (December 1959), p. 774.
[9] *Ibid.*

sonable" people—including charwomen.

In designing a computerized system on the site of a previously existing "manual" social structure, one inevitably must deal with the effects the new system will have on previously existing roles and their incumbents. When the role incumbents are unskilled or semi-skilled workers whose more or less routinized jobs are assumed by the computerized installation, this takes the form of concern with "technological displacement" and consideration of the consequences of "automation." The dialogue may proceed along lines of "these displaced workers must be trained for new skills—like computer programming; however, some people are untrainable and they constitute the core of the social problem accompanying automation. This is something like what happened when the automobile replaced the horse and buggy—new jobs will emerge for which people can be trained —the blacksmiths will simply have to face reality, and so forth."

In terms of social stratification, the human, low-skilled workers are simply eliminated. They are not just placed at the bottom of the status and economic-reward ladder; they are removed from it.

But this removal inevitably has direct consequences for those who remain. The middle-level bureaucrat whose value consisted primarily of the uncodified information in his desk, file, or head now finds that he has been asked to furnish all relevant information to a central repository. Much of the prior basis of his unequal reward has been removed. The second- or third-level executive whose value consisted of an ability to analyze large quantities of data and come up with significant policy recommendations now finds his data analysis can be done more effectively according to predetermined analytical schemes. The highly skilled and psychologically demanding positions become those relating to operations of the computer and the formulation of computer programs.

All this, of course, shakes the foundations of existing stratification realities. Former "key decision makers" begin to feel, and indeed are regarded, as anachronistic hangers-on. Experienced computer experts have many techniques for dealing with this problem. One approach is to point out that the locus of decision making still rests with the former executive or manager. This, of course, is not really true. Disbelievers see the light when they ask for a given set of figures or ask that a pet procedure be implemented.

The answer, all too frequently, becomes "but the program can't handle it." Or, "We can't do that just yet, but in about six months, after these immediate problems are ironed out, I'm sure we can get that for you." Or, "This set of figures will cover about 98 percent of all the cases you could possibly be interested in; it just wouldn't be economical to try to get 100 percent of all the cases," and so on.

To an executive accustomed to getting his own way from human employees, even if they have to work overtime or develop ulcers in the process, this may all sound like an unpardonable affront to managerial prerogatives. He is thus inexorably driven to the next step in the process—the "I want a computer course" step. The feeling seems to be: "If I could only learn a little about computer programming, I could keep those snotty kids from being in a position to tell me how to run my business."

But, unfortunately, computer courses for executives seldom provide enduring solutions. At best, the executive learns to deal with his frustrations by accepting the frame of reference of the computer expert and adjusting his sights accordingly. The exercise of power, which formerly was mediated through conventions of law, custom, "what the union will stand still for," or "principles of human relations"—now must be mediated through the current state of computer technology.

To proceed in this fashion (that is, through technology-screened power) is to adopt an orientation that is essentially formalist in nature (although the work of Newell, Simon, and Shaw in the area of heuristic programming provides the promise of creative alternatives). The specification of future and current system states within this orientation characteristically requires an insistence upon a uniformity of perspective, a standardization of language, and a consensus of values that is characteristic of highly authoritarian social structures. Nonconforming perspectives, language, and values can be and, indeed, must be excluded as system elements.

All this is a familiar pattern in classical utopias. Although the inhabitants of utopian societies were frequently prepared to deal with external threats, internal dissension was almost invariably taboo. The tradition of specifying functions within computer-based systems enhances the points of structural correspondence of these systems and classical utopias. In this connection, Ralf Dahrendorf's summary of the structural features of utopian societies provides some useful insights. He points out that: (1) Utopias do not grow out of familiar reality or follow realistic patterns of development. (2) Utopias characteristically have universal consensus on values and institutional arrangements; that is, they are highly uniform throughout. (3) Utopias are characterized by an absence of internal conflict; that is, they are characterized by social harmony, which helps to account for their stability. (4) All processes within utopian societies follow recurrent patterns

and occur as part of the design of the whole. (5) Utopias are characteristically isolated in time and space from other parts of the world.[10]

The simple fact of the matter seems to be that classically designed computer-based systems, like classical utopias, resolve problems of conflict, consensus, and reality by simple fiat. But these old problems do not thereby simply fade away. Environments change. Internal conditions change. Systems and utopias alike must be ready and able to change if they are to survive. But crucial types of change originate *within* systems—out of the contradictions and conflicts existing between two or more opposing sets of values, ideologies, roles, institutions, or groups.[11]

To insist that social structures must always be shaped and controlled from "topside," is to reinforce maladaptive tendencies in systems and to help to ensure their ultimate collapse. A façade of value homogeneity cannot resolve the internal stresses, conflicts, and dilemmas that arise in any system designed to cope effectively with the fact of change.

Power and Bureaucracy

The problem of understanding what it is that makes human societies "stick together" or cohere has been studied by philosophers and social theorists for thousands of years. In general, two different kinds of explanation are offered. The first of these emphasizes the role of *consensus*—the existence of a general agreement on values within the society. The second explanation empha-

[10] Cf. Ralf Dahrendorf, "Out of Utopia: Toward a Reorientation of Sociological Analysis," *American Journal of Sociology*, 64:2 (September 1958), pp. 116–117.

[11] Cf. Pierre L. Van Den Berghe, "Dialetic and Functionalism: Toward a Theoretical Synthesis," *American Sociological Review*, 28:5 (October 1963), p. 699.

sizes the role of *coercion*—the use of force and constraint to hold a society together.[12]

One of the interesting limitations of traditional utopias is the relative lack of detailed concern they reflect about the composition of the glue used to hold things together.

In the *consensus* formula for social glue, people with common values voluntarily associate to help ensure more effective cooperation. In the *coercion* formula, positions within the system are defined to ensure effective application of force and constraints.[13] To understand the operation of any system, it is crucial to understand the distribution of authority and power within it. Differences in system design may, in the last analysis, involve little more than different allocations of power and authority throughout the system. Indeed, alternate arguments about the merits of different system design formats may well involve little beyond implicit rationalizations for alternate modes of power distribution.

Each of these formulas is based upon a set of assumptions about the nature of society or social systems. The consensus formula assumes that society is a relatively stable and well-integrated structure of elements, each of which has a well-defined function. Throughout the system itself, there exists a consensus of values among its various members. The coercion formula assumes that every society is at every point subject to both processes of change and social conflict. It further assumes that every element in a society contributes to the system's disintegration and change. And finally, the coercion formula assumes that every society is based on the coercion of some of its members by others. . . .[14]

The point to be stressed here, however, is the importance of specifying the exact nature of the particular glue to be used in a specific system design. Perhaps the easiest error to make is the one that assumes that a consensus glue exists, when in point of fact the design either requires, or has surreptitiously imposed, a coercion formula.

To clarify this somewhat, it may be helpful to note how power, in the sociological sense, is differentiated from force on the one hand and authority on the other.

Force, in this context, refers to the reduction, limitation, closure, or total elimination of alternatives to the social action of one person or group by another person or group. For example, "Your money or your life," symbolizes a situation in which the alternatives have been reduced to two. Hanging a convicted criminal exemplifies the total elimination of alternatives. Dismissal or demotion of personnel in an organization illustrates the closure of alternatives. An army may successively place limitations upon the social action of its enemy until only two alternatives remain—to surrender or die.[15]

Power refers to the ability to apply force, rather than to its actual application. It is the "predisposition or prior capacity which makes the application of force possible." [16]

Authority refers to institutionalized power. In an idealized organization, power and authority become equivalent to each other. The right to use force is attached to certain statuses within the organization. "It is . . . authority in virtue of which persons in an association exercise command or control over other persons in the same association." [17] Examples of the use of authority include: the bishop who trans-

---

[12] Ralf Dahrendorf, *Class and Class Conflict in Industrial Society* (Stanford, Calif.: Stanford Univ. Press, 1959), pp. 157–159.
[13] Cf. *ibid.*, p. 169.
[14] Cf. *ibid.*, pp. 161–162.

[15] Cf. Robert Bierstedt, "An Analysis of Social Power," *American Sociological Review*, 15:6 (December 1950), p. 733.
[16] *Ibid.*
[17] *Ibid.*, 734.

fers a priest from his parish, the commanding officer who assigns a subordinate to a post of duty, a baseball team manager who changes a pitcher in the middle of an inning, and a factory superintendent who requires that an employee complete a task by a given time.[18]

"Your money or your life," constitutes what in the computer trade would be called a binary choice. If the alternatives available were extended to include, let us say, "the twenty-dollar bill you now have in your pocket," "room and board at your home for two days," "a serviceable overcoat," "the three bottles of scotch you have in your closet," or "a friendly chat over a good meal," then the intensity of the force being applied might be seen as somewhat diminished. This is simply another way of noting that the exercise of force is related to the range of action alternatives made available. The person with the ability to specify the alternatives— in this case, the person with the gun— is the one who possesses power.

And so it is that a designer of systems, who has the de facto prerogative to specify the range of phenomena that his system will distinguish, clearly is in possession of enormous degrees of power (depending, of course, upon the nature of the system being designed). It is by no means necessary that this power be formalized through the allocation of specific authority to wield nightsticks or guns.

The strength of high-speed computers lies precisely in their capacity to process binary choice data rapidly. But to process these data, the world of reality must at some point in time be reduced to binary form. This occurs initially through operational specifications handed to a computer programmer. These specifications serve as the basis for more detailed reductions to binary choices. The range of possibilities is

ultimately set by the circuitry of the computer, which places finite limits on alternatives for data storage and processing. The structure of the language used to communicate with the computer places additional restrictions on the range of alternatives. The programmer himself, through the specific sets of data he uses in his solution to a programming problem and the specific techniques he uses for his solution, places a final set of restrictions on action alternatives available within a computer-based system.

It is in this sense that computer programmers, the designers of computer equipment, and the developers of computer languages possess power. To the extent that decisions made by each of these participants in the design process serve to reduce, limit, or totally eliminate action alternatives, they are applying force and wielding power in the precise sociological meaning of these terms. . . .

As computer-based systems become increasingly more significant in shaping the realistic terms of existence in contemporary society, it becomes increasingly more relevant to inquire about the implications contained for expression of individual values. The process of obtaining representation for individual values is one of the specific notions contained in popular conceptions of democracy. However, the central idea of democracy has been penetratingly described as "one particular way in which the authority to govern is acquired and held." [19] Thus,

A man may be said to hold authority democratically when he has been freely chosen to hold such authority by those who must live under it, when they have had, and will have, the alternative of choosing somebody

18 *Ibid.*

19 Charles Frankel, "Bureaucracy and Democracy in the New Europe," *Daedalus* (Proceedings of the American Academy of Arts and Sciences), 93:1 (Winter 1964), p. 476.

else, and when he is accountable to them for the way in which he exercises this authority.[20]

It is, of course, clear that there are limits on the democratic principle and that legal and institutional safeguards must exist to protect values other than those of democracy itself. It is equally clear that at best the democratic principle can be only approximated. No one in our society seriously suggests that every person must be absolutely equal to every other person in power and influence.[21] But,

the working touchstone of a "democratic" system of authority is simply the degree to which it gives individuals legitimate instruments for reaching those who make the decisions that affect them, and for bringing influence to bear upon them. A system is more or less "democratic" depending on the number, availability, and effectiveness of these instruments, and on the proportion of

the population entitled and able to use them.[22]

Now, whether the "masses" are denied legitimate access to decision makers by reason of despotism, bureaucratic deviousness, or simple technical obfuscation, the resultant erosion of democratic process can be much the same. To the extent that decisions made by equipment manufacturers, computer programmers, or system designers are enshrouded in the mystery of "technical" detail, the persons most affected by these decisions (including customers, publics, and employees) will be denied the opportunity to participate or react to the decision made. The spectrum of values represented in the new decision-making order can and is being increasingly more circumscribed by fiat disguised as technological necessity. The paramount issues to be raised in connection with the design of our new computerized utopias are not technological—they are issues of values and the power through which these values become translated into action.

[20] Ibid.
[21] Cf. ibid., pp. 476–477.

[22] Ibid., p. 477.

49

The Role of the Legislator

EDWARD A. SHILS

In the United States, as in any other large democratic government, the burden on the legislator is great. The volume of legislation is vast and its complexity beyond the judgment of lay-

Reprinted by permission of the publisher from *The Torment of Secrecy* by Edward A. Shils. Copyright 1956 by The Free Press, A Corporation.

men. Even an expert could not hope to understand and master fully all the bills which are produced. In Great Britain, where the party leadership strictly controls the introduction of legislation and private members' bills are the exceptions, the detailed mastery of all proposed legislation is beyond the power of all Members of Parliament. In the

United States, where so many nearly similar bills are produced on the same subject, where the number of subjects on which legislation is proposed is vast, and where individual legislators often have their own legislative ambitions in addition to the program of their party leaders and of the Executive, the burden is especially great. The legislator is overwhelmed by his legislative work alone. He frequently votes on measures on which he has not formed his own judgment and on which he has not had his judgment authoritatively and reassuringly formed for him by his party organization. The fact that he leaves so much uncovered has a disquieting effect on him; it causes him to feel that matters are slipping beyond his control. The American legislator does not inherit a tradition of a political class who have a sense of having been born to rule. American legislators come from a great diversity of backgrounds, but for a long time they have come from moderate provincial circumstances in which there was no sense of a natural affinity to authority. The self-esteem of a traditional political class has been lacking in the tradition of American politics, and the effects of the absence have been aggravated by the prestige of the "people."

The discipline of the British parliamentary party and the power of the national headquarters lightens the burden of judgment and worry for the British M.P. If he behaves himself reasonably well, he can count on the support of his party for re-election. The decentralized structure of the American party system and absence of disciplinary power of the party leadership in Congress accentuate, on the contrary, the strains on the American legislator. He is very much on his own. The national party does not arrange his candidacy; it has little control over the machine on which the Congressman depends for his re-election; and its financial aid for the conduct of his campaign is much less than adequate. He must keep his machine going. Like an ambassador who is uneasy that his enemies at home are undoing his work and undermining his position while he is away, the legislator must always keep his eye on the machine at home—fearing that it might break out of his control during his absence in Washington.

American constituents, at least a sector of them, are often very outspoken in their demands. The American legislator is moreover hypersensitive to the faintest whisper of a constituent's voice. Unable to depend on the national party for re-election, he must cultivate and nurture the more active elements in his constituency more than legislators in Great Britain where constituents are less clamorous and parties are stronger at the center.

To satisfy the demands of some of his constituents the American legislator expends much of his time and energy running errands for them in Washington and receiving them when they visit the capital for business or for sightseeing purposes. He himself is often quite pleased to have this opportunity for personal contact with his constituents, even though it distracts him from his job in Washington.

In addition to trying to please those whom he sees, he is constantly harried in his mind's eye by those whom he does not see. His remoteness from them does not make him less sensitive to their sentiments or less fearful of their displeasure. The distance from the voters and their anonymity make the sensitivity even greater and more delicate. The nature of the recruitment process favors the man with a delicate ear for the voters' sentiments and an eagerness to gain their approbation. The populistic ethos of the American electorate and the traditions of American politics favor the person who can present himself as a man of the people, who is proud of the fact that he deviates from them in no significant way and who fears that any known deviations would be interpreted as snobbery or standoffishness.

This eagerness to gratify an unseen constituency and to rank high in their favor helps us to understand why it is that legislators who have no strong convictions on a given topic might sometimes be among its most fervent investigators. They do so simply because they believe it will appeal to their constituents and because they cannot allow any rival for the affection and votes of their constituents to preempt this theme.

Far from his home base and insecure about his tenure and support, he is hard put to find a procedure for keeping in touch with his constituents and fixing himself in their minds. The press conference, the cultivation of newspapermen, the radio and the television program, and the congressional investigation are often the best-suited instruments for the legislator's need to remind his constituents of his existence. That is the reason why investigations often involve such unseemly uses of the organs of publicity. By giving material to the press, he pleases the journalists and reaches the eyes of his constituents. Publicity is the next best thing to the personal contact which the legislator must forego. It is his substitute offering by which he tries to counteract the personal contact which his rivals at home have with his constituents.

The frequent recourse to personal intervention on behalf of individual constituents has greater consequences than the maintenance of a sensitive attachment of the legislator to his audible constituency and the wasteful expenditure of his time. It encourages in him expectation of personal service by the bureaucracy, an expectation long entrenched in the traditions of patronage politics and populism.

The American legislator, whose professional traditions date back to a social order in which government intervention played no great part and in which patronage was the main method of the recruitment of civil servants, tends to look on the administrator's role and tasks as properly the legislator's own responsibility—which are only transiently delegated to the administrator. He draws no fine line between legislation and administration and he likes to cooperate in and assist in administration as well as to specify, scrutinize, and control the administrator's tasks and powers. The modern separation of powers is indeed often felt as an implicit rebuff.

To these particular strains in the vocational life of an American legislator should be added the more general strains. For one thing, the career of the professional politician is full of hazards. In all democracies the legislator is recurrently in danger of not being re-elected. In the event of being unsuccessful he must go back to a career which he has neglected. In the United States very few of our professional politicians are recruited from the classes which live from inherited wealth. If he is in the professions or business, he will, if defeated for re-election, have to make up the distance which his contemporaries have gained on him. Although he might have improved certain "connections," some of his skill other than political skill might well have deteriorated. He will probably have allowed some of his professional connections to lapse. Whatever the effect on his skill he often faces the humiliation of return as a political failure, and the need to begin at a lower level than those who were his equals a few years before. Moreover, since our politicians do not come from classes which have as part of their tradition a normal expectation of entering a political career, they tend to a greater extent to be selected from among persons who enjoy the game of politics, to whom it has a special psychological appeal. For such persons, the threat of exclusion from politics through failure is especially unsatisfactory. Thus the situation of the political career in the United States makes legislators faced with the possibility of failure take eager refuge in devices which will recommend them to their constituents and reassure their continuation in office. Activity as a member of an investigative committee bathed in publicity is one of these devices.

Even when successful, however, the professional politician in the United States cannot always have the unalloyed pleasure and comfort of feeling that he is participating in a highly honored profession. The fact that he is so often made into an errand boy or a handmaiden to his constituents is indicative of their attitude towards him and of his attitude towards himself. Government in the United States, where established institutions are not usually objects of deep reverence, is far from the most esteemed of institutions. Living from the public treasury, from the taxpayer's money, whether as legislator or administrator, has until recently been rather looked down upon by the hardworking taxpayer and his journalistic spokesmen. This view is still alive in American public opinion. The image of the politician in the organs of mass communication is not a laudatory one. Pomposity, vanity, an unbalanced sense of importance and occasionally sheer dishonesty are part of the traditional American concept of the professional politician—although the reality has been far different. Even though this popular image has been changing in the past decades, the term "politician" still has a derogatory overtone.

It is significant that there is no word in current usage to describe the legislator which is free from either cant or delegation. The word "politician" in the United States brings a wrinkle—and scarcely a smiling one—to the nose. There is no other word save "statesman" for the job, and it always evokes uneasiness and visions of diplomatic chancelleries and of elegant gentlemen who have a rather hard time at the hands of the politicians. The fact that the United States is simultaneously the freest of great states and at the same time the scene of some of the most unworthy departures from the principles of liberty and the rule of law is closely connected with the devaluation of the politician in American life.

The occasional outbursts of an excessive desire to please on the one hand, and of vindictive aggressiveness on the other, are both products of this perception by the professional politician of his ambiguous status. The legislator's suspicion of the administrator as one who lives wastefully on the taxpayer's money is also an expression of the discomfiture which arises from the uneasy feeling that he himself is doing exactly that. Congressional investigations often provide favorable occasions for the manifestations of this deep-lying distrust.

It is not only the social status of politics that influences the legislator's mood. The geographical location of the center of national political life also has its effect. The almost exclusive position of politics as the chief preoccupation of Washington has an influence on the life of the legislator. It means that he is forced to live almost entirely in an atmosphere of politics. It is true, of course, that many enjoy this type of life with its incessant stress on influence, rivalry, ambition and frustration—it sharpens political wits and has a brilliance of its own. It does, however, strengthen and even overdevelop the political orientation of men who have already entered voluntarily upon such a career. It aggravates the exclusive preoccupation with political events to the point where every human activity becomes evaluated not in terms of its intrinsic value in its own appropriate sphere, but in terms of its political significance.

In London, a legislator can carry on his own profession if he is fortunate, which is more frequently the case than in Washington. He can also associate more easily with persons in other professions, with businessmen, scientists, writers, clergymen, in fact with all the groups which the diversified life of a great city which is not merely the political and administrative capital of a great country makes possible. A diversity of interests and a reduction of the primacy of politics is more practicable in this kind of situation.

In Washington, however, legislators must associate in their leisure hours almost entirely with other legislators or with journalists, administrators, and businessmen whose presence in Washington is almost always evidence of their own predominantly political interests. In such a society, where the talk is invariably centered about who is getting what from whom, both the sensitivity and the insecurity of the legislator are increased. It strengthens his tendency to interpret everything in political terms and to look on the world as engaged at every moment in arranging political combinations, intended to advance some individual or group and to ruin another. This type of social life offers no respite from the tensions and anxieties of the individual legislator's own political career. It provides a stimulant rather than a soothing calm. The gossip and rumors agitate him and cause him to worry more about his own political fortunes. Hearing so much of what others are doing or are having done for them to secure their political

fortunes, he feels he must exert himself more to establish and advance his own prestige. Whoever blocks him is his enemy. Whoever has a deficiency, real or imputable, which can be attacked in the name of a major political value, becomes a fair target in the competition to keep oneself politically afloat. He is more susceptible to excitation by rumors and by the passing currents of opinion.

As a result of these factors—not all of which operate equally for all legislators—the life of the American politician holding a seat in the Senate or in the House of Representatives is far from an easy one. He is always confronted with more demands on him than he can satisfy. He is always in danger of displeasing some people and he is never sure of just what it will take to please them or how he can do it when he knows what it is. He is always dependent on someone else's judgment for his equanimity and for his security, and he tends to be a person with a desire to please. The result is a state of stress and disquiet, often flaring up into rage and sometimes into vindictiveness.

If we bear in mind the populistic atmosphere in which the political career is conducted, and the populistic dispositions which many of our political leaders carry with them as a product of their own spontaneous outlook and as a product of the need to read and please their constituents' minds, we begin to understand why political life in the United States is often so stormy, and why so many politicians seek their salvation in publicity. We also begin to see why politicians have conspiracies on their minds and why they are preoccupied with secrecy. . . .

50

The Rhythm of Democratic Politics

DENNIS H. WRONG

Democratic societies with universal suffrage and competing political parties experience a cyclical alternation of periods dominated by protest from the Left and retrenchment by the Right. The notion that politics conform to such cyclical periodicity is scarcely a new one: it is implicit in the most commonplace language of political journalism, which regularly uses such metaphors as "swing of the pendulum," "rising and ebbing tides," or "waxing and waning" forces, to describe events.

The conception of a Left/Right continuum along which parties, movements, regimes, and ideologies can be located has often been justly criticized,[1] yet some such conception seems indispensable and invariably creeps back in hidden guise when the conventional categories are repudiated. I shall use "Left" to refer to programmatic demands for planned or enacted social change toward a more equal distribution of economic benefits, social status, and power, or, in unpropitious times, to the defense of an existing, achieved degree of equality against advocates of increased inequality. The classic Left demand is to realize for all men the French revolutionary slogan of "liberté, egalité, fraternité." Since the Left is an established and permanent political tendency came into being at the time of the French Revolution, the "Right"

is best defined residually as resistance, on whatever grounds, to any further movement toward equality in the distribution of material satisfactions, status, and/or power, or as the demand for restoration of a (usually idealized) *status quo ante* in which greater inequality prevailed.

Obviously, these sparse definitions raise all sorts of problems if they are applied to the rich diversity of past and present political movements. Yet they embody the most common, minimal understanding of the Left/Right distinction. In emphasizing the broad *content* of political demands, they avoid the difficulties raised by classifying political groups as Left or Right according to their social base—whether they are supported by or direct their appeals to the victims or the beneficiaries of the existing distribution of rewards and privileges. Thus Peronism in the 1940s and '50s was not necessarily a leftist movement because its main following was among industrial workers; nor must New Left student movements of the '60s be considered "really" rightist because their members were disproportionately drawn from upper-middle-class backgrounds.

Nor need the actual structure of a party or regime determine its classification as Left or Right: parties of the Left may be led and controlled by tiny, self-perpetuating elites, while parties of the Right may be organized in a loose, decentralized, "populistic" manner. Communist dictatorships appeal, at least outside their borders, to supporters of the demands of the Left, although, since my primary concern is with the politics of democracies, the problem of how to classify nondemo-

Reprinted from *Dissent* (Winter 1974), by permission of the publisher, *Dissent Magazine*, New York, N. Y.

[1] For a useful recent critique, see Giovanni Sartori, "From the Sociology of Politics to Political Sociology," in Seymour Martin Lipset, ed., *Politics and the Social Sciences* (New York: Oxford University Press, 1969), pp. 77–80.

cratic regimes that claim legitimacy through an identification with the Left can be safely put aside.

Before the Enlightenment a "Left" in the modern sense of a vision of a more egalitarian future society to be created by organized political effort did not exist. Nor was there an identifiable "Right": conservative ideologies and organizations emerged only in response to the challenge of the Left. Citing Hegel's famous "owl of Minerva" metaphor, Karl Mannheim defined conservatism as traditionalism become conscious of itself and wrote: "Goaded on by opposing theories, conservative mentality discovers its *idea* only *ex post facto*." [2] Since most societies through most of history have been traditionalist, claiming their legitimacy from continuity with the past rather than from a vision of the future, classical conservatives, viewing the world *sub specie aeternitatas*, have dismissed the outlook of the Left as the expression of Enlightenment naiveté over the perfectability of man, as presumptuous intervention in the workings of "providential forces" (Burke), or as an attempt, necessarily tyrannical in its outcome, to destroy "organically" evolved societies and rebuild them according to an imposed design.

The more subtle conservative thinkers, from Burke to Michael Oakeshott, have repudiated efforts to construct a conservative ideology, recognizing that the strength of conservatism lies in the emotional attachment of mortal men to the world as they have known it, in an only apparently irrational conviction that "what is, is right," which actually implies the unspoken major premise that it is right *because it is*. All men, including men of the Left, cannot help

forming emotional attachments to what has the inestimable advantage and power of actually existing. Even prisoners have learned to love their bars, and most of us feel nostalgic about the places and people of our childhood no matter how unhappy it may have been. This is the existential root of conservatism—of the "eternal Right." Its strength has been habitually underestimated by the Left, even within the Left's own constituency of the deprived and oppressed; the naturalness of conservative emotions is too often facilely dismissed as indoctrination by the ruling class (these days as "brainwashing by the mass media"), or, more pretentiously, as "false consciousness," a term that carries a heavy burden of responsibility not merely for ideological delusions but for actual political crimes.

Contemporary technocrats, of course, are committed to the planned application of scientific knowledge. Their anti-ideological animus seems very remote indeed from classical conservatism with its religious piety and preference for faith over reason, its aura of knights and ladies and agrarian life—and, for that matter, remote too, from the free market of 19th-century capitalism. But there is a curious continuity between a technocratic outlook favoring a "pragmatic" politics engaged in by the representatives of established organizations and the implicit pragmatism of such conservatives as Oakeshott, who fear rational abstractions and universal principles and affirm instead their trust in the implicit truths of "experience."

But there is an "eternal Left" too, as deeply rooted in the human condition as the eternal Right even if it only became a conscious political tendency after the Enlightenment. The vision of the Left derives from the Vichean insight that man makes his own history, or "socially constructs his reality," in today's fashionable sociological parlance. Once this insight enters general

[2] *Ideology and Utopia* (New York: Harcourt, Brace, 1946), p. 207. See also Mannheim, *Essays on Sociology and Social Psychology* (New York: Oxford University Press, 1953), pp. 98–101.

awareness, the social world is demystified and classical conservative veneration of a fixed social order sanctified by the past loses meaning. Men feel "alienated" precisely because they know that theirs is a man-made world of arbitrary, makeshift social arrangements which they can imagine quite otherwise. We have learned only too well that they may respond to this alienation with frenzied efforts to remystify the world, to press the genie back into the bottle, rather than by embracing the challenge to try to create the now possible free and egalitarian community envisioned by the Left.

Political democracy makes actual the eternal Left in time and history. By giving a voice to the voiceless, mobilizing the apathetic, and organizing the unorganized it introduces planned and directed social change as a principal of historical movement. The voice of the people need not be sanctified as the voice of God, but democracy requires that it at least be heard and taken into account. Democratic politics legitimizes demands for reform and, introduced into societies that remain highly unequal and create new inequalities in the course of their economic and technological growth, is therefore incurably ideological. The end of ideology would mean the end of the Left as a political force and the end of democracy itself —either by the restoration or creation of an authoritarian or totalitarian regime, or by the achievement of utopia.

The institutionalization of the Left in democratic politics initiates a long-term movement toward realization of the goals of the Left, a movement inherent in the workings of political democracy. However, all firmly established groups, including parties of the Left, become committed defensively to their own continued survival within a system that has permitted them to develop and even flourish. Michels called this the "iron law of oligarchy"; it has recently been described more accurately and renamed the "iron law of decadence" by Theodore Lowi. As organized groups become frozen in defense of their own internal structure, the stasis of Lowi's "interest-group pluralism" threatens; the spirit of the Left seeks to reactivate not only itself but the very power of majoritarian democracy through those nascent rather than fully organized groups we call "social movements." [3] But the resistance offered by the Right —as organized minority power, as inarticulate mass sentiment, as metaphysical reflection of the human condition—produces the oscillating pattern I have called the rhythm of democratic politics. How does this rhythm manifest itself and what is its source?

The periodicity of Left and Right in democratic political life is not necessarily equivalent to an alternation of parties in power, nor of governments actually pursuing more or less egalitarian or conservative policies. Political leaders, in office or out, frequently talk one way and act another, or follow inconsistent policies whatever their rhetoric. The achievements of politics are often symbolic ones—which is not to minimize their significance. The rhythm or cycle is rather one of the *kinds of issues* that dominate political debate, and often intellectual and cultural life as well. Nor is this rhythm the sole, or even always the major, substance of democratic politics. If the division between Left and Right is the most enduring focus of political conflict, it is nevertheless often obscured by ethnic, religious, and racial cleavages within particular polities. In the past,

[3] *The Politics of Disorder* (New York: Basic Books, 1971), pp. 3–61. Lowi mentions the civil rights movement of the early '60s as an example of such a social movement outside of the established parties and interest organizations (p. 60). See also Lowi's earlier book, *The End of Liberalism* (New York: W. W. Norton, 1969).

Marxists in particular have been predisposed to deny the autonomy and irreducibility of such "subcultural" cleavages, although their domination of the political life of a large number of countries is by now fully clear. One can nevertheless abstract out of the welter of the democratic political experience a discernible rhythm—or dialectic—of Left/Right conflict, which represents at least *one* major theme of their politics. Perhaps there is also a rhythm in the development over time of ethnic or religious struggles, a rhythm intersecting or superimposed upon that of Left/Right conflict. But my concern here is solely with the latter.

The cyclical rhythm is not the effect of a mysterious cosmic law; it rather reflects a pattern of change that is inherent in the working of a democratic political system in a class-divided society. Political democracy based on universal suffrage was itself originally a demand of the Left introduced into previously authoritarian and hierarchical social orders. In European countries, though not in the United States, it was the central issue around which new working-class and socialist parties organized in the closing decades of the 19th century. For the formal, i.e., the legal and constitutional, redistribution of power achieved by universal suffrage to have any consequences in reducing social inequalities, a long period of political mobilization of the lower classes had to take place, a process that is scarcely complete even today in many countries, including the United States. Once, however, parties of the Left have been organized, or the lower classes have been successfully mobilized by older parties, some crisis such as an economic depression, defeat in war, or a split in the ranks of the Right is bound to give the parties of the Left the opportunity to win office, whether on their own or as part of a coalition. They are then able to carry out reforms

that constitute at least their minimum program. But the crisis passes or is resolved; the Right regroups while conflicts between moderates and radicals on the Left become more acute; and the discontent of the Left's electoral constituency is temporarily appeased by the limited gains, actual or symbolic, that have been won. The Right then returns to office after successfully persuading a sizable segment of the Left's regular following that a conservative government will not wipe out these gains.

Although American political history has often been regarded as uniquely "consensual" and free of ideological conflict, it fits rather neatly into a pattern of oscillation between periods in which demands from the Left dominate, and those given over to periods of reaction. In any case, whatever truth there may have been in the past to the view that American politics reflected the historical peculiarities of American origins and destiny—the doctrine of American "exceptionalism" as it has sometimes been called—the idea has increasingly lost plausibility. Richard Rovere, one of the more astute observers of American politics, remarked in 1970 that "the Europeanization of American politics proceeds . . . apace."

The periodization of American politics into successive Left and Right eras was presented at length by Arthur Schlesinger, Sr., in a 1939 article, "Tides of American Politics," revised and expanded in his 1949 book *Paths to the Present*,[4] which attracted a good deal of attention at the time. His son, Arthur Schlesinger, Jr., revived and updated his father's thesis in the late 1950s to argue that the '60s were destined to be a period of reform and innovation favorable to the liberal wing

[4] *Paths to the Present* (New York: Macmillan, 1949), pp. 77–92.

of the Democratic party, in which he himself was an active figure.

The elder Schlesinger divided American history into 11 periods of alternating Right and Left ascendancy—he used the labels "conservative" and "liberal"—from 1765 to 1947, each one averaging 16.5 years with very slight deviations around the mean, except in the period from the Civil War to the end of the 19th century. Schlesinger's inferences or "predictions" for the years ahead have been borne out to a surprising degree.

In this century, if we carry Schlesinger's periodization up to the present and modify it very slightly, there are five distinct periods. The progressive era is usually seen as beginning with Theodore Roosevelt's accession to the presidency in 1901 and ending with American entrance into World War I, or, at least, with Wilson's congressional losses in 1918. The period from 1918 until Franklin D. Roosevelt's election in 1932, or, perhaps, until the stock-market crash in 1929, was a period of war-inspired patriotism, postwar reaction (the "Red Scare"), return to "normalcy" under Harding and Coolidge, and complacent prosperity. The decline in the momentum of the New Deal is often dated from Democratic losses in the mid-term elections of 1938, but World War II prolonged and partially revived the ideological climate of the '30s. (Someone has remarked that 1948 was the last year of the '30s.) The Cold War, Korea, Republican victories, and the years of McCarthyism to which these events contributed gave a conservative cast to the '50s. The Left began to recapture some political initiative with the civil rights movement in the South in the late '50s, shortly followed by the rhetoric of the New Frontier and the resounding electoral repudiation of a militant right-wing presidential candidate in 1964. A few years later the "radicalization" of large

segments of college youth and intellectuals in response to the Vietnam War created a mood of left-wing insurgency on a variety of fronts. Since 1968, however, reaction or "backlash" against the black, student, and peace movements has been a salient theme of our politics, exploited by George Wallace's candidacy in the 1968 and 1972 election campaigns, and very closely identified with the Vice-President and the Attorney-General who were the most publicized figures of the first Nixon administration. The mentality that led to Watergate fed off the mood of backlash.

Wars often appear to mark the beginning or the end of the intensification of particular phases of the cycle. Schlesinger denied that there was "a correlation between foreign wars and the mass drift of sentiments," maintaining that "these conflicts have taken place about equally in conservative and liberal periods, sometimes coming at the start, sometimes at the end and sometimes midway." But surely foreign wars differ in the ideological significance they possess for domestic currents of opinion. Also, their significance has certainly increased since the 1930s. Moreover, as Robert Nisbet has cogently argued, neither nations, continents, nor even units as large as civilizations can be treated as isolated, self-contained "systems" obeying their own internal laws.[5] They are parts of a large international or supra-civilizational environment that interpenetrates them. Wars, international crises, and the issues of foreign policy to which they give rise can therefore neither be ignored as shaping agents of the domestic political process nor invoked as *dei ex machina* to account for internal political shifts. Theories of American exceptionalism, on the one hand, and some Marxist

[5] *Social Change and History* (New York: Oxford University Press, 1969), pp. 240–262.

Sociology of Contemporary Society

analyses, on the other, have unduly minimized this fact.

In general, the ideological coloration of the perceived national enemy has complicated the impact of wars on the Left/Right dialectic. World War I divided the American Left; the Russian Revolution not only further divided it but gave impetus to the period of postwar reaction and repression that ended the Progressive era. World War II, on the other hand, was fought against nations seen as the very incarnation of the values most bitterly opposed by the Left and did not therefore displace New Deal liberalism and its radical allies. The Cold War and Korea, fought against an enemy laying total claim to the ideological heritage of the Left, not only delegitimated the American Left but almost completely obliterated its radical wing. In the '60s, however, the failure and unpopularity of the Vietnam War revived American radicalism and discredited the Cold War. But the fact that responsibility for the Vietnam disaster rested on a liberal Democratic administration created a split on the Left that permitted Nixon's victory in 1968.

The Left, of course, is itself invariably divided into reformist and radical wings, and the shifting balance of unity and conflict achieved by its factions constitutes another dialectic within the larger dialectic of Left and Right. Obviously, the Right is also usually divided between militants and moderates, reactionaries and conservatives, although such divisions have not, I think, played as important a role in the United States as in some European countries.

Metaphors of pendular or tidal movements are misleading when applied to the cyclical rhythm of politics. For the pattern has not been one of a mere repetitive oscillation between fixed points. In Schlesinger's words, "a more appropriate figure than the pendulum is the spiral, in which the alternation proceeds at successively higher levels." The classic Marxist conception of the movement of history has also been described as a spiral, combining a cyclical with a developmental or unilinear motion. But to disclose such a pattern in historical events is not to explain *why* it prevails, or *how* transitions from one stage to the next come about. No one who has read Robert Nisbet's brilliant book *Social Change and History* can retain any illusions on this score.[6] One must always ask, "What makes the wheels go around?" in the case of a cyclical motion, or, "What propels mankind upward and onward?" —or, at least, forward in a given direction—if a unilinear trend is exhibited. Neither recurrent cycles, unilinear evolution, nor a spiral course combining them amount to self-sufficient, self-explaining "laws" of change. Schlesinger recognized this in his cyclical account of American politics, but his own explanations of the cycle were brief and vague, scarcely going beyond the assertion of inevitable "changes in mass psychology" resulting from boredom or disappointment with the prevailing phase of the cycle. In trying to account for the cyclical rhythm, Schlesinger also referred to alleged peculiarities of the American people, such as their preference for "empiricism" rather than "preconceived theory," and their belief in the virtues of competition—although he also acknowledged the existence of a similar rhythm in the Western European democracies.

In his autobiography, published in 1963 just two years before his death, Schlesinger reported that Franklin D. Roosevelt's adviser, David Niles, once told him that FDR was influenced in his decision to run for reelection in 1944 by Schlesinger's calculation that liberalism would remain dominant until 1948 (based on his figure of a 16.5

[6] *Ibid.*, pp. 284–304.

years' average duration of each phase of the cycle).[7] Schlesinger also mentioned a preelection column by James Reston in 1960 maintaining that John F. Kennedy "based his campaign on the assumption," derived from Schlesinger's "theory," that a turn to the Left was in the offing within a year or two.[8]

If these stories are true, Roosevelt and Kennedy would seem to have understood the cyclical pattern in far too mechanical a fashion that is vulnerable to Nisbet's strictures. Such efforts to predict the exact duration of periods of the cyclical or spiral rhythm, while they possess a dangerous fascination, do not increase our understanding of it. For a description of the rhythm, however accurate, *explains* nothing whatsoever: in the language of logicians, the rhythm is an *explanandum* rather than an *explanans*—an effect of underlying causes rather than a causal agency itself. Moreover, it is highly likely that in recent decades the rhythm has accelerated as a result of the increasing saturation of modern populations by the mass media. Nowadays a "new" generation seems to come along every five years or so.

An explanation of the rhythm of democratic politics must necessarily be historically specific, because party politics under conditions of mass suffrage are less than a century old even in most of the stable, "advanced" constitutional democracies of the West. Yet it may be possible to formulate explanatory generalizations that transcend the historical uniqueness of particular nations. Furthermore, it is at least worth observing in passing that there is some evidence of a similar periodicity in nondemocratic states. Despotic rulers of absolutist monarchies have often been followed by rulers more responsive to pressures from below. Totalitarian dictatorships undertake "great leaps forward" that are succeeded by periods of relaxed discipline in which "a hundred flowers" are encouraged to bloom. An analyst of Stalin's rule has written of the "artificial dialectic" imposed by the dictator on Soviet society, where rigorous demands for total ideological conformity and the use of terror to deter even the mildest dissent abruptly alternated with periods of greater permissiveness or "thaw."[9]

But an explanation of the rhythm of democratic politics must necessarily be specific to constitutional mass democracies. I shall try to summarize schematically the elements of such an explanation.

(1) The political mobilization of the previously disenfranchised lower classes is a long and slow process, still incomplete in many of the major Western democracies, as indicated by higher-middle- and upper-class as against working-class rates of voting, higher working- and lower-class support for parties of the Right than of upper- and middle-class support for parties of the Left, and the occasional survival of formal and informal barriers to voting imposed on some low-status groups, such as blacks in the American South. Thus even after the winning of full citizenship rights, including the right to vote, by groups previously subject to legal discrimination, "conservative government," in Woodrow Wilson's words, "is in the saddle most of the time."

(2) But Left parties and movements

---

[7] *In Retrospect: The History of a Historian* (New York: Harcourt, Brace & World, 1963), p. 108.

[8] *Ibid.*, pp. 190–191.

[9] O. Utis, "Generalissimo Stalin and the Art of Government," *Foreign Affairs*, 30 (January 1952): 197–214. The author writes: "This—the 'artificial dialectic'—is Generalissimo Stalin's most original invention, his major contribution to the art of government . . ." p. 210. ("O. Utis," which means "nobody" in classical Greek, was a pseudonym here adopted by Isaiah Berlin.)

succeed in mobilizing a large enough proportion of their potential constituency to become leading opposition parties, sometimes displacing older parties as in the rise of Labour at the expense of the Liberals in Britain. Sometimes they emerge as the first and largest organized mass parties confronting electoral or governmental coalitions of smaller parties of the Right, as on the European continent. Sometimes they partially transform an older, heterogeneous, and factionalized party into a vehicle for the demands of newly mobilized lower-class groups, as in the United States. Sooner or later the Left party wins office, often as a result of a severe economic crisis or the impact of a war (especially a lost one) that discredits an existing government.

It has often been the fate of the Left parties to come to power at a time of such acute crisis for the entire society that they are forced to concentrate on improvised short-run policies to restore or maintain internal peace, with the result that their long-range goals of social reconstruction have to be shelved or severely modified, inspiring accusations of "class betrayal" from their more militant followers. The Social Democracy in the first and last years of the Weimar Republic is the classic case. Nevertheless, by coming to office the Left party wins a kind of legitimacy in the eyes of the electorate that it previously lacked and it is usually able to carry out at least a part of its minimum program. But failure to resolve the crisis that brought the party to office, or the passing of the crisis whether or not the government's measures are given credit for this; splits between the party's or government's radical and moderate reformist wings once the minimum program has been passed; the retrenchment of the Right during a period in opposition; and a constant factor—what George Bernard Shaw called "the damned wantlessness

of the poor"—all result in electoral defeat or the "co-optation" of prominant leaders before the Left party has done more than institute "incremental," or "token," reforms.

(3) The return of the Right, however, is conditional on its persuading the electorate that it will not "turn the clock back" on the reforms achieved by the Left. Old issues bitterly contested in the past by the parties suddenly become obsolescent and periods of "Butskellism," or even Grand Coalitions between the rivals, become the order of the day, isolating and infuriating the more militant partisans on each side who may break away and create splinter or "ginger" groups within legislatures, or "extraparliamentary opposition" movements outside. The Right party, in an effort to enhance or consolidate its appeal to the constituency of the Left, may adopt new hybrid, apparently contradictory, names or slogans designed to suggest that it has outgrown past hostility to Left policies now in effect, such as "Tory Socialism," "Progressive Conservatism," "Christian Democracy," or "Moderate Republicanism"—this last a label favored by President Eisenhower shortly after his first election.

This recurrent sequence of events is the rhythm, or the "dialectic," of politically directed change in a democracy. It falls far short of realizing either the far-reaching hopes of the advocates or the apocalyptic fears of the opponents of universal suffrage in the 19th century. Why do parties of the Left become so pallidly reformist and achieve so little in the way of fundamental "structural change" in the direction of their egalitarian ideals? Machiavelli gave the most general answer long before the establishment of democratic institutions:

It must be considered that there is nothing more difficult to carry out, nor more doubtful of success nor more dangerous to handle, than to initiate a new order of things. For the reformer has enemies in all those who profit by the old order, and only lukewarm defenders in all those who would profit by the new order, this lukewarmness arising partly from fear of their adversaries, who have the laws in their favor; and partly from the incredulity of mankind, who do not truly believe in anything new until they have actual experience of it. Thus it arises that on every opportunity for attacking the reformer, his opponents do so with the zeal of partisans, the others only defend him halfheartedly, so that between them he runs great danger.[10]

The contemporary social scientist would doubtless put it in different and far less elegant language, but his conclusion would be much the same as Machiavelli's.

Yet the potential electoral constituency of the Left in modern democracies is larger than that of the Right—"God must love the poor people for he made so many of them," Lincoln once remarked. Popular elections based on universal suffrage give decisive weight to the one political resource with which the lower classes are amply endowed—numbers. How does the Right counter this demographic superiority of their opponents? In the first place, the Right possesses a massive advantage with respect to other political resources—wealth, education, social status, traditional legitimacy—and is able to throw these into the balance in election campaigns as well as employing them on an enormous scale to influence government policy between elections. In confronting the electorate, however, the most regular and reliable strategy of the Right is to appeal to nationalist sentiment. Modern nationalism is itself, of course, a product of democratic ideology, born in the wake of the French

and American Revolutions. But this very fact has served to enhance its appeal in opposition to the class and anticlitist populist appeals of the Left, which has so repeatedly and tragically underestimated the strength of national loyalties in this century.

The Right lays claim to the symbols of legitimacy identified with the past of the nation, indeed with its very existence in a world of competing nation-states, an existence usually achieved by wars of conquest or revolts against foreign domination which usually, though not in the United States, antedated the creation of democratic institutions and the extension of the franchise. Thus parties of the Right tend to wave the flag, to nominate generals who stand "above politics" as candidates for office, and to invoke the need for national unity, in contrast to the divisive appeals of the Left. National leaders of the Right have sometimes engaged in foreign adventurism and even embarked upon limited expansionist wars in order to overcome internal tensions generated by the domestic class struggle. War has often in this sense been "the health of the state," in Randolph Bourne's famous dictum. Parties of the Left, on the other hand, have traditionally been isolationist in the United States, internationalist and anti-imperialist on the European continent, and Little Englanders in Britain.

If events ensure that sooner or later reformist parties of the Left will come to office, and if the return to office of conservative parties is partly conditional on their leaving untouched the popular reforms carried out by Left administrations, then there is *an unmistakable "leftward drift" inherent in the functioning over time of democratic politics.* The existence of such a drift alarms and enrages militants of the Right; its slowness and the many counterpressures to which it is subject disillusions and

---

[10] *The Prince,* chap. VI. See pp. 21–22 in the Modern Library Edition (New York: Random House, 1940).

radicalizes utopians of the Left, who then dismiss parliament as a "talking-shop," the major parties as "Tweedle-dum" and "Tweedledee," and "the system" itself as a fraud in professing to offer opportunities for change. Militants of both Right and Left are disposed to conclude with Machiavelli that

Thus it comes about that all armed prophets have conquered and unarmed ones failed; for . . . the character of peoples varies, and it is easy to persuade them of a thing, but difficult to keep them in that persuasion. And so it is necessary to order things so that when they no longer believe, they can be made to believe by force.[11]

Segments of both Right and Left, in short, are attracted by violent revolutionary or counterrevolutionary short-cuts: in the case of the Right, to arrest and even reverse the leftward drift; in the case of the Left, to accelerate and complete it. The Right calls for a government of "national unity" that will not hesitate to suspend constitutional liberties and suppress the opposition parties, while the Left succumbs to a mood of revolutionary impatience, or "utopian greed." In periods of acute national crisis and distress, a "dialectic of the extremes," to use a phrase of Raymond Aron's,[12] in which each side violently confronts the other, often enough in the streets, may take center stage and threaten the survival of democratic institutions themselves. The last years of the Weimar Republic are, of course, the classic example of such a confrontation.

But even in less critical situations, this dialectic is visible at the periphery rather than at the center of the political arena and often seems to be gaining momentum through the enlistment of growing numbers of partisans on each side. The tactic of Left militants is to attack the entire political system as part of a repressive "Establishment" moving toward "fascism," and the most plausible evidence for this is found in the efforts of militants on the Right to brand their customary political opponents as Communist sympathizers, or dangerous radicals encouraging disrespect for law, insurrectionary violence, treason, or all three. The Left calls for a "popular front" against "repression" and incipient "fascism." The Right reaffirms traditional values and calls for a closing of ranks against the fomenters of public disorder. At the level of rhetoric and public demonstrations, this kind of ultimatist ideological politics was fairly visible in the United States during the late '60s. That it may become at least a permanent sideshow of American politics is one implication of the notion of the Europeanization of American politics to which I previously referred. The dialectic of the extremes reflects an effort, conscious or unconscious, to short-circuit the "normal" pattern of alternating periods of protest and stabilization with its built-in tendency toward a glacially slow "leftward drift."

Democratic conservatives, or "moderates," frequently reject "ideological politics" in favor of a "pragmatic politics" based on bargaining, compromise, and consensus on the rules of political competition. Their suspicion of those on both the Left and the Right who out of impatience with the stately rhythm of democratic politics wish to fracture it by making a forward "leap to socialism" or a restoration of an idealized status quo ante is surely well-founded. But the "ideological" demands of idealists, visionaries, "extremists," prophets, and seers are also part of the democratic political process—sources of "input," as some political scientists

11 Ibid., p. 22.
12 The Century of Total War (Garden City: Doubleday, 1954), pp. 241–261. I am much indebted to Aron's brilliant discussion.

would gracelessly say. Without them, the professional politicians would have little to bargain about and strike compromises over. The major political philosopher of democracy, John Stuart Mill, recognized this when he wrote of his brief period of service in the House of Commons:

If . . . there were any intermediate course which had a claim to a trial, I well knew that to propose something which would be called extreme was the true way not to impede but to facilitate a more moderate experiment. . . . It is the character of the British people, or at least of the higher and middle classes who pass muster for the British people, that to induce them to approve of any change, it is necessary that they should look upon it as a middle course: they think every proposal extreme and violent unless they hear of some other proposal going still further, upon which their antipathy to extreme views may discharge itself.[13]

Mill's tone reflects the relatively serene and civil politics of Britain in the Victorian age when the franchise was still restricted. Out of the experience of the disorder and violence of European mass politics in this century, Albert Camus observed: "Heads must roll, and blood must flow like rivers in the streets, merely to bring about a minor amendment to the Constitution." This is easily read as a despairing or cynical rejection of political effort. But

recall that Camus' heroic exemplar of the human condition was Sisyphus. The task of the Left is always Sisyphean. Movement toward its goals is at best asymptotic. Disappointment is inevitable over the "wantlessness" and fickleness—often sourly labeled "false consciousness"—of the suffering and oppressed the Left seeks to serve. Committed neither in principle nor pragmatically to the world as it is, defined rather by its "project" in the Sartrean sense, the Left is inherently prone to bitter internal struggles over which ends, means, and agencies advance or hinder that project.

The Left is often proclaimed to be obsolete as a result of the very establishment of political democracy, since the voice of the people at any given time so rarely fully affirms the aspirations of the Left. The actual role of the Left is usually the undramatic one, as Barrington Moore, Jr., has recently defined it, of keeping "radical fire" under liberal reforms.[14] The Left might well attribute to political democracy as an ironic motto Galileo's famous aside when forced to recant his belief in the Copernican theory: *eppur si muove*— "and yet it still moves." But unlike the mechanical force of the sun's gravity, the effort and will of men and women on the Left are what keep the system of democratic politics in motion.

[13] *Autobiography* (London: Longmans, Green, 1908), p. 168.

[14] *Reflections on the Causes of Human Misery* (Boston: Beacon Press, 1972), pp. 156–168.

51

Revolution and Evolution in Modern Society

CHRISTOPHER LASCH

I

The contributors to *The New American Revolution* and its companion, *National Liberation: Revolution in the Third World*, use the term "revolution" in a variety of ways. Some equate revolution with any profound social and political change, as when Manfred Halpern speaks of the "world-wide revolution of modernization." Richard M. Pfeffer uses the word in the same broad sense when he writes that "in advanced industrial societies, permanent revolution [that is, permanent radical change] is a fact." Defined in this way, revolution is not necessarily willed by anyone; it may take the form of "unintended, incoherent change," in Halpern's words, extending over a long period of time.

When Franz Schurmann observes that "today, America and other countries of the advanced capitalist world *are* in revolution," he uses the term in a somewhat more restrictive sense, as an attack on "the moral-political order and the traditional hierarchy of class statuses," which succeeds when existing structures lose their legitimacy and can no longer function without wholesale repression. This conception of revolution is still very broad, however, since it extends not only to the culminating phase of the struggle to overthrow an established order—the revolutionary crisis itself—but to the whole series of events that brought the crisis into being.

Both of these definitions embrace much more than the traditional conception of revolution, which I shall adopt for the purpose of the following discussion, as an attempt—sometimes successful, sometimes unsuccessful—to seize state power on the part of political forces avowedly opposed not merely to the existing regime but to the existing social order as a whole. This definition has the advantage of distinguishing revolution, not merely from deep and sudden change in general, but more specifically from the *coup d'état* on the one hand and from rebellion on the other. A *coup d'état* is not necessarily revolutionary, since those who carry it out may have no quarrel with the existing order, proposing merely to overthrow "the rule of the politicians" and to run the existing machinery in a more forceful manner. This applies not only to reactionary generals but also to fascists and other "revolutionary" right-wingers, even though the latter may have strong popular support. Rebellions, on the other hand, can express deep social antagonisms and even class conflicts; but they do not become revolutionary so long as they confine themselves to attacks on feudal overlords, the police, or other agents or symbols of oppression. Revolution is a direct attack—not necessarily violent —on the state. . . .

If revolution is defined as an attack on the state, this suggests at the outset that revolution is a distinctively modern occurrence, associated with the emergence of nation-states. The same centralization of economic and political life that made possible the modern state also exposed the state to revolutionary attack from below. The very strength of the state, its command of a centralized network of political and judicial institutions, proved to be a source of weakness, in times of crisis, particularly since the new administrative bureaucracy often had its center in the capital city of the realm—a vast but delicate organism dependent for its existence on supplies from the surrounding countryside and, more generally, on regular communications with the entire nation. Barrington Moore, Jr., in the important essay cited (in other connections) by many of the contributors to these volumes, has recently called attention to the close relation between this vulnerability of the city, in societies still overwhelmingly agrarian, and the creation of the revolutionary urban mass, which in turn—as the studies of George Rudé and others have begun to demonstrate —has played a central role in so many modern revolutions.[1] Twentieth-century radicals, including Marxists, have tended to minimize the importance of the revolutionary crowd in bringing on the final spasms of the state. Thus Louis Boudin, in *The Theoretical System of Karl Marx*, ridiculed those "who imagine the great revolution as the work of a hungry and desperate mob driven to distraction and destruction by the immediate lack of work, food and shelter."[2]

It is true that no mob ever made a revolution. As Eric Wolf and other scholars represented in these volumes point out, utterly desperate people lack the will to contemplate or to carry out an attack on the fundamental institutions of society. Moreover, social change on such a scale presupposes a revolutionary class—as distinct from a mass —with an ideology and culture of its own that it perceives to be threatened or hemmed in by the existing order. Without such a class, closely tied to production but radically alienated from existing social and political structures, even a collapse of the state does not necessarily lead to revolution; it may only lead to its replacement by a more efficient regime presiding over a reformed version of the old order. Bread riots do not provide the infallible signal that a revolutionary crisis is at hand. All the same, it is hard to imagine a modern revolution without them. The "hungry mob" may not constitute a revolutionary class, but it provides the troops for class warfare, and "the immediate lack of work, food and shelter" therefore cannot be ignored as an indispensable element of the revolutionary situation—at least as we have known it in the past.

In the same essay in which he calls attention to the vulnerability of the city as a factor in the classic European revolutions, Moore distinguishes another type of revolution characteristic of recent upheavals in backward countries. Here the state is attacked not at its center but on its periphery. Through protracted civil and guerrilla warfare, the revolutionary forces, which can survive for long periods of time because they control and even administer parts of the realm, gradually erode the state's capacity for repression and eventually defeat it. This distinction between urban revolutions in Europe and peasant revolutions in Asia, Africa, and Latin America seems somewhat overdrawn, however, for a number of reasons. In the first place, civil war has also been a feature of the major European revolutions, and usually for the same reason that explains its prominence elsewhere. A successful revolution or a revolutionary movement seemingly on the point of success usually invites the intervention of foreign powers bent on reestablishing the status quo. Thus the French

[1] Barrington Moore, Jr., "Revolution in America?" *The New York Review of Books*, Vol. XII, No. 2 (January 30, 1969), pp. 6–12.
[2] *The Theoretical System of Karl Marx* (Chicago, 1907), p. 240.

had to defend their revolution against the combined monarchies of Europe, just as the Chinese Communists in our own time have had to defeat the Japanese, and the Vietnamese defeat the United States.

It is possible, moreover, to exaggerate the importance of events in the capital city, in contrasting "urban" revolutions in Europe with peasant revolutions elsewhere. Recent studies of the French Revolution have disclosed a great deal of revolutionary activity in the provinces as well. In seventeenth-century England, the revolution eventually succeeded, in part, because the Puritans had established a secure territorial basis in outlying parts of the country, notably in East Anglia.

Moore stresses the importance, in non-European revolutions, of the revolutionaries' ability to function as an alternative government in those parts of the country that it militarily controls. Once again, something of the same pattern can be seen in many European revolutions. Before the Jacobin seizure of power in France, the Jacobin clubs had already begun to exercise many of the functions of local government. The same thing is true of the Russian soviets or, for that matter, of the committees of correspondence in the eighteenth-century British colonies of North America. To be sure, this usurpation of governmental functions by revolutionary organizations is not precisely the same thing as the establishment of liberated areas in recent peasant revolutions. In both cases, however, the revolutionary movement grows because it effectively supplants the state in parts of its jurisdiction.

Even the distinction between urban and rural types of revolutions can be overdrawn. It is probably true, as Moore contends, that during the first wave of modern revolution—which embraced England, America, France, all of western and central Europe in 1848,

Paris in 1870, and Russia in 1905–1917 —the principal source of revolutionary energy came from the urban masses (except in the case of England); while the second wave—China, Algeria, Cuba, Vietnam—reflects the dominant influence of the peasantry. Yet the latter revolutions are no more exclusively rural and peasant movements than the former were strictly urban. Eric Wolf suggests that "peasant" revolutions owe much to "the development of an industrial work force still closely geared to life in the villages." This observation would seem to apply also to the earlier revolutions and abortive revolutions in Europe. E. P. Thompson's work on the English working class demonstrates that in the early nineteenth century the most radical elements in English society were those workers, often artisans, who still retained a lively memory of the village past and consciously appealed to preindustrial traditions in their agitation. There is good reason to think that the same pattern can be found in other European countries undergoing the initial stages of industrialization.

Both European and non-European revolutions, in short, seem to have had a number of things in common, and it may be possible to formulate generalizations broad enough to embrace both. Allowing for national and cultural variations, one might view modern revolutions in general as a type of historical event peculiar to societies still predominantly rural and preindustrial, in which traditional social relations, however, are subject to severe stress by the commercialization of agriculture, the introduction of new modes of industrial production, and the centralization of political authority. These changes throw peasants off the land in great numbers, proletarianize many of those who remain, bring about the destruction of artisans as a class, and produce sharp divisions in the ruling class itself. They also create new classes, notably the bourgeoisie and the industrial working class; but these elements, although they furnish leadership and ideology to revolutionary movements and although in the last analysis their presence may account for whatever is progressive and democratic in modern revolutions, do not appear to give them their main impetus. It is the older classes, still rooted in traditions of preindustrial paternalism but directly exposed to the withering blasts of change, that have given to modern revolutions their explosive power, particularly those strata —"middle peasants" and artisans— whose position in the old order was fairly secure. I find highly suggestive Moore's remark, in *Social Origins of Dictatorship and Democracy*, that revolutions are set in motion not by emerging classes but by classes over whom the wheel of progress is about to roll— classes doomed to extinction partly by the very revolutions they set in motion.

All modern revolutions, whether European or non-European, have occurred in predominantly rural societies undergoing rapid change, but it is important to note that precisely because these societies are rural and technologically backward, the pace of change has not itself become "revolutionary," as in advanced societies today. Revolutionary movements articulate new ideas of liberty and equality, but these are firmly rooted in traditional concepts that still retain much force in preindustrial society. Revolutions are directed against powerful states that have arisen on the ruins of seigneurialism but have not yet perfected the methods of repression and control available to the industrial state. In this transitional stage of its development, the state has achieved a sufficient degree of centralization (as I have already suggested) to render it vulnerable to attack, without achieving anything like the awesome power, both military and ideological, wielded by

advanced industrial states today. A further source of the weakness of early modern states is their authoritarianism. Even in Europe, where parliamentary forms had made some headway during the later Middle Ages, the early modern state, as exemplified by the Stuart regime in England and the Bourbon regime in France, ruled not so much through civil institutions—church, schools, courts, parliaments—as through the direct imposition of bureaucratic authority and military force. The same thing is true, to an even greater degree, of the right-wing dictatorships in modern China, Vietnam, and Cuba. An important result of this underdevelopment of civil society and authoritarian state control is that opposition to the state and to the existing order—indeed, opposition of any kind—has to take revolutionary form. Absolutism almost inevitably nourishes a revolutionary negation of itself and forces the state to rely more and more on naked force, thus undermining its own pretensions to divine right or, in the end, to any other form of legitimacy.

II

The foregoing considerations help to explain why there has never been a revolution in an advanced country. (I do not except *"les événéments"* in France in May 1968. Neither the students nor the workers proposed to seize state power, and they would not have known what to do with it even if they had. The "revolution" of May was a student uprising or rebellion, in which large sections of the working class joined for reformist reasons of their own.) Industrial society has not eliminated poverty, but it has eliminated the hungry mob as a force in history. The industrial working class no longer constitutes a revolutionary proletariat. Neither does the so-called "new working class" of clerks, bureaucrats, technicians, and intellectual workers, even if we could agree to call these groups a working class at all. The industrial state represents a far greater concentration of military power than its predecessors. It rules, moreover, not through force alone but through an elaborate network of civil institutions. Opposition movements, instead of being driven underground, are permitted and even encouraged to struggle for control of these institutions; accordingly, they become reformist rather than revolutionary in character. Through its control of mass communications, the ruling class coopts dissident styles of culture and politics and identifies them with its own version of the good life. Preindustrial paternalism, which provided an alternative model of community during the early stages of industrialism, survives as a faint memory only in the urban "culture of poverty" and in isolated backwaters of the western world.

Nor does the culture of the ruling class contain elements subversive of itself, as was the case during earlier periods of western history, when revolutionary movements could appeal not only to the legacy of paternalism but to ideals of human dignity and freedom implicit in ruling-class ideology itself. One of the most important developments of recent years is that the ruling class in advanced countries has largely outgrown its earlier dependence on general culture and a unified world view and relies instead on an instrumental culture resting its claims to legitimacy, not on the elaboration of a world view that purports to explain the meaning of life, but purely on its capacity to solve technological problems and thereby to enlarge the supply of material goods. The ruling class has abandoned its own humanist traditions, which once served not merely to legitimize its own pretensions but, paradoxically, to nourish alternative social visions. As a result, advanced capitalist society, at the very moment it has laid the material basis for a socialism of abundance, more than ever appears to represent, in the eyes of those who live under its sway, the furthest limits of social development.

For all these reasons, revolutions of the traditional type seem a remote possibility in industrial society. Yet the revolutionary tradition persists and exerts a powerful attraction on the American left. How is this persistence, in the face of repeated discouragements, to be explained?

In the course of the nineteenth century, and particularly after the failure of the Paris Commune, the socialist movement gradually ceased to regard the insurrectionary seizure of power as the inevitable and proper goal of radical activity. In its earlier stages the movement consciously modeled itself on French revolutionary examples. By 1900, however, it had largely abandoned hope of overthrowing capitalist society by means of a direct assault on the state. Meanwhile the partial democratization of political life opened up the possibility of achieving socialism through trade unionism and parliamentary politics. This does not mean that socialists had come to agree on every detail of strategy and tactics, or even on fundamental issues. Revisionists like Bernstein argued that capitalism had overcome its "contradictions" and that therefore, in effect, socialist objectives could be achieved within capitalism; orthodox Marxists like Eugene Debs, on the other hand, took the position that capitalist institutions would have to be destroyed before socialism could become a reality. But not even the latter any longer advocated the destruction of state power through a frontal assault or questioned the importance of an electoral strategy. They ridiculed the view, still popular among anarchists and other ultra-leftists, that capitalism would end in "a sudden crash" and, indeed, they went so far as to argue that "this cataclysmic conception of the breakdown of capitalism," as Louis Boudin put it in 1907 (in a book largely devoted to an attack on revisionism), "is not part of the Marxian theory." The socialist movement had evolved, in short, from communism to social democracy, but social democracy had not yet become identified exclusively with timid reformism. Many social democrats retained a commitment to revolutionary objectives even after they had implicitly abandoned the revolutionary strategies deriving from early modern revolutions. The latter, they correctly perceived, were based on social conditions that had ceased to exist—ceased to exist at any rate, in western Europe and the United States.

The First World War and the Russian Revolution profoundly altered the history of the socialist movement. The major social democratic parties' capitulation to the war discredited social democracy, while at the same time, the Russian Revolution gave the insurrectionary tradition a new lease on life. The socialist movement has never recovered from this crisis. The more recent revolutions in China, Vietnam, Cuba, and Algeria have developed ideologies and institutions appropriate to the problems of predominantly agrarian societies, while the social democratic movements have continued to degenerate until in recent years they have become outright accomplices of imperialism disguised as a world-wide crusade against Communist "totalitarianism." The early twentieth century had seen promising steps toward a theoretical synthesis of the insurrectionary and social democratic traditions, particularly in the works of Antonio Gramsci. These efforts, however, have come to nothing. As a result, the socialist movement finds itself lacking either a theory or a practice appropriate to the realities of advanced industrial so-

ciety. The most militant elements cling to an antiquated theory of revolution, while the rest have embraced the Democratic Party, the Labor Party, or their continental equivalents.

Several essays in this book attempt in one way or another to contend with the collapse of socialist theory and its consequences. Some of them try to rescue the idea of revolution from irrelevance by dissociating it from the traditional view that socialism can emerge only from the struggles of the proletariat, and by pointing instead to new classes or groups that allegedly have developed revolutionary potential. But these (and other) writers manage this feat, it seems to me, either by stretching the term revolution out of all resemblance to its original meaning or else by exaggerating the revolutionary consequences that are likely to flow from the activities of blacks, students, and intellectuals. They argue that while the working class has ceased to play a revolutionary role, new social groups are ready to leap into the breach—in particular, the blacks and the students. I wish I found this idea convincing. Moreover, they often contend that "the blacks demand revolution," but in fact the black community is far from united in demanding any such thing. Moreover, the essays by James Turner and by W. E. Perkins and J. E. Higginson show that even black men who regard themselves as revolutionaries do not agree among themselves, let alone with groups like SDS, about what they mean by revolution.

In addition to the blacks, students and "professionals" are often described as a revolutionary force. In the case of students, this conclusion rests more on wishful thinking than on careful analysis. A large minority of students, and possibly even a majority on a few campuses, may well sympathize with radical attacks on the university or

with aspects of those attacks. The
attacks themselves, however, are not
revolutionary, whatever the accompanying rhetoric. As Perkins and
Higginson point out, many black demands can be accommodated without
altering the structure or content of
higher education, and the same thing
is true of white demands for student
power. Many writers on the student
movement are able to make a case for
its revolutionary potential only by
drawing a labored analogy between the
university and the corporation, which
enables them to equate the position of
students in the "knowledge factory"
with that of workers in General Motors
or International Harvester. But students do not work for the universities
in the sense that auto workers work for
General Motors; as Schurmann observes in a footnote, blacks and youth
"are useless classes [that is, they are
economically superfluous] having little
to contribute to economy and society."

After their graduation, however,
most students do go to work—not for
the university but, directly or indirectly,
for the corporations—as technicians,
functionaries, low-level bureaucrats,
teachers, and welfare workers. This fact
does create the possibility that the university in time might come to play an
important role in the development of a
new kind of "working-class" consciousness; but the student movement, in
spite of its revolutionary pretensions,
has not yet addressed itself to that
possibility. Instead it demands power
for students, under the double illusion
that students constitute a class in their
own right and that the demand for
student power is therefore similar to
the demands of industrial workers for
a share in the power of management.
Even when such demands come from
workers, incidentally, they are not revolutionary if they serve only to tie the
workers more firmly than ever to the
corporations and to the corporate-
owned and corporate-dominated ma-

chinery of credit. In the case of students, demands for a share in the power
of management are not revolutionary
under any circumstances. It is true that
corporations use the universities to train
a docile and intellectually stultified
working force, but this condition can
be combated only by identifying the
reform of the university not with student power, but with the long-term interests of the entire working class,
broadly defined to include much of the
so-called new middle class as well.

The third group often seen as
potentially revolutionary is the "professionals"—scientists, technicians, teachers, and functionaries. This is an
interesting suggestion, for it implies
that a broad-based movement for social
change has to rest for the most part on
people engaged in productive work, and
that such a movement, moreover, will
never make any headway until it is able
to show that socialism can be reconciled with law and order in the broadest
sense—not merely with physical safety
and economic security but with a new
cultural synthesis that will bring order
and stability out of the chaos of modern
life. "Professionals" are politically important not because they, together with
blacks and students, have achieved intellectual detachment from industrial
society, but on the contrary because as
brain workers forced to put their talents
at the service of war, "urban renewal,"
and other socially destructive programs,
they represent the higher strata of a
new "working class," the needs of
which, like the needs of the traditional
working class, are increasingly ill-served
by a system that depends on war and
waste for its survival, thereby generating
uncontrollable material and spiritual
disorder.

III

Instead of looking closely at the real
plight of the producing classes, in order
to ascertain whether it might eventually

cause those classes to look with favor on a socialism capable of reconciling the need for change with the need for order, many analysts interpret the need for order as incipient fascism. They argue that productive workers are so strongly committed to the existing industrial system that they will gladly opt for fascism to preserve it. Not only does this view confuse a commitment to order and economic security with a commitment to capitalism as such, but it seems to imply, when coupled with an analysis that insists on the revolutionary potential of blacks and students, that economic expendability alone can serve as a basis for revolutionary discontent. From this we can only conclude that any revolution likely to occur in advanced countries will be, by definition, a minority revolution imposed on the rest of society by a self-appointed vanguard whose economic superfluity liberates it from "false consciousness."

In the face of such analysis it is necessary to insist, with Richard Flacks, that unless a movement for change enlists the active support of the great majority, it is unlikely to accomplish anything that would be recognizable as democratic socialism. This means, among other things, that the student movement will have to transcend its character as a student movement and forge links with those who work in the main institutions of industrial society. Whether it does this has become one of the most important political questions of our day. If it is to succeed, the movement will not only have to abandon the obsolete Leninism that the various factions of SDS have embraced for lack of a better theory, and that Flacks correctly identifies as one of the major obstacles to its success; it will also have to abandon those attitudes and postures of the New Left that betray its upper middle-class origins. I have in mind particularly those attitudes that have led so many radicals to

confuse the search for personal "authenticity" with the search for cultural alternatives to capitalism, and to define personal liberation, moreover, as freedom from work-discipline and from authority in general. The trouble with this definition of the "cultural revolution" is that it tends to divert attention from the realm of work to the realm of leisure, thereby reinforcing one of the strongest and most dangerous tendencies of advanced capitalist society—the attempt to compensate for the meaninglessness of work by holding out the possibility of spiritual fulfillment through consumption. Contrary to a widespread cliché of popular sociology, "the challenge of leisure" is not the most important issue in advanced society. The most important issue remains work—the loss of autonomy on the job, the collapse of high standards of workmanship, the pervasive demoralization that results from the mass production of goods that are widely recognized as intrinsically worthless by those who produce them, and the general crisis of a culture historically oriented around the dignity of labor. As temporary members of a leisure class, students do not experience any of these evils directly; and because students tend to be drawn, moreover, from the more affluent sectors of society, they are likely to be attracted to political and cultural perspectives that define liberation, in effect, as the creative use of leisure or, worse, as the search for ever more sophisticated, shocking, and "radical" styles of consumption in sex, drugs, culture, and politics.

As prospective workers, however, students do experience the many-faceted crisis of work, and it is not only their enforced leisure but also the knowledge that they are being trained for meaningless work that underlies their rebellion. In addition, much of their academic training is itself meaningless, either because it has no recognizable relation to the process of qualification for work or because it makes so few demands on the critical intelligence. Exploration of these issues might serve as the initial steps toward building a genuine student-worker alliance, based on an awareness that intellectual workers, like other workers, are victims of the social processes that have proletarianized workers in general by reducing even intellectual work to a set of disconnected processes that not only offer no satisfaction in themselves but lead to socially disastrous results.

One of the major tasks confronting the left is to show how the urban crisis and the more general "environmental crisis" originate in capitalist production. It is highly encouraging that students—many of whom are not radical by any of the current definitions—are beginning to concern themselves with ecological issues, because these are precisely the issues best calculated to create a common consciousness of deprivation among students, workers, and members of the "new middle class" by showing that the industrial system victimizes *everybody*—except the very rich, who can provide themselves with means of escape from the environmental devastation their own policies have brought about. Much more than imperialism, war, and racism, the burdens of which fall disproportionately on the poor, the evils of pollution, noise, congestion, violence, crime, the physical and moral destruction of the city in the interests of developers, the ravaging of the landscape, suburban sprawl, and the deterioration of the schools are socially less partial in their effects. They have already created widespread fear, resentment, and anger in the working and middle classes; but this anger, instead of venting itself against the corporations, too often finds secondary targets —the blacks, liberals, radical students, "bureaucracy," "government interference." The left then misinterprets the symptoms of popular resentment as in-

corrigible racism, devotion to the status quo, and proto-fascism, and writes off the working class and new middle class as a force for social change. Instead the left should be trying to demonstrate that the deterioration of the environment and the collapse of public services, which people experience most acutely in their capacity as consumers and citizens, must be attributed not to the blacks or to the state but to the corporations and to a system of production that has outlived its economic and social utility. Deprivations and anxieties experienced as community issues, in other words, or as a generalized misery that seemingly defies class analysis must be shown to have their origin in the realm of work and in the class relations that arise from the existing system of production.

I think it is misleading to imply, however, that a mass movement for change may not emerge until the kinds of tensions and strains now experienced chiefly by students become generalized throughout the population—that is, until the population as a whole experiences "the irrelevance . . . of ideologies based on scarcity" (Flacks). This assumes that capitalism itself is capable of generalizing affluence—a dubious proposition. It also assumes that the working and middle class have at present no interest in social change, whereas in fact they suffer from a whole variety of fears and anxieties that might even attract these classes to socialism if they could be convinced that socialism meant something more than a search for "a less repressed, more human, more spontaneous life-style." The so-called cultural revolution identified with one wing of the New Left contains many promising possibilities, but in its present form it does not represent an alternative social vision capable of attracting large masses to its support. In saying this, I do not mean to align myself with those who argue that cultural questions are secondary and that the cultural revolution will have to wait for the political revolution. On the contrary, I believe that cultural questions are central to any movement for socialism. But the "counter-culture" of the sixties denies the possibility of satisfaction through work and envisions utopia as generalized leisure, thereby reaffirming, instead of contradicting, the vision of industrial society itself—one that it cannot realize but which it holds up as the highest good, in the face of centuries of experience that have taught us that work is one of the deepest of man's needs. The cultural task confronting the left is not to overthrow the work ethic, which is already under attack from within capitalist society, but to invest it with new meaning. The left has not yet addressed itself to that question.

One of the reasons for this failure is the influence of an obsolete revolutionary tradition on leftist thought and action. The persistence of that tradition either obscures the importance of cultural questions altogether by encouraging the illusion that a revolutionary seizure of power, at some unspecified point in the future, will automatically usher in the golden age; or else it encourages radicals to define the cultural problem in purely negative terms, as an all-out assault on "middle-class"

values. The revolutionary tradition effectively conceals the fact that in most modern revolutions, the overthrow of the old regime took place only after alternative patterns of culture had established themselves side by side with the dominant ones. (Where this did not happen, as in Russia, the revolution ended in a cultural disaster.) The new cultures themselves, furthermore, drew heavily on older values which the ruling classes were in the process of gradually discarding. In our own time, the ruling class has broken the last ties to its own cultural traditions and has imposed on society a technological anticulture characterized by its ruthless disregard of the past. The agent of the new anticulture is a bulldozer, which destroys familiar landmarks, liquidates entire communities, and breaks down every form of continuity. Under these conditions the idea of revolution as a sharp, sudden, and total break with the past loses the meaning it had in societies on which, for all their restless movement, the past still lay as a dead weight. "Revolution" today may represent, among other things, the only hope of preserving what is worth preserving from the past, including man's natural habitat itself; but if that is the case, it is time that the nineteenth-century idea of revolution be drastically revised or abandoned altogether.

H The Effects of Social Change

INTRODUCTION

Many sociologists, both classical and contemporary, have described and analyzed the tendency of urban-industrial societies to become organized into larger and larger social units. Auguste Comte and Ferdinand Tonnies, for example, pointed to the importance of studying the large cities and nation-states into which the European populations were being organized in the nineteenth century, whereas Karl Marx and Max Weber called attention to the significance of increasing size in industry, business, and government. The processes of metropolitanization and bureaucratization and trends in the political economy discussed in previous sections illustrate the pattern of largeness and complexity in the organization of modern social life. The importance of the individual undoubtedly is reduced in the larger and more complex social organizations. People gradually are forced to adjust to these changes in their life situation and to evolve beliefs, values, and personalities compatible with the new forms of social organization.

Alexis de Tocqueville, in his classic nineteenth-century study, *Democracy in America*, pointed to the increasing size of government and the enlargement of its areas of activity as a "kind of despotism" that he felt "democratic nations have to fear." Americans today have witnessed the growth of government activity in many areas of life, including business, health, education, communication, and even recreation. Such activity does lead to centralization of political power. Many Americans also fear that it reduces individual initiative and creates complacency in the population by seeming to provide for most men's needs without calling for assertive action on their part. On the other hand, the struggles of the working class for effective unions in the 1930's and the black struggle for equality today indicate that disadvantaged groups in the population can and do still fight to assert their interests.

The tendency toward bigness and complexity is to be found in the organization of most areas of modern social life, including, for example, education, health and medical care, and even recreation. Modern man's social life is, therefore, enacted within the context of large-scale organizations. Harry Gracey, in his brief essay, points to one kind of adjustment people make to gaining a living in large-scale bureaucracies. He calls this the development of an "exploitative orientation," and points out that people on all levels of the social structure—upper class, middle class, and working class—and in many different occupations come

542

to regard the organizations they work for as great impersonal units that they can exploit freely for their own benefit whenever the opportunity arises. Gracey rejects the view that this is to be regarded as an outbreak of individual immorality, and instead suggests it is a rational adaptation of individuals to their new social environment.

David Riesman's conception of the "other-directed man" makes sense in the context of the developing total organization of modern society. The other-directed man is socialized to develop great sensitivity to the demands of others and an anxious desire to please them by conforming to their wishes. This man has few firm standards of conduct or inflexible values of his own and is, instead, willing to adjust his actions and beliefs to those prevalent in his social groups. Riesman claims that other-direction is an adaptive personality structure for people living in a highly mobile, rapidly changing society such as ours. It is also adaptive —it should be added here—for people who will spend their lives interacting with others in great impersonal social organizations that require continued association with large numbers of little-known people to whose demands the individual must be ready to accommodate himself. Kingsley Davis deals with a process of social change that, in contrast to political revolution, has been so slow and gradual throughout most of human history that its effects have been almost invisible—the growth of population. In the last two hundred years, and especially in the last twenty, however, world population has grown at unprecedented rates as a result of a worldwide decline in death rates. Such rates of growth cannot continue without bringing about even more widespread poverty than at present and ultimately reversing the drop in death rates, with famines and mass starvation again becoming the major checks on population increase. Davis reviews the alternative possibility of ending the population explosion by adopting successful policies to reduce fertility or the birth rate. His conclusions are far from optimistic.

52
What Sort of Despotism Democratic Nations Have to Fear

ALEXIS DE TOCQUEVILLE

I had remarked during my stay in the United States that a democratic state of society, similar to that of the Americans, might offer singular facilities for

From *Democracy in America* by Alexis de Tocqueville, Volume II, Book IV, Chapter VI. First published in English in 1840.

the establishment of despotism; and I perceived, upon my return to Europe, how much use had already been made, by most of our rulers, of the notions, the sentiments, and the wants created by this same social condition, for the purpose of extending the circle of their power. This led me to think that the nations of Christendom would perhaps eventually undergo some oppression like that which hung over several of the nations of the ancient world.

A more accurate examination of the subject, and five years of further meditation, have not diminished my fears, but have changed their object.

No sovereign ever lived in former ages so absolute or so powerful as to undertake to administer by his own agency, and without the assistance of intermediate powers, all the parts of a great empire; none ever attempted to subject all his subjects indiscriminately to strict uniformity of regulation and personally to tutor and direct every member of the community. The notion of such an undertaking never occurred to the human mind; and if any man had conceived it, the want of information, the imperfection of the administrative system, and, above all, the natural obstacles caused by the inequality of conditions would speedily have checked the execution of so vast a design.

When the Roman emperors were at the height of their power, the different nations of the empire still preserved usages and customs of great diversity; although they were subject to the same monarch, most of the provinces were separately administered; they abounded in powerful and active municipalities; and although the whole government of the empire was centered in the hands of the Emperor alone and he always remained, in case of need, the supreme arbiter in all matters, yet the details of social life and private occupations lay for the most part beyond his control. The emperors possessed, it is true, an immense and unchecked power, which allowed them to gratify all their whimsical tastes and to employ for that purpose the whole strength of the state. They frequently abused that power arbitrarily to deprive their subjects of property or of life; their tyranny was extremely onerous to the few, but it did not reach the many; it was confined to some few main objects and neglected the rest; it was violent, but its range was limited.

It would seem that if despotism were to be established among the democratic nations of our days, it might assume a different character; it would be more extensive and more mild; it would degrade men without tormenting them. I do not question that, in an age of instruction and equality like our own, sovereigns might more easily succeed in collecting all political power into their own hands and might interfere more habitually and decidedly with the circle of private interests than any sovereign of antiquity could ever do. But this same principle of equality which facilitates despotism tempers its rigor. We have seen how the customs of society become more humane and gentle in proportion as men become more equal and alike. When no member of the community has much power or much wealth, tyranny is, as it were, without opportunities and a field of action. As all fortunes are scanty, the passions of men are naturally circumscribed, their imagination limited, their pleasures simple. This universal moderation moderates the sovereign himself and checks within certain limits the inordinate stretch of his desires.

Independently of these reasons, drawn from the nature of the state of society itself, I might add many others arising from causes beyond my subject; but I shall keep within the limits I have laid down.

Democratic governments may become violent and even cruel at certain periods of extreme effervescence or of great danger, but these crises will be rare and brief. When I consider the petty passions of our contemporaries, the mildness of their manners, the extent of their education, the purity of their religion, the gentleness of their morality, their regular and industrious habits, and the restraint which they almost all observe in their vices no less than in their virtues, I have no fear that they will meet with tyrants in their rulers, but rather with guardians.

I think, then, that the species of oppression by which democratic nations are menaced is unlike anything that ever before existed in the world; our contemporaries will find no prototype of it in their memories. I seek in vain for an expression that will accurately convey the whole of the idea I have formed of it; the old words *despotism* and *tyranny* are inappropriate: the thing itself is new, and since I cannot name, I must attempt to define it.

I seek to trace the novel features under which despotism may appear in the world. The first thing that strikes the observation is an innumerable multitude of men, all equal and alike, incessantly endeavoring to procure the petty and paltry pleasures with which they glut their lives. Each of them, living apart, is as a stranger to the fate of all the rest; his children and his private friends constitute to him the whole of mankind. As for the rest of his fellow citizens, he is close to them, but he does not see them; he touches them, but he does not feel them; he exists only in himself and for himself alone; and if his kindred still remain to him, he may be said at any rate to have lost his country.

Above this race of men stands an immense and tutelary power, which takes upon itself alone to secure their gratifications and to watch over their fate. That power is absolute, minute, regular, provident, and mild. It would be like the authority of a parent if, like that authority, its object was to prepare men for adulthood; but it seeks, on the contrary, to keep them in perpetual childhood: it is well content that the people should rejoice, provided they think of nothing but rejoicing.

For their happiness such a government willingly labors, but it chooses to be the sole agent and the only arbiter of that happiness; it provides for their security, foresees and supplies their necessities, facilitates their pleasures, manages their principle concerns, directs their industry, regulates the descent of property, and subdivides their inheritances: what remains, but to spare them all the care of thinking and all the trouble of living?

Thus it every day renders the exercise of the free agency of man less useful and less frequent; it circumscribes the will within a narrower range and gradually robs a man of all the uses of himself. The principle of equality has prepared men for these things; it has predisposed men to endure them and often to look on them as benefits.

After having thus successively taken each member of the community in its powerful grasp and fashioned him at will, the supreme power then extends its arm over the whole community. It covers the surface of society with a network of small complicated rules, minute and uniform, through which the most original minds and the most energetic characters cannot penetrate, to rise above the crowd. The will of man is not shattered, but softened, bent, and guided; men are seldom forced by it to act, but they are constantly restrained from acting. Such a power does not destroy, but it prevents existence; it does not tyrannize, but it compresses, enervates, extinguishes, and stupefies a people, till each nation is reduced to nothing better than a flock of timid and industrious animals, of which the government is the shepherd.

I have always thought that servitude of the regular, quiet, and gentle kind which I have just described might be combined more easily than is commonly believed with some of the outward forms of freedom, and that it might even establish itself under the wing of the sovereignty of the people.

Our contemporaries are constantly excited by two conflicting passions: they want to be led, and they wish to remain free. As they cannot destroy either the one or the other of these contrary propensities, they strive to satisfy them both at once. They devise a sole, tutelary, and all-powerful form of government, but elected by the people. They combine the principle of centralization and that of popular sovereignty; this gives them a respite: they console themselves for being in tutelage by the reflection that they have chosen their own guardians. Every man allows himself to be put in leading-strings, because he sees that it is not a person or a class of persons, but the people at large who hold the end of his chain.

By this system the people shake off their state of dependence just long enough to select their master and then relapse into it again. A great many persons at the present day are quite contented with this sort of compromise between administrative despotism and the sovereignty of the people; and they think they have done enough for the protection of individual freedom when they have surrendered it to the power of the nation at large. This does not satisfy me: the nature of him I am to obey signifies less to me than the fact of extorted obedience.

I do not deny, however, that a constitution of this kind appears to me to be infinitely preferable to one which, after having concentrated all the powers of government, should vest them in the hands of an irresponsible person or body of persons. Of all the forms that democratic despotism could assume, the latter would assuredly be the worst.

When the sovereign is elective, or narrowly watched by a legislature which is really elective and independent, the oppression that he exercises over individuals is sometimes greater, but it is always less degrading; because every man, when he is oppressed and disarmed, may still imagine that, while he yields obedience, it is to himself he yields it, and that it is to one of his own inclinations that all the rest give way. In like manner, I can understand that when the sovereign represents the nation and is dependent upon the people, the rights and the power of which every citizen is deprived serve not only the head of the state, but the state itself; and that private persons derive some return from the sacrifice of their independence which they have made to the public. To create a representation of the people in every centralized country is, therefore, to diminish the evil that extreme centralization may produce, but not to get rid of it.

I admit that, by this means, room is left for the intervention of individuals in the more important affairs; but it is not the less suppressed in the smaller and more private ones. It must not be forgotten that it is especially dangerous to enslave men in the minor details of life. For my own part, I should be inclined to think freedom less necessary in great things than in little ones, if it were possible to be secure of the one without possessing the other.

Subjection in minor affairs breaks out every day and is felt by the whole community indiscriminately. It does not drive men to resistance, but it crosses them at every turn, till they are led to surrender the exercise of their own will. Thus their spirit is gradually broken and their character enervated; whereas that obedience which is exacted on a few important but rare occasions only exhibits servitude at certain intervals and throws the burden of it upon a small number of men. It is in vain to summon a people who have been rendered so dependent on the central power to choose from time to time the representatives of that power; this rare and brief exercise of their free choice, however important it may be, will not prevent them from gradually losing the faculties of thinking, feeling, and acting for themselves, and thus gradually falling below the level of humanity.

I add that they will soon become incapable of exercising the great and only privilege which remains to them. The democratic nations that have introduced freedom into their political constitution at the very time when they were augmenting the despotism of their administrative constitution have been led into strange paradoxes. To manage those minor affairs in which good sense is all that is wanted, the people are held to be unequal to the task; but when the government of the country is at stake, the people are invested with immense powers; they are alternately made the playthings of their ruler, and his masters, more than kings and less than men. After having exhausted all the different modes of election without finding one to suit their purpose, they are still amazed and still bent on seeking further; as if the evil they notice did not originate in the constitution of the country far more than in that of the electoral body.

It is indeed difficult to conceive how men who have entirely given up the habit of self-government should succeed in making a proper choice of those by whom they are to be governed; and no one will ever believe that a liberal, wise, and energetic government can spring from the suffrages of a subservient people.

A constitution republican in its head and ultra-monarchical in all its other parts has always appeared to me to be a shortlived monster. The vices of rulers and the ineptitude of the people would speedily bring about its ruin; and the nation, weary of its representatives and of itself, would create freer institutions or soon return to stretch itself at the feet of a single master.

53

Morality in the Organized Society

HARRY L. GRACEY

During the past decade the investigating units of various governmental bodies have brought to light illegal and unethical practices in almost all areas of organized social life. These "scandals," which have been exposed in industry, labor, government, entertainment, and other institutions of society, with such regularity that they periodically chase one another across the pages of the daily press, share the common feature of individuals acting solely or primarily to secure for themselves as much money, power, and prestige as they can. Their behavior is regarded as "scandalous" when they employ illegal and unethical means to exploit the social institutions for their own ends.

This behavior has been popularly interpreted as an outbreak of "immorality" among individual Americans. Public discussion of the problem consists primarily of moral condemnation and pleas for individual moral rehabilitation. *The New York Times*, for example, editorializes on the "moral decline" of the United States and, as a solution, urges Americans to throw off "the moral slothfulness that makes success more important than the methods for achieving it." A major religious body took the same line when it proclaimed recently, "the nation's life is marked by a disintegration of moral and ethical behavior" and urged "every American to adopt personal integrity and morality as part of his code of life."

By posing the problem as one of individual misbehavior, the popular discussion avoids the crucial question of what it is about life in our society which produces such a widespread exploitative orientation. To paraphrase C. Wright Mills, if a few people showed this exploitative orientation toward social institutions we would look to their character for the explanation, but when many people from all social levels show this orientation we must examine the structure and functioning of social institutions to find the causes of their behavior.

This exploitative orientation is one important part of the malaise which seems to infect the social organism today, and is therefore worth a serious effort at understanding.

Recent investigations by the Kefauver Committee and the Justice Department have shown that corporations manufacturing such diverse products as electrical equipment, autos, steel, drugs, and bread engage in illegal price fixing to the end of securing a constantly increasing profit. These policies are, of course, set by responsible top executives and board members of the corporations (regardless of who takes the rap when they are discovered) whose wealth, status, and corporate privileges are enhanced by ever-increasing company profits. When caught at their illegal activities, company executives justify their actions as having been in the best interests of their companies, and seem to regret only the

damage they have done to their companies' reputations—and thus the danger to their own privileged positions in society. The stockholders also seem to feel that the companies should pursue any policies which assure them of ever-increasing monetary returns. At the year's annual meetings, the majority of General Electric stockholders present, whose dividends have been increasing with the annual increases in GE's profits, jeered anyone who tried to question top management policy and voted down all motions condemning illegal practices.

The exploitative orientation of middle-level bureaucrats is regularly documented in the case of government employees charged with inspecting the work of private contractors. Often it is the rule, rather than the exception, that people in such positions accept and even demand money from the contractors for passing on work which either does or does not meet the legal specifications. The petty bureaucrats in government are probably not getting rich on this graft, but it does contribute to their ability to live up to the middle-class consumption standards upon which their families' status depends. Bribery and graft, therefore, seem to provide middle-level bureaucrats with the means for living the middle-class version of the good life.

It has long been known that the people at the bottom of the American status heap, the blue-collar workers, regard their routine, monotonous, and dehumanizing jobs solely as sources of income. It has recently been shown that members of the teamsters' union have the same orientation toward their union. The attitude of the teamsters is essentially the same as that of the GE stockholders—they support their organization as long as it provides them with an ever-increasing income. The fact that their president, James Hoffa, has been accused of illegal and unethical practices seems to be unimportant to the majority of union members, so long as he brings home the annual wage increases.

The exploitative orientation toward social institutions is not confined to business, government, and labor. It can be found in almost any institution of contemporary society. In higher education, for example, we have witnessed the much-publicized basketball scandals. Equally unethical, but unpublicized, is the politics of academic grant-getting by which university faculty members use research funds from the government and private foundations for purposes other than those for which they were allocated. In many cases, the administrators of the grants know that the money will be misused. Everyone is involved in the status function of academic grant-getting, which is to build the prestige of the faculty member and the university as a basis for getting more grants, and thus providing a means for increasing the wealth of both.

The majority of Americans today live in urban communities in which most aspects of their lives are organized by large bureaucratic structures. The exploitative orientation, I shall contend, is a product of the mass bureaucratic nature of contemporary society.

The small community in the preindustrial, or early industrial, society was a social organization on a more personal scale. It was a static place with a rigid social structure, but it provided many opportunities for intimate, emotionally fulfilling social relations. Few aspects of one's life were free from the scrutiny of neighbors, but most people had a secure place in a network of informal social relations in which they were assigned status on the basis of their family background, size and source of income, community activities, and conformity to community morality.

Today the metropolis is replacing the small community as the home of the majority of people. In metropolitan life social relations tend to become limited, formal, and rationally calculating in nature. Opportunities for lasting, comprehensive, and intimate associations tend to decrease, though they continue to exist in some stable neighborhoods of large cities and in suburban communities in which the population has become stabilized over a period of time. As the opportunity for intimate associations decreases, people have less knowledge of one another upon which to base their judgments of each other. Under these conditions, material possessions, signifying varying expenditures of money, become an important basis upon which people judge and rank one another. Accurate knowledge of how the money has been obtained is difficult to get, and therefore cannot be easily subject to judgment. The urban mass society thus provides opportunities for personal privacy impossible in small rural communities at the same time that it isolates people from intimate contact with each other.

Upon this base of an individuated urban mass have arisen the great bureaucratic structures which organize almost all areas of social life outside of the family and small friendship groups. Bureaucracy is the product of two major trends in industrial society: the trend toward greater functional specialization and the trend toward larger organizations. It is the only form of social organization yet invented for coordinating the work of many specialists in the accomplishment of many interrelated tasks in large business, government, education, and other areas of modern life. All important decision-making power is vested in the top offices of bureaucracies and in the private bureaucracies of business and industry, the manipulation of the organization by those at the top to maximize their own gain is the accepted and expected behavior under the profit system. Laws, ethics, and "social responsibility" must be viewed in a pragmatic and utilitarian light by those who would succeed in such positions. The lower bureaucratic employees, both blue collar and white collar, in both public and private bureaucracies have little control over organization policy and thus over their own futures. This powerlessness of bureaucratic employees to influence organizational policy makes it rational for them to exploit their present positions to gain whatever wealth, power, or prestige they can.

Morals are products of social life and can be expected to change as the life experiences of people in their society change. Man in the mass society —isolated from much intimate contact with others, relying heavily on conspicuous consumption for his social standing and self-respect, and for the

most part powerless in the organizations which determine his own future —has little reason to regard the organizations in which he participates as anything other than sources of private gain. The mass-bureaucratic nature of social life today, in other words, probably produces so many individuals with the exploitative orientation toward modern social organizations. Without significant primary groups to enforce traditional moral standards in these organizations, there is no reason to expect the mass man to reject any means which are convenient for attaining his own end. Finally, individuals living in such a society cannot be expected to feel much responsibility for anyone's welfare but their own and certainly cannot be expected to "rise in indignation" when others are shown to be exploiting the social institutions too.

54

The Other-Directed Man

DAVID RIESMAN

Types of Social Character

. . . The typology of character set forth in *The Lonely Crowd* is at the same time a typology of societies. In terms of models, we speak of a society depending on *tradition-direction* if in it conformity to tradition is the characteristic achievement both of institutions and of individuals; this conformity is assured by a type of character we term

From *Faces in the Crowd* by David Riesman. Copyright © 1952 by the Yale University Press. Reprinted by permission of the Yale University Press.

tradition-directed. We posit such a society and such a character type as typical for preliterate and peasant cultures in most of the world, while recognizing that there may be instances (such as the Manus of the Admiralty Islands, as described by Margaret Mead) where "primitives" are anything but traditional in outlook. In the Western world as a whole we see emerging over the course of the post-medieval period an expanding and dynamic form of society which we speak of as depending on *inner-direction*—one in which individuals are trained to conform not to external tradition but to internalized norms; this conformity is assured by a type of character we term inner-directed. This type must still be considered the dominant mode of conformity of the dominant classes of the West; hence we cannot speak as yet of a whole society depending on *other-direction*, a third form of conformity; we can only say that adumbrations of such a society appear in contemporary America, especially in the larger metropolitan areas, and in the middle and, notably, the upper-middle strata. In such areas and groups individuals are trained to conform neither to tradition nor to internalized goals but to the ever-changing expectations of ever-changing contemporaries; this conformity is assured by a type of character we term other-directed.

It will be seen that it is through the concept of the mode of conformity that character and society are linked in our analysis, for each type of society is seen as instilling a particular mode of conformity in its members, who then perpetuate the society as they go about its business, including the rearing of the young. I shall postpone discussion of some of the more or less obvious difficulties presented by such a formulation and turn first to a brief picture of each of the three character types.

The Tradition-Directed Type. In the type of society depending on tradition-direction, social change is at a minimum, though upsets in personal life may be violent and catastrophic. Conformity is assured by inculcating in the young a near-automatic obedience to tradition, as this is defined for the particular social role toward which the individual is headed by his sex and station at birth. That obedience, with all its gratifying rewards, is taught by the large circumambient clan and, after childhood, usually by members of one's own sex group. In this way one learns

to master increasingly admired and difficult techniques and to avoid the shame that befalls the violator of the given norms. Since this type in its pristine form is almost nonexistent in today's America, it is not necessary to say more about it at this point.

The Inner-Directed Type. In historical sequence, the tradition-directed type gave way to a new pattern of conformity resting less on continuously encouraged obedience to customs and more on obedience to internalized controls instilled in childhood by the individual's parents and other adult authorities. This change in the source of direction was both cause and consequence of the creation, in western Europe and its conquered territories, of historically new social roles for which children could not possibly be prepared by rigorous or amiable attention to traditional mores. Hence the parent—and, for the first time, there *is* a parent in control, rather than an extended family ménage—equipped his child with an inflexible determination to achieve any of the possible goals which an expanding society seemed to suggest.

The inner-directed type can be described by a related congeries of attitudes toward work, toward the self, toward leisure, toward children, toward history, and so on. Among these no one readily isolable criterion is definitive. What is central, however, to the concept of inner-direction is that one's whole life is guided, for good or ill, by very generalized goals—such as wealth, fame, goodness, achievement—which were implanted early by identification with the modeling upon one's parents and other influential adults. One may be torn among these goals, fail to achieve them, or fight their tug; but one never doubts that life is goal-directed and that the inner voice is the principal source of that direction. Metaphorically, one may think of such people as *gyroscopically* driven—the gyroscope being implanted by adults and serving to stabilize the young even in voyages occupationally, socially, or geographically far from the ancestral home.

The Other-Directed Type. The inner-directed type, as just indicated, is prepared to cope with fairly rapid social change, and to exploit it in pursuance of individualistic ends. But the very possession of these ends makes the type less resilient, in the face of exceedingly quick change, than the other directed type whose conformity rests not so much on the incorporation of adult authority as on sensitive attention to the expectations of contemporaries. In the place of lifelong goals toward which one is steered as by a gyroscope, the other-directed person obeys a fluctuating series of short-run goals picked up (to continue with metaphor) by a *radar*. This radar, to be sure, is also installed in childhood, but the parents and other adults encourage the child to tune in to the people around him at any given time and share his preoccupation with their reactions to him and his to them.

The development of this character type, with its mode of sensitivity to others, is both cause and consequence of sweeping and accelerated changes in the social structure of contemporary industrial society: the rise of the "new" middle class; the preoccupation with consumption rather than production, and, within the sphere of production, with the "human factor"; the weakening of parental assurance and control over children; and so on down a long list. Again, a new congeries of attitudes toward all major spheres of life—toward work, consumption, sex, politics, and the self—reflect and confirm the shifts in character structure and in social structure. The world of interpersonal relations almost obscures from view the world of physical nature and the supernatural as the setting for the human drama.

Other-direction makes its appearance in a society in which the problem not only of mere subsistence but also of large-scale industrial organization and production have been for the most part surmounted, freeing for other concerns both the small leisure class and the large leisure masses. In such a society the customer can only be wrong if he remains an ascetic Puritan, haunted by ideas of thrift and fears of scarcity. Outside of America such a state of affairs has only been spottily attained —in parts of Sweden, in Australia and New Zealand, and perhaps in a few other centers. But even within America other-direction has not yet become equivalent to "the American way" and inner-directed types are still important.

Some Essential Qualifications. We are a long way from being able to say that other-direction can be equated with contemporary metropolitan America, or that the people of this or that preliterate society actually have been found to be tradition-directed. And doubtless, by the time such empirical tests are made we shall have better models to work with. Meanwhile it should be clear that the very nature of the typology, which is overlapping rather than discrete in its categories, implies the necessity of going through a number of further steps before such concrete test, against individuals or against societies, could even be fruitfully undertaken. In human affairs one seldom deals with all-or-none situations, and our typology is designed to grapple with the interrelationships rather than with the discontinuities in social life; this commitment, at least at the present stage of the work, rules out any neat litmus-paper test for character.

In fact, the discerning reader may already have realized that in the nature of the case there can be no such thing as a society or a person wholly dependent on tradition-direction, inner-direction, or other-direction: each of these modes of conformity is universal, and the question is always one of the degree to which an individual or a social group places principal reliance on one or the other of the three available mechanisms. Thus, all human beings are inner-directed in the sense that, brought up as they are by people older than they, they have acquired and internalized some permanent orientations from them. And, conversely, all human beings are other-directed in the sense that they are oriented to the expectations of their peers and to the "field situation" (Kurt Lewin) or "definition of the situation" (W. I. Thomas) that these peers at any moment help create. . . .

An Example of Other-Direction

Inner-direction and other-direction, as leading contenders for American allegiance, set up crosscurrents which are nicely illustrated by the fact that one of the radio programs to which the inner-directed Mr. Burns listens is written (along with others) by a Hollywood script-writer whom I have chosen as an example of other-direction; I shall call him Shelton. This writer, in his thirties, was too busy to allow the interview to be completed, but enough transpired to show how constant is his need to be liked and reassured about himself. Though claiming to be bored by his $1000-a-week job, he could not help overplaying his role as clever comic; nor does he appear to relax his stance even in the midst of his own family; and, though often anxious when he is with others, he cannot bear to be alone.

Indeed, for him the separation of work and play is almost nonexistent.[1]

[1] True, he tells us: "I go to wrestling matches very occasionally, but only for a source of amusement," commenting also that "I dislike boxing matches—fights—unless they're really top fighters." . . . But here as elsewhere it is clear that he is concerned with the status of his leisure pursuits, and in that sense he works at them.

Asked what movies he prefers, he states:

[Repeated question out loud to himself.] I enjoy a comedy because I'm in that branch of the writing business. [Much more of this, then:] I like pictures with a pertinent theme. Pictures like *Possessed*, with Joan Crawford, a psychiatric study, is the best of its kind in the last couple of years. It gave me a feeling of realism. I always considered movies a form of escapism, but when you get realism in them you become more aware of the cares of the world.

Asked about his reading tastes, he declares:

If someone has given me a book or I hear of something entertaining, I'll read it. [He mentioned a book about Colonel Evans Carlson—"great admiration for the man"— and *Wind in the Olive Trees*—"pertinent to Spain."] In other words, if they are significant books. On the other hand, I have had *Inside U.S.A.* for some months and haven't finished it.

But he does "scan the newspaper at home every day"—mainly for columnists, including show-business ones; he adds: "Now and again I glance at a column like Pegler's to see who he is attacking and the reasons; to see how the other half lives. I used to read sports a lot." Who are his heroes?

Well, how far back can I go? Colonel Evans Carlson—I'll start early. Wendell Willkie. Franklin Roosevelt. Henry Wallace. Eugene Debs. Lincoln. A man like Edison. Da Vinci. There's quite a list. Collectively they have foresight, ingenuity, humanity, perseverance—the main things collectively.

In these responses the manner quite as much as the matter gives indications of the self-consciousness, the concern with the other's reaction, the tendency to rate one's experiences, and the lack of long-term aims that are among the criteria for other-direction. The political section of the interview exhibits Shelton as a not exceptional Hollywood "lib-lab" without real conviction, with that combination of cynicism about "what really goes on" and idealism about the heroes just named which can so readily be manipulated by Stalinist commissars in the writers' guilds. His cultural judgments are held with like deference to opinion leaders: timid toward the supposedly highbrow milieu of the interviewer, he is yet drawn to his own vulgarities by an equal fear of losing the common touch.

In one of those "real-life" encounters that are worth more than any number of questions, Shelton invites the interviewer to have dinner with him and his family at a night club. Here he is described as the genial host—so genial as never to relax for a moment; his generosity, which he mentions in the interview—and which may be a show-business convention as much as an individual character trait [2]—is borne out in his treatment of waiters and guests. In the interview, asked what he would do if he had six months to live and could do just as he pleased [3]—a question which was frequently productive— Shelton has said: "I'd probably travel for a good part of it. Then I would like to write something that would be profound enough to live a while." Even in this hypothetical crisis Shelton sees himself as aimless, hoping both to

travel—a frequent, and usually aimless, answer to this question—and still find time to write something of moment. However, at the night club he gives additional reasons for his desire to write a novel or serious play: he wants to lift himself out of the group of more or less anonymous and hence insecure script-writers—an effort, that is, at "marginal differentiation"; [4] beyond such pressing competitive needs, the unwritten opus seems to stand as a kind of culturally accepted symbol for the deficiencies Shelton senses in his way of life. Yet it develops that in his job he always works in tandem with other writers, jealousy of whom he represses in bursts of generosity which he then resents.

Leaving the night club, he jokes about an abstract painting to hide his self-consciousness about "art"—but, as with so much else he does, the very act of hiding is revealing, and the interviewer suspects that he *wants* to reveal, to share, to be warm and intimate. Asked in the interview about guilt feelings, he had said that he more than lives up to his community obligations but that "I've been told I've neglected obligations to myself." He seems unwilling to make this claim, or confession, on his own behalf, and the interview is devoid of strong complaints; he declares drably: "My past few years have been happy ones. I survived a war. I came back—after a short period of struggle I regained my position. I'm content with my wife."

In Shelton's case, character, Hollywood culture (on one of its levels), and occupational role all seem to reinforce one another. (We can also see that, as an influential writer, he will

[2] To put matters this way, of course, polarizes the individual from his milieu in a way which is usually unjustified. For it is "no accident" that Shelton is in show business: occupations have differential appeals to different character types, and their traditions are carried not only in surface behavior but also in the character structure of many, though not all, of those who are drawn to and remain in the given roles.

[3] This question in our interview, like a number of others, was taken from preliminary reports of the Berkeley study which eventuated in The Authoritarian Personality. We adapted other questions (particularly concerning work attitudes) from long interviews by C. Wright Mills which were preparatory to his White Collar (New York, Oxford University Press, 1951).

[4] For a description of this phenomenon, see the portrait of Higgins, p. 577, n. 5; also my article, "Some Observations Concerning Marginality," Phylon, 12 (1951), 113, 116 ff.

tend, as a media model, to spread the ethos characteristic of other-directed types even when—as in his preference for "message" films—he may appear to react against "entertainment" or the consumer outlook.) More than metaphorically, he lives by his radar, and the interview shows that the scanning never stops. And yet even this man, who seems successful and "adjusted," has strivings of another sort—some generosity, perhaps, which transcends (or is rationalized by) what others expect of him; some deeply repressed desires for fulfillment of obligations to himself, which bespeak his "humanistic conscience" (in Erich Fromm's sense), his wish for autonomy.

And we can also see that were such a man to be put in another milieu— say, a Hartford insurance office or a southern university—his very sensitivity might enable him to wear, on short notice, a seemly cloak of inner-directed attitudes.[5] By the same token, of course, the *content* of his answers, especially when taken one by one, does not demonstrate that Shelton is, in fact, other-directed; as always, it is the Gestalt, the total mechanism, which counts. Furthermore, the fact that Shelton may strike many readers as, in comparison with Burns, an unattractive "character" (as Shelton himself would be the first to anticipate) should not lead them to a hasty verdict on other-direction per se; for here again a wide gamut of individuals could be brought together under that designation. And Shelton's all-too-evident insecurities can be laid at the door of his occupation, the excess of his income (which includes his child-

5 Cf. Theodore Newcomb, *Personality and Social Change* (New York, Dryden Press, 1943), a study of the ways in which the attitudes and values of Bennington College girls shifted during the four-year course in a "liberal" direction, in consonance with the atmosphere created by the faculty and older students.

less wife's high earnings as an interior decorator) over his inherited capital and cultural background, and perhaps his very strivings toward less ephemeral accomplishment, quite as much as to the defects inherent in other-direction as a conformity-mechanism. Many observers would be inclined to say that Shelton handles his "high income guilt" in a distinctly more graceful way than many, and that his other-directed effortfulness succeeds in achieving genuine hospitalities quite beyond Burns' ken.

Turning again to our collection of interviews we find a very different type of other-direction in the case of a thirty-eight-year-old navy commander, home on a visit from his Honolulu headquarters station. Son of a Vermont small-town contractor, he took an advanced agronomist degree at the University of Vermont, got a commission in 1939, and has remained in the navy since. Yet there is nothing stereotypically "rural" or "braid" in his very urbane interview. His friendly, calm responses aim to show him as cosmopolitan and tolerant. In his unusually well-informed political remarks he emphasizes the insincerity of the Russians as the basis of international discord. In his navy command his interests seem to be entirely in the sphere of human relations, divorced from any technical matters; speaking of his pep talks to junior officers, he observes:

Sometimes it was good to fly into a rage or sometimes to say well, we're all good friends, and we want to do the best we can, and we're all in this together. If I used the same method it would have lost its effectiveness. In fact it was good to change the method by throwing them off balance—especially if they thought I would rant and rage and then I was friendly—that threw them off balance until they were working in the right direction.

As his best trait he names "ability to see the other person's side," and as his worst a certain intolerance when "he doesn't see yours." The whole interview shows him as amiably people-oriented and consumption-oriented rather than job-oriented.

Yet here again it is necessary to distinguish between the content and the mechanisms of direction. An interest in personnel, as an occupational matter, is not necessarily a sign of other-direction in character. I recall the dismay of one of my students who discovered that a group of personnel men in a large company were, in the main, inner-directed rather than other-directed. She had assumed that, since such work involved concern for morale and group mood, it would draw only other directed types; she overlooked (among many other possibilities which in any given case can quite reverse "normal" expectations of this sort) the fact that personnel work has for many years been a crusade as well as a career for many inner-directed people—whose organizational zeal later on made places in industry available for men of a different mold.

To return to our naval officer, we cannot be sure, then, about his character. It is striking that he has made with such apparent ease the transition from small-town Vermont and soil science to the "smooth" and worldly executive. Just such transitions of role and locale, however, are characteristic of these still very fluid United States, and the high-school and university system is the navigational lock ordinarily used to by-pass the rapids of becoming a self-made man. Thus, the fact of transition says nothing about whether a person is inner-directed or other-directed; many types can make it, and

their character influences the form and style of ascent rather than the ascent itself. It is again the whole quality of the interview which leads to an interpretation that the commander is, on the whole, governed by the mechanism of other-direction.

Save in rare cases, however, such an interpretation must remain tentative. In the study of lengthy interviews the experience I often have is to come upon an answer for which I am totally unprepared, one which fits neither my own nor any other frame of interpretation known to me. We can therefore never be sure that, had the army officer said more, or been asked questions of a different genre, he might not have compelled the interpreter to realign all the rest of the answers. Thus, studying an interview with a highly cultivated, skeptical, and intelligent clubwoman, we say to ourselves: yes, here is a person, on the whole other-directed, typical of her suburban set in the League of Women Voters (in which she is active)—until we come to her answer to the question whether she would like to have been born in some other age, and we see her matter-of-fact declaration that she probably has been—she believes in reincarnation! There is, so far as I can see, nothing in the previous answers to prepare for this; on the contrary, everything else makes it most unlikely. And then, in interpreting such an interview, in trying to find clues to character and social orientation, we may be led to see this as not only more salient but more significant, for this particular person, than the general schematic question of the degrees of inner-direction or other-direction. . . .

55

Population Policy: Stemming the Human Tide

KINGSLEY DAVIS

One of the most crucial issues in the world today is that of population control. Faced with the undesired consequences of unprecedented and accelerating human multiplication, many countries are currently trying to curb their birthrates by supporting family-planning programs. For *Homo sapiens*, with his unique sociocultural apparatus, has suddenly achieved such a preeminent place in the organic world that he threatens to drive out all species except those he pets or eats.

In man's history, there have probably been two major jumps in the rate of population increase. One of these came with the invention of agriculture and animal husbandry some several thousand years ago; the other came with the Industrial Revolution beginning around 1750. Of the two jumps, the second is by far the greater. Over one-fifth of the earth's entire human increase has occurred in the last 220 years—less than one-tenth of 1% of man's history. In those 220 years the population has multiplied itself more than four and one-half times. Even within the modern era, the most recent periods have seen the most rapid growth. Nearly 40% of the increase after 1750 has occurred in 10% of the time, the two decades between 1950 and 1970. The number of people added in those 20 years is equal to the entire population of the world in 1825.

It takes little skill at arithmetic to see that this trend, if allowed to continue, will give the world an unworkable population within a short time. In only 150 years the total would be 57,000,000,000.

From *1971 Britannica Yearbook of Science and the Future*. Encyclopedia Britannica, Inc. (Chicago), pp. 400–411.

Since the 3,600,000,000 on earth today are far too many—judging by the hundreds of millions who are impoverished, illiterate, unskilled, crowded, and plagued by deteriorating air, water, and soil—the question is not will the growth stop, but how. One hopes that this can be accomplished by drastically reducing fertility. If that should fail, the inevitable result will be a calamitous resurgence of the death rate.

The Failure of Population Control

It is obvious that current efforts to curb population are not succeeding. Between 1960 and 1970, world population rose by approximately 600 million, a 20% increase in 10 years. This eclipsed the 488 million increase (19%) of the prior decade. Even in countries that have had a population-control policy, no appreciable decline in population growth can be demonstrated. In India, for example, the government began a population-control program in 1952, but the growth of the Indian population has been more rapid since that time than before. In Taiwan the long-time downward trend in population growth, which had occurred as a result of urban-industrial development, diminished after 1964, when a huge private program became fully operational.

According to some critics, current population policies are not succeeding because they are inadequate. If so, it is an old story; these are not the first population policies to be tried, nor are they the first to fail.

In the industrially advanced nations, the 19th century was a period of rapid population growth; economic success was accompanied by demographic expansion. The peoples of northwestern Europe and their offshoots overseas multiplied faster than the rest of the world. Whereas in 1750 they had represented approximately 21% of the world's population, by 1900 they accounted for about 32%. There was much debate over this growth, but on the whole it was academic; no real effort was made to stop the increase.

Around 1870, however, the birthrate in industrial countries began a long decline that lasted until about 1933. During the depression of the 1930s, fertility reached such a low point that, had it continued at that level, the populations of the urban-industrial nations would eventually have failed to replace themselves. This virtual cessation of population growth brought widespread alarm, and deliberate government policies to raise the birthrate were instituted in several developed countries, among them Germany, Italy, Japan, Sweden, and France. These policies failed; it cannot be demonstrated that any of the measures had a significant positive effect. Beginning in the late 1930s birthrates began to rise, but they rose in countries that had no special pronatalist measures as well as in those with them.

In the meantime, the locus of population growth had shifted from the industrialized nations to the less developed countries. The reason was that advanced health techniques were being exported to the poorer nations. Mortality declined far more rapidly in the less developed two-thirds of the world than it had ever done in the industrial countries; it also declined at an earlier stage of economic development and independently of local economic advance or stagnation. This was especially marked after World War II, when large-scale international aid made it possible to bring machine-age medicine even to Stone Age aborigines.

In recent decades, the population in less developed areas has been growing almost twice as fast, on the average, as the population of the industrial nations. This does not mean that the industrial nations themselves have not been growing; they all had a baby boom after World War II that contributed to the recent acceleration of world population growth. However, by far the most spectacular increase has been in the less developed countries.

In these countries the skyrocketing population is a major obstacle to economic development. But the industrial countries are not exempt from the problems of population growth. Their lesser but still rapid increase robs their economic development of a large part of its value, since an increasing share of per capita income must be spent simply in coping with the nuisances and dangers created by a rising population multiplied by a rising use of material goods.

Table 1
Modern Growth of World's Population

YEAR	POPULATION (IN 000,000)	DOUBLING TIME (IN YEARS)
1750	791	
1850	1,262	148
1900	1,650	129
1950	2,515	82
1970	3,628	38

Sources: Durand, *op. cit.,* except for 1970 estimate, which is by the author.

Beginnings of Action

In the 1950s world leaders began to advocate population control, cautiously at first but with increasing vigor. Their aim was to get governments to act in three ways. First, for the sake of population control, old rules outlawing contraceptive information were to be eliminated. Second, governments in less developed countries were urged to undertake programs to spread knowledge and use of advanced contraceptive techniques. Third, the governments of industrial nations were asked to pour money into research on improved contraceptives, to install birth-control clinics for their own poor, to use part of their economic-aid funds to finance family-planning programs in less developed countries, and to influence such international agencies as the United Nations to further similar programs.

Although Puerto Rico passed enabling legislation in 1937 for the installation of contraceptive services in public health clinics, India was the first independent nation to start a national population-control program. In December 1952, Prime Minister Jawaharlal Nehru presented to Parliament India's first five-year plan, which called for $1 million to establish family-planning clinics throughout the country. Pakistan started a similar program in 1957, followed by South Korea in 1961, the United Arab Republic in 1966, and several other countries at more recent dates. The industrial nations proved anxious to help. Sweden, for example, after a nationwide fund-raising campaign in 1955–56, donated $77,360 to help start a family-planning scheme in Ceylon, with Swedish doctors investigating local birth-control attitudes and then teaching methods. An agreement was signed between the two governments in 1958.

Private U.S. foundations had long been active in assisting family-planning programs. As early as 1952, the Population Council was set up as an intermediary organization through which funds could be channeled for this purpose. Increasingly, however, the U.S. government was being put under pressure to help. In 1959, after a committee appointed by Pres. Dwight D. Eisenhower to review the activities of the Agency for International Development had recommended inclusion of family planning in AID's work, the president responded that birth control was not a proper concern for government. Although Eisenhower later changed his mind, this remark, together with a statement by the Catholic bishops of America opposing any use of public funds for birth control abroad, forced a showdown on the issue. The politicians of the day generally equivocated by misinterpreting the question as one of "compelling" other countries to adopt birth control, but the leaders of the movement were in no mood to be sidetracked. As a result of their persistent efforts in February 1965 AID finally sent instructions to its missions abroad to provide assistance in family planning, although this assistance did not include contraceptive devices or equipment for their manufacture. Nevertheless, in only six years, U.S. officials had completely reversed themselves, going from political fear of mentioning birth control to an endeavor to join with those advocating such a policy.

During this period the subject of population growth also became an issue in the United Nations. After the administration of Pres. John F. Kennedy had joined with Sweden in urging the UN to discuss the question, the General Assembly concluded its first debate devoted entirely to population on Dec. 18, 1962. It then adopted a resolution calling for intensified international cooperation "in the population field," but birth control and population limitation were not actually mentioned. A year later, however, the UN sponsored an Asian population conference—the first such conference of governments ever held—with a mandate to make recommendations for population policies. Then, in his June 1965 speech to the UN commemorating the 20th anniversary of that organization, Pres. Lyndon B. Johnson made the now-famous statement, "Let us act on the fact that less than five dollars invested in population control is worth a hundred dollars invested in economic growth." Subsequently in December 1966, UN Sec-

Table 2

Population Growth in Developed Regions Versus Less Developed Regions

DECADE	Percentage of World's Population		Rate of Increase per Decade	
	DEVELOPED	LESS DEVELOPED	DEVELOPED	LESS DEVELOPED
1920–40	26.0	74.0	8.3	12.4
1940–60	29.7	70.3	8.9	18.5
1960–70	30.8	69.2	12.6	22.9

Note: Derived from data on populations of each country every 10 years, as given in the United Nations, *Demographic Yearbook*. The countries making up the "developed" and "less developed" categories are held constant for each decade but are allowed to change from one decade to another if their developmnt justifies it. In 1920–30 the "developed" category included Canada, the United States, Australia, New Zealand, northwest Europe, and parts of central Europe. The U.S.S.R. was added in 1930; Czechoslovakia and Japan in 1940; Argentina, Israel, Italy, and Uruguay in 1950; and Chile, Poland, South Africa, Spain, Venezuela, and Yugoslavia in 1960. The "less developed" category includes the rest of the world in each decade.

retary-General U Thant endorsed a Declaration on Population signed by 12 heads of state (later joined by 18 others) that called attention to the seriousness of the problem and approved family planning.

Meanwhile, in the same month as President Johnson's 20th anniversary speech to the UN, the U.S. Congress began public hearings on legislation that would give to federal agencies direct responsibilities in providing birth-control facilities. This was followed, on July 18, 1969, by Pres. Richard Nixon's historic population message to Congress, in which he pointed out that "many already impoverished nations are struggling under a handicap of intense population increase." He not only offered the cooperation of the United States in strengthening population and family programs abroad but also recommended that contraceptive services in the United States be expanded. Thus, by 1969 the advocates of a U.S. government population policy that had been rejected only 10 years before had achieved victory. Official programs to control fertility were amazingly popular.

Just at the moment of success, however, doubt was raised that this type of action would prove effective. An article, "Population Policy: Will Current Programs Succeed?" in the Nov. 10, 1967, issue of *Science*, pointed out that, if the goal is population control, family planning is not the means. This criticism rapidly gained wide assent.

Family Planning: Is It Enough?

Essentially, family planning is the use of contraceptives to ensure the desired number and spacing of births. The planned parenthood movement has concentrated on research to find a 100% effective contraceptive, clinics to supply contraceptive materials and instruction, and education to induce couples to use contraception so they will have only as many children as they want. Viewed from the standpoint of population control, however, family-planning programs have a fundamental flaw: they provide control for couples but not for societies. There has been considerable confusion over this distinction. Thus, the Declaration on Population, signed by 30 world leaders and endorsed by Secretary-General U Thant, says that a "great problem threatens the world. . . . the problem of unplanned population growth."

One then expects the declaration to call for *population* planning, but actually it calls only for *family* planning, stating that "the opportunity [of parents] to decide the number and spacing of children is a basic human right."

According to the critics of the family-planning approach, undesired population growth is a collective rather than an individual problem. The number of children that a couple wants is not necessarily the number that, from society's point of view, it should have. To make individual decisions add up to a desirable population trend, a nation must find ways to influence those decisions in accordance with an overall plan. Otherwise, individual planning will merely result in collective nonplanning.

To demonstrate the ineffectiveness of family-planning programs for population control, the critics cite many surveys, taken all over the world, which show that the number of offspring couples want is enough to guarantee rapid population growth. In the United States, for example, polls taken since the 1930s indicate that white women, on the average, want more than three children, and that there is a tendency for the number to rise. In 1961 the average white female under age 30 considered 3.6 children to be the ideal family size, while 52% of the women questioned said they wanted four or more. If these desires were achieved—if couples had as many children as they say they want—the U.S. population would be growing even more rapidly than it is. And this holds true for the industrialized countries generally.

In less developed societies, the desire for children is even greater. In Taiwan in 1967, for instance, 42% of the women under 40 who already had three children said they wanted more. A 1963 survey in Turkey found that over 42% of the women wanted four or more children. In an eastern Javan village, the average size for an "ideal" family was thought to be 4.3 children; in a Delhi, India, village, 4 children; and in a Mysore, India, village, 4.2. Furthermore, urbanization in the less developed countries brought only slight reductions in the desired number of children. In Bangalore, India, a city of over a million, the number of children desired by wives was 3.7; in seven capital cities of Latin America, it averaged 3.4.

This being the case, critics of family planning see no evidence that merely furnishing couples with efficient contraceptives will control population. If nothing is done beyond making contraceptives available, the birthrate will usually be well above the zero-population-growth level and, particularly in industrialized societies, will tend to rise when economic conditions are good. Couples can "plan" big families as well as small ones.

The defenders of the family-planning approach claim that it represents a first step in population control, that it has the advantage of being religiously and politically acceptable, and that, as societies modernize, couples will voluntarily bring down fertility to a reasonable level. To this, the critics reply that family planning is a way to avoid facing up to the revolutionary social changes required to bring fertility into balance with low mortality. Obviously, people must have some means to control their fertility, but the object of that control —the desired number of children— depends on other factors.

If people are sufficiently motivated, the argument continues, they will lower their fertility even without a government program to help them. The steady fall in birthrates in industrial countries between 1870 and 1932 occurred while governments were trying to suppress birth control. In the teeth of official opposition, people reduced their fertility by postponing marriage, by not marrying at all, by getting abortions, or

by using such simple contraceptive techniques as coitus interruptus, douches,
and condoms, none of which requires
the services of a clinic. They did this in
order to take advantage of the opportunities of an industrializing society,
where social position increasingly depended on education and achievement
and where children were becoming
economic liabilities rather than assets.

When the depression came in the
1930s, prospects seemed so poor that
people postponed marriage and child-
bearing to a point where the population
was in imminent danger of decreasing
—but still without government-spon-
sored birth-control services. Thus, the
post-World War II baby boom cannot
be interpreted as the result of a decline
in contraceptive technology or services.
Rather, it was due to economic prosperity, which led people to plan larger
families. In short, therefore, human
fertility is directly related, not to the
availability of contraceptive services or
technology, but to social and economic
conditions. And while couples may
lower their fertility if conditions become bad enough, one of the goals of
population policy is to prevent the uncontrolled population growth that will
make conditions so bad that having a
family seems pointless.

A further argument against the
family-planning approach is that it is
peculiarly unsuited to less developed
countries. With its emphasis on a
100% sure, medically certified and
supervised contraceptive, it requires a
highly organized and expensive bureaucratic apparatus, deflects attention from
institutional changes that would reduce
the motivation to have large families,
and makes contraception itself too cum-
bersome. In India, for example, the program of inserting intrauterine devices
was a failure. In the absence of sufficient medical personnel, side effects
went untreated and were magnified, in
the popular mind, by rumors. Reliable

follow-up and research were impossible.
Even in the United States, this emphasis on the "perfect contraceptive"
led to hasty introduction of the Pill, the
medical wisdom of which is only now
being questioned.

New Solutions

The proponents of the family-planning approach stress that their policy
has the advantage of being purely
voluntary, but its critics say it is they,
not the family planners, who wish to
free people from the compulsions built
into the old system. The old institutions were designed to ensure that
people would have enough children to
offset the high death rate. If population
control is to be achieved, the institutions themselves must be altered.

The general principle underlying such
changes should be to release people,
especially women, from the social and
economic coercion to marry and reproduce, and to offer them new opportunities outside the family. Suppose a
Pakistani woman is given a perfect contraceptive and advised to have only two
children. What then? For thousands of
years the Oriental woman's mission in
life has been to bear and rear children.
Unless she is given an attractive alternative, her life after bearing two children
will be so empty that she will crave
more.

There are many possibilities for
change. Among the old compulsions is
the ban on abortions, which forces
women to bear children once they are
conceived. Lifting the ban and subsi-
dizing the costs of abortion would automatically provide a birth-control
method that is 100% effective, regardless of the kind of contraceptive used, if
any. The traditional discrimination
against women in educational and occupational spheres has the effect of forcing them back into a family role for

economic and emotional satisfaction. Removal of this discrimination would enable women to develop the same absorbing career interests and outside contacts that are now available to men. Again, instead of taxing single people more heavily than married individuals, and instead of taxing families in which the wife works more heavily than those in which she does not work, the taxing authorities could do the opposite. The military authorities could cease exempting men because they are fathers.

Positive incentives by advocates of effective population control include paying people to become sterilized (now practiced in some states of India); giving couples a bond or some other payment for each year they refrain from having children; offering career fellowships to men and women who remain single; providing tax incentives and child-care facilities for the working wife; providing recreational facilities and social life around the place of work; and giving special housing, recreational, and other advantages to childless people.

It is to be hoped that, if the traditional compulsions were removed and new and attractive alternatives to reproduction were provided, the birthrate could be reduced sufficiently to avoid the need for direct compulsory measures. If compulsory measures had to be adopted, they could be of two kinds: those relating to marriage and those relating specifically to reproduction. Couples might be required to furnish evidence of economic ability to support a family before being allowed to marry —a condition that would cause many marriages to be postponed or avoided. In addition, illegitimate pregnancy could be penalized, the girl being required to secure an abortion and the father being punished. Finally, women might be forbidden to have more than four children. In the United States during the four years 1965–68, nearly 15% of all births were of the fifth or higher order. If no woman with four children had been allowed to have another, the birthrate would have been 15.6 per 1,000 population instead of the actual 18.3, and the net reproduction rate—the generation replacement rate—would have been only 8% above unity instead of 27%.

Mention of such policies, whether of the positive or the punitive variety, seems immoral to many people. This is because traditional morality encourages reproduction. It is a system of inducing people to marry, rear children, and value family life. Any policy that will effectively discourage reproduction is therefore revolutionary. This is why no government, as yet, has seriously tried to achieve zero population growth.

The critics of the purely family-planning approach to population control are probably right, but the family planners, because they advocate only minimum changes in existing institutions and because they generally go along with religious beliefs and dogmas, are more readily accepted. It may be that, in the long run, the problems of population growth will force the adoption of effective control policies. As things stand, however, one can only conclude that any efforts likely to be made in the foreseeable future will be too feeble to avoid catastrophic rises in the death rate brought on by overpopulation.

For Additional Reading

1. BERELSON, BERNARD, et al. (ed.), *Family Planning and Population Programs* (University of Chicago Press, 1966).

2. BLAKE, JUDITH, "Population Policy for Americans: Is the Government Being Misled?," *Science* (May 2, 1969, pp. 522–529).
3. DAVIS, KINGSLEY, "Population Policy: Will Current Programs Succeed?," *Science* (Nov. 10, 1967, pp. 730–739).
4. DURAND, JOHN D., "The Modern Expansion of World Population," *Proceedings of the American Philosophical Society*, vol. iii, no. 3 (June 1967).
5. ERLICH, PAUL R., and ERLICH, ANNE H., *Population, Resources, Environment* (W. H. Freeman, 1970).
6. NAM, CHARLES B. (ed.), *Population and Society: A Textbook of Reading* (Houghton Mifflin, 1968).
7. PETERSON, WILLIAM, *Population*, 2nd ed. (Macmillan, 1969).